PHILIP'S

SCHOOL ATLAS

Bounty BOOKS

Text: Richard Widdows
Picture acknowledgement: page 16, Tony Stone Images

First published in 2000 by Chancellor Press,
an imprint of Bounty Books, a division of Octopus Publishing Group Ltd,
2-4 Heron Quays, London E14 4JP

Reprinted 2001, 2002, 2004

Copyright © 2000 Octopus Publishing Group Ltd
Maps and index © 2000 George Philip Ltd
Cartography by Philip's

ISBN 0 7537 0995 3

A CIP catalogue record for this book is available
from the British Library

Produced by Toppan Printing Co., (HK) Ltd
Printed in Hong Kong

Contents

● The Physical Earth

The Earth in Motion	4–5	Shaping the Landscape	10–11
Oceans	6–7	Climate	12–13
The Unstable Earth	8–9	Water and Vegetation	14–15

● Maps

General Reference	1	Arabia and the Horn of Africa	32
The World: Political	2–3	The Near East	33
Arctic Ocean	4	Northern Africa	34–35
Antarctica	5	Central and Southern Africa	36–37
Scandinavia	6–7	Australia and Oceania: Physical and Political	38
England and Wales	8–9	New Zealand	39
The British Isles	10	Western Australia	40–41
Netherlands, Belgium and Luxembourg	11	Eastern Australia	42–43
Middle Europe	12–13	Pacific Ocean	44–45
France	14	Canada	46–47
Spain and Portugal	15	Eastern Canada	48–49
Italy and the Balkan States	16–17	Western Canada	50–51
Eastern Europe and Turkey	18–19	Eastern United States	52–53
Russia and Central Asia	20–21	Middle United States	54–55
Japan	22–23	Western United States	56–57
China and Korea	24–25	Mexico	58–59
Indonesia and the Philippines	26–27	Central America and the West Indies	60–61
South Asia	28–29	South America – North	62–63
The Middle East	30–31	South America – South	64

● Index

65–112

The Earth in Motion

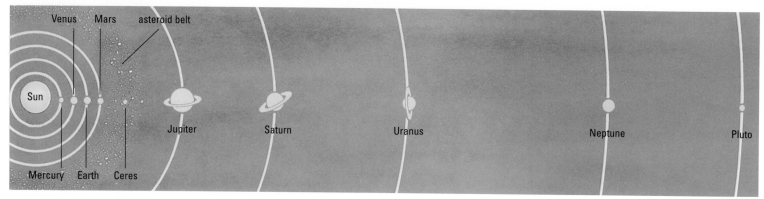

Venus Mars asteroid belt
Sun
Jupiter Saturn Uranus Neptune Pluto
Mercury Earth Ceres

The solar system

A tiny part of one of the billions of galaxies (collections of stars) that make up the universe, the solar system lies about 27,000 light-years from the centre of our own galaxy, "the Milky Way". At least 4,700 million years old – and possibly far more – it comprises a central sun with nine planets revolving around it, attracted by its strong gravitational pull (above).

The Sun's diameter is 109 times that of Earth's 12,756 kilometres, and the temperature at its core – caused by continuous fusions of hydrogen into helium – is estimated to be 15,000°C. The Sun accounts for almost 99.9% of the total mass of the solar system (Jupiter contains most of the remainder), and is its only source of light and heat.

By composition as well as distance, the planets divide neatly into two groups: an inner system of four small solid planets, and an outer system of four huge gas giants. Between the two groups lies a scattering of asteroids, perhaps as many as 40,000. The ninth and smallest planet, Pluto (discovered only in 1930), appears to be a rocky world of the "inner" type.

All the planets orbit the sun in the same direction and almost in the same plane. Only Mercury and Pluto follow paths that deviate noticeably from a circular one. Near perihelion (its closest approach to the Sun) Pluto actually passes inside the orbit of Neptune, a situation that last occurred between 1983 and 1999.

Time

Year The time taken by the Earth to revolve around the Sun, or 365.24 days.
Month The approximate time taken by the Moon to revolve around the Earth; the 12 months of the year in fact vary from 28 (29 in a Leap Year) to 31 days.
Week An artificial period of 7 days; unlike days, months and years, it is not based on astronomical time.
Day The time taken by the Earth to complete one rotation on its axis.
Hour One day comprises 24 hours, which are usually divided into hours AM (ante meridiem, or before noon) and PM (post meridiem, or after noon), though timetables use the 24-hour system from midnight to midnight.

The seasons

The Earth revolves around the Sun once a year, always "tilted" an angle of 66½°. In June (far left), the northern hemisphere is tilted towards the Sun, and as a result it receives more hours of sunshine during a day and enjoys its warmest season, summer. By December the Earth has rotated halfway round the Sun, so that the southern hemisphere is now tilted towards the sun and has its warmest season, while the hemisphere that is tilted away from the Sun has its coldest season, winter.

On 21 June the Sun is directly overhead at the Tropic of Cancer (23½°N), representing midsummer in the northern hemisphere; midsummer in the southern hemisphere occurs on 21 December, when the Sun is directly overhead at the Tropic of Capricorn (23½°S). These are the solstices; the equinox occur in spring and autumn.

Northern Spring Equinox
Southern Autumn Equinox

Equinox is one of the two times in the year when day and night are of equal length due to the Sun being overhead at the Equator.

Northern Summer Solstice
21 March
Northern Winter Solstice
21 June
SUN
21 December
Southern Winter Solstice
21 September
Southern Summer Solstice
Southern Spring Equinox
Northern Spring Equinox

Solstice is one of the two times in the year when the Sun is overhead at one of the Tropics 23½° north or south of the Equator.

Day and night

The Sun appears to "rise" in the east, reach its highest point at noon, and then "set" in the west, to be followed by night. In reality it is not the Sun that is moving but the Earth, rotating ("spinning" on its axis) from west to east. Due to the tilting of the Earth, the length of day and night varies from place to place and month to month (left).

At the summer solstice in the northern hemisphere (21 June), the area inside the Arctic Circle has total daylight and the area inside the Antarctic Circle has total darkness. The opposite occurs at the winter solstice on 21 December. At latitude 50° the length of day and night varies from about 16 hours to about 8 hours; at latitude 30° it varies from about 14 to 10 hours; at the Equator, the length of day and night are almost equal all year round.

The Earth rotates through 360° in one day, and moves 15° every hour. As a result the world is divided into 24 official time zones (right), each centred on lines of longitude at 15° intervals. The Greenwich meridian lies at the centre of the "first" zone.

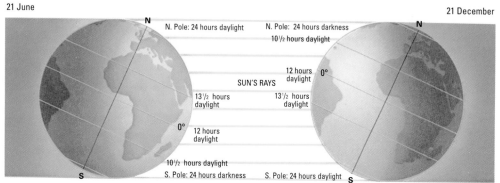

21 June 21 December

N. Pole: 24 hours daylight
N
N. Pole: 24 hours darkness
10½ hours daylight
12 hours daylight 0°
SUN'S RAYS
13½ hours daylight 13½ hours daylight
0°
12 hours daylight
10½ hours daylight
S. Pole: 24 hours darkness S. Pole: 24 hours daylight
S S
N

The Moon

The Moon rotates more slowly than the Earth, making one complete turn on its axis in just over 27 days. Since this corresponds to its period of revolution around the Earth, the Moon always presents the same hemisphere to us on Earth, and we never see "the dark side".

The interval between one full Moon and the next (and thus also between two new Moons) is about 29½ days – a lunar month. The apparent changes in the shape of the Moon are caused by its changing position in relation to the Earth *(right)*; like the planets, the Moon produces no light of its own and shines only by reflecting the rays of the Sun.

Distance from Earth The Moon orbits the Earth at a mean distance of 384,199 kilometres, at an average speed of 3,683 kilometres per hour in relation to the Earth.
Size and mass The average diameter of the Moon is 3,475 kilometres. It is 400 times smaller than the Sun but about 400 times closer to the Earth, so we see them as the same size. The Moon has a mass of about ¹/₈₁ that of Earth, and its surface gravity is one-sixth that of Earth.
Visibility Only 59% of the Moon's surface is directly visible from Earth; reflected light takes 1.25 seconds to reach Earth – compared to 8 minutes 27.3 seconds for light from the Sun.
Temperature With the Sun overhead the temperature on the lunar equator can reach 117.2°C, and at night it can sink to -162.7°C.

Tides

The daily rise and fall of the ocean's tides are the result of the gravitational pull of the Moon and that of the Sun, though the effect of the latter is less than half that of the Moon. The effect is greatest on the hemisphere of the Earth facing the Moon and causes a tidal "bulge".

When lunar and solar forces pull together, with Sun, Earth and Moon in line (near new and full Moons), higher spring tides and lower low tides occur, creating a greater tidal range; when lunar and solar forces are least coincidental, with the Moon and Sun at an angle (near the Moon's first and third quarters) "neap tides" occur, which have a small tidal range.

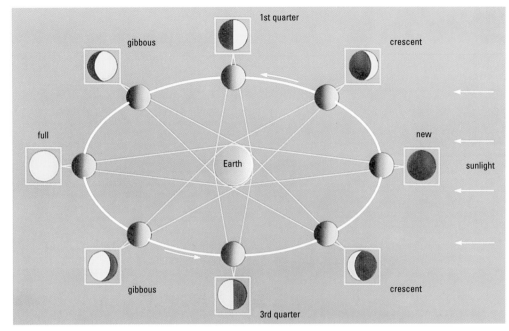

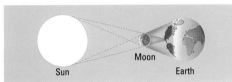

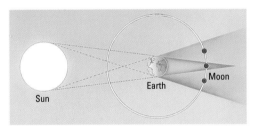

A solar eclipse *(left)* occurs when the Moon passes between the Sun and the Earth. It will cause a partial eclipse of the Sun if the Earth passes through the Moon's outer shadow, or a total eclipse if the inner cone shadow crosses the Earth's surface. A total solar eclipse was visible in many parts of the northern hemisphere in the summer of 1999.

In a lunar eclipse *(left)* the Earth's shadow crosses the Moon and, as with the solar version, provides either a partial or total eclipse. Eclipses do not occur every month because of the 5° difference between the plane of the Moon's orbit and the plane in which the Earth moves. In the 1990s, for example, only 14 eclipses were possible – seven partial and seven total – and each was visible only from certain parts of the world which vary with every eclipse. The same period witnessed 13 solar eclipses, six partial (or annular) and seven total.

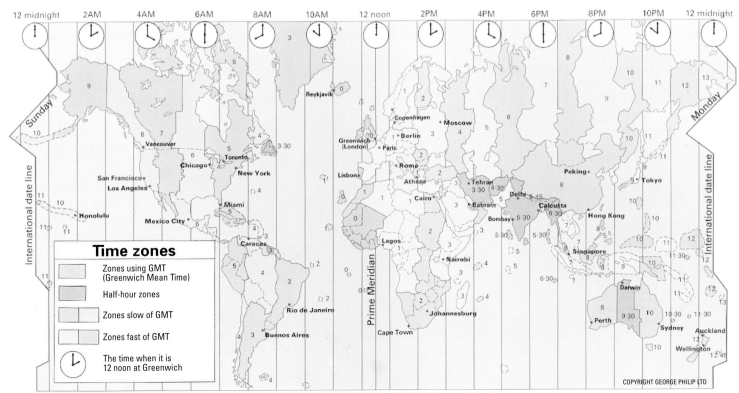

Time zones

- Zones using GMT (Greenwich Mean Time)
- Half-hour zones
- Zones slow of GMT
- Zones fast of GMT
- The time when it is 12 noon at Greenwich

Oceans

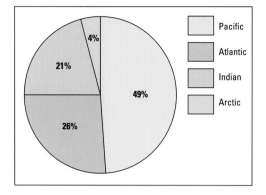

- Pacific
- Atlantic
- Indian
- Arctic

4%
21%
49%
26%

● The great oceans

The Earth is a watery planet: almost 71% of its surface is covered by its oceans and seas. This great liquid cloak gives our planet its characteristic and beautiful blue appearance from space, and is one of the two obvious differences between the Earth and its two near-neighbours, Venus and Mars. The other difference is the presence of life – and the two are closely linked.

In a strict geographical sense the Earth has only three oceans – Atlantic, Indian and Pacific. The legendary "Seven Seas" would require these to be divided at the Equator and the addition of the smaller Arctic Ocean. Geographers do not recognise the Antarctic Ocean (much less the "Southern Ocean") as a separate entity.

Over 360 million sq km of the Earth's surface area are covered by oceans and seas, with the Pacific accounting for nearly 36% of the total.

Winter in Northern Hemisphere

Ocean currents

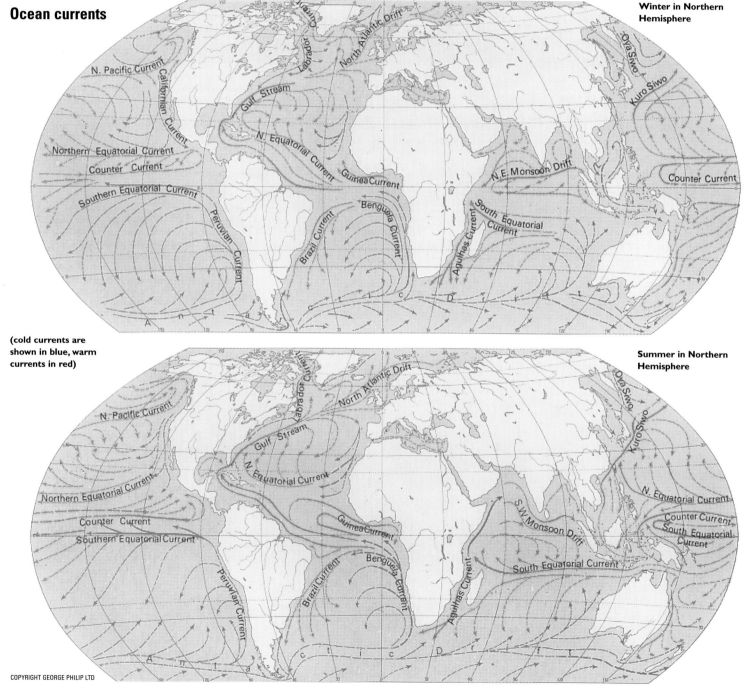

(cold currents are shown in blue, warm currents in red)

Summer in Northern Hemisphere

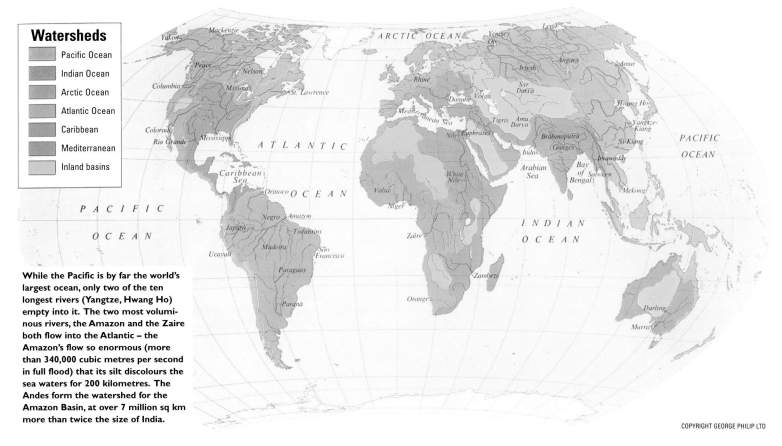

Watersheds

- Pacific Ocean
- Indian Ocean
- Arctic Ocean
- Atlantic Ocean
- Caribbean
- Mediterranean
- Inland basins

While the Pacific is by far the world's largest ocean, only two of the ten longest rivers (Yangtze, Hwang Ho) empty into it. The two most voluminous rivers, the Amazon and the Zaire both flow into the Atlantic – the Amazon's flow so enormous (more than 340,000 cubic metres per second in full flood) that its silt discolours the sea waters for 200 kilometres. The Andes form the watershed for the Amazon Basin, at over 7 million sq km more than twice the size of India.

● The ocean currents

Moving immense quantities of energy as well as billions of tonnes of water every hour, the ocean currents (left) are a vital part of the heat engine that drives the Earth's climate. The currents are produced by a twofold mechanism: at the surface winds push masses of water before them, while in the deeper ocean variations in density cause slow vertical movements.

The pattern of circulation of the major surface currents is determined by the displacement caused by the Earth's rotation. The deflection is most obvious near the Equator, where the Earth's surface is spinning eastwards at 1,700 kilometres per hour; currents moving towards the polar regions are "curved" clockwise in the northern hemisphere and anti-clockwise in the southern hemisphere.

The result of this displacement (known as the Coriolis Effect) is a system of spinning circles called gyres (below). The Coriolis Effect piles water up on the left of each gyre, creating a narrow, fast-moving flow that is matched by.a slower, broader returning current on the right.

North and south of the Equator, the fastest currents are located in the west and east respectively. In each case, warm water moves from the Equator and cold water returns to it. Cold currents often bring an upwelling of nutrients, supporting the world's most economically important fisheries; the Peruvian Current is an example.

It is this upwelling that is suppressed by El Niño, the phenomenon caused by the eastward movement of warm water from the western Pacific, thus depriving the fishing areas of nutrients. In an El Niño year the water is warmed by as much as 7°C, disturbing the tropical atmospheric circulation and causing climatic havoc in areas thousands of kilometres away – including heavy rainfall in the USA, rainforest fires in south-east Asia and drought in Australia.

Depending on the prevailing winds, some currents on or near the Equator may reverse their direction in the course of a year – a seasonal variation on which Asian monsoon rains depend. If the reversal fails, it can mean disaster for millions of people on the Indian subcontinent.

While the depths of the major oceans are not far apart (below), the sea-floor is no more uniform than the surface of the continents, featuring plains, hills, mid-ocean ridges and seamounts (underwater volcanoes). Trenches also slice dramatically into the Earth's crust – especially in the Pacific, where eight trenches reach down more than the height of Everest. Life is scarce in the deep ocean, but a few organisms have been found, even in the abysmal darkness of the great trenches.

NORTH
Arctic
Atlantic Ocean
SOUTH
Antarctic

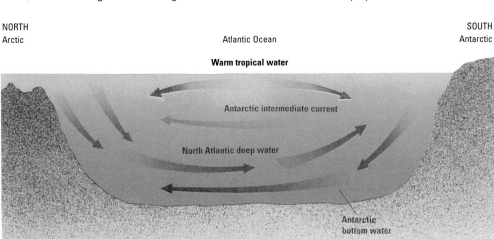

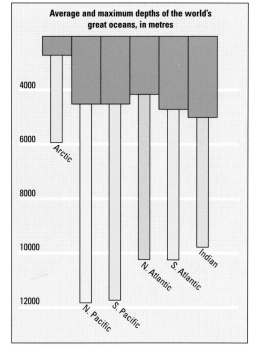

Average and maximum depths of the world's great oceans, in metres

The Unstable Earth

Profile of the Earth

While the origin of the Earth is still open to debate, the most widely accepted theory is that it was formed 4,700 billion years ago – and possibly far more, from a solar cloud consisting mainly of hydrogen. The cloud condensed, forming the planets.

The lighter elements floated to the surface of the Earth, where they cooled to form a crust, but the inner material remained hot and molten. Although the first rocks were formed over 3,500 billion years ago, the Earth's surface has been constantly altered – from inside as well as outside forces – ever since.

The brittle, low-density crust accounts for only 1.5% of the Earth's volume. The rigid upper mantle extends to about 1,000 km, below which is a more viscous mantle 1,900 km thick. The molten outer core is 2,100 km thick, and a liquid transition zone about 5,000 km below the surface separates it from the solid inner core, a sphere 2,700 km across where rock is three times as dense as in the crust. The temperature here is probably about 5,000°C.

The moving continents

The migration of the continents is a feature which, as far as we know, is unique to the planet Earth. The jigsaw puzzle fit of the coastlines on each side of the Atlantic Ocean led the German meteorologist Alfred Wegener to propose his theory of continental drift at the beginning of the 20th century (right). The theory suggests that an ancient super-continent, which he called Pangaea, once incorporated all the land masses and gradually split up to form the continents we see today.

Geological evidence that the continents once formed a single land mass is provided by distinctive rock formations that can be assembled into continuous belts when South America and Africa are lined up next to each other. There are also the processes of mountain building, notably India "colliding" with Asia and crumpling up sediments to form the Himalayas. Distribution of some plants and animals in the past, as well as ancient climatic zones, can only be explained by the theory of continental drift. There is nothing to suggest the process will not continue.

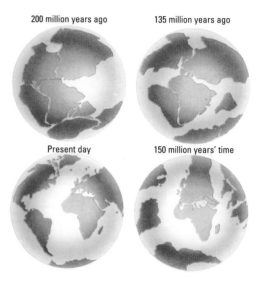

200 million years ago | 135 million years ago

Present day | 150 million years' time

Plate tectonics

The original debate about continental drift was a prelude to a more radical idea developed since the 1960s: plate tectonics. The basic theory is that the Earth's crust is made up of a series of rigid plates (left) which float on a soft layer of the mantle, and are moved about by continental convection currents within the Earth's interior. These plates diverge and converge along margins marked by seismic (earthquake) activity. Plates diverge from mid-ocean ridges, where molten lava pushes upwards and forces the plates apart; converging plates form trenches or mountain ranges.

Earthquakes

Earthquakes are a series of rapid vibrations originating from the slipping or faulting parts of the Earth's crust, when stresses build to breaking point. They usually occur at depths varying from 8 to 30 kilometres.

The magnitude of earthquakes is rated according to the Richter or the Mercalli scale. The former measures absolute earthquake power with mathematical precision, each step representing a tenfold increase in shockwave amplitude, and in theory there is no upper limit. Based on observed effects, Mercalli is more meaningful, ranging from I (recorded by seismologists) to XII (total destruction).

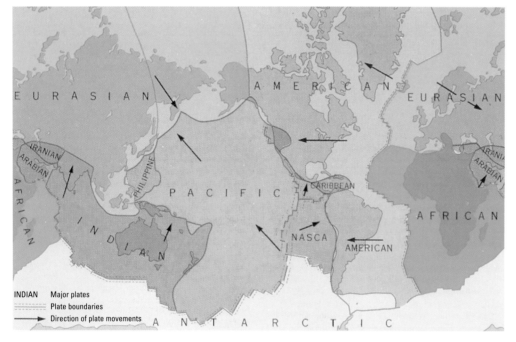

INDIAN — Major plates
- - - - Plate boundaries
——→ Direction of plate movements

Earthquakes

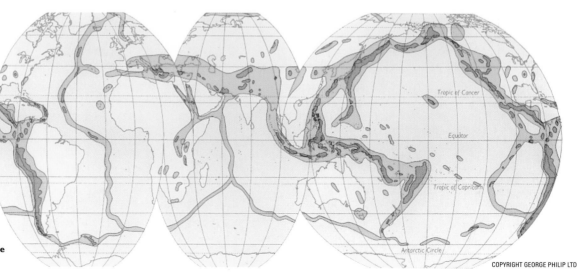

Major earthquake zones

Areas experiencing frequent earthquakes

The highest magnitude recorded on the Richter scale is 8.9, on 2 March 1933, for a quake that killed 2,990 people in Japan. The most devastating earthquake ever affected three provinces of central China, on 2 February 1556, when it is believed that about 830,000 people perished. The highest toll in modern times was at Tangshan, eastern China, on 28 July 1976: the original figure of over 655,000 deaths has since been twice revised to stand at 242,000.

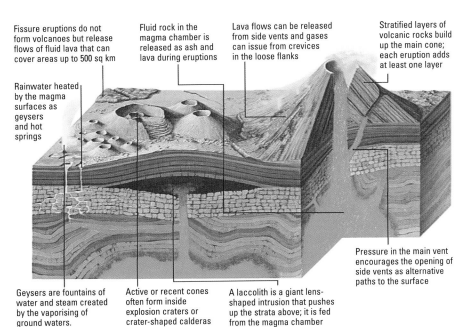

Fissure eruptions do not form volcanoes but release flows of fluid lava that can cover areas up to 500 sq km

Rainwater heated by the magma surfaces as geysers and hot springs

Fluid rock in the magma chamber is released as ash and lava during eruptions

Lava flows can be released from side vents and gases can issue from crevices in the loose flanks

Stratified layers of volcanic rocks build up the main cone; each eruption adds at least one layer

Geysers are fountains of water and steam created by the vaporising of ground waters.

Active or recent cones often form inside explosion craters or crater-shaped calderas

A laccolith is a giant lens-shaped intrusion that pushes up the strata above; it is fed from the magma chamber

Pressure in the main vent encourages the opening of side vents as alternative paths to the surface

1

2

3

Volcanic eruptions take various forms. Fissure eruptions [1] release the most basic and runny lava; in Hawaiian eruptions [2] the lava is less fluid and produces

low cones; Vulcanian eruptions [3] are more violent and eject solid lava; Stombolian eruptions [4] blow out incandescent material; in the Peléean type [5]

a blocked vent is cleared explosively; and a Plinian eruption [6] is a continuous blast of gas that rises to immense heights.

4

5

6

● Volcanoes

Volcanoes occur when hot liquefied rock beneath the Earth's crust is pushed up by pressure to the surface as molten lava. They are found in places where the crust is weak – the mid-ocean ridges and their continental continuations, and along the collision edges of crustal plates. Some volcanoes erupt in an explosive way, throwing out rocks and ash, while others are effusive and lava flows out of the vent. There are examples, such as Mount Fuji in Japan, which are both.

An accumulation of lava and cinders creates cones of various sizes and shapes. As a result of many eruptions over centuries, for example, Mount Etna in Sicily has a circumference of more than 120 kilometres. Craters at rest are often filled by a lake – and the mudflow caused by an eruption can be as destructive as a lava flow and, because of its speed, even more lethal.

Despite the increasingly sophisticated technololgy available volcanoes – like earthquakes – remain both dramatic and unpredictable. In 1991 Mount Pinatubo, located 100 kilometres north of the Philippines capital Manila, suddenly burst into life without warning after lying dormant for no fewer than six centuries.

Most of the world's active volcanoes are located in a belt round the Pacific Ocean, on the edge of the Pacific crustal plate, called the "Ring of Fire" – a circle of fear that threatens over 400 million people. However, the soils formed by the weathering of volcanic rocks are usually

exceptionally fertile, and despite the dangers large numbers of people have always lived in the shadows of volcanoes.

Indonesia has the greatest concentration with 90, 12 of which are active. The 1815 eruption of Tambora in Indonesia ranks as the greatest volcanic disaster in history: 10,000 people were killed by the eruption itself, and over 80,000 more died later of disease and starvation.

Climatologists believe that volcanic ash, if ejected high into the atmosphere, can influence temperature and weather conditions generally over a massive area and for several years afterwards. It has been estimated that the 1991 eruption of Mount Pinatubo in the Philippines threw up more than 20 million tonnes of dust and ash over 30 kilometres into the atmosphere, and it is widely believed that this accelerated the depletion of the ozone layer over large parts of the globe.

There are far more volcanoes on the sea-floor than on the land, however. Known as seamounts, they exist because the oceanic crust is thin and easily pierced by the underlying magma. The Pacific alone is thought to have more than 10,000 underwater volcanoes above 3,000 metres high.

The Hawaiian volcanoes were caused by hotspots in the Earth's mantle, which gave rise to a string of volcanoes as the crust moved slowly over them. Mount Loa, on Hawaii itself, is the world's largest active volcano, measuring 120 kilometres long and 50 kilometres wide; of its total volume, more than 84% is below sea level.

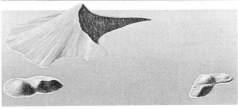

Situated in the Sunda Strait of Indonesia, west of Java, Krakatau (above) was a small volcanic island which had been inactive for over 200 years when, in August 1883, two-thirds of it was destroyed by a violent natural explosion. The eruption was so powerful that the resulting tidal wave killed 36,000 people, and tremors were felt as far away as Australia.

Volcanoes

- Volcanoes
- Sea floor spreading centre
- Ocean trench
- Continental shelf

Structure

- Pre-Cambrian
- Caledonian folding
- Hercynian folding
- Tertiary folding
- Great Rift Valley
- // // Main trend lines

Of the 850 volcanoes to produce recorded eruptions, nearly three-quarters lie in the "Ring of Fire" that surrounds the Pacific Ocean on the edge of the Pacific plate.

Shaping the Landscape

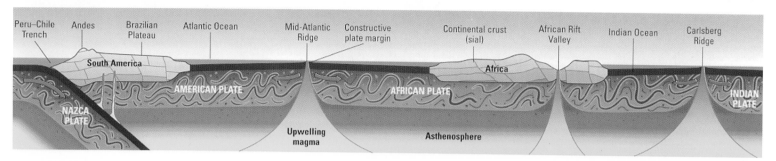

● Sea-floor spreading

The vast ridges that divide the Earth beneath the world's oceans mark the boundaries between tectonic plates that are gradually moving in opposite directions. As the plates shift apart (above), molten magma rises from the mantle to seal the rift and the sea-floor spreads towards the land masses. The rate of spreading has been calculated at about 40mm a year in the North Atlantic Ocean.

Near the ocean shore, underwater volcanoes mark the lines where the continental rise begins. As the plates meet, much of the denser oceanic crust dips beneath the continental plate and melts back to the magma.

● Mountain building

Mountains are formed when pressures on the Earth's crust become so intense that the surface buckles or cracks. This happens where oceanic crust is subducted by continental crust, or where two tectonic plates collide: the Rockies, Andes, Alps, Urals and Himalayas all resulted from such impacts. These are known as fold mountains because they were formed by the compression of the rocks, forcing the surface to bend and fold like a crumpled rug.

The other main mountain-building process occurs when the crust fractures to create faults, allowing rock to be forced upwards in large blocks; or when the pressure of magma inside the crust forces the surface to bulge into a dome, or erupts to form a volcano. Large mountain ranges may well reveal a combination of these features.

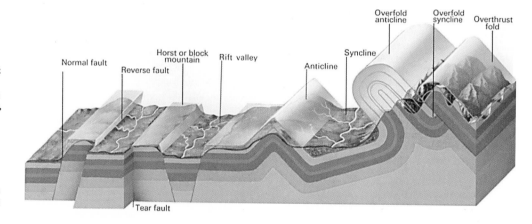

Faults occur where the crust is being stretched or compressed so violently that the rock strata breaks (above). A normal fault results when vertical movement causes the surface to break apart, while compression causes a reverse fault. Horizontal movement causes shearing, known as a tear or strike-slip fault. When the rock breaks in two places, the central block may be pushed up in a horst, or sink in a rift valley. Folds occur when rock strata are squeezed and compressed (above right). Layers bending up form an anticline, those bending down form a syncline.

● Agents of erosion

Destruction of the landscape, however, begins as soon as it is formed. Wind, ice, water and sea, the main agents of erosion, maintain a constant assault that even the hardest rocks cannot withstand. Mountain peaks may dwindle by only a few millimetres a year, but if they are not uplifted by further movements of the Earth's crust they will eventually disappear. Over millions of years, even great mountain ranges can be reduced to a low rugged landscape.

Water is the most powerful destroyer: it has been estimated that 100 billion tonnes of rock are washed into the oceans each year. Three Asian rivers alone account for a fifth of this total – the Hwang Ho in China, and the Ganges and the Brahmaputra in Bangladesh.

When water freezes, its volume increases by about 9%, and no rock is strong enough to resist this pressure. Where water has penetrated fissures or seeped into softer rock, a freeze followed by a thaw may result in rockfalls or earthslides, creating major destruction in minutes.

Over much longer periods, acidity in rain water breaks down the chemical composition of porous rocks such as limestone, eating away the rock to form deep caves and tunnels. Chemical decomposition also occurs in river beds and glacier valleys, hastening the process of mechanical erosion.

Like the sea, rivers and glaciers generate much of their effect through abrasion, pounding or tearing the land with the debris they carry. Yet as well as destroying existing landforms they also create new ones, many of them spectacular. Prominent examples are the vast deltas of the Mississippi and the Nile, the rock arches and stacks off the south coast of Australia, and the deep fjords cut by glaciers in British Columbia, Norway and New Zealand.

While landscapes evolve from a "young" mountainous stage, through a "mature" hilly stage to an "old age" of lowland plain, this long-term cycle of erosion is subject to interruption by a number of crucial factors, including the effects of plate tectonics and climate change.

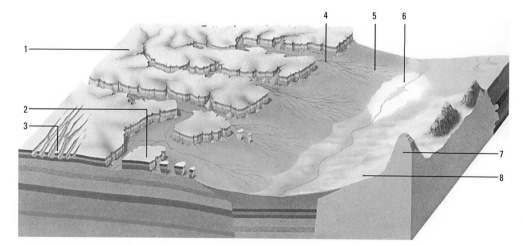

The topography of a desert is characterised by the relative absence of the chemical weathering associated with water, and most erosion takes place mechanically through wind abrasion and the effect of heat.

Mesas [1] are large flat-topped areas with steep sides, while the butte [2] is an isolated version of it. Elongated in the direction of the wind, yardangs [3] comprise tabular masses of resistant rock resting on undercut pillars of softer material. Alluvial fans [5] are pebble-mounds deposited in desert deltas by flash floods, usually at the end of a wadi [4]. A saltpan [6] is a temporary lake of brackish water also formed by flash floods. An inselberg [7] is an isolated hill rising from the plain, and a pediment [8] is an inclining rock surface.

● Shaping forces: ice

Many of the world's most dramatic landscapes have been carved by ice-sheets and glaciers. During the ice ages of the Pleistocene Epoch (over 10,000 years ago) up to a third of the land surface was glaciated; even today a tenth is covered in ice – the vast majority locked up in vast ice-sheets and ice-caps. The world's largest ice-sheet covers most of Antarctica and is up to 4,800 metres thick. It is extremely slow moving – unlike valley glaciers, which can move at rates of between a few centimetres and several metres a day.

Valley glaciers are found in mountainous regions throughout the world, except Australia. In the relatively short geological time scale of the recent ice ages, glaciers accomplished far more carving of the topography than rivers and wind. They are formed from compressed snow, called névé, accumulating in a valley head or cirque. Slowly the glacier moves downhill *(right)*, scraping away debris from the mountains and valleys through which it passes. The debris, or moraine, adds to the abrasive power of the ice. The sediments are transported by the ice to the edge of the glacier, where they are deposited or carried away by meltwater streams.

● Shaping forces: rivers

From their origins as small upland rills and streams channelling rainfall, or as springs releasing water that has seeped into the ground, all rivers are incessantly at work cutting and shaping the landscape on their way to the sea *(right)*.

In highland regions flow may be rapid and turbulent, pounding rocks to cut deep gorges and V-shaped valleys through softer rocks, or tumble as waterfalls over harder ones. Rocks and pebbles move along the bed by saltation (bouncing) or traction (rolling), while lighter sediments are carried in suspension or dissolved in solution.

As they reach more gentle slopes, rivers release some of the pebbles and heavier sediments they have carried downstream, flow more slowly and broaden out. Levées or ridges are raised along their banks by the deposition of mud and sand during floods. In lowland plains the river drifts into meanders, depositing layers of sediment, especially on the inside of bends where the flow is weakest. As the river reaches the sea it deposits its remaining load, and estuaries are formed where the tidal currents are strong enough to remove them; if not, the debris creates a delta.

● Shaping forces: the sea

Under the constant assault from tides and currents, wind and waves, coastlines *(right)* change faster than most landscape features, both by erosion and by the building up of sand and pebbles carried by the sea. In severe storms, giant waves pound the shoreline with rocks and boulders; but even in much quieter conditions, the sea steadily erodes cliffs and headlands, creating new features in the form of sand dunes, spits and salt marshes. Beaches, where sand and shingle have been deposited, form a buffer zone between the erosive power of the waves and the coast. Because it is composed of loose materials, a beach can rapidly adapt its shape to changes in wave energy.

Where the coastline is formed from soft rocks such as sandstones, debris may fall evenly and be carried away by currents from shelving beaches. In areas with harder rock, the waves may cut steep cliffs and wave-cut platforms; eroded debris is deposited as a terrace. Bays are formed when sections of soft rock are carved away between headlands of harder rock. These are then battered by waves from both sides, until the headlands are eventually reduced to rock arches and stacks.

A number of factors affect the rate of erosion in coastal environments. These vary from rock type and structure, beach width and supply of beach materials to the more complex fluid dynamics of the waves, namely the breaking point, steepness and length of fetch.

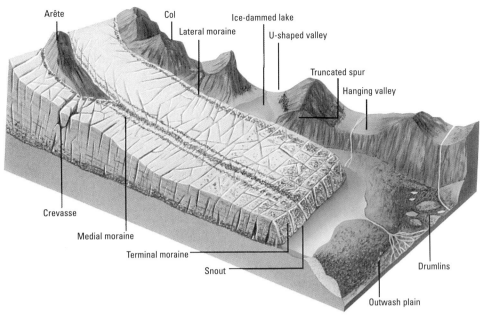

Arête • Col • Lateral moraine • Ice-dammed lake • U-shaped valley • Truncated spur • Hanging valley • Crevasse • Medial moraine • Terminal moraine • Snout • Drumlins • Outwash plain

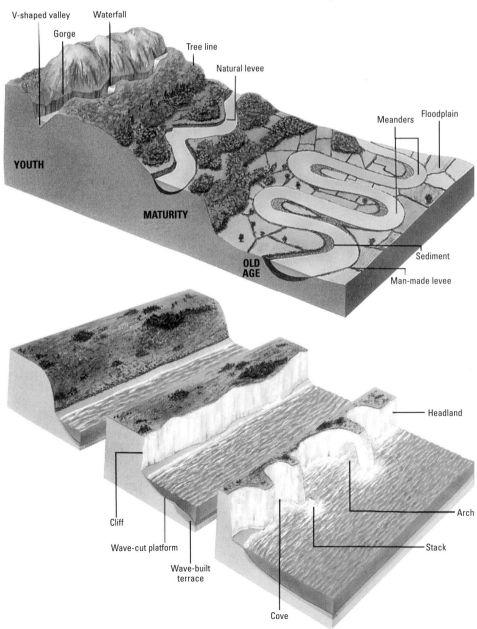

V-shaped valley • Gorge • Waterfall • Tree line • Natural levee • Meanders • Floodplain • YOUTH • MATURITY • OLD AGE • Sediment • Man-made levee • Headland • Cliff • Wave-cut platform • Wave-built terrace • Cove • Arch • Stack

Climate

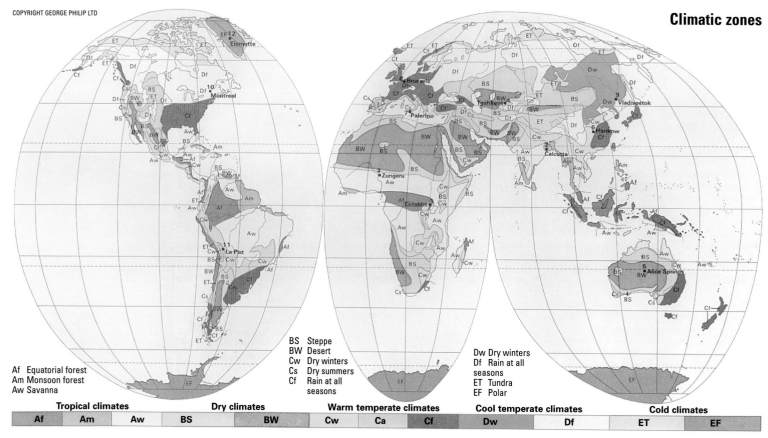

Af Equatorial forest
Am Monsoon forest
Aw Savanna

BS Steppe
BW Desert
Cw Dry winters
Cs Dry summers
Cf Rain at all seasons

Dw Dry winters
Df Rain at all seasons
ET Tundra
EF Polar

Tropical climates			Dry climates		Warm temperate climates			Cool temperate climates		Cold climates	
Af	Am	Aw	BS	BW	Cw	Ca	Cf	Dw	Df	ET	EF

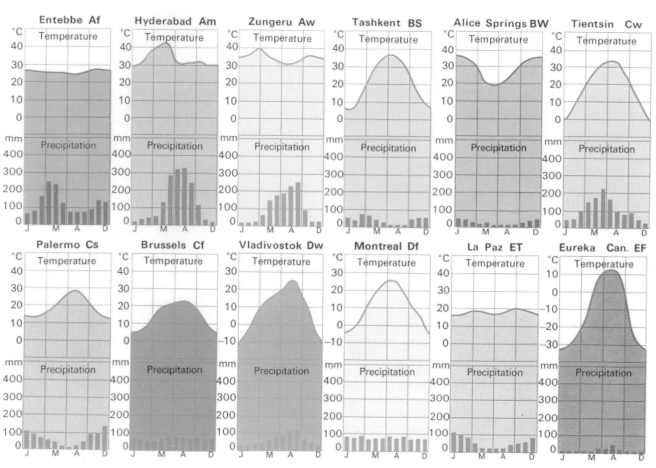

CLIMATE TERMS

Cyclone Violent storm called hurricane in N. America, typhoon in Far East

Depression Area of low pressure

Frost Dew when air temperature falls below freezing point

Hail Frozen rain

Humidity Amount of moisture in air

Isobar Line on map connecting places of equal pressure

Isotherm Line connecting places of equal temperatutre

Precipitation Measurable rain, snow, sleet or hail

Rain Precipitation of liquid particles with diameter larger than 0.5mm

Sleet Partially melted snow

Snow Formed when water vapour condenses below freezing point

Tornado Severe funnel-shaped storm that twists as hot air spins vertically; a waterspout at sea

● Definition of climate

Climate is weather in the long term – the seasonal pattern of hot and cold, wet and dry, averaged over time (usually 30 years). At the simplest level, it is caused by the uneven heating of the Earth. Surplus heat at the Equator passes towards the poles, levelling out the energy differential. Its passage is marked by a ceaseless churning of the atmosphere and the oceans, further agitated by the Earth's daily spin and the motion it imparts to moving air and water.

The heat's means of transport – by winds and ocean currents, by the continual evaporation and recondensation of water molecules – is the weather itself. There are four basic types of climate, each of which can be further sub-divided: tropical, desert (dry), temperate and polar.

● Climate records

Temperature
Highest recorded shade temperature: Al Aziziyah, Libya, 58°C [136.4°F], 13 September 1922.

Highest mean annual temperature: Dallol, Ethiopia, 34.4°C [94°F], 1960–66.

Longest heatwave: Marble Bar, W. Australia, 162 days over 38°C [100°F], 23 October 1923 to 7 April 1924.

Lowest recorded temperature (outside poles): Verkhoyansk, Siberia, -68°C [-90°F], 6 February 1933.

Lowest mean annual temperature: Plateau Station, Antarctica, -56.6°C [-72.0°F].

Precipitation
Longest drought: Calama, N. Chile, no recorded rainfall in 400 years to 1971.

Wettest place (12 months): Cherrapunji, Meghalaya, N. E. India, 26,470 mm [1,040 in], August 1860 to August 1861; Cherrapunji also holds the record for the most rainfall in one month: 2,930 mm [115 in], July 1861.

Wettest place (average): Mawdsynram, India, mean annual rainfall 11,873 mm [467.4 in].

Wettest place (24 hours): Cilaos, Réunion, Indian Ocean, 1,870 mm [73.6 in], 15–16 March 1952.

Heaviest hailstones: Gopalganj, Bangladesh, up to 1.02 kg [2.25 lb], 14 April 1986 (killed 92 people)

Heaviest snowfall (continuous): Bessans, Savoie, France, 1,730 mm [68 in] in 19 hours, 5–6 April 1969.

Heaviest snowfall (season/year): Paradise Ranger Station, Mt Rainier, Washington, USA, 31,102 mm [1,224.5 in], 19 February 1971 to 18 February 1972.

Pressure and winds
Highest barometric pressure: Agata, Siberia (at 262 m [862 ft] altitude), 1,083.8 millibars, 31 December 1968.

Lowest barometric pressure: Typhoon Tip, Guam, Pacific Ocean, 870 millibars, 12 October 1979.

Highest recorded wind speed: Mt Washington, New Hampshire, USA, 371 km/h [231 mph], 12 April 1934; this is three times as strong as hurricane force on the Beaufort Scale.

Windiest place: Commonwealth Bay, Antarctica, where gales frequently reach over 320 km/h [200 mph].

Conversions
°C = (°F -32) x ⁵/₉; °F = (°C x ⁹/₅) + 32; 0°C = 32°F
1 mm = 0.0394 in (100 mm = 3.94 in); 1 in = 25.4 mm

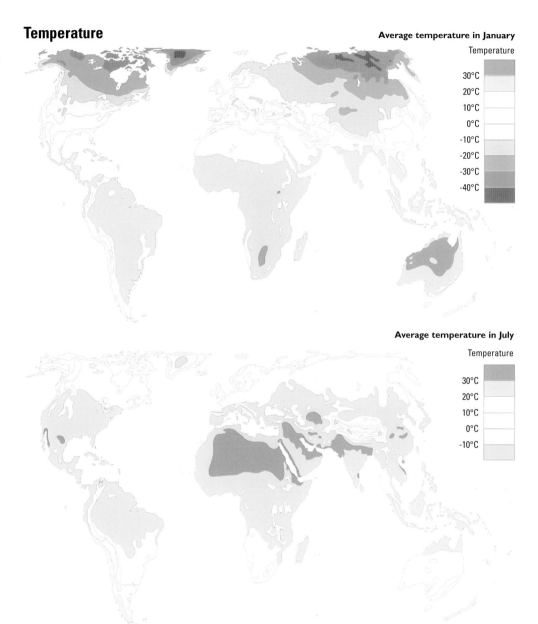

Temperature

Average temperature in January

Temperature
30°C
20°C
10°C
0°C
-10°C
-20°C
-30°C
-40°C

Average temperature in July

Temperature
30°C
20°C
10°C
0°C
-10°C

Rainfall

Average annual precipitation

3,000mm
2,000mm
1,000mm
500mm
250mm

Water and Vegetation

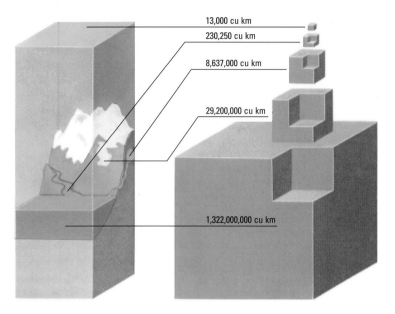

13,000 cu km

230,250 cu km

8,637,000 cu km

29,200,000 cu km

1,322,000,000 cu km

The total water supply of the world *(left)* is estimated to be about 1,360,000,000 cubic kilometres, and some 97% of it is accounted for by the oceans. Of the total water on land more than 75% is frozen in ice-sheets and glaciers, as in Greenland and Antarctica. Most of the rest, about 22%, is water collected below the Earth's surface and called ground water. Comparatively small quantities are in lakes and rivers (0.017% of the total), while water vapour represents only 0.001%. Without this, however, there would be no life on land.

● The water of life

Fresh water is essential to all life on Earth, from the humblest bacterium to the most advanced technological society. Yet freshwater resources form a minute fraction of the Earth's 1.36 billion cubic kilometres of water: most human needs must be met from the 2,000 cubic kilometres circulating in rivers at any one time.

Agriculture accounts for huge quantities: without large-scale irrigation, most of the world's people would starve. Since fresh water is just as essential for most industrial processes, the combination of growing population and advancing industry has put supplies under increasing strain.

Fortunately water is seldom used up: the planet's water cycle circulates it with efficiency, at least on a global scale. More locally, however, human activity can cause severe shortages: water for industry and agriculture is being withdrawn from many river basins and underground aquifers faster than natural recirculation can replace it.

The demand for water has led to tensions between nations as supplies are diverted or horded. Both Iraq and Syria, for example, have protested at Turkey's dam-building programme, which they claim drastically reduces the flow of the Tigris and Euphrates rivers.

● The water cycle

Oceanic water is salty and unsuitable for drinking or farming. In some desert regions, where fresh sources are in short supply, seawater is desalinated to make fresh water, but most of the world is constantly supplied with fresh water by the natural process of the water or hydrological cycle *(left)*, which relies on the action of two factors: gravity and the Sun's heat.

Over the oceans, which cover almost 71% of the Earth's surface, the Sun's heat causes evaporation. Water vapour rises on air currents and winds; some of this vapour condenses and returns directly to the oceans as rain, but because of the circulation of the atmosphere, air bearing large amounts of water vapour is carried over land, where it falls as rain or snow.

Much of this precipitation is quickly re-evaporated by the Sun. Some soaks into the soil, where it is absorbed by plants and partly returned to the air through transpiration; some flows over the land surface as run-off, which flows into streams and rivers; and some rain and melted snow seeps through the soil into the rocks beneath. All the water that does not return directly to the atmosphere gradually returns to the sea to complete the water cycle.

Precip-
itation
on land

Precipitation
on ocean

Evaporation
from
vegetation

Evaporation
from soil

Evaporation from
lakes and ponds

Evaporation from
vegetation and
streams

Evaporation
from ocean

Intercepted by vegetation
Ground water to soil

Ground water to lakes and streams

Ground water to vegetation

Ground water to ocean

The lowest level of the water-table, reached at the driest time of year, is called the permanent water-table, and wells must be drilled to this level if they are to supply water throughout the year. In artesian wells *(right)* water is forced to the surface by hydrostatic pressure.

The water-table [1] in the confined aquifer [2] lies near the top of the dipping layers. A well [4] drilled through the top impervious layer [3] is not an artesian well because the head of hydrostatic pressure [6] is not sufficient to force water to the surface. In such wells the water must be pumped or drawn to the surface.

The top of an artesian well [5] lies below the level of the head of hydrostatic pressure and so water gushes to the surface. Artesian springs [8] may occur along joints or faults [7] where the head of hydrostatic pressure is sufficient to force the water up along the fault. Areas with artesian wells, such as the Great Basin of Australia, are called artesian basins. In the London and Paris artesian basins, the water has been so heavily tapped that the water level has dropped below the level of the well heads.

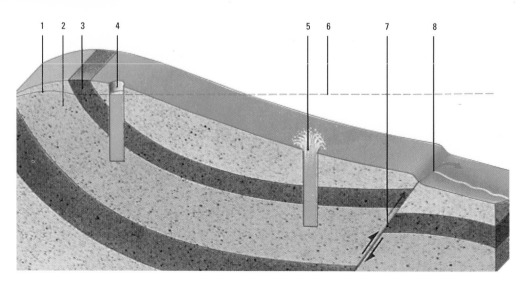

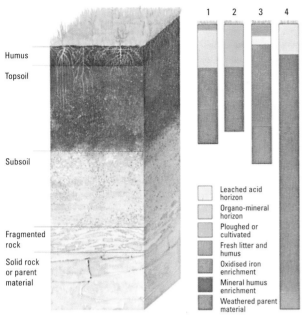

Humus
Topsoil
Subsoil
Fragmented rock
Solid rock or parent material

1 2 3 4

Leached acid horizon
Organo-mineral horizon
Ploughed or cultivated
Fresh litter and humus
Oxidised iron enrichment
Mineral humus enrichment
Weathered parent material

Profile 1 (left) is of acid brown earth found in temperate climates – this one on sandy rock – and 2 is a cultivated brown earth of the same climatic region. Grey leached podzol [3] is typical of wet, cool climates – for example, the taiga in Russia – while oxisol [4], a thick red soil containing iron compounds, is found in humid, tropical lands where chemical and biological activity are both high.

The composition and colour of a soil (right) identifies it to a pedologist. This tundra soil [1] has a dark, peaty surface. Light-coloured desert soil [2] is coarse and poor in organic matter. Chestnut-brown soil [3] and chernozem [4] – the Russian for "black earth" – are humus-rich grassland soils typical of the central Asian steppes and prairies of North America. The reddish, leached latosol [5] of tropical savannas has a very thin but rich humus layer. Podzolic soils [6,7,8,9] are typical of northern climates where rainfall is heavy but evaporation is slow.

● The living soil

The whole structure of life on Earth, with its enormous diversity of plant and animal types, is utterly dependent on a mantle of soil which is rich in moisture and nutrients.

Soil is a result of all the processes of physical and chemical weathering on the barren, underlying rock mass of the Earth that it covers, and varies in depth from a few centimetres to several metres. The depth of soil is measured either by the distance to which plants send down

their roots or by the depth of soil directly influencing their systems. In some places only a very thin layer is necessary to support life.

Formation of soil is the result of the interaction of five major elements – the parent rock, land relief, time, climate and decay. However, by far the most single important factor in the development of soil is climate, with water essential to all chemical and biological change in soil.

The map below illustrates the natural "climax" vegetation of a region, as dictated by its climate and typography. In the vast majority of cases, however, human agricultural activity has drastically altered the pattern of vegetation. Western Europe, for example, lost most of its broadleaf forest many centuries ago, and in other areas irrigation has gradually turned natural semi-desert into productive land.

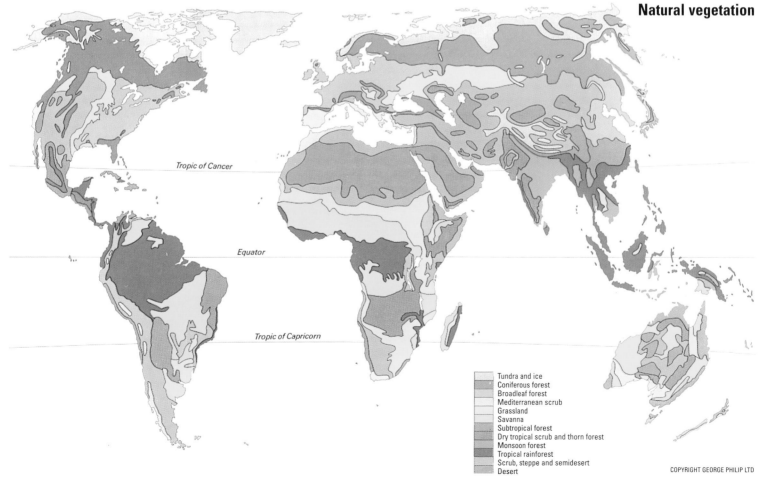

Natural vegetation

Tropic of Cancer

Equator

Tropic of Capricorn

Tundra and ice
Coniferous forest
Broadleaf forest
Mediterranean scrub
Grassland
Savanna
Subtropical forest
Dry tropical scrub and thorn forest
Monsoon forest
Tropical rainforest
Scrub, steppe and semidesert
Desert

WORLD MAPS

SETTLEMENTS

■ PARIS   ■ Berne   ◉ Livorno   ◉ Brugge   ◎ Algeciras   ○ Frejus   ○ Oberammergau   ○ Thira

Settlement symbols and type styles vary according to the scale of each map and indicate the importance
of towns on the map rather than specific population figures

∴   Ruins or Archæological Sites   Wells in Desert

ADMINISTRATION

—— International Boundaries	National Parks	Administrative Area Names
– – – – International Boundaries (Undefined or Disputed)	Country Names NICARAGUA	KENT CALABRIA
·········· Internal Boundaries		

International boundaries show the *de facto* situation where there are rival claims to territory

COMMUNICATIONS

—— Principal Roads	⊕ Airfields	—— Other Railways
—— Other Roads	—— Principal Railways	⌐··⌐ Railway Tunnels
⌐··⌐ Road Tunnels	– ∿ – Railways Under Construction	·········· Principal Canals
⋈ Passes		

PHYSICAL FEATURES

—— Perennial Streams	Intermittent Lakes	▲ 8848 Elevations in metres
– – – Intermittent Streams	Swamps and Marshes	▼ 8500 Sea Depths in metres
Perennial Lakes	Permanent Ice and Glaciers	*1134* Height of Lake Surface Above Sea Level in metres

ARCTIC OCEAN

10 11 12 13 14 15 16 17 18

Svalbard *(Norw.)*
gian
rth
ea

Barents Sea
Novaya Zemlya
Kara Sea
Severnaya Zemlya
Laptev Sea
New Siberian Is.
East Siberian Sea
Wrangel I.
A

Murmansk
Arkhangelsk
Salekhard
Norilsk
Yenisey
Lena
Verkhoyansk
Yakutsk
Arctic Circle

NORWAY SWEDEN FINLAND Helsinki
Oslo
Stockholm EST.
Copenhagen
DENMARK LATVIA LITH.
Hamburg
Amsterdam POLAND BELARUS
Berlin
Brussels Prague Warsaw Kiev
PARIS GERMANY CZECH SLOVAK.
Minsk
UKRAINE
Odessa
Bucharest
Milan ITALY CROATIA HUNG. ROMANIA
Marseilles
Rome YUG. Sofia BULGARIA
Barcelona Naples Black Sea GEORGIA Tbilisi
Sardinia GREECE TURKEY Yerevan
Algiers Tunis MALTA Athens Izmir CYPRUS SYRIA
TUNISIA Mediterranean Sea Beirut LEB. Damascus
Tripoli Benghazi Jerusalem ISR. Amman
Alexandria JORDAN IRAQ IRAN
GERIA CAIRO KUWAIT

St. PETERSBURG
Perm Yekaterinburg Tomsk Krasnoyarsk
MOSCOW Kazan Omsk Novosibirsk
Volga Samara Chelyabinsk Irkutsk Ulan Ude
Saratov Astana Barnaul L. Baikal
Volgograd KAZAKSTAN
Astrakhan
Caspian Sea
L. Balkhash
Aral Sea
Almaty
Bishkek KYRGYZSTAN
UZBEKISTAN Tashkent
AZER. Baku Samarkand TAJIKISTAN
TURKMENISTAN Dushanbe
ARM. Ashkhabad
TEHRĀN Mashhad
Tabrīz
Baghdād Eşfahān Kābul
AFGHANISTAN
Shīrāz Islamabad
Lahore
PAKISTAN DELHI
Riyadh QATAR Abu Dhabi New Delhi
BAHRAIN U.A.E. Muscat KARACHI
Mecca OMAN Ahmadabad INDIA
SAUDI ARABIA Arabian Sea MUMBAI (Bombay)

RUSSIA

Okhotsk Sea of Okhotsk Magadan Bering Sea
Petropavlovsk-Kamchatskiy
Sakhalin Komsomolsk
Khabarovsk
Amur Kuril Is.
International Date Line
B

MONGOLIA
Ulan Bator
Harbin Vladivostok Sapporo
Changchun
SHENYANG NORTH KOREA
BEIJING TIANJIN Pyongyang
Dalian SEOUL JAPAN
CHINA SOUTH KOREA Osaka TŌKYŌ
Lanzhou Taiyuan Xi'an Huang He Nanjing Kitakyūshū
Chengdu Wuhan SHANGHAI
TIBET Lhasa CHONGQING East China Sea
Kathmandu BHU. Kunming Fuzhou
NEPAL Kanpur Ganges Yangtze Guangzhou Taipei Ryukyu Is.
BANGLA-DESH DACCA HONG KONG TAIWAN
CALCUTTA BURMA Hanoi
Nagpur MYANMAR Hainan
Bay of Bengal Rangoon South China Sea
Hyderabad VIET-NAM
CHENNAI THAILAND
(Madras) BANGKOK CAMBODIA MANILA
Bangalore Andaman Is. (India) Phnom Penh PHILIPPINES
SRI LANKA Ho Chi Minh City
Colombo Nicobar Is. (India)
MALDIVES
MALAYSIA

PACIFIC OCEAN
C

Bonin Is. (Japan) Tropic of Cancer
Volcano Is. (Japan) Marcus I. (Japan) Wake I. (U.S.A.)
NORTHERN MARIANAS (U.S.A.)
GUAM (U.S.A.)
D
MARSHALL IS.
Yap FEDERATED STATES Pohnpei
Truk Caroline Is.
PALAU OF MICRONESIA
Gilbert Is.
NAURU KIRIBATI

LIBYA EGYPT
NIGER CHAD SUDAN
Omdurmān ERITREA Asmara YEMEN Sana
Niamey Kano Khartoum DJIBOUTI Aden G. of Aden Socotra (Yemen)
Ndjamena CENTRAL AFRICAN REP. Addis Ababa SOMALI REP.
NIGERIA Abuja ETHIOPIA
BENIN Ibadan CAMEROON Bangui
Lagos Douala L. Turkana
Yaoundé UGANDA Mogadishu
EQUATORIAL GUINEA Kisangani Kampala
uinea Libreville GABON Victoria KENYA
SÃO TOMÉ & PRÍNCIPE CONGO DEM.REP.OF THE Kigali RWANDA Nairobi
Brazzaville Kinshasa CONGO Bujumbura BURUNDI Mombasa
CABINDA (Angola) Kananga Dodoma Zanzibar
Luanda TANZANIA Dar es Salaam
ANGOLA Lubumbashi
Benguela ZAMBIA Malawi
Lusaka MALAWI Lilongwe
NAMIBIA ZIMBABWE MOZAMBIQUE MADAGASCAR
Windhoek Harare Antananarivo
BOTSWANA Bulawayo
Gaborone Pretoria
Johannesburg SWAZILAND Maputo
SOUTH LESOTHO Durban
AFRICA
Cape Town C. of Good Hope Port Elizabeth

Medan SABAH
Kuala Lumpur BRUNEI
PEN. MALAYSIA
SINGAPORE Borneo
Sumatra IRIAN JAYA
Palembang Banjarmasin PAPUA New Ireland
INDONESIA New Guinea
JAKARTA Ujung Pandang Port Moresby New Britain
Bandung EAST Arafura Sea C. York SOLOMON IS.
Java Surabaya TIMOR
Timor Santa Cruz Is.
E
Darwin VANUATU FIJI
Cairns Suva
Townsville NEW CALEDONIA (Fr.)

Equator
INDIAN OCEAN
SEYCHELLES
Amirante Is.
Chagos Arch. (U.K.)
Diego Garcia
Aldabra Is.
Agalega Is. (Fr.)
Cargados Carajos
COMOROS Mayotte (Fr.)
Rodriguez MAURITIUS
RÉUNION I. (Fr.)
Cocos Is. (Austral.)
Christmas I. (Austral.)

Tropic of Capricorn

AUSTRALIA
Port Hedland Alice Springs Rockhampton
Geraldton Brisbane
Perth Kalgoorlie-Boulder Lord Howe I. (Austral.)
Fremantle Darling Newcastle Norfolk I. (Austral.)
Great Australian Bight Adelaide Sydney
Amsterdam I. (Fr.) Canberra Auckland
St. Paul (Fr.) Melbourne North I. F
Tasman Sea NEW ZEALAND
Tasmania Wellington
Prince Edward Is. (S. Africa) Crozet Is. (Fr.) Kerguelen (Fr.) Hobart Christchurch South I.
McDonald Is. (Austral.) Heard I. (Austral.) Stewart I. Dunedin
Bounty Is. (N.Z.)
Bouvet I. (Norw.) Antipodes Is. (N.Z.)
Campbell I. (N.Z.) Auckland Is. (N.Z.)
G

OUTHERN OCEAN

c t i c a

East from Greenwich
20 40 60 80 100
12 13 14 15 16 17 18
10 11

Ross Sea
H

Antarctic Circle

Hanoi ● Capital Cities

COPYRIGHT GEORGE PHILIP LTD.

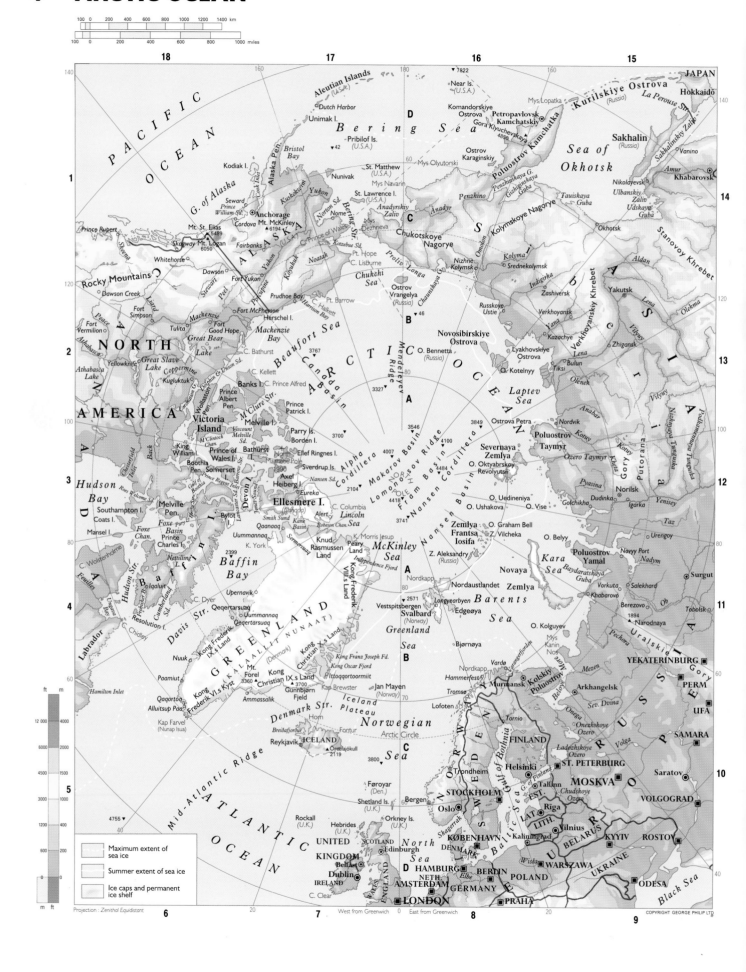

Projection : Zenithal Equidistant

West from Greenwich   East from Greenwich

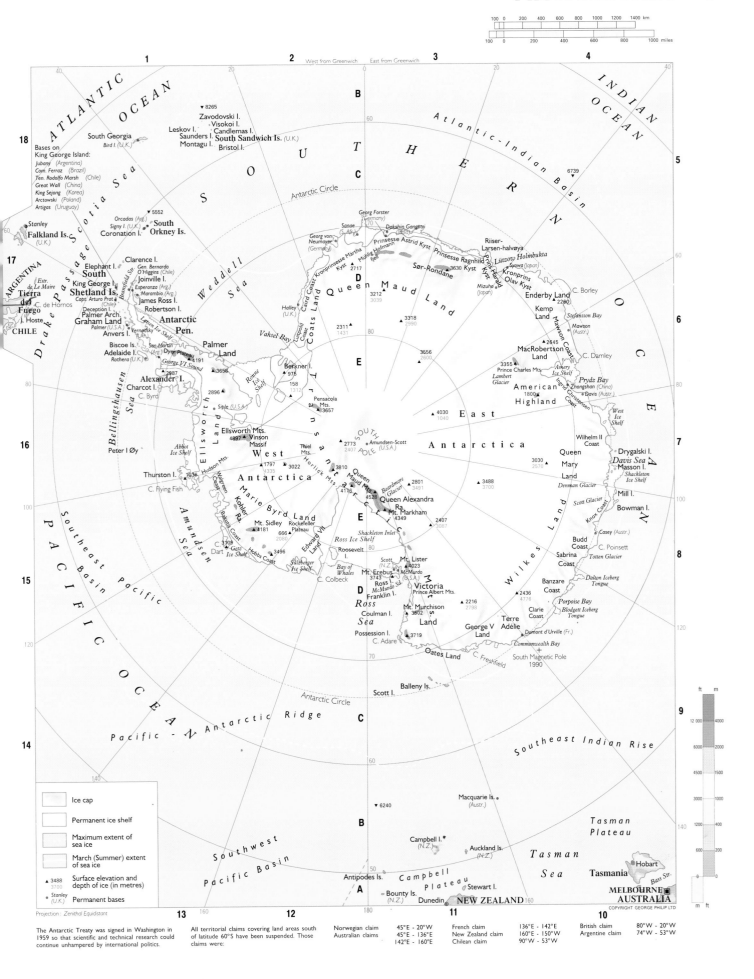

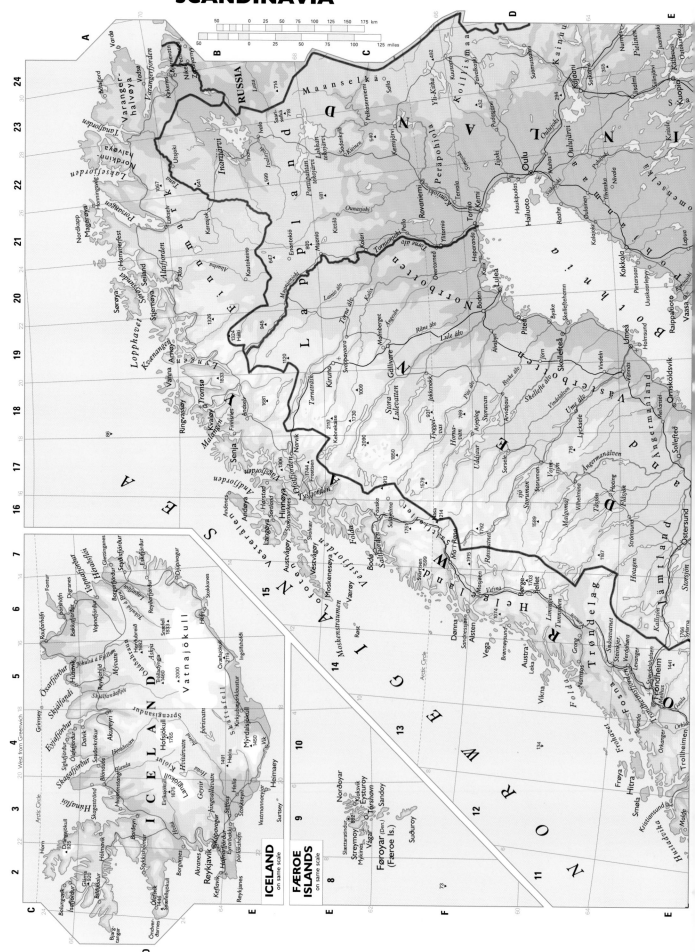

50 0 25 50 75 100 125 150 175 km
50 0 25 50 75 100 125 miles

ICELAND
on same scale

FÆROE ISLANDS
on same scale

Føroyar (Den.)
(Faeroe Is.)

East from Greenwich

Projection: Conic with two standard parallels

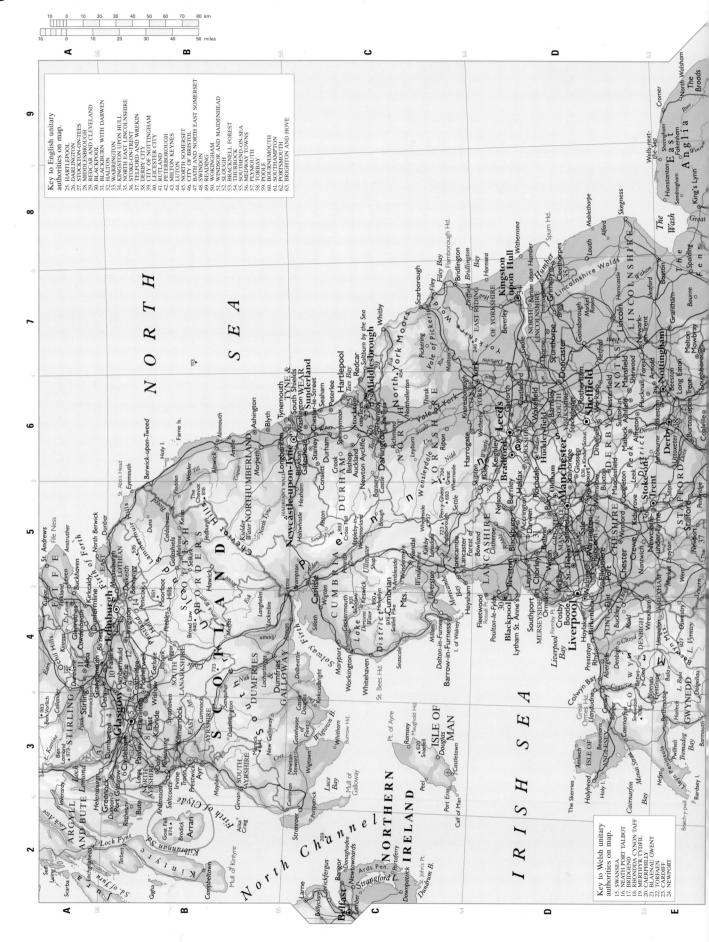

Key to English unitary authorities on map.

25. HARTLEPOOL
26. DARLINGTON
27. STOCKTON-ON-TEES
28. MIDDLESBROUGH
29. REDCAR AND CLEVELAND
30. BLACKPOOL
31. BLACKBURN WITH DARWEN
32. HALTON
33. WARRINGTON
34. KINGSTON UPON HULL
35. NORTH EAST LINCOLNSHIRE
36. STOKE-ON-TRENT
37. TELFORD AND WREKIN
38. DERBY CITY
39. CITY OF NOTTINGHAM
40. LEICESTER CITY
41. RUTLAND
42. PETERBOROUGH
43. MILTON KEYNES
44. LUTON
45. NORTH SOMERSET
46. CITY OF BRISTOL
47. BATH AND NORTH EAST SOMERSET
48. SWINDON
49. READING
50. WOKINGHAM
51. WINDSOR AND MAIDENHEAD
52. SLOUGH
53. BRACKNELL FOREST
54. THURROCK
55. SOUTHEND-ON-SEA
56. MEDWAY TOWNS
57. PLYMOUTH
58. TORBAY
59. POOLE
60. BOURNEMOUTH
61. SOUTHAMPTON
62. PORTSMOUTH
63. BRIGHTON AND HOVE

Key to Welsh unitary authorities on map.

15. SWANSEA
16. NEATH PORT TALBOT
17. BRIDGEND
18. RHONDDA CYNON TAFF
19. MERTHYR TYDFIL
20. CAERPHILLY
21. BLAENAU GWENT
22. TORFAEN
23. CARDIFF
24. NEWPORT

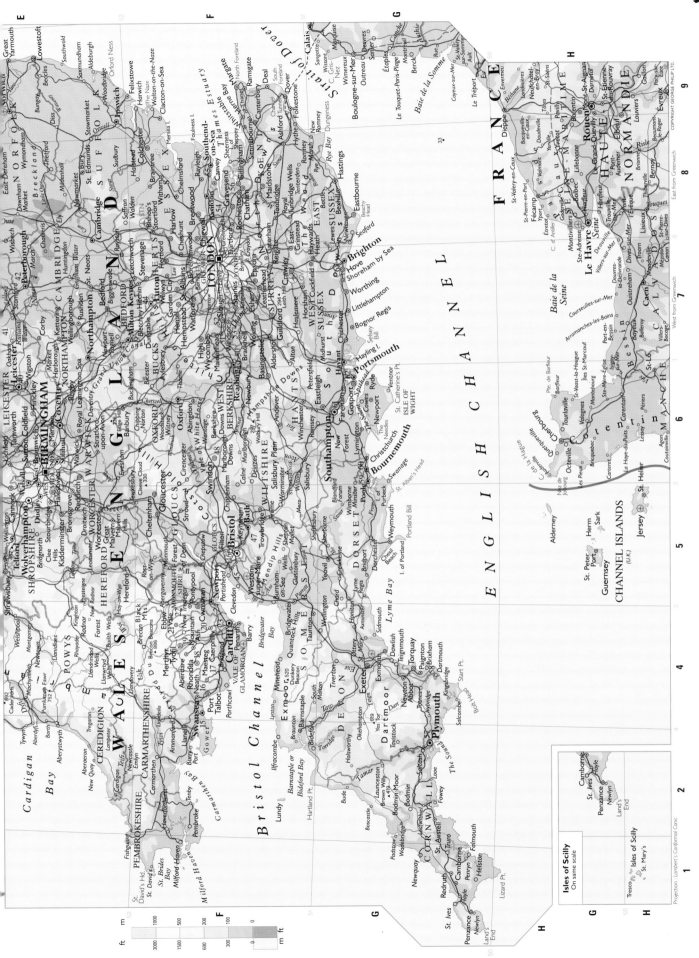

Projection: Conical with two standard parallels

West from Greenwich

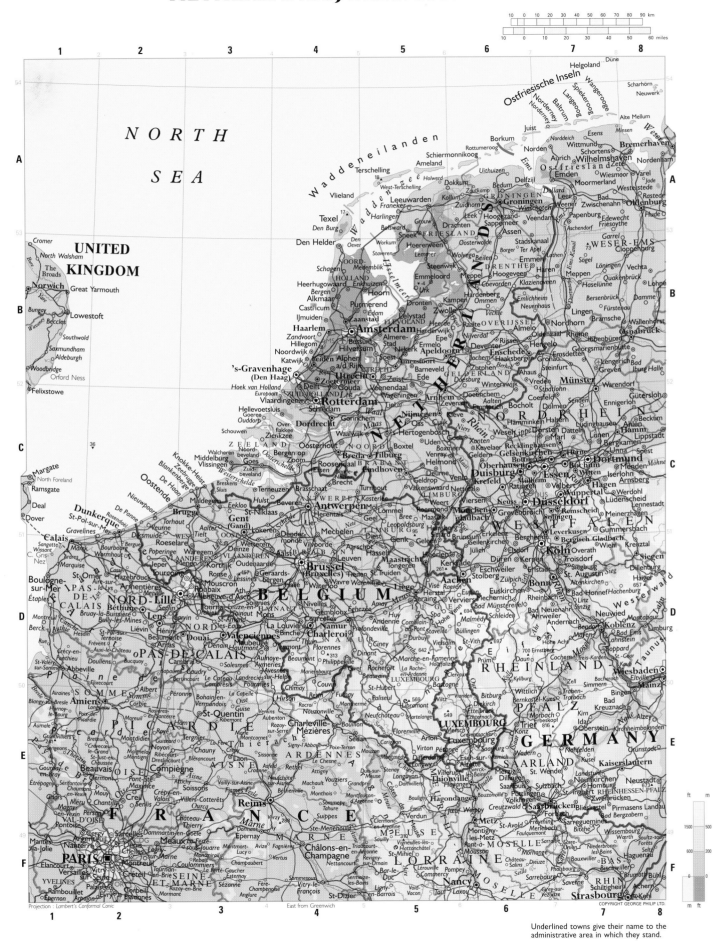

Projection : Lambert's Conformal Conic

East from Greenwich

COPYRIGHT GEORGE PHILIP LTD.

Underlined towns give their name to the
administrative area in which they stand.

Corse (Corsica)

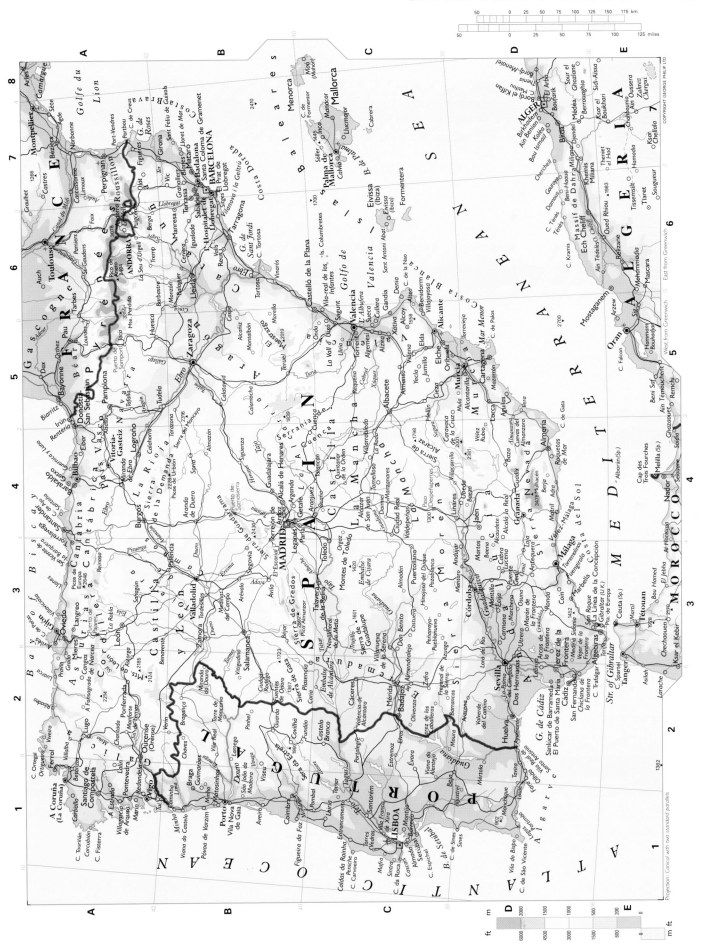

8   9   10   11   12   13

HUNGARY

Kaposvár   Kalocsa   Kiskőrös   Kiskunhalas   Oroszháza   Orosháza   Hódmezővásárhely Crişul Alb   Muntii Bihor   1848   Odorheiu Secuiesc   Miercurea Ciuc   Oneşti   Siret   Bârlad   Tatarbunary

Szekszárd   Makó   Brad   Abrud   Alba-Iulia   Târnăveni   Sighişoara   Sfântu Gheorghe   1783   Focşani   Vulcăneşti   Bolhrad   Kiliya   **UKRAINE**

Pécs   Baja   Szeged   Subotica   Arad   **R O M Â N I A**   Mediaş   Tecuci   Cahul   Reni   Izmail   Vylkove   Ozero Sasyk

Mohács   Sânnicolau Mare   Deva   Simeria   Sibiu   Făgăraş   Braşov   Vulcăneşti   Galaţi   B

Sombor   Bečej   Kikinda   Timişoara   Lugoj   1380   Hunedoara   Petroşani   Câmpulung   2543   2507   Râmnicu Sărat   Brăila   Sulina

Osijek   **Vojvodina**   Zrenjanin   Caransebeş   Vf. Peleaga 2509   Vulcan   2518   Parângul Mare   Vf. Omul   Câmpina   Buzău   Babadag

Vukovar   Novi Sad   Petrovaradin   Reşiţa   Porta Orientalis   Curtea de Argeş   Târgovişte   Ploieşti   Lacul Razelm

Slavonski Brod   Sremska Mitrovica   Pančevo   Bela Crkva   1226   Portile de Fier   Drobeta-Turnu-Severin   Drăgăşani   Piteşti   Slobozia   Dobruja

Doboj   Vinkovci   Zemun   (Dunav)   Orşova   **V**   Slatina   **BUCUREŞTI** (Bucharest)   Feteşti   Medgidia   Năvodari

Brčko   Bijeljina   Tuzla   Šabac   **BEOGRAD** (Belgrade)   Smederevo   Požarevac   Craiova   Roşiori-de-Vede   Olteniţa   Silistra   Constanţa

BOSNIA-   943   Zepče   Zenica   **YUGOSLAVIA**   1366   Negotin   Băileşti   Caracal   Turnu Măgurele   Alexandria   Giurgiu   Tutrakan   Mangalia

ZEGOVINA   2112   Travnik   Srebrenica   Valjevo   Kragujevac   Jagodina   Bor   Corabia   Zimnicea   Ruse   Dobrich   Balchik

Sarajevo   Han Pijesak   Užice   Čačak   Vidin   Lom   Oryakhovo   Svishtov   Razgrad   Nos Kaliakra

Konjic   Goražde   Višegrad   Kraljevo   Kruševac   Zaječar   Montana   Pleven   Shūmen   Varna   C

Mostar   1969   Plevlja   **SERBIA**   Niš   2168   Midžor   Vratsa   Lovech   Gorna Oryakhovitsa   Veliko Tūrnovo   Tūrgovishte

Stolac   2522   Durmitor   Novi Pazar   1833   2017   Prokuplje   Pirot   P. Dragoman   Teteven   Sevlievo   Gabrovo   Sliven   Aytos

Trebinje   Nikšić   Leskovac   1409   Suva Planina   2198   Vezhen   Shipchenski P.   1536   Burgas   **B L A C K**

Dubrovnik   **MONTENEGRO**   Kosovska Mitrovica   Priština   Vranje   Pernik   **SOFIYA**   Karlovo   Kazanlŭk   **BULGARIA**   Yambol   **S E A**

Herceg-Novi   Podgorica   Peć   Uroševac   Dūpnitsa   Samokov   Stara Zagora   Nova Zagora   Elkhovo   Michurin

Kotor   2693   Đakovica   **Kosovo**   Kumanovo   2252   Kyustendil   **Pazardzhik**   Dimitrovgrad   Nos Emine

1210   Skadarsko Jezero   Drin   Prizren   Plovdiv   Asenovgrad   Khaskovo   1018   İğneada Burnu

Bar   Shkodër   Kukës   Tetovo   Skopje   Kočani   Štip   Blagoevgrad   Kŭrdzhali   Kırklareli   Demirköy   İstanbul Boğazı (Bosporus)

Ulcinj   2925   Musala   **Rhodopi Planina**   Smilyan   Arda   Momchilgrad   Edirne   Pınarhisar   Saray   Kerkezköy

Peshkopi   2764   Solunska Glava 2540   Veles   Sandanski   2186   **Pirin Planina**   Zlatograd   Orestiás   Babaeski   Lüleburgaz   Çorlu   **İSTANBUL**   Kartal

Lezhë   Korab   Debar   Prilep   Strumica   Petrich   2031   Hayrabolu   Muratlı   Silivri   1220 Gebze   Darıca   D

Durrës   **Tiranë**   **MACEDONIA**   Valandovo   **M**   Xánthi   Komotini   **T**   Uzunköprü   Tekirdağ   Çerkezköy   Yalova   Orhangazi

Elbasan   Ohrid   Bitola   Préspansko Jezero   Dráma   Malkara   Marmara   Marmara Denizi (Sea of Marmara)   Gemlik   İznik Gölü

Shkumbin   Ohridsko Jezero   Florina   Kilkis   Kaválla   Ipsala   Keşan   Enez   Gelibolu   Lâpseki   Erdek   Bandırma   Mudanya   Bursa   2543

Lushnjë   Berat   Édhessa   Yiannitsá   Sérrai   Alexandroúpolis   Saros Körfezi   Éceabat   Çanakkale   Biga   Gönen   Karacabey   Uludağ   2543

Vlorë   Fier   Ptolemaïs   Véroia   Strimonikós Kólpos   1127   Thásos   Samothráki   (Dardanelles)   Çan   Yenice   Mustafakemalpaşa   Orhaneli

Vjosë   2520   Kastoria   Kozáni   **Thessaloniki**   Polyiros   Áthos 2033   Gökçeada   TROY   **M y s**   Balya   Dursunbey   Emet

Gjirokastër   Smólikas 2637   Kólpos   Thermaïkós Kólpos   Toroneos Kólpos   Ákra Pinnes   Moúdhros   Bozcaada   Ezine   Bayramiç   1766   Edremit   Balıkesir

Delvinë   Olimbos 2917 (Mt. Olympus)   Singitikós Kólpos   Ákra Palioúrion   Límnos   Baba Burnu   Ayvacık   Edremit Körfezi   Burhaniye   Bigadiç   Alaçam Dağları   2089   Simav

Mathráki   Óssa 1978   Ávios Evstrátios   Ayvalık   Bergama   Soma   Demirci   Simav   E

Kérkira (Corfu)   Ioánnina   Tírnavos   Lárisa   1280   **Lésvos**   Mitilíni   968   **TURKEY**   **Lydia**

Igoumenítsa   2469   Trikkala   **G**   Vólos   Vóriai Sporádhes   Alioğa   Akhisar   Manisa

Páxoi   Párga   Árta   Kardhítsa   Fársala   Pagastikós Kólpos   Skiathos   Skópelos   Skiros   Karaburun   Foça   Gediz   Menemen   Turgutlu   Salihli   Alaşehir   Eşme

Préveza   2315   Lamía   Istiaía   **Æ**   SARDIS   İZMİR (Smyrna)   Torbalı   Ödemiş   Sarıgöl

Levkás   Agrinion   Óros Gióna 2510   Thermopylae P.   Psará   Çeşme   Urla   **Boz Dağları**   1297   Seferihisar   Selçuk   Tire   Nazilli

1158   Mesolóngion   Párnassós 2457   Leváidhia   Khios   1297   Khios   EPHESUS   Aydın   Büyük Menderes   Sarayköy

Kefallinía   Ithåki   Návpaktos   1413   **Æ**   Kuşadası   İncirliova Karacasu   Buldan

Argostólion   1628   Patraïkós Kólpos   Korinthiakós Kólpos   Khalkís   Ákra Kafirévs   1398   Sámos   Söke   Çine   Bozdoğan

Pátrai   Aiyion   Killíni   **Mégara**   Akharnai   **ATHÍNAI (Athens)**   **Ándros**   MILETUS   Milas   Yatağan

Zákinthos   Zákinthos   Erimanthos   2224   Kórinthos   2376   **Piraiévs**   Salamís   Saronikós Kólpos   Kéa   Tínos   Andros   Güllük   Muğla   **C**   Kale

Amaliás   OLYMPIA   Árgos   Návplion   MYCENÆ   **Peloponnisos**   Ídhra   Kíthnos   Síros   Míkonos   Bodrum   Ören   Gölgeli Dağları

Pírgos   Tripolis   Argolikós Kólpos   **E**   Sérifos   Páros   Náxos   Patmos   Gökova Körfezi   Marmaris   Köyceğiz   Ortaca

Kiparissiakós Kólpos   Kiparissia   Filiatrá   Messini   Spárti   Sifnos   Náxos 1001   Ios   Amorgós   **Dhodhekánisos**   Kos   Datça   Bozburun

Pílos   Kalámai   Taíyetos Óros   Sérifos   Síkinos   Astipálaia   Kálimnos   Tilos   Sími   **Ródhos**

Messiniakós Kólpos   Lakonikós Kólpos   2407   Yíthion   Milos   Thíra   1215   Ródhos (Rhodes)   Líndhos

Ákra Ákritas   Ákra Maléa   Ákra Taínaron   Kíthira   **Kárpathos**   G

4070   Andikíthira   Ákra Spátha   1480   Kólpos Khanion   Kólpos Soúdhas   **Kríti**   Kólpos Mirabéllou   1215   Kásos

Khaniá   2453   Lévka Óri   Réthimnon   Iráklion   KNOSSOS   Ídhi Óros 2456   Dhíkti Óros 2148   Ákra Pláka   Sitía

Khóra Sfakíon   Ákra Lithínon   Ierápetra   Gávdhos

R A N E A N   S E A   **B L A C K   S E A**   **I O N I A N   S E A**   **Str. of Otranto**   **Iónioi Nísoi**

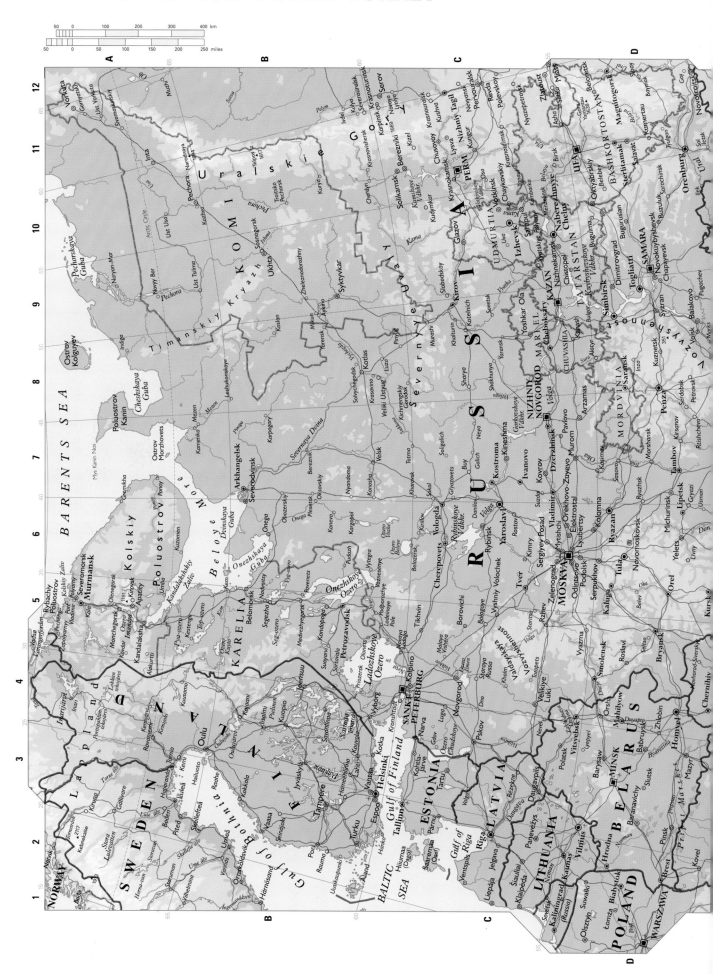

Projection: Conical with two standard parallels

East from Greenwich

CASPIAN SEA

BLACK SEA

MEDITERRANEAN SEA

Sea of Azov

KAZAKSTAN

Kirgiziy a Steppe

Caspian Depression

TURKMENISTAN

UKRAINE

MOLDOVA

ROMANIA

BULGARIA

CRIMEA

RUSSIA

Caucasus Mountains

GEORGIA

ABKHAZIA

ADJARIA

AZERBAIJAN

ARMENIA

DAGESTAN

CHECHENIA

KALMYKIA

NORTH OSSETIA

INGUSHETIA

KABARDINO-BALKARIA

KARACHEVO-CHERKESSIA

KAZAKSTAN

TURKEY

Anadolu

Kuzey Anadolu Dağları

Toros Dağları

Aladağ

SYRIA

LEBANON

CYPRUS

IRAQ

Kurdistan

IRAN

Zagros

Reshteh-ye Kühhā-ye Alborz

Dasht-e Kavir

TEHRĀN

BAYRŪT

DIMASHQ

TBILISI

YEREVAN

BAKI

VOLGOGRAD

ROSTOV

DONETSK

KHARKIV

DNIPROPETROVSK

KYYIV

ODESA

CHIŞINĂU

BUCUREŞTI

İSTANBUL

ANKARA

KONYA

ADANA

TABRĪZ

Black Sea

Mediterranean Sea

ft
12 000
9000
6000
4500
3000
1500
0

m
4000
3000
2000
1500
1000
500
200
0

RUSSIA
1 Adygea
2 Karachey-Cherkessia
3 Kabardino-Balkaria
4 North Ossetia
5 Ingushetia
6 Chechenia
7 Dagestan
8 Mordvinia
9 Chuvashia
10 Mari El
11 Tatarstan
12 Udmurtia
13 Khakassia

AZERBAIJAN
14 Naxçıvan

GEORGIA   **UKRAINE**
15 Ajaria   17 Crimea
16 Abkhazia

Projection: Conical Orthomorphic with two standard parallels

East from Greenwich

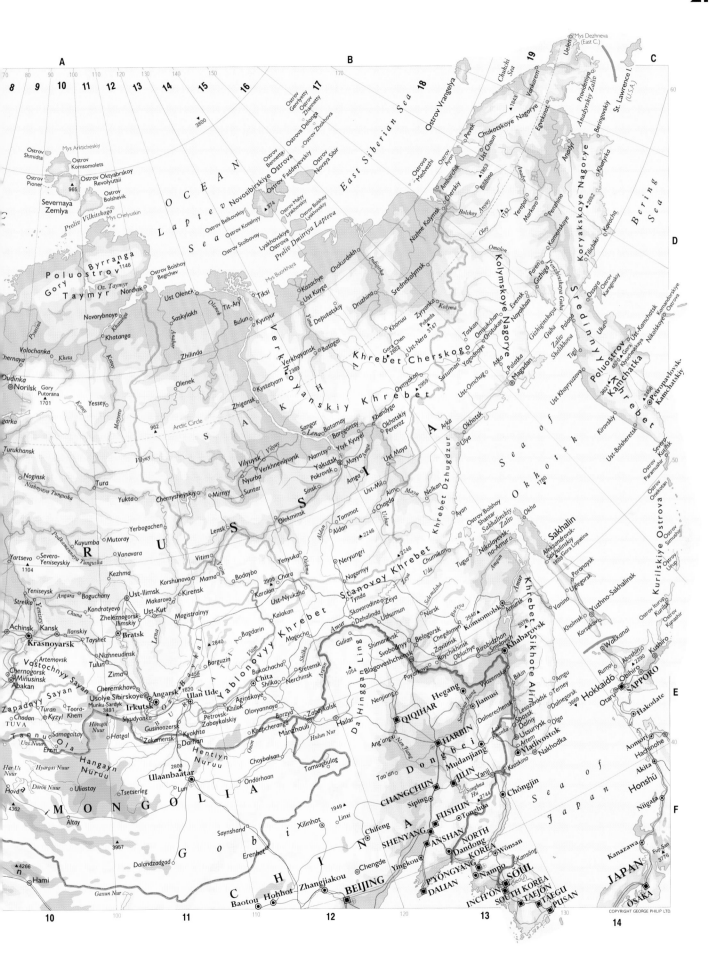

JAPAN

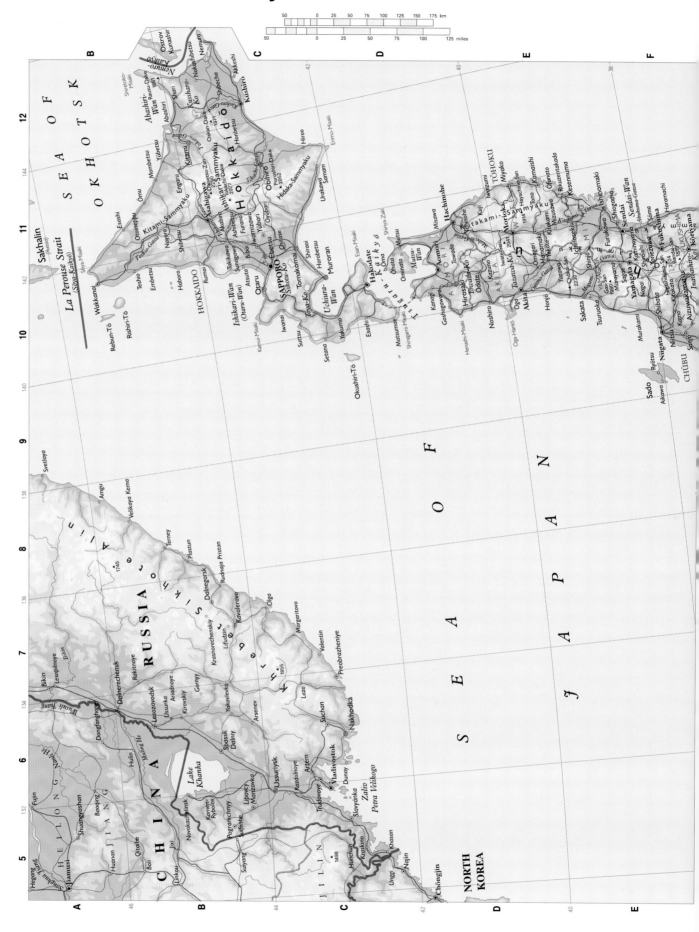

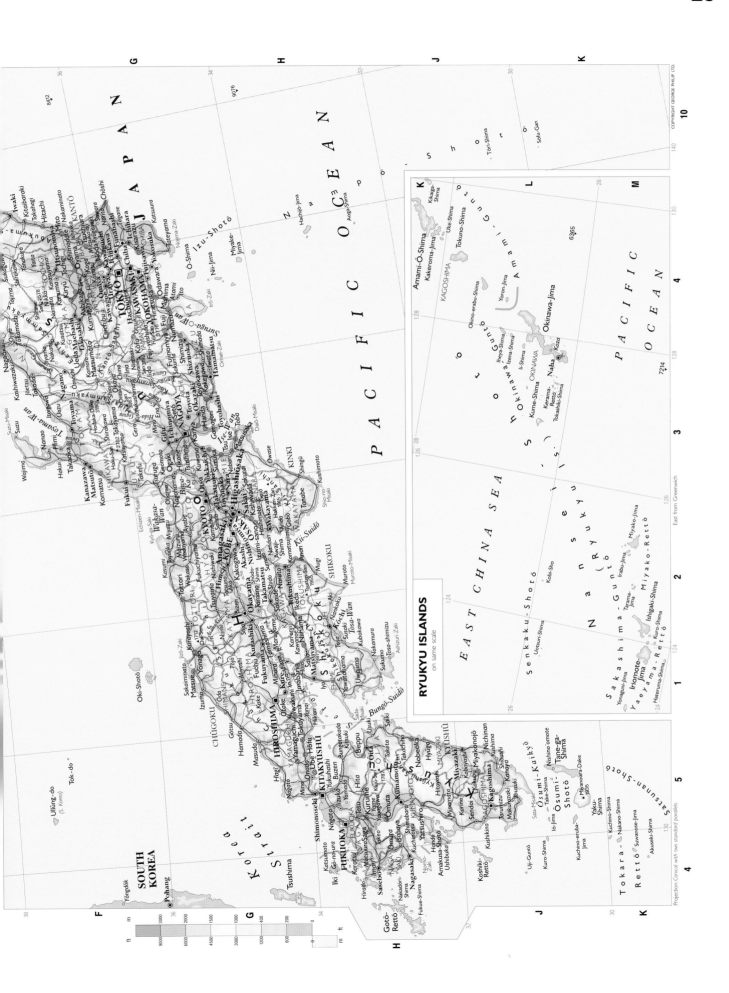

JAPAN

RYUKYU ISLANDS
on same scale

PACIFIC OCEAN

EAST CHINA SEA

SOUTH KOREA

Korea Strait

Nansyukyu-Guntō (RYUKYU)

Sakashima-Guntō

Projection: Conical with two standard parallels

East from Greenwich

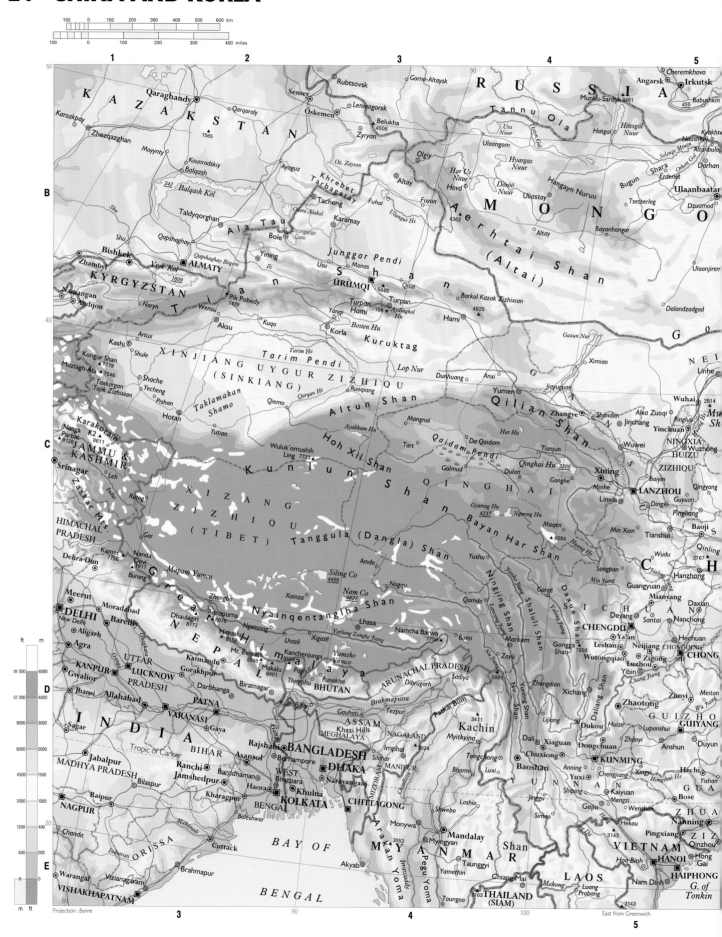

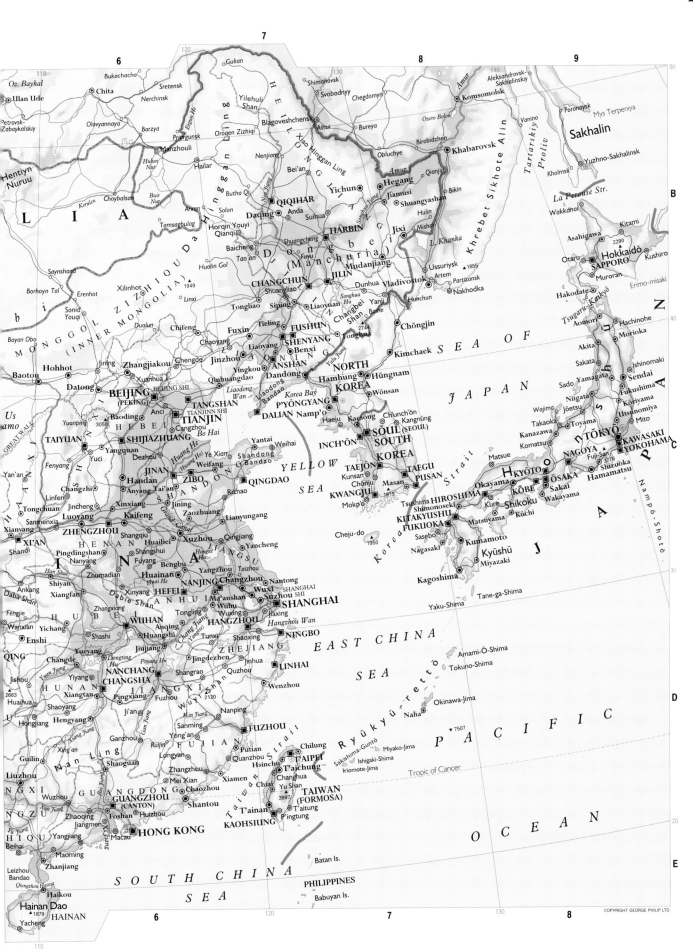

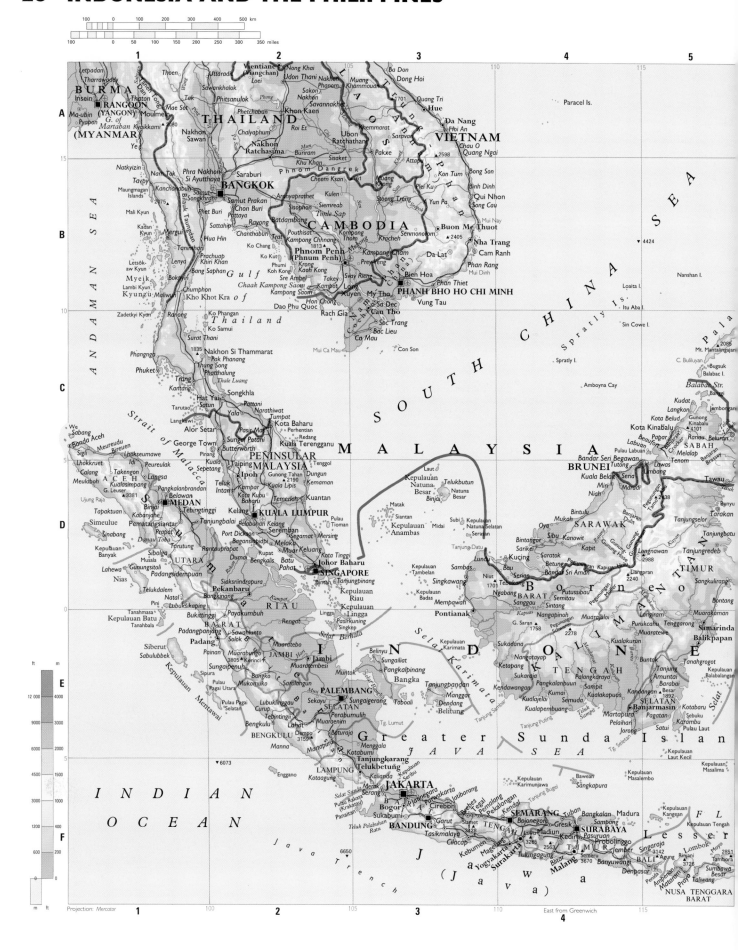

Projection: Mercator

East from Greenwich

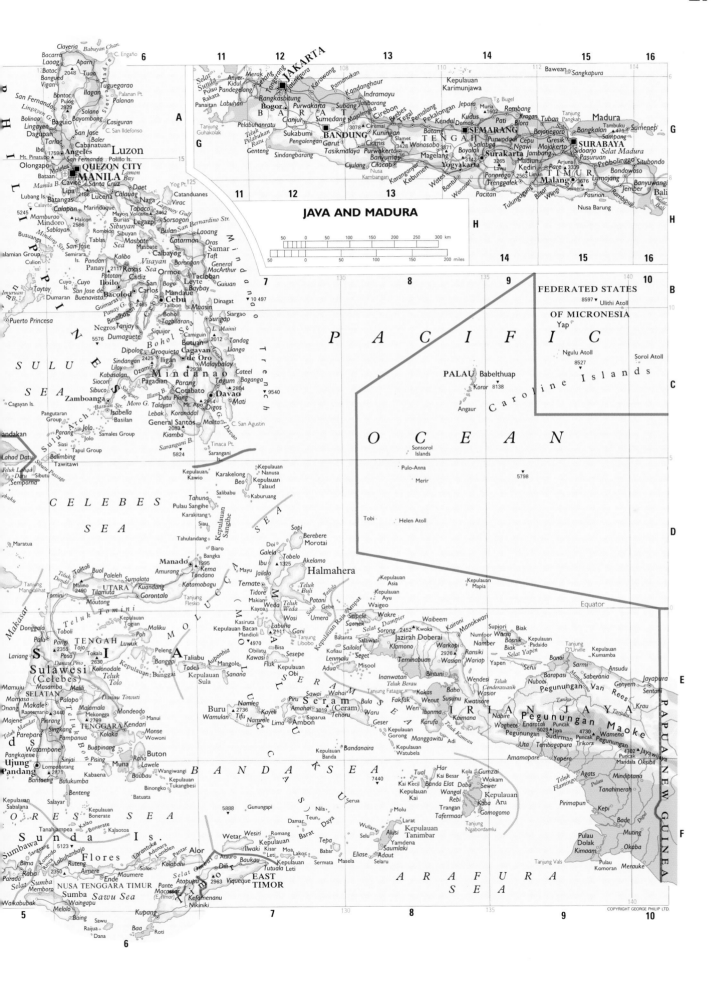

JAVA AND MADURA

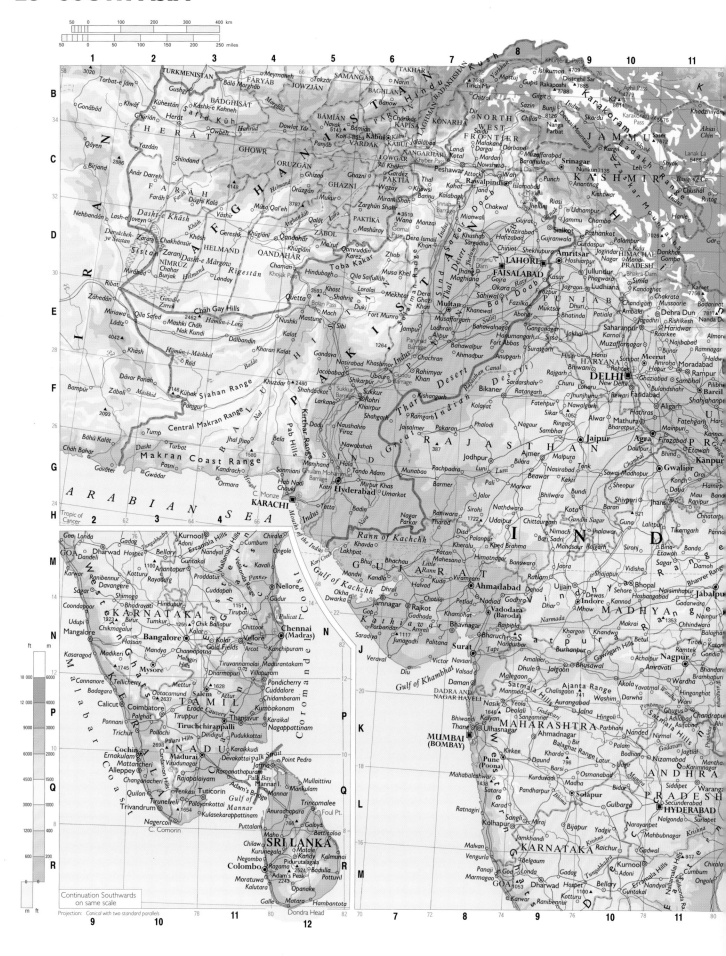

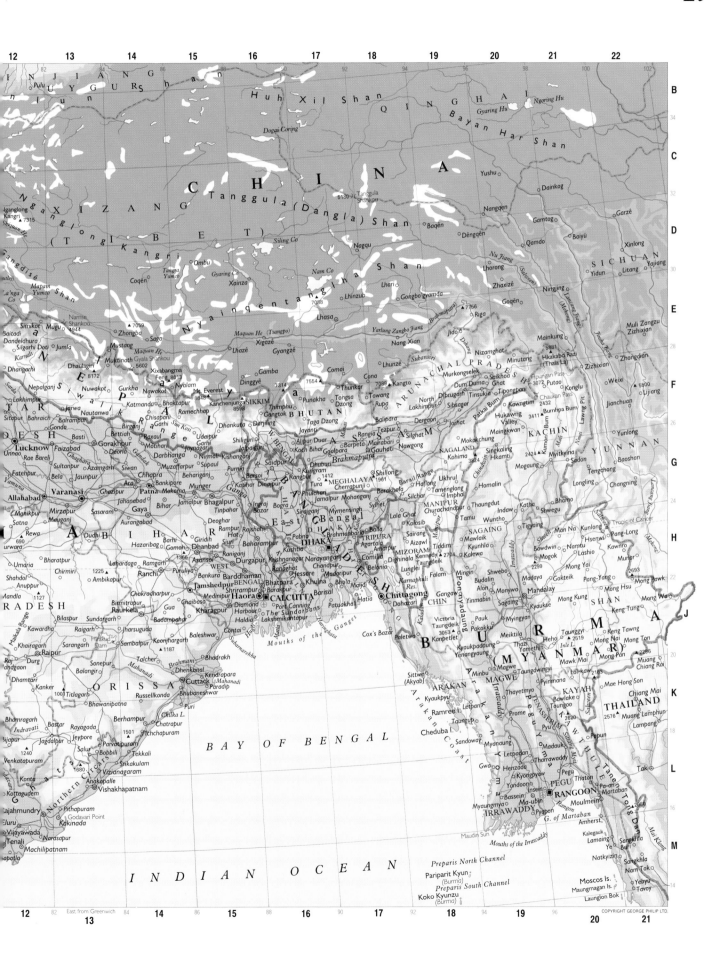

XIN JIANG
UYGUR Shan
Pulu
Hun
Huh Xil Shan
QINGHAI
Gyaring Hu
Ngoring Hu
Dogai Coring
Bayan Har Shan
Yushu
Dainkog
C H I N A
Gamtog
Garzê
Tanggula (Dangla) Shan
Nangqen
Baiyü
X I Z A N G
Tangula Shankou
Dênggên
Xinlong
Iganglong
Kangri
Shiquan He
Tangra
Qamdo
SICHUAN
Siling Co
Nagqu
Qamdo
Yidun
Litang
Yajiang
Ombu
Gangdisê
Nam Co
Nyainqentanglha Shan
Lhorong
Ningjing
Mapam
Yumco Shan
Coqên
Xainza
Gyaring Co
Lhari
Gongbo gyamda
Zhaxizê
Gogên
Muli Zangzu
Zizhixian
La'nga
Co
Namse
Shankou
Zhongba
Saga
Lhasa
Xigazê
Lhazê
Gyangzê
Gamba
Yarlung Zangbo Jiang
Riga
Mainkung
Zhongdian
Simikot
Mugu
7059
1944
Maquan He (Tsangpo)
Nang Xian
5881
Weixi
Baitadi
Dandeldhura
Zhongba
Mustang
Dinggyê
Comai
Cona
7088 Kangto
Murkongselek
Nizamghat
Hkakabo Razi
(Thala La)
5900
Lijiang
Silgarhi Doti
Jumla
Nepalganj
Muktinath Gyala Shankou
5602
Xixabangma
Feng, 8013
Nyalam
7314
7554
Thunkar
Towang
Tongsa
ARUNACHAL PRADESH
Putao
Konglu
Zizhixian
Jianchuan
Dhaulagiri 8172
Mt. Everest
8848
Kangto
Rupa
North
Lakhimpur
Dibrugarh
Tinsukia
Tipongpani
Hpungan Pass
3072 Putao
Kawngtim
2432
Yunlong
NEPAL
Nuwakot
Gurkha
Kanchenjunga
8598
SIKKIM
Punakha
Taga Dzong
Sibsagar
Parkai Bum
Bumhpa Bum
Baoshan
Katmandu
Bhaktapur
Gangtok
BHUTAN
Tezpur
Jorhat
Hukawng
Valley
3411 Tengchong
Lokhimpur
Jarwa
Nautanwa
Ramechhap
Darjiling
Alipur Duar
Koch Bihar
Rangia
Silghat
Dergaon
Mokokchung
Maingkwan
KACHIN
Myitkyina
Sadon
Yunlong
Nepalganj
Jayanti
Jalpaiguri
Goalpara
Gauhati
Nowgong
NAGALAND
Singkaling
Hkamti
2424 Kumon Bum
Mogaung
Longling
Changning
TAR
Sitapur
Bahraich
Gonda
Basti
Gorakhpur
Faizabad
Bettiah
Raxaul
Motihari
Garhi
Udaipur
Dhankuta
Shiliguri
W. BENGAL
Jolpaiguri
Dhubri
Barpeta
Mairabari
A S S A M
Kohima
3824 Chindwin
Mogok
Shwegu
Bhamo
Longling
DESH
Lucknow
Rae Bareli
Jaunpur
Chhapra
Siwan
Muzaffarpur
Supaul
Purnia
Saidpur
Rangpur
Katihar
Dinajpur
MEGHALAYA
Cherrapunji
1961
Ukhrul
Tamenglong
Imphal
MANIPUR
Homalin
Indaw
Katha
Shwegu
Tigyaing
Mong Yai
Sadon
Munar
Mong Pawk
Fatehpur
Allahabad
Varanasi
Ghazipur
Patna
Mokama
Bihar
Jamalpur Bhagalpur
Tinpahar
Ingraj
Bazar
Bogra
Siraganj
Phulchari
Barkhola
Barail Range
Haflong
Silchar
Churachandpur
Thaungdut
Tamu
Wuntho
Mingin
Shwebo
Budalin
Alon
Madaya
Gokteik
Mong Yai
2693
Manikpur
Mirzapur
Satna
Rewa
Gaya
Jahanabad
Aurangabad
Deoghar
Barhi
Rampur
Hat
Rajshahi
Pabna
Brahmanbaria
Balla
BANGLADESH
Sylhet
TRIPURA
Agartala
Lala Ghat
Kolosib
Aizawl
Sairang
Tiddim
Kennedy 2704
Falam
Mawlaik
Kyunhla
Kalewa
Bowdwin
Namtu
Lashio
Kawnro
Mandalay
Urwara
Dudhi
B I H A R
Giridih
Gomoh
Dhanbad
Hazaribag
1366
Asansol
Raniganj
Durgapur
DHAKA
Kushtia
Narayanganj
Chandpur
Comilla
Belonia
MIZORAM
Dighinala
Lunglei
2299
Mingin
Monywa
Sagaing
Kyaukse
Mong Kung
Kawng
Keng Tung
Mong Hsu
Mong Wa
690
Rewa
Umaria
Bharatpur
Lohardaga
Ramgarh
1225
Ranchi
Puruliya
Bankura
WEST
Barddhaman
Bhatpara
Barrackpur
Jessore
Khulna
Madaripur
Bhola
Barisal
Maijdi
Hatia
CHIN
Pakokku
Myingyan
Meiktila
Thazi
Inle L.
2183
Mong Pan
Mong Ton
Muang
Chiang Rai
Shahdol
Anuppur
Ambikapur
Chakradharpur
Jamshedpur
BENGAL
Medinipur
Haora
CALCUTTA
Port Canning
Diamond
Harbour
Barisal
Patuakhali
Chittagong
Dohazari
Gangaw
Pauk
Kanpetlet
3053
Victoria
Taungdeik
Heho
Taunggyi 2519
Keng Tawng
Mong Nai
Mandla 1127
RADESH
Bilaspur
Raurkela
Gua
Chaibasa
Kharagpur
Shrirampur
Haldia
Lakshmikantapur
The Sundarbans
Cox's Bazar
Paletwa
Yenangyaung
Yamethin
Pyinmana
Loikaw
KAYAH
2576
Chiang Mai
Mong Pan
Khairagarh
Raipur
Durg
Bhawanipatna
Raigarh
Sarangarh
Sambalpur
1187
Keonjhargarh
Baleshwar
Contai
Mouths of the Ganges
Sittwe
(Akyab)
ARAKAN
Kyaukpyu
Minbu
Magwe
MAGWE
Taungdwingyi
Prome
Thayetmyo
KAYAH
Toungoo
2620
THAILAND
Muang Lamphun
Lampang
Raj
andgaon
Dhamtari
Kanker
Titlagarh 1001
Balangir
Sonepur
Talcher
Dhenkanal
Bhadrakh
ORISSA
Russellkonda
Puri
Bhubaneswar
Cuttack
Kendrapara
Paradip
Mahanadi
Brahmani
Chilka L.
Chatrapur
Berhampur
BAY OF BENGAL
Ramree I.
Cheduba I.
Sandoway
Myanaung
Letpadan
ARAKAN
YOMA
Taungup
Arakan Coast
Gwa
Henzada
Kyongpyau
Yandoon
Bassein
Ma-ubin
Pyapon
Tharrawaddy
PEGU
Pegu
Insein
RANGOON
Thaton
Martaban
Moulmein
TENASSERIM
Amherst
Madauk
Bhamragarh
Indravati
Bastar
Rayagada
Jeypore
Parvatipuram
Bobbili
Srikakulam
Vizianagaram
1240
Salur
Jagdalpur
1680
Konta
Anakapalle
Vishakhapatnam
Northern Circars
IRRAWADDY
Myaungmya
Mouths of the Irrawaddy
Maudin Sun
G. of Martaban
Kalegauk
Lamaing
Ye
Sangkla Buri
Sangkhla
Nam Tok
Bijapur
Venkatapuram
Pithapuram
Kottagudem
Rajahmundry
Godavari Point
Kakinada
INDIAN OCEAN
Preparis North Channel
Pariparit Kyun
(Burma)
Preparis South Channel
Koko Kyunzu
(Burma)
Moscos Is.
Maungmagan Is.
Launglon Bok
Yebyu
Tavoy
Eluru
Vijayawada
Tenali
Machilipatnam

East from Greenwich
COPYRIGHT GEORGE PHILIP LTD.

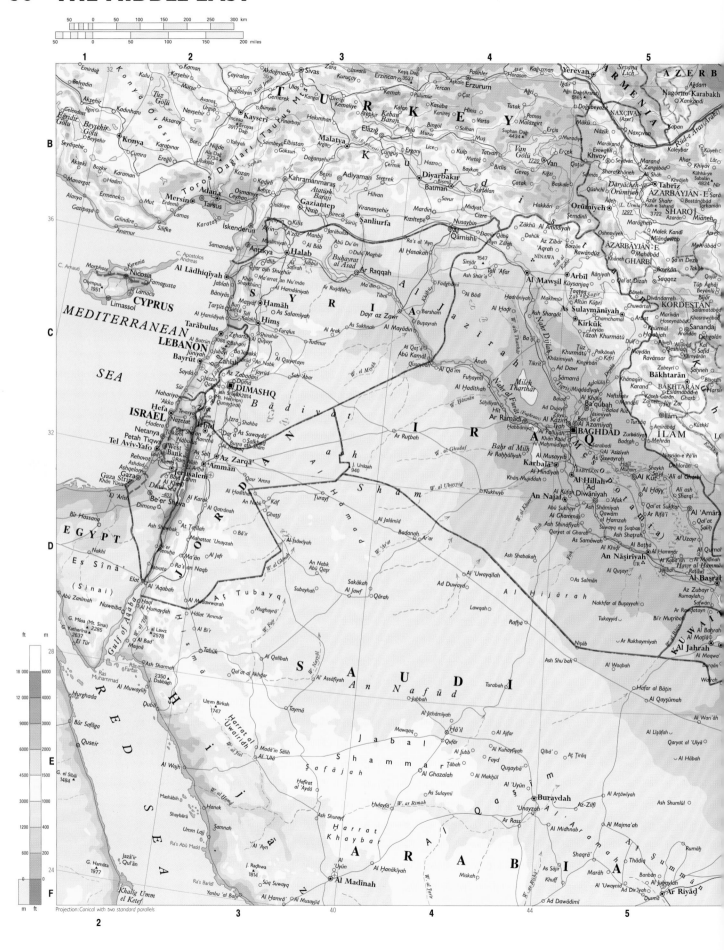

Projection: Conical with two standard parallels

CASPIAN SEA

TURKMENISTAN

Kara Kum

Kopet Dagh

Ashgabat

Mary

BAKİ

Rasht

GILAN

MAZANDARAN

TEHRĀN

MARKAZİ

SEMNĀN

KHORĀSĀN

HERĀT

AFGHANISTAN

FARĀH

HAMADĀN

Qom

Mashhad

Neyshābūr
Sabzevār

I R Ā N

ESFAHĀN

YAZD

Yazd

Kermān

KERMĀN

PAKISTAN

Zāhedān

KHUZESTĀN

CHAHĀR MAHĀLL
VA BAKHTIĀRİ

KOHKILŪYEH
VA
BUYER AHMADİ

Ahvāz

FARS

Shīrāz

BUSHEHR

SĪSTĀN
VA BALŪCHESTĀN

Al Kuwayt

BAHRAIN

Manāmah

QATAR

THE GULF

HORMOZGĀN

Bandar 'Abbās

Kūhhā-ye Bashākerd

Gulf of Oman

Dubayy

Abū Zāby

OMAN

UNITED ARAB EMIRATES

East from Greenwich

COPYRIGHT GEORGE PHILIP LTD.

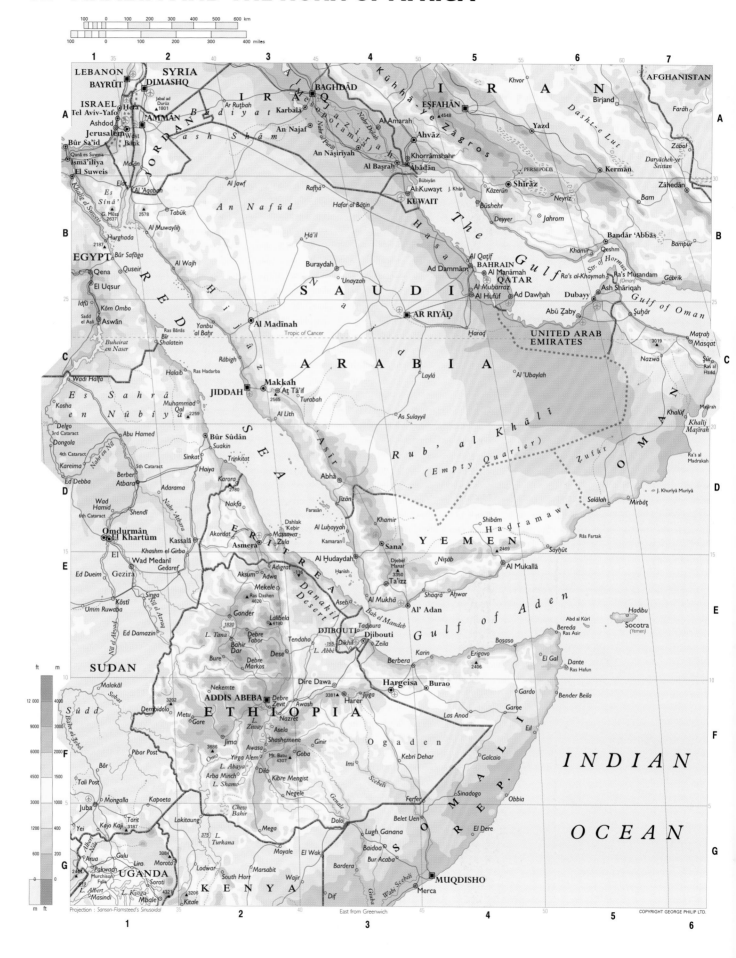

Projection : Sanson-Flamsteed's Sinusoidal East from Greenwich

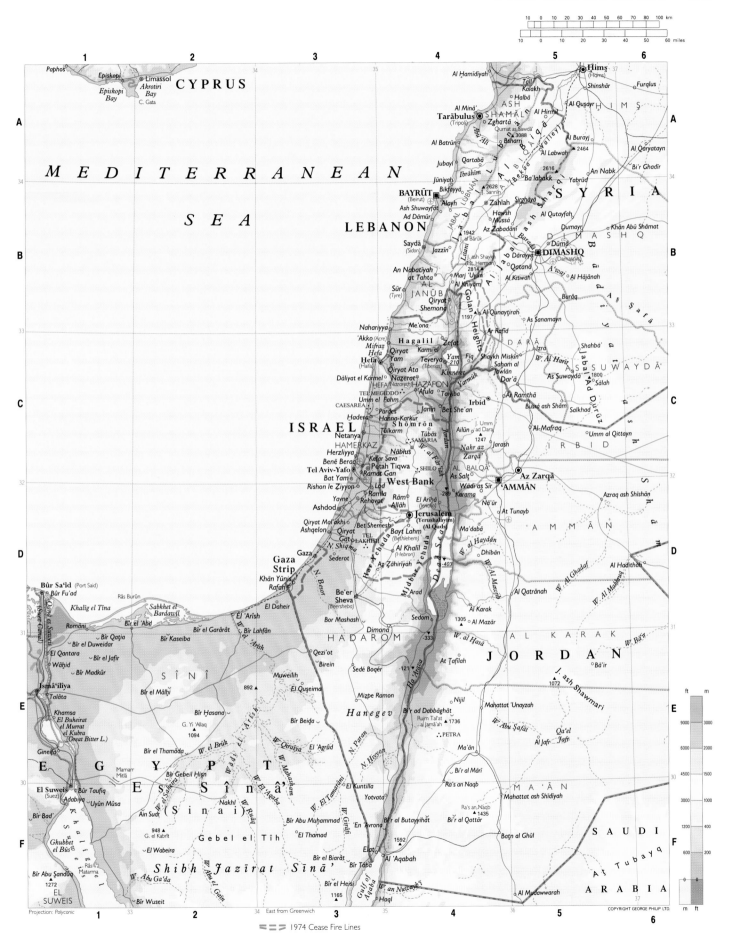

10 0 10 20 30 40 50 60 70 80 100 km
10 0 10 20 30 40 50 60 miles

1   **2**   **3**   **4**   **5**   **6**

Paphos
Episkopi
Episkopi
Bay   Limassol
Akrotiri   Akrotiri
Bay   C. Gata

CYPRUS

A

Al Hamidiyah
Al Mina'
Tarābulus
(Tripoli)   Zgharta
Al Batrūn   Qurnat as Sawdā'
               3088
Jubayl   Bsharri
Qartabā
Ibrāhīm

Tāll
Kalakh   Hims
Halbā   (Homs)
            Shinshār   Furqlus
Al Hirmil
Al Qusayr
            2464   Al Qaryatayn
Al Labwah   Bi'r Ghadīr
An Nabk

ASH SHAMĀL

HIMS

MEDITERRANEAN

BAYRŪT
(Beirut)   Bikfayyā
Jūniyah   2628 Sannīn
Alayh   Zahlah
Ash Shuwayfāt Sirghāyā
Ad Dāmūr   Hawsh
               Mūssā   Al Qutayfah
1942   Az Zabadānī
al Bārūk

2616
Ba'labakk   Yabrūd

SYRIA

Dumayr   Khān Abū Shāmat

Dūmā
DIMASHQ
(Damascus)
Dārayyā
A'waj   Al Hājānah

LEBANON

JABAL LUBNĀN

DIMASHQ

SEA

B

Saydā
(Sidon)   Jazzīn
An Nabatīyah
at Tahta   Marj 'Uyūn
Sūr   Al Khiyām
(Tyre)   2814
Qiryat   ash Shaykh (Mt. Hermon)
Shemona   1197

AL JANŪB

Al Kiswah
Qatanā
Burāq   As Safā

Golan Heights

Al Qunaytirah
Ar Rafīd   As Sanamayn

DARʿĀ

Shahbā'   1800
             Sālah
As Suwaydā'
Dar'ā

AD DURŪZ

AS SUWAYDĀ'

33

Nahariyyā
Me'ona   Izra
'Akko (Acre)
Mifraz   Karmi'el
Hefa   Qiryat   Yam
Hefa   Yam   Teverya   Fiq   Shaykh Miskīn
(Haifa)   Qiryat Ata (Tiberias) Saham al
Dāliyat el Karmel   Kinneret Jawlān
             Nazerat   Yarmūk Dar'ā
TEL MEGIDDO (Nazareth) Taiyiba
Umm el Fahm Afula
             Bet She'an

Hagalil

Zefat

-210 Yam

Būsrá ash Shām
Salkhad

Jabal ad Durūz

Al-Mafraq
Umm al Qittayn

HAZAFON

IRBID

C

CAESAREA
Hadera   Jenin
Pardes   Shōmrōn
Hanna-Karkur
Netanya   Tulkarm
             Tūbās
             SAMARIA
Herzliyya   Nāblus
Benē Beraq
Kefar Sava   SHILO
Petah Tiqwa
Tel Aviv-Yafo Ramat Gan
Bat Yam   West Bank
Rishon le Ziyyon
             Rām
Yavne   Allāh
Rehovot
Ashdod   El Arīhā
             (Jericho)

ISRAEL

HAMERKAZ

Ailūn   1247
Bet She'an   Nahr az
             Zarqā'   Jarash
AL BALQĀ'
Wadi as Sīr **AMMĀN**
             Az Zarqā
Karama
-289
Na'ūr   Azraq ash Shīshān
At Tunayb

'AMMĀN

Sahh

D

Qiryat Mal'akhi
Ashqelon   Bet Shemesh
Qiryat   Bayt Lahm
Gat   (Bethlehem)
TEL LAKHISH
N. Shiqma   Al Khalīl
             (Hebron)
Gaza   Sederot
Gaza
Strip
Khān Yūnis   Az Zāhirīyah
Rafah   Arad

Ma'dabā   Al Haydān
             Dhibān
Sedom
             W. al Mūjib
1305   Al Hadītha
Al Mazār
             Al Qatrānah

Har Yehuda

Mijbar Yehuda

-403 Dead Sea

Bûr Sa'īd (Port Said)
Bûr Fu'ad
             Rās Burūn
Khalig el Tīna
Sabkhet el   El 'Arīsh
Bardawîl
Romāni   Bîr el 'Abd
Bîr el Garârât
Bîr Qatia   Bîr Lahfān
Bîr el Duweidar
El Qantara   Bîr Kaseiba
Wâhid   Bîr el Jafîr
Bîr Madkûr

Be'er
Sheva
(Beersheba)
             El Daheir
Bor Mashash

HADAROM

-333
Sedom

Al Karak   W. al Hasā
             JORDAN
             Bā'ir

AL KARAK

W. Bā'ir

EGYPT

Ismâ'ilîya
Talâta
Khamsa   892
El Buheirat
el Murrat
el Kubra
(Great Bitter L.)
Gineifa

SÎNÎ

Bîr el Mâlhi
Muweilih
El Quşeima
Birein
Qezi'ot   Sedé Boqér
Mizpe Ramon

Dimona   1305
-121
At Tafīlah

Mahattat 'Unayzah

MA'ĀN

E

1094
G. Yi 'Allaq

Bîr Hasana
Bîr Beiqa
             Bîr el 'Arîsh
Wâdi el   W. Qraîya   El 'Agrûd
Brûk
             Hanegev
Be'er ad Dabbâghât
Rujm Tal'at   1736
al Jamâ'ah
             PETRA
Ma'ān

Al Jafr   Qa'el
             Jafr

W. Abu Safât

9000 3000
6000 2000
4500 1500
3000 1000
1200   400
600   200

El Suweis
(Suez)   Bûr Taufiq
Adabiya   Uyûn Mûsa
Bîr Bad'

Ain Sudr   948
             G. el Kabrît
             El Wabeira
Nakhl
W. el Aqaba

Gebel el Tîh

N. Paran
N. Hiyyon
'En 'Avrona
             Yotvata
El Kuntilla
Ra's an Naqb 1435
Bi'r al Butayyihât
Bi'r al Qattâr

Mahattat ash Shidîyah

SAUDI

F

Ghubbet
el Bûs
Bîr Abu Sandûq
1272
EL
SUWEIS
Bîr Wuseit

Shibh Jazîrat Sînâ'

Bîr el Biarât
             El Thamad
W. Abu Ga'da Bîr el Heisi
             1165
Elat
Al 'Aqabah
Haql
Gulf of Aqaba
W. an Nuwayb

1592
Batn al Ghûl

Al Mudawwarah

At Tubayq

ARABIA

m **ft**

═══ 1974 Cease Fire Lines

100 0 100 200 300 400 500 600 km
100 0 100 200 300 400 miles

| | 1 | | 20 | | 2 | | 15 | | 3 | | | 10 | | 4 | | | 5 | | | 5 | | | 6 | | 7 |

A

A T L A N T I C

Azores *(Port.)*

SPAIN
Cabo de São Vicente
Cádiz
Málaga Almería
Str. of Gibraltar Gibraltar *(U.K.)*
Ceuta *(Sp.)* Al Hoceïma Melilla *(Sp.)*
Tanger Tétouan Mostaganem
Ksar el Kebir Ouezzane Nador
Kenitra Taza
Salé Fès
Rabat Meknès Khémisset
Mohammedia
CASABLANCA
El Jadida Settat Khouribga
Ras Beddouza Safi
Marrakech Beni Mellal Atlas
Essaouira MOROCCO
C. Rhir Dj. Toubkal 4165
Agadir Taroudannt Ouarzazate Ar Rachidiya
2359 Anti Atlas
Ifni Goulimine
Tan-tan

O C E A N

Madeira *(Port.)* Funchal
Porto Santo

B

35

ALGER Tizi-Ouzou Skikda Annaba
Ech Cheliff Blida Bejaia
Oran Mascara Médéa M'sila Sétif Constantine
Sidi-bel-Abbès Tlemcen Batna 2328 Tébessa Khenchela
Oujda Mecheria Chott ech Chergui Djelfa Aflou Messad Laghouat Chott Melrhir Tozeur Chott Djérid
Bouârfa Ain-Sefra El Bayadh Berriane El Oued
Béchar Ghardaïa Ouargla Touggourt
Abadla 2235 El Goléa Hassi Messaoud
Figuig Grand Erg Occidental Grand Erg Oriental
Kerzaz Timimoun Ohanet
Plateau du Tademaït Bordj Omar Driss
In Salah Illizi
Bordj Fly Ste. Marie Arak Tassili n' Ajjer 2158
Zaouiet Reggane Djanet
Ouallene
Bordj-in-Eker
Tanezrouft A h a g g a r Tahat 2918
Tamanrasset

M a g h r e b

A L G E R I A

S a h a r a

C

30

Islas Canarias *(Sp.)*
La Palma Lanzarote
Santa Cruz de Tenerife Arrecife
Gomera 3718 Las Palmas Fuerteventura
Hierro Tenerife Gran Canaria
C. Juby Tarfaya
El Aaiún
Bu Craa Smara
C. Bojador
WESTERN

Bir Moghreïn

SAHARA

Dakhla

D

Tropic of Cancer

Ras Nouâdhibou Nouâdhibou
Atâr Chinguetti
Zouîrât
Fdérik
Adrar

MAURITANIA
Akjoujt
Ras Timirist
Rachid Tidjikja
Nouakchott
Aleg Aoukâr
Rosso Kaédi Kiffa
St. Louis Dagana 'Ayoûn el 'Atroûs Néma
Mboro Louga Linguère Nioro du Sahel
Louga Matam Sélibabi Nara
C. Thiès Tivaouane
Vert Bakel
DAKAR SENEGAL
Kaolack Bafoulabé
Banjul GAMBIA Georgetown Kayes
Sédhiou Tambacounda
Ziguinchor GUINEA Satadougou
BISSAU Fouta
Bissau Djalon Siguiri
Arq. dos Gaoual Labé
Bijagós Dalaba
C. Verga GUINEA Kankan
Dubréka Mamou Faranah Fabala
Kindia Dabola
Conakry Kabala 1948 Kissidougou
Port Loko SIERRA Kindia
Freetown LEONE Faranah
Yonibana Koidu Bo Kenema
Sherbro I. Bonthe Kailahun
Sulima Zimmi
Monrovia Buchanan
LIBERIA Tapeta
Grain River Cess Coast
Harper C. Palmas Tabou

S a h e l

Tessalit Adrar 598
des Iforas
Kidal
Arlit Iférouâne
Aïr 1900
I-n-Gall Agadez
Téné...
N I G E R

M a l i

Tombouctou Bourem
Niger Gao
Hombori Ansongo Ménaka
Famalé Tahoua Tanout
Mopti Filingué Birni Nkonni Zinder
Diafarabé Dori Niamey Sokoto Maradi Katsina
Ségou Kaya Tougan Botou Dosso Birnin Kebbi Gusau Gumel Hadejia
San BURKINA Gaya Jega Funtua Kano Azare
Bamako Ouagadougou FASO Bena Zaria
Koudougou Fada-n-Gourma Kandi Shanga Kontagora Kaduna Bauchi
Bougouni Bobo-Dioulasso Bawku Dapaong Mango Bembéréké Minna Jos NIGERIA Shendam
Sikasso Gaoua Tumu Natitingou Parakou Kainji Abuja Kafanchan
Tingréla Savelugu Salaga Savalou Res. Keffi Lafia
Odienné Korhogo Bouna Tamale Sokodé Bida Baro Makurdi Wukari
Boundiali Ferkéssédougou Kong Wenchi Benue
Séguéla Kong Koro Oyo Ogbomosho Offa Lokoja Oturkpo
Man Katiola GHANA Lake Ilorin Iwo Ilesha Ife Owo Benin
Danané Bouaflé Volta Oshogbo Akure City Enugu Bamenda
IVORY L. de Berekum Abengourou Kumasi Kibi IBADAN Ijebu-Ode Bafoussam
Nzérékoré Kossou Bouaké Obuasi Asamankese Koforidua Abeokuta LAGOS Benin Onitsha
Ganta COAST Daloa Gagnoa Agboville Koforidua Lomé Cotonou Porto-Novo Sapele CAMEROON
Sanniquellie Gagnoa Divo Grand Accra Slave Warri Aba Uyo
Yamoussoukro Lakota Bassam Sekondi-Takoradi Coast Buruti Calabar Kumba
ABIDJAN Sassandra C. Three Points Bight of Port Harcourt Mt. Cameroun 4070 Limbe Dou...
Axim Gold Benin Rey Malabo Bioko 2850

E

25

F

15

G

10

H

5

ft m
12 000 4000
9000 3000
6000 2000
4500 1500
3000 1000
1200 400
600 200
0
m ft

Projection : Sanson-Flamsteed's Sinusoidal

West from Greenwich East from Greenwich

| 3 | | 10 | | 4 | | 5 | 5 | | 6 | | | 5 | | 7 | | 10 |

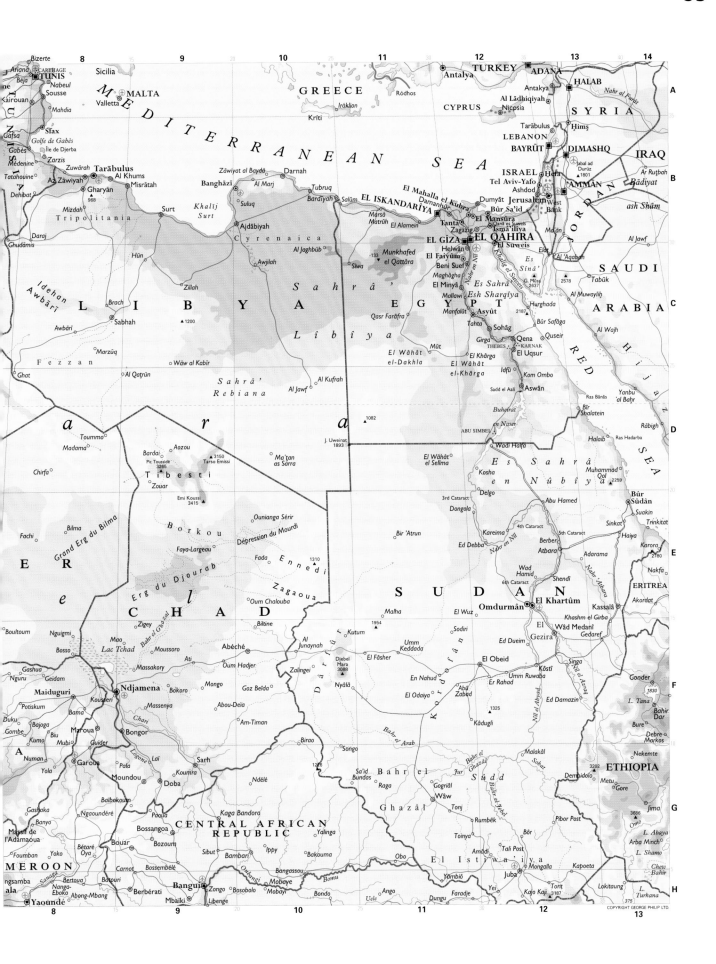

Bizerte
Ariana
TUNIS
CARTHAGE
Beja
Nabeul
Sousse
Kairouan
Mahdia
Sicilia
MALTA
Valletta
GREECE
Iráklion
Kríti
Ródhos
TURKEY
Antalya
ADANA
Antakya
HALAB
Nahr al Furat
CYPRUS
Al Lādhiqiyah
Nicosia
SYRIA

Sfax
Golfe de Gabès
Île de Djerba
Gafsa
Gabès
Médenine
Zarzis
Tarābulus
Himş
DIMASHQ
LEBANON
BAYRŪT
Jabal ad Durūz
Ar Ruţbah
IRAQ

Tataouine
Dehibat
Zuwārah **Tarābulus**
Al Khums
Zāwiyat al Baydā
Darnah
ISRAEL
Tel Aviv-Yafo
Ashdod
Hefa
AMMĀN
Bādiyat

Az Zāwiyah
Gharyān
968
Misrātah
Banghāzī
Al Marj
Suluq
Tubruq
Bardīyah
Salūm
El Mahalla el Kubra
Damanhûr
Dumyât
Jerusalem
West Bank
ash Shām

Mizdah
Surt
Khalīj Surt
Ajdābiyah
EL ISKANDARĪYA
Marsâ Matrûh
El Alamein
Tanta
Zagazig
El Mansûra
Ismā'īlīya
Bûr Sa'id
Qanā es Suweis
Al Jawf

Daraj
Ghudāmis
Tripolitania
Cyrenaica
Al Jaghbūb
Munkhafed el Qattâra
-133
Siwa
EL GĪZA
EL QAHIRA
Helwân
El Suweis
El Faiyûm
Beni Suef
Es Sînâ'
2637
2578
Al 'Aqabah
Elat
Ma'ān
SAUDI

Hūn
Zillah
Mizdah
Maghâgha
El Minyâ
Mallawi
Es Sahrâ'
Esh Sharqîya
Hurghada
Tabûk
Al Muwaylih

L I B Y A
Brach
Awbārī
Sabhah
1200
Sahrâ'
E G Y P T
Lîbîya
Manfalût
Asyût
Tahta
Sohâg
Girga
Qena
2187
Bûr Safâga
Quseir
Al Wajh
A R A B I A

Marzūq
Waw al Kabīr
Qasr Farâfra
THEBES KARNAK
El Khârga
El Uqsur
Idfû
Kom Ombo
Aswân
Yanbu' al Baḩr

Fezzan
Ghat
Al Qatrūn
Sahrâ' Rebiana
Al Kufrah
Al Jawf
El Wâhât el-Dakhla
El Wâhât el-Khârga
Sadd el Aali
Bîr Shalatein
Ras Bânâs
RED
HIJĀZ
Rābigh

1082
J. Uweinat 1893
ABU SIMBEL
Buheirat en Naser
Halaib
Ras Hadarba
SEA

Toummo
Madama
Bardai
Pic Toussidé 3265
3150
Tarso Emissi
Ma'tan as Sârra
El Wâhât el Selîma
Wadi Halfa
Es Sahrâ en Nûbîya
Kosha
Muhammad Qol
2259
Bûr Sûdân

Chirfa
Tibesti
Zouar
Emi Koussi 3415
3rd Cataract
Dongola
Abu Hamed
Suakin
Sinkat
Trinkitat

Fachi
Bilma
Borkou
Ounianga Sérir
Dépression du Mourdi
Fada
Ennedi
1310
Bir 'Atrun
Ed Debba
Kareima
Nahr en Nil
4th Cataract
Berber
5th Cataract
Atbara
Adarama
Haiya
Karora
2780
ERITREA
Nakfa
Akordat

Grand Erg du Bilma
E R E
Erg du Djourab
Zagaoua
Wad Hamid
6th Cataract
Shendî
Nafkat

Boultoum
Nguigmi
Bosso
Gashua
CHAD
Zigey
Bahr el Ghazal
Moussoro
Ati
Abéché
Oum Hadjer
Al Junaynah
Kutum
1954
Malha
Sodiri
Umm Keddada
El Wuz
Omdurmân
El Khartûm
Khashm el Girba
Kassalâ
Gedaref

Nguru
Geidam
Mao
Lac Tchad
Massakory
Bokoro
Mongo
Goz Beïda
Zalingei
Djebel Mara 3088
Nyâlâ
El Fâsher
En Nahud
Umm Ruwaba
Er Rahad
El Obeid
Kôstî
Singa
1830
Gonder
L. Tana

Maiduguri
Kousséri
Ndjamena
Massenya
Abou-Deïa
Am-Timan
Dârfûr
Birao
El Odaiya
Abû Zabad
1325
El
Wâd Medanî
Ed Damazin
L. Tana

Potiskum
Bama
Chari
Bongor
Kordofân
Kâdugli
Bahir Dar
Debre Markos

Buku
Bajoga
Biu
Maroua
Guider
Logone
Birao
Songo
Bahr el Arab
Jur
Raga
Bahr el Ghazal
Malakâl
Sobat
Nekemte
Nekemte

Gombe
Kumo
Mubi
Garoua
Pala
Laï
Sarh
Ndélé
1235
Sa'id Bundas
Bahr el
Ghazâl
Waw
Gogriâl
3202
Dembidolo
ETHIOPIA
Metu
Gore

Numan
Yola
Moundou
Doba
Kaga Bandora
Yalinga
Ippy
Raga
Tonj
Rumbêk
Pibor Post
3686
Jima

Gashaka
Baibokoum
Bouar
Bozoum
CENTRAL AFRICAN
REPUBLIC
Bambari
Bakouma
Obo
El Istiwa'îya
Toinya
Tali Post
Bôr
Amâdi
Juba
Mongalla
Kapoeta
L. Abaya
Arba Minch
L. Shamo

Banyo
Ngaoundéré
Bossangoa
Sibut
Bétaré Oya
Yoko
Foumban
Massif de l'Adamaoua
Bangassou
Bomu
Yambîo
Yei
Kajo Kaji 3187
Torit
Lokitaung
Chew Bahir

MEROON
Foumban
Nanga-Eboko
Bertoua
Batouri
Bangui
Zongo
Bosobolo
Mobaye
Mobayi
Bondo
Uele
Dungu
Faradje
375
L. Turkana

ngsamba
ala
Yaoundé
Abong-Mbang
Berbérati
Mbaïki
Libenge
Ango

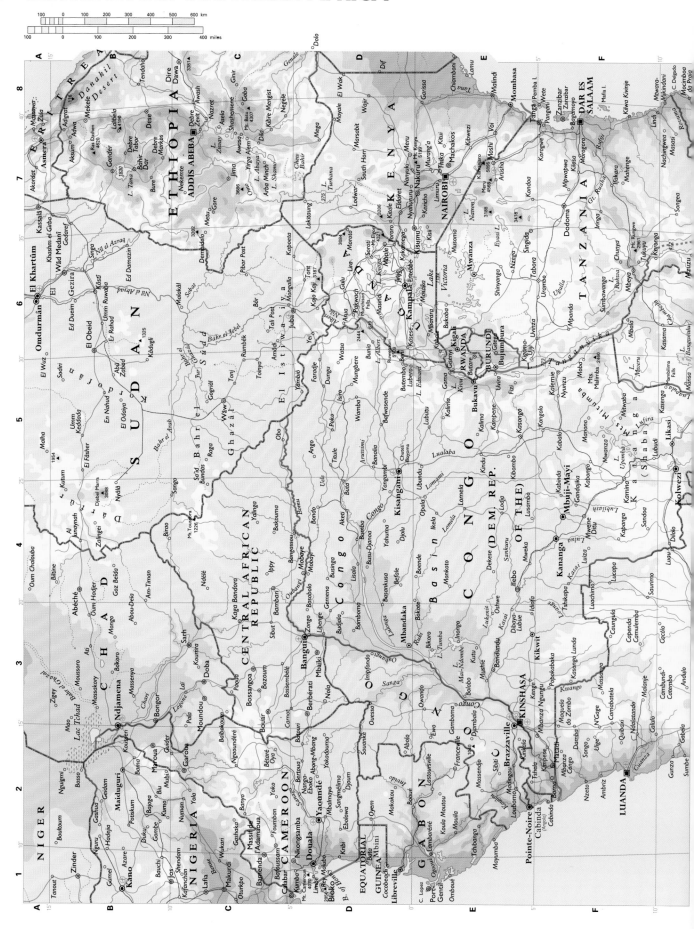

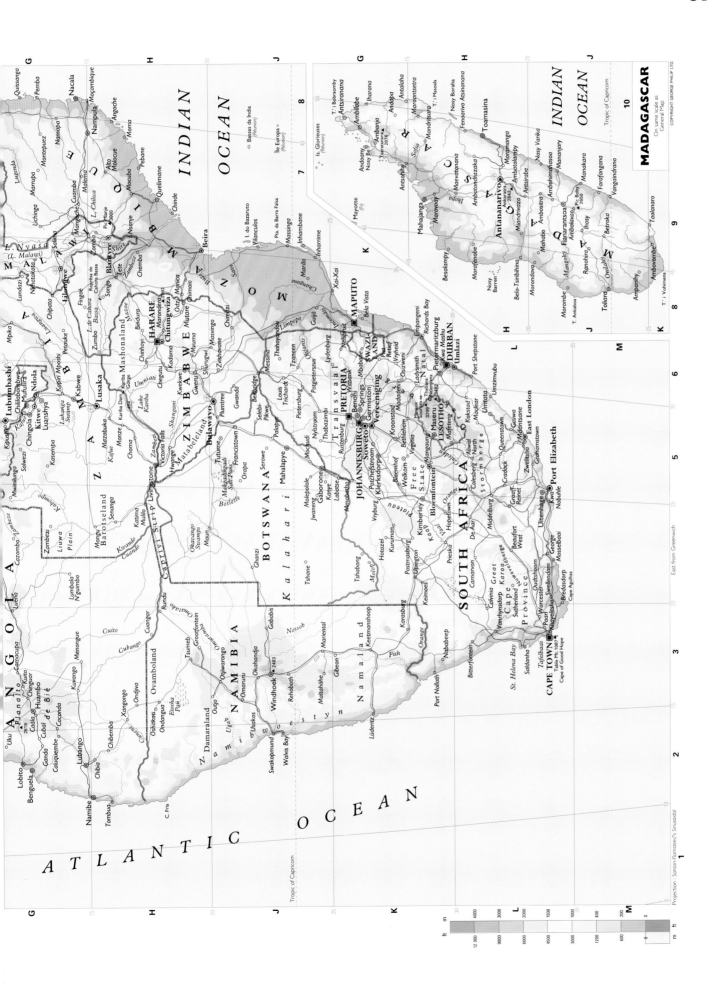

MADAGASCAR

On same scale as
General Map

COPYRIGHT GEORGE PHILIP LTD.

INDIAN

OCEAN

INDIAN

OCEAN

Tropic of Capricorn

10

ATLANTIC OCEAN

Projection: Sanson-Flamsteed's Sinusoidal

Tropic of Capricorn

East from Greenwich

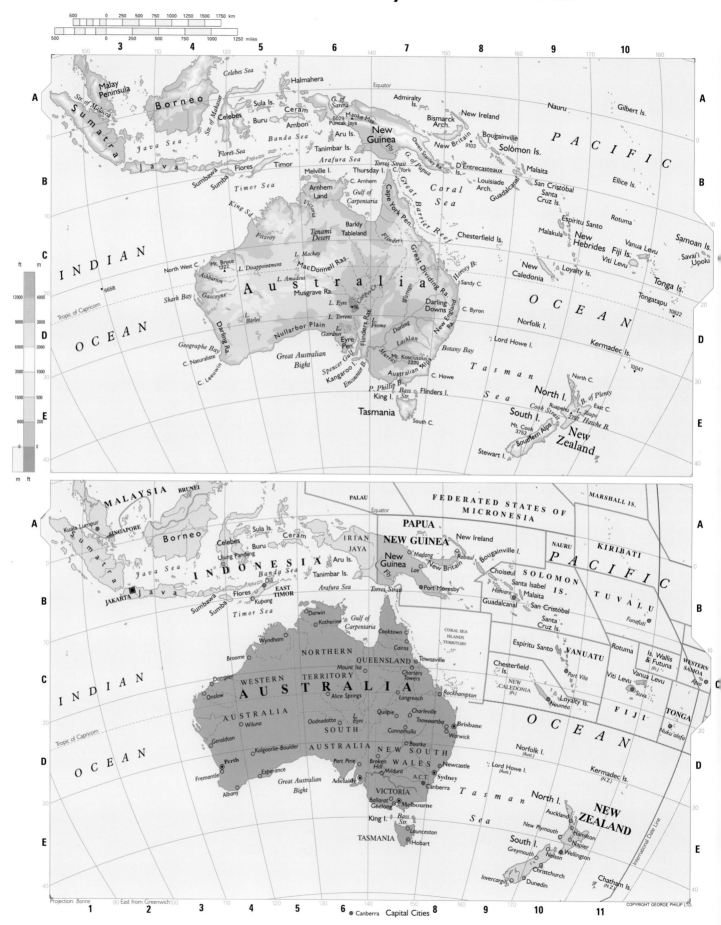

Physical map (top):

500   0   250 500 750 1000 1250 1500 1750 km
500   0   250 500 750 1000 1250 miles

ft   m

Malay Peninsula
Str. of Malacca
Sumatra
Borneo
Celebes Sea
Halmahera
Celebes
Str. of Makassar
Sula Is.
Ceram
Buru
Ambon
Equator
G. of Sarera
Maoke Mts.
5029 Puncak Jaya
New Guinea
Admiralty Is.
New Ireland
Bismarck Arch.
New Britain
Bougainville
9103
Solomon Is.
Nauru
Gilbert Is.
PACIFIC

Java Sea
Banda Sea
Flores Sea
Aru Is.
Owen Stanley Ra.
D'Entrecasteaux Is.
Malaita
Ellice Is.

Java
Sumbawa
Sumba
Flores
Timor
Arafura Sea
Tanimbar Is.
G. of Papua
Fly
Torres Strait
C. York
Thursday I.
Coral Sea
Louisiade Arch.
San Cristóbal
Santa Cruz Is.
Guadalcanal

Timor Sea
Melville I.
Arnhem Land
Victoria
C. Arnhem
Gulf of Carpentaria
Cape York Pen.
Great Barrier Reef
Chesterfield Is.
Espíritu Santo
Malakula
Rotuma
Samoan Is.
Savai'i
Upolu

King Sd.
Fitzroy
Tanami Desert
Barkly Tableland
Flinders R.
Great Dividing Ra.
New Hebrides
Fiji Is.
Viti Levu
Vanua Levu

INDIAN
North West C.
Mt. Bruce 1227
L. Mackay
L. Disappointment
MacDonnell Ras.
Harvey B.
New Caledonia
Loyalty Is.
Tonga Is.

Ashburton
6658
Australia
L. Amadeus
Musgrave Ra.
Warrego
Sandy C.
Tongatapu
10822

Tropic of Capricorn
Shark Bay
Gascoyne
L. Eyre 16
Cooper Cr.
Darling
Darling Downs
C. Byron
New England
OCEAN

OCEAN
L. Barlee
L. Torrens
L. Gairdner
L. Frome
Lachlan
Norfolk I.
Kermadec Is.
10047

Geographe Bay
Nullarbor Plain
Eyre Pen.
Flinders Ras.
Darling
Murray
Botany Bay
Lord Howe I.
Tasman

C. Naturaliste
Great Australian Bight
Spencer Gulf
Kangaroo I.
Encounter B.
Mt. Kosciuszko 2230
Australian Alps
Sea
North C.

C. Leeuwin
P. Phillip B.
Bass Str.
King I.
Flinders I.
C. Howe
North I.
B. of Plenty
East C.
Ruapehu Taupo 2797
Hawke B.

Tasmania
South C.
South I.
Cook Strait
Mt. Cook 3753
Southern Alps
New Zealand
Stewart I.

m ft
12000 4000
9000 3000
6000 2000
3000 1000
1500 500
600 200
0 0

Political map (bottom):

MALAYSIA   BRUNEI
PALAU
FEDERATED STATES OF MICRONESIA
MARSHALL IS.
Kuala Lumpur
SINGAPORE
Sumatra
Borneo
Celebes
Ujung Pandang
Sula Is.
Ceram
Buru
IRIAN JAYA
Equator
PAPUA NEW GUINEA
New Ireland
NAURU
KIRIBATI
PACIFIC

INDONESIA
New Guinea
Madang
Rabaul
Bougainville
Choiseul
Santa Isabel
SOLOMON IS.

Java Sea
Banda Sea
Aru Is.
Fly
Lae
New Britain
TUVALU

JAKARTA
Java
Sumbawa
Sumba
Flores
Dili
EAST TIMOR
Kupang
Arafura Sea
Tanimbar Is.
Port Moresby
Honiara
Malaita
San Cristóbal
Funafuti

Timor Sea
Darwin
Katherine
Torres Strait
Gulf of Carpentaria
Guadalcanal
Santa Cruz Is.
Espíritu Santo
VANUATU
Rotuma
Is. Wallis & Futuna (Fr.)
WESTERN SAMOA

Wyndham
Cooktown
CORAL SEA ISLANDS TERRITORY
Chesterfield Is.
Apia

Broome
NORTHERN TERRITORY
Cairns
Townsville
Port Vila
NEW CALEDONIA (Fr.)

Dampier
Mount Isa
QUEENSLAND
Charters Towers
Vanua Levu
Siva

Onslow
WESTERN AUSTRALIA
AUSTRALIA
Alice Springs
Longreach
Rockhampton
Nouméa
Loyalty Is.
FIJI
Viti Levu

INDIAN
AUSTRALIA
Oodnadatta
L. Eyre
Quilpie
Charleville
Toowoomba
Brisbane
TONGA
Nuku'alofa

Wiluna
SOUTH
Cunnamulla
Warwick
Norfolk I. (Aust.)
OCEAN

Geraldton
Bourke
Mildura
Broken Hill
Lord Howe I. (Aust.)
Kermadec Is. (N.Z.)

Kalgoorlie-Boulder
AUSTRALIA
NEW SOUTH WALES
Newcastle
Tasman

OCEAN
Perth
Port Pirie
Sydney
A.C.T.
Canberra
North I.
NEW ZEALAND

Fremantle
Esperance
Adelaide
VICTORIA
Ballarat
Melbourne
Sea
Auckland

Albany
Great Australian Bight
Geelong
New Plymouth
Hamilton

King I.
Bass Str.
Launceston
South I.
Napier
Wellington

TASMANIA
Hobart
Greymouth
Nelson
Christchurch

Invercargill
Dunedin
Chatham Is. (N.Z.)

Tropic of Capricorn
International Date Line

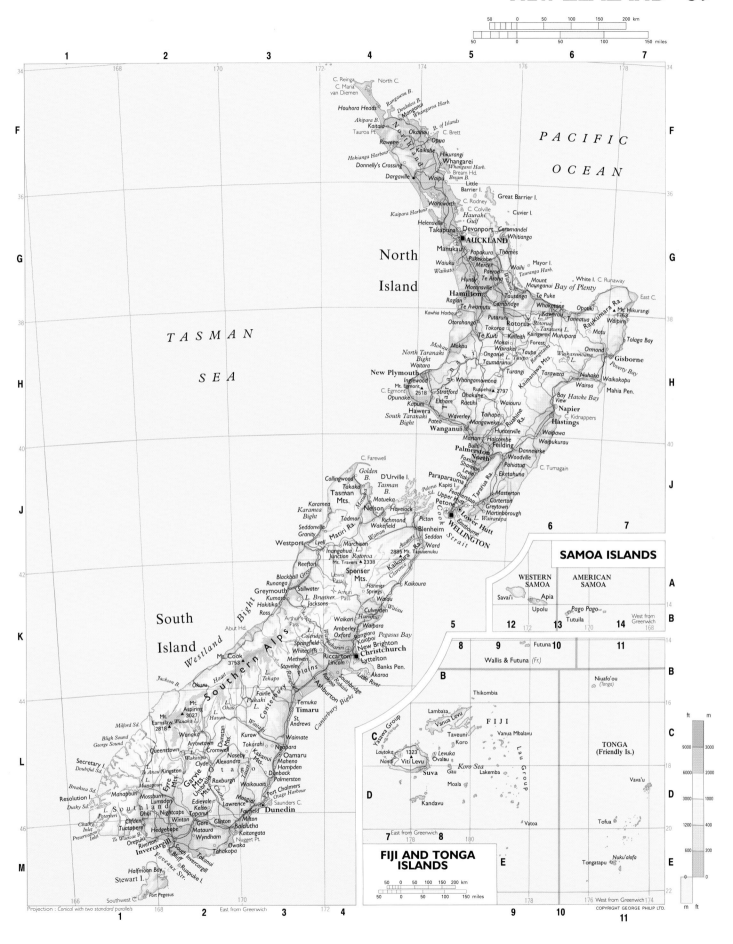

50 0 50 100 150 200 km
50 0 50 100 150 miles

1 **2** **3** **4** **5** **6** **7**

168 170 172 174 176 178

34 34

PACIFIC

F F

C. Reinga
C. Maria
van Diemen
North C.
Rangaunu B.
Houhora Heads
Doubtless B.
Mangonui
Whangaroa Harb.
Ahipara B.
Kaitaia
Kaikohe
Tauroa Pt.
Okaihau
B. of Islands
C. Brett
Rawene
Hikurangi
Opua
Hokianga Harbour
Whangarei
Donnelly's Crossing
Whangarei Harb.
Dargaville
Waipu
Bream Hd.
Bream B.
Little
Barrier I.

OCEAN

36 36
Great Barrier I.
Warkworth
C. Rodney
Kaipara Harbour
C. Colville
Cuvier I.
Helensville
Hauraki
Gulf
Coromandel
Takapuna
Devonport
Whitianga
Manukau
AUCKLAND
Thames

North
Papakura
Waiuku
Pukekohe
Mercer
Mayor I.
Island
Waikato
Paeroa
Waihi
Tauranga Harb.
Huntly
Te Aroha
White I. C. Runaway
Morrinsville
Mount
Maunganui
Bay of Plenty

G G
Hamilton
Tauranga
Te Puke
Whakatane
Raglan
Cambridge
Opotiki
Rau Kumara Ra.
Te Awamutu
Kawerau
Mt. Hikurangi
Kawhia Harbour
Putaruru
Rotorua
Rotorua L.
Taneatua
1753
Waipira
Otorohanga
Tokoroa
Rotorua
Tarawera L.
Murupara
Motu
Tolaga Bay
Mokau
Te Kuiti
Kinleith
Mokai
Taupo
Ruatahuna
Mokau
Wairakei
Waikaremoana
Ormond

H
North Taranaki
Bight
Ongarue
Taupo L.
L.
Gisborne H
Waitara
Taumarunui
Rangitaiki
Waikaremoana
Poverty Bay
New Plymouth
Inglewood
Whangamomona
Turangi
Kaimanawa Mts.
Tarawera
Nuhaka
Waikokopu
Mt. Egmont
Ruapehu
2797
Mahia Pen.
C. Egmont
2518
Stratford
Ohakune
Bay
Hawke Bay
Opunake
Eltham
Raetihi
View
Kapuni
Taihape
Napier
Hawera
Mangaweka
Ruahine
C. Kidnappers
South Taranaki
Waverley
Ra.
Hastings
Bight
Patea
Hunterville
Waipawa
Wanganui
Marton
Halcombe
Waipukurau
Bulls
Feilding
Dannevirke
Palmerston
Woodville
C. Turnagain

40 40
North
Foxton
Shannon
Pohiatua
Levin
Eketahuna
J
D'Urville I.
Paraparaumu
Otaki
Collingwood
Golden
Tasman
Kapiti I.
Tararua Ra.
Masterton
C. Farewell
B.
B.
Featherston
Carterton
Takaka
Pelorus
Upper Hutt
Greytown
Karamea
Tasman
Motueka
Sd.
Petone
Martinborough
Mts.
Nelson
Eastbourne
Wairarapa
Karamea
Havelock
Lower Hutt
Bight
Tadmor
Richmond
Picton
WELLINGTON
Seddonville
Murchison
Wakefield
Blenheim
Granity
Matiri Ra.
Seddon
Westport
Lyell
Inangahua
Rotoroa
Ward
Junction
L.
2885 Mt. Tapuaenuku
Reefton
Mt. Travers 2338

42 42
Blackball
Spenser
Runanga
Greymouth
Mts.
Stillwater
Hanmer
Kumara
L. Brunner
Springs
Hokitika
Jacksons
Arthur's
Ross
Pass
Waikari
Culverden
Waipara
Abut Hd.
Amberley
Pegasus Bay
South
Oxford
Kaiapoi
Island
Springfield
New Brighton
Whitecliffs
Christchurch
Methven
Riccarton
Lyttelton
Staveley
Lincoln
Banks Pen.
Akaroa

44 44
Mt. Cook
Southbridge
Little
3753
River
Temuka
St.
Andrews
Timaru
Fairlie
Waimate
Mt.
Aspiring
3027
Kurow
Ngapara
Earnslaw
Wanaka L.
Tokarahi
Oamaru
2818
Wanaka
Maheno
Milford Sd.
Arrowtown
Cromwell
Hampden
Bligh Sound
Queenstown
Clyde
Palmerston
George Sound
Wakatipu
Alexandra
Dunback
Roxburgh
Port Chalmers

46 46
Secretary I.
Kingston
Waikouaiti
Otago Harbour
Doubtful Sd.
Lawrence
Saunders C.
Te Anau
Edievale
Fairfield
Dunedin
Breaksea Sd.
Mossburn
Kelso
Milton
Resolution I.
Manapouri
Lumsden
Tapanui
Balclutha
Dusky Sd.
Ohai
Nightcaps
Gore
Kaitangata
Winton
Mataura
Owaka
Clinton
Nugget Pt.
Wyndham
Tahakopa
Invercargill
Tokanui
Riverton
South Invercargill
Halfmoon Bay
Ruapuke I.

Foveaux Str.
Stewart I.
Southwest C.
Port Pegasus

TASMAN
SEA

Westland Bight

Southern Alps

Canterbury
Plains

South
Island

166 168 170 172

1 **2** **3** **4**

East from Greenwich

Projection : Conical with two standard parallels

SAMOA ISLANDS

6 **7**

A
WESTERN AMERICAN
SAMOA SAMOA
Savai'i
Apia
14
Upolu
Pago Pago
Tutuila
B
West from
Greenwich
12 **13** **14**
172 170 168

8 **9** **10** **11**
14
Futuna
Wallis & Futuna (Fr.)
B
Niuafo'ou
(Tonga)
16
Thikombia
Lambasa
Vanua Levu
TONGA
C
Yasawa Group
Taveuni
(Friendly Is.) C
Koro
Lautoka
FIJI
Vanua Mbalavu
Nandi
1323
Levuka
Vava'u
Viti Levu
Ovalau
Gau
Suva
Lau Group
Lakemba
D
Moala
Koro Sea
18
Kandavu
Vatoa
Tofua
Vatoa
20
7 East from Greenwich **8**
178 180

FIJI AND TONGA ISLANDS

E
Nuku'alofa
Tongatapu E
22
176 West from Greenwich 174

50 0 50 100 150 200 km
50 0 50 100 150 miles

9 **10** **11**

COPYRIGHT GEORGE PHILIP LTD.

ft m
9000 3000
6000 2000
3000 1000
1200 400
600 200
0 0
m ft

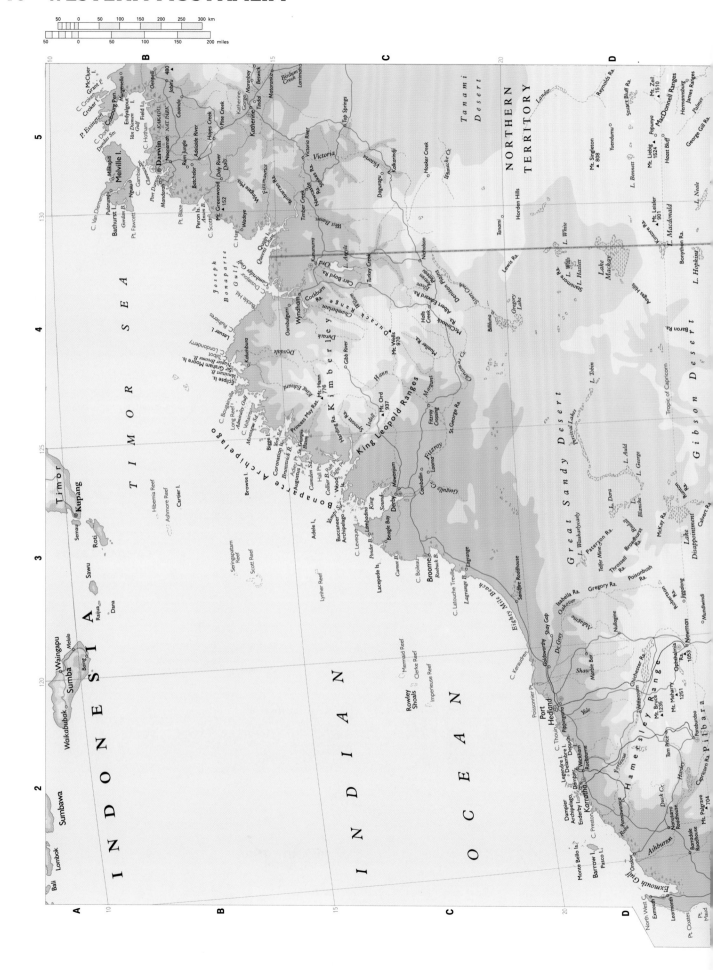

50 0 50 100 150 200 250 300 km
50 0 50 100 150 200 miles

INDONESIA

Bali
Lombok
Sumbawa
Sumba
Waikabubak
Waingapu
Melolo
Boing
Sawu
Raijua
Dana
Roti
Semau
Kupang
Timor

TIMOR SEA

Ashmore Reef
Hibernia Reef
Cartier I.

Seringapatam
Reef
Scott Reef

Mermaid Reef
Clerke Reef
Imperieuse Reef
Rowley
Shoals

Lynher Reef

INDIAN OCEAN

Monte Bello Is.
Barrow I.
Pasco I.

Adele I.
Lacepede Is.

Kimberley

NORTHERN TERRITORY

Tanami Desert

Great Sandy Desert

Gibson Desert

Hamersley Range
Pilbara

WESTERN AUSTRALIA

SOUTH AUSTRALIA

INDIAN OCEAN

SOUTHERN OCEAN

Great Victoria Desert

Great Australian Bight

Nullarbor Plain

Hampton Tableland

PERTH

Kalgoorlie-Boulder

Geraldton

Albany

Esperance

COPYRIGHT GEORGE PHILIP LTD.

East from Greenwich

Projection: Bonne

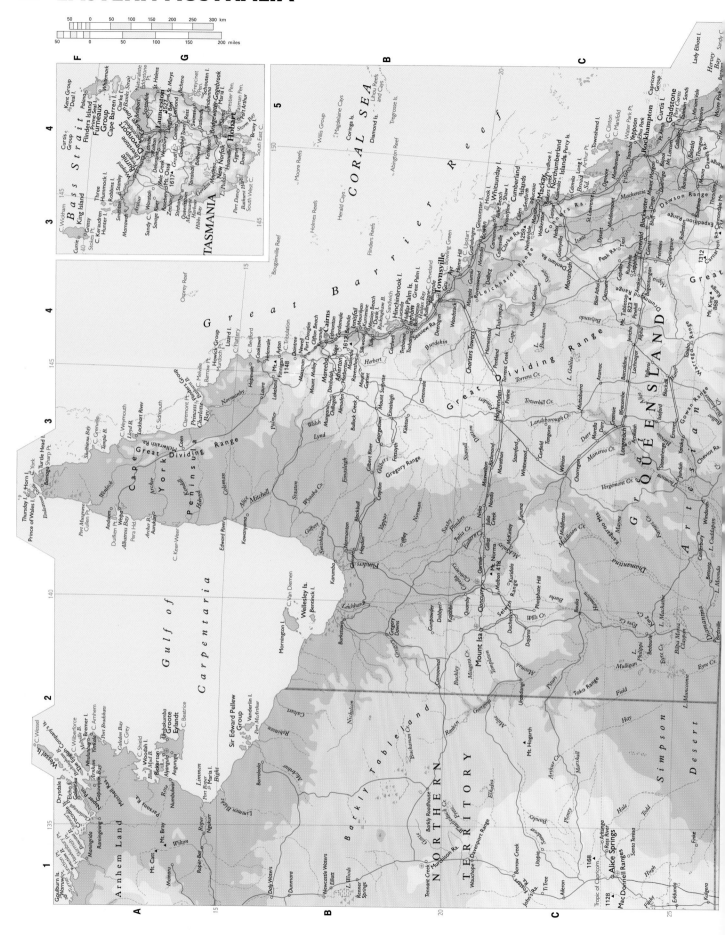

50 0 50 100 150 200 250 300 km
50   100   150   200 miles

TASMANIA

Bass Strait

King Island

CORAL SEA

Willis Group

Magdelaine Cays

Coringa Is.

Lihou Reefs and Cays

Tregrosse Is.

Diamond Is.

Abington Reef

Moore Reefs

Holmes Reefs

Herald Cays

Flinders Reefs

Bougainville Reef

Osprey Reef

Great Barrier Reef

QUEENSLAND

Gulf of Carpentaria

Cape York Peninsula

Great Dividing Range

Arnhem Land

NORTHERN TERRITORY

Simpson Desert

Barkly Tableland

Great Artesian Basin

MacDonnell Ranges

Alice Springs

Tropic of Capricorn

Townsville

Cairns

Mount Isa

Rockhampton

Gladstone

Mackay

Hobart

Launceston

SOUTHERN OCEAN

TASMAN SEA

NEW SOUTH WALES

SOUTH AUSTRALIA

BRISBANE
Gold Coast
Tweed Heads

SYDNEY
Newcastle
Gosford
Campbelltown
Wollongong
Canberra
Penrith

MELBOURNE
Geelong
Ballarat
Bendigo

ADELAIDE
Elizabeth
Gawler
Port Augusta
Port Pirie
Whyalla

Broken Hill

Mildura

Tamworth
Armidale
Dubbo
Orange
Bathurst
Parkes

Wagga Wagga
Albury
Wodonga
Shepparton

Gippsland

Bass Strait
King Island
Flinders Island
Furneaux Group
Cape Barren I.

Projection Bonne

East from Greenwich

m
ft
4500
3000
1500
1200
600
400
200
0
40
m
ft

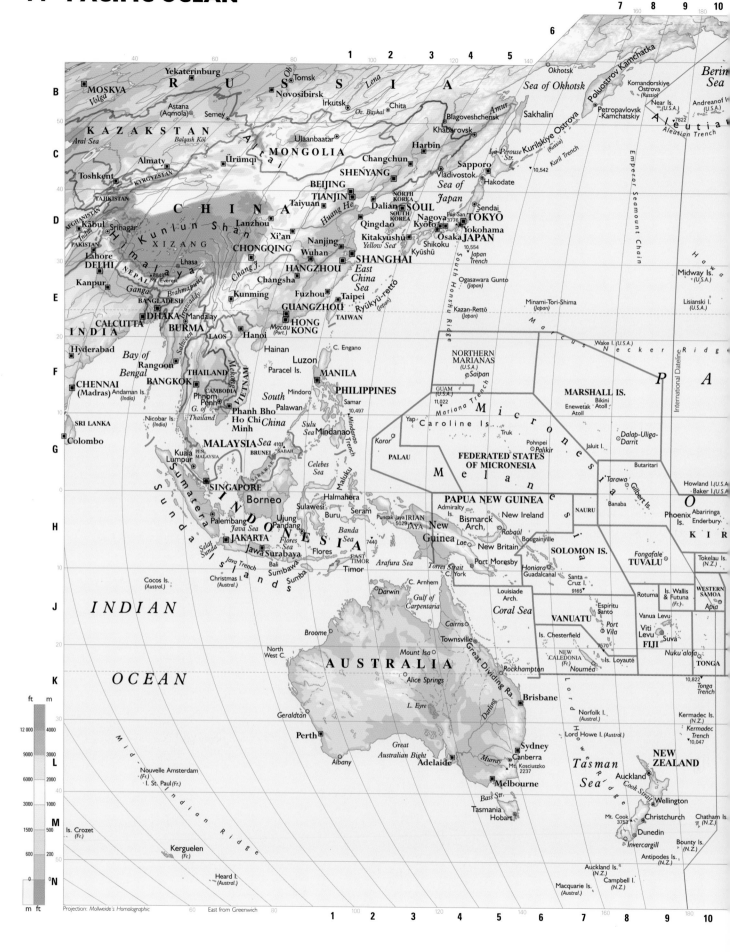

Projection: Mollweide's Homolographic   East from Greenwich

11 12 13 14

15

ALASKA
(U.S.A.)
Anchorage

Arctic Circle

16 17 18 19 20

Bristol Bay

Gulf of Alaska

5959

Juneau

Prince of Wales I.
(U.S.A.) Prince Rupert
Queen Charlotte Is.
(Canada)

Is. (U.S.A.)

C A N A D A

Edmonton

Calgary

Regina

L. Winnipeg

Winnipeg

Newfoundland

NORTH

St. Lawrence

Québec

St. John's

B

Vancouver
Vancouver I. Victoria
Seattle
Portland

Boise

L. Superior

Minneapolis

Missouri

L.
Michigan

Montréal
Ottawa
Toronto
Detroit
L. Huron
L. Ontario
Buffalo
L. Erie

Boston

C

Salt Lake
City

Denver

CHICAGO

Pittsburgh

NEW YORK CITY
PHILADELPHIA
Baltimore
Washington D.C.

ATLANTIC

C. Mendocino

Sacramento

SAN FRANCISCO

Kansas City

UNITED STATES

St. Louis
Cincinnati

4418

D

6741

LOS ANGELES
San Diego

Phoenix

Oklahoma City

Dallas

Memphis

Atlanta

C. Hatteras

Bermuda
(U.K.)

Colorado

Snake

R O C K Y M t s.

Guadalupe
(Mex.)

Ciudad
Juárez

Houston

San Antonio

New
Orleans

Jacksonville

Sargasso Sea

OCEAN

E

Tropic of Cancer

M E X I C O

Gulf of Mexico

Miami

BAHAMAS

Gulf of California

Baja California

Monterrey

La Habana

West Indies

C. San Lucas

Honolulu

Oahu

HAWAIIAN IS.
(U.S.A.)

4205

Hawaii

Guadalajara

Is. Revilla Gigedo
(Mex.)

MEXICO

5700

Puebla

Mérida

Canal de Yucatan

C U B A

Florida Str.

9200

7680

HAITI

DOMINICAN REP.

JAMAICA

Kingston

PUERTO
RICO
(U.S.A.)

Leeward
Is.

Johnston I.
(U.S.A.)

Acapulco

BELIZE

F

C I F I C

GUATEMALA
Guatemala
San Salvador
EL SALVADOR

HONDURAS

NICARAGUA

Caribbean Sea

BARBADOS
Windward Is.

an Ridge

North West Christmas Ridge

Palmyra Is.
(U.S.A.)

I. Clipperton
(Fr.)

Managua

Maracaibo

Caracas

P O L Y N E S I A

Teraina
Tabuaeran
Kiritimati

Barranquilla
San José
COSTA
RICA
Colón
PANAMA
Panamá

Orinoco

VENEZUELA

G

Jarvis I.
(U.S.A.)

C E A N

I. del Coco
(Costa Rica)

Medellín

Bogotá

Cali

COLOMBIA

I B A T I

Malden I.

Starbuck I.

Equator

I. de Malpelo
(Colombia)

Galápagos
(Ecuador)

Quito

ECUADOR

Amazonas

Tongareva

Caroline I.

Guayaquil

Iquitos

BRAZIL

H

Pukapuka Manihiki

Is. Marquises

Vostok I.

Flint I.

C. Paliñas

Trujillo

MER.
AMOA
U.S.A.

Suwarrow Is.

Is. de la
Société

6369

PERU

J

Niue
(N.Z.)

Cook Is.
(N.Z.)

Papeete Tahiti

Is. Tuamotu

LIMA

Cuzco

Arequipa

L. Titicaca

Nevada Ancohuma
6550

Rarotonga

FRENCH POLYNESIA

Mururoa

Is. Tubuai

Tropic of Capricorn

6866

Peru–

Arica

La Paz

BOLIVIA

Ducie I.

East Pacific Ridge

San Felix
(Chile)

San Ambrosio
(Chile)

Iquique

Chile

K

Pitcairn I.
(U.K.)

Sala-y-Gómez
(Chile)

8050
Trench

Antofagasta

PARAGUAY

Asunción

Rapa

I. de Pascua
(Chile)

San Miguel
de Tucumán

Pôrto
Alegre

Arch. de
Juan Fernández
(Chile)

Córdoba
Aconcagua
6960

Rosario

Valparaíso

URUGUAY

L

SANTIAGO

BUENOS
AIRES

Montevideo

Río de la Plata

Concepción

ARGENTINA

Chile Rise

SOUTH

M

Pacific-Antarctic Ridge

ATLANTIC

Patagonian

OCEAN

6212

Punta Arenas

Falkland Is.
(U.K.)

South Georgia
(U.K.)

N

Est. de Magallanes
Tierra del Fuego

C. de Hornos

West from Greenwich

COPYRIGHT GEORGE PHILIP LTD.

11 12 13 14 15 16 17 18 19 20

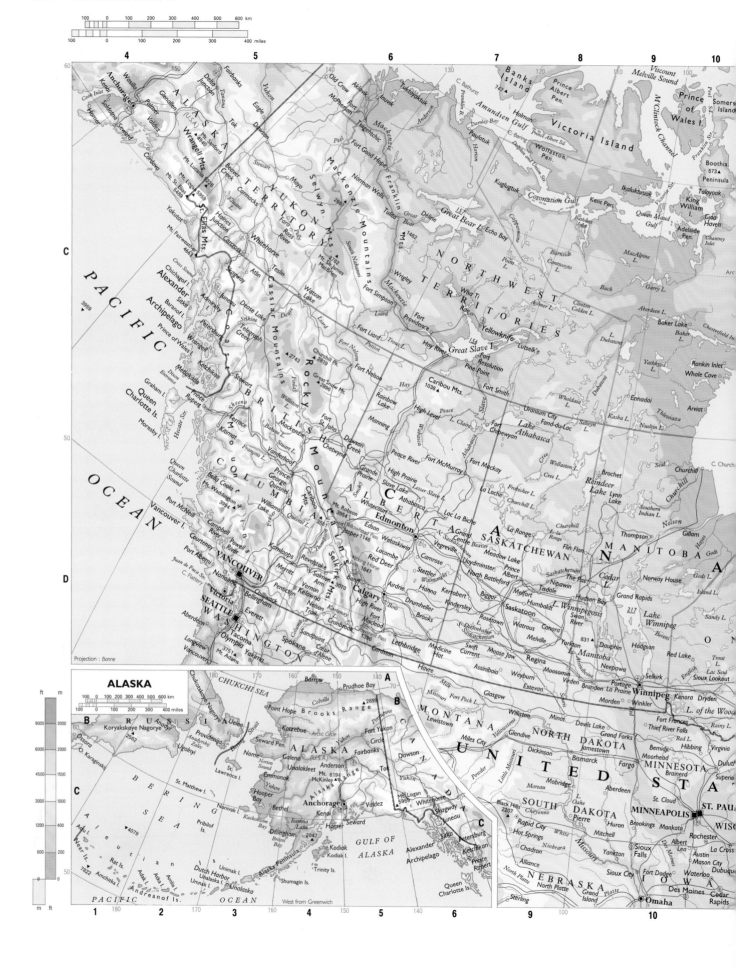

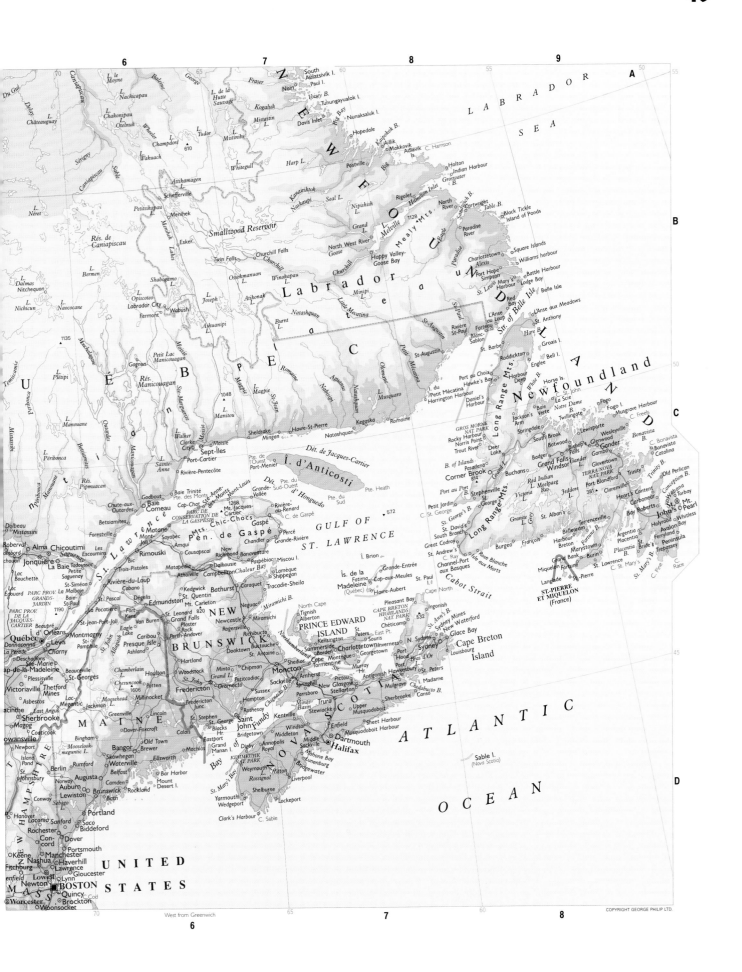

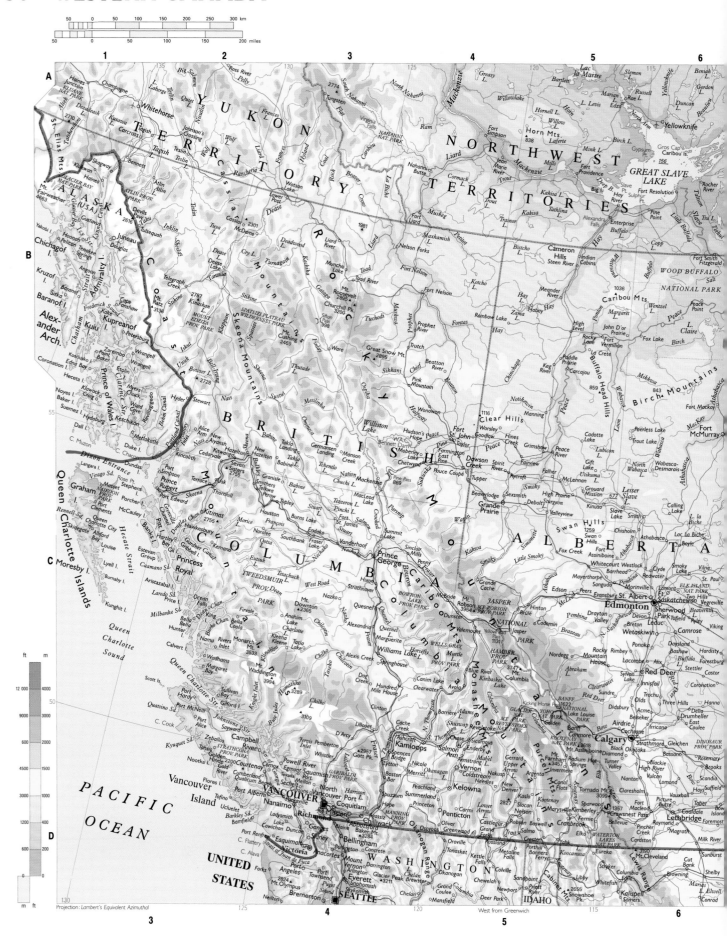

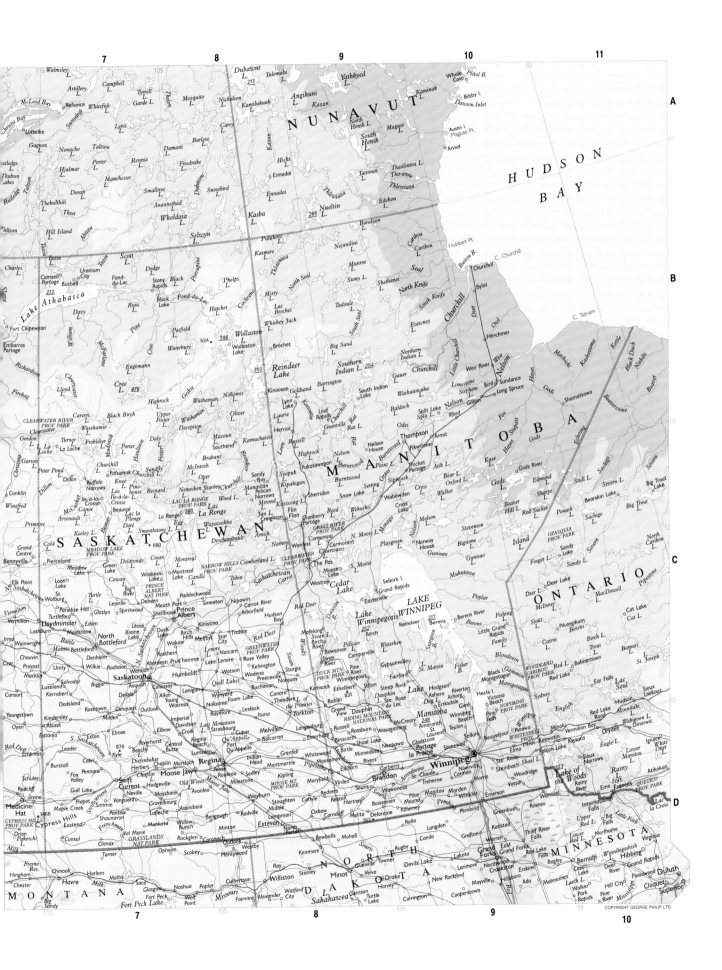

NUNAVUT

HUDSON BAY

MANITOBA

SASKATCHEWAN

ONTARIO

Lake Athabasca

LAKE WINNIPEG

Lake Winnipegosis

Reindeer Lake

Cree L.

Wollaston Lake

Cedar Lake

Southern Indian L.

Churchill

Saskatoon

Regina

Moose Jaw

Swift Current

Winnipeg

Brandon

Prince Albert

North Battleford

Medicine Hat

Lloydminster

MONTANA

NORTH DAKOTA

MINNESOTA

Churchill

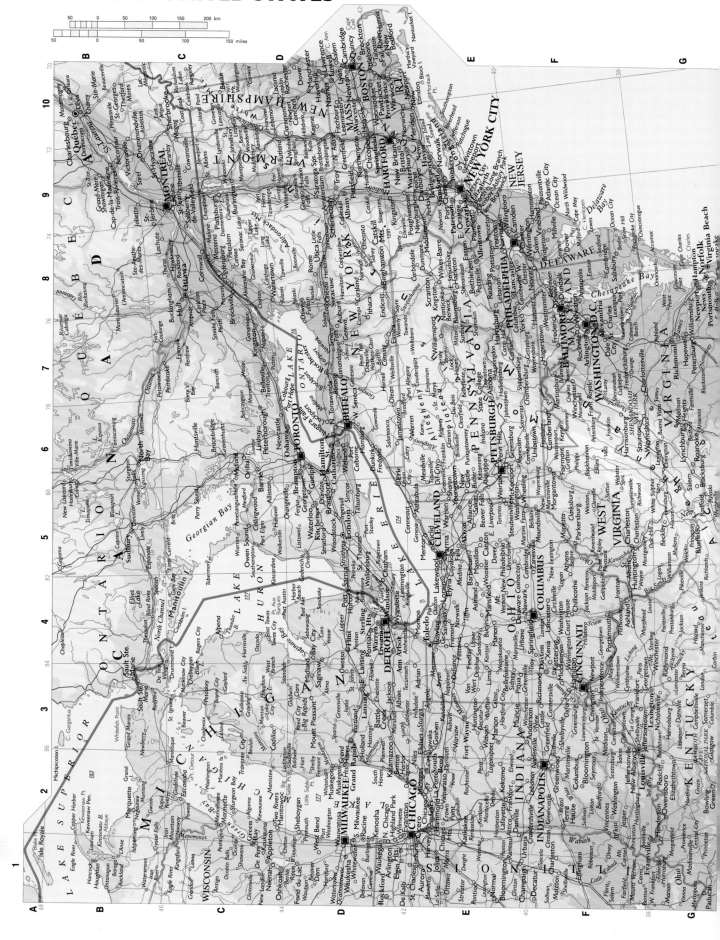

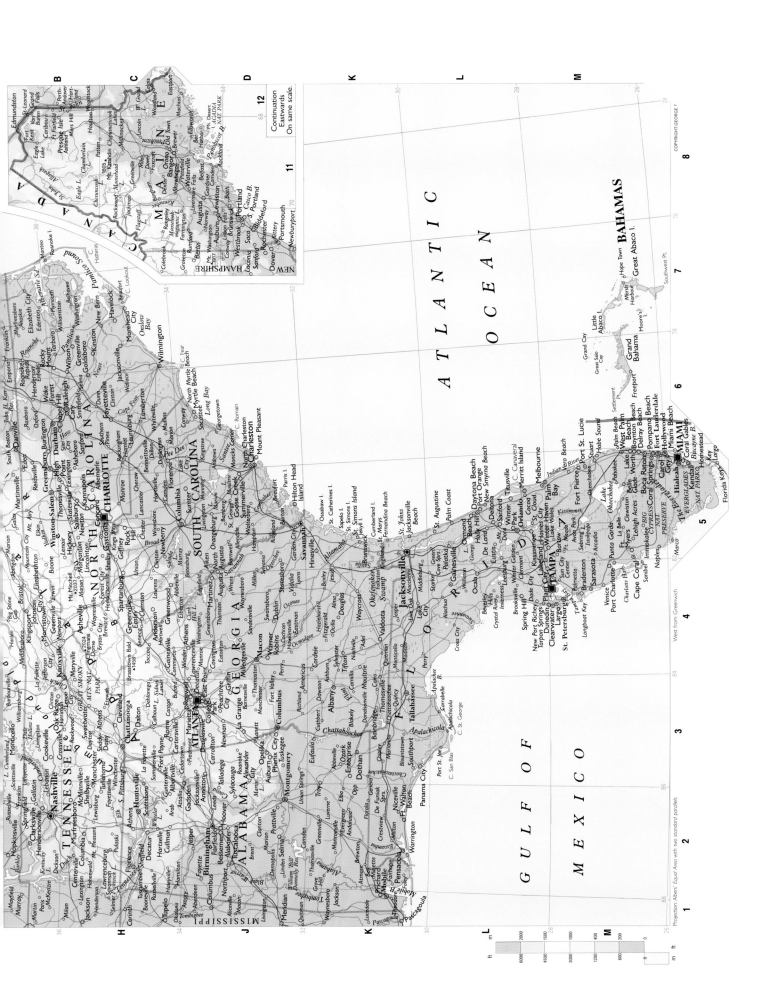

Continuation
Eastwards
On the same scale.

Projection Albers Equal Area with two standard parallels

West from Greenwich

54 MIDDLE UNITED STATES

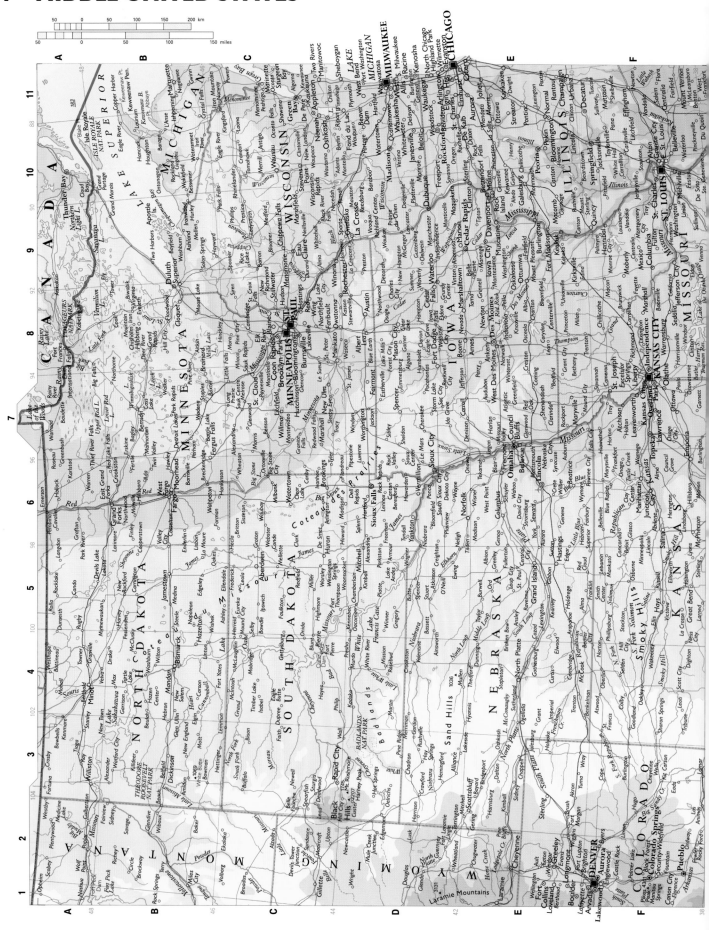

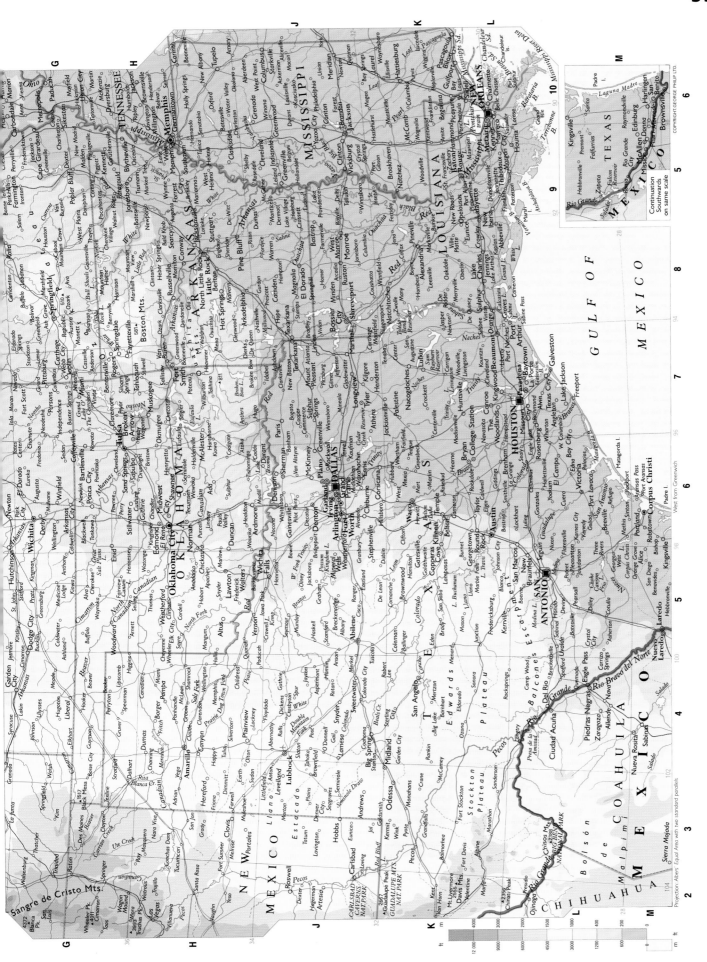

55

57

West from Greenwich

Projection: Albers' Equal Area with two standard parallels

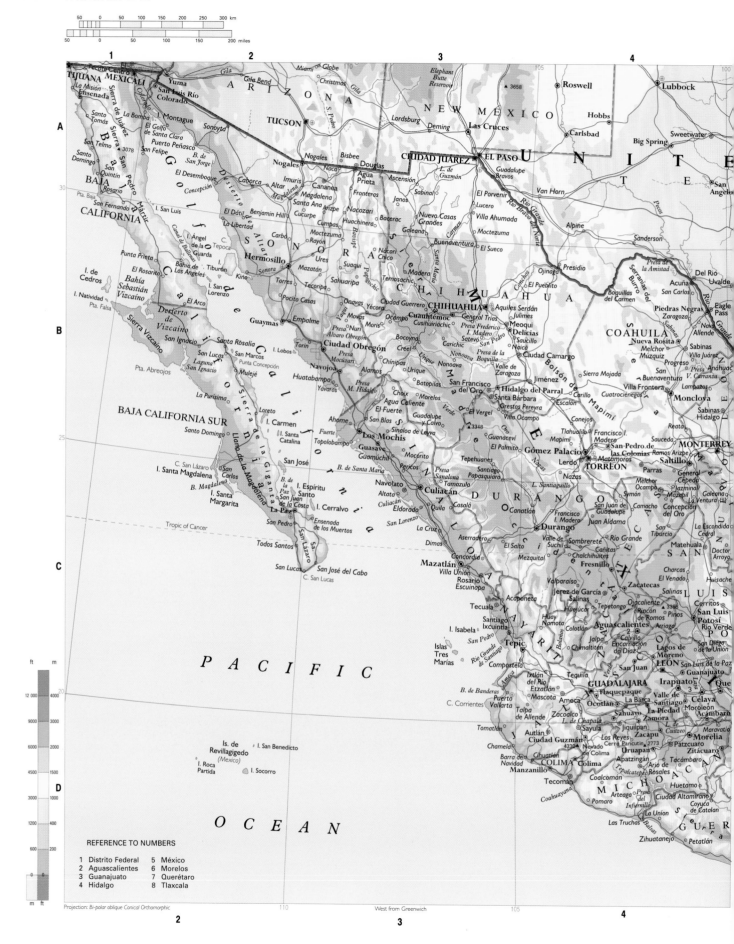

50 0 50 100 150 200 250 300 km
50 0 50 100 150 200 miles

PACIFIC

OCEAN

ft   m
12 000   4000
9000   3000
6000   2000
4500   1500
3000   1000
1200   400
600   200
0   0
m   ft

REFERENCE TO NUMBERS

1 Distrito Federal   5 México
2 Aguascalientes   6 Morelos
3 Guanajuato   7 Querétaro
4 Hidalgo   8 Tlaxcala

Projection: Bi-polar oblique Conical Orthomorphic

West from Greenwich

GULF OF MEXICO

M E X I C O

Tropic of Cancer

Golfo de Campeche

Golfo de Tehuantepec

ARKANSAS

MISSISSIPPI

ALABAMA

GEORGIA

FLORIDA

LOUISIANA

DALLAS

FORT WORTH

HOUSTON

SAN ANTONIO

NEW ORLEANS

MOBILE

Corpus Christi

Nuevo Laredo

Laredo

Matamoros

Reynosa

Laguna Madre

Ciudad Victoria

Tampico

Ciudad Madero

MÉXICO

PUEBLA

Veracruz

Córdoba

Orizaba

TABASCO

Villahermosa

Coatzacoalcos

Minatitlán

CAMPECHE

Campeche

Ciudad del Carmen

Mérida

YUCATÁN

Progreso

Cancún

Puerto Juárez

Cozumel

QUINTANA ROO

Chetumal

BELIZE

Belize City

Belmopan

GUATEMALA

HONDURAS

Tegucigalpa

San Pedro Sula

Oaxaca

OAXACA

CHIAPAS

CUBA

Canal de Yucatán

COPYRIGHT GEORGE PHILIP LTD.

GULF OF MEXICO

PACIFIC OCEAN

Projection: Conical with two standard parallels

MEXICO

GUATEMALA

BELIZE

HONDURAS

EL SALVADOR

NICARAGUA

COSTA RICA

PANAMÁ

CUBA

JAMAICA

BAH

CARIB

U.S.A.

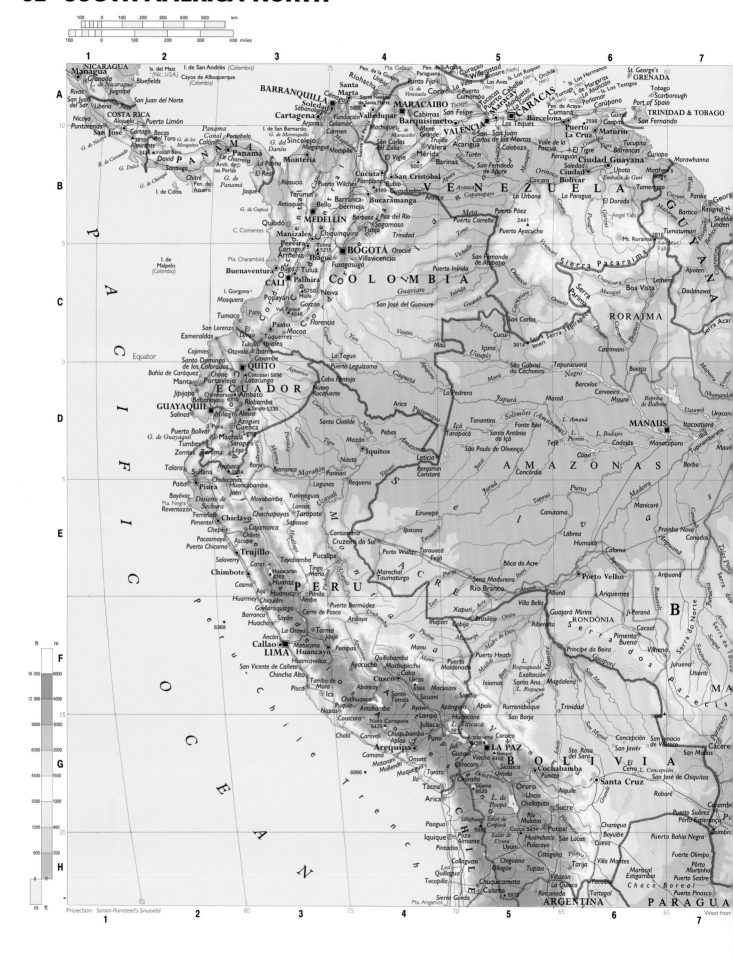

km
100 0 100 200 300 400 500 km
100 0 100 200 300 400 miles

Projection: Sanson-Flamsteed's Sinusoidal

West from

ATLANTIC

OCEAN

FRENCH
GUIANA

SURINAM
△ 1230
Ilianatop

Amsterdam
Nieuw Nickerie
Totness Paramaribo
Nieuw Amsterdam
Kwakoegron Albina
Moengo
Sinnamary
Kourou
Cayenne
Prof. Van
Blommestein-
meer
C. Orange
Kaw
Approuague
Georges
Oiapoque
Camopi

Serra Tumucumaque

AMAPÁ

Meriruma

Serra do
Navio
Araguari

I. de Maracá

Amapá

Macapá

I. Caviana
I. Mexiana

Equator

São Paulo
(Braz.)

C. Maguannho

Mazagão
I. Grande
de Gurupá
Afuá
Chaves
Curuçá
Salinópolis

Marajó BELÉM
Breves
Gurupá
Almeirim
Soure
Vigia
Bragança
Viseu

Santarém
Belterra
Altamira

Óbidos
Monte
Alegre
Prainha
Pôrto de Móz
Curralinho
Cametá
Castanhal
Abaetetuba

Cururupu

Alenquer
Juruti
Aveiro

Parintins

Brasília Legal

Itaituba

P A R Á

Tucuruí

Baião

Santa Inês
Bacabal

Pinheiro
Alcântara
Rosário
Viana
Itapecuru-
Mirim
Brejo
Coroatá

Barreirinhas
Tutóia
Luís Correia
Parnaíba
Piracuruca
Camocim
Granja
Itapipoca
Caucaia

FORTALEZA
Sobral
Maranguape
Cascavel
Acaraú

Rocas

Fernando de Noronha
(Braz.)

B. de São Marcos
São Luís

Codó
Piripiri
Campo
Maior
Ipu
Quixadá
Aracati
Baturité
Russas
Areia Branca
Macau
Mossoró
Ceará Mirim
C. de São Roque

Carnaubais
DO NORTE Natal
RIO GRANDE

Acailândia
Marabá
Tocantins

MARANHÃO
Imperatriz

Carajás
Serra dos Carajás
São João do
Araguaia

Grajaú
Barra
do Corda
Porto Franco

Caxias
Pedreiras
Teresina
Senador Pompeu
Crateús
Caraúbas
Currais
Caicó
Novos

Carolina
Estreito
Tocantinópolis

Colinas
Floriano
Valença
do Piauí
Amarante
Iguatu
Cedro
Sousa
Patos
Cajàzeiras
Juàzeiro
Crato

Novo Iorque
Loreto
Riachão

Oeiras
Picos
PIAUÍ
Uruçuí

Conceição do
Araguaia

Santa
Filomena

São João
do Piauí
Ouricuri
do Norte
Salgueiro
Pesqueira

PARAÍBA
Campina
Grande
João Pessoa
Cabedelo
Canguaretama
Mamanguape
Olinda
RECIFE
Jaboatão

Araguacema

Pedro Afonso

Caracol
Sa. Dois Irmãos
Petrolina
Juàzeiro
Paulo Afonso

Caruaru
PERNAMBUCO
Garanhuns
Palmares
Vitória de Santo Antão

Palmas

Chapada das Mangabeiras

Parnaguá
Novo Remanso
Nova Casa
Nova
Represa de
Sobradinho

Senhor-do-
Bonfim

Palmeira
dos Índios
Propriá
SERGIPE
Rio Largo
Maceió
Arapiraca
ALAGOAS
Penedo

6059 ▼

TOCANTINS

Pôrto Nacional

Gurupi

Santa Isabel
do Morro

I. do Bananal

Xique-Xique
Barra
Jacobina
Mundo
Novo
Queimadas
Serrinha
Capela
Aracaju
São Cristóvão
Estância

RAZIL

Serra Formosa
Serra do Roncador

Taguatinga
Barreiras
BAHIA
Feira de
Santana
Alagoinhas
Santo Amaro
SALVADOR
B. de Todos os Santos

MATO GROSSO
Planalto do

Diamantino
Cuiabá Mato Grosso

Santa Antonio
Rondonópolis
Barra do Garças

Uruaçu

Niquelândia
1678 ▲

Niquelândia

Posse
Campos Belos
São Domingos
Santa Maria
da Vitória
Bom Jesus
da Lapa Serra do Sincorá
Ibotirama
Itaberaba
Cachoeira
Castro
Alves
Valença
Nazaré

Caetité
Brumado
Condeúba
Ubaitaba
Vitória da
Conquista
Jequié
Itabuna
Ilhéus

Carinhanha

MATO GROSSO
DO SUL

Cáceres

Coxim

Aruanã

DIST
FED
Formosa
Januária
São Francisco
Monte Azul
Pedra Azul
Canavieiras
Belmonte
Pôrto Seguro

Goiás
Taguatinga
BRASÍLIA
Luziânia
Montes
Claros
Salinas
Jequitinhonha
Itamaraju
Prado
Caravelas

Anápolis
Goiânia

Vianópolis
Araguari
Morrinhos
Alto Araguaia
GOIÁS
Jataí
Rio Verde
Itumbiara
Quirinópolis
Catalão
Paracatu
Pirapora
Araçuaí
Teófilo Otoni
Nanuque
Mucuri
Diamantina
Governador
Valadares
Conceição da Barra
São Mateus

Patos de
Minas
Corinto
Ipatinga
Nova
Venécia
Linhares
Colatina

Campo
Grande
Três Lagoas
Rio Prêto
Araxá
Ibiá
Uberlândia
MINAS GERAIS
Prata
Uberaba
Curvelo
Sête Lagoas
Itabira
Caratinga
Cariacica
Vitória
Vila Velha
Cachoeiro de Itapemirim

Aquidauana
Miranda
Ribas
do Rio
Pardo
Santa Fé do Sul
Água Clara
São José do Barretos
Frutal
Igarapava
Franca
Divinópolis
BELO HORIZONTE
Sabará
Ponte Nova
Ouro
Prêto
Uba

Trindade
(Braz.)

Dourados
Presidente Epitácio
Araçatuba
Penápolis
Birigui
Catanduva
Ribeirão Prêto
Passos
Poços de
Caldas
Lafaiete
Barbacena
Juiz de Fora
Itapemirim
Campos

Ponta Porã
Presidente
Prudente
Assis
Linssão
Araraquara
SÃO
Poços de
PAULO
São Carlos
del Rei
Três Rios
Nova Friburgo
Pedro Juan
Caballero
Bauru
Jaú
Moji-Mirim
Lourenço
Petrópolis
Cabo Frio

Piracicaba
Limeira
Campinas
Volta
Redonda
Niterói
RIO DE JANEIRO

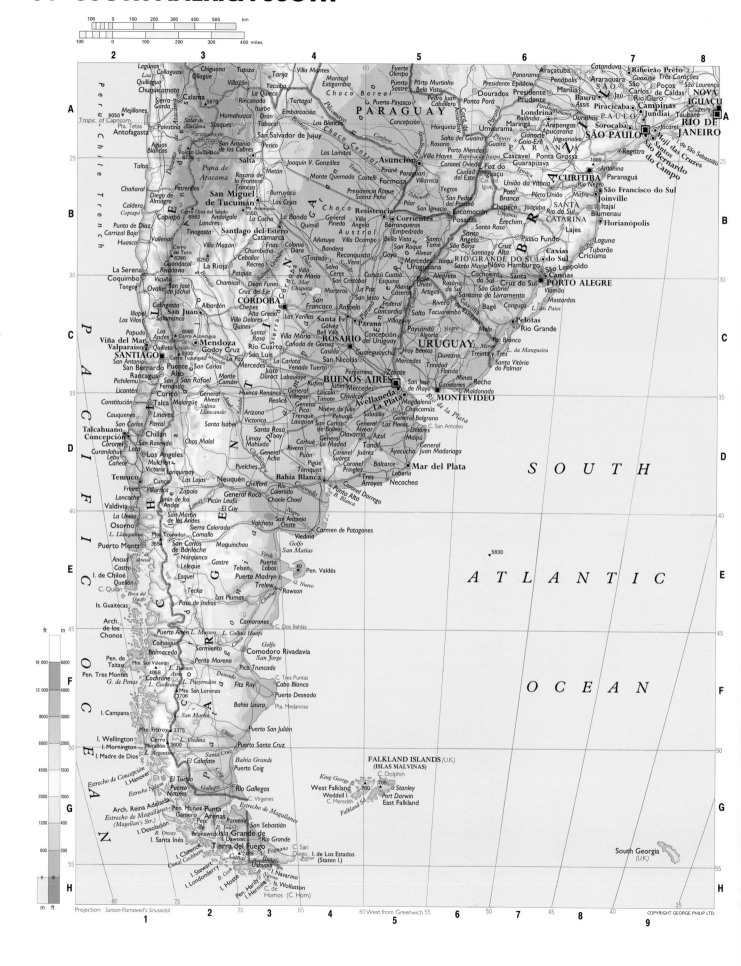

Index to Map Pages

The index contains the names of all principal places and features shown on the maps. Physical features composed of a proper name (Erie) and a description (Lake) are positioned alphabetically by the proper name. The description is positioned after the proper name and is usually abbreviated:

Erie, L., *N. Amer.* **52 D5**

Where a description forms part of a settlement or administrative name however, it is always written in full and put in its true alphabetical position:

Lake Charles, *U.S.A.* **55 K8**

The number in bold type which follows each name in the index refers to the number of the map page where that feature or place will be found. This is usually the largest scale at which the place or feature appears.

The letter and figure which are in bold type immediately after the page number give the grid square on the map page, within which the feature is situated.

Rivers carry the symbol ➤ after their names. A solid square ■ follows the name of a country while an open square □ refers to a first order administrative area.

A Coruña, *Spain* 15 A1
A Estrada, *Spain* 15 A1
A Fonsagrada, *Spain* . . . 15 A2
Aachen, *Germany* 12 C4
Aalborg = Ålborg,
  Denmark 7 H13
Aalen, *Germany* 12 D6
Aalst, *Belgium* 11 D4
Aalten, *Neths.* 11 C6
Aalter, *Belgium* 11 C3
Äänekoski, *Finland* . . . 7 E21
Aarau, *Switz.* 14 C8
Aare ➤, *Switz.* 14 C8
Aarhus = Århus,
  Denmark 7 H14
Aarschot, *Belgium* . . . 11 D4
Aba, *Nigeria* 34 G7
Ābādān, *Iran* 31 D6
Ābādeh, *Iran* 31 D7
Abadla, *Algeria* 34 B5
Abaetetuba, *Brazil* . . . 63 D9
Abakan, *Russia* 21 D10
Abancay, *Peru* 62 F4
Abariringa, *Kiribati* . . 44 H10
Abarqū, *Iran* 31 D7
Abashiri, *Japan* 22 B12
Abashiri-Wan, *Japan* . 22 C12
Åbay = Nîl el
  Azraq ➤, *Sudan* . . 35 E12
Abay, *Kazakstan* 20 E8
Abaya, L., *Ethiopia* . . 32 F2
Abaza, *Russia* 20 D9
'Abbāsābād, *Iran* . . . 31 C8
Abbay = Nîl el
  Azraq ➤, *Sudan* . . 35 E12
Abbaye, Pt., *U.S.A.* . . 52 B1
Abbé, L., *Ethiopia* . . . 32 E3
Abbeville, *France* 14 A4
Abbeville, *Ala., U.S.A.* 53 K3
Abbeville, *La., U.S.A.* . 55 L8
Abbeville, *S.C., U.S.A.* 53 H4
Abbot Ice Shelf,
  Antarctica 5 D16
Abd al Kūrī, *Ind. Oc.* . 32 E5
Ābdar, *Iran* 31 D7
'Abdolābād, *Iran* 31 C8
Abéché, *Chad* 35 F10
Abengourou, *Ivory C.* . 34 G5
Åbenrå, *Denmark* 7 J13
Abeokuta, *Nigeria* . . . 34 G6
Aberaeron, *U.K.* 9 E3
Aberayron = Aberaeron,
  U.K. 9 E3
Abercorn = Mbala,
  Zambia 36 F6
Abercorn, *Australia* . . 43 D5
Aberdare, *U.K.* 9 F4
Aberdeen, *Australia* . . 43 E5
Aberdeen, *Canada* . . . 51 C7
Aberdeen, *U.K.* 10 C5
Aberdeen, *Ala., U.S.A.* 53 J1
Aberdeen, *Idaho, U.S.A.* 56 E7
Aberdeen, *Md., U.S.A.* 52 F7
Aberdeen, *S. Dak.,
  U.S.A.* 54 C5
Aberdeen, *Wash., U.S.A.* 56 C2
Aberdovey = Aberdyfi,
  U.K. 9 E3
Aberdyfi, *U.K.* 9 E3
Abergavenny, *U.K.* . . . 9 F4
Abergele, *U.K.* 8 D4
Abernathy, *U.S.A.* . . . 55 J4
Aberystwyth, *U.K.* . . . 9 E3
Abhā, *Si. Arabia* 32 D3
Abhar, *Iran* 31 B6
Abidjan, *Ivory C.* 34 G5
Abilene, *Kans., U.S.A.* 54 F6
Abilene, *Tex., U.S.A.* . 55 J5
Abingdon, *U.K.* 9 F6
Abingdon, *U.S.A.* . . . 53 G5
Abington Reef, *Australia* 42 B4
Abitau ➤, *Canada* . . 51 B7
Abitibi ➤, *Canada* . . 48 B3
Abitibi, L., *Canada* . . 48 C4
Abkhaz Republic =
  Abkhazia □, *Georgia* 19 F7
Abkhazia □, *Georgia* . 19 F7
Abminga, *Australia* . . 43 D1
Åbo = Turku, *Finland* . 7 F20
Abohar, *India* 28 D9
Abomey, *Benin* 34 G6
Abong-Mbang,
  Cameroon 36 D2
Abou-Deïa, *Chad* . . . 35 F9
Abraham L., *Canada* . 50 C5

Abreojos, Pta., *Mexico* 58 B2
Abrud, *Romania* 13 E12
Absaroka Range, *U.S.A.* 56 D9
Abū al Abyaḍ, *U.A.E.* . 31 E7
Abū al Khaşīb, *Iraq* . . 31 D6
Abū 'Alī, *Si. Arabia* . . 31 E6
Abū 'Alī ➤, *Lebanon* . 33 A4
Abu Dhabi = Abū Ẓāby,
  U.A.E. 31 E7
Abū Du'ān, *Syria* . . . 30 B3
Abu el Gairi, W. ➤,
  Egypt 33 F2
Abu Ga'da, W. ➤,
  Egypt 33 F1
Abū Ḥadrīyah,
  Si. Arabia 31 E6
Abu Hamed, *Sudan* . . 35 E12
Abū Kamāl, *Syria* . . . 30 C4
Abū Madd, Ra's,
  Si. Arabia 30 E3
Abū Mūsā, *U.A.E.* . . . 31 E7
Abū Qaşr, *Si. Arabia* . 30 D3
Abū Şafāt, W. ➤,
  Jordan 33 E5
Abu Simbel, *Egypt* . . 35 D12
Abū Şukhayr, *Iraq* . . 30 D5
Abu Zabad, *Sudan* . . 35 F11
Abū Ẓāby, *U.A.E.* . . . 31 E7
Abū Zeydābād, *Iran* . 31 C6
Abuja, *Nigeria* 34 G7
Abukuma-Gawa ➤,
  Japan 22 E10
Abukuma-Sammyaku,
  Japan 22 F10
Abunã, *Brazil* 62 E5
Abunã ➤, *Brazil* . . . 62 E5
Abut Hd., *N.Z.* 39 K3
Acadia National Park,
  U.S.A. 53 C11
Açailândia, *Brazil* . . . 63 D9
Acajutla, *El Salv.* . . . 60 D2
Acámbaro, *Mexico* . . 58 C4
Acaponeta, *Mexico* . . 58 C3
Acapulco, *Mexico* . . . 59 D5
Acarai, Serra, *Brazil* . 62 C7
Acarigua, *Venezuela* . 62 B5
Acatlán, *Mexico* 59 D5
Acayucan, *Mexico* . . . 59 D6
Accomac, *U.S.A.* . . . 52 G8
Accra, *Ghana* 34 G5
Accrington, *U.K.* 8 D5
Aceh □, *Indonesia* . . 26 D1
Achalpur, *India* 28 J10
Achill I., *Ireland* 10 E1
Achinsk, *Russia* 21 D10
Acireale, *Italy* 16 F6
Ackerman, *U.S.A.* . . . 55 J10
Acklins I., *Bahamas* . 61 B5
Acme, *Canada* 50 C6
Aconcagua, Cerro,
  Argentina 64 C3
Aconquija, Mt.,
  Argentina 64 B3
Açores, Is. dos =
  Azores, Is. dos =
  Azores, Atl. Oc. . . . 34 A1
Acraman, L., *Australia* 43 E2
Acre = 'Akko, *Israel* . 33 C4
Acre □, *Brazil* 62 E4
Acre ➤, *Brazil* 62 E5
Acuña, *Mexico* 58 B4
Ad Dammām, *Si. Arabia* 31 E6
Ad Dāmūr, *Lebanon* . 33 B4
Ad Dawādimī, *Si. Arabia* 30 E5
Ad Dawḥah, *Qatar* . . 31 E6
Ad Dawr, *Iraq* 30 C4
Ad Dir'īyah, *Si. Arabia* 30 E5
Ad Dīwānīyah, *Iraq* . . 30 D5
Ad Dujayl, *Iraq* 30 C5
Ad Duwayd, *Si. Arabia* 30 D4
Ada, *Minn., U.S.A.* . . 54 B6
Ada, *Okla., U.S.A.* . . 55 H6
Adaja ➤, *Spain* 15 B3
Adak I., *U.S.A.* 46 C2
Adamaoua, Massif de l',
  Cameroon 36 C2
Adamawa Highlands =
  Adamaoua, Massif de
  l', *Cameroon* 36 C2
Adamello, Mte., *Italy* . 14 C9
Adaminaby, *Australia* 43 F4
Adams, N.Y., U.S.A. . . 52 D7
Adams, Wis., U.S.A. . . 54 D10
Adam's Bridge,
  Sri Lanka 28 Q11

Adams L., *Canada* . . . 50 C5
Adams Mt., *U.S.A.* . . . 56 C3
Adam's Peak, *Sri Lanka* 28 R12
Adana, *Turkey* 19 G6
Adapazan = Sakarya,
  Turkey 19 F5
Adarama, *Sudan* . . . 35 E12
Adare, C., *Antarctica* . 5 D11
Adaut, *Indonesia* . . . 27 F8
Adavale, *Australia* . . 43 D3
Adda ➤, *Italy* 14 D8
Addis Ababa = Addis
  Abeba, *Ethiopia* . . 32 F2
Addis Abeba, *Ethiopia* . 32 F2
Ādeh, *Iran* 30 B5
Adel, *U.S.A.* 53 K4
Adelaide, *Australia* . . 43 E2
Adelaide, *Bahamas* . . 60 A4
Adelaide I., *Antarctica* 5 C17
Adelaide Pen., *Canada* 46 B10
Adelaide River, *Australia* 40 B5
Adele I., *Australia* . . 40 C3
Adélie, Terre, *Antarctica* 5 C10
Adélie Land = Adélie,
  Terre, *Antarctica* . . 5 C10
Aden = Al 'Adan,
  Yemen 32 E4
Aden, G. of, *Asia* . . . 32 E4
Adh Dhayd, *U.A.E.* . . 31 E7
Adi, *Indonesia* 27 E8
Adieu, C., *Australia* . . 41 F5
Adieu Pt., *Australia* . . 40 C3
Adige ➤, *Italy* 16 B5
Adigrat, *Ethiopia* . . . 32 E2
Adilabad, *India* 28 K11
Adirondack Mts., *U.S.A.* 52 D8
Adlavik Is., *Canada* . . 49 A8
Admiralty G., *Australia* 40 B4
Admiralty I., *U.S.A.* . . 50 B2
Admiralty Is.,
  Papua N. G. 38 B7
Adonara, *Indonesia* . . 27 F6
Adoni, *India* 28 M10
Adour ➤, *France* . . . 14 E3
Adra, *Spain* 15 D4
Adrano, *Italy* 16 F6
Adrar, *Mauritania* . . . 34 D3
Adrian, *Mich., U.S.A.* . 52 E3
Adrian, *Tex., U.S.A.* . . 55 H3
Adriatic Sea, *Medit. S.* 16 C6
Adua, *Indonesia* 27 E7
Adwa, *Ethiopia* 32 E2
Adygea □, *Russia* . . 19 F7
Adzhar Republic =
  Ajaria □, *Georgia* . 19 F7
Adzopé, *Ivory C.* . . . 34 G5
Ægean Sea, *Medit. S.* 17 E11
Aerhtai Shan, *Mongolia* 24 B4
'Afak, *Iraq* 30 C5
Afghanistan ■, *Asia* . 28 C4
Aflou, *Algeria* 34 B6
'Afrīn, *Syria* 30 B3
Afton, *U.S.A.* 56 E8
Afuá, *Brazil* 63 D8
'Afula, *Israel* 33 C4
Afyon, *Turkey* 19 G5
Afyonkarahisar = Afyon,
  Turkey 19 G5
Agadès = Agadez, *Niger* 34 E7
Agadez, *Niger* 34 E7
Agadir, *Morocco* 34 B4
Agartala, *India* 29 H17
Agassiz, *Canada* . . . 50 D4
Agats, *Indonesia* . . . 27 F9
Agboville, *Ivory C.* . . 34 G5
Ağdam, *Azerbaijan* . . 30 B5
Agde, *France* 14 E5
Agen, *France* 14 D4
Āgh Kand, *Iran* 31 B6
Aginskoye, *Russia* . . 21 D12
Agnew, *Australia* . . . 41 E3
Agra, *India* 28 F10
Ağri, *Turkey* 19 G7
Agri ➤, *Italy* 16 D7
Ağrı Dağı, *Turkey* . . . 19 G7
Ağri Karakose = Ağri,
  Turkey 19 G7
Agrigento, *Italy* 16 F5
Agrinion, *Greece* . . . 17 E9
Agua Caliente, *Mexico* 58 B3
Agua Clara, *Brazil* . . 63 H8
Agua Prieta, *Mexico* . 58 A3
Aguadilla, *Puerto Rico* 61 C6
Aguadulce, *Panama* . 60 E3
Aguanish, *Canada* . . 49 B7
Aguanus ➤, *Canada* 49 B7

Aguarico ➤, *Ecuador* 62 D3
Aguas Blancas, *Chile* . 64 A3
Aguascalientes, *Mexico* 58 C4
Aguascalientes □,
  Mexico 58 C4
Aguilas, *Spain* 15 D5
Agulhas, C., *S. Africa* 37 L4
Agung, *Indonesia* . . . 26 F5
Agusan ➤, *Phil.* . . . 27 C7
Ahaggar, *Algeria* . . . 34 D7
Ahar, *Iran* 30 B5
Ahipara B., *N.Z.* 39 F4
Ahiri, *India* 28 K12
Ahmadabad, *India* . . 28 H8
Aḥmadābād, *Khorāsān,
  Iran* 31 C9
Aḥmadābād, *Khorāsān,
  Iran* 31 C8
Ahmadi, *Iran* 31 E8
Ahmadnagar, *India* . . 28 K9
Ahmadpur, *Pakistan* . 28 E7
Ahmedabad =
  Ahmadabad, *India* . 28 H8
Ahmednagar =
  Ahmadnagar, *India* . 28 K9
Ahome, *Mexico* 58 B3
Ahoskie, *U.S.A.* 53 G7
Ahram, *Iran* 31 D6
Āhū, *Iran* 31 C6
Ahuachapán, *El Salv.* 60 D2
Ahvāz, *Iran* 31 D6
Ahvenanmaa = Åland,
  Finland 7 F19
Ahwar, *Yemen* 32 E4
Aichi □, *Japan* 23 G8
Aigues-Mortes, *France* 14 E6
Aihui, *China* 25 A7
Aija, *Peru* 62 E3
Aikawa, *Japan* 22 E9
Aiken, *U.S.A.* 53 J5
Aileron, *Australia* . . . 42 C1
Aillik, *Canada* 49 A8
'Ailūn, *Jordan* 33 C4
Aim, *Russia* 21 D14
Aimere, *Indonesia* . . 27 F6
Ain Ben Tili, *Mauritania* 34 C4
Aïn-Sefra, *Algeria* . . 34 B5
'Ain Sudr, *Egypt* . . . 33 F2
Ainaži, *Latvia* 7 H21
Ainsworth, *U.S.A.* . . 54 D5
Aiquile, *Bolivia* 62 G5
Air, *Niger* 34 E7
Air Force I., *Canada* . 47 B12
Airdrie, *Canada* 50 C6
Aire ➤, *U.K.* 8 D7
Airlie Beach, *Australia* 42 C4
Aisne ➤, *France* . . . 14 B5
Aitkin, *U.S.A.* 54 B8
Aiud, *Romania* 13 E12
Aix-en-Provence, *France* 14 E6
Aix-la-Chapelle =
  Aachen, *Germany* . 12 C4
Aix-les-Bains, *France* . 14 D6
Aíyion, *Greece* 17 E10
Aizawl, *India* 29 H18
Aizkraukle, *Latvia* . . 7 H21
Aizpute, *Latvia* 7 H19
Aizuwakamatsu, *Japan* 22 F9
Ajaccio, *France* 14 F8
Ajalpan, *Mexico* 59 D5
Ajanta Ra., *India* . . . 28 J9
Ajari Rep. = Ajaria □,
  Georgia 19 F7
Ajaria □, *Georgia* . . 19 F7
Ajdābiyah, *Libya* . . . 35 B10
Ajka, *Hungary* 13 E9
'Ajman, *U.A.E.* 31 E7
Ajmer, *India* 28 F9
Ajo, *U.S.A.* 57 K7
Ajo, C. de, *Spain* . . . 15 A4
Akabira, *Japan* 22 C11
Akaroa, *N.Z.* 39 K4
Akashi, *Japan* 23 G7
Akelamo, *Indonesia* . 27 D7
Aketi, *Dem. Rep. of
  the Congo* 36 D4
Akharnaí, *Greece* . . . 17 E10
Akhelóös ➤, *Greece* 17 E9
Akhisar, *Turkey* 17 E12
Akhtyrka = Okhtyrka,
  Ukraine 19 D5
Aki, *Japan* 23 H6
Akimiski I., *Canada* . 48 B3
Akita, *Japan* 22 E10
Akita □, *Japan* 22 E10
Akjoujt, *Mauritania* . . 34 E3

Akkeshi, *Japan* 22 C12
'Akko, *Israel* 33 C4
Aklavik, *Canada* 46 B6
Akmolinsk = Astana,
  Kazakstan 20 D8
Akō, *Japan* 23 G7
Akola, *India* 28 J10
Akordat, *Eritrea* 32 D2
Akpatok I., *Canada* . . 47 B13
Åkrahamn, *Norway* . . 7 G11
Akranes, *Iceland* . . . 6 D2
Akron, *Colo., U.S.A.* . 54 E3
Akron, *Ohio, U.S.A.* . 52 E5
Aksai Chin, *India* . . . 28 B11
Aksaray, *Turkey* 19 G5
Aksay, *Kazakstan* . . . 19 D9
Akşehir, *Turkey* 30 B1
Akşehir Gölü, *Turkey* . 19 G5
Aksu, *China* 24 B3
Aksum, *Ethiopia* 32 E2
Aktogay, *Kazakstan* . 20 E8
Aktsyabrski, *Belarus* . 13 B15
Aktyubinsk = Aqtöbe,
  Kazakstan 19 D10
Akure, *Nigeria* 34 G7
Akureyri, *Iceland* . . . 6 D4
Akuseki-Shima, *Japan* 23 K4
Akyab = Sittwe, *Burma* 29 J18
Al 'Adan, *Yemen* . . . 32 E4
Al Ahsa = Hasa □,
  Si. Arabia 31 E6
Al Ajfar, *Si. Arabia* . . 30 E4
Al Amādīyah, *Iraq* . . 30 B4
Al 'Amārah, *Iraq* . . . 30 D5
Al 'Aqabah, *Jordan* . 33 F4
Al Arak, *Syria* 30 C3
Al 'Aramah, *Si. Arabia* 30 E5
Al Arţāwīyah, *Si. Arabia* 30 E5
Al 'Āşimah =
  'Ammān □, *Jordan* . 33 D5
Al 'Assāfiyah, *Si. Arabia* 30 D3
Al 'Ayn, *Oman* 31 E7
Al 'Ayn, *Si. Arabia* . . 30 E3
Al 'Azamīyah, *Iraq* . . 30 C5
Al 'Azīzīyah, *Iraq* . . . 30 C5
Al Bāb, *Syria* 30 B3
Al Bad', *Si. Arabia* . . 30 D2
Al Bādī, *Iraq* 30 C4
Al Baḩral Mayyit =
  Dead Sea, *Asia* . . 33 D4
Al Balqā' □, *Jordan* . 33 C4
Al Bārūk, J., *Lebanon* 33 B4
Al Başrah, *Iraq* 30 D5
Al Bāţin ➤, *Asia* . . . 30 D5
Al Batrūn, *Lebanon* . . 33 A4
Al Bayḑā, *Libya* 35 B10
Al Biqā, *Lebanon* . . . 33 A5
Al Bi'r, *Si. Arabia* . . . 30 D3
Al Burayj, *Syria* 33 A5
Al Fadilī, *Si. Arabia* . 31 E6
Al Fallūjah, *Iraq* 30 C4
Al Fāw, *Iraq* 31 D6
Al Fujayrah, *U.A.E.* . . 31 E8
Al Ghadaf, W. ➤,
  Jordan 33 D5
Al Ghammās, *Iraq* . . 30 D5
Al Ghazālah, *Si. Arabia* 30 E4
Al Hābah, *Si. Arabia* . 30 E5
Al Ḥadīthah, *Iraq* . . . 30 C4
Al Ḥadīthah, *Si. Arabia* 30 D3
Al Ḩadr, *Iraq* 30 C4
Al Ḥājānah, *Syria* . . 33 B5
Al Hajar al Gharbi,
  Oman 31 E8
Al Ḥamad, *Si. Arabia* 30 D3
Al Ḩamdāniyah, *Syria* 30 C3
Al Ḩamīdīyah, *Syria* . 33 A4
Al Ḩammār, *Iraq* . . . 30 D5
Al Ḩamrā, *Si. Arabia* 30 E3
Al Ḩanākiyah, *Si. Arabia* 30 E4
Al Ḥarīr, W. ➤, *Syria* 33 C4
Al Ḥasā ➤, *Jordan* . 33 D4
Al Ḥasakah, *Syria* . . 30 B4
Al Ḥaydān, W. ➤,
  Jordan 33 D4
Al Ḥayy, *Iraq* 30 C5
Al Ḥijarah, *Asia* 30 D4
Al Ḥillah, *Iraq* 30 C5
Al Hindīyah, *Iraq* . . . 30 C5
Al Hoceïma, *Morocco* 34 A5
Al Ḥudaydah, *Yemen* 32 E3
Al Ḥufūf, *Si. Arabia* . 31 E6
Al Ḥumaydah, *Si. Arabia* 30 D2
Al Ḥunayy, *Si. Arabia* 31 E6

Al Īsāwīyah, *Si. Arabia* 30 D3
Al Jafr, *Jordan* 33 E5
Al Jāfūrah, *Si. Arabia* 31 E7
Al Jaghbūb, *Libya* . . 35 C10
Al Jahrah, *Kuwait* . . . 30 D5
Al Jalāmid, *Si. Arabia* 30 D3
Al Jamalīyah, *Qatar* . 31 E6
Al Janūb □, *Lebanon* 33 B4
Al Jawf, *Libya* 35 D10
Al Jawf, *Si. Arabia* . . 30 D3
Al Jazirah, *Iraq* 30 C5
Al Jithāmiyah,
  Si. Arabia 30 E4
Al Jubayl, *Si. Arabia* . 31 E6
Al Jubaylah, *Si. Arabia* 30 E5
Al Jubb, *Si. Arabia* . . 30 E4
Al Junaynah, *Sudan* . 35 F10
Al Kabā'ish, *Iraq* . . . 30 D5
Al Karak, *Jordan* . . . 33 D4
Al Karak □, *Jordan* . 33 E5
Al Kāzim Tyah, *Iraq* . 30 C5
Al Khābūra, *Oman* . . 31 F8
Al Khafji, *Si. Arabia* . 31 E6
Al Khalīl, *West Bank* . 33 D4
Al Khāliş, *Iraq* 30 C5
Al Kharsāniyah,
  Si. Arabia 31 E6
Al Khaşab, *Oman* . . . 31 E8
Al Khawr, *Qatar* 31 E6
Al Khiḍr, *Iraq* 30 D5
Al Khiyām, *Lebanon* . 33 B4
Al Khums, *Libya* 35 B8
Al Kiswah, *Syria* 33 B5
Al Kūfah, *Iraq* 30 C5
Al Kufrah, *Libya* 35 D10
Al Kuhayfiyah,
  Si. Arabia 30 E4
Al Kūt, *Iraq* 30 C5
Al Kuwayt, *Kuwait* . . 30 D5
Al Labwah, *Lebanon* . 33 A5
Al Lādhiqīyah, *Syria* . 30 C2
Al Līth, *Si. Arabia* . . . 32 C3
Al Liwā', *Oman* 31 E8
Al Luḩayyah, *Yemen* . 32 D3
Al Madīnah, *Iraq* . . . 30 D5
Al Madīnah, *Si. Arabia* 30 E3
Al Mafraq, *Jordan* . . 33 C5
Al Maḩmūdīyah, *Iraq* 30 C5
Al Majma'ah, *Si. Arabia* 30 E5
Al Makhruq, W. ➤,
  Jordan 33 D6
Al Makhūl, *Si. Arabia* 30 E4
Al Manāmah, *Bahrain* 31 E6
Al Maqwa', *Kuwait* . . 30 D5
Al Marj, *Libya* 35 B10
Al Maţlā, *Kuwait* . . . 30 D5
Al Mawjib, W. ➤,
  Jordan 33 D4
Al Mawşil, *Iraq* 30 B4
Al Mayādin, *Syria* . . 30 C4
Al Mazār, *Jordan* . . . 33 D4
Al Midhnab, *Si. Arabia* 30 E5
Al Minā', *Lebanon* . . 33 A4
Al Miqdādīyah, *Iraq* . 30 C5
Al Mubarraz, *Si. Arabia* 31 E6
Al Mudawwarah, *Jordan* 33 F5
Al Mughayrā', *U.A.E.* 31 E7
Al Muharraq, *Bahrain* 31 E6
Al Mukallā, *Yemen* . . 32 E4
Al Mukhā, *Yemen* . . . 32 E3
Al Musayjid, *Si. Arabia* 30 E3
Al Musayyib, *Iraq* . . . 30 C5
Al Muwaylih, *Si. Arabia* 30 E2
Al Qā'im, *Iraq* 30 C4
Al Qalibah, *Si. Arabia* 30 D3
Al Qāmishli, *Syria* . . 30 B4
Al Qaryatayn, *Syria* . 33 A6
Al Qaşim, *Si. Arabia* . 30 E4
Al Qaţ'a, *Syria* 30 C4
Al Qaţif, *Si. Arabia* . . 31 E6
Al Qaţrānah, *Jordan* . 33 D5
Al Qaţrūn, *Libya* . . . 35 D9
Al Qayşūmah, *Si. Arabia* 30 D5
Al Quds = Jerusalem,
  Israel 33 D4
Al Qunayţirah, *Syria* . 33 C4
Al Qurnah, *Iraq* 30 D5
Al Qusayr, *Syria* 33 A5
Al Qutayfah, *Syria* . . 33 B5
Al 'Udaylīyah, *Si. Arabia* 31 E6
Al 'Ulā, *Si. Arabia* . . 30 E3
Al Uqayr, *Si. Arabia* . 31 E6
Al 'Uthmānīyah,
  Si. Arabia 31 E6

Al 'Uwaynid, *Si. Arabia* 30 E5
Al 'Uwayqīlah,
  Si. Arabia 30 D4
Al 'Uyūn, Ḥijāz,
  Si. Arabia 30 E3
Al 'Uyūn, Najd,
  Si. Arabia 30 E4
Al 'Uzayr, *Iraq* 30 D5
Al Wajh, *Si. Arabia* . . . 30 E3
Al Wakrah, *Qatar* 31 E6
Al Wannān, *Si. Arabia* . 31 E6
Al Waqbah, *Si. Arabia* . 30 D5
Al Wari'āh, *Si. Arabia* . 30 D5
Al Wusayl, *Qatar* 31 E6
Ala Dağ, *Turkey* 30 B2
Ala Tau Shankou =
  Dzungarian Gates,
  Asia 24 B3
Alabama □, *U.S.A.* 53 J2
Alabama →, *U.S.A.* . . . 53 K2
Alabaster, *U.S.A.* 53 J2
Alaçam Dağları, *Turkey* 17 E13
Alachua, *U.S.A.* 53 L4
Alagoa Grande, *Brazil* . 63 E11
Alagoas □, *Brazil* 63 E11
Alagoinhas, *Brazil* 63 F11
Alajuela, *Costa Rica* . . 60 D3
Alakurtti, *Russia* 18 A5
Alamarvdasht, *Iran* . . . 31 E7
Alameda, *U.S.A.* 57 J10
Alamo, *U.S.A.* 57 H6
Alamogordo, *U.S.A.* . . 57 K11
Alamos, *Mexico* 58 B3
Alamosa, *U.S.A.* 57 H11
Åland, *Finland* 7 F19
Ålands hav, *Sweden* . . 7 F18
Alania = North
  Ossetia □, *Russia* . . . 19 F7
Alanya, *Turkey* 19 G5
Alapayevsk, *Russia* . . . 20 D7
Alaşehir, *Turkey* 17 E13
Alaska □, *U.S.A.* 46 B5
Alaska, G. of, *Pac. Oc.* . 46 C5
Alaska Peninsula, *U.S.A.* 46 C4
Alaska Range, *U.S.A.* . . 46 B4
Älät, *Azerbaijan* 19 G8
Alatyr, *Russia* 18 D8
Alausi, *Ecuador* 62 D3
Alava, C., *U.S.A.* 56 B1
Alavus, *Finland* 7 E20
Alawoona, *Australia* . . 43 E3
'Alayh, *Lebanon* 33 B4
Alba, *Italy* 14 D8
Alba-Iulia, *Romania* . . 13 E12
Albacete, *Spain* 15 C5
Albacutya, L., *Australia* 43 F5
Albanel, L., *Canada* . . . 48 B5
Albania ■, *Europe* 17 D9
Albany, *Australia* 41 G2
Albany, *Ga., U.S.A.* . . . 53 K3
Albany, *N.Y., U.S.A.* . . 52 D9
Albany, *Oreg., U.S.A.* . 56 D2
Albany, *Tex., U.S.A.* . . 55 J5
Albany →, *Canada* 48 B3
Albardón, *Argentina* . . 64 C3
Albatross B., *Australia* . 42 A3
Albemarle, *U.S.A.* 53 H5
Albemarle Sd., *U.S.A.* . 53 H7
Alberche →, *Spain* . . . 15 C3
Albert, L., *Australia* . . . 43 F2
Albert Edward Ra.,
  Australia 40 C4
Albert L., *Africa* 36 D6
Albert Lea, *U.S.A.* 54 D8
Albert Nile →, *Uganda* 36 D6
Albert Town, *Bahamas* 61 B5
Alberta □, *Canada* 50 C6
Alberton, *Canada* 49 C7
Albertville = Kalemie,
  *Dem. Rep. of
  the Congo* 36 F5
Albertville, *France* 14 D7
Albertville, *U.S.A.* 53 H2
Albi, *France* 14 E5
Albia, *U.S.A.* 54 E8
Albina, *Surinam* 63 B8
Albion, *Mich., U.S.A.* . 52 D3
Albion, *Nebr., U.S.A.* . 54 E6
Ålborg, *Denmark* 7 H13
Alborz, Reshteh-ye
  Kühhā-ye, *Iran* 31 C7
Albuquerque, *U.S.A.* . . 57 J10
Albuquerque, Cayos de,
  Caribbean 60 D3
Albury-Wodonga,
  Australia 43 F4
Alcalá de Henares,
  Spain 15 B4
Alcalá la Real, *Spain* . . 15 D4
Álcamo, *Italy* 16 F5
Alcaniz, *Spain* 15 B5
Alcântara, *Brazil* 63 D10
Alcántara, Embalse de,
  Spain 15 C2
Alcantarilla, *Spain* 15 D5
Alcaraz, Sierra de, *Spain* 15 C4
Alcaudete, *Spain* 15 D3
Alcázar de San Juan,
  Spain 15 C4
Alchevsk, *Ukraine* 19 E6
Alcira = Alzira, *Spain* . 15 C5
Alcova, *U.S.A.* 56 E10
Alcoy, *Spain* 15 C5
Aldabra Is., *Seychelles* . 3 E12

Aldama, *Mexico* 59 C5
Aldan, *Russia* 21 D13
Aldan →, *Russia* 21 C13
Aldeburgh, *U.K.* 9 E9
Alderney, *U.K.* 9 H5
Aldershot, *U.K.* 9 F7
Aledo, *U.S.A.* 54 E9
Aleg, *Mauritania* 34 E3
Alegrete, *Brazil* 64 B5
Aleisk, *Russia* 20 D9
Aleksandriya =
  Oleksandriya, *Ukraine* 13 C14
Aleksandrov Gay,
  Russia 19 D8
Aleksandrovsk-
  Sakhalinskiy, *Russia* . 21 D15
Alençon, *France* 14 B4
Alenquer, *Brazil* 63 D8
Aleppo = Ḥalab, *Syria* . 30 B3
Alès, *France* 14 D6
Alessándria, *Italy* 14 D8
Ålesund, *Norway* 7 E12
Aleutian Is., *Pac. Oc.* . . 46 C2
Aleutian Trench,
  Pac. Oc. 44 C10
Alexander, *U.S.A.* 54 B3
Alexander, Mt.,
  Australia 41 E3
Alexander Arch., *U.S.A.* 46 C6
Alexander City, *U.S.A.* . 53 J3
Alexander I., *Antarctica* 5 C17
Alexandra, *Australia* . . 43 F4
Alexandra, *N.Z.* 39 L2
Alexandra Falls, *Canada* 50 A5
Alexandria = El
  Iskandarîya, *Egypt* . . 35 B11
Alexandria, *B.C., Canada* 50 C4
Alexandria, *Ont.,
  Canada* 48 C5
Alexandria, *Romania* . . 13 G13
Alexandria, *La., U.S.A.* 55 K8
Alexandria, *Minn.,
  U.S.A.* 54 C7
Alexandria, *S. Dak.,
  U.S.A.* 54 D6
Alexandria, *Va., U.S.A.* 52 F7
Alexandria Bay, *U.S.A.* 52 C8
Alexandrina, L.,
  Australia 43 F2
Alexandroúpolis, *Greece* 17 D11
Alexis →, *Canada* 49 B8
Alexis Creek, *Canada* . 50 C4
Alford, *U.K.* 8 D8
Alfreton, *U.K.* 8 D6
Alga, *Kazakhstan* 19 E10
Ålgård, *Norway* 7 G11
Algarve, *Portugal* 15 D1
Algeciras, *Spain* 15 D3
Algemesí, *Spain* 15 C5
Alger, *Algeria* 34 A6
Algeria ■, *Africa* 34 C6
Alghero, *Italy* 16 D3
Algiers = Alger, *Algeria* 34 A6
Algoma, *U.S.A.* 52 C2
Algona, *U.S.A.* 54 D7
Algonquin Prov. Park,
  Canada 48 C4
Algorta, *Uruguay* 64 C5
Alhucemas = Al
  Hoceïma, *Morocco* . . 34 A5
'Alī al Gharbī, *Iraq* . . . 30 C5
'Alī ash Sharqī, *Iraq* . . 30 C5
'Alī Khēl, *Afghan.* 28 C6
Ali Shāh, *Iran* 30 B5
'Alīābād, *Khorāsān, Iran* 31 C8
'Alīābād, *Kordestān, Iran* 30 C5
'Alīābād, *Yazd, Iran* . . . 31 D7
Aliağa, *Turkey* 17 E12
Aliákmon →, *Greece* . . 17 D10
Alicante, *Spain* 15 C5
Alice, *U.S.A.* 55 M5
Alice →, *Queens.,
  Australia* 42 C3
Alice →, *Queens.,
  Australia* 42 B3
Alice Arm, *Canada* . . . 50 B3
Alice Springs, *Australia* 42 C1
Aliceville, *U.S.A.* 53 J1
Aligarh, *India* 28 F11
Alīgūdarz, *Iran* 31 C6
Alingsås, *Sweden* 7 H15
Alipur, *Pakistan* 28 E7
Alipur Duar, *India* 29 F16
Aliquippa, *U.S.A.* 52 E5
Alitus = Alytus,
  Lithuania 7 J21
Aliwal North, *S. Africa* . 37 L5
Alix, *Canada* 50 C6
Aljustrel, *Portugal* 15 D1
Alkmaar, *Neths.* 11 B4
All American Canal,
  U.S.A. 57 K6
Allagash →, *U.S.A.* . . . 53 B11
Allahabad, *India* 29 G12
Allan, *Canada* 51 C7
Allegheny →, *U.S.A.* . . 52 E6
Allegheny Mts., *U.S.A.* 52 G6
Allendale, *U.S.A.* 53 J5
Allende, *Mexico* 58 B4
Allentown, *U.S.A.* 52 E8
Alleppey, *India* 28 Q10
Aller →, *Germany* 12 B5
Alliance, *Nebr., U.S.A.* 54 D3
Alliance, *Ohio, U.S.A.* . 52 E5
Allier →, *France* 14 C5

Alliford Bay, *Canada* . . 50 C2
Alliston, *Canada* 48 D4
Allora, *Australia* 43 D5
Alluitsup Paa,
  Greenland 4 C5
Alma, *Canada* 49 C5
Alma, *Ga., U.S.A.* 53 K4
Alma, *Kans., U.S.A.* . . 54 F6
Alma, *Mich., U.S.A.* . . 52 D3
Alma, *Nebr., U.S.A.* . . 54 E5
Alma Ata = Almaty,
  Kazakstan 20 E8
Almada, *Portugal* 15 C1
Almaden, *Australia* . . . 42 B3
Almadén, *Spain* 15 C3
Almansa, *Spain* 15 C5
Almanzor, Pico, *Spain* . 15 B3
Almanzora →, *Spain* . . 15 D5
Almaty, *Kazakstan* . . . 20 E8
Almazán, *Spain* 15 B4
Almeirim, *Brazil* 63 D8
Almelo, *Neths.* 11 B6
Almendralejo, *Spain* . . 15 C2
Almere-Stad, *Neths.* . . 11 B5
Almería, *Spain* 15 D4
Almirante, *Panama* . . . 60 E3
Almora, *India* 28 E11
Almnouth, *U.K.* 8 B6
Alnwick, *U.K.* 8 B6
Alon, *Burma* 29 H19
Alor, *Indonesia* 27 F6
Alor Setar, *Malaysia* . . 26 C2
Aloysius, Mt., *Australia* 41 E4
Alpena, *U.S.A.* 52 C4
Alpha, *Australia* 42 C4
Alphen aan den Rijn,
  Neths. 11 B4
Alpine, *Ariz., U.S.A.* . . 57 K9
Alpine, *Tex., U.S.A.* . . 55 K3
Alps, *Europe* 14 C8
Alsace, *France* 14 B7
Alsask, *Canada* 51 C7
Alsasua, *Spain* 15 A4
Alsek →, *U.S.A.* 50 B1
Alsten, *Norway* 6 D15
Alston, *U.K.* 8 C5
Alta, *Norway* 6 B20
Alta Gracia, *Argentina* . 64 C4
Altaelva →, *Norway* . . 6 B20
Altafjorden, *Norway* . . 6 A20
Altai = Aerhtai Shan,
  Mongolia 24 B4
Altamaha →, *U.S.A.* . . 53 K5
Altamira, *Brazil* 63 D8
Altamira, *Mexico* 59 C5
Altamura, *Italy* 16 D7
Altanbulag, *Mongolia* . 24 A5
Altar, *Mexico* 58 A2
Altar, Desierto de,
  Mexico 58 B2
Altata, *Mexico* 58 C3
Altavista, *U.S.A.* 52 G6
Altay, *China* 24 B3
Altea, *Spain* 15 C5
Alto Araguaia, *Brazil* . . 63 G8
Alto Cuchumatanes =
  Cuchumatanes, Sierra
  de los, *Guatemala* . . 60 C1
Alto Molocue, *Mozam.* 37 H7
Alton, *U.K.* 9 F7
Alton, *U.S.A.* 54 F9
Altoona, *U.S.A.* 52 E6
Altūn Kūprī, *Iraq* 30 C5
Altun Shan, *China* 24 C3
Alturas, *U.S.A.* 56 F3
Altus, *U.S.A.* 55 H5
Alucra, *Turkey* 19 F6
Alūksne, *Latvia* 7 H22
Alusi, *Indonesia* 27 F8
Alva, *U.S.A.* 55 G5
Alvarado, *Mexico* 59 D5
Alvarado, *U.S.A.* 55 J6
Alvaro Obregón, Presa,
  Mexico 58 B3
Alvear, *Argentina* 64 B5
Alvesta, *Sweden* 7 H16
Alvin, *U.S.A.* 55 L7
Älvkarleby, *Sweden* . . 7 F17
Alvord Desert, *U.S.A.* . 56 E4
Älvsbyn, *Sweden* 6 D19
Alwar, *India* 28 F10
Alxa Zuoqi, *China* 24 C5
Alyangula, *Australia* . . 42 A2
Alyata =
  Azerbaijan* 19 G8
Alytus, *Lithuania* 7 J21
Alzada, *U.S.A.* 54 C2
Alzira, *Spain* 15 C5
Am-Timan, *Chad* 35 F10
Amadeus, L., *Australia* 41 D5
Amâdi, *Sudan* 35 G12
Amadjuak L., *Canada* . 47 B12
Amagasaki, *Japan* 23 G7
Amahai, *Indonesia* . . . 27 E7
Amakusa-Shotō, *Japan* 23 H5
Åmål, *Sweden* 7 G15
Amaliás, *Greece* 17 F9
Amalner, *India* 28 J9
Amamapare, *Indonesia* 27 E9
Amambay, Cordillera
  de, *S. Amer.* 64 A5
Amami-Guntō, *Japan* . 23 L4
Amami-Ō-Shima, *Japan* 23 L4
Amaná, L., *Brazil* 62 D6

Amangeldy, *Kazakstan* 20 D7
Amapá, *Brazil* 63 C8
Amapá □, *Brazil* 63 C8
Amaranth, *Canada* . . . 51 C9
Amarante, *Brazil* 63 E10
Amaranth, *Canada* . . . 51 C9
Amarillo, *U.S.A.* 55 H4
Amaro, Mte., *Italy* 16 C6
Amasya, *Turkey* 19 F6
Amata, *Australia* 41 E5
Amatitlán, *Guatemala* . 60 D1
Amay, *Belgium* 11 D5
Amazon =
  Amazonas →,
  S. Amer. 63 D9
Amazonas □, *Brazil* . . 62 E6
Amazonas →, *S. Amer.* 63 D9
Ambala, *India* 28 D10
Ambalavao, *Madag.* . . 37 J9
Ambanja, *Madag.* 37 G9
Ambarchik, *Russia* . . . 21 C17
Ambato, *Ecuador* 62 D3
Ambatolampy, *Madag.* 37 H9
Ambatondrazaka,
  Madag. 37 H9
Amberg, *Germany* 12 D6
Ambergris Cay, *Belize* . 59 D7
Amberley, *N.Z.* 39 K4
Ambikapur, *India* 29 H13
Ambilobé, *Madag.* . . . 37 G9
Ambleside, *U.K.* 8 C5
Ambo, *Peru* 62 F3
Amboise, *France* 14 C4
Ambon, *Indonesia* 27 E7
Ambositra, *Madag.* . . . 37 J9
Ambovombe, *Madag.* . 37 K9
Amboy, *U.S.A.* 57 J6
Amboyna Cay,
  S. China Sea 26 C4
Ambriz, *Angola* 36 F2
Amchitka I., *U.S.A.* . . . 46 C1
Amderma, *Russia* 20 C7
Ameca, *Mexico* 58 C4
Amecameca, *Mexico* . . 58 C3
Amecameca, *Mexico* . . 59 D5
Ameland, *Neths.* 11 A5
American Falls, *U.S.A.* . 56 E7
American Falls
  Reservoir, *U.S.A.* . . . 56 E7
American Fork, *U.S.A.* . 56 F8
American Highland,
  Antarctica 5 D6
American Samoa ■,
  Pac. Oc. 39 B13
Americus, *U.S.A.* 53 K3
Amersfoort, *Neths.* . . . 11 B5
Amery Ice Shelf,
  Antarctica 5 C6
Ames, *U.S.A.* 54 E8
Amga, *Russia* 21 C14
Amga →, *Russia* 21 C14
Amgu, *Russia* 21 E14
Amgun →, *Russia* 21 D14
Amherst, *Canada* 49 C7
Amherst, *U.S.A.* 52 D2
Amherstburg, *Canada* . 48 D3
Amiata, Mte., *Italy* . . . 16 C4
Amidon, *U.S.A.* 54 B3
Amiens, *France* 14 B5
Amīrābād, *Iran* 30 C5
Amirante Is., *Seychelles* 3 E12
Amisk L., *Canada* 51 C8
Amistad, Presa de la,
  Mexico 58 B4
Amite, *U.S.A.* 55 K9
Amla I., *U.S.A.* 46 C2
Amlwch, *U.K.* 8 D3
'Ammān, *Jordan* 33 D4
'Ammān □, *Jordan* . . . 33 D5
Ammanford, *U.K.* 9 F4
Ammassalik = Tasiilaq,
  Greenland 4 C6
Ammon, *U.S.A.* 56 E8
Åmol, *Iran* 31 B7
Amorgós, *Greece* 17 F11
Amory, *U.S.A.* 53 J1
Amos, *Canada* 48 C4
Åmot, *Norway* 7 G13
Amoy = Xiamen, *China* 25 D6
Ampanihy, *Madag.* . . . 37 J8
Ampenan, *Indonesia* . . 26 F5
Amper →, *Germany* . . . 12 D6
Amqui, *Canada* 49 C6
Amravati, *India* 28 J10
Amreli, *India* 28 J7
Amritsar, *India* 28 D9
Amroha, *India* 28 E11
Amsterdam, *Neths.* . . . 11 B4
Amsterdam, *U.S.A.* . . . 52 D8
Amsterdam, I. =
  Nouvelle-Amsterdam,
  I., *Ind. Oc.* 3 F13
Amstetten, *Austria* . . . 12 D8
Amudarya →,
  Uzbekistan 20 E6
Amundsen Gulf, *Canada* 46 A7
Amundsen Sea,
  Antarctica 5 D15
Amuntai, *Indonesia* . . 26 E5
Amur →, *Russia* 21 D15
Amuri Pass, *N.Z.* 39 K4
Amursk, *Russia* 21 D14
Amyderya =
  Amudarya →,
  Uzbekistan 20 E6

An Nabatīyah at Tahta,
  Lebanon 33 B4
An Nabk, *Si. Arabia* . . 30 D3
An Nabk, *Syria* 33 A5
An Nafūd, *Si. Arabia* . . 30 D4
An Najaf, *Iraq* 30 C5
An Nhon, *Vietnam* . . . 26 B3
An Nāṣirīyah, *Iraq* 30 D5
An Nu'ayrīyah,
  Si. Arabia 31 E6
An Nuwayb'ī, W. →,
  Si. Arabia 33 F3
Anabar →, *Russia* 21 B12
'Anabtā, *West Bank* . . . 33 C4
Anaconda, *U.S.A.* 56 C7
Anacortes, *U.S.A.* 56 B2
Anadarko, *U.S.A.* 55 H5
Anadolu, *Turkey* 19 G5
Anadyr, *Russia* 21 C18
Anadyr →, *Russia* 21 C18
Anadyrskiy Zaliv, *Russia* 21 C19
'Ānah, *Iraq* 30 C4
Anaheim, *U.S.A.* 57 K5
Anahim Lake, *Canada* . 50 C3
Anáhuac, *Mexico* 58 B4
Anakapalle, *India* 29 L13
Anakie, *Australia* 42 C4
Anambas, Kepulauan,
  Indonesia 26 D3
Anambas Is. =
  Anambas, Kepulauan,
  Indonesia 26 D3
Anamosa, *U.S.A.* 54 D9
Anamur, *Turkey* 19 G5
Anan, *Japan* 23 H7
Anantnag, *India* 28 C9
Ananyiv, *Ukraine* 13 E15
Anápolis, *Brazil* 63 G9
Anapu →, *Brazil* 63 D8
Anār, *Iran* 31 D7
Anārak, *Iran* 31 C7
Anatolia = Anadolu,
  Turkey 19 G5
Añatuya, *Argentina* . . . 64 B4
Anaunethad L., *Canada* 51 A8
Anchorage, *U.S.A.* . . . 46 B5
Ancohuma, Nevada,
  Bolivia 62 G5
Ancón, *Peru* 62 F3
Ancona, *Italy* 16 C5
Ancud, *Chile* 64 E2
Ancud, G. de, *Chile* . . . 64 E2
Anda, *China* 25 B7
Andalgalá, *Argentina* . 64 B3
Åndalsnes, *Norway* . . . 7 E12
Andalucía □, *Spain* . . . 15 D3
Andalusia =
  Andalucía □, *Spain* . . 15 D3
Andalusia, *U.S.A.* 53 K2
Andaman Is., *Ind. Oc.* . 3 D14
Andaman Is., *Ind. Oc.* . 3 D14
Andaman Sea, *Ind. Oc.* 26 B1
Andamooka Opal Fields,
  Australia 43 E2
Andapa, *Madag.* 37 G9
Andenes, *Norway* 6 B17
Andenne, *Belgium* . . . 11 D5
Anderson, *Alaska,
  U.S.A.* 46 B5
Anderson, *Calif., U.S.A.* 56 F2
Anderson, *Ind., U.S.A.* 52 E3
Anderson, *Mo., U.S.A.* 55 G7
Anderson, *S.C., U.S.A.* 53 H4
Anderson →, *Canada* . 46 B7
Andes, Cord. de los,
  S. Amer. 62 H5
Andfjorden, *Norway* . . 6 B17
Andhra Pradesh □, *India* 28 L11
Andijon, *Uzbekistan* . . 20 E8
Andikíthira, *Greece* . . . 17 G10
Andizhan = Andijon,
  Uzbekistan 20 E8
Andoany, *Madag.* 37 G9
Andoom, *Australia* . . . 42 A3
Andorra ■, *Europe* . . . 14 E4
Andorra La Vella,
  Andorra 14 E4
Andover, *U.K.* 9 F6
Andøya, *Norway* 6 B16
Andradina, *Brazil* 63 H8
Andreanof Is., *U.S.A.* . 46 C2
Andrews, *S.C., U.S.A.* . 53 J6
Andrews, *Tex., U.S.A.* . 55 J3
Ándria, *Italy* 16 D7
Andropov = Rybinsk,
  Russia 18 C6
Ándros, *Greece* 17 F11
Andros I., *Bahamas* . . . 60 B4
Andros Town, *Bahamas* 60 B4
Andselv, *Norway* 6 B18
Andújar, *Spain* 15 C3
Andulo, *Angola* 36 G3
Anegada Passage,
  W. Indies 61 C7
Aneto, Pico de, *Spain* . 15 A6
Ang Thong, *Thailand* . . 26 B2
Angamos, Punta, *Chile* 62 H4
Angara →, *Russia* 21 D10
Angarsk, *Russia* 21 D11
Angas Hills, *Australia* . 40 D4
Angaston, *Australia* . . 43 E2
Ange, *Sweden* 7 E16

Ángel, Salto = Angel
  Falls, *Venezuela* . . . 62 B6
Ángel de la Guarda, I.,
  Mexico 58 B2
Angel Falls, *Venezuela* 62 B6
Angeles, *Phil.* 27 A6
Ängelholm, *Sweden* . . 7 H15
Angels Camp, *U.S.A.* . . 57 G3
Ångermanälven →,
  Sweden 6 E17
Ångermanland, *Sweden* 6 E18
Angers, *France* 14 C3
Ängesån →, *Sweden* . . 6 C20
Angikuni L., *Canada* . . 51 A9
Anglesey, Isle of □, *U.K.* 8 D3
Angleton, *U.S.A.* 55 L7
Angmagssalik =
  Tasiilaq, *Greenland* . 4 C6
Ango, *Dem. Rep. of
  the Congo* 36 D5
Angoche, *Mozam.* . . . 37 H7
Angola, *U.S.A.* 52 E3
Angola ■, *Africa* 37 G3
Angoulême, *France* . . . 14 D4
Angoumois, *France* . . . 14 D3
Angren, *Uzbekistan* . . 20 E8
Anguilla ■, *W. Indies* . 61 C7
Angurugu, *Australia* . . 42 A2
Anholt, *Denmark* 7 H14
Anhui □, *China* 25 C6
Anhwei = Anhui □,
  China 25 C6
Animas →, *U.S.A.* 57 H9
Anjalankoski, *Finland* . 7 F22
Anjou, *France* 14 C3
Ankaboa, Tanjona,
  Madag. 37 J8
Ankang, *China* 25 C5
Ankara, *Turkey* 19 G5
Ankaratra, *Madag.* . . . 37 H9
Ankeny, *U.S.A.* 54 E8
Ann, C., *U.S.A.* 52 D10
Ann Arbor, *U.S.A.* 52 D4
Anna, *U.S.A.* 55 G10
Annaba, *Algeria* 34 A7
Annan, *U.K.* 10 D5
Annapolis Royal,
  Canada 49 D6
Annean, L., *Australia* . . 41 E2
Annecy, *France* 14 D7
Anning, *China* 24 D5
Anniston, *U.S.A.* 53 J3
Annotto Bay, *Jamaica* . 60 C4
Anqing, *China* 25 C6
Ansbach, *Germany* . . . 12 D6
Anshan, *China* 25 B7
Anshun, *China* 24 D5
Ansley, *U.S.A.* 54 E5
Anson, *U.S.A.* 55 J5
Anson B., *Australia* . . . 40 B5
Ansongo, *Mali* 34 E6
Ansudu, *Indonesia* . . . 27 E9
Antabamba, *Peru* 62 F4
Antakya, *Turkey* 19 G6
Antalaha, *Madag.* 37 G10
Antalya, *Turkey* 19 G5
Antalya Körfezi, *Turkey* 19 G5
Antananarivo, *Madag.* . 37 H9
Antarctic Pen.,
  Antarctica 5 C18
Antarctica 5 E3
Antequera, *Spain* 15 D3
Antero, Mt., *U.S.A.* . . . 57 G10
Anthony, *Kans., U.S.A.* 55 G5
Anthony, N. Mex.,
  U.S.A. 57 K10
Anti Atlas, *Morocco* . . 34 C4
Anti-Lebanon = Ash
  Sharqi, Al Jabal,
  Lebanon 33 B5
Antibes, *France* 14 E7
Anticosti, Î. d', *Canada* 49 C7
Antigo, *U.S.A.* 54 C10
Antigonish, *Canada* . . 49 C7
Antigua, *W. Indies* . . . 61 C7
Antigua & Barbuda ■,
  W. Indies 61 C7
Antigua Guatemala,
  Guatemala 60 D1
Antilla, *Cuba* 60 B4
Antilles = West Indies,
  Cent. Amer. 61 D7
Antioquia, *Colombia* . . 62 B3
Antipodes Is., *Pac. Oc.* 44 M9
Antlers, *U.S.A.* 55 H7
Antofagasta, *Chile* . . . 64 A2
Anton, *U.S.A.* 55 J3
Antonina, *Brazil* 64 B7
Antrim, *U.K.* 10 D3
Antrim Plateau,
  Australia 40 C4
Antsirabe, *Madag.* . . . 37 H9
Antsiranana, *Madag.* . 37 G9
Antsohihy, *Madag.* . . . 37 G9
Antwerp = Antwerpen,
  Belgium 11 C4
Antwerpen, *Belgium* . . 11 C4
Antwerpen □, *Belgium* 11 C4
Anupgarh, *India* 28 E8
Anuradhapura,
  Sri Lanka 28 Q12
Anveh, *Iran* 31 E7
Anvers = Antwerpen,
  Belgium 11 C4

Ayabe

Anvers I., *Antarctica* 5 C17
Anxi, *China* 24 B4
Anxious B., *Australia* 43 E1
Anyang, *China* 25 C6
Anyer-Kidul, *Indonesia* 27 G11
Anzhero-Sudzhensk, *Russia* 20 D9
Ánzio, *Italy* 16 D5
Aoga-Shima, *Japan* 23 H9
Aomen = Macau □, *China* 25 D6
Aomori, *Japan* 22 D10
Aomori □, *Japan* 22 D10
Aoraki Mount Cook, *N.Z.* 39 K3
Aosta, *Italy* 14 D7
Aoukâr, *Mauritania* 34 E4
Aozou, *Chad* 35 D9
Apache, *U.S.A.* 55 H5
Apache Junction, *U.S.A.* 57 K8
Apalachee B., *U.S.A.* 53 L4
Apalachicola, *U.S.A.* 53 L3
Apalachicola →, *U.S.A.* 53 L3
Apaporis →, *Colombia* 62 D5
Aparri, *Phil.* 27 A6
Apatity, *Russia* 18 A5
Apatzingán, *Mexico* 58 D4
Apeldoorn, *Neths.* 11 B5
Apennines = Appennini, *Italy* 16 B4
Apia, *Samoa* 39 A13
Apiacás, Serra dos, *Brazil* 62 E7
Apizaco, *Mexico* 59 D5
Aplao, *Peru* 62 G4
Apo, Mt., *Phil.* 27 C7
Apollo Bay, *Australia* 43 F3
Apolo, *Bolivia* 62 F5
Aporé →, *Brazil* 63 G8
Apostle Is., *U.S.A.* 54 B9
Apostolos Andreas, C., *Cyprus* 30 C2
Apoteri, *Guyana* 62 C7
Appalachian Mts., *U.S.A.* 52 G6
Appennini, *Italy* 16 B4
Appleby-in-Westmorland, *U.K.* 8 C5
Appleton, *U.S.A.* 52 C1
Approuague →, *Fr. Guiana* 63 C8
Aprília, *Italy* 16 D5
Apucarana, *Brazil* 64 A6
Apure →, *Venezuela* 62 B5
Apurimac →, *Peru* 62 F4
Āqā Jarī, *Iran* 31 D6
Aqaba = Al 'Aqabah, *Jordan* 33 F4
Aqaba, G. of, *Red Sea* 30 D2
'Aqabah, Khalīj al = Aqaba, G. of, *Red Sea* 30 D2
'Aqdā, *Iran* 31 C7
Aqmola = Astana, *Kazakstan* 20 D8
'Aqrah, *Iraq* 30 B4
Aqtaū, *Kazakstan* 20 E6
Aqtöbe, *Kazakstan* 19 D10
Aquidauana, *Brazil* 63 H7
Aquiles Serdán, *Mexico* 58 B3
Aquin, *Haiti* 61 C5
Aquitain, Bassin, *France* 14 D3
Aqviligjuaq = Pelly Bay, *Canada* 47 B11
Ar Rachidiya, *Morocco* 34 B5
Ar Rafid, *Syria* 33 C4
Ar Raḥḥālīyah, *Iraq* 30 C4
Ar Ramādī, *Iraq* 30 C4
Ar Ramthā, *Jordan* 33 C5
Ar Raqqah, *Syria* 30 C3
Ar Rass, *Si. Arabia* 30 E4
Ar Rifā'ī, *Iraq* 30 D5
Ar Riyāḍ, *Si. Arabia* 30 E5
Ar Ru'ays, *Qatar* 31 E6
Ar Rukhaymīyah, *Iraq* 30 D5
Ar Ruqayyidah, *Si. Arabia* 31 E6
Ar Ruṣāfah, *Syria* 30 C3
Ar Ruṭbah, *Iraq* 30 C4
Ara, *India* 29 G14
Arab, *U.S.A.* 53 H2
'Arab, Bahr el →, *Sudan* 35 G11
Arab, Shatt al →, *Asia* 31 D6
'Arabābād, *Iran* 31 C8
Arabian Desert = Es Sahrâ' Esh Sharqîya, *Egypt* 35 C12
Arabian Gulf = Gulf, The, *Asia* 31 E6
Arabian Sea, *Ind. Oc.* 3 C13
Arabian Sea, *Ind. Oc.* 3 C13
Aracaju, *Brazil* 63 F11
Aracati, *Brazil* 63 D11
Araçatuba, *Brazil* 63 H8
Aracena, *Spain* 15 D2
Araçuaí, *Brazil* 63 G10
'Arad, *Israel* 33 D4
Arad, *Romania* 13 E11
Arādān, *Iran* 31 C7
Arafura Sea, *E. Indies* 38 B6
Aragón □, *Spain* 15 B5
Aragón →, *Spain* 15 A5
Araguacema, *Brazil* 63 E9
Araguaia →, *Brazil* 63 E9
Araguaína, *Brazil* 63 E9
Araguari, *Brazil* 63 G9
Araguari →, *Brazil* 63 C9
Arak, *Algeria* 34 C6
Arāk, *Iran* 31 C6
Arakan Coast, *Burma* 29 K19
Arakan Yoma, *Burma* 29 K19
Araks = Aras, Rūd-e →, *Asia* 30 B5
Aral, *Kazakstan* 20 E7
Aral Sea, *Asia* 20 E7
Aral Tengizi = Aral Sea, *Asia* 20 E7
Aralsk = Aral, *Kazakstan* 20 E7
Aralskoye More = Aral Sea, *Asia* 20 E7
Aramac, *Australia* 42 C4
Aran I., *Ireland* 10 D2
Aran Is., *Ireland* 10 E2
Aranda de Duero, *Spain* 15 B4
Arandān, *Iran* 30 C5
Aranjuez, *Spain* 15 B4
Aransas Pass, *U.S.A.* 55 M6
Aranyaprathet, *Thailand* 26 B2
Arapahoe, *U.S.A.* 54 E5
Arapgir, *Turkey* 30 B3
Arapiraca, *Brazil* 63 E11
Arapongas, *Brazil* 64 A6
Ar'ar, *Si. Arabia* 30 D4
Araraquara, *Brazil* 63 H9
Ararat, *Australia* 43 F3
Ararat, Mt. = Ağrı Dağı, *Turkey* 19 G7
Araripe, Chapada do, *Brazil* 63 E11
Aras, Rūd-e →, *Asia* 30 B5
Arauca, *Colombia* 62 B4
Arauca →, *Venezuela* 62 B5
Araxá, *Brazil* 63 G9
Araya, Pen. de, *Venezuela* 62 A6
Arba Minch, *Ethiopia* 32 F2
Arbat, *Iraq* 30 C5
Árbatax, *Italy* 16 E3
Arbīl, *Iraq* 30 B5
Arborfield, *Canada* 51 C8
Arborg, *Canada* 51 C9
Arbroath, *U.K.* 10 C5
Arbuckle, *U.S.A.* 56 G2
Arcachon, *France* 14 D3
Arcadia, *Fla., U.S.A.* 53 M5
Arcadia, *La., U.S.A.* 55 J8
Arcata, *U.S.A.* 56 F1
Archangel = Arkhangelsk, *Russia* 18 B7
Archer →, *Australia* 42 A3
Archer B., *Australia* 42 A3
Arches National Park, *U.S.A.* 57 G9
Arckaringa Cr. →, *Australia* 43 D2
Arco, *U.S.A.* 56 E7
Arcos de la Frontera, *Spain* 15 D3
Arcot, *India* 28 N11
Arctic Bay, *Canada* 47 A11
Arctic Ocean, *Arctic* 4 B18
Arctic Red River = Tsiigehtchic, *Canada* 46 B6
Arda →, *Bulgaria* 17 D12
Ardabīl, *Iran* 31 B6
Ardakān = Sepīdān, *Iran* 31 D7
Ardakān, *Iran* 31 C7
Ardenne, *Belgium* 12 D3
Ardennes = Ardenne, *Belgium* 12 D3
Ardestān, *Iran* 31 C7
Ardlethan, *Australia* 43 E4
Ardmore, *U.S.A.* 55 H6
Ardrossan, *Australia* 43 E2
Arecibo, *Puerto Rico* 61 C6
Areia Branca, *Brazil* 63 E11
Arena, Pt., *U.S.A.* 56 G2
Arenal, *Honduras* 60 C2
Arendal, *Norway* 7 G13
Arequipa, *Peru* 62 G4
Arévalo, *Spain* 15 B3
Arezzo, *Italy* 16 C4
Arga, *Turkey* 30 B3
Arganda, *Spain* 15 B4
Argenta, *Canada* 50 C5
Argentan, *France* 14 B3
Argentário, Mte., *Italy* 16 C4
Argentia, *Canada* 49 C9
Argentina ■, *S. Amer.* 64 D3
Argentina Is., *Antarctica* 5 C17
Argentino, L., *Argentina* 64 G2
Argeş →, *Romania* 13 F14
Arghandab →, *Afghan.* 28 D4
Argolikós Kólpos, *Greece* 17 F10
Árgos, *Greece* 17 F10
Argostólion, *Greece* 17 E9
Arguello, Pt., *U.S.A.* 57 J3
Argun →, *Russia* 21 D13
Argyle, L., *Australia* 40 C4
Århus, *Denmark* 7 H14
Ariadnoye, *Russia* 22 B7
Ariana, *Tunisia* 35 A7
Arica, *Chile* 62 G4
Arica, *Colombia* 62 D4
Arid, C., *Australia* 41 F3
Arida, *Japan* 23 G7
Arima, *Trin. & Tob.* 61 D7
Arinos →, *Brazil* 62 F7
Ario de Rosales, *Mexico* 58 D4
Aripuanã, *Brazil* 62 E6
Aripuanã →, *Brazil* 62 E6
Ariquemes, *Brazil* 62 E6
Aristazabal I., *Canada* 50 C3
Arizona, *Argentina* 64 D3
Arizona □, *U.S.A.* 57 J8
Arizpe, *Mexico* 58 A2
Arjeplog, *Sweden* 6 D18
Arjona, *Colombia* 62 A3
Arjuna, *Indonesia* 27 G15
Arka, *Russia* 21 C15
Arkadelphia, *U.S.A.* 55 H8
Arkalyk = Arqalyk, *Kazakstan* 20 D7
Arkansas □, *U.S.A.* 55 H8
Arkansas →, *U.S.A.* 55 J9
Arkansas City, *U.S.A.* 55 G6
Arkaroola, *Australia* 43 E2
Arkhangelsk, *Russia* 18 B7
Arklow, *Ireland* 10 E3
Arktitcheskiy, Mys, *Russia* 21 A10
Arlanzón →, *Spain* 15 A3
Arlbergpass, *Austria* 12 E6
Arles, *France* 14 E6
Arlington, *Oreg., U.S.A.* 56 D3
Arlington, *S. Dak., U.S.A.* 54 C6
Arlington, *Tex., U.S.A.* 55 J6
Arlington, *Va., U.S.A.* 52 F7
Arlington, *Wash., U.S.A.* 56 B2
Arlington Heights, *U.S.A.* 52 D2
Arlit, *Niger* 34 E7
Arlon, *Belgium* 11 E5
Arltunga, *Australia* 42 C1
Armagh, *U.K.* 10 D3
Armavir, *Russia* 19 E7
Armenia, *Colombia* 62 C3
Armenia ■, *Asia* 19 F7
Armidale, *Australia* 43 E5
Armour, *U.S.A.* 54 D5
Armstrong, *B.C., Canada* 50 C5
Armstrong, *Ont., Canada* 48 B2
Arnarfjörður, *Iceland* 6 D2
Arnaud →, *Canada* 47 B12
Arnauti, C., *Cyprus* 30 C2
Arnett, *U.S.A.* 55 G5
Arnhem, *Neths.* 11 C5
Arnhem, C., *Australia* 42 A2
Arnhem B., *Australia* 42 A2
Arnhem Land, *Australia* 42 A1
Arno →, *Italy* 16 C4
Arno Bay, *Australia* 43 E2
Arnold, *U.K.* 8 D6
Arnot, *Canada* 51 B9
Arnøy, *Norway* 6 A19
Arnprior, *Canada* 48 C4
Arnsberg, *Germany* 12 C5
Arqalyk, *Kazakstan* 20 D7
Arrah = Ara, *India* 29 G14
Arran, *U.K.* 10 D4
Arras, *France* 14 A5
Arrecife, *Canary Is.* 34 C3
Arrée, Mts. d', *France* 14 B2
Arriaga, *Chiapas, Mexico* 59 D6
Arriaga, *San Luis Potosí, Mexico* 58 C4
Arrilalah, *Australia* 42 C3
Arrino, *Australia* 41 E2
Arrowtown, *N.Z.* 39 L2
Arroyo Grande, *U.S.A.* 57 J3
Ars, *Iran* 30 B5
Arsenault L., *Canada* 51 B7
Arsenev, *Russia* 22 B6
Árta, *Greece* 17 E9
Arteaga, *Mexico* 58 D4
Artem, *Russia* 22 C6
Artemovsk, *Russia* 21 D10
Artemovsk, *Ukraine* 19 E6
Artesia, *U.S.A.* 55 J2
Arthur →, *Australia* 42 G3
Arthur Cr. →, *Australia* 42 C2
Arthur Pt., *Australia* 42 C5
Arthur River, *Australia* 41 F2
Arthur's Pass, *N.Z.* 39 K3
Arthur's Town, *Bahamas* 61 B4
Artigas, *Uruguay* 64 C5
Artillery L., *Canada* 51 A7
Artois, *France* 14 A5
Artsyz, *Ukraine* 13 E15
Artvin, *Turkey* 19 F7
Aru, Kepulauan, *Indonesia* 27 F8
Aru Is. = Aru, Kepulauan, *Indonesia* 27 F8
Arua, *Uganda* 36 D6
Aruanã, *Brazil* 63 F8
Aruba ■, *W. Indies* 62 A5
Arun →, *U.K.* 9 G7
Arunachal Pradesh □, *India* 29 F19
Arusha, *Tanzania* 36 E7
Aruwimi →, *Dem. Rep. of the Congo* 36 D4
Arvada, *Colo., U.S.A.* 54 F2
Arvada, *Wyo., U.S.A.* 56 D10
Arviat, *Canada* 51 A10
Arvidsjaur, *Sweden* 6 D18
Arvika, *Sweden* 7 G15
Arxan, *China* 25 B6
Arys, *Kazakstan* 20 E7
Arzamas, *Russia* 18 C7
Aş Şadr, *U.A.E.* 31 E7
Aş Şafā, *Syria* 33 B6
As Saffānīyah, *Si. Arabia* 31 E6
As Safīrah, *Syria* 30 B3
Aş Şahm, *Oman* 31 E8
As Sājir, *Si. Arabia* 30 E5
As Salamīyah, *Syria* 30 C3
As Salmān, *Iraq* 30 D5
As Salṭ, *Jordan* 33 C4
As Sal'w'a, *Qatar* 31 E6
As Samāwah, *Iraq* 30 D5
As Sanamayn, *Syria* 33 B5
As Sohar = Şuḥār, *Oman* 31 E8
As Sukhnah, *Syria* 30 C3
As Sulaymānīyah, *Iraq* 30 C5
As Sulaymī, *Si. Arabia* 30 E4
As Sulayyil, *Si. Arabia* 32 C4
As Summān, *Si. Arabia* 30 E5
As Suwaydā', *Syria* 33 C5
As Suwaydā' □, *Syria* 33 C5
As Suwayq, *Oman* 31 F8
Aş Şuwayrah, *Iraq* 30 C5
Asad, Buḥayrat al, *Syria* 30 C3
Asahi-Gawa →, *Japan* 23 G6
Asahigawa, *Japan* 22 C11
Asamankese, *Ghana* 34 G5
Asansol, *India* 29 H15
Asbestos, *Canada* 49 C5
Asbury Park, *U.S.A.* 52 E8
Ascensión, *Mexico* 58 A3
Ascensión, B. de la, *Mexico* 59 D7
Ascension I., *Atl. Oc.* 2 E9
Aschaffenburg, *Germany* 12 D5
Aschersleben, *Germany* 12 C6
Áscoli Piceno, *Italy* 16 C5
Ascope, *Peru* 62 E3
Aseb, *Eritrea* 32 E3
Asela, *Ethiopia* 32 F2
Asenovgrad, *Bulgaria* 17 C11
Aserradero, *Mexico* 58 C3
Ash Fork, *U.S.A.* 57 J7
Ash Grove, *U.S.A.* 55 G8
Ash Shabakah, *Iraq* 30 D4
Ash Shamāl □, *Lebanon* 33 A5
Ash Shāmīyah, *Iraq* 30 D5
Ash Shāriqah, *U.A.E.* 31 E7
Ash Sharmah, *Si. Arabia* 30 D2
Ash Sharqāt, *Iraq* 30 C4
Ash Sharqi, Al Jabal, *Lebanon* 33 B5
Ash Shaṭrah, *Iraq* 30 D5
Ash Shawbak, *Jordan* 30 D2
Ash Shawmari, J., *Jordan* 33 E5
Ash Shināfīyah, *Iraq* 30 D5
Ash Shu'bah, *Si. Arabia* 30 D5
Ash Shumlūl, *Si. Arabia* 30 E5
Ash Shūr'a, *Iraq* 30 C4
Ash Shurayf, *Si. Arabia* 30 E3
Ash Shuwayfāt, *Lebanon* 33 B4
Asha, *Russia* 18 D10
Ashbourne, *U.K.* 8 D6
Ashburn, *U.S.A.* 53 K4
Ashburton, *N.Z.* 39 K3
Ashburton →, *Australia* 40 D1
Ashcroft, *Canada* 50 C4
Ashdod, *Israel* 33 D3
Ashdown, *U.S.A.* 55 J7
Asheboro, *U.S.A.* 53 H6
Ashern, *Canada* 51 C9
Asherton, *U.S.A.* 55 L5
Asheville, *U.S.A.* 53 H4
Asheweig →, *Canada* 48 B2
Ashford, *Australia* 43 D5
Ashford, *U.K.* 9 F8
Ashgabat, *Turkmenistan* 20 F6
Ashibetsu, *Japan* 22 C11
Ashikaga, *Japan* 23 F9
Ashington, *U.K.* 8 B6
Ashizuri-Zaki, *Japan* 23 H6
Ashkhabad = Ashgabat, *Turkmenistan* 20 F6
Āshkhāneh, *Iran* 31 B8
Ashland, *Kans., U.S.A.* 55 G5
Ashland, *Ky., U.S.A.* 52 F4
Ashland, *Mont., U.S.A.* 56 D10
Ashland, *Ohio, U.S.A.* 52 E4
Ashland, *Oreg., U.S.A.* 56 E2
Ashland, *Va., U.S.A.* 52 G7
Ashland, *Wis., U.S.A.* 54 B9
Ashley, *U.S.A.* 54 B5
Ashmore Reef, *Australia* 40 B3
Ashmyany, *Belarus* 7 J21
Ashqelon, *Israel* 33 D3
Ashtabula, *U.S.A.* 52 E5
Ashton, *U.S.A.* 56 D8
Ashuanipi, L., *Canada* 49 B6
Asia, Kepulauan, *Indonesia* 27 D8
Āsīā Bak, *Iran* 31 C6
Asifabad, *India* 28 K11
Asinara, *Italy* 16 D3
Asinara, G. dell', *Italy* 16 D3
Asino, *Russia* 20 D9
Asipovichy, *Belarus* 13 B15
'Asīr □, *Si. Arabia* 32 D3
Asir, Ras, *Somali Rep.* 32 E5
Askersund, *Sweden* 7 G16
Askim, *Norway* 7 G14
Askja, *Iceland* 6 D5
Askøy, *Norway* 7 F11
Asmara = Asmera, *Eritrea* 32 D2
Asmera, *Eritrea* 32 D2
Åsnen, *Sweden* 7 H16
Aspen, *U.S.A.* 57 G10
Aspermont, *U.S.A.* 55 J4
Aspiring, Mt., *N.Z.* 39 L2
Asquith, *Canada* 51 C7
Assam □, *India* 29 G18
Asse, *Belgium* 11 D4
Assen, *Neths.* 11 A6
Assiniboia, *Canada* 51 D7
Assiniboine →, *Canada* 51 D9
Assiniboine, Mt., *Canada* 50 C5
Assis, *Brazil* 63 H8
Assisi, *Italy* 16 C5
Astana, *Kazakstan* 20 D8
Āstāneh, *Iran* 31 B6
Astara, *Azerbaijan* 19 G8
Asti, *Italy* 14 D8
Astipálaia, *Greece* 17 F12
Astorga, *Spain* 15 A2
Astoria, *U.S.A.* 56 C2
Astrakhan, *Russia* 19 E8
Asturias □, *Spain* 15 A3
Asunción, *Paraguay* 64 B5
Asunción Nochixtlán, *Mexico* 59 D5
Aswân, *Egypt* 35 D12
Aswân High Dam = Sadd el Aali, *Egypt* 35 D12
Asyût, *Egypt* 35 C12
At Ṭafilah, *Jordan* 33 E4
Aṭ Ṭā'if, *Si. Arabia* 32 C3
Aṭ Ṭirāq, *Si. Arabia* 30 E5
Aṭ Ṭubayq, *Si. Arabia* 30 D3
Atacama, Desierto de, *Chile* 64 A3
Atacama, Salar de, *Chile* 64 A3
Atalaya, *Peru* 62 F4
Atami, *Japan* 23 G9
Atapupu, *Indonesia* 27 F6
Atâr, *Mauritania* 34 D3
Atascadero, *U.S.A.* 57 J3
Atasu, *Kazakstan* 20 E8
Atatürk Barajı, *Turkey* 19 G6
Atauro, *Indonesia* 27 F7
'Atbara, *Sudan* 35 E12
'Atbara, Nahr →, *Sudan* 35 E12
Atbasar, *Kazakstan* 20 D7
Atchafalaya B., *U.S.A.* 55 L9
Atchison, *U.S.A.* 54 F7
Āteshān, *Iran* 31 C7
Ath, *Belgium* 11 D3
Athabasca, *Canada* 50 C6
Athabasca →, *Canada* 51 B6
Athabasca, L., *Canada* 51 B7
Athens = Athínai, *Greece* 17 F10
Athens, *Ala., U.S.A.* 53 H2
Athens, *Ga., U.S.A.* 53 J4
Athens, *Ohio, U.S.A.* 52 F4
Athens, *Tenn., U.S.A.* 53 H3
Athens, *Tex., U.S.A.* 55 J7
Atherton, *Australia* 42 B4
Athínai, *Greece* 17 F10
Athlone, *Ireland* 10 E3
Atholville, *Canada* 49 C6
Áthos, *Greece* 17 D11
Athy, *Ireland* 10 E3
Ati, *Chad* 35 F9
Atik L., *Canada* 51 B9
Atikameg →, *Canada* 48 B3
Atikokan, *Canada* 48 C1
Atikonak L., *Canada* 49 B7
Atka, *Russia* 21 C16
Atka I., *U.S.A.* 46 C2
Atkinson, *U.S.A.* 54 D5
Atlanta, *Ga., U.S.A.* 53 J3
Atlanta, *Tex., U.S.A.* 55 J7
Atlantic, *U.S.A.* 54 E7
Atlantic City, *U.S.A.* 52 F8
Atlantic Ocean 2 E9
Atlas Mts. = Haut Atlas, *Morocco* 34 B4
Atlin, *Canada* 50 B2
Atlin, L., *Canada* 50 B2
Atlin Prov. Park, *Canada* 50 B2
Atmore, *U.S.A.* 53 K2
Atoka, *U.S.A.* 55 H6
Atrak = Atrek →, *Turkmenistan* 31 B8
Atrek →, *Turkmenistan* 31 B8
Atsuta, *Japan* 22 C10
Attalla, *U.S.A.* 53 H2
Attapu, *Laos* 26 B3
Attawapiskat, *Canada* 48 B3
Attawapiskat →, *Canada* 48 B3
Attawapiskat L., *Canada* 48 B2
Attica, *U.S.A.* 52 E2
Attikamagen L., *Canada* 49 B6
Attleboro, *U.S.A.* 52 E10
Attock, *Pakistan* 28 C8
Attopeu = Attapu, *Laos* 26 B3
Attu I., *U.S.A.* 46 C1
Attur, *India* 28 P11
Atuel →, *Argentina* 64 D3
Åtvidaberg, *Sweden* 7 G17
Atwater, *U.S.A.* 57 H3
Atwood, *U.S.A.* 54 F4
Atyraū, *Kazakstan* 19 E9
Au Sable →, *U.S.A.* 52 C4
Aubagne, *France* 14 E6
Aube →, *France* 14 B5
Auburn, *Ala., U.S.A.* 53 J3
Auburn, *Calif., U.S.A.* 56 G3
Auburn, *Ind., U.S.A.* 52 E3
Auburn, *Maine, U.S.A.* 53 C10
Auburn, *N.Y., U.S.A.* 52 D7
Auburn, *Nebr., U.S.A.* 54 E7
Auburn Ra., *Australia* 43 D5
Auburndale, *U.S.A.* 53 L5
Aubusson, *France* 14 D5
Auch, *France* 14 E4
Auckland, *N.Z.* 39 G5
Auckland Is., *Pac. Oc.* 44 N8
Aude →, *France* 14 E5
Auden, *Canada* 48 B2
Audubon, *U.S.A.* 54 E7
Augathella, *Australia* 43 D4
Augsburg, *Germany* 12 D6
Augusta, *Australia* 41 F2
Augusta, *Italy* 16 F6
Augusta, *Ark., U.S.A.* 55 H9
Augusta, *Ga., U.S.A.* 53 J5
Augusta, *Kans., U.S.A.* 55 G6
Augusta, *Maine, U.S.A.* 47 D13
Augusta, *Mont., U.S.A.* 56 C7
Augustów, *Poland* 13 B12
Augustus, Mt., *Australia* 41 D2
Augustus I., *Australia* 40 C3
Auld, L., *Australia* 40 D3
Ault, *U.S.A.* 54 E2
Aunis, *France* 14 C3
Auponhia, *Indonesia* 27 E7
Aurangabad, *Bihar, India* 29 G14
Aurangabad, *Maharashtra, India* 28 K9
Aurich, *Germany* 12 B4
Aurillac, *France* 14 D5
Aurora, *Colo., U.S.A.* 54 F2
Aurora, *Ill., U.S.A.* 52 E1
Aurora, *Mo., U.S.A.* 55 G8
Aurora, *Nebr., U.S.A.* 54 E6
Aurukun, *Australia* 42 A3
Auschwitz = Oświęcim, *Poland* 13 C10
Austin, *Minn., U.S.A.* 54 D8
Austin, *Nev., U.S.A.* 56 G5
Austin, *Tex., U.S.A.* 55 K6
Austin, L., *Australia* 41 E2
Austin I., *Canada* 51 A10
Austra, *Norway* 6 D14
Austral Is. = Tubuai Is., *Pac. Oc.* 45 K13
Austral Seamount Chain, *Pac. Oc.* 45 K13
Australia ■, *Oceania* 38 D6
Australian Alps, *Australia* 38 E7
Australian Capital Territory □, *Australia* 43 F4
Australind, *Australia* 41 F2
Austria ■, *Europe* 12 E8
Austvågøy, *Norway* 6 B16
Autlán, *Mexico* 58 D4
Autun, *France* 14 C6
Auvergne, *France* 14 D5
Auvergne, Mts. d', *France* 14 D5
Auxerre, *France* 14 C5
Ava, *U.S.A.* 55 G8
Avallon, *France* 14 C5
Avalon Pen., *Canada* 49 C9
Avanos, *Turkey* 30 B2
Aveiro, *Brazil* 63 D7
Aveiro, *Portugal* 15 B1
Āvej, *Iran* 31 C6
Avellaneda, *Argentina* 64 C5
Avellino, *Italy* 16 D6
Aversa, *Italy* 16 D6
Avery, *U.S.A.* 56 C6
Aves, Is. las, *Venezuela* 62 A5
Avesta, *Sweden* 7 F17
Avezzano, *Italy* 16 C5
Aviemore, *U.K.* 10 C5
Avignon, *France* 14 E6
Ávila, *Spain* 15 B3
Avilés, *Spain* 15 A3
Avoca →, *Australia* 43 F3
Avola, *Canada* 50 C5
Avola, *Italy* 16 F6
Avon →, *Australia* 41 F2
Avon →, *Bristol, U.K.* 9 F5
Avon →, *Dorset, U.K.* 9 G6
Avon →, *Warks., U.K.* 9 E5
Avon Park, *U.S.A.* 53 M5
Avonlea, *Canada* 51 D8
Avranches, *France* 14 B3
A'waj →, *Syria* 33 B5
Awaji-Shima, *Japan* 23 G7
'Awālī, *Bahrain* 31 E6
Awasa, *Ethiopia* 32 F2
Awash, *Ethiopia* 32 F3
Awatere →, *N.Z.* 39 J5
Awbārī, *Libya* 35 C8
Awjilah, *Libya* 35 C10
Axe →, *U.K.* 9 F5
Axel Heiberg I., *Canada* 4 B3
Axim, *Ghana* 34 H5
Axiós →, *Greece* 17 D10
Axminster, *U.K.* 9 G4
Ayabaca, *Peru* 62 D3
Ayabe, *Japan* 23 G7

Ayacucho, Argentina .. 64 D5
Ayacucho, Peru 62 F4
Ayaguz, Kazakstan ... 20 E9
Ayamonte, Spain 15 D2
Ayan, Russia 21 D14
Aydin, Turkey 17 F12
Aydın □, Turkey 19 G4
Ayers Rock, Australia . 41 E5
Áyios Evstrátios, Greece 17 E11
Aykino, Russia 18 B8
Aylesbury, U.K. 9 F7
Aylmer, L., Canada .. 46 B8
'Ayn, Wādī al, Oman . 31 F7
Ayn Dār, Si. Arabia .. 31 E7
Ayn Zālah, Iraq 30 B4
Ayon, Ostrov, Russia .. 21 C17
'Ayoûn el 'Atroûs, Mauritania 34 E4
Ayr, Australia 42 B4
Ayr, U.K. 10 D4
Ayre, Pt. of, U.K. ... 8 C3
Ayton, Australia 42 B4
Aytos, Bulgaria 17 C12
Ayu, Kepulauan, Indonesia 27 D8
Ayutla, Guatemala .. 60 D1
Ayutla, Mexico 59 D5
Ayvacık, Turkey 17 E12
Ayvalık, Turkey 17 E12
Az Zabadānī, Syria .. 33 B5
Az Zāhiriyah, West Bank 33 D3
Az Zahrān, Si. Arabia . 31 E6
Az Zarqā, Jordan ... 33 C5
Az Zarqā', U.A.E. ... 31 E7
Az Zibār, Iraq 30 B5
Az Zilfī, Si. Arabia ... 30 E5
Az Zubayr, Iraq 30 D5
Azamgarh, India 29 F13
Azangaro, Peru 62 F4
Āzār Shahr, Iran 30 B5
Azarán, Iran 30 B5
Āzarbāyjān = Azerbaijan ■, Asia . 19 F8
Āzarbāyjān-e Gharbī □, Iran 30 B5
Āzarbāyjān-e Sharqī □, Iran 30 B5
Azare, Nigeria 34 F8
A'zāz, Syria 30 B3
Azbine = Aïr, Niger . 34 E7
Azerbaijan ■, Asia ... 19 F8
Azerbaijchan = Azerbaijan ■, Asia .. 19 F8
Azogues, Ecuador ... 62 D3
Azores, Atl. Oc. 34 A1
Azov, Russia 19 E6
Azov, Sea of, Europe .. 19 E6
Azovskoye More = Azov, Sea of, Europe 19 E6
Azraq ash Shīshān, Jordan 33 D5
Aztec, U.S.A. 57 H10
Azúa de Compostela, Dom. Rep. 61 C5
Azuaga, Spain 15 C3
Azuero, Pen. de, Panama 60 E3
Azul, Argentina 64 D5

Ba Don, Vietnam ... 26 A3
Baa, Indonesia 27 F6
Baarle-Nassau, Belgium 11 C4
Bab el Mandeb, Red Sea 32 E3
Bābā, Koh-i-, Afghan. . 28 B5
Baba Burnu, Turkey .. 17 E12
Bābā Kalū, Iran 31 D6
Babadag, Romania .. 13 F15
Babadayhan, Turkmenistan 20 F7
Babaeski, Turkey ... 17 D12
Babahoyo, Ecuador .. 62 D3
Babar, Indonesia ... 27 F7
Babb, U.S.A. 56 B7
Babelthuap, Pac. Oc. .. 27 C8
Babinda, Australia ... 42 B4
Babine, Canada 50 B3
Babine →, Canada .. 50 B3
Babine L., Canada ... 50 C3
Babo, Indonesia 27 E8
Bābol, Iran 31 B7
Bābol Sar, Iran 31 B7
Babruysk, Belarus .. 13 B15
Babuyan Chan., Phil. . 27 A6
Babylon, Iraq 30 C5
Bac Lieu, Vietnam ... 26 C3
Bacabal, Brazil 63 D10
Bacalar, Mexico 59 D7
Bacan, Kepulauan, Indonesia 27 E7
Bacarra, Phil. 27 A6
Bacău, Romania 13 E14
Bacerac, Mexico 58 A3
Bachelina, Russia ... 20 D7
Back →, Canada 46 B9
Bacolod, Phil. 27 B6
Bād, Iran 31 C7
Bad →, U.S.A. 54 C4
Bad Axe, U.S.A. 52 D4
Bad Ischl, Austria ... 12 E7
Bad Kissingen, Germany 12 C6
Bad Lands, U.S.A. .. 54 D3
Badagara, India 28 P9

Badajós, L., Brazil ... 62 D6
Badajoz, Spain 15 C2
Badalona, Spain 15 B7
Badampahar, India .. 29 H15
Badanah, Si. Arabia .. 30 D4
Badarinath, India ... 28 D11
Badas, Kepulauan, Indonesia 26 D3
Baddo →, Pakistan .. 28 F4
Bade, Indonesia 27 F9
Baden, Austria 12 D9
Baden-Baden, Germany 12 D5
Baden-Württemberg □, Germany 12 D5
Badgastein, Austria .. 12 E7
Badger, Canada 49 C8
Bādghīsāt □, Afghan. . 28 B3
Badin, Pakistan 28 G6
Badlands National Park, U.S.A. 54 D3
Badrah, Iraq 30 C5
Badulla, Sri Lanka ... 28 R12
Baena, Spain 15 D3
Baeza, Spain 15 D4
Baffin B., Canada ... 4 B4
Baffin I., Canada ... 47 B12
Bafing →, Mali 34 F3
Bafliyūn, Syria 30 B3
Bāft, Iran 31 D8
Bafwasende, Dem. Rep. of the Congo 36 D5
Bagamoyo, Tanzania . 36 F7
Baganga, Phil. 27 C7
Bagansiapiapi, Indonesia 26 D2
Bagdarin, Russia ... 21 D12
Bagé, Brazil 64 C6
Baggs, U.S.A. 56 F10
Baghdād, Iraq 30 C5
Bagheria, Italy 16 E5
Baghlān, Afghan. ... 28 A6
Bagley, U.S.A. 54 B7
Bago = Pegu, Burma . 29 L20
Bagrationovsk, Russia . 7 J19
Baguio, Phil. 27 A6
Bahama, Canal Viejo de, W. Indies 60 B4
Bahamas ■, N. Amer. . 61 B5
Baharampur, India .. 29 G16
Bahawalpur, Pakistan . 28 E7
Bahía = Salvador, Brazil 63 F11
Bahía □, Brazil 63 F10
Bahía, Is. de la, Honduras 60 C2
Bahía Blanca, Argentina 64 D4
Bahía de Caráquez, Ecuador 62 D2
Bahía Honda, Cuba .. 60 B3
Bahía Laura, Argentina 64 F3
Bahía Negra, Paraguay 62 H7
Bahir Dar, Ethiopia .. 32 E2
Bahmanzād, Iran ... 31 D6
Bahr el Ghazâl □, Sudan 35 G11
Bahraich, India 29 F12
Bahrain ■, Asia 31 E6
Bāhū Kalāt, Iran 31 E9
Bai Bung, Mui = Ca Mau, Mui, Vietnam . 26 C2
Baia Mare, Romania . 13 E12
Baião, Brazil 63 D9
Baïbokoum, Chad ... 35 G9
Baidoa, Somali Rep. . 32 G3
Baie Comeau, Canada . 49 C6
Baie-St-Paul, Canada . 49 C5
Baie Trinité, Canada . 49 C6
Baie Verte, Canada .. 49 C8
Ba'ījī, Iraq 30 C4
Baikal, L. = Baykal, Oz., Russia 21 D11
Baile Atha Cliath = Dublin, Ireland 10 E3
Băilești, Romania ... 13 F12
Bainbridge, U.S.A. .. 53 K3
Baing, Indonesia ... 27 F6
Ba'ir, Jordan 33 E5
Bairnsdale, Australia . 43 F4
Baitadi, Nepal 29 E12
Baiyin, China 24 C5
Baja, Hungary 13 E10
Baja, Pta., Mexico ... 58 B2
Baja California, Mexico 58 A1
Baja California □, Mexico 58 B2
Baja California Sur □, Mexico 58 B2
Bājgīrān, Iran 31 B8
Bajimba, Mt., Australia 43 D5
Bajo Nuevo, Caribbean 60 C4
Bajoga, Nigeria 35 F8
Bajool, Australia ... 42 C5
Bakala, C.A.R. 32
Bakel, Senegal 34 F3
Baker, Calif., U.S.A. . 57 J5
Baker, Mont., U.S.A. . 54 B2
Baker, L., Canada ... 46 B10
Baker City, U.S.A. .. 56 D5
Baker I., Pac. Oc. ... 44 G10
Baker I., U.S.A. 50 B2
Baker L., Australia .. 41 E4
Baker Lake, Canada .. 46 B10
Baker Mt., U.S.A. ... 56 B3
Bakers Creek, Australia 42 C4

Baker's Dozen Is., Canada 48 A4
Bakersfield, U.S.A. .. 57 J4
Bākhtarān, Iran 30 C5
Bākhtarān □, Iran ... 30 C5
Bakı, Azerbaijan ... 19 F8
Bakkafjörður, Iceland . 6 C6
Bakony, Hungary ... 13 E9
Bakony Forest = Bakony, Hungary ... 13 E9
Bakouma, C.A.R. ... 36 C4
Baku = Bakı, Azerbaijan 19 F8
Bakutis Coast, Antarctica 5 D15
Baky = Bakı, Azerbaijan 19 F8
Bala, U.K. 8 E4
Bala, L., U.K. 8 E4
Balabac I., Phil. 26 C5
Balabac Str., E. Indies . 26 C5
Ba'labakk, Lebanon .. 33 B5
Balabalangan, Kepulauan, Indonesia 26 E5
Balad, Iraq 30 C5
Balad Rūz, Iraq 30 C5
Bālādeh, Fārs, Iran .. 31 D6
Bālādeh, Māzandaran, Iran 31 B6
Balaghat, India 28 J12
Balaghat Ra., India .. 28 K10
Balaguer, Spain 15 B6
Balaklava, Ukraine .. 19 F5
Balakovo, Russia ... 18 D8
Balancán, Mexico ... 59 D6
Balashov, Russia ... 19 D7
Balasore = Baleshwar, India 29 J15
Balaton, Hungary ... 13 E9
Balbina, Reprêsa de, Brazil 62 D7
Balboa, Panama 60 E4
Balcarce, Argentina .. 64 D5
Balcarres, Canada ... 51 C8
Balchik, Bulgaria ... 17 C13
Balclutha, N.Z. 39 M2
Balcones Escarpment, U.S.A. 55 L5
Bald Hd., Australia .. 41 G2
Bald I., Australia ... 41 F2
Bald Knob, U.S.A. .. 55 H9
Baldock L., Canada .. 51 B9
Baldwin, U.S.A. 52 D3
Baldy Mt., U.S.A. ... 56 B9
Baldy Peak, U.S.A. .. 57 K9
Balearic Is. = Baleares, Is., Spain 15 C7
Baleares, Is., Spain .. 15 C7
Balearic Is. = Baleares, Is., Spain 15 C7
Baleine = Whale →, Canada 49 A6
Baler, Phil. 27 A6
Baleshwar, India ... 29 J15
Balfate, Honduras ... 60 C2
Bali □, Indonesia ... 26 F5
Bali, Selat, Indonesia . 27 H16
Balikeşir, Turkey ... 17 E12
Balikpapan, Indonesia . 26 E5
Balimbing, Phil. 27 C5
Balipara, India 29 F18
Balkan Mts. = Stara Planina, Bulgaria . 17 C10
Balkhash = Balqash, Kazakstan 20 E8
Balkhash, Ozero = Balqash Köl, Kazakstan 20 E8
Balla, Bangla. 29 G17
Balladonia, Australia . 41 F3
Ballarat, Australia ... 43 F3
Ballard, L., Australia . 41 E3
Ballater, U.K. 10 C5
Ballenas, Canal de, Mexico 58 B2
Balleny Is., Antarctica . 5 C11
Ballina, Australia ... 43 D5
Ballina, Ireland 10 D2
Ballinasloe, Ireland .. 10 E2
Ballinger, U.S.A. ... 55 K5
Ballymena, U.K. ... 10 D3
Balmaceda, Chile ... 64 F2
Balmertown, Canada . 51 C10
Balmoral, Australia .. 43 F3
Balmorhea, U.S.A. .. 55 K3
Balonne →, Australia 43 D4
Balqash, Kazakstan .. 20 E8
Balqash Köl, Kazakstan 20 E8
Balrampur, India ... 29 F13
Balranald, Australia .. 43 E3
Balsas, Mexico 59 D5
Balsas →, Brazil ... 63 E9
Balsas →, Mexico .. 58 D4
Balta, Ukraine 13 D15
Bălţi, Moldova 13 E14
Baltic Sea, Europe ... 7 H18
Baltimore, U.S.A. ... 52 F7
Baltiysk, Russia 7 J18
Baluchistan □, Pakistan 28 F4
Balvi, Latvia 7 H22
Balya, Turkey 17 E12
Bam, Iran 31 D8
Bama, Nigeria 35 F8
Bamaga, Australia .. 42 A3
Bamaji L., Canada .. 48 B1
Bamako, Mali 34 F4
Bambari, C.A.R. 36 C4
Bambaroo, Australia . 42 B4
Bamberg, Germany .. 12 D6

Bamberg, U.S.A. ... 53 J5
Bamfield, Canada ... 50 D3
Bāmīān □, Afghan. .. 28 B5
Bampūr, Iran 31 E9
Ban Don = Surat Thani, Thailand 26 C1
Ban Kantang, Thailand 26 C1
Ban Mê Thuôt = Buon Ma Thuot, Vietnam . 26 B3
Banaba, Kiribati 44 H8
Banalia, Dem. Rep. of the Congo 36 D5
Bananal, I. do, Brazil . 63 F8
Banaras = Varanasi, India 29 G13
Bânâs, Ras, Egypt ... 35 D13
Banbān, Si. Arabia .. 30 E5
Banbury, U.K. 9 E6
Bancroft, Canada ... 48 C4
Band Boni, Iran 31 E8
Band Qīr, Iran 31 D6
Banda, India 28 G12
Banda, Kepulauan, Indonesia 27 E7
Banda Aceh, Indonesia 26 C1
Banda Banda, Mt., Australia 43 E5
Banda Elat, Indonesia . 27 F8
Banda Is. = Banda, Kepulauan, Indonesia 27 E7
Banda Sea, Indonesia . 27 F7
Bandai-San, Japan .. 22 F10
Bandān, Iran 31 D9
Bandanaira, Indonesia 27 E7
Bandar = Machilipatnam, India 29 L12
Bandar 'Abbās, Iran .. 31 E8
Bandar-e Anzalī, Iran . 31 B6
Bandar-e Bushehr = Büshehr, Iran 31 D6
Bandar-e Chārak, Iran . 31 E7
Bandar-e Deylam, Iran . 31 D6
Bandar-e Khomeyni, Iran 31 D6
Bandar-e Lengeh, Iran . 31 E7
Bandar-e Maqām, Iran . 31 E7
Bandar-e Ma'shur, Iran . 31 D6
Bandar-e Nakhīlū, Iran . 31 E7
Bandar-e Rīg, Iran .. 31 D6
Bandar-e Torkeman, Iran 31 B7
Bandar Maharani = Muar, Malaysia ... 26 D2
Bandar Penggaram = Batu Pahat, Malaysia 26 D2
Bandar Seri Begawan, Brunei 26 C4
Bandar Sri Aman, Malaysia 26 D4
Bandera, Argentina .. 64 B4
Banderas, B. de, Mexico 58 C3
Bandırma, Turkey ... 17 D13
Bandon, Ireland 10 F2
Bandundu, Dem. Rep. of the Congo 36 E3
Bandung, Indonesia . 27 G12
Bāneh, Iran 30 C5
Banes, Cuba 61 B4
Banff, Canada 50 C5
Banff, U.K. 10 C5
Banff Nat. Park, Canada 50 C5
Bang Saphan, Thailand 26 B1
Bangalore, India ... 28 N10
Bangassou, C.A.R. .. 36 D4
Banggai, Indonesia .. 27 E6
Banggai, Kepulauan, Indonesia 27 E6
Banggai Arch. = Banggai, Kepulauan, Indonesia 27 E6
Banggi, Malaysia ... 26 C5
Banghāzī, Libya 35 B10
Bangka, Sulawesi, Indonesia 27 D7
Bangka, Sumatera, Indonesia 26 E3
Bangka, Selat, Indonesia 26 E3
Bangkalan, Indonesia . 27 G15
Bangkinang, Indonesia 26 D2
Bangko, Indonesia .. 26 E2
Bangkok, Thailand .. 26 B2
Bangladesh ■, Asia .. 29 H17
Bangong Co, India .. 28 B11
Bangor, Down, U.K. . 10 D4
Bangor, Gwynedd, U.K. 8 D3
Bangor, U.S.A. 47 D13
Bangued, Phil. 27 A6
Bangui, C.A.R. 36 D3
Bangweulu, L., Zambia 36 G6
Bani, Dom. Rep. 61 C5
Banī Sa'd, Iraq 30 C5
Bāniyās, Syria 30 C3
Banja Luka, Bos.-H. .. 16 B7
Banjarmasin, Indonesia 26 E4
Banjul, Gambia 34 F2
Bankipore, India ... 29 G14
Banks I., B.C., Canada . 50 C3
Banks I., N.W.T., Canada 46 A7
Banks Pen., N.Z. ... 39 K4
Banks Str., Australia . 42 G4
Bankura, India 29 H15
Banning, U.S.A. 57 K5
Banningville = Bandundu, Dem. Rep. of the Congo 36 E3

Bannu, Pakistan 28 C7
Banská Bystrica, Slovak Rep. 13 D10
Banswara, India 28 H9
Bantaeng, Indonesia . 27 F5
Bantry, Ireland 10 F2
Bantul, Indonesia ... 27 G14
Banyak, Kepulauan, Indonesia 26 D1
Banyo, Cameroon ... 36 C2
Banyumas, Indonesia . 27 G13
Banyuwangi, Indonesia 27 H16
Banzare Coast, Antarctica 5 C9
Banzyville = Mobayi, Dem. Rep. of the Congo 36 D4
Baoding, China 25 C6
Baoji, China 24 C5
Baoshan, China 24 D4
Baotou, China 25 B6
Bapatla, India 29 M12
Bāqerābād, Iran ... 31 C6
Ba'qūbah, Iraq 30 C5
Bar, Montenegro, Yug. 17 C8
Bar, Ukraine 13 D14
Bar Harbor, U.S.A. .. 53 C11
Bar-le-Duc, France .. 14 B6
Barabai, Indonesia .. 26 E5
Baraboo, U.S.A. ... 54 D10
Baracoa, Cuba 61 B5
Baradā →, Syria ... 33 B5
Baradine, Australia .. 43 E4
Baraga, U.S.A. 54 B10
Barahona, Dom. Rep. . 61 C5
Barail Range, India .. 29 G18
Barakaldo, Spain ... 15 A4
Barakhola, India ... 29 G18
Barakpur, India 29 H16
Baralaba, Australia .. 42 C4
Baralzon L., Canada . 51 B9
Baramula, India 28 B9
Baran, India 28 G10
Baranavichy, Belarus . 13 B14
Baranof, U.S.A. 50 B2
Baranof I., U.S.A. ... 46 C6
Barapasi, Indonesia . 27 E9
Barat Daya, Kepulauan, Indonesia 27 F7
Barataria B., U.S.A. .. 55 L10
Barbacena, Brazil ... 63 H10
Barbados ■, W. Indies . 61 D8
Barbastro, Spain ... 15 A6
Barberton, U.S.A. .. 52 E5
Barbosa, Colombia .. 62 B4
Barbourville, U.S.A. . 53 G4
Barbuda, W. Indies .. 61 C7
Barcaldine, Australia . 42 C4
Barcellona Pozzo di Gotto, Italy 16 E6
Barcelona, Spain ... 15 B7
Barcelona, Venezuela . 62 A6
Barcelos, Brazil 62 D6
Barcoo →, Australia . 42 D3
Bardaï, Chad 35 D9
Barddhaman, India .. 29 H15
Bardejov, Slovak Rep. . 13 D11
Bardera, Somali Rep. . 32 G3
Bardīyah, Libya 35 B10
Bardsey I., U.K. 8 E3
Bareilly, India 28 E11
Barents Sea, Arctic .. 4 B9
Barfleur, Pte. de, France 14 B3
Bargara, Australia .. 42 C5
Barguzin, Russia ... 21 D11
Barham, Australia .. 43 F3
Barhi, India 29 G14
Bari, Italy 16 D7
Bari Doab, Pakistan . 28 D8
Barīdī, Ra's, Si. Arabia . 30 E3
Barinas, Venezuela .. 62 B4
Baring, C., Canada .. 46 B8
Barisal, Bangla. 29 H17
Barisan, Bukit, Indonesia 26 E2
Barito →, Indonesia . 26 E4
Barkley, L., U.S.A. .. 53 G2
Barkley Sound, Canada 50 D3
Barkly Roadhouse, Australia 42 B2
Barkly Tableland, Australia 42 B2
Barkol Kazak Zizhixian, China 24 B4
Bârlad, Romania ... 13 E14
Bârlad →, Romania . 13 F14
Barlee, L., Australia . 41 E2
Barlee, Mt., Australia . 41 E4
Barletta, Italy 16 D7
Barlow L., Canada .. 51 A8
Barmedman, Australia . 43 E4
Barmer, India 28 G7
Barmera, Australia .. 43 E3
Barmouth, U.K. 8 E3
Barnard Castle, U.K. . 8 C6
Barnaul, Russia 20 D9
Barnesville, U.S.A. .. 53 J3
Barnet □, U.K. 9 F7
Barneveld, Neths. .. 11 B5
Barnhart, U.S.A. ... 55 K4
Barnsley, U.K. 8 D6
Barnstaple, U.K. ... 9 F3
Barnstaple Bay = Bideford Bay, U.K. . 9 F3
Barnsville, U.S.A. .. 54 B6

Barnwell, U.S.A. ... 53 J5
Baro, Nigeria 34 G7
Baroda = Vadodara, India 28 H8
Baron Ra., Australia . 40 D4
Barotseland, Zambia . 37 H4
Barpeta, India 29 F17
Barques, Pt. Aux, U.S.A. 52 C4
Barquisimeto, Venezuela 62 A5
Barr Smith Range, Australia 41 E3
Barra, Brazil 63 F10
Barra, U.K. 10 C3
Barra de Navidad, Mexico 58 D4
Barra do Corda, Brazil . 63 E9
Barra Falsa, Pta. da, Mozam. 37 J7
Barraba, Australia .. 43 E5
Barrackpur = Barakpur, India 29 H16
Barradale Roadhouse, Australia 40 D1
Barraigh = Barra, U.K. 10 C3
Barranca, Lima, Peru . 62 F3
Barranca, Loreto, Peru . 62 D3
Barrancabermeja, Colombia 62 B4
Barrancas, Venezuela . 62 B6
Barrancos, Portugal .. 15 C2
Barranqueras, Argentina 64 B5
Barranquilla, Colombia 62 A4
Barraute, Canada ... 48 C4
Barre, U.S.A. 52 C9
Barreiras, Brazil 63 F10
Barreirinhas, Brazil .. 63 D10
Barretos, Brazil 63 H9
Barrhead, Canada .. 50 C6
Barrie, Canada 48 D4
Barrier Ra., Australia . 43 E3
Barrière, Canada ... 50 C4
Barrington, L., Canada . 51 B8
Barrington Tops, Australia 43 E5
Barringun, Australia . 43 D4
Barro do Garças, Brazil 63 G8
Barron, U.S.A. 54 C9
Barrow, U.S.A. 46 A4
Barrow Creek, Australia 42 C1
Barrow I., Australia . 40 D2
Barrow-in-Furness, U.K. 8 C4
Barrow Pt., Australia . 42 A3
Barrow Ra., Australia . 41 E4
Barrow Str., Canada . 4 B3
Barry, U.K. 9 F4
Barry's Bay, Canada . 48 C4
Barsham, Syria 30 C4
Barsi, India 28 K9
Barsoi, India 29 G15
Barstow, U.S.A. 57 J5
Bartica, Guyana 62 B7
Bartlesville, U.S.A. .. 55 G7
Bartlett, L., Canada . 50 A5
Barton upon Humber, U.K. 8 D7
Bartow, U.S.A. 53 M5
Barú, Volcan, Panama . 60 E3
Barysaw, Belarus ... 13 A15
Barzān, Iraq 30 B5
Bāsa'idū, Iran 31 E7
Basankusa, Dem. Rep. of the Congo 36 D3
Basarabeasca, Moldova 13 E15
Basel, Switz. 14 C7
Bashäkerd, Kühhä-ye, Iran 31 E8
Bashaw, Canada ... 50 C6
Bāshī, Iran 31 D6
Bashkir Republic = Bashkortostan □, Russia 18 D10
Bashkortostan □, Russia 18 D10
Basilan I., Phil. 27 C6
Basilan Str., Phil. ... 27 C6
Basildon, U.K. 9 F8
Basim = Washim, India 28 J10
Basin, U.S.A. 56 D9
Basingstoke, U.K. .. 9 F6
Baskatong, Rés., Canada 48 C4
Basle = Basel, Switz. . 14 C7
Basque Provinces = País Vasco □, Spain . 15 A4
Basra = Al Başrah, Iraq 30 D5
Bass Str., Australia .. 42 F4
Bassano, Canada ... 50 C6
Bassano del Grappa, Italy 16 B4
Bassas da India, Ind. Oc. 37 J7
Basse-Terre, Guadeloupe 61 C7
Bassein, Burma 29 L19
Basseterre, St. Kitts & Nevis . 61 C7
Bassett, U.S.A. 54 D5
Bastak, Iran 31 E7
Baştām, Iran 31 B7
Bastar, India 29 K12
Basti, India 29 F13
Bastia, France 14 E8
Bastogne, Belgium .. 11 D5
Bastrop, La., U.S.A. . 55 J9
Bastrop, Tex., U.S.A. . 55 K6
Bat Yam, Israel 33 C3
Bata, Eq. Guin. 36 D1

Bilbao

Bataan □, *Phil.* 27 B6
Batabanó, *Cuba* 60 B3
Batabanó, G. de, *Cuba* 60 B3
Batac, *Phil.* 27 A6
Batagai, *Russia* 21 C14
Batamay, *Russia* 21 C13
Batang, *Indonesia* 27 G13
Batangafo, *C.A.R.* 32
Batangas, *Phil.* 27 B6
Batanta, *Indonesia* 27 E8
Batavia, *U.S.A.* 52 D6
Batchelor, *Australia* 40 B5
Batdambang, *Cambodia* 26 B2
Bateman's B., *Australia* 43 F5
Batemans Bay, *Australia* 43 F5
Bates Ra., *Australia* 41 E3
Batesburg-Leesville, *U.S.A.* 53 J5
Batesville, *Ark., U.S.A.* 55 H9
Batesville, *Miss., U.S.A.* 55 H10
Batesville, *Tex., U.S.A.* 55 L5
Bath, *U.K.* 9 F5
Bath, *Maine, U.S.A.* 53 D11
Bath, *N.Y., U.S.A.* 52 D7
Bath & North East Somerset □, *U.K.* 9 F5
Bathurst = Banjul, *Gambia* 34 F2
Bathurst, *Australia* 43 E4
Bathurst, *Canada* 49 C6
Bathurst, C., *Canada* 46 A7
Bathurst B., *Australia* 42 A3
Bathurst Harb., *Australia* 42 G4
Bathurst I., *Australia* 40 B5
Bathurst I., *Canada* 4 B2
Bathurst Inlet, *Canada* 46 B9
Batlow, *Australia* 43 F4
Batman, *Turkey* 19 G7
Baṭn al Ghūl, *Jordan* 33 F4
Batna, *Algeria* 34 A7
Baton Rouge, *U.S.A.* 55 K9
Batopilas, *Mexico* 58 B3
Batouri, *Cameroon* 36 D2
Båtsfjord, *Norway* 6 A23
Battambang = Batdambang, *Cambodia* 26 B2
Batticaloa, *Sri Lanka* 28 R12
Battipáglia, *Italy* 16 D6
Battle, *U.K.* 9 G8
Battle →, *Canada* 51 C7
Battle Creek, *U.S.A.* 52 D3
Battle Harbour, *Canada* 49 B8
Battle Lake, *U.S.A.* 54 B7
Battle Mountain, *U.S.A.* 56 F5
Battleford, *Canada* 51 C7
Batu, *Ethiopia* 32 F2
Batu, Kepulauan, *Indonesia* 26 E1
Batu Is. = Batu, Kepulauan, *Indonesia* 26 E1
Batu Pahat, *Malaysia* 26 D2
Batuata, *Indonesia* 27 F6
Batumi, *Georgia* 19 F7
Baturaja, *Indonesia* 26 E2
Baturité, *Brazil* 63 D11
Bau, *Malaysia* 26 D4
Baubau, *Indonesia* 27 F6
Bauchi, *Nigeria* 34 F7
Baudette, *U.S.A.* 54 A7
Bauer, C., *Australia* 43 E1
Bauhinia, *Australia* 42 C4
Baukau, *Indonesia* 27 F7
Bauld, C., *Canada* 47 C14
Bauru, *Brazil* 63 H9
Bauska, *Latvia* 7 H21
Bautzen, *Germany* 12 C8
Bavānāt, *Iran* 31 D7
Bavaria = Bayern □, *Germany* 12 D6
Bavispe →, *Mexico* 58 B3
Bawdwin, *Burma* 29 H20
Bawean, *Indonesia* 26 F4
Bawku, *Ghana* 34 F5
Bawlake, *Burma* 29 K20
Baxley, *U.S.A.* 53 K4
Baxter, *U.S.A.* 54 B7
Baxter Springs, *U.S.A.* 55 G7
Bay City, *Mich., U.S.A.* 52 D4
Bay City, *Tex., U.S.A.* 55 L7
Bay Minette, *U.S.A.* 53 K2
Bay Roberts, *Canada* 49 C9
Bay St. Louis, *U.S.A.* 55 K10
Bay Springs, *U.S.A.* 55 K10
Bay View, *N.Z.* 39 H6
Bayamo, *Cuba* 60 B4
Bayamón, *Puerto Rico* 61 C6
Bayan Har Shan, *China* 24 C4
Bayan Hot = Alxa Zuoqi, *China* 24 C5
Bayanaŭyl, *Kazakstan* 20 D8
Bayanhongor, *Mongolia* 24 B5
Bayard, *N. Mex., U.S.A.* 57 K9
Bayard, *Nebr., U.S.A.* 54 E3
Baybay, *Phil.* 27 B6
Bayern □, *Germany* 12 D6
Bayeux, *France* 14 B3
Bayfield, *U.S.A.* 54 B9
Bayındır, *Turkey* 17 E12
Baykal, Oz., *Russia* 21 D11
Baykan, *Turkey* 30 B4
Baykonur = Bayqongyr, *Kazakstan* 20 E7
Baymak, *Russia* 18 D10
Bayombong, *Phil.* 27 A6
Bayonne, *France* 14 E3
Bayovar, *Peru* 62 E2
Bayqongyr, *Kazakstan* 20 E7
Bayram-Ali = Bayramaly, *Turkmenistan* 20 F7
Bayramaly, *Turkmenistan* 20 F7
Bayramiç, *Turkey* 17 E12
Bayreuth, *Germany* 12 D6
Bayrūt, *Lebanon* 33 B4
Bayt Lahm, *West Bank* 33 D4
Baytown, *U.S.A.* 55 L7
Baza, *Spain* 15 D4
Bazaruto, I. do, *Mozam.* 37 J7
Bazmān, Kūh-e, *Iran* 31 D9
Beach, *U.S.A.* 54 B3
Beachport, *Australia* 43 F3
Beachy Hd., *U.K.* 9 G8
Beacon, *Australia* 41 F2
Beacon, *U.S.A.* 52 E9
Beaconsfield, *Australia* 42 G4
Beagle, Canal, *S. Amer.* 64 H3
Beagle Bay, *Australia* 40 C3
Beals Cr. →, *U.S.A.* 55 J4
Bear L., *Canada* 51 B9
Bear L., *U.S.A.* 56 F8
Beardmore, *Canada* 48 C2
Beardmore Glacier, *Antarctica* 5 E11
Beardstown, *U.S.A.* 54 F9
Béarn, *France* 14 E3
Bearpaw Mts., *U.S.A.* 56 B9
Bearskin Lake, *Canada* 48 B1
Beata, C., *Dom. Rep.* 61 C5
Beata, I., *Dom. Rep.* 61 C5
Beatrice, *U.S.A.* 54 E6
Beatrice, C., *Australia* 42 A2
Beatton →, *Canada* 50 B4
Beatton River, *Canada* 50 B4
Beatty, *U.S.A.* 57 H5
Beauce, Plaine de la, *France* 14 B4
Beauceville, *Canada* 49 C5
Beaudesert, *Australia* 43 D5
Beaufort, *Malaysia* 26 C5
Beaufort, *N.C., U.S.A.* 53 H7
Beaufort, *S.C., U.S.A.* 53 J5
Beaufort Sea, *Arctic* 4 B1
Beaufort West, *S. Africa* 37 L4
Beaulieu →, *Canada* 50 A6
Beaumaris, *U.K.* 8 D3
Beaumont, *Belgium* 11 D4
Beaumont, *U.S.A.* 55 K7
Beaune, *France* 14 C6
Beaupré, *Canada* 49 C5
Beauraing, *Belgium* 11 D4
Beauséjour, *Canada* 51 C9
Beauvais, *France* 14 B5
Beauval, *Canada* 51 B7
Beaver, *Okla., U.S.A.* 55 G4
Beaver, *Utah, U.S.A.* 57 G7
Beaver →, *B.C., Canada* 50 B4
Beaver →, *Ont., Canada* 48 A2
Beaver →, *Sask., Canada* 51 B7
Beaver →, *U.S.A.* 55 G5
Beaver City, *U.S.A.* 54 E5
Beaver Creek, *Canada* 46 B5
Beaver Dam, *U.S.A.* 54 D10
Beaver Falls, *U.S.A.* 52 E5
Beaver Hill L., *Canada* 51 C10
Beaver I., *U.S.A.* 52 C3
Beaverhill L., *Canada* 50 C6
Beaverlodge, *Canada* 50 B5
Beaverstone →, *Canada* 48 B2
Beaverton, *U.S.A.* 56 D2
Beawar, *India* 28 F9
Beccles, *U.K.* 9 E9
Bečej, *Serbia, Yug.* 17 B9
Béchar, *Algeria* 34 B5
Beckley, *U.S.A.* 52 G5
Beddouza, Ras, *Morocco* 34 B4
Bedford, *U.K.* 9 E7
Bedford, *Ind., U.S.A.* 52 F2
Bedford, *Iowa, U.S.A.* 54 E7
Bedford, *Va., U.S.A.* 52 G6
Bedford, C., *Australia* 42 B4
Bedfordshire □, *U.K.* 9 E7
Bedourie, *Australia* 42 C2
Bedum, *Neths.* 11 A6
Beenleigh, *Australia* 43 D5
Be'er Menuḥa, *Israel* 30 D2
Be'er Sheva, *Israel* 33 D3
Beersheba = Be'er Sheva, *Israel* 33 D3
Beeston, *U.K.* 8 E6
Beeville, *U.S.A.* 55 L6
Befale, *Dem. Rep. of the Congo* 36 D4
Bega, *Australia* 43 F4
Behābād, *Iran* 31 C8
Behbehān, *Iran* 31 D6
Behm Canal, *U.S.A.* 50 B2
Behshahr, *Iran* 31 B7
Bei Jiang →, *China* 25 D6
Bei'an, *China* 25 B7
Beihai, *China* 25 D5
Beijing, *China* 25 C6
Beilen, *Neths.* 11 B6
Beilpajah, *Australia* 43 E3
Beinn na Faoghla = Benbecula, *U.K.* 10 C3
Beira, *Mozam.* 37 H6
Beirut = Bayrūt, *Lebanon* 33 B4
Beiseker, *Canada* 50 C6
Beitbridge, *Zimbabwe* 37 J6
Beja, *Portugal* 15 C2
Béja, *Tunisia* 35 A7
Bejaia, *Algeria* 34 A7
Béjar, *Spain* 15 B3
Bejestān, *Iran* 31 C8
Békéscsaba, *Hungary* 13 E11
Bela, *India* 29 G13
Bela, *Pakistan* 28 F5
Bela Crkva, *Serbia, Yug.* 17 B9
Bela Vista, *Brazil* 63 H7
Bela Vista, *Mozam.* 37 K6
Belarus ■, *Europe* 13 B14
Belau = Palau ■, *Pac. Oc.* 38 A6
Belawan, *Indonesia* 26 D1
Belaya →, *Russia* 18 C9
Belaya Tserkov = Bila Tserkva, *Ukraine* 13 D16
Belcher Is., *Canada* 48 A3
Belebey, *Russia* 18 D9
Belém, *Brazil* 63 D9
Belen, *U.S.A.* 57 J10
Belet Uen, *Somali Rep.* 32 G4
Belev, *Russia* 18 D6
Belfast, *U.K.* 10 D4
Belfast, *U.S.A.* 53 C11
Belfield, *U.S.A.* 54 B3
Belfort, *France* 14 C7
Belfry, *U.S.A.* 56 D9
Belgaum, *India* 28 M9
Belgium ■, *Europe* 11 D4
Belgorod, *Russia* 19 D6
Belgorod-Dnestrovskiy = Bilhorod-Dnistrovskyy, *Ukraine* 19 E5
Belgrade = Beograd, *Serbia, Yug.* 17 B9
Belgrade, *U.S.A.* 56 D8
Belhaven, *U.S.A.* 53 H7
Beli Drim →, *Europe* 17 C9
Belinyu, *Indonesia* 26 E3
Beliton Is. = Belitung, *Indonesia* 26 E3
Belitung, *Indonesia* 26 E3
Belize ■, *Cent. Amer.* 59 D7
Belize City, *Belize* 59 D7
Belkovskiy, Ostrov, *Russia* 21 B14
Bell →, *Canada* 48 C4
Bell I., *Canada* 49 B8
Bell-Irving →, *Canada* 50 B3
Bell Peninsula, *Canada* 47 B11
Bell Ville, *Argentina* 64 C4
Bella Bella, *Canada* 50 C3
Bella Coola, *Canada* 50 C3
Bella Unión, *Uruguay* 64 C5
Bella Vista, *Argentina* 64 B5
Bellaire, *U.S.A.* 52 E5
Bellary, *India* 28 M10
Bellata, *Australia* 43 D4
Belle-Chasse, *U.S.A.* 55 L10
Belle Fourche, *U.S.A.* 54 C3
Belle Fourche →, *U.S.A.* 54 C3
Belle Glade, *U.S.A.* 53 M5
Belle-Île, *France* 14 C2
Belle Isle, *Canada* 49 B8
Belle Isle, Str. of, *Canada* 49 B8
Belle Plaine, *U.S.A.* 54 E8
Bellefontaine, *U.S.A.* 52 E4
Bellefonte, *U.S.A.* 52 E7
Belleoram, *Canada* 49 C8
Belleville, *Canada* 48 D4
Belleville, *Ill., U.S.A.* 54 F10
Belleville, *Kans., U.S.A.* 54 F6
Bellevue, *Canada* 50 D6
Bellevue, *Idaho, U.S.A.* 56 E6
Bellevue, *Nebr., U.S.A.* 54 E7
Bellin = Kangirsuk, *Canada* 47 B13
Bellingen, *Australia* 43 E5
Bellingham, *U.S.A.* 46 D7
Bellingshausen Sea, *Antarctica* 5 C17
Bellinzona, *Switz.* 14 C8
Bello, *Colombia* 62 B3
Bellows Falls, *U.S.A.* 52 D9
Belluno, *Italy* 16 A5
Belmonte, *Brazil* 63 G11
Belmopan, *Belize* 59 D7
Belo Horizonte, *Brazil* 63 G10
Belo-Tsiribihina, *Madag.* 37 H8
Belogorsk, *Russia* 21 D13
Beloit, *Kans., U.S.A.* 54 F5
Beloit, *Wis., U.S.A.* 54 D10
Belokorovichi, *Ukraine* 13 C15
Belomorsk, *Russia* 18 B5
Belonia, *India* 29 H17
Beloretsk, *Russia* 18 D10
Belorussia = Belarus ■, *Europe* 13 B14
Belovo, *Russia* 20 D9
Beloye, Ozero, *Russia* 18 B6
Beloye More, *Russia* 18 A6
Belozersk, *Russia* 18 B6
Belpre, *U.S.A.* 52 F5
Belt, *U.S.A.* 56 C8
Beltana, *Australia* 43 E2
Belterra, *Brazil* 63 D8
Belton, *U.S.A.* 55 K6
Belton L., *U.S.A.* 55 K6
Beltsy = Bălţi, *Moldova* 13 E14
Belukha, *Russia* 20 E9
Beluran, *Malaysia* 26 C5
Belvidere, *U.S.A.* 54 D10
Belyando →, *Australia* 42 C4
Belyy, Ostrov, *Russia* 20 B8
Belyy Yar, *Russia* 20 D9
Belzoni, *U.S.A.* 55 J9
Bembéréke, *Benin* 34 F6
Bemidji, *U.S.A.* 54 B7
Ben, *Iran* 31 C6
Ben Lomond, *N.S.W., Australia* 43 E5
Ben Lomond, *Tas., Australia* 42 G4
Ben Nevis, *U.K.* 10 C4
Bena, *Nigeria* 34 F7
Benalla, *Australia* 43 F4
Benares = Varanasi, *India* 29 G13
Benavente, *Spain* 15 A3
Benavides, *U.S.A.* 55 M5
Benbecula, *U.K.* 10 C3
Benbonyathe, *Australia* 43 E2
Bend, *U.S.A.* 56 D3
Bendemeer, *Australia* 43 E5
Bender Beila, *Somali Rep.* 32 F5
Bendery = Tighina, *Moldova* 13 E15
Bendigo, *Australia* 43 F3
Benē Beraq, *Israel* 33 C3
Benevento, *Italy* 16 D6
Bengal, Bay of, *Ind. Oc.* 29 M17
Bengbu, *China* 25 C6
Benghazi = Banghāzī, *Libya* 35 B10
Bengkalis, *Indonesia* 26 D2
Bengkulu, *Indonesia* 26 E2
Bengkulu □, *Indonesia* 26 E2
Bengough, *Canada* 51 D7
Benguela, *Angola* 37 G2
Beni, *Dem. Rep. of the Congo* 36 D5
Beni →, *Bolivia* 62 F5
Beni Mellal, *Morocco* 34 B4
Beni Suef, *Egypt* 35 C12
Beniah L., *Canada* 50 A6
Benidorm, *Spain* 15 C5
Benin ■, *Africa* 34 G6
Benin, Bight of, *W. Afr.* 34 H6
Benin City, *Nigeria* 34 G7
Benjamin Constant, *Brazil* 62 D4
Benjamin Hill, *Mexico* 58 A2
Benkelman, *U.S.A.* 54 E4
Bennett, *Canada* 50 B2
Bennett, L., *Australia* 40 D5
Bennetta, Ostrov, *Russia* 21 B15
Bennettsville, *U.S.A.* 53 H6
Bennington, *U.S.A.* 52 D9
Benoni, *S. Africa* 37 K5
Benque Viejo, *Belize* 59 D7
Benson, *Ariz., U.S.A.* 57 L8
Benson, *Minn., U.S.A.* 54 C7
Bent, *Iran* 31 E8
Benteng, *Indonesia* 27 F6
Bentinck I., *Australia* 42 B2
Benton, *Ark., U.S.A.* 55 H8
Benton, *Ill., U.S.A.* 54 G10
Benton Harbor, *U.S.A.* 52 D2
Bentonville, *U.S.A.* 55 G7
Benue →, *Nigeria* 34 G7
Benxi, *China* 25 B7
Beo, *Indonesia* 27 D7
Beograd, *Serbia, Yug.* 17 B9
Beppu, *Japan* 23 H5
Beqaa Valley = Al Biqā, *Lebanon* 33 A5
Berat, *Albania* 17 D8
Berati = Berat, *Albania* 17 D8
Berau, Teluk, *Indonesia* 27 E8
Berber, *Sudan* 35 E12
Berbera, *Somali Rep.* 32 E4
Berbérati, *C.A.R.* 36 D3
Berbice →, *Guyana* 62 B7
Berdichev = Berdychiv, *Ukraine* 13 D15
Berdsk, *Russia* 20 D9
Berdyansk, *Ukraine* 19 E6
Berdychiv, *Ukraine* 13 D15
Berea, *U.S.A.* 52 G3
Berebere, *Indonesia* 27 D7
Bereda, *Somali Rep.* 32 E5
Berehove, *Ukraine* 13 D12
Berekum, *Ghana* 34 G5
Berens →, *Canada* 51 C9
Berens I., *Canada* 51 C9
Berens River, *Canada* 51 C9
Beresford, *U.S.A.* 54 D6
Berestechko, *Ukraine* 13 C13
Bereza = Byaroza, *Belarus* 13 B13
Berezhany, *Ukraine* 13 D13
Berezina = Byarezina →, *Belarus* 13 B16
Berezniki, *Russia* 18 B7
Berezniki, *Russia* 18 C10
Berezovo, *Russia* 20 C7
Berga, *Spain* 15 A6
Bergama, *Turkey* 17 E12
Bérgamo, *Italy* 14 D8
Bergen, *Neths.* 11 B4
Bergen, *Norway* 7 F11
Bergen op Zoom, *Neths.* 11 C4
Bergerac, *France* 14 D4
Bergisch Gladbach, *Germany* 11 D7
Berhala, Selat, *Indonesia* 26 E2
Berhampore = Baharampur, *India* 29 G16
Berhampur = Brahmapur, *India* 29 K14
Bering Sea, *Pac. Oc.* 46 C1
Bering Strait, *Pac. Oc.* 46 B3
Beringovskiy, *Russia* 21 C18
Berja, *Spain* 15 D4
Berkeley, *U.S.A.* 56 H2
Berkner I., *Antarctica* 5 D18
Berkshire Downs, *U.K.* 9 F6
Berlin, *Germany* 12 B7
Berlin, *Md., U.S.A.* 52 F8
Berlin, *N.H., U.S.A.* 52 C10
Berlin, *Wis., U.S.A.* 52 D1
Bermejo →, *Formosa, Argentina* 64 B5
Bermejo →, *San Juan, Argentina* 64 C3
Bermen, L., *Canada* 49 B6
Bermuda ■, *Atl. Oc.* 2 C6
Bern, *Switz.* 14 C7
Bernalillo, *U.S.A.* 57 J10
Bernburg, *Germany* 12 C6
Berne = Bern, *Switz.* 14 C7
Bernier I., *Australia* 41 D1
Bernina, Piz, *Switz.* 14 C8
Beroun, *Czech Rep.* 12 D8
Berri, *Australia* 43 E3
Berriane, *Algeria* 34 B6
Berrigan, *Australia* 43 F4
Berry, *Australia* 43 E5
Berry, *France* 14 C5
Berry Is., *Bahamas* 60 A4
Berryville, *U.S.A.* 55 G8
Bershad, *Ukraine* 13 D15
Berthold, *U.S.A.* 54 A4
Berthoud, *U.S.A.* 54 E2
Bertoua, *Cameroon* 36 D2
Berwick, *U.S.A.* 52 E7
Berwick-upon-Tweed, *U.K.* 8 B6
Berwyn Mts., *U.K.* 8 E4
Besalampy, *Madag.* 37 H8
Besançon, *France* 14 C7
Besar, *Indonesia* 26 E5
Besnard L., *Canada* 51 B7
Besni, *Turkey* 30 B3
Besor, N. →, *Egypt* 33 D3
Bessarabiya, *Moldova* 13 E15
Bessarabka = Basarabeasca, *Moldova* 13 E15
Bessemer, *Ala., U.S.A.* 53 J2
Bessemer, *Mich., U.S.A.* 54 B9
Beswick, *Australia* 40 B5
Bet She'an, *Israel* 33 C4
Bet Shemesh, *Israel* 33 D4
Betanzos, *Spain* 15 A1
Bétaré Oya, *Cameroon* 36 C2
Bethany, *U.S.A.* 54 E7
Bethel, *U.S.A.* 46 B3
Bethlehem = Bayt Lahm, *West Bank* 33 D4
Bethlehem, *S. Africa* 37 K5
Bethlehem, *U.S.A.* 52 E8
Béthune, *France* 14 A5
Betoota, *Australia* 42 D3
Betroka, *Madag.* 37 J9
Betsiamites, *Canada* 49 C6
Betsiamites →, *Canada* 49 C6
Bettendorf, *U.S.A.* 54 E9
Bettiah, *India* 29 F14
Betul, *India* 28 J10
Betung, *Malaysia* 26 D4
Betws-y-Coed, *U.K.* 8 D4
Beulah, *Mich., U.S.A.* 52 C2
Beulah, *N. Dak., U.S.A.* 54 B4
Beveren, *Belgium* 11 C4
Beverley, *Australia* 41 F2
Beverley, *U.K.* 8 D7
Beverley Hills, *U.S.A.* 53 L4
Beverly Hills, *U.S.A.* 57 J4
Bexhill, *U.K.* 9 G8
Beyānlū, *Iran* 30 C5
Beyneu, *Kazakstan* 19 E10
Beypazarı, *Turkey* 19 F5
Beyşehir Gölü, *Turkey* 19 G5
Béziers, *France* 14 E5
Bezwada = Vijayawada, *India* 29 L12
Bhachau, *India* 28 H7
Bhadrakh, *India* 29 J15
Bhadravati, *India* 28 N9
Bhagalpur, *India* 29 G15
Bhakra Dam, *India* 28 D10
Bhamo, *Burma* 29 G20
Bhandara, *India* 28 J11
Bhanrer Ra., *India* 28 H11
Bharat = India ■, *Asia* 28 K11
Bharatpur, *India* 28 F10
Bhatpara, *India* 29 H16
Bhaunagar = Bhavnagar, *India* 28 J8
Bhavnagar, *India* 28 J8
Bhilsa = Vidisha, *India* 28 H10
Bhilwara, *India* 28 G9
Bhima →, *India* 28 L10
Bhind, *India* 28 F11
Bhiwandi, *India* 28 K8
Bhiwani, *India* 28 E10
Bhola, *Bangla.* 29 H17
Bhopal, *India* 28 H10
Bhubaneshwar, *India* 29 J14
Bhuj, *India* 28 H6
Bhusaval, *India* 28 J9
Bhutan ■, *Asia* 29 F17
Biafra, B. of = Bonny, Bight of, *Africa* 36 D1
Biak, *Indonesia* 27 E9
Biała Podlaska, *Poland* 13 B12
Białogard, *Poland* 12 A8
Białystok, *Poland* 13 B12
Bīārjmand, *Iran* 31 B7
Biaro, *Indonesia* 27 D7
Biarritz, *France* 14 E3
Bibai, *Japan* 22 C10
Bibby I., *Canada* 51 A10
Biberach, *Germany* 12 D5
Bic, *Canada* 49 C6
Bicester, *U.K.* 9 F6
Bicheno, *Australia* 42 G4
Bickerton I., *Australia* 42 A2
Bida, *Nigeria* 34 G7
Bidar, *India* 28 L10
Biddeford, *U.S.A.* 53 D10
Bideford, *U.K.* 9 F3
Bideford Bay, *U.K.* 9 F3
Bié, Planalto de, *Angola* 37 G3
Bieber, *U.S.A.* 56 F3
Biel, *Switz.* 14 C7
Bielefeld, *Germany* 12 B5
Biella, *Italy* 14 D8
Bielsk Podlaski, *Poland* 13 B12
Bielsko-Biała, *Poland* 13 D10
Bien Hoa, *Vietnam* 26 B3
Bienne = Biel, *Switz.* 14 C7
Bienville, L., *Canada* 48 A5
Big →, *Canada* 49 B8
Big B., *Canada* 49 A7
Big Belt Mts., *U.S.A.* 56 C8
Big Bend National Park, *U.S.A.* 55 L3
Big Black →, *U.S.A.* 55 K9
Big Blue →, *U.S.A.* 54 F6
Big Cypress National Preserve, *U.S.A.* 53 M5
Big Cypress Swamp, *U.S.A.* 53 M5
Big Falls, *U.S.A.* 54 A8
Big Fork →, *U.S.A.* 54 A8
Big Horn Mts. = Bighorn Mts., *U.S.A.* 56 D10
Big I., *Canada* 50 A5
Big Lake, *U.S.A.* 55 K4
Big Muddy Cr. →, *U.S.A.* 54 A2
Big Pine, *U.S.A.* 57 H4
Big Piney, *U.S.A.* 56 E8
Big Rapids, *U.S.A.* 52 D3
Big River, *Canada* 51 C7
Big Sable Pt., *U.S.A.* 52 C2
Big Salmon →, *Canada* 50 A2
Big Sand L., *Canada* 51 B9
Big Sandy, *U.S.A.* 56 B8
Big Sandy →, *U.S.A.* 52 F4
Big Sandy Cr. →, *U.S.A.* 54 F3
Big Sioux →, *U.S.A.* 54 D6
Big Spring, *U.S.A.* 55 J4
Big Stone City, *U.S.A.* 54 C6
Big Stone Gap, *U.S.A.* 53 G4
Big Stone L., *U.S.A.* 54 C6
Big Timber, *U.S.A.* 56 D9
Big Trout L., *Canada* 48 B2
Big Trout Lake, *Canada* 48 B2
Biğa, *Turkey* 17 D12
Bigadiç, *Turkey* 17 E13
Biggar, *Canada* 51 C7
Bigge I., *Australia* 40 B4
Biggenden, *Australia* 43 D5
Biggleswade, *U.K.* 9 E7
Bighorn, *U.S.A.* 56 C10
Bighorn →, *U.S.A.* 56 C10
Bighorn L., *U.S.A.* 56 D9
Bighorn Mts., *U.S.A.* 56 D10
Bigstone L., *Canada* 51 C9
Bihać, *Bos.-H.* 12 F8
Bihar, *India* 29 G14
Bihar □, *India* 29 G15
Bihor, Munţii, *Romania* 13 E12
Bijagós, Arquipélago dos, *Guinea-Biss.* 34 F2
Bijapur, *Karnataka, India* 28 L9
Bijapur, *Mad. P., India* 29 K12
Bījār, *Iran* 30 C5
Bijeljina, *Bos.-H.* 17 B8
Bijnor, *India* 28 E11
Bikaner, *India* 28 E8
Bikfayyā, *Lebanon* 33 B4
Bikin, *Russia* 21 E14
Bikin →, *Russia* 22 A7
Bikini Atoll, *Marshall Is.* 44 F8
Bila Tserkva, *Ukraine* 13 D16
Bilara, *India* 28 F8
Bilaspur, *India* 29 H13
Bilauk Taungdan, *Thailand* 26 B1
Bilbao, *Spain* 15 A4

Bilbo

Bilbo = Bilbao, *Spain* 15 A4
Bíldudalur, *Iceland* 6 D2
Bílé Karpaty, *Europe* 13 D9
Bilecik, *Turkey* 19 F5
Bilhorod-Dnistrovskyy, *Ukraine* 19 E5
Bilibino, *Russia* 21 C17
Billabalong Roadhouse, *Australia* 41 E2
Billiluna, *Australia* 40 C4
Billings, *U.S.A.* 56 D9
Billiton Is. = Belitung, *Indonesia* 26 E3
Bilma, *Niger* 35 E8
Biloela, *Australia* 42 C5
Biloxi, *U.S.A.* 55 K10
Bilpa Morea Claypan, *Australia* 42 D3
Biltine, *Chad* 35 F10
Bima, *Indonesia* 27 F5
Bimini Is., *Bahamas* 60 A4
Bina-Etawah, *India* 28 G11
Bināb, *Iran* 31 B6
Binalbagan, *Phil.* 27 B6
Binalong, *Australia* 43 E4
Bīnālūd, Kūh-e, *Iran* 31 B8
Binatang = Bintangor, *Malaysia* 26 D4
Binche, *Belgium* 11 D4
Bindura, *Zimbabwe* 37 H6
Bingara, *Australia* 43 D5
Bingham, *U.S.A.* 53 C11
Binghamton, *U.S.A.* 52 D8
Bingöl, *Turkey* 30 B4
Binh Dinh = An Nhon, *Vietnam* 26 B3
Binh Son, *Vietnam* 26 A3
Binjai, *Indonesia* 26 D3
Binnaway, *Australia* 43 E4
Binongko, *Indonesia* 27 F6
Binscarth, *Canada* 51 C8
Bintan, *Indonesia* 26 D2
Bintangor, *Malaysia* 26 D4
Bintulu, *Malaysia* 26 D4
Bintuni, *Indonesia* 27 E8
Binzert = Bizerte, *Tunisia* 35 A7
Bioko, *Eq. Guin.* 36 D1
Bir, *India* 28 K9
Bîr Abu Muḥammad, *Egypt* 33 F3
Bi'r ad Dabbāghāt, *Jordan* 33 E4
Bi'r al Butayyihāt, *Jordan* 33 F4
Bi'r al Mārī, *Jordan* 33 E4
Bi'r al Qattār, *Jordan* 33 F4
Bir Atrun, *Sudan* 35 E11
Bîr Beiḍa, *Egypt* 33 E3
Bîr el 'Abd, *Egypt* 33 D2
Bîr el Biarât, *Egypt* 33 F3
Bîr el Duweidar, *Egypt* 33 E1
Bîr el Garârât, *Egypt* 33 D2
Bîr el Heisi, *Egypt* 33 F3
Bîr el Jafir, *Egypt* 33 E1
Bîr el Mâlḥi, *Egypt* 33 E2
Bîr el Thamâda, *Egypt* 33 E2
Bîr Gebeil Ḥiṣn, *Egypt* 33 E2
Bi'r Ghadīr, *Syria* 33 A6
Bîr Ḥasana, *Egypt* 33 E2
Bîr Kaseiba, *Egypt* 33 E2
Bîr Lahfân, *Egypt* 33 E2
Bîr Madkûr, *Egypt* 33 E1
Bîr Mogreïn, *Mauritania* 34 C3
Bi'r Muṭribah, *Kuwait* 30 D5
Bîr Qaṭia, *Egypt* 33 E1
Bîr Shalatein, *Egypt* 35 D13
Birch →, *Canada* 50 B6
Birch Hills, *Canada* 51 C7
Birch I., *Canada* 51 C9
Birch L., *N.W.T., Canada* 50 A5
Birch L., *Ont., Canada* 48 B1
Birch Mts., *Canada* 50 B6
Birch River, *Canada* 51 C8
Birchip, *Australia* 43 F3
Bird, *Canada* 51 B10
Bird I. = Las Aves, Is., *W. Indies* 61 C7
Birdsville, *Australia* 42 D2
Birdum Cr., *Australia* 40 C5
Birecik, *Turkey* 30 B3
Birein, *Israel* 33 E3
Bireuen, *Indonesia* 26 C1
Birjand, *Iran* 31 C8
Birkenhead, *U.K.* 8 D4
Bîrlad = Bârlad, *Romania* 13 E14
Birmingham, *U.K.* 9 E6
Birmingham, *U.S.A.* 53 J2
Birmitrapur, *India* 29 H14
Birni Nkonni, *Niger* 34 F7
Birnin Kebbi, *Nigeria* 34 F6
Birobidzhan, *Russia* 21 E14
Birr, *Ireland* 10 E3
Birrie →, *Australia* 43 D4
Birsk, *Russia* 18 C10
Birtle, *Canada* 51 C8
Birur, *India* 28 N9
Biržai, *Lithuania* 7 H21
Bisa, *Indonesia* 27 E7
Bisbee, *U.S.A.* 57 L9
Biscay, B. of, *Atl. Oc.* 14 D1
Biscayne B., *U.S.A.* 53 N5
Biscoe Bay, *Antarctica* 5 D13
Biscoe Is., *Antarctica* 5 C17
Biscostasing, *Canada* 48 C3
Bishkek, *Kyrgyzstan* 20 E8
Bishop, *Calif., U.S.A.* 57 H4
Bishop, *Tex., U.S.A.* 55 M6
Bishop Auckland, *U.K.* 8 C6
Bishop's Falls, *Canada* 49 C8
Bishop's Stortford, *U.K.* 9 F8
Biskra, *Algeria* 34 B7
Bismarck, *U.S.A.* 54 B4
Bismarck Arch., *Papua N. G.* 38 B7
Bison, *U.S.A.* 54 C3
Bīsotūn, *Iran* 30 C5
Bissagos = Bijagós, Arquipélago dos, *Guinea-Biss.* 34 F2
Bissau, *Guinea-Biss.* 34 F2
Bistcho L., *Canada* 50 B5
Bistrița, *Romania* 13 E13
Bistrița →, *Romania* 13 E14
Bitlis, *Turkey* 30 B4
Bitola, *Macedonia* 17 D9
Bitolj = Bitola, *Macedonia* 17 D9
Bitter Creek, *U.S.A.* 56 F9
Bitterfontein, *S. Africa* 37 L3
Bitterroot →, *U.S.A.* 56 C6
Bitterroot Range, *U.S.A.* 56 D6
Biu, *Nigeria* 35 F8
Biwa-Ko, *Japan* 23 G8
Biwabik, *U.S.A.* 54 B8
Bixby, *U.S.A.* 55 H7
Biysk, *Russia* 20 D9
Bizen, *Japan* 23 G7
Bizerte, *Tunisia* 35 A7
Bjargtangar, *Iceland* 6 D1
Bjelovar, *Croatia* 16 B7
Bjørnevatn, *Norway* 6 B23
Bjørnøya, *Arctic* 4 B8
Black →, *Ariz., U.S.A.* 57 K8
Black →, *Ark., U.S.A.* 55 H9
Black →, *Wis., U.S.A.* 54 D9
Black Bay Pen., *Canada* 48 C2
Black Birch L., *Canada* 51 B7
Black Diamond, *Canada* 50 C6
Black Duck →, *Canada* 48 A2
Black Forest = Schwarzwald, *Germany* 12 D5
Black Forest, *U.S.A.* 54 F2
Black Hills, *U.S.A.* 54 D3
Black I., *Canada* 51 C9
Black L., *Canada* 51 B7
Black L., *U.S.A.* 52 C3
Black Lake, *Canada* 51 B7
Black Mesa, *U.S.A.* 55 G3
Black Mt. = Mynydd Du, *U.K.* 9 F4
Black Mts., *U.K.* 9 F4
Black Range, *U.S.A.* 57 K10
Black River, *Jamaica* 60 C4
Black River Falls, *U.S.A.* 54 C9
Black Sea, *Eurasia* 19 F6
Black Tickle, *Canada* 49 B8
Black Volta →, *Africa* 34 G5
Black Warrior →, *U.S.A.* 53 J2
Blackall, *Australia* 42 C4
Blackball, *N.Z.* 39 K3
Blackbull, *Australia* 42 B3
Blackburn, *U.K.* 8 D5
Blackburn with Darwen □, *U.K.* 8 D5
Blackfoot, *U.S.A.* 56 E7
Blackfoot →, *U.S.A.* 56 C7
Blackfoot River Reservoir, *U.S.A.* 56 E8
Blackie, *Canada* 50 C6
Blackpool, *U.K.* 8 D4
Blackpool □, *U.K.* 8 D4
Blacks Harbour, *Canada* 49 C6
Blacksburg, *U.S.A.* 52 G5
Blackstone, *U.S.A.* 52 G7
Blackstone Ra., *Australia* 41 E4
Blackwater, *Australia* 42 C4
Blackwater →, *Ireland* 10 E3
Blackwell, *U.S.A.* 55 G6
Blaenau Ffestiniog, *U.K.* 8 E4
Blaenau Gwent □, *U.K.* 9 F4
Blagodarnoye = Blagodarnyy, *Russia* 19 E7
Blagodarnyy, *Russia* 19 E7
Blagoevgrad, *Bulgaria* 17 C10
Blagoveshchensk, *Russia* 21 D13
Blaine, *Minn., U.S.A.* 54 C8
Blaine, *Wash., U.S.A.* 56 B2
Blaine Lake, *Canada* 51 C7
Blair, *U.S.A.* 54 E6
Blair Athol, *Australia* 42 C4
Blake Pt., *U.S.A.* 54 A10
Blakely, *U.S.A.* 53 K3
Blanc, Mont, *Alps* 14 D7
Blanc-Sablon, *Canada* 49 B8
Blanca, B., *Argentina* 64 D4
Blanca Peak, *U.S.A.* 57 H11
Blanche, C., *Australia* 43 E1
Blanche, L., *S. Austral., Australia* 43 D2
Blanche, L., *W. Austral., Australia* 40 D3
Blanco, *U.S.A.* 55 K5
Blanco, C., *Costa Rica* 60 E2
Blanco, C., *U.S.A.* 56 E1
Blanda →, *Iceland* 6 D3
Blandford Forum, *U.K.* 9 G5
Blanding, *U.S.A.* 57 H9
Blanes, *Spain* 15 B7
Blankenberge, *Belgium* 11 C3
Blanquilla, I., *Venezuela* 61 D7
Blantyre, *Malawi* 37 H6
Blåvands Huk, *Denmark* 7 J13
Blaydon, *U.K.* 8 C6
Blayney, *Australia* 43 E4
Blaze, Pt., *Australia* 40 B5
Blekinge, *Sweden* 7 H16
Blenheim, *N.Z.* 39 J4
Bletchley, *U.K.* 9 F7
Blida, *Algeria* 34 A6
Bligh Sound, *N.Z.* 39 L1
Blind River, *Canada* 48 C3
Bliss, *U.S.A.* 56 E6
Blitar, *Indonesia* 27 H15
Block I., *U.S.A.* 52 E10
Blodgett Iceberg Tongue, *Antarctica* 5 C9
Bloemfontein, *S. Africa* 37 K5
Bloemhof, *S. Africa* 37 K5
Blois, *France* 14 C4
Blönduós, *Iceland* 6 D3
Bloodvein →, *Canada* 51 C9
Bloomer, *U.S.A.* 54 C9
Bloomfield, *Iowa, U.S.A.* 54 E8
Bloomfield, *N. Mex., U.S.A.* 57 H10
Bloomfield, *Nebr., U.S.A.* 54 D6
Bloomington, *Ill., U.S.A.* 54 E10
Bloomington, *Ind., U.S.A.* 52 F2
Bloomington, *Minn., U.S.A.* 54 C8
Bloomsburg, *U.S.A.* 52 E7
Blora, *Indonesia* 27 G14
Blountstown, *U.S.A.* 53 K3
Blue Earth, *U.S.A.* 54 D8
Blue Mesa Reservoir, *U.S.A.* 57 G10
Blue Mts., *U.S.A.* 56 D4
Blue Mud B., *Australia* 42 A2
Blue Nile = Nîl el Azraq →, *Sudan* 35 E12
Blue Rapids, *U.S.A.* 54 F6
Blue Ridge Mts., *U.S.A.* 53 G5
Blue River, *Canada* 50 C5
Bluefield, *U.S.A.* 52 G5
Bluefields, *Nic.* 60 D3
Bluff, *Australia* 42 C4
Bluff, *N.Z.* 39 M2
Bluff, *U.S.A.* 57 H9
Bluff Knoll, *Australia* 41 F2
Bluff Pt., *Australia* 41 E1
Bluffton, *U.S.A.* 52 E3
Blumenau, *Brazil* 64 B7
Blunt, *U.S.A.* 54 C5
Bly, *U.S.A.* 56 E3
Blyth, *U.K.* 8 B6
Blythe, *U.S.A.* 57 K6
Blytheville, *U.S.A.* 55 H10
Bo, *S. Leone* 34 G3
Bo Hai, *China* 25 C6
Boa Vista, *Brazil* 62 C6
Boaco, *Nic.* 60 D2
Bobadah, *Australia* 43 E4
Bobbili, *India* 29 K13
Bobcaygeon, *Canada* 48 D4
Bobo-Dioulasso, *Burkina Faso* 34 F5
Bóbr →, *Poland* 12 B8
Bobraomby, Tanjon' i, *Madag.* 37 G9
Bobruysk = Babruysk, *Belarus* 13 B15
Boby, Pic, *Madag.* 37 J9
Bôca do Acre, *Brazil* 62 E5
Boca Raton, *U.S.A.* 53 M5
Bocaranga, *C.A.R.* 32
Bocas del Toro, *Panama* 60 E3
Bochnia, *Poland* 13 D11
Bochum, *Germany* 12 C4
Bocoyna, *Mexico* 58 B3
Bodaybo, *Russia* 21 D12
Boddington, *Australia* 41 F2
Boden, *Sweden* 6 D19
Bodensee, *Europe* 14 C8
Bodhan, *India* 28 K10
Bodmin, *U.K.* 9 G3
Bodmin Moor, *U.K.* 9 G3
Bodø, *Norway* 6 C16
Bodrog →, *Hungary* 13 D11
Bodrum, *Turkey* 17 F12
Boende, *Dem. Rep. of the Congo* 36 E4
Boerne, *U.S.A.* 55 L5
Bogalusa, *U.S.A.* 55 K10
Bogan →, *Australia* 43 D4
Bogan Gate, *Australia* 43 E4
Bogantungan, *Australia* 42 C4
Bogata, *U.S.A.* 55 J7
Boggabilla, *Australia* 43 D5
Boggabri, *Australia* 43 E5
Boglan = Solhan, *Turkey* 30 B4
Bognor Regis, *U.K.* 9 G7
Bogo, *Phil.* 27 B6
Bogong, Mt., *Australia* 43 F4
Bogor, *Indonesia* 27 G12
Bogotá, *Colombia* 62 C4
Bogotol, *Russia* 20 D9
Bogra, *Bangla.* 29 G16
Boguchany, *Russia* 21 D10
Bohemian Forest = Böhmerwald, *Germany* 12 D7
Böhmerwald, *Germany* 12 D7
Bohol □, *Phil.* 27 C6
Bohol Sea, *Phil.* 27 C6
Bohuslän, *Sweden* 7 G14
Boiaçu, *Brazil* 62 D6
Boileau, C., *Australia* 40 C3
Boise, *U.S.A.* 56 E5
Boise City, *U.S.A.* 55 G3
Boissevain, *Canada* 51 D8
Bojador C., *W. Sahara* 34 C3
Bojana →, *Albania* 17 D8
Bojnūrd, *Iran* 31 B8
Bojonegoro, *Indonesia* 27 G14
Bokhara →, *Australia* 43 D4
Boknafjorden, *Norway* 7 G11
Bokoro, *Chad* 35 F9
Bokpyin, *Burma* 26 B1
Bolan Pass, *Pakistan* 28 E5
Bolaños →, *Mexico* 58 C4
Bolbec, *France* 14 B4
Boldājī, *Iran* 31 D6
Bole, *China* 24 B3
Bolekhiv, *Ukraine* 13 D12
Bolesławiec, *Poland* 12 C8
Bolgrad = Bolhrad, *Ukraine* 13 F15
Bolhrad, *Ukraine* 13 F15
Bolivar, *Mo., U.S.A.* 55 G8
Bolivar, *Tenn., U.S.A.* 55 H10
Bolivia ■, *S. Amer.* 62 G6
Bollnäs, *Sweden* 7 F17
Bollon, *Australia* 43 D4
Bolmen, *Sweden* 7 H15
Bolobo, *Dem. Rep. of the Congo* 36 E3
Bologna, *Italy* 16 B4
Bologoye, *Russia* 18 C5
Bolonchenticul, *Mexico* 59 D7
Bolsena, L. di, *Italy* 16 C4
Bolshevik, Ostrov, *Russia* 21 B11
Bolshoi Kavkas = Caucasus Mountains, *Eurasia* 19 F7
Bolshoy Anyuy →, *Russia* 21 C17
Bolshoy Begichev, Ostrov, *Russia* 21 B12
Bolshoy Lyakhovskiy, Ostrov, *Russia* 21 B15
Bolshoy Tyuters, Ostrov, *Russia* 7 G22
Bolsward, *Neths.* 11 A5
Bolt Head, *U.K.* 9 G4
Bolton, *U.K.* 8 D5
Bolu, *Turkey* 19 F5
Bolungavík, *Iceland* 6 C2
Bolvadin, *Turkey* 19 G5
Bolzano, *Italy* 16 A4
Bom Jesus da Lapa, *Brazil* 63 F10
Boma, *Dem. Rep. of the Congo* 36 F2
Bombala, *Australia* 43 F4
Bombay = Mumbai, *India* 28 K8
Bomboma, *Dem. Rep. of the Congo* 36 D3
Bømlo, *Norway* 7 G11
Bomu →, *C.A.R.* 36 D4
Bonaire, *Neth. Ant.* 62 A5
Bonang, *Australia* 43 F4
Bonanza, *Nic.* 60 D3
Bonaparte Arch., *Australia* 40 B3
Bonaventure, *Canada* 49 C6
Bonavista, *Canada* 49 C9
Bonavista, C., *Canada* 49 C9
Bonavista B., *Canada* 49 C9
Bondo, *Dem. Rep. of the Congo* 36 D4
Bondoukou, *Ivory C.* 34 G5
Bondowoso, *Indonesia* 27 G15
Bone, Teluk, *Indonesia* 27 E6
Bonerate, *Indonesia* 27 F6
Bonerate, Kepulauan, *Indonesia* 27 F6
Bong Son = Hoai Nhon, *Vietnam* 26 B3
Bongor, *Chad* 35 F9
Bonham, *U.S.A.* 55 J6
Bonifacio, *France* 14 F8
Bonifacio, Bouches de, *Medit. S.* 16 D3
Bonin Is. = Ogasawara Gunto, *Pac. Oc.* 44 E6
Bonn, *Germany* 12 C4
Bonne Terre, *U.S.A.* 55 G9
Bonners Ferry, *U.S.A.* 56 B5
Bonney, L., *Australia* 43 F3
Bonnie Rock, *Australia* 41 F2
Bonny, Bight of, *Africa* 36 D1
Bonnyville, *Canada* 51 C6
Bonoi, *Indonesia* 27 E9
Bontang, *Indonesia* 26 D5
Bonthe, *S. Leone* 34 G3
Bontoc, *Phil.* 27 A6
Bonython Ra., *Australia* 40 D4
Bookabie, *Australia* 41 F5
Booker, *U.S.A.* 55 G4
Booligal, *Australia* 43 E3
Boonah, *Australia* 43 D5
Boone, *Iowa, U.S.A.* 54 D8
Boone, *N.C., U.S.A.* 53 G5
Booneville, *Ark., U.S.A.* 55 H8
Booneville, *Miss., U.S.A.* 53 H1
Boonville, *Ind., U.S.A.* 52 F2
Boonville, *Mo., U.S.A.* 54 F8
Boonville, *N.Y., U.S.A.* 52 D8
Boorindal, *Australia* 43 E4
Boorowa, *Australia* 43 E4
Boothia, Gulf of, *Canada* 47 A11
Boothia Pen., *Canada* 46 A10
Bootle, *U.K.* 8 D4
Booué, *Gabon* 36 E2
Boquete, *Panama* 60 E3
Boquilla, Presa de la, *Mexico* 58 B3
Boquillas del Carmen, *Mexico* 58 B4
Bor, *Serbia, Yug.* 17 B10
Bôr, *Sudan* 35 G12
Bor Mashash, *Israel* 33 D3
Borah Peak, *U.S.A.* 56 D7
Borås, *Sweden* 7 H15
Borāzjān, *Iran* 31 D6
Borba, *Brazil* 62 D7
Bord Khūn-e Now, *Iran* 31 D6
Borda, C., *Australia* 43 F2
Bordeaux, *France* 14 D3
Borden, *Australia* 41 F2
Borden, *Canada* 49 C7
Borden I., *Canada* 4 B2
Borden Pen., *Canada* 47 A11
Bordertown, *Australia* 43 F3
Borðeyri, *Iceland* 6 D3
Bordj Fly Ste. Marie, *Algeria* 34 C5
Bordj-in-Eker, *Algeria* 34 D7
Bordj Omar Driss, *Algeria* 34 C7
Borehamwood, *U.K.* 9 F7
Borgå = Porvoo, *Finland* 7 F21
Borgarfjörður, *Iceland* 6 D7
Borgarnes, *Iceland* 6 D3
Børgefjellet, *Norway* 6 D15
Borger, *Neths.* 11 B6
Borger, *U.S.A.* 55 H4
Borgholm, *Sweden* 7 H17
Borhoyn Tal, *Mongolia* 25 B6
Borisoglebsk, *Russia* 19 D7
Borisov = Barysaw, *Belarus* 13 A15
Borja, *Peru* 62 D3
Borkou, *Chad* 35 E9
Borkum, *Germany* 12 B4
Borlänge, *Sweden* 7 F16
Borley, C., *Antarctica* 5 C5
Borneo, *E. Indies* 26 D5
Bornholm, *Denmark* 7 J16
Borogontsy, *Russia* 21 C14
Borongan, *Phil.* 27 B7
Borovichi, *Russia* 18 C5
Borroloola, *Australia* 42 B2
Borşa, *Romania* 13 E13
Borth, *U.K.* 9 E3
Borūjerd, *Iran* 31 C6
Boryslav, *Ukraine* 13 D12
Borzya, *Russia* 21 D12
Bosa, *Italy* 16 D3
Bosanska Gradiška, *Bos.-H.* 16 B7
Bosaso, *Somali Rep.* 32 E4
Boscastle, *U.K.* 9 G3
Boshrūyeh, *Iran* 31 C8
Bosna →, *Bos.-H.* 17 B8
Bosna i Hercegovina = Bosnia-Herzegovina ■, *Europe* 16 B7
Bosnia-Herzegovina ■, *Europe* 16 B7
Bosnik, *Indonesia* 27 E9
Bosobolo, *Dem. Rep. of the Congo* 36 D3
Bosporus = İstanbul Boğazı, *Turkey* 17 D13
Bosque Farms, *U.S.A.* 57 J10
Bossangoa, *C.A.R.* 36 C3
Bossier City, *U.S.A.* 55 J8
Bosso, *Niger* 35 F8
Bostānābād, *Iran* 30 B5
Bosten Hu, *China* 24 B3
Boston, *U.K.* 8 E7
Boston, *U.S.A.* 52 D10
Boston Bar, *Canada* 50 D4
Boston Mts., *U.S.A.* 55 H8
Boswell, *Canada* 50 D5
Botany B., *Australia* 38 E8
Bothnia, G. of, *Europe* 6 E19
Bothwell, *Australia* 42 G4
Botletle →, *Botswana* 37 J4
Botoşani, *Romania* 13 E14
Botou, *Burkina Faso* 34 F6
Botswana ■, *Africa* 37 J4
Bottineau, *U.S.A.* 54 A4
Bottrop, *Germany* 11 C6
Botucatu, *Brazil* 63 H9
Botwood, *Canada* 49 C8
Bouaflé, *Ivory C.* 34 G4
Bouaké, *Ivory C.* 34 G4
Bouar, *C.A.R.* 36 C3
Bouârfa, *Morocco* 34 B5
Bouca, *C.A.R.* 32
Boucaut B., *Australia* 42 A1
Bougainville, C., *Australia* 40 B4
Bougainville I., *Papua N. G.* 38 B8
Bougainville Reef, *Australia* 42 B4
Bougie = Bejaia, *Algeria* 34 A7
Bougouni, *Mali* 34 F4
Bouillon, *Belgium* 11 E5
Boulder, *Colo., U.S.A.* 54 E2
Boulder, *Mont., U.S.A.* 56 C7
Boulder City, *U.S.A.* 57 J6
Boulder Dam = Hoover Dam, *U.S.A.* 57 J6
Boulia, *Australia* 42 C2
Boulogne-sur-Mer, *France* 14 A4
Boultoum, *Niger* 35 F8
Bouna, *Ivory C.* 34 G5
Boundiali, *Ivory C.* 34 G4
Bountiful, *U.S.A.* 56 F8
Bounty Is., *Pac. Oc.* 44 M9
Bourbonnais, *France* 14 C5
Bourdel L., *Canada* 48 A5
Bourem, *Mali* 34 E5
Bourg-en-Bresse, *France* 14 C6
Bourg-St-Maurice, *France* 14 D7
Bourges, *France* 14 C5
Bourgogne, *France* 14 C6
Bourke, *Australia* 43 E4
Bourne, *U.K.* 8 E7
Bournemouth, *U.K.* 9 G6
Bournemouth □, *U.K.* 9 G6
Bouvet I. = Bouvetøya, *Antarctica* 3 G10
Bouvetøya, *Antarctica* 3 G10
Bovill, *U.S.A.* 56 C5
Bow →, *Canada* 50 C6
Bow Island, *Canada* 50 D6
Bowbells, *U.S.A.* 54 A3
Bowdle, *U.S.A.* 54 C5
Bowelling, *Australia* 41 F2
Bowen, *Australia* 42 C4
Bowen Mts., *Australia* 43 F4
Bowie, *Ariz., U.S.A.* 57 K9
Bowie, *Tex., U.S.A.* 55 J6
Bowkān, *Iran* 30 B5
Bowland, Forest of, *U.K.* 8 D5
Bowling Green, *Ky., U.S.A.* 52 G2
Bowling Green, *Ohio, U.S.A.* 52 E4
Bowling Green, C., *Australia* 42 B4
Bowman, *U.S.A.* 54 B3
Bowman I., *Antarctica* 5 C8
Bowral, *Australia* 43 E5
Bowraville, *Australia* 43 E5
Bowron →, *Canada* 50 C4
Bowron Lake Prov. Park, *Canada* 50 C4
Bowser L., *Canada* 50 B3
Bowsman, *Canada* 51 C8
Box Cr. →, *Australia* 43 E3
Boxmeer, *Neths.* 11 C5
Boxtel, *Neths.* 11 C5
Boyce, *U.S.A.* 55 K8
Boyd L., *Canada* 48 B4
Boyle, *Canada* 50 C6
Boyne →, *Ireland* 10 E3
Boyne City, *U.S.A.* 52 C3
Boynton Beach, *U.S.A.* 53 M5
Boyolali, *Indonesia* 27 G14
Boysen Reservoir, *U.S.A.* 56 E9
Boyuibe, *Bolivia* 62 G6
Boyup Brook, *Australia* 41 F2
Boz Dağları, *Turkey* 17 E13
Bozburun, *Turkey* 17 F13
Bozcaada, *Turkey* 17 E12
Bozdoğan, *Turkey* 17 F13
Bozeman, *U.S.A.* 56 D8
Bozen = Bolzano, *Italy* 16 A4
Bozoum, *C.A.R.* 36 C3
Bra, *Italy* 14 D7
Brabant □, *Belgium* 11 D4
Brabant L., *Canada* 51 B8
Brač, *Croatia* 16 C7
Bracciano, L. di, *Italy* 16 C5
Bracebridge, *Canada* 48 C4
Brach, *Libya* 35 C8
Bräcke, *Sweden* 7 E16
Brackettville, *U.S.A.* 55 L4
Bracknell, *U.K.* 9 F7
Bracknell Forest □, *U.K.* 9 F7
Brad, *Romania* 13 E12
Bradenton, *U.S.A.* 53 M4
Bradford, *U.K.* 8 D6
Bradford, *U.S.A.* 52 E6
Bradley, *U.S.A.* 55 J8
Brady, *U.S.A.* 55 K5
Braga, *Portugal* 15 B1
Bragança, *Brazil* 63 D9
Bragança, *Portugal* 15 B2
Brahmanbaria, *Bangla.* 29 H17
Brahmani →, *India* 29 J15
Brahmapur, *India* 29 K14
Brahmaputra →, *India* 29 H16
Braich-y-pwll, *U.K.* 8 E3
Braidwood, *Australia* 43 F4
Brăila, *Romania* 13 F14
Brainerd, *U.S.A.* 54 B7
Braintree, *U.K.* 9 F8
Brampton, *Canada* 48 D4

Brampton, U.K. 8 C5
Branco →, Brazil 62 D6
Brandenburg =
  Neubrandenburg,
  Germany 12 B7
Brandenburg, Germany 12 B7
Brandenburg □,
  Germany 12 B6
Brandon, Canada 51 D9
Braniewo, Poland 13 A10
Bransfield Str.,
  Antarctica 5 C18
Branson, U.S.A. 55 G8
Brantford, Canada . . . 48 D3
Bras d'Or L., Canada . . 49 C7
Brasiléia, Brazil 62 F5
Brasília, Brazil 63 G9
Brasília Legal, Brazil . . 63 D7
Braslaw, Belarus 7 J22
Braşov, Romania 13 F13
Brasschaat, Belgium . . 11 C4
Brastad, Sweden 7 G14
Bratislava, Slovak Rep. 13 D9
Bratsk, Russia 21 D11
Brattleboro, U.S.A. . . . 52 D9
Braunau, Austria 12 D7
Braunschweig, Germany 12 B6
Braunton, U.K. 9 F3
Bravo del Norte, Rio =
  Grande, Rio →,
  U.S.A. 55 N6
Brawley, U.S.A. 57 K6
Bray, Ireland 10 E3
Bray, Mt., Australia . . 42 A1
Bray, Pays de, France . 14 B4
Brazeau →, Canada . . 50 C5
Brazil, U.S.A. 52 F2
Brazil ■, S. Amer. . . . 63 F9
Brazos →, U.S.A. 55 L7
Brazzaville, Congo 36 E3
Brčko, Bos.-H. 17 B8
Breaden, L., Australia . 41 E4
Breaksea Sd., N.Z. . . . 39 L1
Bream B., N.Z. 39 F5
Bream Hd., N.Z. 39 F5
Brebes, Indonesia 27 G13
Brecht, Belgium 11 C4
Breckenridge, Colo.,
  U.S.A. 56 G10
Breckenridge, Minn.,
  U.S.A. 54 B6
Breckenridge, Tex.,
  U.S.A. 55 J5
Breckland, U.K. 9 E8
Brecon, U.K. 9 F4
Brecon Beacons, U.K. . 9 F4
Breda, Neths. 11 C4
Bredasdorp, S. Africa . 37 L4
Bree, Belgium 11 C5
Bregenz, Austria 12 E5
Breiðafjörður, Iceland . 6 D2
Brejo, Brazil 63 D10
Bremen, Germany 12 B5
Bremer Bay, Australia . 41 F2
Bremer I., Australia . . 42 A2
Bremerhaven, Germany 12 B5
Bremerton, U.S.A. 56 C2
Brenham, U.S.A. 55 K6
Brennerpass, Austria . . 12 E6
Brent, U.S.A. 53 J2
Brentwood, U.K. 9 F8
Bréscia, Italy 14 D9
Breskens, Neths. 11 C3
Breslau = Wrocław,
  Poland 13 C9
Bressanone, Italy 16 A4
Brest, Belarus 13 B12
Brest, France 14 B1
Brest-Litovsk = Brest,
  Belarus 13 B12
Bretagne, France 14 B2
Breton, Canada 50 C6
Breton Sd., U.S.A. . . . 55 L10
Brett, C., N.Z. 39 F5
Brevard, U.S.A. 53 H4
Breves, Brazil 63 D8
Brewarrina, Australia . 43 E4
Brewer, U.S.A. 53 C11
Brewster, U.S.A. 56 B4
Brewster, Kap =
  Kangikajik, Greenland 4 B6
Brewton, U.S.A. 53 K2
Brezhnev =
  Naberezhnyye Chelny,
  Russia 18 C9
Bria, C.A.R. 32
Briançon, France 14 D7
Bribie I., Australia . . . 43 D5
Bribri, Costa Rica 60 E3
Bridgend, U.K. 9 F4
Bridgend □, U.K. 9 F4
Bridgeport, Calif., U.S.A. 57 G4
Bridgeport, Conn.,
  U.S.A. 52 E9
Bridgeport, Nebr.,
  U.S.A. 54 E3
Bridgeport, Tex., U.S.A. 55 J6
Bridger, U.S.A. 56 D9
Bridgeton, U.S.A. 52 F8
Bridgetown, Australia . 41 F2
Bridgetown, Barbados . 61 D8

Bridgetown, Canada . . 49 D6
Bridgewater, Canada . . 49 D7
Bridgewater, C.,
  Australia 43 F3
Bridgewater-Gagebrook,
  Australia 42 G4
Bridgnorth, U.K. 9 E5
Bridgwater, U.K. 9 F5
Bridgwater B., U.K. . . . 9 F4
Bridlington, U.K. 8 C7
Bridlington B., U.K. . . . 8 C7
Bridport, Australia . . . 42 G4
Bridport, U.K. 9 G5
Brig, Switz. 14 C7
Brigg, U.K. 8 D7
Brigham City, U.S.A. . . 56 F7
Bright, Australia 43 F4
Brighton, Australia . . . 43 F2
Brighton, U.K. 9 G7
Brighton, U.S.A. 54 F2
Brindisi, Italy 17 D7
Brinkley, U.S.A. 55 H9
Brion, I., Canada 49 C7
Brisbane, Australia . . . 43 D5
Brisbane →, Australia . 43 D5
Bristol, U.K. 9 F5
Bristol, Conn., U.S.A. . 52 E9
Bristol, Tenn., U.S.A. . 53 G4
Bristol, City of □, U.K. . 9 F5
Bristol B., U.S.A. 46 C4
Bristol Channel, U.K. . 9 F3
Bristol I., Antarctica . . 5 B1
Bristol L., U.S.A. 57 J5
Bristow, U.S.A. 55 H6
Britain = Great Britain,
  Europe 10 D5
Britain = Great Britain,
  Europe 10 D5
British Columbia □,
  Canada 50 C3
British Indian Ocean
  Terr. = Chagos Arch.,
  Ind. Oc. 3 E13
British Indian Ocean
  Terr. = Chagos Arch.,
  Ind. Oc. 3 E13
British Isles, Europe . . 10 D5
British Isles, Europe . . 10 D5
Britt, Canada 48 C3
Brittany = Bretagne,
  France 14 B2
Britton, U.S.A. 54 C6
Brive-la-Gaillarde,
  France 14 D4
Brixen = Bressanone,
  Italy 16 A4
Brixham, U.K. 9 G4
Brno, Czech Rep. 13 D9
Broad →, U.S.A. 53 J5
Broad Arrow, Australia 41 E3
Broad Sd., Australia . . 42 C4
Broadback →, Canada 48 B4
Broadford, Australia . . 43 F4
Broadhurst Ra.,
  Australia 40 D3
Broads, The, U.K. 8 E9
Broadus, U.S.A. 54 C2
Brochet, Canada 51 B8
Brochet, L., Canada . . 51 B8
Brocken, Germany . . . 12 C6
Brockport, U.S.A. 52 D7
Brockton, U.S.A. 52 D10
Brockville, Canada . . . 48 D4
Brockway, U.S.A. 54 B2
Brodeur Pen., Canada . 47 A11
Brodnica, Poland 13 B10
Brody, Ukraine 13 C13
Brogan, U.S.A. 56 D5
Broken Arrow, U.S.A. . 55 G7
Broken Bow, Nebr.,
  U.S.A. 54 E5
Broken Bow, Okla.,
  U.S.A. 55 H7
Broken Bow Lake,
  U.S.A. 55 H7
Broken Hill = Kabwe,
  Zambia 37 G5
Broken Hill, Australia . . 43 E3
Bromley □, U.K. 9 F8
Bromsgrove, U.K. 9 E5
Brønderslev, Denmark . 7 H13
Brønnøysund, Norway . 6 C16
Brookhaven, U.S.A. . . . 55 K9
Brookings, Oreg., U.S.A. 56 E1
Brookings, S. Dak.,
  U.S.A. 54 C6
Brooklyn Park, U.S.A. . 54 C8
Brooks, Canada 50 C6
Brooks Range, U.S.A. . 46 B5
Brooksville, U.S.A. . . . 53 L4
Brookton, Australia . . . 41 F2
Brookville, U.S.A. 52 E6
Broome, Australia 40 C3
Brothers, U.S.A. 56 E3
Brough, U.K. 8 C5
Broughton Island =
  Qikiqtarjuaq, Canada 47 B13
Brown, L., Australia . . 41 F2
Brown, Pt., Australia . . 43 E1
Brown Willy, U.K. 9 G3
Brownfield, U.S.A. 55 J3
Browning, U.S.A. 56 B7
Brownsville, Oreg.,
  U.S.A. 56 D2

Brownsville, Tenn.,
  U.S.A. 55 H10
Brownsville, Tex., U.S.A. 55 N6
Brownwood, U.S.A. . . . 55 K5
Browse I., Australia . . . 40 B3
Bruay-la-Buissière,
  France 14 A5
Bruce, Mt., Australia . . 40 D2
Bruce Rock, Australia . 41 F2
Bruck an der Leitha,
  Austria 13 D9
Bruck an der Mur,
  Austria 12 E8
Brue →, U.K. 9 F5
Bruges = Brugge,
  Belgium 11 C3
Brugge, Belgium 11 C3
Brûlé, Canada 50 C5
Brumado, Brazil 63 F10
Brumunddal, Norway . 7 F14
Bruneau, U.S.A. 56 E6
Bruneau →, U.S.A. . . 56 E6
Brunei = Bandar Seri
  Begawan, Brunei . . . 26 C4
Brunei ■, Asia 26 D4
Brunner, L., N.Z. 39 K3
Brunssum, Neths. 11 D5
Brunswick =
  Braunschweig,
  Germany 12 B6
Brunswick, Ga., U.S.A. 53 K5
Brunswick, Maine,
  U.S.A. 53 D11
Brunswick, Md., U.S.A. 52 F7
Brunswick, Mo., U.S.A. 54 F8
Brunswick, Pen. de,
  Chile 64 G2
Brunswick B., Australia 40 C3
Brunswick Junction,
  Australia 41 F2
Bruny I., Australia 42 G4
Brus Laguna, Honduras 60 C3
Brush, U.S.A. 54 E3
Brussel, Belgium 11 D4
Brussels = Brussel,
  Belgium 11 D4
Bruthen, Australia . . . 43 F4
Bruxelles = Brussel,
  Belgium 11 D4
Bryan, Ohio, U.S.A. . . . 52 E3
Bryan, Tex., U.S.A. . . . 55 K6
Bryan, Mt., Australia . . 43 E2
Bryansk, Russia 18 D4
Bryce Canyon National
  Park, U.S.A. 57 H7
Bryne, Norway 7 G11
Bryson City, U.S.A. . . . 53 H4
Bsharri, Lebanon 33 A5
Bū Baqarah, U.A.E. . . . 31 E8
Bu Craa, W. Sahara . . 34 C3
Bū Ḥasā, U.A.E. 31 F7
Buapinang, Indonesia . 27 E6
Būbiyān, Kuwait 31 D6
Bucaramanga, Colombia 62 B4
Bucasia, Australia 42 C4
Buccaneer Arch.,
  Australia 40 C3
Buchach, Ukraine 13 D13
Buchan, U.K. 10 D6
Buchanan, Canada . . . 51 C8
Buchanan, Liberia 34 G3
Buchanan, L., Queens.,
  Australia 42 C4
Buchanan, L.,
  W. Austral., Australia 41 E3
Buchanan, L., U.S.A. . . 55 K5
Buchanan Cr. →,
  Australia 42 B2
Buchans, Canada 49 C8
Bucharest = Bucureşti,
  Romania 13 F14
Buckeye, U.S.A. 57 K7
Buckhannon, U.S.A. . . 52 F5
Buckie, U.K. 10 C5
Buckingham, Canada . . 48 C4
Buckingham, U.K. 9 F7
Buckingham B.,
  Australia 42 A2
Buckinghamshire □,
  U.K. 9 F7
Buckle Hd., Australia . . 40 B4
Buckleboo, Australia . . 43 E2
Buckley, U.K. 8 D4
Buckley →, Australia . 42 C2
Bucklin, U.S.A. 55 G5
Buctouche, Canada . . . 49 C7
Bucureşti, Romania . . . 13 F14
Bucyrus, U.S.A. 52 E4
Budalin, Burma 29 H19
Budapest, Hungary . . . 13 E10
Budd Coast, Antarctica 5 C8
Bude, U.K. 9 G3
Budennovsk, Russia . . 19 F7
Budgewoi, Australia . . 43 E5
Budjala, Dem. Rep. of
  the Congo 36 D3
Buena Vista, Colo.,
  U.S.A. 57 G10
Buena Vista, Va., U.S.A. 52 G6
Buena Vista Lake Bed,
  U.S.A. 57 J4
Buenaventura, Colombia 62 C3
Buenaventura, Mexico . 58 B3
Buenos Aires, Argentina 64 C5
Buenos Aires,
  Costa Rica 60 E3

Buenos Aires, L., Chile 64 F2
Buffalo, Mo., U.S.A. . . 55 G8
Buffalo, N.Y., U.S.A. . . 52 D6
Buffalo, Okla., U.S.A. . 55 G5
Buffalo, S. Dak., U.S.A. 54 C3
Buffalo, Wyo., U.S.A. . 56 D10
Buffalo →, Canada . . 50 A5
Buffalo Head Hills,
  Canada 50 B5
Buffalo L., Alta., Canada 50 C6
Buffalo L., N.W.T.,
  Canada 50 A5
Buffalo Narrows,
  Canada 51 B7
Buford, U.S.A. 53 H4
Bug = Buh →, Ukraine 19 E5
Bug →, Poland 13 B11
Buga, Colombia 62 C3
Bugel, Tanjung,
  Indonesia 27 G14
Bugsuk, Phil. 26 C5
Bugulma, Russia 18 D9
Bugun Shara, Mongolia 24 B5
Buguruslan, Russia . . . 18 D9
Buh →, Ukraine 19 E5
Buhl, U.S.A. 56 E6
Builth Wells, U.K. 9 E4
Buir Nur, Mongolia . . . 25 B6
Bujumbura, Burundi . . 36 E5
Bukachacha, Russia . . 21 D12
Bukavu, Dem. Rep. of
  the Congo 36 E5
Bukhara = Bukhoro,
  Uzbekistan 20 F7
Bukhoro, Uzbekistan . . 20 F7
Bukittinggi, Indonesia . 26 E2
Bukoba, Tanzania 36 E6
Būl, Kuh-e, Iran 31 D7
Bula, Indonesia 27 E8
Bulahdelah, Australia . 43 E5
Bulan, Phil. 27 B6
Bulandshahr, India . . . 28 E10
Bulawayo, Zimbabwe . 37 J5
Buldan, Turkey 17 E13
Bulgar, Russia 18 D8
Bulgaria ■, Europe . . . 17 C11
Buli, Teluk, Indonesia . 27 D7
Buliluyan, C., Phil. . . . 26 C5
Bulkley →, Canada . . 50 B3
Bull Shoals L., U.S.A. . 55 G8
Bullhead City, U.S.A. . 57 J6
Büllingen, Belgium . . . 11 D6
Bullock Creek, Australia 42 B3
Bulloo →, Australia . . 43 D3
Bulloo L., Australia . . . 43 D3
Bulls, N.Z. 39 J5
Bulsar = Valsad, India . 28 J8
Bulukumba, Indonesia . 27 F6
Bulun, Russia 21 B13
Bumba, Dem. Rep. of
  the Congo 36 D4
Bumhpa Bum, Burma . 29 F20
Bunbury, Australia . . . 41 F2
Buncrana, Ireland 10 D3
Bundaberg, Australia . . 43 C5
Bundey →, Australia . 42 C2
Bundi, India 28 G9
Bundoran, Ireland 10 D2
Bungatakada, Japan . . 23 H5
Bungay, U.K. 9 E9
Bungil Cr. →, Australia 43 D4
Bungo-Suidō, Japan . . 23 H6
Bunia, Dem. Rep. of
  the Congo 36 D6
Bunji, Pakistan 28 B9
Bunkie, U.S.A. 55 K8
Bunnell, U.S.A. 53 L5
Buntok, Indonesia 26 E4
Bunyu, Indonesia 26 D5
Buol, Indonesia 27 D6
Buon Ma Thuot,
  Vietnam 26 B3
Buorkhaya, Mys, Russia 21 B14
Buqayq, Si. Arabia . . . 31 E6
Bur Acaba, Somali Rep. 32 G3
Bûr Safâga, Egypt . . . 30 E2
Bûr Sa'îd, Egypt 35 B12
Bûr Sûdân, Sudan . . . 35 E13
Burakin, Australia 41 F2
Burao, Somali Rep. . . . 32 F4
Burāq, Syria 33 B5
Buraydah, Si. Arabia . . 30 E4
Burbank, U.S.A. 57 J4
Burdekin →, Australia 42 B4
Burdur, Turkey 19 G5
Burdwan =
  Barddhaman, India . 29 H15
Bure, Ethiopia 32 E2
Bure →, U.K. 8 E9
Bureya →, Russia . . . 21 E13
Burgas, Bulgaria 17 C12
Burgeo, Canada 49 C8
Burges, Mt., Australia . 41 F3
Burgos, Spain 15 A4
Burgsvik, Sweden 7 H18
Burgundy = Bourgogne,
  France 14 C6
Burhaniye, Turkey 17 E12
Burhanpur, India 28 J10
Burias I., Phil. 27 B6
Burica, Pta., Costa Rica 60 E3
Buriram, Thailand 26 A2
Burin, Canada 49 C8
Burj Säfītā, Syria 30 C3
Burkburnett, U.S.A. . . . 55 H5

Burke →, Australia . . 42 C2
Burke Chan., Canada . 50 C3
Burketown, Australia . . 42 B2
Burkina Faso ■, Africa 34 F5
Burk's Falls, Canada . . 48 C4
Burley, U.S.A. 56 E7
Burlington, Canada . . . 48 D4
Burlington, Colo., U.S.A. 54 F3
Burlington, Iowa, U.S.A. 54 E9
Burlington, Kans.,
  U.S.A. 54 F7
Burlington, N.C., U.S.A. 53 G6
Burlington, Vt., U.S.A. . 52 C9
Burlington, Wash.,
  U.S.A. 56 B2
Burlington, Wis., U.S.A. 52 D1
Burlyu-Tyube, Kazakstan 20 E8
Burma ■, Asia 29 J20
Burnaby I., Canada . . . 50 C2
Burnet, U.S.A. 55 K5
Burney, U.S.A. 56 F3
Burnham-on-Sea, U.K. 9 F5
Burnie, Australia 42 G4
Burnley, U.K. 8 D5
Burns, U.S.A. 56 E4
Burns Lake, Canada . . 50 C3
Burnside →, Canada . 46 B9
Burnside, L., Australia . 41 E3
Burnsville, U.S.A. 54 C8
Burnt L., Canada 49 B7
Burntwood →, Canada 51 B9
Burntwood L., Canada . 51 B8
Burqān, Kuwait 30 D5
Burra, Australia 43 E2
Burren Junction,
  Australia 43 E4
Burrinjuck Res.,
  Australia 43 F4
Burro, Serranías del,
  Mexico 58 B4
Burruyacú, Argentina . 64 B4
Burry Port, U.K. 9 F3
Bursa, Turkey 17 D13
Burstall, Canada 51 C7
Burton, U.S.A. 53 J5
Burton, L., Canada . . . 48 B4
Burton upon Trent, U.K. 8 E6
Buru, Indonesia 27 E7
Burûn, Râs, Egypt . . . 33 D2
Burundi ■, Africa 36 E5
Burutu, Nigeria 34 G7
Burwell, U.S.A. 54 E5
Bury, U.K. 8 D5
Bury St. Edmunds, U.K. 9 E8
Buryatia □, Russia . . . 21 D11
Buşayrah, Syria 30 C4
Büshehr, Iran 31 D6
Büshehr □, Iran 31 D6
Bushell, Canada 51 B7
Bushire = Büshehr, Iran 31 D6
Businga, Dem. Rep. of
  the Congo 36 D4
Buşra ash Shām, Syria 33 C5
Busselton, Australia . . 41 F2
Bussum, Neths. 11 B5
Busto Arsizio, Italy . . . 14 D8
Busu-Djanoa, Dem. Rep.
  of the Congo 36 D4
Busuanga I., Phil. 27 B5
Buta, Dem. Rep. of
  the Congo 36 D4
Butare, Rwanda 36 E5
Butaritari, Kiribati 44 G9
Bute Inlet, Canada . . . 50 C4
Butembo, Dem. Rep. of
  the Congo 36 D5
Butha Qi, China 25 B7
Butler, Mo., U.S.A. . . . 54 F7
Butler, Pa., U.S.A. . . . 52 E6
Buton, Indonesia 27 E6
Butte, Mont., U.S.A. . . 56 C7
Butte, Nebr., U.S.A. . . 54 D5
Butterworth = Gcuwa,
  S. Africa 37 L5
Butterworth, Malaysia . 26 C2
Buttfield, Mt., Australia 41 D4
Button B., Canada . . . 51 B10
Butty Hd., Australia . . 41 F3
Butuan, Phil. 27 C7
Butung = Buton,
  Indonesia 27 E6
Buturlinovka, Russia . . 19 D7
Buxtehude, Germany . . 12 B5
Buxton, U.K. 8 D6
Buy, Russia 18 C7
Büyük Menderes →,
  Turkey 17 F12
Büyükçekmece, Turkey 17 D13
Büzău, Romania 13 F14
Büzău →, Romania . . 13 F14
Buzen, Japan 23 H5
Buzi →, Mozam. 37 H6
Buzuluk, Russia 18 D9
Byarezina →, Belarus . 13 B16
Byaroza, Belarus 13 B13
Bydgoszcz, Poland . . . 13 B9
Byelarus = Belarus ■,
  Europe 13 B14
Byelorussia =
  Belarus ■, Europe . . 13 B14
Byers, U.S.A. 54 F2
Byford, Australia 41 F2
Bykhaw, Belarus 13 B16
Bykhov = Bykhaw,
  Belarus 13 B16

Bylas, U.S.A. 57 K8
Bylot, Canada 51 B10
Bylot I., Canada 47 A12
Byrd, C., Antarctica . . 5 C17
Byrock, Australia 43 E4
Byron, C., Australia . . 38 D8
Byron Bay, Australia . . 43 D5
Byrranga, Gory, Russia 21 B11
Byrranga Mts. =
  Byrranga, Gory,
  Russia 21 B11
Byske, Sweden 6 D19
Byske älv →, Sweden . 6 D19
Bytom, Poland 13 C10
Bytów, Poland 13 A9

Ca Mau, Vietnam 26 C3
Ca Mau, Mui, Vietnam . 26 C2
Caála, Angola 37 G3
Caamaño Sd., Canada . 50 C3
Cabanatuan, Phil. 27 A6
Cabano, Canada 49 C6
Cabedelo, Brazil 63 E12
Cabimas, Venezuela . . 62 A4
Cabinda, Angola 36 F2
Cabinda □, Angola . . . 36 F2
Cabinet Mts., U.S.A. . . 56 C6
Cabo Blanco, Argentina 64 F3
Cabo Frio, Brazil 63 H10
Cabo Pantoja, Peru . . 62 D3
Cabonga, Réservoir,
  Canada 48 C4
Cabool, U.S.A. 55 G8
Caboolture, Australia . 43 D5
Cabora Bassa Dam =
  Cahora Bassa,
  Reprêsa de, Mozam. 37 H6
Caborca, Mexico 58 A2
Cabot Str., Canada . . . 49 C8
Cabra, Spain 15 D3
Cabrera, Spain 15 C7
Cabri, Canada 51 C7
Cabriel →, Spain 15 C5
Čačak, Serbia, Yug. . . 17 C9
Cáceres, Brazil 62 G7
Cáceres, Spain 15 C2
Cache Bay, Canada . . . 48 C4
Cache Creek, Canada . 50 C4
Cachimbo, Serra do,
  Brazil 63 E7
Cachoeira, Brazil 63 F11
Cachoeira de
  Itapemirim, Brazil . . 63 H10
Cachoeira do Sul, Brazil 64 C6
Cacoal, Brazil 62 F6
Cacólo, Angola 36 G3
Caconda, Angola 37 G3
Cader Idris, U.K. 9 E4
Cadereyta, Mexico . . . 58 B5
Cadibarrawirracanna, L.,
  Australia 43 D2
Cadillac, U.S.A. 52 C3
Cadiz, Phil. 27 B6
Cádiz, Spain 15 D2
Cádiz, G. de, Spain . . . 15 D2
Cadiz L., U.S.A. 57 J6
Cadney Park, Australia 43 D1
Cadomin, Canada 50 C5
Cadotte Lake, Canada . 50 B5
Cadoux, Australia 41 F2
Caen, France 14 B3
Caernarfon, U.K. 8 D3
Caernarfon B., U.K. . . . 8 D3
Caernarvon =
  Caernarfon, U.K. . . . 8 D3
Caerphilly, U.K. 9 F4
Caerphilly □, U.K. 9 F4
Caesarea, Israel 33 C3
Caetité, Brazil 63 F10
Cagayan de Oro, Phil. . 27 C6
Cagayan Is., Phil. 27 C5
Cágliari, Italy 16 E3
Cágliari, G. di, Italy . . 16 E3
Caguán →, Colombia . 62 D4
Caguas, Puerto Rico . . 61 C6
Cahora Bassa, Reprêsa
  de, Mozam. 37 H6
Cahors, France 14 D4
Cahul, Moldova 13 F15
Caibarién, Cuba 60 B4
Caicara, Venezuela . . . 62 B5
Caicó, Brazil 63 E11
Caicos Is., W. Indies . . 61 B5
Caicos Passage,
  W. Indies 61 B5
Caird Coast, Antarctica 5 D1
Cairns, Australia 42 B4
Cairns L., Canada 51 C10
Cairo = El Qâhira, Egypt 35 B12
Cairo, Ga., U.S.A. 53 K3
Cairo, Ill., U.S.A. 55 G10
Cajamarca, Peru 62 E3
Cajàzeiras, Brazil 63 E11
Calabar, Nigeria 34 H7
Calabozo, Venezuela . . 62 B5
Calábria □, Italy 16 E7
Calafate, Argentina . . 64 G2
Calahorra, Spain 15 A5
Calais, France 14 A4
Calais, U.S.A. 53 C12
Calama, Brazil 62 E6
Calama, Chile 62 H5
Calamar, Colombia . . . 62 A4

Calamian Group, *Phil.* . 27 B5
Calamocha, *Spain* 15 B5
Calang, *Indonesia* 26 D1
Calapan, *Phil.* 27 B6
Călărași, *Romania* .. 13 F14
Calatayud, *Spain* 15 B5
Calauag, *Phil.* 27 B6
Calavite, C., *Phil.* 27 B6
Calbayog, *Phil.* 27 B6
Calca, *Peru* 62 F4
Calcasieu L., *U.S.A.* . 55 L8
Calcutta = Kolkata, *India* 29 H16
Caldas da Rainha,
  Portugal 15 C1
Calder →, *U.K.* 8 D6
Caldera, *Chile* 64 B2
Caldwell, *Idaho, U.S.A.* 56 E5
Caldwell, *Kans., U.S.A.* 55 G6
Caldwell, *Tex., U.S.A.* . 55 K6
Caledon →, *S. Africa* . 37 L3
Caledon B., *Australia* . 42 A2
Calen, *Australia* 42 C4
Calexico, *U.S.A.* 57 K6
Calf of Man, *U.K.* 8 C3
Calgary, *Canada* 50 C6
Calhoun, *U.S.A.* 53 H3
Cali, *Colombia* 62 C3
Calicut, *India* 28 P9
Caliente, *U.S.A.* 57 H6
California, *U.S.A.* 54 F8
California, Baja, *Mexico* 58 A1
California, Baja, T.N. =
  Baja California □,
  Mexico 58 B2
California, Baja, T.S. =
  Baja California Sur □,
  Mexico 58 B2
California, G. de, *Mexico* 58 B2
Calingasta, *Argentina* . 64 C3
Calipatria, *U.S.A.* 57 K6
Calistoga, *U.S.A.* 56 G2
Callabonna, L., *Australia* 43 D3
Callao, *Peru* 62 F3
Calles, *Mexico* 59 C5
Calling Lake, *Canada* . 50 B6
Calliope, *Australia* ... 42 C5
Calne, *U.K.* 9 F6
Caloundra, *Australia* . 43 D5
Calstock, *Canada* 48 C3
Caltagirone, *Italy* 16 F6
Caltanissetta, *Italy* ... 16 F6
Calulo, *Angola* 36 G2
Calvert →, *Australia* . 42 B2
Calvert I., *Canada* ... 50 C3
Calvert Ra., *Australia* . 40 D3
Calvi, *France* 14 E8
Calviá, *Spain* 15 C7
Calvillo, *Mexico* 58 C4
Calvinia, *S. Africa* ... 37 L3
Cam →, *U.K.* 9 E8
Cam Ranh, *Vietnam* . 26 B3
Camabatela, *Angola* . 36 F3
Camacha, *Mexico* ... 58 C4
Camacupa, *Angola* ... 37 G3
Camagüey, *Cuba* 60 B4
Camaná, *Peru* 62 G4
Camargo, *Mexico* ... 59 B5
Camargue, *France* ... 14 E6
Camarón, C., *Honduras* 60 C2
Camarones, *Argentina* . 64 E3
Camas, *U.S.A.* 56 D2
Camas Valley, *U.S.A.* . 56 E2
Camballin, *Australia* . 40 C3
Cambay = Khambhat,
  India 28 H8
Cambay, G. of =
  Khambhat, G. of, *India* 28 J8
Cambodia ■, *Asia* ... 26 B3
Camborne, *U.K.* 9 G2
Cambrai, *France* 14 A5
Cambria, *U.S.A.* 57 J3
Cambrian Mts., *U.K.* . 9 E4
Cambridge, *Canada* . 48 D3
Cambridge, *Jamaica* . 60 C4
Cambridge, *N.Z.* 39 G5
Cambridge, *U.K.* 9 E8
Cambridge, *Mass.,*
  U.S.A. 52 D10
Cambridge, *Minn.,*
  U.S.A. 54 C8
Cambridge, *Nebr.,*
  U.S.A. 54 E4
Cambridge, *Ohio, U.S.A.* 52 E5
Cambridge Bay =
  Ikaluktutiak, *Canada* . 46 B9
Cambridge G., *Australia* 40 B4
Cambridgeshire □, *U.K.* 9 E7
Cambundi-Catembo,
  Angola 36 G3
Camden, *Ala., U.S.A.* . 53 K2
Camden, *Ark., U.S.A.* . 55 J8
Camden, *Maine, U.S.A.* 53 C11
Camden, *N.J., U.S.A.* . 52 F8
Camden, *S.C., U.S.A.* . 53 H5
Camden Sd., *Australia* . 40 C3
Camdenton, *U.S.A.* ... 54 F8
Cameron, *Ariz., U.S.A.* 57 J8
Cameron, *La., U.S.A.* . 55 L8
Cameron, *Mo., U.S.A.* . 54 F7
Cameron, *Tex., U.S.A.* . 55 K6
Cameron Hills, *Canada* 50 B5
Cameroon ■, *Africa* . 36 C2
Cameroun, Mt.,
  Cameroon 36 D1

Cametá, *Brazil* 63 D9
Camiguin I., *Phil.* 27 C6
Camilla, *U.S.A.* 53 K4
Caminha, *Portugal* ... 15 B1
Camino, *U.S.A.* 56 G3
Camira Creek, *Australia* 43 D5
Camocim, *Brazil* 63 D10
Camooweal, *Australia* . 42 B2
Camopi, *Fr. Guiana* .. 63 C8
Camp Hill, *U.S.A.* ... 52 E7
Camp Verde, *U.S.A.* . 57 J8
Camp Wood, *U.S.A.* . 55 L5
Campana, I., *Chile* ... 64 F1
Campana, *U.S.A.* 53 D6
Campánia □, *Italy* ... 16 D6
Campbell, I., *Pac. Oc.* . 5 N8
Campbell L., *Canada* . 51 A7
Campbell River, *Canada* 50 C3
Campbell Town,
  Australia 42 G4
Campbellsville, *U.S.A.* . 52 G3
Campbellton, *Canada* . 49 C6
Campbelltown, *Australia* 43 E5
Campbeltown, *U.K.* .. 10 D4
Campeche, *Mexico* .. 59 D6
Campeche □, *Mexico* . 59 D6
Campeche, Golfo de,
  Mexico 59 D6
Camperdown, *Australia* 43 F3
Camperville, *Canada* . 51 C8
Câmpina, *Romania* .. 13 F13
Campina Grande, *Brazil* 63 E11
Campinas, *Brazil* 63 H9
Campo Grande, *Brazil* . 63 H8
Campo Maior, *Brazil* . 63 D10
Campobasso, *Italy* ... 16 D6
Campos, *Brazil* 63 H10
Campos Belos, *Brazil* . 63 F9
Câmpulung, *Romania* . 13 F13
Camrose, *Canada* 50 C6
Camsell Portage,
  Canada 51 B7
Çan, *Turkey* 17 D12
Can Tho, *Vietnam* ... 26 B3
Canada ■, *N. Amer.* . 46 C10
Cañada de Gómez,
  Argentina 64 C4
Canadian, *U.S.A.* 55 H4
Canadian →, *U.S.A.* . 55 H7
Çanakkale, *Turkey* .. 17 D12
Çanakkale Boğazı,
  Turkey 17 D12
Canal Flats, *Canada* . 50 C5
Canandaigua, *U.S.A.* . 52 D7
Cananea, *Mexico* 58 A2
Canarias, Is., *Atl. Oc.* . 34 C2
Canarreos, Arch. de los,
  Cuba 60 B3
Canary Is. = Canarias,
  Is., *Atl. Oc.* 34 C2
Canatlán, *Mexico* 58 C4
Canaveral, C., *U.S.A.* . 53 L5
Canavieiras, *Brazil* ... 63 G11
Canberra, *Australia* .. 43 F4
Canby, *Calif., U.S.A.* . 56 F3
Canby, *Minn., U.S.A.* . 54 C6
Canby, *Oreg., U.S.A.* . 56 D2
Cancún, *Mexico* 59 C7
Candelo, *Australia* ... 43 F4
Candia = Iráklion,
  Greece 17 G11
Candle L., *Canada* ... 51 C7
Candlemas I., *Antarctica* 5 B1
Cando, *U.S.A.* 54 A5
Canea = Khaniá, *Greece* 17 G11
Canelones, *Uruguay* .. 64 C5
Cañete, *Chile* 64 D2
Cañete, *Peru* 62 F3
Cangas de Narcea,
  Spain 15 A2
Canguaretama, *Brazil* . 63 E11
Canguçu, *Brazil* 64 C6
Caniapiscau →,
  Canada 49 A6
Caniapiscau Rés. de,
  Canada 49 B6
Canicattì, *Italy* 16 F5
Canim Lake, *Canada* . 50 C4
Cañitas, *Mexico* 58 C4
Çankırı, *Turkey* 19 F5
Canmore, *Canada* ... 50 C5
Cann River, *Australia* . 43 F4
Cannanore, *India* 28 P9
Cannes, *France* 14 E7
Cannock, *U.K.* 9 E5
Cannon Ball →, *U.S.A.* 54 B4
Cannondale Mt.,
  Australia 42 D4
Cannonvale, *Australia* . 42 C4
Canoas, *Brazil* 64 B6
Canoe L., *Canada* ... 51 B7
Canon City, *U.S.A.* .. 54 F2
Canora, *Canada* 51 C8
Canowindra, *Australia* . 43 E4
Canso, *Canada* 49 C7
Cantabria □, *Spain* .. 15 A4
Cantabrian Mts. =
  Cantábrica, Cordillera,
  Spain 15 A3
Cantábrica, Cordillera,
  Spain 15 A3
Cantal, Plomb du,
  France 14 D5
Canterbury, *Australia* . 42 D3
Canterbury, *U.K.* 9 F9
Canterbury Bight, *N.Z.* 39 L3

Canterbury Plains, *N.Z.* 39 K3
Canton = Guangzhou,
  China 25 D6
Canton, *Ga., U.S.A.* .. 53 H3
Canton, *Ill., U.S.A.* ... 54 E9
Canton, *Miss., U.S.A.* . 55 J9
Canton, *Mo., U.S.A.* .. 54 E9
Canton, *N.Y., U.S.A.* . 52 C8
Canton, *Ohio, U.S.A.* . 52 E5
Canton, *S. Dak., U.S.A.* 54 D6
Canton L., *U.S.A.* 55 G5
Canudos, *Brazil* 62 E7
Canumã →, *Brazil* .. 62 D7
Canutama, *Brazil* 62 E6
Canutillo, *U.S.A.* 57 L10
Canvey, *U.K.* 9 F8
Canyon, *U.S.A.* 55 H4
Canyonlands National
  Park, *U.S.A.* 57 G9
Canyonville, *U.S.A.* .. 56 E2
Cap-aux-Meules,
  Canada 49 C7
Cap-Chat, *Canada* ... 49 C6
Cap-de-la-Madeleine,
  Canada 48 C5
Cap-Haïtien, *Haiti* ... 61 C5
Capanaparo →,
  Venezuela 62 B5
Cape →, *Australia* .. 42 C4
Cape Barren I., *Australia* 42 G4
Cape Breton Highlands
  Nat. Park, *Canada* . 49 C7
Cape Breton I., *Canada* 49 C7
Cape Charles, *U.S.A.* . 52 G8
Cape Coast, *Ghana* .. 34 G5
Cape Coral, *U.S.A.* .. 53 M5
Cape Dorset, *Canada* . 47 B12
Cape Fear →, *U.S.A.* 53 H6
Cape Girardeau, *U.S.A.* 55 G10
Cape May, *U.S.A.* ... 52 F8
Cape May Point, *U.S.A.* 52 F8
Cape Province, *S. Africa* 37 L3
Cape Tormentine,
  Canada 49 C7
Cape Town, *S. Africa* . 37 L3
Cape Verde Is. ■,
  Atl. Oc. 2 D8
Cape York Peninsula,
  Australia 42 A3
Capela, *Brazil* 63 F11
Capella, *Australia* 42 C4
Capim →, *Brazil* 63 D9
Capitan, *U.S.A.* 57 K11
Capitol Reef National
  Park, *U.S.A.* 57 G8
Capraia, *Italy* 14 E8
Capreol, *Canada* 48 C3
Capri, *Italy* 16 D6
Capricorn Group,
  Australia 42 C5
Capricorn Ra., *Australia* 40 D2
Caprivi Strip, *Namibia* . 37 H4
Captain's Flat, *Australia* 43 F4
Caquetá →, *Colombia* 62 D5
Caracal, *Romania* 13 F13
Caracas, *Venezuela* .. 62 A5
Caracol, *Brazil* 63 E10
Carajas, *Brazil* 63 E8
Carajás, Serra dos,
  Brazil 63 E8
Caransebeş, *Romania* . 13 F12
Caraquet, *Canada* ... 49 C6
Caras, *Peru* 62 E3
Caratasca, L., *Honduras* 60 C3
Caratinga, *Brazil* 63 G10
Caraúbas, *Brazil* 63 E11
Caravaca = Caravaca de
  la Cruz, *Spain* 15 C5
Caravaca de la Cruz,
  Spain 15 C5
Caravelas, *Brazil* 63 G11
Caraveli, *Peru* 62 G4
Carballo, *Spain* 15 A1
Carberry, *Canada* 51 D9
Carbó, *Mexico* 58 B2
Carbonara, C., *Italy* .. 16 E3
Carbondale, *Colo.,*
  U.S.A. 56 G10
Carbondale, *Ill., U.S.A.* 55 G10
Carbondale, *Pa., U.S.A.* 52 E8
Carbonear, *Canada* .. 49 C9
Carbónia, *Italy* 16 E3
Carcajou, *Canada* ... 50 B5
Carcasse, C., *Haiti* ... 61 C5
Carcassonne, *France* . 14 E5
Carcross, *Canada* 50 A2
Cardamon Hills, *India* . 28 Q10
Cárdenas, *Cuba* 60 B3
Cárdenas,
  San Luis Potosí,
  Mexico 59 C5
Cárdenas, *Tabasco,*
  Mexico 59 D6
Cardiff, *U.K.* 9 F4
Cardiff □, *U.K.* 9 F4
Cardigan, *U.K.* 9 E3
Cardigan B., *U.K.* ... 9 E3
Cardston, *Canada* ... 50 D6
Cardwell, *Australia* ... 42 B4
Careen L., *Canada* ... 51 B7
Carei, *Romania* 13 E12
Careme = Ciremai,
  Indonesia 27 G13
Carey, *U.S.A.* 56 E7
Carey, L., *Australia* .. 41 E3

Carey L., *Canada* 51 A8
Carhué, *Argentina* ... 64 D4
Caria, *Turkey* 17 F13
Cariacica, *Brazil* 63 H10
Caribbean Sea,
  W. Indies 61 D5
Cariboo Mts., *Canada* . 50 C4
Caribou, *U.S.A.* 53 B12
Caribou →, *Man.,*
  Canada 51 B10
Caribou →, *N.W.T.,*
  Canada 50 A3
Caribou Is., *Canada* .. 50 A6
Caribou L., *Man.,*
  Canada 51 B9
Caribou L., *Ont., Canada* 48 B2
Caribou Mts., *Canada* . 50 B5
Carichic, *Mexico* 58 B3
Carillo, *Mexico* 58 B4
Carinda, *Australia* ... 43 E4
Carinhanha, *Brazil* ... 63 F10
Carinhanha →, *Brazil* 63 F10
Carinthia = Kärnten □,
  Austria 12 E8
Caripito, *Venezuela* .. 62 A6
Carleton, Mt., *Canada* . 49 C6
Carleton Place, *Canada* 48 C4
Carlin, *U.S.A.* 56 F5
Carlinville, *U.S.A.* ... 54 F10
Carlisle, *U.K.* 8 C5
Carlisle, *U.S.A.* 52 E7
Carlow, *Ireland* 10 E3
Carlsbad, *Calif., U.S.A.* 57 K5
Carlsbad, *N. Mex.,*
  U.S.A. 55 J2
Carlsbad Caverns
  National Park, *U.S.A.* 55 J2
Carlyle, *Canada* 51 D8
Carmacks, *Canada* .. 46 B6
Carman, *Canada* 51 D9
Carmarthen, *U.K.* ... 9 F3
Carmarthen B., *U.K.* . 9 F3
Carmarthenshire □, *U.K.* 9 F3
Carmaux, *France* 14 D5
Carmen, *Colombia* ... 62 B3
Carmen →, *Mexico* . 58 A3
Carmen, I., *Mexico* .. 58 B2
Carmen de Patagones,
  Argentina 64 E4
Carmi, *Canada* 50 D5
Carmi, *U.S.A.* 52 F1
Carmila, *Australia* ... 42 C4
Carmona, *Costa Rica* . 60 E2
Carmona, *Spain* 15 D3
Carnac, *France* 14 C2
Carnamah, *Australia* . 41 E2
Carnarvon, *Australia* . 41 D1
Carnarvon, *S. Africa* . 37 L4
Carnarvon Ra., *Queens.,*
  Australia 42 D4
Carnarvon Ra.,
  W. Austral., Australia 41 E3
Carndonagh, *Ireland* . 10 D3
Carnduff, *Canada* 51 D8
Carnegie, L., *Australia* . 41 E3
Carnic Alps = Karnische
  Alpen, *Europe* 12 E7
Carniche Alpi =
  Karnische Alpen,
  Europe 12 E7
Carnot, *C.A.R.* 36 D3
Carnot, C., *Australia* . 43 E2
Carnot B., *Australia* .. 40 C3
Caro, *U.S.A.* 52 D4
Carol City, *U.S.A.* ... 53 N5
Carolina, *Brazil* 63 E9
Carolina, *Puerto Rico* . 61 C6
Caroline I., *Kiribati* .. 45 H12
Caroline Is., *Micronesia* 44 G7
Caroni →, *Venezuela* . 62 B6
Caronie = Nébrodi,
  Monti, *Italy* 16 F6
Caroona, *Australia* ... 43 E5
Carpathians, *Europe* . 13 D11
Carpaţii Meridionali,
  Romania 13 F13
Carpentaria, G. of,
  Australia 42 A2
Carpentras, *France* ... 14 D6
Carpi, *Italy* 16 B4
Carpinteria, *U.S.A.* .. 57 J4
Carr Boyd Ra., *Australia* 40 C4
Carrabelle, *U.S.A.* ... 53 L3
Carranza, Presa V.,
  Mexico 58 B4
Carrara, *Italy* 14 D9
Carrauntoohill, *Ireland* . 10 E2
Carrick-on-Suir, *Ireland* 10 E3
Carrieton, *Australia* .. 43 E2
Carrington, *U.S.A.* ... 54 B5
Carrizal Bajo, *Chile* .. 64 B2
Carrizo →, *U.S.A.* .. 58 B4
Carrizo Springs, *U.S.A.* 55 L5
Carrizozo, *U.S.A.* 57 K11
Carroll, *U.S.A.* 54 D7
Carrollton, *Ga., U.S.A.* 53 J3
Carrollton, *Ill., U.S.A.* . 54 F9
Carrollton, *Ky., U.S.A.* 52 F3
Carrollton, *Mo., U.S.A.* 54 F8
Carrot →, *Canada* ... 51 C8
Carrot River, *Canada* . 51 C8
Carruthers, *Canada* .. 51 C7
Carson, *U.S.A.* 54 B4
Carson City, *U.S.A.* .. 56 G4
Carson Sink, *U.S.A.* .. 56 G4

Cartagena, *Colombia* . 62 A3
Cartagena, *Spain* 15 D5
Cartago, *Colombia* ... 62 C3
Cartago, *Costa Rica* .. 60 E3
Cartersville, *U.S.A.* .. 53 H3
Carterton, *N.Z.* 39 J5
Carthage, *Tunisia* 35 A8
Carthage, *Ill., U.S.A.* . 54 E9
Carthage, *Mo., U.S.A.* 55 G7
Carthage, *N.Y., U.S.A.* 52 D8
Carthage, *Tex., U.S.A.* 55 J7
Cartier I., *Australia* ... 40 B3
Cartwright, *Canada* .. 49 B8
Caruaru, *Brazil* 63 E11
Carúpano, *Venezuela* . 62 A6
Caruthersville, *U.S.A.* . 55 G10
Carvoeiro, *Brazil* 62 D6
Carvoeiro, C., *Portugal* 15 C1
Cary, *U.S.A.* 53 H6
Casa Grande, *U.S.A.* . 57 K8
Casablanca, *Morocco* . 34 B4
Casas Grandes, *Mexico* 58 A3
Cascade, *Idaho, U.S.A.* 56 D5
Cascade, *Mont., U.S.A.* 56 C8
Cascade Locks, *U.S.A.* 56 D3
Cascade Ra., *U.S.A.* . 56 C3
Cascade Reservoir,
  U.S.A. 56 D5
Cascais, *Portugal* 15 C1
Cascavel, *Brazil* 63 H8
Cáscina, *Italy* 16 C4
Casco B., *U.S.A.* 53 D10
Caserta, *Italy* 16 D6
Casiguran, *Phil.* 27 A6
Casilda, *Argentina* ... 64 C4
Casino, *Australia* 43 D5
Casiquiare →,
  Venezuela 62 C5
Casma, *Peru* 62 E3
Caspe, *Spain* 15 B5
Caspian Depression,
  Eurasia 19 E8
Caspian Sea, *Eurasia* . 19 F9
Cass Lake, *U.S.A.* ... 54 B7
Casselton, *U.S.A.* 54 B6
Cassiar, *Canada* 50 B3
Cassiar Mts., *Canada* . 50 B2
Cassino, *Italy* 16 D5
Cassville, *U.S.A.* 55 G8
Castanhal, *Brazil* 63 D9
Castellammare di
  Stábia, *Italy* 16 D6
Castelli, *Argentina* ... 64 D5
Castelló de la Plana,
  Spain 15 C5
Castelo Branco, *Portugal* 15 C2
Castelsarrasin, *France* . 14 E4
Castelvetrano, *Italy* .. 16 F5
Casterton, *Australia* .. 43 F3
Castilla-La Mancha □,
  Spain 15 C4
Castilla y Leon □, *Spain* 15 B3
Castle Dale, *U.S.A.* .. 56 G8
Castle Rock, *U.S.A.* .. 54 F2
Castlebar, *Ireland* ... 10 E2
Castleblaney, *Ireland* . 10 D3
Castleford, *U.K.* 8 D6
Castlegar, *Canada* ... 50 D5
Castlemaine, *Australia* . 43 F3
Castlereagh →,
  Australia 43 E4
Castlereagh B., *Australia* 42 A2
Castletown, *U.K.* 8 C3
Castletown, *Canada* .. 50 C6
Castres, *France* 14 E5
Castricum, *Neths.* ... 11 B4
Castries, *St. Lucia* ... 61 D7
Castro, *Chile* 64 E2
Castro Alves, *Brazil* .. 63 F11
Castuera, *Spain* 15 C3
Cat I., *Bahamas* 61 B4
Cat L., *Canada* 48 B1
Cat Lake, *Canada* ... 48 B1
Catacamas, *Honduras* . 60 D2
Catalão, *Brazil* 63 G9
Çatalca, *Turkey* 17 D13
Catalina, *Canada* 49 C9
Catalina, *U.S.A.* 57 K8
Catalonia = Cataluña □,
  Spain 15 B6
Cataluña □, *Spain* ... 15 B6
Catamarca, *Argentina* . 64 B3
Catanduanes □, *Phil.* . 27 B6
Catanduva, *Brazil* 63 H9
Catánia, *Italy* 16 F6
Catanzaro, *Italy* 16 E7
Catarman, *Phil.* 27 B6
Cateel, *Phil.* 27 C7
Caterham, *U.K.* 9 F7
Cathcart, *S. Africa* ... 37 L5
Cathlamet, *U.S.A.* ... 56 C2
Catlettsburg, *U.S.A.* .. 52 F4
Catoche, C., *Mexico* .. 59 C7
Catriman, *Brazil* 62 C6
Catrimani →, *Brazil* .. 62 C6
Catskill, *U.S.A.* 52 D9
Catskill Mts., *U.S.A.* . 52 D8
Catt, Mt., *Australia* .. 42 A1
Cauca →, *Colombia* . 62 B4
Caucaia, *Brazil* 63 D11
Caucasus Mountains,
  Eurasia 19 F7
Caungula, *Angola* 36 F3
Cauquenes, *Chile* 64 D2
Caura →, *Venezuela* . 62 B6

Causapscal, *Canada* .. 49 C6
Cauvery →, *India* .. 28 P11
Caux, Pays de, *France* . 14 B4
Cavalier, *U.S.A.* 54 A6
Cavan, *Ireland* 10 D3
Cave Creek, *U.S.A.* .. 57 K7
Cavenagh Ra., *Australia* 41 E4
Cavendish, *Australia* . 43 F3
Caviana, I., *Brazil* 63 C8
Cavite, *Phil.* 27 B6
Cawndilla L., *Australia* . 43 E3
Cawnpore = Kanpur,
  India 28 F12
Caxias, *Brazil* 63 D10
Caxias do Sul, *Brazil* . 64 B6
Cay Sal Bank, *Bahamas* 60 B4
Cayambe, *Ecuador* ... 62 C3
Cayenne, *Fr. Guiana* . 63 B8
Cayman Brac,
  Cayman Is. 60 C4
Cayman Is. ■, *W. Indies* 60 C3
Cayo Romano, *Cuba* . 60 B4
Cayuga L., *U.S.A.* ... 52 D7
Cazombo, *Angola* 37 G4
Ceanannus Mor, *Ireland* 10 E3
Ceará = Fortaleza, *Brazil* 63 D11
Ceará □, *Brazil* 63 E11
Ceará Mirim, *Brazil* .. 63 E11
Cebaco, I. de, *Panama* . 60 E3
Cebollar, *Argentina* .. 64 B3
Cebu, *Phil.* 27 B6
Cecil Plains, *Australia* . 43 D5
Cedar →, *U.S.A.* 54 E9
Cedar City, *U.S.A.* ... 57 H7
Cedar Creek Reservoir,
  U.S.A. 55 J6
Cedar Falls, *U.S.A.* ... 54 D8
Cedar Key, *U.S.A.* ... 53 L4
Cedar L., *Canada* ... 51 C9
Cedar Rapids, *U.S.A.* . 54 E9
Cedartown, *U.S.A.* ... 53 H3
Cedarvale, *Canada* ... 50 B3
Cedral, *Mexico* 58 C4
Cedro, *Brazil* 63 E11
Cedros, I. de, *Mexico* . 58 B1
Ceduna, *Australia* 43 E1
Cefalù, *Italy* 16 E6
Cegléd, *Hungary* 13 E10
Celaya, *Mexico* 58 C4
Celebes = Sulawesi,
  Indonesia 27 E6
Celebes = Sulawesi □,
  Indonesia 27 E6
Celebes Sea, *Indonesia* 27 D6
Celina, *U.S.A.* 52 E3
Celje, *Slovenia* 12 E8
Celle, *Germany* 12 B6
Celtic Sea, *Atl. Oc.* .. 10 F2
Cenderwasih, Teluk,
  Indonesia 27 E9
Center, *N. Dak., U.S.A.* 54 B4
Center, *Tex., U.S.A.* .. 55 K7
Centerville, *Iowa, U.S.A.* 54 E8
Centerville, *Tenn.,*
  U.S.A. 53 H2
Centerville, *Tex., U.S.A.* 55 K7
Central, *Cordillera,*
  Colombia 62 C4
Central, *Cordillera,*
  Costa Rica 60 D3
Central, *Cordillera,*
  Dom. Rep. 61 C5
Central African Rep. ■,
  Africa 36 C4
Central Butte, *Canada* . 51 C7
Central City, *Colo.,*
  U.S.A. 56 G11
Central City, *Ky., U.S.A.* 52 G2
Central City, *Nebr.,*
  U.S.A. 54 E6
Central Makran Range,
  Pakistan 28 F4
Central Patricia, *Canada* 48 B1
Central Point, *U.S.A.* . 56 E2
Centralia, *Ill., U.S.A.* . 54 F10
Centralia, *Mo., U.S.A.* 54 F8
Centralia, *Wash., U.S.A.* 56 C2
Cephalonia = Kefallinía,
  Greece 17 E9
Cepu, *Indonesia* 27 G14
Ceram = Seram,
  Indonesia 27 E7
Ceram Sea = Seram
  Sea, *Indonesia* 27 E7
Ceredigion □, *U.K.* .. 9 E3
Ceres, *Argentina* 64 B4
Cerignola, *Italy* 16 D6
Cerigo = Kíthira, *Greece* 17 F10
Çerkezköy, *Turkey* .. 17 D12
Cerralvo, I., *Mexico* .. 58 C3
Cerritos, *Mexico* 58 C4
Cervantes, *Australia* .. 41 F2
Cervera, *Spain* 15 B6
Cesena, *Italy* 16 B5
Cēsis, *Latvia* 7 H21
Česke Budějovice,
  Czech Rep. 12 D8
Českomoravská
  Vrchovina, *Czech Rep.* 12 D8
Çeşme, *Turkey* 17 E12
Cessnock, *Australia* .. 43 E5
Cetinje,
  Montenegro, Yug. .. 17 C8
Cetraro, *Italy* 16 E6
Ceuta, *N. Afr.* 15 E3

Cévennes, France 14 D5
Ceyhan, Turkey 30 B2
Ceylon = Sri Lanka ■, Asia 28 R12
Chachapoyas, Peru . . 62 E3
Chachran, Pakistan . . 28 E7
Chaco →, U.S.A. 57 H9
Chaco Austral, S. Amer. 64 B4
Chaco Boreal, S. Amer. 62 H6
Chaco Central, S. Amer. 64 A4
Chacon, C., U.S.A. . . . 50 C2
Chad ■, Africa 35 E9
Chad, L. = Tchad, L., Chad 35 F8
Chadan, Russia 21 D10
Chadileuvú →, Argentina 64 D3
Chadron, U.S.A. 54 D3
Chadyr-Lunga = Ciadâr-Lunga, Moldova . . . 13 E15
Chagai Hills = Chāh Gay, Afghan. 28 E3
Chagda, Russia 21 D14
Chagos Arch., Ind. Oc. . 3 E13
Chagos Arch., Ind. Oc. . 3 E13
Chāh Ākhvor, Iran . . . 31 C8
Chāh Bahar, Iran 31 E9
Chāh-e Kavīr, Iran . . . 31 C8
Chāh Gay, Afghan. . . . 28 E3
Chahar Burjak, Afghan. 28 D3
Chahār Mahāll va Bakhtīarī □, Iran . . 31 C6
Chaibasa, India 29 H14
Chakhānsūr, Afghan. . . 28 D3
Chakonipau, L., Canada 49 A6
Chakradharpur, India . 29 H14
Chakwal, Pakistan . . . 28 C8
Chala, Peru 62 G4
Chalchihuites, Mexico . 58 C4
Chalcis = Khalkís, Greece 17 E10
Chaleur B., Canada . . . 49 C6
Chalhuanca, Peru . . . 62 F4
Chalisgaon, India . . . 28 J9
Chalk River, Canada . . 48 C4
Chalky Inlet, N.Z. 39 M1
Challapata, Bolivia . . . 62 G5
Challis, U.S.A. 56 D6
Chalmette, U.S.A. . . . 55 L10
Chalon-sur-Saône, France 14 C6
Châlons-en-Champagne, France 14 B6
Chalyaphum, Thailand 26 A2
Chama, U.S.A. 57 H10
Chaman, Pakistan . . . 28 D5
Chamba, India 28 C10
Chambal →, India . . . 28 F11
Chamberlain, U.S.A. . . 54 D5
Chamberlain →, Australia 40 C4
Chamberlain L., U.S.A. 53 B11
Chambers, U.S.A. . . . 57 J9
Chambersburg, U.S.A. 52 F7
Chambéry, France . . . 14 D6
Chambeshi →, Zambia 36 G6
Chambord, Canada . . 49 C5
Chamchamal, Iraq . . . 30 C5
Chamela, Mexico . . . 58 D3
Chamical, Argentina . 64 C3
Chamonix-Mont Blanc, France 14 D7
Chamouchouane →, Canada 48 C5
Champagne, Canada . 50 A1
Champagne, France . . 14 B6
Champaign, U.S.A. . . 52 E1
Champdoré, L., Canada 49 A6
Champlain, U.S.A. . . . 52 C9
Champlain, L., U.S.A. . 52 C9
Champotón, Mexico . . 59 D6
Chañaral, Chile 64 B2
Chanārān, Iran 31 B8
Chandeleur Is., U.S.A. 55 L10
Chandeleur Sd., U.S.A. 55 L10
Chandigarh, India . . . 28 D10
Chandler, Australia . . 43 D1
Chandler, Canada . . . 49 C7
Chandler, Ariz., U.S.A. 57 K8
Chandler, Okla., U.S.A. 55 H6
Chandpur, Bangla. . . . 29 H17
Chandrapur, India . . . 28 K11
Chānf, Iran 31 E9
Chang, Ko, Thailand . . 26 B2
Ch'ang Chiang = Chang Jiang →, China . . . 25 C7
Chang Jiang →, China . 25 C7
Changanacheri, India . 28 Q10
Changane →, Mozam. 37 J6
Changchiak'ou = Zhangjiakou, China . 25 B6
Ch'angchou = Changzhou, China . . 25 C6
Changchun, China . . . 25 B7
Changde, China 25 D6
Changhai = Shanghai, China 25 C7
Changhua, Taiwan . . . 25 D7
Changsha, China 25 D6
Changzhi, China 25 C6
Changzhou, China . . . 25 C6
Channapatna, India . . 28 N10
Channel Is., U.K. 9 H5
Channel Is., U.S.A. . . . 57 K4

Channel Islands National Park, U.S.A. 57 J3
Channel-Port aux Basques, Canada . . 49 C8
Channel Tunnel, Europe 9 F9
Channing, U.S.A. 55 H3
Chantada, Spain 15 A2
Chanthaburi, Thailand 26 B2
Chantrey Inlet, Canada 46 B10
Chanute, U.S.A. 55 G7
Chao Phraya →, Thailand 26 B2
Chaozhou, China . . . 25 D6
Chapais, Canada . . . 48 C5
Chapala, L. de, Mexico 58 C4
Chapayev, Kazakstan . 19 D9
Chapayevsk, Russia . . 18 D8
Chapecó, Brazil 64 B6
Chapel Hill, U.S.A. . . . 53 H6
Chapleau, Canada . . . 48 C3
Chaplin, Canada 51 C7
Chaplin L., Canada . . . 51 C7
Chappell, U.S.A. 54 E3
Chapra = Chhapra, India 29 G14
Chara, Russia 21 D12
Charagua, Bolivia . . . 62 G6
Charambirá, Punta, Colombia 62 C3
Charaña, Bolivia 62 G5
Charcas, Mexico 58 C4
Chard, U.K. 9 G5
Chardzhou = Chärjew, Turkmenistan 20 F7
Charente →, France . . 14 D3
Chari →, Chad 35 F8
Chārīkār, Afghan. . . . 28 B6
Chariton →, U.S.A. . . 54 F8
Chärjew, Turkmenistan 20 F7
Charleroi, Belgium . . . 11 D4
Charles, C., U.S.A. . . . 52 G8
Charles City, U.S.A. . . 54 D8
Charles L., Canada . . . 51 B6
Charles Town, U.S.A. . 52 F7
Charleston, Ill., U.S.A. . 52 F1
Charleston, Miss., U.S.A. 55 H9
Charleston, Mo., U.S.A. 55 G10
Charleston, S.C., U.S.A. 53 J6
Charleston, W. Va., U.S.A. 52 F5
Charlestown, U.S.A. . . 52 F3
Charleville, Australia . . 43 D4
Charleville-Mézières, France 14 B6
Charlevoix, U.S.A. . . . 52 C3
Charlotte, Mich., U.S.A. 52 D3
Charlotte, N.C., U.S.A. . 53 H5
Charlotte Amalie, Virgin Is. 61 C7
Charlotte Harbor, U.S.A. 53 M4
Charlotte L., Canada . . 50 C3
Charlottesville, U.S.A. . 52 F6
Charlottetown, Nfld., Canada 49 B8
Charlottetown, P.E.I., Canada 49 C7
Charlton, Australia . . . 43 F3
Charlton, U.S.A. 54 E8
Charlton I., Canada . . 48 B4
Charny, Canada 49 C5
Charolles, France . . . 14 C6
Charters Towers, Australia 42 C4
Chartres, France 14 B4
Chascomús, Argentina 64 D5
Chāt, Iran 31 B7
Châteaubriant, France . 14 C3
Châteauguay, L., Canada 49 A5
Châteaulin, France . . . 14 B1
Châteauroux, France . . 14 C4
Châtellerault, France . . 14 C4
Chatham = Miramichi, Canada 49 C6
Chatham, Canada . . . 48 D3
Chatham, U.K. 9 F8
Chatham Is., Pac. Oc. . 44 M10
Chatrapur, India 29 K14
Chattahoochee, U.S.A. 53 K3
Chattahoochee →, U.S.A. 53 K3
Chattanooga, U.S.A. . . 53 H3
Chatteris, U.K. 9 E8
Chaukan Pass, Burma . 29 F20
Chaumont, France . . . 14 B6
Chauvin, Canada 51 C6
Chaves, Brazil 63 D9
Chaves, Portugal 15 B2
Chaykovskiy, Russia . . 18 C9
Cheb, Czech Rep. . . . 12 C7
Cheboksary, Russia . . 18 C8
Cheboygan, U.S.A. . . . 52 C3
Chech, Erg, Africa . . . 34 D5
Chechenia □, Russia . 19 F8
Checheno-Ingush Republic = Chechenia □, Russia 19 F8
Chechnya = Chechenia □, Russia 19 F8
Checotah, U.S.A. 55 H7
Chedabucto B., Canada 49 C7
Cheduba I., Burma . . . 29 K18
Cheepie, Australia . . . 43 D4
Chegdomyn, Russia . . 21 D14

Chegga, Mauritania . . . 34 C4
Chegutu, Zimbabwe . . 37 H6
Chehalis, U.S.A. 56 C2
Cheju do, S. Korea . . . 25 C7
Chekiang = Zhejiang □, China 25 D7
Chelan, U.S.A. 56 C4
Chelan, L., U.S.A. . . . 56 B3
Cheleken, Turkmenistan 19 G9
Cheleken Yarymadasy, Turkmenistan 31 B7
Chelforó, Argentina . . 64 D3
Chelkar = Shalqar, Kazakstan 20 E6
Chelkar Tengiz, Solonchak, Kazakstan 20 E7
Chełm, Poland 13 C12
Chełmno, Poland . . . 13 B10
Chelmsford, U.K. 9 F8
Cheltenham, U.K. . . . 9 F5
Chelyabinsk, Russia . . 20 D7
Chemba, Mozam. . . . 37 H6
Chemnitz, Germany . . 12 C7
Chemult, U.S.A. 56 E3
Chen, Gora, Russia . . 21 C15
Chenab →, Pakistan . 28 D7
Chengchou = Zhengzhou, China . . 25 C6
Chengde, China 25 B6
Chengdu, China 24 C5
Chengjiang, China . . . 24 D5
Ch'engtu = Chengdu, China 24 C5
Chenkán, Mexico . . . 59 D6
Chennai, India 28 N12
Cheo Reo, Vietnam . . 26 B3
Cheom Ksan, Cambodia 26 B2
Chepén, Peru 62 E3
Chepes, Argentina . . . 64 C3
Chepo, Panama 60 E4
Chepstow, U.K. 9 F5
Chequamegon B., U.S.A. 54 B9
Cher →, France 14 C4
Cheraw, U.S.A. 53 H6
Cherbourg, France . . . 14 B3
Cherdyn, Russia 18 B10
Cheremkhovo, Russia . 21 D11
Cherepanovo, Russia . 20 D9
Cherepovets, Russia . 18 C6
Chergui, Chott ech, Algeria 34 B6
Cherikov = Cherykaw, Belarus 13 B16
Cherkasy, Ukraine . . . 19 E5
Cherkessk, Russia . . . 19 F7
Cherlak, Russia 20 D8
Chernaya, Russia . . . 21 B9
Chernigov = Chernihiv, Ukraine 18 D5
Chernihiv, Ukraine . . . 18 D5
Chernivtsi, Ukraine . . 13 D13
Chernobyl = Chornobyl, Ukraine 13 C16
Chernogorsk, Russia . 21 D10
Chernovtsy = Chernivtsi, Ukraine . 13 D13
Chernyakhovsk, Russia 7 J19
Chernysheyskiy, Russia 21 C12
Cherokee, Iowa, U.S.A. 54 D7
Cherokee, Okla., U.S.A. 55 G5
Cherokee Village, U.S.A. 55 G9
Cherokees, Grand Lake O' The, U.S.A. 55 G7
Cherrapunji, India . . . 29 G17
Cherskiy, Russia 21 C17
Cherskogo Khrebet, Russia 21 C15
Cherven, Belarus 13 B15
Chervonohrad, Ukraine 13 C13
Cherwell →, U.K. . . . 9 F6
Cherykaw, Belarus . . . 13 B16
Chesapeake, U.S.A. . . 52 G7
Chesapeake B., U.S.A. 52 G7
Cheshire □, U.K. 8 D5
Cheshskaya Guba, Russia 18 A8
Cheshunt, U.K. 9 F7
Chesil Beach, U.K. . . . 9 G5
Chester, U.K. 8 D5
Chester, Calif., U.S.A. . 56 F3
Chester, Ill., U.S.A. . . 55 G10
Chester, Mont., U.S.A. . 56 B8
Chester, Pa., U.S.A. . . 52 F8
Chester, S.C., U.S.A. . 53 H5
Chester-le-Street, U.K. . 8 C6
Chesterfield, U.K. . . . 8 D6
Chesterfield, Is., N. Cal. 38 C8
Chesterfield Inlet, Canada 46 B10
Chesterton Ra., Australia 43 D4
Chesuncook L., U.S.A. 53 C11
Chéticamp, Canada . . 49 C7
Chetumal, Mexico . . . 59 D7
Chetumal, B. de, Mexico 59 D7
Chetwynd, Canada . . . 50 B4
Cheviot, The, U.K. . . . 8 B5
Cheviot Hills, U.K. . . . 8 B5
Cheviot Ra., Australia . 42 D3
Chew Bahir, Ethiopia . 32 G2
Chewelah, U.S.A. . . . 56 B5
Cheyenne, Okla., U.S.A. 55 H5
Cheyenne, Wyo., U.S.A. 54 E2

Cheyenne →, U.S.A. . . 54 C4
Cheyenne Wells, U.S.A. 54 F3
Cheyne B., Australia . . 41 F2
Chhapra, India 29 G14
Chhatarpur, India . . . 28 G11
Chhindwara, India . . . 28 H11
Chi →, Thailand 26 A3
Chiai, Taiwan 25 D7
Chiamboni, Somali Rep. 36 E8
Chiamussu = Jiamusi, China 25 B8
Chiapa →, Mexico . . . 59 D6
Chiapa de Corzo, Mexico 59 D6
Chiapas □, Mexico . . . 59 D6
Chiautla, Mexico 59 D5
Chiávari, Italy 14 D8
Chiavenna, Italy 14 C8
Chiba, Japan 23 G10
Chiba □, Japan 23 G10
Chibemba, Angola . . . 37 H2
Chibia, Angola 37 H2
Chibougamau, Canada 48 C5
Chibougamau, L., Canada 48 C5
Chic-Chocs, Mts., Canada 49 C6
Chicacole = Srikakulam, India 29 K13
Chicago, U.S.A. 52 E2
Chicago Heights, U.S.A. 52 E2
Chichagof I., U.S.A. . . 46 C6
Chichén-Itzá, Mexico . 59 C7
Chichester, U.K. 9 G7
Chichester Ra., Australia 40 D2
Chichibu, Japan 23 F9
Ch'ich'iaerh = Qiqihar, China 21 E13
Chickasha, U.S.A. . . . 55 H6
Chiclana de la Frontera, Spain 15 D2
Chiclayo, Peru 62 E3
Chico, U.S.A. 56 G3
Chico →, Chubut, Argentina 64 E3
Chico →, Santa Cruz, Argentina 64 G3
Chicontepec, Mexico . 59 C5
Chicopee, U.S.A. 52 D9
Chicoutimi, Canada . . 49 C5
Chidambaram, India . . 28 P11
Chidley, C., Canada . . 47 B13
Chiemsee, Germany . . 12 E7
Chiese →, Italy 14 D9
Chieti, Italy 16 C6
Chignecto B., Canada . 49 C7
Chiguana, Bolivia . . . 62 H5
Chigwell, U.K. 9 F8
Chihli, G. of = Bo Hai, China 25 C6
Chihuahua, Mexico . . 58 B3
Chihuahua □, Mexico . 58 B3
Chiili, Kazakstan 20 E7
Chik Bollapur, India . . 28 N10
Chilac, Mexico 59 D5
Chilapa, Mexico 59 D5
Chilas, Pakistan 28 B9
Chilaw, Sri Lanka . . . 28 R11
Chilcotin →, Canada . 50 C4
Childers, Australia . . . 43 D5
Childress, U.S.A. 55 H4
Chile ■, S. Amer. 64 D2
Chile Rise, Pac. Oc. . . 45 L18
Chilete, Peru 62 E3
Chililabombwe, Zambia 37 G5
Chilin = Jilin, China . . 25 B7
Chilka L., India 29 K14
Chilko →, Canada . . . 50 C4
Chilko L., Canada . . . 50 C4
Chillagoe, Australia . . 42 B3
Chillán, Chile 64 D2
Chillicothe, Ill., U.S.A. . 54 E10
Chillicothe, Mo., U.S.A. 54 F8
Chillicothe, Ohio, U.S.A. 52 F4
Chilliwack, Canada . . 50 D4
Chiloé, I. de, Chile . . . 64 E2
Chilpancingo, Mexico . 59 D5
Chiltern Hills, U.K. . . . 9 F7
Chilton, U.S.A. 52 C1
Chilung, Taiwan 25 D7
Chilwa, L., Malawi . . . 37 H7
Chimaltitán, Mexico . . 58 C4
Chimán, Panama 60 E4
Chimay, Belgium 11 D4
Chimayo, U.S.A. 57 H11
Chimbay, Uzbekistan . 20 E6
Chimborazo, Ecuador . 62 D3
Chimbote, Peru 62 E3
Chimkent = Shymkent, Kazakstan 20 E7
Chimoio, Mozam. . . . 37 H6
Chin □, Burma 29 J18
China, Mexico 59 B5
China ■, Asia 24 C5
Chinan = Jinan, China 25 C6
Chinandega, Nic. . . . 60 D2
Chinati Peak, U.S.A. . . 55 L2
Chincha Alta, Peru . . 62 F3
Chinchaga →, Canada 50 B5
Chinchilla, Australia . . 43 D5
Chinchorro, Banco, Mexico 59 D7
Chinchou = Jinzhou, China 25 B7

Chincoteague, U.S.A. . 52 G8
Chinde, Mozam. 37 H7
Chindwin →, Burma . . 29 J19
Chingola, Zambia . . . 37 G5
Ch'ingtao = Qingdao, China 25 C7
Chinguetti, Mauritania . 34 D3
Chinhoyi, Zimbabwe . . 37 H6
Chiniot, Pakistan 28 D8
Chinípas, Mexico . . . 58 B3
Chinle, U.S.A. 57 H9
Chinnampo = Namp'o, N. Korea 25 C7
Chino, Japan 23 G9
Chino Valley, U.S.A. . . 57 J7
Chinon, France 14 C4
Chinook, U.S.A. 56 B9
Chióggia, Italy 16 B5
Chíos = Khíos, Greece 17 E12
Chipata, Zambia 37 G6
Chipley, U.S.A. 53 K3
Chipman, Canada . . . 49 C6
Chippenham, U.K. . . . 9 F5
Chippewa →, U.S.A. . . 54 C8
Chippewa Falls, U.S.A. 54 C9
Chipping Norton, U.K. . 9 F6
Chiputneticook Lakes, U.S.A. 53 C11
Chiquián, Peru 62 F3
Chiquimula, Guatemala 60 D2
Chiquinquira, Colombia 62 B4
Chirala, India 28 M12
Chirawa, India 28 E9
Chirchiq, Uzbekistan . 20 E7
Chiredzi, Zimbabwe . . 37 J6
Chirfa, Niger 35 D8
Chiricahua Peak, U.S.A. 57 L9
Chiriquí, G. de, Panama 60 E3
Chiriquí, L. de, Panama 60 E3
Chirmiri, India 29 H13
Chirripó Grande, Cerro, Costa Rica 60 E3
Chisapani Garhi, Nepal 29 F14
Chisasibi, Canada . . . 48 B4
Chisholm, Canada . . . 50 C6
Chisholm, U.S.A. 54 B8
Chișinău, Moldova . . . 13 E15
Chisos Mts., U.S.A. . . 55 L3
Chistopol, Russia . . . 18 C9
Chita, Russia 21 D12
Chitose, Japan 22 C10
Chitral, Pakistan 28 B7
Chitré, Panama 60 E3
Chittagong, Bangla. . . 29 H17
Chittagong □, Bangla. . 29 G17
Chittaurgarh, India . . . 28 G9
Chittoor, India 28 N11
Chitungwiza, Zimbabwe 37 H6
Chiusi, Italy 16 C4
Chivasso, Italy 14 D7
Chivilcoy, Argentina . . 64 C5
Chkalov = Orenburg, Russia 18 D10
Chocolate Mts., U.S.A. 57 K6
Choctawhatchee →, U.S.A. 53 K3
Choele Choel, Argentina 64 D3
Choiseul, Solomon Is. . 38 B8
Choix, Mexico 58 B3
Chojnice, Poland 13 B9
Chōkai-San, Japan . . . 22 E10
Choke Canyon L., U.S.A. 55 L5
Chokurdakh, Russia . . 21 B15
Cholet, France 14 C3
Choluteca, Honduras . 60 D2
Choluteca →, Honduras 60 D2
Choma, Zambia 37 H5
Chomutov, Czech Rep. . 12 C7
Chon Buri, Thailand . . 26 B2
Chone, Ecuador 62 D3
Chŏngjin, N. Korea . . 25 B7
Chongqing, China . . . 24 D5
Chongqing □, China . . 24 C5
Chŏnju, S. Korea 25 C7
Chonos, Arch. de los, Chile 64 F2
Chop, Ukraine 13 D12
Chorley, U.K. 8 D5
Chornobyl, Ukraine . . 13 C16
Chorregon, Australia . 42 C3
Chortkiv, Ukraine . . . 13 D13
Chorzów, Poland 13 C10
Chos-Malal, Argentina . 64 D2
Choszczno, Poland . . 12 B8
Choteau, U.S.A. 56 C7
Chotila, India 28 H7
Chowchilla, U.S.A. . . . 57 H3
Choybalsan, Mongolia . 25 B6
Christchurch, N.Z. . . . 39 K4
Christchurch, U.K. . . . 9 G6
Christiansted, Virgin Is. 61 C7
Christie B., Canada . . 51 A6
Christina →, Canada . 51 B6
Christmas Cr. →, Australia 40 C4
Christmas I. = Kiritimati, Kiribati 45 G12
Christmas I., Ind. Oc. . 44 J2
Christopher L., Australia 41 D4
Chu = Shu, Kazakstan 20 E8
Ch'uanchou = Quanzhou, China . . 25 D6
Chubbuck, U.S.A. . . . 56 E7
Chūbu □, Japan 23 F8
Chubut →, Argentina . 64 E3

Chuchi L., Canada . . . 50 B4
Chudskoye, Ozero, Russia 7 G22
Chūgoku □, Japan . . . 23 G6
Chūgoku-Sanchi, Japan 23 G6
Chugwater, U.S.A. . . . 54 E2
Chukchi Sea, Russia . 21 C19
Chukotskoye Nagorye, Russia 21 C18
Chula Vista, U.S.A. . . 57 K5
Chulucanas, Peru . . . 62 E2
Chulym →, Russia . . . 20 D9
Chumbicha, Argentina . 64 B3
Chumikan, Russia . . . 21 D14
Chumphon, Thailand . 26 B1
Chuna →, Russia . . . 21 D10
Ch'unch'ŏn, S. Korea . 25 C7
Chungking = Chongqing, China . . 24 D5
Chunya, Tanzania . . . 36 F6
Chuquibamba, Peru . . 62 G4
Chuquicamata, Chile . 62 H5
Chur, Switz. 14 C8
Churachandpur, India . 29 G18
Churchill, Canada . . . 51 B10
Churchill →, Man., Canada 51 B10
Churchill →, Nfld., Canada 49 B7
Churchill, C., Canada . 51 B10
Churchill Falls, Canada 49 B7
Churchill L., Canada . . 51 B7
Churchill Pk., Canada . 50 B3
Churu, India 28 E9
Chushal, India 28 C11
Chuska Mts., U.S.A. . . 57 H9
Chusovoy, Russia . . . 18 C10
Chute-aux-Outardes, Canada 49 C6
Chuvash Republic = Chuvashia □, Russia 18 C8
Chuvashia □, Russia . 18 C8
Chuwärtah, Iraq 30 C5
Ciadâr-Lunga, Moldova 13 E15
Ciamis, Indonesia . . . 27 G13
Cianjur, Indonesia . . . 27 G12
Cianorte, Brazil 64 A6
Cicero, U.S.A. 52 E2
Ciechanów, Poland . . 13 B11
Ciego de Avila, Cuba . 60 B4
Ciénaga, Colombia . . 62 A4
Cienfuegos, Cuba . . . 60 B3
Cieszyn, Poland 13 D10
Cieza, Spain 15 C5
Cijara, Embalse de, Spain 15 C3
Cijulang, Indonesia . . 27 G13
Cilacap, Indonesia . . . 27 G13
Cill Chainnigh = Kilkenny, Ireland . . 10 E3
Cilo Daği, Turkey . . . 19 G7
Cimarron, Kans., U.S.A. 55 G4
Cimarron, N. Mex., U.S.A. 55 G2
Cimarron →, U.S.A. . . 55 G6
Cimişlia, Moldova . . . 13 E15
Cimone, Mte., Italy . . 16 B4
Cinca →, Spain 15 B6
Cincar, Bos.-H. 16 C7
Cincinnati, U.S.A. . . . 52 F3
Çine, Turkey 17 F13
Ciney, Belgium 11 D5
Cinto, Mte., France . . 14 E8
Circle, Alaska, U.S.A. . 46 B5
Circle, Mont., U.S.A. . 54 B2
Circleville, U.S.A. . . . 52 F4
Cirebon, Indonesia . . 27 G13
Ciremai, Indonesia . . 27 G13
Cirencester, U.K. . . . 9 F6
Cisco, U.S.A. 55 J5
Citlaltépetl, Mexico . . 59 D5
Città di Castello, Italy . 16 C5
Ciudad Altamirano, Mexico 58 D4
Ciudad Bolívar, Venezuela 62 B6
Ciudad Camargo, Mexico 58 B3
Ciudad de Valles, Mexico 59 C5
Ciudad del Carmen, Mexico 59 D6
Ciudad del Este, Paraguay 64 B6
Ciudad Delicias = Delicias, Mexico . . 58 B3
Ciudad Guayana, Venezuela 62 B6
Ciudad Guerrero, Mexico 58 B3
Ciudad Guzmán, Mexico 58 D4
Ciudad Juárez, Mexico 58 A3
Ciudad Madero, Mexico 59 C5
Ciudad Mante, Mexico 59 C5
Ciudad Obregón, Mexico 58 B3
Ciudad Real, Spain . . 15 C4
Ciudad Rodrigo, Spain 15 B2
Ciudad Trujillo = Santo Domingo, Dom. Rep. 61 C6
Ciudad Victoria, Mexico 59 C5
Civitanova Marche, Italy 16 C5

Civitavécchia, *Italy* 16 C4
Cizre, *Turkey* 19 G7
Clacton-on-Sea, *U.K.* ... 9 F9
Claire, L., *Canada* 50 B6
Clanton, *U.S.A.* 53 J2
Clare, *Australia* 43 E2
Clare, *U.S.A.* 52 D3
Claremont, *U.S.A.* 52 D9
Claremont Pt., *Australia* 42 A3
Claremore, *U.S.A.* 55 G7
Clarence →, *Australia* . 43 D5
Clarence →, *N.Z.* 39 K4
Clarence, I., *Chile* 64 G2
Clarence I., *Antarctica* . 5 C18
Clarence Str., *Australia* 40 B5
Clarence Town,
 Bahamas 61 B5
Clarendon, *U.S.A.* 55 H4
Clarenville, *Canada* 49 C9
Claresholm, *Canada* 50 D6
Clarie Coast, *Antarctica* 5
Clarinda, *U.S.A.* 54 E7
Clarion, *U.S.A.* 54 D8
Clark, *U.S.A.* 54 C6
Clark Fork, *U.S.A.* 56 B5
Clark Fork →, *U.S.A.* .. 56 B5
Clarkdale, *U.S.A.* 57 J7
Clarke City, *Canada* 49 B6
Clarke I., *Australia* 42 G4
Clarke Ra., *Australia* ... 42 C4
Clark's Fork →, *U.S.A.* . 56 D9
Clark's Harbour, *Canada* 49 D6
Clarks Hill L., *U.S.A.* .. 53 J4
Clarksburg, *U.S.A.* 52 F5
Clarksdale, *U.S.A.* 55 H9
Clarksville, *Ark., U.S.A.* 55 H8
Clarksville, *Tenn., U.S.A.* 53 G2
Clarksville, *Tex., U.S.A.* 55 J7
Claude, *U.S.A.* 55 H4
Claveria, *Phil.* 27 A6
Clay Center, *U.S.A.* 54 F6
Claypool, *U.S.A.* 57 K8
Clayton, *N. Mex., U.S.A.* 55 G3
Clayton, *N.Y., U.S.A.* .. 52 C7
Clear, C., *Ireland* 10 F2
Clear Hills, *Canada* 50 B5
Clear, L., *U.S.A.* 56 G2
Clear Lake, *Iowa, U.S.A.* 54 D8
Clear Lake, *S. Dak.,*
 U.S.A. 54 C6
Clear Lake Reservoir,
 U.S.A. 56 F3
Clearfield, *Pa., U.S.A.* . 52 E6
Clearfield, *Utah, U.S.A.* 56 F8
Clearlake, *U.S.A.* 56 G2
Clearwater, *Canada* 50 C4
Clearwater, *U.S.A.* 53 M4
Clearwater →, *Alta.,*
 Canada 50 C6
Clearwater →, *Alta.,*
 Canada 51 B6
Clearwater L., *Canada* . 51 C9
Clearwater Mts., *U.S.A.* 56 C6
Clearwater Prov. Park,
 Canada 51 C8
Clearwater River Prov.
 Park, *Canada* 51 B7
Cleburne, *U.S.A.* 55 J6
Clee Hills, *U.K.* 9 E5
Cleethorpes, *U.K.* 8 D7
Cleeve Cloud, *U.K.* 9 F6
Clemson, *U.S.A.* 53 H4
Clerke Reef, *Australia* . 40 C2
Clermont, *Australia* 42 C4
Clermont, *U.S.A.* 53 L5
Clermont-Ferrand,
 France 14 D5
Clervaux, *Lux.* 11 D6
Cleve, *Australia* 43 E2
Clevedon, *U.K.* 9 F5
Cleveland, *Miss., U.S.A.* 55 J9
Cleveland, *Ohio, U.S.A.* 52 E5
Cleveland, *Okla., U.S.A.* 55 G6
Cleveland, *Tenn., U.S.A.* 53 H3
Cleveland, *Tex., U.S.A.* 55 K7
Cleveland, C., *Australia* 42 B4
Cleveland, Mt., *U.S.A.* . 56 B7
Clewiston, *U.S.A.* 53 M5
Clifden, *N.Z.* 39 M1
Cliffy Hd., *Australia* ... 41 G2
Clifton, *Australia* 43 D5
Clifton, *Ariz., U.S.A.* .. 57 K9
Clifton, *Colo., U.S.A.* .. 57 G9
Clifton, *Tex., U.S.A.* ... 55 K6
Clifton Beach, *Australia* 42 B4
Climax, *Canada* 51 D7
Clinch →, *U.S.A.* 53 H3
Clingmans Dome,
 U.S.A. 53 H4
Clint, *U.S.A.* 57 L10
Clinton, *B.C., Canada* .. 50 C4
Clinton, *Ont., Canada* .. 48 D3
Clinton, *N.Z.* 39 M2
Clinton, *Ark., U.S.A.* ... 55 H8
Clinton, *Ill., U.S.A.* 54 E10
Clinton, *Ind., U.S.A.* ... 52 F2
Clinton, *Iowa, U.S.A.* ... 54 E9
Clinton, *Miss., U.S.A.* .. 55 J9
Clinton, *Mo., U.S.A.* ... 54 F8
Clinton, *N.C., U.S.A.* ... 53 H6
Clinton, *Okla., U.S.A.* .. 55 H5
Clinton, *S.C., U.S.A.* ... 53 H5
Clinton, *Tenn., U.S.A.* .. 53 G3
Clinton C., *Australia* ... 42 C5

Clinton Colden L.,
 Canada 46 B9
Clintonville, *U.S.A.* 54 C10
Clipperton, I., *Pac. Oc.* . 45 F17
Clitheroe, *U.K.* 8 D5
Cloates, Pt., *Australia* . 40 D1
Cloncurry, *Australia* ... 42 C3
Cloncurry →, *Australia* 42 B3
Clones, *Ireland* 10 D3
Clonmel, *Ireland* 10 E3
Cloquet, *U.S.A.* 54 B8
Cloud Bay, *Canada* ... 48 C2
Cloud Peak, *U.S.A.* ... 56 D10
Cloudcroft, *U.S.A.* 57 K11
Cloverdale, *U.S.A.* 56 G2
Clovis, *Calif., U.S.A.* .. 57 H4
Clovis, *N. Mex., U.S.A.* 55 H3
Cluj-Napoca, *Romania* . 13 E12
Clunes, *Australia* 43 F3
Clutha →, *N.Z.* 39 M2
Clwyd □, *U.K.* 8 D4
Clwyd →, *U.K.* 8 D4
Clyde, *Canada* 50 C6
Clyde, *N.Z.* 39 L2
Clyde →, *U.K.* 10 D4
Clyde, Firth of, *U.K.* ... 10 D4
Clyde River, *Canada* ... 47 A13
Coachella, *U.S.A.* 57 K5
Coachella Canal, *U.S.A.* 57 K6
Coahoma, *U.S.A.* 55 J4
Coahuayana →,
 Mexico 58 D4
Coahuila □, *Mexico* ... 58 B4
Coal →, *Canada* 50 B3
Coalcomán, *Mexico* ... 58 D4
Coaldale, *Canada* 50 D6
Coalgate, *U.S.A.* 55 H6
Coalinga, *U.S.A.* 57 H3
Coalville, *U.K.* 8 E6
Coalville, *U.S.A.* 56 F8
Coari, *Brazil* 62 D6
Coast Mts., *Canada* ... 50 C3
Coast Ranges, *U.S.A.* . 56 F2
Coatepec, *Mexico* 59 D5
Coatepeque, *Guatemala* 60 D1
Coatesville, *U.S.A.* 52 F8
Coaticook, *Canada* 49 C5
Coats I., *Canada* 47 B11
Coats Land, *Antarctica* 5
Coatzacoalcos, *Mexico* 59 D6
Cobalt, *Canada* 48 C4
Cobán, *Guatemala* 60 C1
Cobar, *Australia* 43 E4
Cóbh, *Ireland* 10 F2
Cobija, *Bolivia* 62 F5
Cobleskill, *U.S.A.* 52 D8
Cobourg, *Canada* 48 D4
Cobourg Pen., *Australia* 40 B5
Cobram, *Australia* 43 F4
Coburg, *Germany* 12 C6
Cocanada = Kakinada,
 India 29 L13
Cochabamba, *Bolivia* .. 62 G5
Cochin, *India* 28 Q10
Cochin China = Nam-
 Phan, *Vietnam* 26 B3
Cochran, *U.S.A.* 53 J4
Cochrane, *Alta., Canada* 50 C6
Cochrane, *Ont., Canada* 48 C3
Cochrane, *Chile* 64 F2
Cochrane →, *Canada* . 51 B8
Cochrane, L., *Chile* 64 F2
Cockburn, *Australia* ... 43 E3
Cockburn, Canal, *Chile* 64 G2
Cockburn I., *Canada* ... 48 C3
Cockburn Ra., *Australia* 40 C4
Cockermouth, *U.K.* 8 C4
Cocklebiddy, *Australia* . 41 F4
Coco →, *Cent. Amer.* .. 60 D3
Coco, I. del, *Pac. Oc.* .. 45 G19
Cocoa, *U.S.A.* 53 L5
Cocobeach, *Gabon* 36 D1
Cocos Is., *Ind. Oc.* 44 J1
Cod, C., *U.S.A.* 52 D10
Codajás, *Brazil* 62 D6
Codó, *Brazil* 63 D10
Cody, *U.S.A.* 56 D9
Coen, *Australia* 42 A3
Cœur d'Alene, *U.S.A.* . 56 C5
Cœur d'Alene L., *U.S.A.* 56 C5
Coevorden, *Neths.* 11 B6
Coffeyville, *U.S.A.* 55 G7
Coffin B., *Australia* 43 E2
Coffin Bay, *Australia* ... 43 E2
Coffin Bay Peninsula,
 Australia 43 E2
Coffs Harbour, *Australia* 43 E5
Cognac, *France* 14 D3
Cohuna, *Australia* 43 F3
Coiba, I., *Panama* 60 E3
Coig →, *Argentina* 64 G3
Coihaique, *Chile* 64 F2
Coimbatore, *India* 28 P10
Coimbra, *Brazil* 62 G7
Coimbra, *Portugal* 15 B1
Coin, *Spain* 15 D3
Coipasa, Salar de,
 Bolivia 62 G5
Cojimíes, *Ecuador* 62 C3
Cojutepequé, *El Salv.* . 60 D2
Colac, *Australia* 43 F3
Colatina, *Brazil* 63 G10
Colbeck, C., *Antarctica* 5 D13
Colby, *U.S.A.* 54 F4

Colchester, *U.K.* 9 F8
Cold L., *Canada* 51 C7
Coldstream, *Canada* ... 50 C5
Coldwater, *Kans., U.S.A.* 55 G5
Coldwater, *Mich., U.S.A.* 52 E3
Coleambally, *Australia* 43 E4
Colebrook, *U.S.A.* 52 C10
Coleman, *U.S.A.* 55 K5
Coleman →, *Australia* 42 B3
Coleraine, *Australia* ... 43 F3
Coleraine, *U.K.* 10 D3
Coleridge, L., *N.Z.* 39 K3
Colesberg, *S. Africa* ... 37 L5
Colfax, *La., U.S.A.* 55 K8
Colfax, *Wash., U.S.A.* . 56 C5
Colhué Huapi, L.,
 Argentina 64 F3
Colima, *Mexico* 58 D4
Colima □, *Mexico* 58 D4
Colima, Nevado de,
 Mexico 58 D4
Colinas, *Brazil* 63 E10
Coll, *U.K.* 10 C3
Collaguasi, *Chile* 62 H5
Collarenebri, *Australia* 43 D4
College Park, *U.S.A.* ... 53 J3
College Station, *U.S.A.* 55 K6
Collie, *Australia* 41 F2
Collier B., *Australia* ... 40 C3
Collier Ra., *Australia* ... 41 D2
Collina, Passo di, *Italy* . 16 B4
Collingwood, *Canada* . 48 D3
Collingwood, *N.Z.* 39 J4
Collins, *Canada* 48 B2
Collinsville, *Australia* .. 42 C4
Colmar, *France* 14 B7
Colo →, *Australia* 43 E5
Cologne = Köln,
 Germany 12 C4
Colomb-Béchar =
 Béchar, *Algeria* 34 B5
Colombia ■, *S. Amer.* . 62 C4
Colombo, *Sri Lanka* ... 28 R11
Colón, *Cuba* 60 B3
Colón, *Panama* 60 E4
Colonia Dora, *Argentina* 64 B4
Colonial Beach, *U.S.A.* 52 F7
Colonsay, *Canada* 51 C7
Colonsay, *U.K.* 10 C3
Colorado □, *U.S.A.* ... 57 G10
Colorado →, *Argentina* 64 D4
Colorado →, *N. Amer.* 55 L6
Colorado →, *U.S.A.* .. 55 L7
Colorado City, *U.S.A.* . 55 J4
Colorado Plateau, *U.S.A.* 57 H8
Colorado River
 Aqueduct, *U.S.A.* ... 57 J6
Colorado Springs,
 U.S.A. 54 F2
Colotlán, *Mexico* 58 C4
Colstrip, *U.S.A.* 56 D10
Columbia, *Ky., U.S.A.* . 52 G3
Columbia, *La., U.S.A.* . 55 J8
Columbia, *Miss., U.S.A.* 55 K10
Columbia, *Mo., U.S.A.* 54 F8
Columbia, *Pa., U.S.A.* . 52 E7
Columbia, *S.C., U.S.A.* 53 J5
Columbia, *Tenn., U.S.A.* 53 H2
Columbia →, *N. Amer.* 56 C1
Columbia, C., *Canada* . 4 A4
Columbia, District of □,
 U.S.A. 52 F7
Columbia, Mt., *Canada* 50 C5
Columbia Basin, *U.S.A.* 56 C4
Columbia Falls, *U.S.A.* 56 B6
Columbia Mts., *Canada* 50 C5
Columbia Plateau,
 U.S.A. 56 D5
Columbretes, Is., *Spain* 15 C6
Columbus, *Ga., U.S.A.* 53 J3
Columbus, *Ind., U.S.A.* 52 F3
Columbus, *Kans., U.S.A.* 55 G7
Columbus, *Miss., U.S.A.* 53 J1
Columbus, *Mont.,*
 U.S.A. 56 D9
Columbus, *N. Mex.,*
 U.S.A. 57 L10
Columbus, *Nebr., U.S.A.* 54 E6
Columbus, *Ohio, U.S.A.* 52 F4
Columbus, *Tex., U.S.A.* 55 L6
Colusa, *U.S.A.* 56 G2
Colville, *U.S.A.* 56 B5
Colville →, *U.S.A.* 46 A4
Colville, C., *N.Z.* 39 G5
Colwyn Bay, *U.K.* 8 D4
Comácchio, *Italy* 16 B5
Comalcalco, *Mexico* ... 59 D6
Comallo, *Argentina* ... 64 E2
Comanche, *U.S.A.* 55 K5
Comayagua, *Honduras* 60 D2
Combahee →, *U.S.A.* . 53 J5
Comblain-au-Pont,
 Belgium 11 D5
Comet, *Australia* 42 C4
Comilla, *Bangla.* 29 H17
Comino, C., *Italy* 16 D3
Comitán, *Mexico* 59 D6
Commerce, *Ga., U.S.A.* 53 H4
Commerce, *Tex., U.S.A.* 55 J7
Committee B., *Canada* . 47 B11
Commonwealth B.,
 Antarctica 5 C10
Commoron Cr. →,
 Australia 43 D5

Communism Pk. =
 Kommunizma, Pik,
 Tajikistan 20 F8
Como, *Italy* 14 D8
Como, Lago di, *Italy* .. 14 D8
Comodoro Rivadavia,
 Argentina 64 F3
Comorin, C., *India* 28 Q10
Comoro Is. =
 Comoros ■, *Ind. Oc.* 3 E12
Comoros ■, *Ind. Oc.* . 3 E12
Comox, *Canada* 50 D4
Compiègne, *France* ... 14 B5
Compostela, *Mexico* .. 58 C4
Comrat, *Moldova* 13 E15
Con Son, *Vietnam* 26 C3
Conakry, *Guinea* 34 G3
Conara, *Australia* 42 G4
Concarneau, *France* ... 14 C2
Conceição da Barra,
 Brazil 63 G11
Conceição do Araguaia,
 Brazil 63 E9
Concepción, *Argentina* 64 B3
Concepción, *Bolivia* ... 62 G6
Concepción, *Chile* 64 D2
Concepción, *Mexico* .. 59 D6
Concepción, *Paraguay* 64 A5
Concepción →, *Mexico* 58 A2
Concepción, Est. de,
 Chile 64 G2
Concepción, L., *Bolivia* 62 G6
Concepción, Punta,
 Mexico 58 B2
Concepción del Oro,
 Mexico 58 C4
Concepción del
 Uruguay, *Argentina* 64 C5
Conception, Pt., *U.S.A.* 57 J3
Conception B., *Canada* 49 C9
Conception I., *Bahamas* 61 B4
Conchas Dam, *U.S.A.* . 55 H2
Concho, *U.S.A.* 57 J9
Concho →, *U.S.A.* 55 K5
Conchos →,
 Chihuahua, Mexico . 58 B4
Conchos →,
 Tamaulipas, Mexico . 59 B5
Concord, *Calif., U.S.A.* 56 H2
Concord, *N.C., U.S.A.* 53 H5
Concord, *N.H., U.S.A.* . 52 D10
Concordia, *Argentina* . 64 C5
Concórdia, *Brazil* 62 D5
Concordia, *Mexico* 58 C3
Concordia, *U.S.A.* 54 F6
Concrete, *U.S.A.* 56 B3
Condamine, *Australia* . 43 D5
Conde, *U.S.A.* 54 C5
Condeúba, *Brazil* 63 F10
Condobolin, *Australia* . 43 E4
Condon, *U.S.A.* 56 D3
Conegliano, *Italy* 16 B5
Conejos, *Mexico* 58 B4
Confuso →, *Paraguay* 64 B5
Congleton, *U.K.* 8 D5
Congo (Kinshasa) =
 Congo, Dem. Rep. of
 the ■, *Africa* 36 E4
Congo ■, *Africa* 36 E3
Congo →, *Africa* 36 F2
Congo, Dem. Rep. of
 the ■, *Africa* 36 E4
Congo Basin, *Africa* .. 36 E4
Congress, *U.S.A.* 57 J7
Coniston, *Canada* 48 C3
Conjeeveram =
 Kanchipuram, *India* . 28 N11
Conklin, *Canada* 51 B6
Conn, L., *Ireland* 10 D2
Connacht □, *Ireland* .. 10 E2
Conneaut, *U.S.A.* 52 E5
Connecticut □, *U.S.A.* 52 E9
Connecticut →, *U.S.A.* 52 E9
Connell, *U.S.A.* 56 C4
Connellsville, *U.S.A.* .. 52 E6
Connemara, *Ireland* ... 10 E2
Connersville, *U.S.A.* ... 52 F3
Connors Ra., *Australia* 42 C4
Conquest, *Canada* 51 C7
Conrad, *U.S.A.* 56 B8
Conran, C., *Australia* .. 43 F4
Conroe, *U.S.A.* 55 K7
Conselheiro Lafaiete,
 Brazil 63 H10
Consett, *U.K.* 8 C6
Consort, *Canada* 51 C6
Constance = Konstanz,
 Germany 12 E5
Constance, L. =
 Bodensee, *Europe* .. 14 C8
Constanța, *Romania* .. 13 F15
Constantine, *Algeria* .. 34 A7
Constitución, *Chile* ... 64 D2
Consul, *Canada* 51 D7
Contact, *U.S.A.* 56 F6
Contai, *India* 29 J15
Contamana, *Peru* 62 E4
Contas →, *Brazil* 63 F11
Contwoyto L., *Canada* 46 B8
Conway = Conwy, *U.K.* 8 D4
Conway,
 U.K. 8 D4
Conway, *Ark., U.S.A.* .. 55 H8
Conway, *N.H., U.S.A.* . 52 D10
Conway, *S.C., U.S.A.* .. 53 J6

Conway, L., *Australia* . 43 D2
Conwy, *U.K.* 8 D4
Conwy □, *U.K.* 8 D4
Conwy →, *U.K.* 8 D4
Coober Pedy, *Australia* 43 D1
Cooch Behar = Koch
 Bihar, *India* 29 F16
Cooinda, *Australia* 40 B5
Cook, *Australia* 41 F5
Cook, *U.S.A.* 54 B8
Cook, B., *Chile* 64 H3
Cook, C., *Canada* 50 C3
Cook, Mt. = Aoraki
 Mount Cook, *N.Z.* .. 39 K3
Cook Inlet, *U.S.A.* 46 C4
Cook Is., *Pac. Oc.* 45 J12
Cook Strait, *N.Z.* 39 J5
Cookeville, *U.S.A.* 53 G3
Cookhouse, *S. Africa* . 37 L4
Cooktown, *Australia* .. 42 B4
Coolabah, *Australia* ... 43 E4
Cooladdi, *Australia* ... 43 D4
Coolah, *Australia* 43 E4
Coolamon, *Australia* .. 43 E4
Coolgardie, *Australia* . 41 F3
Coolidge, *U.S.A.* 57 K8
Coolidge Dam, *U.S.A.* 57 K8
Cooma, *Australia* 43 F4
Coon Rapids, *U.S.A.* .. 54 C8
Coonabarabran,
 Australia 43 E4
Coonalpyn, *Australia* . 43 F2
Coonamble, *Australia* . 43 E4
Coonana, *Australia* ... 41 F3
Coondapoor, *India* 28 N9
Cooninie, L., *Australia* 43 D2
Cooper, *U.S.A.* 55 J7
Cooper Cr. →,
 Australia 43 D2
Cooperstown, *N. Dak.,*
 U.S.A. 54 B5
Cooperstown, *N.Y.,*
 U.S.A. 52 D8
Coorabie, *Australia* ... 41 F5
Coorow, *Australia* 41 E2
Coos Bay, *U.S.A.* 56 E1
Cootamundra, *Australia* 43 E4
Copainalá, *Mexico* 59 D6
Copán, *Honduras* 60 D2
Cope, *U.S.A.* 54 F3
Copenhagen =
 København, *Denmark* 7 J15
Copiapó, *Chile* 64 B2
Copiapó →, *Chile* 64 B2
Copp L., *Canada* 50 A6
Copper Harbor, *U.S.A.* 52 B2
Copperas Cove, *U.S.A.* 55 K6
Coppermine =
 Kugluktuk, *Canada* . 46 B8
Coppermine →,
 Canada 46 B8
Coquet →, *U.K.* 8 B6
Coquilhatville =
 Mbandaka, *Dem. Rep.*
 of the Congo 36 D3
Coquille, *U.S.A.* 56 E1
Coquimbo, *Chile* 64 C2
Corabia, *Romania* 13 G13
Coracora, *Peru* 62 G4
Coraki, *Australia* 43 D5
Coral Gables, *U.S.A.* .. 53 N5
Coral Harbour = Salliq,
 Canada 47 B11
Coral Sea, *Pac. Oc.* ... 38 C8
Coral Sea Islands
 Terr. □, *Australia* .. 38 C8
Coral Springs, *U.S.A.* . 53 M5
Corato, *Italy* 16 D7
Corbin, *U.S.A.* 52 G3
Corby, *U.K.* 9 E7
Corcaigh = Cork, *Ireland* 10 F2
Corcoran, *U.S.A.* 57 H4
Corcubión, *Spain* 15 A1
Cordele, *U.S.A.* 53 K4
Cordell, *U.S.A.* 55 H5
Córdoba, *Argentina* ... 64 C4
Córdoba, *Mexico* 59 D5
Córdoba, *Spain* 15 D3
Córdoba, Sierra de,
 Argentina 64 C4
Cordova, *U.S.A.* 46 C5
Corella →, *Australia* .. 42 B3
Corfield, *Australia* 42 C3
Corfu = Kérkira, *Greece* 17 E8
Coria, *Spain* 15 C2
Corigliano Cálabro, *Italy* 16 E7
Coringa Is., *Australia* .. 42 B4
Corinth = Kórinthos,
 Greece 17 F10
Corinth, *U.S.A.* 53 H1
Corinth, G. of =
 Korinthiakós Kólpos,
 Greece 17 E10
Corinto, *Brazil* 63 G10
Corinto, *Nic.* 60 D2
Cork, *Ireland* 10 F2
Çorlu, *Turkey* 17 D12
Cormack L., *Canada* .. 50 A4
Cormorant, *Canada* ... 51 C8
Corn Is. = Maíz, Is. del,
 Nic. 60 D3

Corner Brook, *Canada* . 49 C8
Cornești, *Moldova* 13 E15
Corning, *Ark., U.S.A.* .. 55 G9
Corning, *Calif., U.S.A.* . 56 G2
Corning, *Iowa, U.S.A.* . 54 E7
Corning, *N.Y., U.S.A.* .. 52 D7
Cornwall, *Canada* 48 C5
Cornwall □, *U.K.* 9 G3
Corny Pt., *Australia* ... 43 E2
Coro, *Venezuela* 62 A5
Coroatá, *Brazil* 63 D10
Corocoro, *Bolivia* 62 G5
Coroico, *Bolivia* 62 G5
Coromandel, *N.Z.* 39 G5
Coromandel Coast, *India* 28 N12
Corona, *Calif., U.S.A.* . 57 K5
Corona, *N. Mex., U.S.A.* 57 J11
Coronach, *Canada* 51 D7
Coronado, B. de,
 Costa Rica 60 E3
Coronation, *Canada* .. 50 C6
Coronation Gulf, *Canada* 46 B8
Coronation I., *Antarctica* 5 C18
Coronation Is., *Australia* 40 B3
Coronel, *Chile* 64 D2
Coronel Dorrego,
 Argentina 64 D4
Coronel Oviedo,
 Paraguay 64 B5
Coronel Pringles,
 Argentina 64 D4
Coronel Suárez,
 Argentina 64 D4
Coropuna, Nevado, *Peru* 62 G4
Corowa, *Australia* 43 F4
Corozal, *Belize* 59 D7
Corpus Christi, *U.S.A.* . 55 M6
Corpus Christi, L.,
 U.S.A. 55 L6
Corrib, L., *Ireland* 10 E2
Corrientes, *Argentina* . 64 B5
Corrientes →, *Peru* ... 62 D4
Corrientes, C., *Colombia* 62 B3
Corrientes, C., *Cuba* .. 60 B3
Corrientes, C., *Mexico* 58 C3
Corrigan, *U.S.A.* 55 K7
Corrigin, *Australia* 41 F2
Corry, *U.S.A.* 52 E6
Corryong, *Australia* ... 43 F4
Corse, *France* 14 F8
Corse, C., *France* 14 E8
Corsica = Corse, *France* 14 F8
Corsicana, *U.S.A.* 55 J6
Corte, *France* 14 E8
Cortez, *U.S.A.* 57 H9
Cortland, *U.S.A.* 52 D7
Çorum, *Turkey* 19 F5
Corumbá, *Brazil* 62 G7
Corunna = A Coruña,
 Spain 15 A1
Corvallis, *U.S.A.* 56 D2
Corvette, L. de la,
 Canada 48 B5
Corydon, *U.S.A.* 54 E8
Cosalá, *Mexico* 58 C3
Cosamaloapan, *Mexico* 59 D5
Cosenza, *Italy* 16 E7
Coshocton, *U.S.A.* 52 E5
Cosmo Newberry,
 Australia 41 E3
Costa Blanca, *Spain* ... 15 C5
Costa Brava, *Spain* ... 15 B7
Costa del Sol, *Spain* .. 15 D3
Costa Dorada, *Spain* .. 15 B6
Costa Rica ■,
 Cent. Amer. 60 E3
Cotabato, *Phil.* 27 C6
Cotagaita, *Bolivia* 62 H5
Côte d'Azur, *France* ... 14 E7
Côte-d'Ivoire = Ivory
 Coast ■, *Africa* 34 G4
Coteau des Prairies,
 U.S.A. 54 C6
Coteau du Missouri,
 U.S.A. 54 B4
Cotentin, *France* 14 B3
Cotonou, *Benin* 34 G6
Cotopaxi, *Ecuador* 62 D3
Cotswold Hills, *U.K.* .. 9 F5
Cottage Grove, *U.S.A.* 56 E2
Cottbus, *Germany* 12 C8
Cottonwood, *U.S.A.* .. 57 J7
Cotulla, *U.S.A.* 55 L5
Coudersport, *U.S.A.* .. 52 E6
Couedic, C. du, *Australia* 43 F2
Coulee City, *U.S.A.* ... 56 C4
Coulman I., *Antarctica* . 5 D11
Coulonge →, *Canada* . 48 C4
Council, *U.S.A.* 56 D5
Council Bluffs, *U.S.A.* . 54 E7
Council Grove, *U.S.A.* 54 F6
Courantyne →,
 S. Amer. 62 B7
Courcelles, *Belgium* .. 11 D4
Courtenay, *Canada* ... 50 D4
Courtrai = Kortrijk,
 Belgium 11 D3
Coushatta, *U.S.A.* 55 J8
Coutts Crossing,
 Australia 43 D5
Couvin, *Belgium* 11 D4
Coventry, *U.K.* 9 E6
Covilhã, *Portugal* 15 B2
Covington, *Ga., U.S.A.* 53 J4
Covington, *Ky., U.S.A.* 52 F3

Covington, *Okla., U.S.A.* 55 G6
Covington, *Tenn., U.S.A.* 55 H10
Covington, *Va., U.S.A.* . 52 G5
Cowal, L., *Australia* . . . 43 E4
Cowan, L., *Australia* . . 41 F3
Cowan L., *Canada* 51 C7
Cowangie, *Australia* . . 43 F3
Cowansville, *Canada* . . 48 C5
Coward Springs,
  Australia 43 D2
Cowcowing Lakes,
  Australia 41 F2
Cowell, *Australia* 43 E2
Cowes, *U.K.* 9 G6
Cowra, *Australia* 43 E4
Coxim, *Brazil* 63 G8
Cox's Bazar, *Bangla.* . . 29 J17
Coyuca de Benítez,
  Mexico 59 D4
Coyuca de Catalan,
  Mexico 58 D4
Cozad, *U.S.A.* 54 E5
Cozumel, *Mexico* 59 C7
Cozumel, Isla, *Mexico* . 59 C7
Cracow = Kraków,
  Poland 13 C10
Cracow, *Australia* 43 D5
Cradock, *Australia* . . . 43 E2
Cradock, *S. Africa* . . . 37 L5
Craig, *U.S.A.* 56 F10
Craigavon, *U.K.* 10 D3
Craik, *Canada* 51 C7
Crailsheim, *Germany* . . 12 D6
Craiova, *Romania* . . . 13 F12
Cramsie, *Australia* . . . 42 C3
Cranberry Portage,
  Canada 51 C8
Cranbrook, *Australia* . . 41 F2
Cranbrook, *Canada* . . . 50 D5
Crandon, *U.S.A.* 54 C10
Crane, *Oreg., U.S.A.* . 56 E4
Crane, *Tex., U.S.A.* . . 55 K3
Crater L., *U.S.A.* 56 E2
Crater Lake National
  Park, *U.S.A.* 56 E2
Crateús, *Brazil* 63 E10
Crato, *Brazil* 63 E11
Craven, L., *Canada* . . . 48 B4
Crawford, *U.S.A.* 54 D3
Crawfordsville, *U.S.A.* . 52 E2
Crawley, *U.K.* 9 F7
Crazy Mts., *U.S.A.* . . . 56 C8
Crean L., *Canada* 51 C7
Cree →, *Canada* 51 B7
Cree L., *Canada* 51 B7
Creede, *U.S.A.* 57 H10
Creel, *Mexico* 58 B3
Creighton, *Canada* . . . 51 C8
Creighton, *U.S.A.* . . . 54 D6
Crema, *Italy* 14 D8
Cremona, *Italy* 14 D9
Cres, *Croatia* 12 F8
Crescent City, *U.S.A.* . 56 F1
Creston, *Canada* 50 D5
Creston, *U.S.A.* 54 E7
Crestview, *U.S.A.* . . . 53 K2
Crete = Kríti, *Greece* . 17 G11
Crete, *U.S.A.* 54 E6
Créteil, *France* 14 B5
Creus, C. de, *Spain* . . 15 A7
Creuse →, *France* . . . 14 C4
Crewe, *U.K.* 8 D5
Crewkerne, *U.K.* 9 G5
Criciúma, *Brazil* 64 B7
Crimea □, *Ukraine* . . . 19 E5
Crimean Pen. =
  Krymskyy Pivostriv,
  Ukraine 19 F5
Crişul Alb →, *Romania* 13 E11
Crişul Negru →,
  Romania 13 E11
Crna →, *Macedonia* . . 17 D9
Crna Gora =
  Montenegro □,
  Yugoslavia 17 C8
Crna Gora, *Macedonia* 17 C9
Crna Reka = Crna →,
  Macedonia 17 D9
Croatia ■, *Europe* . . . 12 F9
Crocker, Banjaran,
  Malaysia 26 C5
Crockett, *U.S.A.* 55 K7
Crocodile Is., *Australia* 42 A1
Croix, L. La, *Canada* . . 48 C1
Croker, C., *Australia* . . 40 B5
Croker I., *Australia* . . . 40 B5
Cromer, *U.K.* 8 E9
Cromwell, *N.Z.* 39 L2
Crook, *U.K.* 8 C6
Crooked →, *Canada* . 50 C4
Crooked →, *U.S.A.* . . 56 D3
Crooked I., *Bahamas* . . 61 B5
Crooked Island Passage,
  Bahamas 61 B5
Crookston, *Minn., U.S.A.* 54 B6
Crookston, *Nebr., U.S.A.* 54 D4
Crookwell, *Australia* . . 43 E4
Crosby, *U.K.* 8 D4
Crosby, *U.S.A.* 54 A3
Crosbyton, *U.S.A.* . . . 55 J4
Cross City, *U.S.A.* . . . 53 L4
Cross Fell, *U.K.* 8 C5
Cross L., *Canada* 51 C9
Cross Lake, *Canada* . . 51 C9
Cross Sound, *U.S.A.* . . 46 C6

Crossett, *U.S.A.* 55 J9
Crossville, *U.S.A.* 53 G3
Crotone, *Italy* 16 E7
Crow →, *Canada* . . . 50 B4
Crow Agency, *U.S.A.* . . 56 D10
Crowell, *U.S.A.* 55 J5
Crowley, *U.S.A.* 55 K8
Crown Point, *U.S.A.* . . 52 E2
Crownpoint, *U.S.A.* . . . 57 J9
Crows Nest, *Australia* . 43 D5
Crowsnest Pass, *Canada* 50 D6
Croydon, *Australia* . . . 42 B3
Croydon □, *U.K.* 9 F7
Crozet, Is., *Ind. Oc.* . . . 3 G12
Cruz, C., *Cuba* 60 C4
Cruz Alta, *Brazil* 64 B6
Cruz del Eje, *Argentina* 64 C4
Cruzeiro, *Brazil* 64 A8
Cruzeiro do Sul, *Brazil* . 62 E4
Cry L., *Canada* 50 B3
Crystal Brook, *Australia* 43 E2
Crystal City, *U.S.A.* . . . 55 L5
Crystal Falls, *U.S.A.* . . 52 B1
Crystal River, *U.S.A.* . . 53 L4
Crystal Springs, *U.S.A.* 55 K9
Csongrád, *Hungary* . . 13 E11
Cuamba, *Mozam.* 37 G7
Cuando →, *Angola* . . 37 H4
Cuatrociénegas, *Mexico* 58 B4
Cuauhtémoc, *Mexico* . . 58 B3
Cuba, *U.S.A.* 57 J10
Cuba ■, *W. Indies* 60 B4
Cubango →, *Africa* . . 37 H4
Cuchumatanes, Sierra
  de los, *Guatemala* . . 60 C1
Cuckfield, *U.K.* 9 F7
Cucuí, *Brazil* 62 C5
Cucurpe, *Mexico* 58 A2
Cúcuta, *Colombia* 62 B4
Cuddalore, *India* 28 P11
Cuddapah, *India* 28 M11
Cuddapan, L., *Australia* 42 D3
Cue, *Australia* 41 E2
Cuenca, *Ecuador* 62 D3
Cuenca, *Spain* 15 B4
Cuenca, Serranía de,
  Spain 15 C5
Cuernavaca, *Mexico* . . 59 D5
Cuero, *U.S.A.* 55 L6
Cuevas del Almanzora,
  Spain 15 D5
Cuevo, *Bolivia* 62 H6
Cuiabá, *Brazil* 63 G7
Cuiabá →, *Brazil* . . . 63 G7
Cuijk, *Neths.* 11 C5
Cuilco, *Guatemala* 60 C1
Cuillin Hills, *U.K.* 10 D2
Cuillin Sd., *U.K.* 10 D2
Cuito →, *Angola* 37 H4
Cuitzeo, L. de, *Mexico* . 58 D4
Culbertson, *U.S.A.* . . . 54 A2
Culcairn, *Australia* . . . 43 F4
Culgoa →, *Australia* . . 43 D4
Culiacán, *Mexico* 58 C3
Culiacán →, *Mexico* . . 58 C3
Culion, *Phil.* 27 B6
Cullarin Ra., *Australia* . 43 E4
Cullen Pt., *Australia* . . 42 A3
Cullera, *Spain* 15 C5
Cullman, *U.S.A.* 53 H2
Culpeper, *U.S.A.* 52 F7
Culuene →, *Brazil* . . . 63 F8
Culver, Pt., *Australia* . . 41 F3
Culverden, *N.Z.* 39 K4
Cumaná, *Venezuela* . . 62 A6
Cumberland, *Canada* . . 50 D4
Cumberland, *U.S.A.* . . 52 F6
Cumberland →, *U.S.A.* 53 G2
Cumberland, L., *U.S.A.* 53 G3
Cumberland I., *U.S.A.* . 53 K5
Cumberland Is.,
  Australia 42 C4
Cumberland L., *Canada* 51 C8
Cumberland Pen.,
  Canada 47 B13
Cumberland Plateau,
  U.S.A. 53 H3
Cumberland Sd.,
  Canada 47 B13
Cumborah, *Australia* . . 43 D4
Cumbria □, *U.K.* 8 C5
Cumbrian Mts., *U.K.* . . 8 C5
Cumbum, *India* 28 M11
Cuminá →, *Brazil* . . . 63 D7
Cummins, *Australia* . . . 43 E2
Cumnock, *Australia* . . . 43 E4
Cumpas, *Mexico* 58 B3
Cunco, *Chile* 64 D2
Cunderdin, *Australia* . . 41 F2
Cunene →, *Angola* . . 37 H2
Cúneo, *Italy* 14 D7
Çüngüş, *Turkey* 30 B3
Cunnamulla, *Australia* . 43 D4
Cupar, *Canada* 51 C8
Cupica, G. de, *Colombia* 62 B3
Curaçao, *Neth. Ant.* . . 62 A5
Curanilahue, *Chile* . . . 64 D2
Curaray →, *Peru* 62 D4
Curiapo, *Venezuela* . . 62 B6
Curicó, *Chile* 64 C2
Curitiba, *Brazil* 64 B7
Currabubula, *Australia* 43 E5
Currais Novos, *Brazil* . 63 E11
Curralinho, *Brazil* 63 D9
Current →, *U.S.A.* . . . 56 G6
Current →, *U.S.A.* . . . 55 G9
Currie, *Australia* 42 F3

Currie, *U.S.A.* 56 F6
Curtea de Argeş,
  Romania 13 F13
Curtis, *U.S.A.* 54 E4
Curtis Group, *Australia* 42 F4
Curtis I., *Australia* . . . 42 C5
Curuápanema →,
  Brazil 63 D7
Curuçá, *Brazil* 63 D9
Curup, *Indonesia* 26 E2
Cururupu, *Brazil* 63 D10
Curuzú Cuatiá,
  Argentina 64 B5
Curvelo, *Brazil* 63 G10
Cushing, *U.S.A.* 55 H6
Cushing, Mt., *Canada* . 50 B3
Cusihuiriáchic, *Mexico* 58 B3
Custer, *U.S.A.* 54 D3
Cut Bank, *U.S.A.* 56 B7
Cuthbert, *U.S.A.* 53 K3
Cuttaburra →,
  Australia 43 D3
Cuttack, *India* 29 J14
Cuvier, C., *Australia* . . 41 D1
Cuvier I., *N.Z.* 39 G5
Cuxhaven, *Germany* . . 12 B5
Cuyahoga Falls, *U.S.A.* 52 E5
Cuyo, *Phil.* 27 B6
Cuyuni →, *Guyana* . . 62 B7
Cuzco, *Bolivia* 62 H5
Cuzco, *Peru* 62 F4
Cwmbran, *U.K.* 9 F4
Cyclades = Kikládhes,
  Greece 17 F11
Cygnet, *Australia* 42 G4
Cynthiana, *U.S.A.* . . . 52 F3
Cypress Hills, *Canada* . 51 D7
Cypress Hills Prov. Park,
  Canada 51 D7
Cyprus ■, *Asia* 30 C2
Cyrenaica, *Libya* . . . 35 C10
Cyrene, *Libya* 35 B10
Czar, *Canada* 51 C6
Czech Rep. ■, *Europe* . 12 D8
Częstochowa, *Poland* . 13 C10

Da Hinggan Ling, *China* 25 B7
Da Lat, *Vietnam* 26 B3
Da Nang, *Vietnam* . . . 26 A3
Da Qaidam, *China* . . . 24 C4
Daba Shan, *China* . . . 25 C5
Dabbagh, Jabal,
  Si. Arabia 30 E2
Dabo = Pasirkuning,
  Indonesia 26 E2
Dabola, *Guinea* 34 F3
Dacca = Dhaka, *Bangla.* 29 H17
Dacca = Dhaka □,
  Bangla. 29 G17
Dachau, *Germany* . . . 12 D6
Dadanawa, *Guyana* . . 62 C7
Dade City, *U.S.A.* . . . 53 L4
Dadra & Nagar
  Haveli □, *India* 28 J8
Dadu, *Pakistan* 28 F5
Daet, *Phil.* 27 B6
Dagana, *Senegal* 34 E2
Dagestan □, *Russia* . . 19 F8
Daghestan Republic =
  Dagestan □, *Russia* . 19 F8
Dağlıq Qarabağ =
  Nagorno-Karabakh,
  Azerbaijan 19 F8
Dagö = Hiiumaa,
  Estonia 7 G20
Dagupan, *Phil.* 27 A6
Daguragu, *Australia* . . 40 C5
Dahlak Kebir, *Eritrea* . 32 D3
Dahlonega, *U.S.A.* . . . 53 H4
Dahod, *India* 28 H9
Dahomey = Benin ■,
  Africa 34 G6
Dahûk, *Iraq* 30 B3
Dai-Sen, *Japan* 23 G6
Daintree, *Australia* . . . 42 B4
Daiō-Misaki, *Japan* . . 23 G8
Daisetsu-Zan, *Japan* . 22 C11
Dajarra, *Australia* . . . 42 C2
Dakar, *Senegal* 34 F2
Dakhla, *W. Sahara* . . . 34 D2
Dakhla, El Wâhât el-,
  Egypt 35 C11
Dakota City, *U.S.A.* . . 54 D6
Đakovica, *Kosovo, Yug.* 17 C9
Đakovica, *Kosovo, Yug.* 17 C9
Đalaki, *Iran* 31 D6
Dalälven, *Sweden* 7 F17
Dalaman →, *Turkey* . . 17 F13
Dalandzadgad,
  Mongolia 24 B5
Dalap-Uliga-Darrit,
  Marshall Is. 44 G9
Dalarna, *Sweden* 7 F16
Dālbandīn, *Pakistan* . . 28 E4
Dalby, *Australia* 43 D5
Dale City, *U.S.A.* 52 F7
Dale Hollow L., *U.S.A.* . 53 G3
Dalgán, *Iran* 31 E8
Dalhart, *U.S.A.* 55 G3
Dalhousie, *Canada* . . . 49 C6
Dali, *China* 24 D5
Dalian, *China* 25 C7
Daliang Shan, *China* . . 24 D5
Dāliyat el Karmel, *Israel* 33 C4
Dallas, *Oreg., U.S.A.* . 56 D2

Dallas, *Tex., U.S.A.* . . 55 J6
Dalmā, *U.A.E.* 31 E7
Dalmacija, *Croatia* . . . 16 C7
Dalmas, L., *Canada* . . 49 B5
Dalmatia = Dalmacija,
  Croatia 16 C7
Dalnegorsk, *Russia* . . 21 E14
Dalnerechensk, *Russia* 21 E14
Daloa, *Ivory C.* 34 G4
Dalrymple, L., *Australia* 42 C4
Dalsland, *Sweden* 7 G14
Dalton, *Ga., U.S.A.* . . 53 H3
Dalton, *Nebr., U.S.A.* . 54 E3
Dalton Iceberg Tongue,
  Antarctica 5 C9
Dalton-in-Furness, *U.K.* 8 C4
Dalvík, *Iceland* 6 D4
Dalwallinu, *Australia* . . 41 F2
Daly →, *Australia* . . . 40 B5
Daly L., *Canada* 51 B7
Daly River, *Australia* . . 40 B5
Daly Waters, *Australia* . 42 B1
Daman, *India* 28 J8
Dāmaneh, *Iran* 31 C6
Damanhûr, *Egypt* . . . 35 B12
Damant L., *Canada* . . 51 A7
Damar, *Indonesia* . . . 27 F7
Damaraland, *Namibia* . 37 J2
Damascus = Dimashq,
  Syria 33 B5
Damāvand, *Iran* 31 C7
Damāvand, Qolleh-ye,
  Iran 31 C7
Damba, *Angola* 36 F3
Dâmboviţa →,
  Romania 13 F14
Dame Marie, *Haiti* . . . 61 C5
Damiel, *Spain* 15 C4
Damietta = Dumyât,
  Egypt 35 B12
Damir Qâbû, *Syria* . . 30 B4
Dammam = Ad
  Dammām, *Si. Arabia* 31 E6
Damoh, *India* 28 H11
Dampier, *Australia* . . . 40 D2
Dampier, Selat,
  Indonesia 27 E8
Dampier Arch., *Australia* 40 D2
Dana, *Indonesia* 27 F6
Dana, L., *Canada* . . . 48 B4
Danakil Desert, *Ethiopia* 32 E3
Danané, *Ivory C.* 34 G4
Danau Poso, *Indonesia* 27 E6
Danbury, *U.S.A.* 52 E9
Danby L., *U.S.A.* 57 J6
Dandeldhura, *Nepal* . . 29 E12
Dandeli, *India* 28 M9
Dandenong, *Australia* . 43 F4
Dandong, *China* 25 B7
Danger Is. = Pukapuka,
  Cook Is. 45 J11
Dangla Shan =
  Tanggula Shan, *China* 24 C4
Dangriga, *Belize* 59 D7
Daniel, *U.S.A.* 56 E8
Daniel's Harbour,
  Canada 49 B8
Danilov, *Russia* 18 C7
Dank, *Oman* 31 F8
Dankhar Gompa, *India* 28 C11
Danli, *Honduras* 60 D2
Dannemora, *U.S.A.* . . 52 C9
Dannevirke, *N.Z.* 39 J6
Dansville, *U.S.A.* 52 D7
Dante, *Somali Rep.* . . 32 E5
Danube = Dunărea →,
  Europe 13 F15
Danville, *Ill., U.S.A.* . . 52 E2
Danville, *Ky., U.S.A.* . . 52 G3
Danville, *Va., U.S.A.* . . 53 G6
Danzig = Gdańsk,
  Poland 13 A10
Dapaong, *Togo* 34 F6
Dar el Beida =
  Casablanca, *Morocco* 34 B4
Dar es Salaam, *Tanzania* 36 F7
Dar Mazār, *Iran* 31 D8
Dar'ā, *Syria* 33 C5
Dar'ā □, *Syria* 33 C5
Dārāb, *Iran* 31 D7
Daraj, *Libya* 35 B8
Dayr az Zawr, *Syria* . . 30 C4
Dārayyā, *Syria* 33 B5
Darband, *Pakistan* . . . 28 B8
Darband, Küh-e, *Iran* . 31 D8
Darbhanga, *India* . . . 29 F14
D'Arcy, *Canada* 50 C4
Dardanelle, *U.S.A.* . . . 55 H8
Dardanelles =
  Çanakkale Boğazı,
  Turkey 17 D12
Dārestān, *Iran* 31 D8
Dârfûr, *Sudan* 35 F10
Dargai, *Pakistan* 28 B7
Dargan Ata, *Uzbekistan* 20 E7
Dargaville, *N.Z.* 39 F4
Darhan, *Mongolia* . . . 24 B5
Danca, *Turkey* 17 D13
Darién, G. del, *Colombia* 62 B3
Darjeeling = Darjiling,
  India 29 F16
Darjiling, *India* 29 F16
Darkan, *Australia* 41 F2
Darkhazineh, *Iran* . . . 31 D6

Darling →, *Australia* . 43 E3
Darling Downs,
  Australia 43 D5
Darling Ra., *Australia* . 41 F2
Darlington, *U.K.* 8 C6
Darlington, *U.S.A.* . . . 53 H6
Darlington □, *U.K.* 8 C6
Darlington Point,
  Australia 43 E4
Darlot, L., *Australia* . . 41 E3
Darłowo, *Poland* 12 A9
Darmstadt, *Germany* . . 12 D5
Darnah, *Libya* 35 B10
Darnley, C., *Antarctica* . 5 C6
Darnley B., *Canada* . . 46 B7
Darr →, *Australia* . . . 42 C3
Darrington, *U.S.A.* . . . 56 B3
Dart, C., *Antarctica* . . 5 D14
Dartford, *U.K.* 9 F8
Dartmoor, *U.K.* 9 G4
Dartmouth, *Canada* . . 49 D7
Dartmouth, *U.K.* 9 G4
Dartmouth, L., *Australia* 43 D4
Darvaza, *Turkmenistan* 20 E6
Darvel, Teluk = Lahad
  Datu, Teluk, *Malaysia* 27 D5
Darwen, *U.K.* 8 D5
Darwha, *India* 28 J10
Darwin, *Australia* 40 B5
Daryoi Amu =
  Amudarya →,
  Uzbekistan 20 E6
Dās, *U.A.E.* 31 E7
Dashen, Ras, *Ethiopia* . 32 E2
Dashhowuz,
  Turkmenistan 20 E6
Dashköpri,
  Turkmenistan 31 B9
Dasht, *Iran* 31 B8
Dasht →, *Pakistan* . . 28 G2
Daţça, *Turkey* 17 F12
Datia, *India* 28 G11
Datong, *China* 25 B6
Datu, Tanjung,
  Indonesia 26 D3
Datu Piang, *Phil.* 27 C6
Datuk, Tanjong = Datu,
  Tanjung, *Indonesia* . 26 D3
Daugava →, *Latvia* . . 7 H21
Daugavpils, *Latvia* . . . 7 J22
Daulpur, *India* 28 F10
Dauphin, *Canada* . . . 51 C8
Dauphin L., *Canada* . . 51 C9
Dauphiné, *France* . . . 14 D6
Davangere, *India* . . . 28 M9
Davao, *Phil.* 27 C7
Davao G., *Phil.* 27 C7
Davenport, Iowa, U.S.A. 54 E9
Davenport, Wash.,
  U.S.A. 56 C4
Davenport Ra., *Australia* 42 C1
Daventry, *U.K.* 9 E6
David, *Panama* 60 E3
David City, *U.S.A.* . . . 54 E6
David Gorodok = Davyd
  Haradok, *Belarus* . . 13 B14
Davidson, *Canada* . . . 51 C7
Davis, *U.S.A.* 56 G3
Davis Dam, *U.S.A.* . . . 57 J6
Davis Inlet, *Canada* . . 49 A7
Davis Mts., *U.S.A.* . . . 55 K2
Davis Sea, *Antarctica* . 5 C7
Davis Str., *N. Amer.* . . 47 B14
Davos, *Switz.* 14 C8
Davy L., *Canada* 51 B7
Davyd Haradok, *Belarus* 13 B14
Dawei, *Burma* 26 B1
Dawes Ra., *Australia* . 42 C5
Dawlish, *U.K.* 9 G4
Dawson, *Canada* 46 B6
Dawson, *U.S.A.* 53 K3
Dawson, I., *Chile* 64 G2
Dawson B., *Canada* . . 51 C8
Dawson Creek, *Canada* 50 B4
Dawson Inlet, *Canada* . 51 A10
Dawson Ra., *Australia* . 42 C4
Dax, *France* 14 E3
Daxian, *China* 24 C5
Daxue Shan, *China* . . 24 C5
Daylesford, *Australia* . 43 F3
Daysland, *Canada* . . . 50 C6
Dayton, *Ohio, U.S.A.* . 52 F3
Dayton, *Tenn., U.S.A.* . 53 H3
Dayton, *Wash., U.S.A.* 56 C4
Dayton, *Wyo., U.S.A.* . 56 D10
Daytona Beach, *U.S.A.* 53 L5
Dayville, *U.S.A.* 56 D4
De Aar, *S. Africa* 37 L4
De Funiak Springs,
  U.S.A. 53 K2
De Grey →, *Australia* 40 D2
De Haan, *Belgium* . . . 11 C3
De Kalb, *U.S.A.* 54 E10
De Land, *U.S.A.* 53 L5
De Leon, *U.S.A.* 55 J5
De Panne, *Belgium* . . 11 C2
De Queen, *U.S.A.* . . . 55 H7
De Quincy, *U.S.A.* . . . 55 K8
De Ridder, *U.S.A.* . . . 55 K8
De Smet, *U.S.A.* 54 C6
De Soto, *U.S.A.* 54 F9

De Tour Village, *U.S.A.* 52 C4
De Witt, *U.S.A.* 55 H9
Dead Sea, *Asia* 33 D4
Deadwood, *U.S.A.* . . . 54 C3
Deadwood L., *Canada* . 50 B3
Deal, *U.K.* 9 F9
Deal I., *Australia* 42 F4
Dean →, *Canada* . . . 50 C3
Dean, Forest of, *U.K.* . 9 F5
Dean, C., *Canada* . . . 50 C3
Deán Funes, *Argentina* 64 C4
Dease →, *Canada* . . 50 B3
Dease L., *Canada* . . . 50 B2
Dease Lake, *Canada* . 50 B2
Death Valley, *U.S.A.* . . 57 H5
Death Valley Junction,
  U.S.A. 57 H5
Death Valley National
  Park, *U.S.A.* 57 H5
Debar, *Macedonia* . . . 17 D9
Debden, *Canada* 51 C7
Dębica, *Poland* 13 C11
Debolt, *Canada* 50 B5
Deborah East, L.,
  Australia 41 F2
Deborah West, L.,
  Australia 41 F2
Debre Markos, *Ethiopia* 32 E2
Debre Tabor, *Ethiopia* . 32 E2
Debre Zeyit, *Ethiopia* . 32 F2
Debrecen, *Hungary* . . 13 E11
Decatur, *Ala., U.S.A.* . 53 H2
Decatur, *Ga., U.S.A.* . 53 J3
Decatur, *Ill., U.S.A.* . . 54 F10
Decatur, *Ind., U.S.A.* . 52 E3
Decatur, *Tex., U.S.A.* . 55 J6
Deccan, *India* 28 L11
Deception Bay, *Australia* 43 D5
Deception L., *Canada* . 51 B8
Děčín, *Czech Rep.* . . . 12 C8
Decorah, *U.S.A.* 54 D9
Dedéagach =
  Alexandroúpolis,
  Greece 17 D11
Dee →, *Aberds., U.K.* 10 C5
Dee →, *Wales, U.K.* . 8 D4
Deep B., *Canada* 50 A5
Deepwater, *Australia* . 43 D5
Deer →, *Canada* . . . 51 B10
Deer L., *Canada* 51 C10
Deer Lake, *Nfld., Canada* 49 C8
Deer Lake, *Ont., Canada* 51 C10
Deer Lodge, *U.S.A.* . . 56 C7
Deer Park, *U.S.A.* . . . 56 C5
Deer River, *U.S.A.* . . . 54 B8
Deeragun, *Australia* . . 42 B4
Defiance, *U.S.A.* 52 E3
Dégelis, *Canada* 49 C6
Deggendorf, *Germany* . 12 D7
Deh Bīd, *Iran* 31 D7
Deh-e Shīr, *Iran* 31 D7
Dehaj, *Iran* 31 D7
Dehak, *Iran* 31 E9
Dehdez, *Iran* 31 D6
Dehestān, *Iran* 31 D7
Dehgolān, *Iran* 30 C5
Dehibat, *Tunisia* 35 B8
Dehlorān, *Iran* 30 C5
Dehnow-e Kühestān,
  Iran 31 E8
Dehra Dun, *India* . . . 28 D11
Deinze, *Belgium* 11 D3
Dej, *Romania* 13 E12
Dekese, *Dem. Rep. of
  the Congo* 36 E4
Del Norte, *U.S.A.* . . . 57 H10
Del Rio, *U.S.A.* 55 L4
Delambre I., *Australia* . 40 D2
Delano, *U.S.A.* 57 J4
Delano Peak, *U.S.A.* . . 57 G7
Delavan, *U.S.A.* 54 D10
Delaware, *U.S.A.* 52 E4
Delaware □, *U.S.A.* . . 52 F8
Delaware →, *U.S.A.* . 52 F8
Delay →, *Canada* . . . 49 A5
Delegate, *Australia* . . 43 F4
Delft, *Neths.* 11 B4
Delfzijl, *Neths.* 11 A6
Delgado, *Mozam.* . . . 36 G8
Delgo, *Sudan* 35 D12
Delhi, *India* 28 E10
Delhi, *U.S.A.* 55 J9
Delia, *Canada* 50 C6
Delice, *Turkey* 19 G5
Delicias, *Mexico* 58 B3
Delījān, *Iran* 31 C6
Déline, *Canada* 46 B7
Delisle, *Canada* 51 C7
Dell City, *U.S.A.* 57 L11
Dell Rapids, *U.S.A.* . . 54 D6
Delmenhorst, *Germany* 12 B5
Delonga, Ostrova,
  Russia 21 B15
Deloraine, *Australia* . . 42 G4
Deloraine, *Canada* . . . 51 D8
Delphi, *U.S.A.* 52 E2
Delphos, *U.S.A.* 52 E3
Delray Beach, *U.S.A.* . 53 M5
Delta, *Colo., U.S.A.* . . 57 G9
Delta, *Utah, U.S.A.* . . 56 G7
Delta Junction, *U.S.A.* . 46 B5
Deltona, *U.S.A.* 53 L5
Delungra, *Australia* . . 43 D5
Delvinë, *Albania* 17 E9

Demak, *Indonesia* 27 G14
Demanda, Sierra de la, *Spain* 15 A4
Demavand = Damāvand, *Iran* 31 C7
Dembidolo, *Ethiopia* .. 32 F1
Demer →, *Belgium* .. 11 D4
Deming, *U.S.A.* 57 K10
Demini →, *Brazil* ... 62 D6
Demirci, *Turkey* 17 E13
Demirköy, *Turkey* ... 17 D12
Demopolis, *U.S.A.* ... 53 J2
Dempo, *Indonesia* 26 E2
Den Burg, *Neths.* 11 A4
Den Haag = 's-Gravenhage, *Neths.* .. 11 B4
Den Helder, *Neths.* ... 11 B4
Den Oever, *Neths.* 11 B5
Denau, *Uzbekistan* ... 20 F7
Denbigh, *U.K.* 8 D4
Denbighshire □, *U.K.* .. 8 D4
Dendang, *Indonesia* ... 26 E3
Dendermonde, *Belgium* 11 C4
Denham, *Australia* 41 E1
Denham Ra., *Australia* . 42 C4
Denham Sd., *Australia* . 41 E1
Denholm, *Canada* 51 C7
Denia, *Spain* 15 C6
Denial B., *Australia* ... 43 E1
Deniliquin, *Australia* .. 43 F3
Denison, *Iowa, U.S.A.* . 54 E7
Denison, *Tex., U.S.A.* .. 55 J6
Denison Plains, *Australia* 40 C4
Denizli, *Turkey* 19 G4
Denman Glacier, *Antarctica* 5 C7
Denmark, *Australia* ... 41 F2
Denmark ■, *Europe* ... 7 J13
Denmark Str., *Atl. Oc.* . 4 C6
Denpasar, *Indonesia* .. 26 F5
Denton, *Mont., U.S.A.* . 56 C9
Denton, *Tex., U.S.A.* .. 55 J6
D'Entrecasteaux, Pt., *Australia* 41 F2
D'Entrecasteaux Is., *Papua N. G.* 38 B8
Denver, *U.S.A.* 54 F2
Denver City, *U.S.A.* ... 55 J3
Deoghar, *India* 29 G15
Deolali, *India* 28 K8
Deoria, *India* 29 F13
Deosai Mts., *Pakistan* . 28 B9
Depuch I., *Australia* ... 40 D2
Deputatskiy, *Russia* ... 21 C14
Dera Ghazi Khan, *Pakistan* 28 D7
Dera Ismail Khan, *Pakistan* 28 D7
Derbent, *Russia* 19 F8
Derby, *Australia* 40 C3
Derby, *U.K.* 8 E6
Derby, *U.S.A.* 55 G6
Derby City □, *U.K.* 8 E6
Derbyshire □, *U.K.* 8 D6
Derg, L., *Ireland* 10 E2
Dergaon, *India* 29 F19
Dermott, *U.S.A.* 55 J9
Derry = Londonderry, *U.K.* 10 D3
Derwent →, *Cumb., U.K.* 8 C4
Derwent →, *Derby, U.K.* 8 E6
Derwent →, *N. Yorks., U.K.* 8 D7
Derwent Water, *U.K.* .. 8 C4
Des Moines, *Iowa, U.S.A.* 54 E8
Des Moines, *N. Mex., U.S.A.* 55 G3
Des Moines →, *U.S.A.* 54 E9
Desaguadero →, *Bolivia* 62 G5
Deschaillons, *Canada* . 49 C5
Deschambault L., *Canada* 51 C8
Deschutes →, *U.S.A.* . 56 D3
Dese, *Ethiopia* 32 E2
Deseado →, *Argentina* 64 F3
Desert Center, *U.S.A.* . 57 K6
Desna →, *Ukraine* ... 13 C16
Desolación, I., *Chile* .. 64 G2
Despeñaperros, Paso, *Spain* 15 C4
Dessau, *Germany* 12 C7
Dessye = Dese, *Ethiopia* 32 E2
D'Estrees B., *Australia* . 43 F2
Detmold, *Germany* ... 12 C5
Detour, Pt., *U.S.A.* ... 52 C2
Detroit, *U.S.A.* 52 D4
Detroit Lakes, *U.S.A.* . 54 B7
Deurne, *Neths.* 11 C5
Deutsche Bucht, *Germany* 12 A5
Deva, *Romania* 13 F12
Devakottai, *India* 28 Q11
Deventer, *Neths.* 11 B6
Devils Lake, *U.S.A.* ... 54 A5
Devils Paw, *Canada* .. 50 B2
Devils Tower Junction, *U.S.A.* 54 C2
Devine, *U.S.A.* 55 L5
Devizes, *U.K.* 9 F6
Devon, *Canada* 50 C6

Devon □, *U.K.* 9 G4
Devon I., *Canada* 4 B3
Devonport, *Australia* .. 42 G4
Devonport, *N.Z.* 39 G5
Dewas, *India* 28 H10
Dexter, *Maine, U.S.A.* . 53 C11
Dexter, *Mo., U.S.A.* ... 55 G10
Dexter, *N. Mex., U.S.A.* 55 J2
Dey-Dey, L., *Australia* . 41 E5
Deyhūk, *Iran* 31 C8
Deyyer, *Iran* 31 E6
Dezadeash L., *Canada* . 50 A1
Dezfūl, *Iran* 31 C6
Dezhneva, Mys, *Russia* 21 C19
Dhahiriya = Aẓ Ẓāhiriyah, *West Bank* 33 D3
Dhahran = Aẓ Ẓahrān, *Si. Arabia* 31 E6
Dhaka, *Bangla.* 29 H17
Dhaka □, *Bangla.* 29 G17
Dhamtari, *India* 29 J12
Dhanbad, *India* 29 H15
Dhangarhi, *Nepal* 29 E12
Dhankuta, *Nepal* 29 F15
Dhar, *India* 28 H9
Dharmapuri, *India* ... 28 N11
Dharwad, *India* 28 M9
Dhaulagiri, *Nepal* 29 E9
Dhenkanal, *India* 29 J14
Dhībān, *Jordan* 33 D4
Dhíkti Óros, *Greece* .. 17 G11
Dhírfis = Dhírfis Óros, *Greece* 17 E10
Dhírfis Óros, *Greece* .. 17 E10
Dhodhekánisos, *Greece* 17 F12
Dhrol, *India* 28 H7
Dhuburi, *India* 29 F16
Dhule, *India* 28 J9
Diafarabé, *Mali* 34 F5
Diamantina, *Brazil* ... 63 G10
Diamantina →, *Australia* 43 D2
Diamantino, *Brazil* ... 63 F7
Diamond Harbour, *India* 29 H16
Diamond Is., *Australia* . 42 B5
Diamond Mts., *U.S.A.* . 56 G6
Dibā, *Oman* 31 E8
Dibaya-Lubue, *Dem. Rep. of the Congo* 36 E3
Dibrugarh, *India* 29 F19
Dickens, *U.S.A.* 55 J4
Dickinson, *U.S.A.* 54 B3
Dickson = Dikson, *Russia* 20 B9
Dickson, *U.S.A.* 53 G2
Didiéni, *Mali* 34 F4
Didsbury, *Canada* ... 50 C6
Diefenbaker, L., *Canada* 51 C7
Diego de Almagro, *Chile* 64 B2
Diego Garcia, *Ind. Oc.* . 3 E13
Diekirch, *Lux.* 11 E6
Dieppe, *France* 14 B4
Dierks, *U.S.A.* 55 H8
Diest, *Belgium* 11 D5
Dif, *Somali Rep.* 32 G3
Differdange, *Lux.* 11 E5
Digby, *Canada* 49 D6
Dighinala, *Bangla.* ... 29 H18
Dighton, *U.S.A.* 54 F4
Digne-les-Bains, *France* 14 D7
Digos, *Phil.* 27 C7
Digranes, *Iceland* 6 C6
Digul →, *Indonesia* .. 27 F9
Dihang →, *India* 29 F19
Dijlah, Nahr →, *Asia* . 30 D5
Dijon, *France* 14 C6
Dikhil, *Djibouti* 32 E3
Dikkil = Dikhil, *Djibouti* 32 E3
Diksmuide, *Belgium* .. 11 C2
Dikson, *Russia* 20 B9
Dila, *Ethiopia* 32 F2
Dili, *Indonesia* 27 F7
Dilley, *U.S.A.* 55 L5
Dillingham, *U.S.A.* ... 46 C4
Dillon, *Canada* 51 B7
Dillon, *Mont., U.S.A.* .. 56 D7
Dillon, *S.C., U.S.A.* ... 53 H6
Dillon →, *Canada* ... 51 B7
Dilolo, *Dem. Rep. of the Congo* 36 G4
Dimas, *Mexico* 58 C3
Dimashq, *Syria* 33 B5
Dimashq □, *Syria* ... 33 B5
Dimboola, *Australia* .. 43 F3
Dîmbovița →, *Romania* 13 F14
Dimbulah, *Australia* .. 42 B4
Dimitrovgrad, *Bulgaria* 17 C11
Dimitrovgrad, *Russia* . 18 D8
Dimitrovo = Pernik, *Bulgaria* 17 C10
Dimmitt, *U.S.A.* 55 H3
Dimona, *Israel* 33 D4
Dinagat, *Phil.* 27 B7
Dinajpur, *Bangla.* ... 29 G16
Dinan, *France* 14 B2
Dīnān Āb, *Iran* 31 C8
Dinant, *Belgium* 11 D4
Dīnār, Kūh-e, *Iran* ... 31 D6
Dinara Planina, *Croatia* 16 C7
Dinard, *France* 14 B2
Dinaric Alps = Dinara Planina, *Croatia* ... 16 C7

Dindigul, *India* 28 P11
Dingle, *Ireland* 10 E1
Dingo, *Australia* 42 C4
Dingwall, *U.K.* 10 C4
Dinh, Mui, *Vietnam* .. 26 B3
Dinorwic, *Canada* ... 51 D10
Dinosaur National Monument, *U.S.A.* .. 56 F9
Dinosaur Prov. Park, *Canada* 50 C6
Dinuba, *U.S.A.* 57 H4
Dipolog, *Phil.* 27 C6
Dir, *Pakistan* 28 B7
Dire Dawa, *Ethiopia* .. 32 F3
Diriamba, *Nic.* 60 D2
Dirk Hartog I., *Australia* 41 E1
Dirranbandi, *Australia* . 43 D4
Disa, *India* 28 G8
Disappointment, C., *U.S.A.* 56 C2
Disappointment, L., *Australia* 40 D3
Disaster B., *Australia* .. 43 F4
Discovery B., *Australia* 43 F3
Disko = Qeqertarsuaq, *Greenland* 4 C5
Disko Bugt, *Greenland* . 4 C5
Disteghil Sar, *Pakistan* . 28 A9
Distrito Federal □, *Brazil* 63 G9
Distrito Federal □, *Mexico* 59 D5
Diu, *India* 28 J7
Divándarreh, *Iran* 30 C5
Divide, *U.S.A.* 56 D7
Dividing Ra., *Australia* . 41 E2
Divinópolis, *Brazil* ... 63 H10
Divnoye, *Russia* 19 E7
Divo, *Ivory C.* 34 G4
Dixon, *U.S.A.* 54 E10
Dixon Entrance, *U.S.A.* 46 C6
Diyālā →, *Iraq* 30 C5
Diyarbakır, *Turkey* ... 19 G7
Djakarta = Jakarta, *Indonesia* 27 G12
Djambala, *Congo* 36 E2
Djanet, *Algeria* 34 D7
Djawa = Jawa, *Indonesia* 27 G14
Djelfa, *Algeria* 34 B6
Djerba, I. de, *Tunisia* .. 35 B8
Djerid, Chott, *Tunisia* . 34 B7
Djibouti, *Djibouti* 32 E3
Djibouti ■, *Africa* 32 E3
Djolu, *Dem. Rep. of the Congo* 36 D4
Djoum, *Cameroon* ... 36 D2
Djourab, Erg du, *Chad* . 35 E9
Djugu, *Dem. Rep. of the Congo* 36 D4
Djúpivogur, *Iceland* .. 6 D6
Dmitriya Lapteva, Proliv, *Russia* 21 B15
Dnepr →= Dnipro →, *Ukraine* 19 E5
Dneprodzerzhinsk = Dniprodzerzhynsk, *Ukraine* 19 E5
Dnepropetrovsk = Dnipropetrovsk, *Ukraine* 19 E6
Dnestr →= Dnister →, *Europe* 13 E16
Dnestrovski = Belgorod, *Russia* 19 D6
Dnieper = Dnipro →, *Ukraine* 19 E5
Dniester = Dnister →, *Europe* 13 E16
Dnipro →, *Ukraine* .. 19 E5
Dniprodzerzhynsk, *Ukraine* 19 E5
Dnipropetrovsk, *Ukraine* 19 E6
Dnister →, *Europe* .. 13 E16
Dnistrovskyy Lyman, *Ukraine* 13 E16
Dno, *Russia* 18 C4
Dnyapro = Dnipro →, *Ukraine* 19 E5
Doaktown, *Canada* .. 49 C6
Doba, *Chad* 35 G9
Dobbyn, *Australia* ... 42 B3
Dobele, *Latvia* 7 H20
Doberai, Jazirah, *Indonesia* 27 E8
Dobo, *Indonesia* 27 F8
Doboj, *Bos.-H.* 17 B8
Dobreta-Turnu Severin, *Romania* 13 F12
Dobrich, *Bulgaria* 13 F14
Dobruja, *Europe* 13 F15
Dobrush, *Belarus* 13 B16
Docker River, *Australia* 41 D4
Doctor Arroyo, *Mexico* 58 C4
Doda, L., *Canada* 48 C4
Dodecanese = Dhodhekánisos, *Greece* 17 F12
Dodge City, *U.S.A.* ... 55 G5
Dodge L., *Canada* ... 51 B7
Dodgeville, *U.S.A.* ... 54 D9
Dodoma, *Tanzania* .. 36 F7
Dodsland, *Canada* ... 51 C7
Dodson, *U.S.A.* 56 B9
Doesburg, *Neths.* 11 B6
Doetinchem, *Neths.* .. 11 C6
Dog Creek, *Canada* .. 50 C4

Dog L., *Man., Canada* . 51 C9
Dog L., *Ont., Canada* . 48 C2
Doğubayazıt, *Turkey* .. 30 B5
Doha = Ad Dawḥah, *Qatar* 31 E6
Dohazari, *Bangla.* 29 H18
Doi, *Indonesia* 27 D7
Dois Irmãos, Sa., *Brazil* 63 E10
Dokkum, *Neths.* 11 A5
Dolak, Pulau, *Indonesia* 27 F9
Dolbeau, *Canada* 49 C5
Dole, *France* 14 C6
Dolgellau, *U.K.* 8 E4
Dolgelley = Dolgellau, *U.K.* 8 E4
Dollard, *Neths.* 11 A7
Dolo, *Ethiopia* 32 G3
Dolomites = Dolomiti, *Italy* 16 A4
Dolomiti, *Italy* 16 A4
Dolores, *Argentina* ... 64 D5
Dolores, *U.S.A.* 57 H9
Dolphin, C., *Falk. Is.* .. 64 G5
Dolphin and Union Str., *Canada* 46 B8
Dombarovskiy, *Russia* . 20 D6
Dombås, *Norway* 7 E13
Domel I. = Letsôk-aw Kyun, *Burma* 26 B1
Dominica ■, *W. Indies* 61 C7
Dominica Passage, *W. Indies* 61 C7
Dominican Rep. ■, *W. Indies* 61 C5
Domodóssola, *Italy* .. 14 C8
Domville, Mt., *Australia* 43 D5
Don →, *Russia* 19 E6
Don →, *Aberds., U.K.* 10 C5
Don →, *S. Yorks., U.K.* 8 D7
Don, C., *Australia* 40 B5
Don Benito, *Spain* ... 15 C3
Donald, *Australia* 43 F3
Donaldsonville, *U.S.A.* 55 K9
Donalsonville, *U.S.A.* . 53 K3
Donau = Dunărea →, *Europe* 13 F15
Donau →, *Austria* ... 11 D3
Donauwörth, *Germany* 12 D6
Doncaster, *U.K.* 8 D6
Dondo, Teluk, *Indonesia* 27 D6
Dondra Head, *Sri Lanka* 28 S12
Donegal, *Ireland* 10 D2
Donets →, *Russia* ... 19 E7
Donetsk, *Ukraine* 19 E6
Dong Hoi, *Vietnam* .. 26 A3
Dongara, *Australia* ... 41 E1
Dongbei, *China* 25 B7
Dongchuan, *China* ... 24 D5
Donggala, *Indonesia* . 27 E5
Dongola, *Sudan* 35 E12
Dongting Hu, *China* .. 25 D6
Donington, C., *Australia* 43 E2
Doniphan, *U.S.A.* ... 55 G9
Dønna, *Norway* 6 C15
Donna, *U.S.A.* 55 M5
Donnaconna, *Canada* . 49 C5
Donnelly's Crossing, *N.Z.* 39 F4
Donnybrook, *Australia* 41 F2
Donostia = Donostia-San Sebastián, *Spain* 15 A5
Donostia-San Sebastián, *Spain* 15 A5
Dora, L., *Australia* 40 D3
Dora Báltea →, *Italy* . 14 B8
Doran L., *Canada* 51 A7
Dorchester, *U.K.* 9 G5
Dorchester, C., *Canada* 47 B12
Dordogne →, *France* 14 D3
Dordrecht, *Neths.* ... 11 C4
Doré, L., *Canada* 51 B7
Doré Lake, *Canada* .. 51 C7
Dori, *Burkina Faso* ... 34 F5
Dornbirn, *Austria* 12 E5
Dorohoi, *Romania* ... 13 E14
Döröö Nuur, *Mongolia* 24 B4
Dorr, *Iran* 31 C6
Dorre I., *Australia* 41 E1
Dorrigo, *Australia* ... 43 E5
Dorris, *U.S.A.* 56 F3
Dorset □, *U.K.* 9 G5
Dortmund, *Germany* . 12 C4
Dorūneh, *Iran* 31 C8
Dos Bahías, C., *Argentina* 64 E3
Dos Hermanas, *Spain* . 15 D3
Dosso, *Niger* 34 F6
Dothan, *U.S.A.* 53 K3
Douai, *France* 14 A5
Douala, *Cameroon* ... 36 D1
Douarnenez, *France* .. 14 B1
Double Island Pt., *Australia* 43 D5
Double Mountain Fork →, *U.S.A.* .. 55 J4
Doubs →, *France* ... 14 C6
Doubtful, Sd., *N.Z.* ... 39 L1
Doubtless B., *N.Z.* ... 39 F4
Douglas, *U.K.* 8 C3
Douglas, *Ariz., U.S.A.* . 57 L9
Douglas, *Wyo., U.S.A.* 56 D2
Douglas Chan., *Canada* 50 C3
Douglasville, *U.S.A.* .. 53 J3

Dourada, Serra, *Brazil* . 63 F9
Dourados, *Brazil* 63 H8
Douro →, *Europe* ... 15 B1
Dove →, *U.K.* 8 E6
Dove Creek, *U.S.A.* .. 57 H9
Dover, *Australia* 42 G4
Dover, *U.K.* 9 F9
Dover, *Del., U.S.A.* ... 52 F8
Dover, *N.H., U.S.A.* .. 52 D10
Dover, *Ohio, U.S.A.* .. 52 E5
Dover, Pt., *Australia* .. 41 F4
Dover, Str. of, *Europe* . 9 G9
Dover-Foxcroft, *U.S.A.* 53 C11
Dovey = Dyfi →, *U.K.* 9 E3
Dovrefjell, *Norway* ... 7 E13
Dow Rūd, *Iran* 31 C6
Dowagiac, *U.S.A.* 52 E2
Dowerin, *Australia* ... 41 F2
Dowgha'i, *Iran* 31 B8
Dowlatābād, *Iran* 31 D8
Downey, *U.S.A.* 56 E7
Downham Market, *U.K.* 9 E8
Downieville, *U.S.A.* ... 56 G3
Downpatrick Hd., *Ireland* 10 D2
Downton, Mt., *Canada* 50 C4
Dowsārī, *Iran* 31 D8
Dozois, Rés., *Canada* . 48 C4
Drachten, *Neths.* 11 A6
Drăgăşani, *Romania* .. 13 F13
Dragichyn, *Belarus* ... 13 B13
Dragoman, Prokhod, *Bulgaria* 17 C10
Draguignan, *France* .. 14 E7
Drain, *U.S.A.* 56 E2
Drake, *U.S.A.* 54 B4
Drake Passage, *S. Ocean* 5 B17
Drakensberg, *S. Africa* 37 L5
Dráma, *Greece* 17 D11
Drammen, *Norway* ... 7 G14
Drangajökull, *Iceland* . 6 C2
Drau = Drava →, *Croatia* 17 B8
Drava →, *Croatia* ... 17 B8
Drayton Valley, *Canada* 50 C6
Drenthe □, *Neths.* .. 11 B6
Dresden, *Germany* .. 12 C7
Dreux, *France* 14 B4
Driffield, *U.K.* 8 C7
Driggs, *U.S.A.* 56 E8
Drin →, *Albania* 17 C8
Drina →, *Bos.-H.* ... 17 B8
Drini = Drin →, *Albania* 17 C8
Drøbak, *Norway* 7 G14
Drochia, *Moldova* ... 13 D14
Drogheda, *Ireland* ... 10 E3
Drogichin = Dragichyn, *Belarus* 13 B13
Drogobych = Drohobych, *Ukraine* 13 D12
Drohobych, *Ukraine* .. 13 D12
Droichead Atha = Drogheda, *Ireland* .. 10 E3
Droitwich, *U.K.* 9 E5
Dromedary, C., *Australia* 43 F5
Dronfield, *U.K.* 8 D6
Dronten, *Neths.* 11 B5
Drumheller, *Canada* .. 50 C6
Drummond, *U.S.A.* .. 56 C7
Drummond I., *U.S.A.* . 52 C4
Drummond Pt., *Australia* 43 E2
Drummond Ra., *Australia* 42 C4
Drummondville, *Canada* 48 C5
Drumright, *U.S.A.* ... 55 H6
Druskininkai, *Lithuania* 7 J20
Drut →, *Belarus* 13 B16
Druzhina, *Russia* 21 C15
Dry Tortugas, *U.S.A.* . 60 B3
Dryden, *Canada* 51 D10
Drygalski I., *Antarctica* . 5 C7
Drysdale →, *Australia* 40 B4
Drysdale I., *Australia* .. 42 A2
Du Bois, *U.S.A.* 52 E6
Du Gué →, *Canada* . 48 A5
Du Quoin, *U.S.A.* ... 54 G10
Duaringa, *Australia* .. 42 C4
Quḅā, *Si. Arabia* 30 E3
Dubai = Dubayy, *U.A.E.* 31 E7
Dubāsari, *Moldova* ... 13 E15
Dubāsari Vdkhr., *Moldova* 13 E15
Dubawnt →, *Canada* . 51 A8
Dubawnt, L., *Canada* . 51 A8
Dubayy, *U.A.E.* 31 E7
Dubbo, *Australia* 43 E4
Dublin, *Ireland* 10 E3
Dublin, *Ga., U.S.A.* .. 53 J4
Dublin, *Tex., U.S.A.* .. 55 J5
Dublin □, *Ireland* 10 E3
Dubno, *Ukraine* 13 C13
Dubois, *U.S.A.* 56 D7
Dubossary = Dubāsari, *Moldova* 13 E15
Dubossary Vdkhr. = Dubāsari Vdkhr., *Moldova* 13 E15
Dubréka, *Guinea* 34 G3
Dubrovitsa = Dubrovytsya, *Ukraine* 13 C14
Dubrovnik, *Croatia* ... 17 C8
Dubrovytsya, *Ukraine* . 13 C14
Dubuque, *U.S.A.* 54 D9

Duchess, *Australia* ... 42 C2
Ducie I., *Pac. Oc.* 45 K15
Duck →, *U.S.A.* 53 G2
Duck Cr. →, *Australia* 40 D2
Duck Lake, *Canada* .. 51 C7
Duck Mountain Prov. Park, *Canada* 51 C8
Dudhi, *India* 29 G13
Dudinka, *Russia* 21 C9
Dudley, *U.K.* 9 E5
Duero = Douro →, *Europe* 15 B1
Dūghī Kalā, *Afghan.* .. 28 C3
Dugi Otok, *Croatia* ... 12 G8
Duifken Pt., *Australia* . 42 A3
Duisburg, *Germany* .. 12 C4
Dūkdamīn, *Iran* 31 C8
Dukelský Průsmyk, *Slovak Rep.* 13 D11
Dukhān, *Qatar* 31 E6
Duki, *Pakistan* 28 D6
Duku, *Nigeria* 35 F8
Dulce, *U.S.A.* 57 H10
Dulce →, *Argentina* . 64 C4
Dulce, G., *Costa Rica* . 60 E3
Dulf, *Iraq* 30 C5
Dulit, Banjaran, *Malaysia* 26 D4
Dulq Maghār, *Syria* .. 30 B3
Duluth, *U.S.A.* 54 B8
Dum Duma, *India* ... 29 F19
Dūmā, *Syria* 33 B5
Dumaguete, *Phil.* 27 C6
Dumai, *Indonesia* ... 26 D2
Dumaran, *Phil.* 27 B5
Dumas, *Ark., U.S.A.* .. 55 J9
Dumas, *Tex., U.S.A.* .. 55 H4
Qumayr, *Syria* 33 B5
Dumbleyung, *Australia* 41 F2
Dumfries, *U.K.* 10 D5
Dumoine →, *Canada* . 48 C4
Dumoine, L., *Canada* . 48 C4
Dumyât, *Egypt* 35 B12
Dún Dealgan = Dundalk, *Ireland* ... 10 E3
Dun Laoghaire, *Ireland* 10 E3
Duna = Dunărea →, *Europe* 13 F15
Dunaj = Dunărea →, *Europe* 13 F15
Dunakeszi, *Hungary* .. 13 E10
Dunărea →, *Europe* . 13 F15
Dunaújváros, *Hungary* 13 E10
Dunav = Dunărea →, *Europe* 13 F15
Dunay, *Russia* 22 C6
Dunback, *N.Z.* 39 L3
Dunbar, *U.K.* 10 C5
Duncan, *Canada* 50 D4
Duncan, *Ariz., U.S.A.* . 57 K9
Duncan, *Okla., U.S.A.* . 55 H6
Duncan, L., *Canada* .. 48 B4
Duncan L., *Canada* .. 50 A6
Duncan Town, *Bahamas* 60 B4
Dundalk, *Ireland* 10 E3
Dundalk, *U.S.A.* 52 F7
Dundas, L., *Canada* .. 48 D5
Dundas, L., *Australia* . 41 F3
Dundas I., *Canada* ... 50 C2
Dundas Str., *Australia* . 40 B5
Dundee, *U.K.* 10 C5
Dunedin, *N.Z.* 39 L3
Dunedin, *U.S.A.* 53 L4
Dunedoo, *Australia* .. 43 E4
Dunfermline, *U.K.* ... 10 C5
Dungarvan, *Ireland* .. 10 E3
Dungeness, *U.K.* 9 G8
Dungog, *Australia* ... 43 E5
Dungu, *Dem. Rep. of the Congo* 36 D5
Dunhua, *China* 25 C15
Dunhuang, *China* 24 B4
Dunk I., *Australia* 42 B4
Dunkeld, *Australia* ... 43 E4
Dunkerque, *France* .. 14 A5
Dunkery Beacon, *U.K.* 9 F4
Dunkirk = Dunkerque, *France* 14 A5
Dunkirk, *U.S.A.* 52 D6
Dúnlary = Dun Laoghaire, *Ireland* . 10 E3
Dunmara, *Australia* .. 42 B1
Dunmore, *U.S.A.* 52 E8
Dunmore Town, *Bahamas* 60 A4
Dunnellon, *U.S.A.* ... 53 L4
Dunning, *U.S.A.* 54 E4
Dunolly, *Australia* ... 43 F3
Dunphy, *U.S.A.* 56 F5
Dunseith, *U.S.A.* 54 A4
Dunsmuir, *U.S.A.* ... 56 F2
Dunstable, *U.K.* 9 F7
Dunstan Mts., *N.Z.* .. 39 L2
Dunster, *Canada* 50 C5
Dunvegan L., *Canada* . 51 A7
Dupree, *U.S.A.* 54 C4
Dupuyer, *U.S.A.* 56 B7
Durack →, *Australia* . 40 C4
Durack Ra., *Australia* . 40 C4
Durance →, *France* .. 14 E6
Durand, *U.S.A.* 54 C9
Durango, *Mexico* 58 C4
Durango, *U.S.A.* 57 H10
Durango □, *Mexico* .. 58 C4
Durant, *Miss., U.S.A.* . 55 J10
Durant, *Okla., U.S.A.* . 55 J6

Durazno, *Uruguay* 64 C5
Durazzo = Durrës,
  Albania 17 D8
Durban, *S. Africa* ... 37 K6
Durbuy, *Belgium* ... 11 D5
Düren, *Germany* 12 C4
Durg, *India* 29 J12
Durgapur, *India* 29 H15
Durham, *Canada* 48 D3
Durham, *U.K.* 8 C6
Durham, *U.S.A.* 53 H6
Durham □, *U.K.* 8 C6
Durmā, *Si. Arabia* ... 30 E5
Durmitor,
  Montenegro, Yug. .. 17 C8
Durrës, *Albania* 17 D8
Durrësi = Durrës,
  Albania 17 D8
Dursunbey, *Turkey* .. 17 E13
Durūz, Jabal ad, *Jordan* 33 C5
D'Urville, Tanjung,
  Indonesia 27 E9
D'Urville I., *N.Z.* ... 39 J4
Dushak, *Turkmenistan* . 20 F7
Dushanbe, *Tajikistan* .. 20 F7
Dusky Sd., *N.Z.* 39 L1
Dussejour, C., *Australia* 40 B4
Düsseldorf, *Germany* .. 12 C4
Dutch Harbor, *U.S.A.* .. 46 C3
Dutton →, *Australia* .. 42 C3
Duwayhin, Khawr,
  U.A.E. 31 E6
Duyun, *China* 24 D7
Duzdab = Zāhedān, *Iran* 31 D9
Dvina, Severnaya →,
  Russia 18 B7
Dvinsk = Daugavpils,
  Latvia 7 J22
Dvinskaya Guba, *Russia* 18 B6
Dwarka, *India* 28 H6
Dwellingup, *Australia* . 41 F2
Dwight, *U.S.A.* 52 E1
Dyatlovo = Dzyatlava,
  Belarus 13 B13
Dyer, C., *Canada* 47 B13
Dyer Plateau, *Antarctica* 5 D17
Dyersburg, *U.S.A.* 55 G10
Dyfi →, *U.K.* 9 E3
Dymer, *Ukraine* 13 C16
Dysart, *Australia* 42 C4
Dzamin Üüd = Borhoyn
  Tal, *Mongolia* 25 B6
Dzerzhinsk, *Russia* ... 18 C7
Dzhalinda, *Russia* ... 21 D13
Dzhambul = Zhambyl,
  Kazakstan 20 E8
Dzhankoy, *Ukraine* ... 19 E5
Dzhezkazgan =
  Zhezqazghan,
  Kazakstan 20 E7
Dzhizak = Jizzakh,
  Uzbekistan 20 E7
Dzhugdzur, Khrebet,
  Russia 21 D14
Dzhungarskiye Vorota =
  Dzungarian Gates,
  Asia 24 B3
Działdowo, *Poland* 13 B11
Dzibilchaltun, *Mexico* . 59 C7
Dzierżoniów, *Poland* .. 13 C9
Dzilam de Bravo,
  Mexico 59 C7
Dzungaria = Junggar
  Pendi, *China* 24 B3
Dzungarian Gates, *Asia* 24 B3
Dzuumod, *Mongolia* ... 24 B5
Dzyarzhynsk, *Belarus* . 13 B14
Dzyatlava, *Belarus* ... 13 B13

Eabamet L., *Canada* ... 48 B2
Eads, *U.S.A.* 54 F3
Eagar, *U.S.A.* 57 J9
Eagle, *Alaska, U.S.A.* . 46 B5
Eagle, *Colo., U.S.A.* .. 56 G10
Eagle →, *Canada* ... 49 B8
Eagle Butte, *U.S.A.* ... 54 C4
Eagle Grove, *U.S.A.* .. 54 D8
Eagle L., *Canada* 51 D10
Eagle L., *Calif., U.S.A.* 56 F3
Eagle L., *Maine, U.S.A.* 53 B11
Eagle Lake, *Maine,*
  U.S.A. 53 B11
Eagle Lake, *Tex., U.S.A.* 55 L6
Eagle Nest, *U.S.A.* ... 57 H11
Eagle Pass, *U.S.A.* ... 55 L4
Eagle Pt., *Australia* ... 40 C3
Eagle River, *Mich.,*
  U.S.A. 52 B1
Eagle River, *Wis., U.S.A.* 54 C10
Eaglehawk, *Australia* . 43 F3
Ealing □, *U.K.* 9 F7
Ear Falls, *Canada* 51 C10
Earle, *U.S.A.* 55 H9
Earlimart, *U.S.A.* 57 J4
Earnslaw, Mt., *N.Z.* .. 39 L2
Earth, *U.S.A.* 55 H3
Easley, *U.S.A.* 53 H4
East Anglia, *U.K.* 8 E9
East Angus, *Canada* .. 49 C5
East Bengal, *Bangla.* . 29 H17
East Beskids =
  Vychodné Beskydy,
  Europe 13 D11
East C., *N.Z.* 39 G7

East Chicago, *U.S.A.* .. 52 E2
East China Sea, *Asia* . 25 D7
East Coulee, *Canada* .. 50 C6
East Dereham, *U.K.* ... 9 E8
East Falkland, *Falk. Is.* 64 G5
East Grand Forks, *U.S.A.* 54 B6
East Grinstead, *U.K.* .. 9 F8
East Helena, *U.S.A.* ... 56 C8
East Kilbride, *U.K.* ... 10 D4
East Lansing, *U.S.A.* .. 52 D3
East Liverpool, *U.S.A.* . 52 E5
East London, *S. Africa* . 37 L5
East Main = Eastmain,
  Canada 48 B4
East Orange, *U.S.A.* ... 52 E8
East Pacific Ridge,
  Pac. Oc. 45 J17
East Pine, *Canada* 50 B4
East Point, *U.S.A.* 53 J3
East Pt., *Canada* 49 C7
East Retford = Retford,
  U.K. 8 D7
East Riding of
  Yorkshire □, *U.K.* .. 8 D7
East St. Louis, *U.S.A.* . 54 F9
East Schelde =
  Oosterschelde →,
  Neths. 11 C4
East Siberian Sea,
  Russia 21 B17
East Stroudsburg,
  U.S.A. 52 E8
East Sussex □, *U.K.* .. 9 G8
East Tawas, *U.S.A.* ... 52 C4
East Timor
  Indonesia . 27 F7
East Toorale, *Australia* 43 E4
Eastbourne, *N.Z.* 39 J5
Eastbourne, *U.K.* 9 G8
Eastend, *Canada* 51 D7
Easter I. = Pascua, I. de,
  Pac. Oc. 45 K17
Eastern Cr. →,
  Australia 42 C3
Eastern Ghats, *India* .. 28 N11
Eastern Group = Lau
  Group, *Fiji* 39 C9
Eastern Group, *Australia* 41 F3
Easterville, *Canada* ... 51 C9
Eastland, *U.S.A.* 55 J5
Eastleigh, *U.K.* 9 G6
Eastmain, *Canada* 48 B4
Eastmain →, *Canada* . 48 B4
Eastman, *U.S.A.* 53 J4
Easton, *Md., U.S.A.* .. 52 F7
Easton, *Pa., U.S.A.* ... 52 E8
Eastport, *U.S.A.* 53 C12
Eaton, *U.S.A.* 54 E2
Eatonia, *Canada* 51 C7
Eatonton, *U.S.A.* 53 J4
Eau Claire, *U.S.A.* 54 C9
Eau Claire, L. à l',
  Canada 48 A5
Ebbw Vale, *U.K.* 9 F4
Ebeltoft, *Denmark* ... 7 H14
Eberswalde-Finow,
  Germany 12 B7
Ebetsu, *Japan* 22 C10
Ebolowa, *Cameroon* .. 36 D2
Ebro →, *Spain* 15 B6
Eceabat, *Turkey* 17 D12
Ech Cheliff, *Algeria* ... 34 A6
Echigo-Sammyaku,
  Japan 23 F9
Echizen-Misaki, *Japan* . 23 G7
Echo Bay, *N.W.T.,*
  Canada 46 B8
Echo Bay, *Ont., Canada* 48 C3
Echoing →, *Canada* .. 48 B1
Echternach, *Lux.* 11 E6
Echuca, *Australia* 43 F3
Ecija, *Spain* 15 D3
Eclipse Is., *Australia* .. 40 B4
Eclipse Sd., *Canada* .. 47 A11
Ecuador ■, *S. Amer.* . 62 D3
Ed Damazin, *Sudan* ... 35 F12
Ed Debba, *Sudan* 35 E12
Ed Dueim, *Sudan* 35 F12
Edam, *Canada* 51 C7
Edam, *Neths.* 11 B5
Eddystone Pt., *Australia* 42 G4
Ede, *Neths.* 11 B5
Edehon L., *Canada* ... 51 A9
Eden, *Australia* 43 F4
Eden, *N.C., U.S.A.* ... 53 G6
Eden, *Tex., U.S.A.* ... 55 K5
Eden →, *U.K.* 8 C4
Edenhope, *Australia* .. 43 F3
Edenton, *U.S.A.* 53 G7
Eder →, *Germany* ... 12 C5
Edgar, *U.S.A.* 54 E6
Edge Hill, *U.K.* 9 E6
Edgefield, *U.S.A.* 53 J5
Edgeley, *U.S.A.* 54 B5
Edgemont, *U.S.A.* 54 D3
Edgeøya, *Svalbard* ... 4 B9
Édhessa, *Greece* 17 D10
Edievale, *N.Z.* 39 L2
Edina, *U.S.A.* 54 E8
Edinburg, *U.S.A.* 55 M5
Edinburgh, *U.K.* 10 D5
Edineț, *Moldova* 13 D14
Edirne, *Turkey* 17 D12
Edithburgh, *Australia* . 43 F2
Edmond, *U.S.A.* 55 H6

Edmonds, *U.S.A.* 56 C2
Edmonton, *Australia* .. 42 B4
Edmonton, *Canada* ... 50 C6
Edmund L., *Canada* .. 48 B1
Edmundston, *Canada* . 49 C6
Edna, *U.S.A.* 55 L6
Edremit, *Turkey* 17 E12
Edremit Körfezi, *Turkey* 17 E12
Edson, *Canada* 50 C5
Edward →, *Australia* . 43 F3
Edward, L., *Africa* 36 E5
Edward River, *Australia* 42 A3
Edward VII Land,
  Antarctica 5 E13
Edwards Plateau, *U.S.A.* 55 K4
Edzo, *Canada* 50 A5
Eeklo, *Belgium* 11 C3
Effingham, *U.S.A.* 52 F1
Égadi, Ísole, *Italy* ... 16 F5
Egan Range, *U.S.A.* .. 56 G6
Eganville, *Canada* 48 C4
Eger = Cheb,
  Czech Rep. 12 C7
Eger, *Hungary* 13 E11
Egersund, *Norway* ... 7 G12
Egg L., *Canada* 51 B7
Éghezée, *Belgium* 11 D4
Egmont, *Canada* 50 D4
Egmont, C., *N.Z.* 39 H4
Egmont, Mt. = Taranaki,
  Mt., *N.Z.* 39 H5
Eğridir, *Turkey* 19 G5
Eğridir Gölü, *Turkey* .. 19 G5
Egvekinot, *Russia* 21 C19
Egypt ■, *Africa* 35 C12
Ehime □, *Japan* 23 H6
Eibar, *Spain* 15 A4
Eidsvold, *Australia* ... 43 D5
Eidsvoll, *Norway* 7 F14
Eifel, *Germany* 12 C4
Eigg, *U.K.* 10 C3
Eighty Mile Beach,
  Australia 40 C3
Eil, *Somali Rep.* 32 F4
Eildon, *Australia* 43 F4
Eildon, L., *Australia* .. 43 F4
Einasleigh, *Australia* .. 42 B3
Einasleigh →, *Australia* 42 B3
Eindhoven, *Neths.* ... 11 C5
Eire = Ireland ■, *Europe* 10 E2
Eiríksjökull, *Iceland* .. 6 D3
Eirunepé, *Brazil* 62 E5
Eisenach, *Germany* ... 12 C6
Eisenerz, *Austria* 12 E8
Eivissa, *Spain* 15 C6
Ejutla, *Mexico* 59 D5
Ekalaka, *U.S.A.* 54 C2
Eketahuna, *N.Z.* 39 J5
Ekibastuz, *Kazakstan* . 20 D8
Eksjö, *Sweden* 7 H16
Ekwan →, *Canada* ... 48 B3
Ekwan Pt., *Canada* ... 48 B3
El 'Agrûd, *Egypt* 33 E3
El Aaiún, *W. Sahara* . 34 C3
El Alamein, *Egypt* ... 35 B11
El 'Aqaba, W. →,
  Egypt 33 E2
El Arīḥā, *West Bank* .. 33 D4
El 'Arîsh, *Egypt* 33 D2
El 'Arîsh, W. →, *Egypt* 33 D2
El Asnam = Ech Cheliff,
  Algeria 34 A6
El Bayadh, *Algeria* ... 34 B6
El Bluff, *Nic.* 60 D3
El Brûk, W. →, *Egypt* . 33 E2
El Cajon, *U.S.A.* 57 N10
El Campo, *U.S.A.* 55 L6
El Centro, *U.S.A.* 57 K6
El Cerro, *Bolivia* 62 G6
El Cuy, *Argentina* 64 D3
El Cuyo, *Mexico* 59 C7
El Daheir, *Egypt* 33 D3
El Dátil, *Mexico* 58 B2
El Dere, *Somali Rep.* . 32 G4
El Desemboque, *Mexico* 58 A2
El Diviso, *Colombia* .. 62 C3
El Djouf, *Mauritania* .. 34 D4
El Dorado, *Ark., U.S.A.* 55 J8
El Dorado, *Kans., U.S.A.* 55 G6
El Dorado, *Venezuela* . 62 B6
El Escorial, *Spain* 15 B3
El Faiyûm, *Egypt* 35 C12
El Fâsher, *Sudan* 35 F11
El Ferrol = Ferrol, *Spain* 15 A1
El Fuerte, *Mexico* 58 B3
El Gal, *Somali Rep.* .. 32 E5
El Geneina = Al
  Junaynah, *Sudan* ... 35 F10
El Gîza, *Egypt* 35 C12
El Goléa, *Algeria* 34 B6
El Iskandarîya, *Egypt* . 35 B11
El Istiwa'iya, *Sudan* .. 35 G11
El Jadida, *Morocco* ... 34 B4
El Jardal, *Honduras* .. 60 D2
El Kabrît, G., *Egypt* .. 33 F2
El Khârga, *Egypt* 35 C12
El Khartûm, *Sudan* ... 35 E12
El Kuntilla, *Egypt* 33 E3
El Maestrazgo, *Spain* . 15 B5
El Mahalla el Kubra,
  Egypt 35 B12
El Mansûra, *Egypt* ... 35 B12
El Minyâ, *Egypt* 35 C12
El Obeid, *Sudan* 35 F12
El Odaiya, *Sudan* 35 F11

El Oro, *Mexico* 59 D4
El Oued, *Algeria* 34 B7
El Palmito, Presa,
  Mexico 58 B3
El Paso, *U.S.A.* 57 L10
El Porvenir, *Mexico* .. 58 A3
El Prat de Llobregat,
  Spain 15 B7
El Progreso, *Honduras* 60 C2
El Pueblito, *Mexico* .. 58 B3
El Puerto de Santa
  María, *Spain* 15 D2
El Qâhira, *Egypt* 35 B12
El Qantara, *Egypt* 33 E1
El Quseima, *Egypt* ... 33 E3
El Real, *Panama* 62 B3
El Reno, *U.S.A.* 55 H6
El Rosarito, *Mexico* .. 58 B2
El Saheira, W. →,
  Egypt 33 E2
El Salto, *Mexico* 58 C3
El Salvador ■,
  Cent. Amer. 60 D2
El Sauce, *Nic.* 60 D2
El Sueco, *Mexico* 58 B3
El Suweis, *Egypt* 35 C12
El Tamarâni, W. →,
  Egypt 33 E3
El Thamad, *Egypt* ... 33 F3
El Tigre, *Venezuela* .. 62 B6
El Tîh, Gebal, *Egypt* .. 33 F2
El Tîna, Khalîg, *Egypt* . 33 D1
El Tûr, *Egypt* 30 D2
El Turbio, *Argentina* .. 64 G2
El Uqsur, *Egypt* 35 C12
El Venado, *Mexico* ... 58 C4
El Vergel, *Mexico* 58 B3
El Vigia, *Venezuela* .. 62 B4
El Wabeira, *Egypt* ... 33 F2
El Wak, *Kenya* 36 D8
El Wuz, *Sudan* 35 E12
Elat, *Israel* 33 F3
Elâzığ, *Turkey* 19 G6
Elba, *Italy* 16 C4
Elba, *U.S.A.* 53 K2
Elbasan, *Albania* 17 D9
Elbasani = Elbasan,
  Albania 17 D9
Elbe →, *Europe* 12 B5
Elbert, Mt., *U.S.A.* ... 57 G10
Elberton, *U.S.A.* 53 H4
Elbeuf, *France* 14 B4
Elbidtan, *Turkey* 30 B3
Elbing = Elbląg, *Poland* 13 A10
Elbląg, *Poland* 13 A10
Elbow, *Canada* 51 C7
Elbrus, *Asia* 19 F7
Elburz Mts. = Alborz,
  Reshteh-ye Kühhã-ye,
  Iran 31 C7
Elche, *Spain* 15 C5
Elcho I., *Australia* 42 A2
Elda, *Spain* 15 C5
Elde →, *Germany* ... 12 B6
Eldon, *U.S.A.* 54 F8
Eldora, *U.S.A.* 54 D8
Eldorado, *Mexico* 58 C3
Eldorado, *Ill., U.S.A.* . 52 G1
Eldorado, *Tex., U.S.A.* 55 K4
Eldorado Springs,
  U.S.A. 55 G8
Eldoret, *Kenya* 36 D7
Eleanora, Pk., *Australia* 41 F3
Elektrostal, *Russia* ... 18 C6
Elephant Butte
  Reservoir, *U.S.A.* .. 57 K10
Elephant I., *Antarctica* . 5 C18
Eleuthera, *Bahamas* .. 60 B4
Elgin, *U.K.* 10 C5
Elgin, *Ill., U.S.A.* 52 D1
Elgin, *N. Dak., U.S.A.* 54 B4
Elgin, *Oreg., U.S.A.* .. 56 D5
Elgin, *Tex., U.S.A.* ... 55 K6
Elgon, Mt., *Africa* ... 36 D6
Eliase, *Indonesia* 27 F8
Elisabethville =
  Lubumbashi,
  Dem. Rep. of
  the Congo 37 G5
Elista, *Russia* 19 E7
Elizabeth, *Australia* .. 43 E2
Elizabeth, *U.S.A.* 52 E8
Elizabeth City, *U.S.A.* . 53 G7
Elizabethton, *U.S.A.* .. 53 G4
Elizabethtown, *U.S.A.* . 52 G3
Elk, *Poland* 13 B12
Elk →, *Canada* 50 C5
Elk →, *U.S.A.* 53 H2
Elk City, *U.S.A.* 55 H5
Elk Island Nat. Park,
  Canada 50 C6
Elk Lake, *Canada* 48 C3
Elk Point, *Canada* ... 51 C6
Elk River, *Idaho, U.S.A.* 56 C5
Elk River, *Minn., U.S.A.* 54 C8
Elkedra →, *Australia* . 42 C2
Elkhart, *Ind., U.S.A.* . 52 E3
Elkhart, *Kans., U.S.A.* 55 G4
Elkhorn, *Canada* 51 D8
Elkhorn →, *U.S.A.* .. 54 E6
Elkhovo, *Bulgaria* ... 17 C12
Elkins, *U.S.A.* 52 F6
Elko, *Canada* 50 D5
Elko, *U.S.A.* 56 F6

Ell, L., *Australia* 41 E4
Elef Ringnes I., *Canada* 4 B2
Ellendale, *U.S.A.* 54 B5
Ellensburg, *U.S.A.* ... 56 C3
Ellenville, *U.S.A.* 52 E8
Ellery, Mt., *Australia* . 43 F4
Ellesmere, L., *N.Z.* ... 39 M4
Ellesmere I., *Canada* . 4 B4
Ellesmere Port, *U.K.* .. 8 D5
Ellice Is. = Tuvalu ■,
  Pac. Oc. 38 B10
Elliot, *Australia* 42 B1
Elliot Lake, *Canada* .. 48 C3
Ellis, *U.S.A.* 54 F5
Elliston, *Australia* ... 43 E1
Ellisville, *U.S.A.* 55 K10
Ellore = Eluru, *India* .. 29 L12
Ellsworth, *Kans., U.S.A.* 54 F5
Ellsworth, *Maine, U.S.A.* 53 C11
Ellsworth Land,
  Antarctica 5 D16
Ellsworth Mts.,
  Antarctica 5 D16
Elma, *Canada* 51 D9
Elma, *U.S.A.* 56 C2
Elmalı, *Turkey* 19 G4
Elmhurst, *U.S.A.* 52 E2
Elmira, *U.S.A.* 52 D7
Elmore, *Australia* 43 F3
Elmshorn, *Germany* .. 12 B5
Eloy, *U.S.A.* 57 K8
Elrose, *Canada* 51 C7
Elsinore = Helsingør,
  Denmark 7 H15
Eltham, *N.Z.* 39 H5
Eluru, *India* 29 L12
Elvas, *Portugal* 15 C2
Elverum, *Norway* 7 F14
Elvire →, *Australia* .. 40 C4
Elvire, Mt., *Australia* . 41 E2
Elwell, L., *U.S.A.* 56 B8
Elwood, *Ind., U.S.A.* .. 52 E3
Elwood, *Nebr., U.S.A.* 54 E5
Elx = Elche, *Spain* ... 15 C5
Ely, *U.K.* 9 E8
Ely, *Minn., U.S.A.* ... 54 B9
Ely, *Nev., U.S.A.* 56 G6
Elyria, *U.S.A.* 52 E4
Emāmrūd, *Iran* 31 B7
Emba, *Kazakstan* 20 E6
Emba →, *Kazakstan* . 19 E9
Embarcación, *Argentina* 64 A4
Embarras Portage,
  Canada 51 B6
Embetsu, *Japan* 22 B10
Embi = Emba,
  Kazakstan 20 E6
Embí = Emba →,
  Kazakstan 19 E9
Embrun, *France* 14 D7
Emden, *Germany* 12 B4
Emerald, *Australia* ... 42 C4
Emerson, *Canada* ... 51 D9
Emet, *Turkey* 17 E13
Emi Koussi, *Chad* ... 35 E9
Emine, Nos, *Bulgaria* . 17 C12
Emmeloord, *Neths.* .. 11 B5
Emmen, *Neths.* 11 B6
Emmet, *Australia* 42 C3
Emmetsburg, *U.S.A.* . 54 D7
Emmett, *U.S.A.* 56 E5
Emmonak, *U.S.A.* ... 46 B3
Emo, *Canada* 51 D10
Empalme, *Mexico* ... 58 B2
Empangeni, S. *Africa* . 37 K6
Empedrado, *Argentina* 64 B5
Emperor Seamount
  Chain, *Pac. Oc.* ... 44 D9
Emporia, *Kans., U.S.A.* 54 F6
Emporia, *Va., U.S.A.* . 53 G7
Emporium, *U.S.A.* ... 52 E6
Empress, *Canada* 51 C7
Empty Quarter = Rub'
  al Khālī, *Si. Arabia* . 32 D4
Ems →, *Germany* ... 12 B4
Emu Park, *Australia* .. 42 C5
'En 'Avrona, *Israel* ... 33 F4
En Nahud, *Sudan* 35 F11
Ena, *Japan* 23 G8
Enaratoli, *Indonesia* .. 27 E9
Enard B., *U.K.* 10 C3
Encarnación, *Paraguay* 64 B5
Encarnación de Diaz,
  Mexico 58 C4
Encino, *U.S.A.* 57 J11
Encounter B., *Australia* 43 F2
Endako, *Canada* 50 C3
Ende, *Indonesia* 27 F6
Endeavour Str.,
  Australia 42 A3
Enderby I., *Kiribati* ... 44 H10
Enderby, *Canada* 50 C5
Enderby I., *Australia* .. 40 D2
Enderby Land,
  Antarctica 5 C5
Enderlin, *U.S.A.* 54 B6
Endicott, *U.S.A.* 52 D7
Endyalgout I., *Australia* 40 B5
Eneabba, *Australia* ... 41 E2
Enewetak Atoll,
  Marshall Is. 44 F8
Enez, *Turkey* 17 D12
Enfield, *Canada* 49 D7

Engadin, *Switz.* 14 C9
Engaño, C., *Dom. Rep.* 61 C6
Engaño, C., *Phil.* 27 A6
Engaru, *Japan* 22 B11
Engels, *Russia* 19 D8
Engemann L., *Canada* 51 B7
Enggano, *Indonesia* .. 26 F2
England, *U.S.A.* 55 H9
England □, *U.K.* 8 D7
Englee, *Canada* 49 B8
Englehart, *Canada* ... 48 C4
Englewood, *U.S.A.* ... 54 F2
English →, *Canada* .. 51 C10
English Bazar = Ingraj
  Bazar, *India* 29 G16
English Channel, *Europe* 9 G6
English River, *Canada* . 48 C1
Enid, *U.S.A.* 55 G6
Enkhuizen, *Neths.* ... 11 B5
Enna, *Italy* 16 F6
Ennadai, *Canada* 51 A8
Ennadai L., *Canada* .. 51 A8
Ennedi, *Chad* 35 E10
Enngonia, *Australia* .. 43 D4
Ennis, *Ireland* 10 E2
Ennis, *Mont., U.S.A.* . 56 D8
Ennis, *Tex., U.S.A.* .. 55 J6
Enniskillen, *U.K.* 10 D3
Enns →, *Austria* 12 D8
Enontekiö, *Finland* ... 6 B20
Enriquillo, L., *Dom. Rep.* 61 C5
Enschede, *Neths.* 11 B6
Ensenada, *Mexico* ... 58 A1
Ensenada de los
  Muertos, *Mexico* ... 58 C2
Entebbe, *Uganda* 36 D6
Enterprise, *Canada* .. 50 A5
Enterprise, *Ala., U.S.A.* 53 K3
Enterprise, *Oreg., U.S.A.* 56 D5
Entre Rios, *Bolivia* ... 64 A4
Entroncamento,
  Portugal 15 C1
Enugu, *Nigeria* 34 G7
Eólie, Ís., *Italy* 16 E6
Epe, *Neths.* 11 B5
Épernay, *France* 14 B5
Ephesus, *Turkey* 17 F12
Ephraim, *U.S.A.* 56 G8
Ephrata, *U.S.A.* 56 C4
Épinal, *France* 14 B7
Epsom, *U.K.* 9 F7
Equatorial Guinea ■,
  Africa 36 D1
Er Rahad, *Sudan* 35 F12
Er Rif, *Morocco* 34 A5
Erāwadī Myit =
  Irrawaddy →, *Burma* 29 M19
Erbil = Arbil, *Iraq* 30 B5
Erçek, *Turkey* 30 B4
Erciyaş Dağı, *Turkey* . 19 G6
Érd, *Hungary* 13 E10
Erdek, *Turkey* 17 D12
Erebus, Mt., *Antarctica* 5 D11
Erechim, *Brazil* 64 B6
Ereğli, *Konya, Turkey* . 19 G5
Ereğli, *Zonguldak,*
  Turkey 19 F5
Eresma →, *Spain* ... 15 B3
Erewadi Myitwanya =
  Irrawaddy, Mouths of
  the, *Burma* 29 M19
Erfurt, *Germany* 12 C6
Erg Iguidi, *Africa* 34 C4
Ergani, *Turkey* 30 B3
Ergeni Vozvyshennost,
  Russia 19 E7
Ērgli, *Latvia* 7 H21
Érice, *Italy* 16 E5
Erie, *U.S.A.* 52 D5
Erie, L., *N. Amer.* 52 D5
Erigavo, *Somali Rep.* . 32 E4
Eriksdale, *Canada* ... 51 C9
Erímanthos, *Greece* .. 17 F9
Erimo-misaki, *Japan* . 22 D11
Eritrea ■, *Africa* 32 D2
Erlangen, *Germany* ... 12 D6
Erldunda, *Australia* .. 42 D1
Ermelo, *Neths.* 11 B5
Ermenek, *Turkey* 30 B2
Ermoúpolis = Síros,
  Greece 17 F11
Ernakulam = Cochin,
  India 28 Q10
Erne, Lower L., *U.K.* .. 10 D3
Ernest Giles Ra.,
  Australia 41 E3
Erode, *India* 28 P10
Eromanga, *Australia* .. 43 D3
Erramala Hills, *India* . 28 M11
Erskine, *U.S.A.* 54 B7
Ertis = Irtysh →,
  Russia 20 C7
Erwin, *U.S.A.* 53 G4
Erzgebirge, *Germany* . 12 C7
Erzin, *Russia* 21 D10
Erzincan, *Turkey* 19 G6
Erzurum, *Turkey* 19 G7
Es Sahrâ' Esh Sharqîya,
  Egypt 35 C12
Es Sînâ', *Egypt* 33 E2
Esan-Misaki, *Japan* .. 22 D10
Esashi, *Hokkaidō, Japan* 22 B11
Esashi, *Hokkaidō, Japan* 22 D10
Esbjerg, *Denmark* 7 J13
Escalante, *U.S.A.* 57 H8

Escalante ➝, *U.S.A.* 57 H8
Escalón, *Mexico* 58 B4
Escambia ➝, *U.S.A.* 53 K2
Escanaba, *U.S.A.* 52 C2
Esch-sur-Alzette, *Lux.* 14 B6
Escondido, *U.S.A.* 57 K5
Escuinapa, *Mexico* 58 C4
Escuintla, *Guatemala* 60 D1
Esenguly, *Turkmenistan* 20 F6
Eşfahān, *Iran* 31 C6
Eşfahān □, *Iran* 31 C6
Esfarāyen, *Iran* 31 B8
Esfideh, *Iran* 31 C8
Esh Sham = Dimashq, *Syria* 33 B5
Esher, *U.K.* 9 F7
Esil = Ishim ➝, *Russia* 20 D8
Esk ➝, *U.K.* 8 C7
Eskān, *Iran* 31 E9
Esker, *Canada* 49 B6
Eskifjörður, *Iceland* 6 D7
Eskilstuna, *Sweden* 7 G17
Eskimo Pt., *Canada* 46 B10
Eskişehir, *Turkey* 19 G5
Esla ➝, *Spain* 15 B2
Eslāmābād-e Gharb, *Iran* 30 C5
Eslāmshahr, *Iran* 31 C6
Eşme, *Turkey* 17 E13
Esmeraldas, *Ecuador* 62 C3
Esnagi L., *Canada* 48 C3
Espanola, *Canada* 48 C3
Espanola, *U.S.A.* 57 H10
Esparta, *Costa Rica* 60 E3
Esperance, *Australia* 41 F3
Esperance B., *Australia* 41 F3
Espichel, C., *Portugal* 15 C1
Espinazo, Sierra del = Espinhaço, Serra do, *Brazil* 63 G10
Espinhaço, Serra do, *Brazil* 63 G10
Espírito Santo □, *Brazil* 63 H10
Espíritu Santo, *Vanuatu* 38 C9
Espíritu Santo, B. del, *Mexico* 59 D7
Espíritu Santo, I., *Mexico* 58 C2
Espita, *Mexico* 59 C7
Espoo, *Finland* 7 F21
Esquel, *Argentina* 64 E2
Esquimalt, *Canada* 50 D4
Esquina, *Argentina* 64 C5
Essaouira, *Morocco* 34 B4
Essen, *Belgium* 11 C4
Essen, *Germany* 12 C4
Essendon, Mt., *Australia* 41 E3
Essequibo ➝, *Guyana* 62 B7
Essex □, *U.K.* 9 F8
Esslingen, *Germany* 12 D5
Estados, I. de Los, *Argentina* 64 G4
Eşţahbānāt, *Iran* 31 D7
Estância, *Brazil* 63 F11
Estancia, *U.S.A.* 57 J10
Estārm, *Iran* 31 D8
Estelí, *Nic.* 60 D2
Esterhazy, *Canada* 51 C8
Estevan, *Canada* 51 D8
Estevan Group, *Canada* 50 C3
Estherville, *U.S.A.* 54 D7
Eston, *Canada* 51 C7
Estonia ■, *Europe* 7 G21
Estreito, *Brazil* 63 E9
Estrela, Serra da, *Portugal* 15 B2
Estremoz, *Portugal* 15 C2
Estrondo, Serra do, *Brazil* 63 E9
Esztergom, *Hungary* 13 E10
Étampes, *France* 14 B5
Etawah, *India* 28 F11
Etawney L., *Canada* 51 B9
Ethelbert, *Canada* 51 C8
Ethiopia ■, *Africa* 32 F3
Etna, *Italy* 16 F6
Etosha Pan, *Namibia* 37 H3
Etowah, *U.S.A.* 53 H3
Ettelbruck, *Lux.* 11 E6
Etzatlán, *Mexico* 58 C4
Etzná, *Mexico* 59 D7
Euboea = Évvoia, *Greece* 17 E11
Eucla, *Australia* 41 F4
Euclid, *U.S.A.* 52 E5
Eucumbene, L., *Australia* 43 F4
Eudora, *U.S.A.* 55 J9
Eufaula, *Ala., U.S.A.* 53 K3
Eufaula, *Okla., U.S.A.* 55 H7
Eufaula L., *U.S.A.* 55 H7
Eugene, *U.S.A.* 56 E2
Eugowra, *Australia* 43 E4
Eulo, *Australia* 43 D4
Eunice, *La., U.S.A.* 55 K8
Eunice, *N. Mex., U.S.A.* 55 J3
Eupen, *Belgium* 11 D6
Euphrates = Furāt, Nahr al ➝, *Asia* 30 D5
Eureka, *Canada* 4 B3
Eureka, *Calif., U.S.A.* 56 F1
Eureka, *Kans., U.S.A.* 55 G6
Eureka, *Mont., U.S.A.* 56 B6
Eureka, *Nev., U.S.A.* 56 G5
Eureka, *S. Dak., U.S.A.* 54 C5

Eureka, Mt., *Australia* 41 E3
Euroa, *Australia* 43 F4
Europa, Île, *Ind. Oc.* 37 J8
Europa, Picos de, *Spain* 15 A3
Europa, Pta. de, *Gib.* 15 D3
Europoort, *Neths.* 11 C4
Eustis, *U.S.A.* 53 L5
Euston, *Australia* 43 E3
Eutsuk L., *Canada* 50 C3
Evans, *U.S.A.* 54 E2
Evans, L., *Canada* 48 B4
Evans Head, *Australia* 43 D5
Evansburg, *Canada* 50 C5
Evanston, *Ill., U.S.A.* 52 E2
Evanston, *Wyo., U.S.A.* 56 F8
Evansville, *U.S.A.* 52 G2
Evaz, *Iran* 31 E7
Eveleth, *U.S.A.* 54 B8
Evensk, *Russia* 21 C16
Everard, L., *Australia* 43 E2
Everard Ranges, *Australia* 41 E5
Everest, Mt., *Nepal* 29 E15
Everett, *U.S.A.* 56 C2
Everglades, The, *U.S.A.* 53 N5
Everglades City, *U.S.A.* 53 N5
Everglades National Park, *U.S.A.* 53 N5
Evergreen, *Ala., U.S.A.* 53 K2
Evergreen, *Mont., U.S.A.* 56 B6
Evesham, *U.K.* 9 E6
Evje, *Norway* 7 G12
Évora, *Portugal* 15 C2
Evowghlī, *Iran* 30 B5
Évreux, *France* 14 B4
Évros ➝, *Bulgaria* 17 D12
Évry, *France* 14 B5
Évvoia, *Greece* 17 E11
Ewing, *U.S.A.* 54 D5
Ewo, *Congo* 36 E2
Exaltación, *Bolivia* 62 F5
Excelsior Springs, *U.S.A.* 54 F7
Exe ➝, *U.K.* 9 G4
Exeter, *U.K.* 9 G4
Exeter, *U.S.A.* 57 H4
Exmoor, *U.K.* 9 F4
Exmouth, *Australia* 40 D1
Exmouth, *U.K.* 9 G4
Exmouth G., *Australia* 40 D1
Expedition Ra., *Australia* 42 C4
Extremadura □, *Spain* 15 C2
Exuma Sound, *Bahamas* 60 B4
Eyasi, L., *Tanzania* 36 E6
Eyjafjörður, *Iceland* 6 C4
Eyre (North), L., *Australia* 43 D2
Eyre (South), L., *Australia* 43 D2
Eyre, L., *Australia* 38 D6
Eyre, L., *Australia* 43 D2
Eyre Mts., *N.Z.* 39 L2
Eyre Pen., *Australia* 43 E2
Eysturoy, *Færoe Is.* 6 E9
Eyvānkī, *Iran* 31 C6
Ezine, *Turkey* 17 E12

F.Y.R.O.M. =
Macedonia ■, *Europe* 17 D9
Fabala, *Guinea* 34 G4
Fabens, *U.S.A.* 57 L10
Fabriano, *Italy* 16 C5
Fachi, *Niger* 35 E8
Fada, *Chad* 35 E10
Fada-n-Gourma, *Burkina Faso* 34 F6
Faddeyevskiy, Ostrov, *Russia* 21 B15
Fadghāmī, *Syria* 30 C4
Faenza, *Italy* 16 B4
Færoe Is. = Føroyar, *Atl. Oc.* 6 F9
Făgăras, *Romania* 13 F13
Fagersta, *Sweden* 7 F16
Fagnano, L., *Argentina* 64 G3
Fahliān, *Iran* 31 D6
Fahraj, *Kermān, Iran* 31 D8
Fahraj, *Yazd, Iran* 31 D7
Fair Haven, *U.S.A.* 52 D9
Fair Isle, *U.K.* 10 B6
Fairbanks, *U.S.A.* 46 B5
Fairbury, *U.S.A.* 54 E6
Fairfield, *Ala., U.S.A.* 53 J2
Fairfield, *Calif., U.S.A.* 56 G2
Fairfield, *Idaho, U.S.A.* 56 E6
Fairfield, *Ill., U.S.A.* 52 F1
Fairfield, *Iowa, U.S.A.* 54 E9
Fairfield, *Tex., U.S.A.* 55 K7
Fairford, *Canada* 51 C9
Fairhope, *U.S.A.* 53 K2
Fairlie, *N.Z.* 39 L3
Fairmont, *Minn., U.S.A.* 54 D7
Fairmont, *W. Va., U.S.A.* 52 F5
Fairplay, *U.S.A.* 57 G11
Fairport, *U.S.A.* 52 D7
Fairview, *Canada* 50 B5
Fairview, *Mont., U.S.A.* 54 B2
Fairview, *Okla., U.S.A.* 55 G5
Fairweather, Mt., *U.S.A.* 50 C6
Faisalabad, *Pakistan* 28 D8
Faith, *U.S.A.* 54 C3
Faizabad, *India* 29 F13
Fajardo, *Puerto Rico* 61 C6
Fajr, W. ➝, *Si. Arabia* 30 D3

Fakenham, *U.K.* 8 E8
Fakfak, *Indonesia* 27 E8
Falaise, *France* 14 B3
Falam, *Burma* 29 H18
Falcón, Presa, *Mexico* 59 B5
Falcon Lake, *Canada* 51 D9
Falcon Reservoir, *U.S.A.* 55 M5
Falconara Maríttima, *Italy* 16 C5
Falcone, C. del, *Italy* 16 D3
Faleshty = Fălești, *Moldova* 13 E14
Fălești, *Moldova* 13 E14
Falfurrias, *U.S.A.* 55 M5
Falher, *Canada* 50 B5
Falkenberg, *Sweden* 7 H15
Falkirk, *U.K.* 10 F5
Falkland Is. □, *Atl. Oc.* 64 G5
Falkland Sd., *Falk. Is.* 64 G5
Falköping, *Sweden* 7 G15
Fall River, *U.S.A.* 52 E10
Fallon, *U.S.A.* 56 G4
Falls City, *U.S.A.* 54 E7
Falmouth, *Jamaica* 60 C4
Falmouth, *U.K.* 9 G2
Falsa, Pta., *Mexico* 58 B1
Falso, C., *Honduras* 60 C3
Falster, *Denmark* 7 J14
Falsterbo, *Sweden* 7 J15
Fălticeni, *Romania* 13 E14
Falun, *Sweden* 7 F16
Famagusta, *Cyprus* 30 C2
Famalé, *Niger* 34 F6
Family L., *Canada* 51 C9
Fannūj, *Iran* 31 E8
Fanø, *Denmark* 7 J13
Fano, *Italy* 16 C5
Fao = Al Fāw, *Iraq* 31 D6
Faradje, *Dem. Rep. of the Congo* 36 D5
Farafangana, *Madag.* 37 J9
Farāh, *Afghan.* 28 C3
Farāh □, *Afghan.* 28 C3
Faranah, *Guinea* 34 F3
Farasān, Jazā'ir, *Si. Arabia* 32 D3
Farasan Is. = Farasān, Jazā'ir, *Si. Arabia* 32 D3
Fareham, *U.K.* 9 G6
Farewell, C., *N.Z.* 39 J4
Farewell C. = Nunap Isua, *Greenland* 4 D5
Farghona, *Uzbekistan* 20 E8
Fargo, *U.S.A.* 54 B6
Fār'iah, W. al ➝, *West Bank* 33 C4
Faribault, *U.S.A.* 54 C8
Faridabad, *India* 28 E10
Farīmān, *Iran* 31 C8
Farina, *Australia* 43 E2
Farmerville, *U.S.A.* 55 J8
Farmington, *Canada* 50 B4
Farmington, *Maine, U.S.A.* 53 C10
Farmington, *Mo., U.S.A.* 55 G9
Farmington, *N. Mex., U.S.A.* 57 H9
Farmington, *Utah, U.S.A.* 56 F8
Farmville, *U.S.A.* 52 G6
Farne Is., *U.K.* 8 B6
Farnham, Mt., *Canada* 50 C5
Faro, *Brazil* 63 D7
Faro, *Canada* 46 B6
Faro, *Portugal* 15 D2
Fårö, *Sweden* 7 H18
Farquhar, C., *Australia* 41 D1
Farrars Cr. ➝, *Australia* 42 D3
Farrāshband, *Iran* 31 D7
Farrokhī, *Iran* 31 C8
Fārs □, *Iran* 31 D7
Fársala, *Greece* 17 E10
Farson, *U.S.A.* 56 E9
Farsund, *Norway* 7 G12
Fartak, Râs, *Si. Arabia* 30 D2
Fartak, Ra's, *Yemen* 32 D5
Fārūj, *Iran* 31 B8
Farvel, Kap = Nunap Isua, *Greenland* 4 D5
Farwell, *U.S.A.* 55 H3
Fasā, *Iran* 31 D7
Fasano, *Italy* 16 D7
Fastiv, *Ukraine* 13 C15
Fastov = Fastiv, *Ukraine* 13 C15
Fatagar, Tanjung, *Indonesia* 27 E8
Fatehgarh, *India* 28 F11
Fatehpur, *Raj., India* 28 F9
Fatehpur, *Ut. P., India* 29 G12
Fatima, *Canada* 49 C7
Faulkton, *U.S.A.* 54 C5
Faure I., *Australia* 41 E1
Fauske, *Norway* 6 C16
Favara, *Italy* 16 F5
Favignana, *Italy* 16 F5
Fawcett, Pt., *Australia* 40 B5
Fawn ➝, *Canada* 48 A2
Faxaflói, *Iceland* 6 D2
Faya-Largeau, *Chad* 35 E9
Fayd, *Si. Arabia* 30 E4
Fayette, *Mo., U.S.A.* 54 F8
Fayette, *Ala., U.S.A.* 53 J2
Fayetteville, *Ark., U.S.A.* 55 G7
Fayetteville, *N.C., U.S.A.* 53 H6

Fayetteville, *Tenn., U.S.A.* 53 H2
Fazilka, *India* 28 D9
Fdérik, *Mauritania* 34 D3
Fear, C., *U.S.A.* 53 J7
Feather ➝, *U.S.A.* 56 G3
Featherston, *N.Z.* 39 J5
Fécamp, *France* 14 B4
Fedala = Mohammedia, *Morocco* 34 B4
Féderal, *Argentina* 64 C5
Fedeshkūh, *Iran* 31 D7
Fehmarn, *Germany* 12 A6
Fehmarn Bælt, *Europe* 7 J14
Fehmarn Belt = Fehmarn Bælt, *Europe* 7 J14
Feijó, *Brazil* 62 E4
Feilding, *N.Z.* 39 J5
Feira de Santana, *Brazil* 63 F11
Feldkirch, *Austria* 12 E5
Felipe Carrillo Puerto, *Mexico* 59 D7
Felixstowe, *U.K.* 9 F9
Femer Bælt = Fehmarn Bælt, *Europe* 7 J14
Femunden, *Norway* 7 E14
Fenoarivo Atsinanana, *Madag.* 37 H9
Fens, The, *U.K.* 8 E7
Fenton, *U.S.A.* 52 D4
Fenyang, *China* 25 C6
Feodosiya, *Ukraine* 19 E6
Ferdows, *Iran* 31 C8
Ferfer, *Somali Rep.* 32 F4
Fergana = Farghona, *Uzbekistan* 20 E8
Fergus Falls, *U.S.A.* 54 B6
Ferkéssédougou, *Ivory C.* 34 G4
Ferland, *Canada* 48 B2
Fermo, *Italy* 16 C5
Fermont, *Canada* 49 B6
Fernandina Beach, *U.S.A.* 53 K5
Fernando de Noronha, *Brazil* 63 D12
Fernando Póo = Bioko, *Eq. Guin.* 36 D1
Ferndale, *U.S.A.* 56 B2
Fernie, *Canada* 50 D5
Fernlees, *Australia* 42 C4
Fernley, *U.S.A.* 56 G4
Ferozepore = Firozpur, *India* 28 D9
Ferrara, *Italy* 16 B4
Ferreñafe, *Peru* 62 E3
Ferret, C., *France* 14 D3
Ferriday, *U.S.A.* 55 K9
Ferrol, *Spain* 15 A1
Ferron, *U.S.A.* 57 G8
Ferryland, *Canada* 49 C9
Fertile, *U.S.A.* 54 B6
Fès, *Morocco* 34 B5
Fessenden, *U.S.A.* 54 B5
Festus, *U.S.A.* 54 F9
Feteşti, *Romania* 13 F14
Fethiye, *Turkey* 19 G4
Fetlar, *U.K.* 10 A6
Feuilles ➝, *Canada* 47 C12
Fez = Fès, *Morocco* 34 B5
Fezzan, *Libya* 35 C8
Fianarantsoa, *Madag.* 37 J9
Field ➝, *Australia* 42 C2
Field I., *Australia* 40 B5
Fier, *Albania* 17 D8
Fier, *Albania* 17 D8
Fifth Cataract, *Sudan* 35 E12
Figeac, *France* 14 D5
Figueira da Foz, *Portugal* 15 B1
Figueres, *Spain* 15 A7
Figuig, *Morocco* 34 B5
Fiji ■, *Pac. Oc.* 39 C8
Filey, *U.K.* 8 C7
Filey B., *U.K.* 8 C7
Filiatrá, *Greece* 17 F9
Filingué, *Niger* 34 F6
Filipstad, *Sweden* 7 G16
Fillmore, *U.S.A.* 57 G7
Findlay, *U.S.A.* 52 E4
Finger L., *Canada* 48 B1
Fíngoè, *Mozam.* 37 G6
Finisterre, C. = Fisterra, C., *Spain* 15 A1
Finke, *Australia* 42 D1
Finland ■, *Europe* 6 E22
Finland, G. of, *Europe* 7 G21
Finlay ➝, *Canada* 50 B3
Finley, *Australia* 43 F4
Finley, *U.S.A.* 54 B6
Finnigan, Mt., *Australia* 42 B4
Finniss, C., *Australia* 43 E1
Finnmark, *Norway* 6 B20
Finnsnes, *Norway* 6 B18
Finspång, *Sweden* 7 G16
Fiora ➝, *Italy* 16 C4
Fiq, *Syria* 33 C4
Firat = Furāt, Nahr al ➝, *Asia* 30 D5
Firebag ➝, *Canada* 51 B6
Firedrake L., *Canada* 51 A8
Firenze, *Italy* 16 C4
Firk ➝, *Iraq* 30 D5
Firozabad, *India* 28 F11
Firozpur, *India* 28 D9

Firūzābād, *Iran* 31 D7
Firūzkūh, *Iran* 31 C7
Firvale, *Canada* 50 C3
Fish ➝, *Namibia* 37 K3
Fisher, *Australia* 41 F5
Fisher B., *Canada* 51 C9
Fishguard, *U.K.* 9 E3
Fishing L., *Canada* 51 C9
Fisterra, C., *Spain* 15 A1
Fitchburg, *U.S.A.* 52 D10
Fitz Roy, *Argentina* 64 F3
Fitzgerald, *Canada* 50 B6
Fitzgerald, *U.S.A.* 53 K4
Fitzmaurice ➝, *Australia* 40 B5
Fitzroy ➝, *Queens., Australia* 42 C5
Fitzroy ➝, *W. Austral., Australia* 40 C3
Fitzroy, Mte., *Argentina* 64 F2
Fitzroy Crossing, *Australia* 40 C4
Fiume = Rijeka, *Croatia* 12 F8
Fizi, *Dem. Rep. of the Congo* 36 E5
Flagstaff, *U.S.A.* 57 J8
Flagstaff L., *U.S.A.* 53 C10
Flaherty I., *Canada* 48 A4
Flåm, *Norway* 7 F12
Flambeau ➝, *U.S.A.* 54 C9
Flamborough Hd., *U.K.* 8 C7
Flaming Gorge Reservoir, *U.S.A.* 56 F9
Flamingo, Teluk, *Indonesia* 27 F9
Flanders = Flandre, *Europe* 10 F8
Flandre, *Europe* 10 F8
Flandre Occidentale = West-Vlaanderen □, *Belgium* 11 D2
Flandre Orientale = Oost-Vlaanderen □, *Belgium* 11 C3
Flandreau, *U.S.A.* 54 C6
Flåsjön, *Sweden* 6 D16
Flat ➝, *Canada* 50 A3
Flathead L., *U.S.A.* 56 C7
Flattery, C., *Australia* 42 A4
Flattery, C., *U.S.A.* 56 B1
Flatwoods, *U.S.A.* 52 F4
Fleetwood, *U.K.* 8 D4
Flekkefjord, *Norway* 7 G12
Flensburg, *Germany* 12 A5
Flers, *France* 14 B3
Flesko, Tanjung, *Indonesia* 27 D6
Fleurieu Pen., *Australia* 43 F2
Flevoland □, *Neths.* 11 B5
Flin Flon, *Canada* 51 C8
Flinders ➝, *Australia* 42 B3
Flinders B., *Australia* 41 F2
Flinders Group, *Australia* 42 A3
Flinders I., *S. Austral., Australia* 43 E1
Flinders I., *Tas., Australia* 42 G4
Flinders Ranges, *Australia* 43 E2
Flinders Reefs, *Australia* 42 B4
Flint, *U.K.* 8 D4
Flint, *U.S.A.* 52 D4
Flint ➝, *U.S.A.* 53 K3
Flint I., *Kiribati* 45 J12
Flintshire □, *U.K.* 8 D4
Flodden, *U.K.* 8 B5
Floodwood, *U.S.A.* 54 B8
Flora, *U.S.A.* 52 F1
Florala, *U.S.A.* 53 K2
Florence = Firenze, *Italy* 16 C4
Florence, *Ala., U.S.A.* 53 H2
Florence, *Ariz., U.S.A.* 57 K8
Florence, *Colo., U.S.A.* 54 F2
Florence, *Oreg., U.S.A.* 56 E1
Florence, *S.C., U.S.A.* 53 H6
Florence, L., *Australia* 43 D2
Florencia, *Colombia* 62 C3
Florennes, *Belgium* 11 D4
Florenville, *Belgium* 11 E5
Flores, *Guatemala* 60 C2
Flores, *Indonesia* 27 F6
Flores I., *Australia* 43 D2
Flores Sea, *Indonesia* 27 F6
Floreşti, *Moldova* 13 E15
Floriano, *Brazil* 63 E10
Florianópolis, *Brazil* 64 B7
Florida, *Cuba* 60 B4
Florida, *Uruguay* 64 C5
Florida □, *U.S.A.* 53 L5
Florida B., *U.S.A.* 60 B4
Florida Keys, *U.S.A.* 53 N5
Florida, Straits of, *U.S.A.* 60 B4
Flórina, *Greece* 17 D9
Florø, *Norway* 7 F11
Fluk, *Indonesia* 27 E7
Flushing = Vlissingen, *Neths.* 11 C3
Fly ➝, *Papua N. G.* 38 B7
Flying Fish, C., *Antarctica* 5 D15
Foam Lake, *Canada* 51 C8

Foça, *Turkey* 17 E12
Focşani, *Romania* 13 F14
Fóggia, *Italy* 16 D6
Fogo, *Canada* 49 C9
Fogo I., *Canada* 49 C9
Föhr, *Germany* 12 A5
Foix, *France* 14 E4
Folda, *Nord-Trøndelag, Norway* 6 D14
Folda, *Nordland, Norway* 6 C16
Foley, *U.S.A.* 53 K2
Foleyet, *Canada* 48 C3
Folgefonni, *Norway* 7 F12
Foligno, *Italy* 16 C5
Folkestone, *U.K.* 9 F9
Folkston, *U.S.A.* 53 K5
Fond-du-Lac, *Canada* 51 B7
Fond du Lac, *U.S.A.* 54 D10
Fond-du-Lac ➝, *Canada* 51 B7
Fondi, *Italy* 16 D5
Fongafale, *Tuvalu* 44 H9
Fonsagrada = A Fonsagrada, *Spain* 15 A2
Fonseca, G. de, *Cent. Amer.* 60 D2
Fontainebleau, *France* 14 B5
Fontas ➝, *Canada* 50 B4
Fonte Boa, *Brazil* 62 D5
Fontenay-le-Comte, *France* 14 C3
Fontenelle Reservoir, *U.S.A.* 56 E8
Fontur, *Iceland* 6 C6
Foochow = Fuzhou, *China* 25 D6
Forbes, *Australia* 43 E4
Førde, *Norway* 7 F11
Ford's Bridge, *Australia* 43 D4
Fordyce, *U.S.A.* 55 J8
Forel, Mt., *Greenland* 4 C6
Foremost, *Canada* 50 D6
Forest, *U.S.A.* 55 J10
Forest City, *Iowa, U.S.A.* 54 D8
Forest City, *N.C., U.S.A.* 53 H5
Forest Grove, *U.S.A.* 56 D2
Forestburg, *Canada* 50 C6
Forestier Pen., *Australia* 42 G4
Forestville, *Canada* 49 C6
Forfar, *U.K.* 10 C5
Forks, *U.S.A.* 56 C1
Forlì, *Italy* 16 B5
Forman, *U.S.A.* 54 B6
Formby Pt., *U.K.* 8 D4
Formentera, *Spain* 15 C6
Formentor, C. de, *Spain* 15 C7
Former Yugoslav Republic of Macedonia = Macedonia ■, *Europe* 17 D9
Fórmia, *Italy* 16 D5
Formosa = Taiwan ■, *Asia* 25 D7
Formosa, *Argentina* 64 B5
Formosa, *Brazil* 63 G9
Formosa, Serra, *Brazil* 63 F8
Føroyar, *Atl. Oc.* 6 F9
Forrest, *Australia* 41 F4
Forrest, Mt., *Australia* 41 D4
Forrest City, *U.S.A.* 55 H9
Forsayth, *Australia* 42 B3
Forssa, *Finland* 7 F20
Forst, *Germany* 12 C8
Forsyth, *U.S.A.* 56 C10
Fort Albany, *Canada* 48 B3
Fort Assiniboine, *Canada* 50 C6
Fort Benton, *U.S.A.* 56 C8
Fort Bragg, *U.S.A.* 56 G2
Fort Bridger, *U.S.A.* 56 F8
Fort Chipewyan, *Canada* 51 B6
Fort Collins, *U.S.A.* 54 E2
Fort-Coulonge, *Canada* 48 C4
Fort Davis, *U.S.A.* 55 K3
Fort-de-France, *Martinique* 61 D7
Fort Defiance, *U.S.A.* 57 J9
Fort Dodge, *U.S.A.* 54 D7
Fort Fairfield, *U.S.A.* 53 B12
Fort Frances, *Canada* 51 D10
Fort Garland, *U.S.A.* 57 H11
Fort George = Chisasibi, *Canada* 48 B4
Fort Good-Hope, *Canada* 46 B7
Fort Hancock, *U.S.A.* 57 L11
Fort Hertz = Putao, *Burma* 29 F20
Fort Hope, *Canada* 48 B2
Fort Jameson = Chipata, *Zambia* 37 G6
Fort Kent, *U.S.A.* 53 B11
Fort Klamath, *U.S.A.* 56 E3
Fort-Lamy = Ndjamena, *Chad* 35 F8
Fort Laramie, *U.S.A.* 54 D2
Fort Lauderdale, *U.S.A.* 53 M5
Fort Liard, *Canada* 50 A4
Fort Liberté, *Haiti* 61 C5
Fort Lupton, *U.S.A.* 54 E2
Fort Mackay, *Canada* 50 B6
Fort Macleod, *Canada* 50 D6
Fort McMurray, *Canada* 50 B6
Fort McPherson, *Canada* 46 B6

Fort Madison, U.S.A. . . 54 E9
Fort Meade, U.S.A. . . . 53 M5
Fort Morgan, U.S.A. . . 54 E3
Fort Myers, U.S.A. . . . 53 M5
Fort Nelson, Canada . . 50 B4
Fort Nelson →, Canada 50 B4
Fort Norman = Tulita,
Canada 46 B7
Fort Payne, U.S.A. . . . 53 H3
Fort Peck, U.S.A. 56 B10
Fort Peck Dam, U.S.A. . 56 C10
Fort Peck L., U.S.A. . . 56 C10
Fort Pierce, U.S.A. . . . 53 M5
Fort Pierre, U.S.A. . . . 54 C4
Fort Providence, Canada 50 A5
Fort Qu'Appelle, Canada 51 C8
Fort Resolution, Canada 50 A6
Fort Rosebery = Mansa,
Zambia 36 G5
Fort Rupert =
Waskaganish, Canada 48 B4
Fort St. James, Canada 50 C4
Fort St. John, Canada . 50 B4
Fort Sandeman = Zhob,
Pakistan 28 D6
Fort Saskatchewan,
Canada 50 C6
Fort Scott, U.S.A. 55 G7
Fort Severn, Canada . . 48 A2
Fort Shevchenko,
Kazakstan 19 F9
Fort Simpson, Canada . 50 A4
Fort Smith, Canada . . . 50 B6
Fort Smith, U.S.A. . . . 55 H7
Fort Stockton, U.S.A. . . 55 K3
Fort Sumner, U.S.A. . . 55 H2
Fort Thompson, U.S.A. . 54 C5
Fort Trinquet = Bir
Mogreïn, Mauritania 34 C3
Fort Valley, U.S.A. . . . 53 J4
Fort Vermilion, Canada . 50 B5
Fort Walton Beach,
U.S.A. 53 K2
Fort Wayne, U.S.A. . . . 52 E3
Fort William, U.K. 10 C4
Fort Worth, U.S.A. . . . 55 J6
Fort Yates, U.S.A. 54 B4
Fort Yukon, U.S.A. . . . 46 B5
Fortaleza, Brazil 63 D11
Forteau, Canada 49 B8
Fortescue →, Australia 40 D2
Fortuna, Calif., U.S.A. . 56 F1
Fortuna, N. Dak., U.S.A. 54 A3
Fortune, Canada 49 C8
Fortune B., Canada . . . 49 C8
Forūr, Iran 31 E7
Foshan, China 25 D6
Fosna, Norway 6 E14
Fosnavåg, Norway 7 E11
Fossano, Italy 14 D7
Fossil, U.S.A. 56 D3
Foster, Australia 43 F4
Foster →, Canada . . . 51 B7
Fostoria, U.S.A. 52 E4
Fougères, France 14 B3
Foul Pt., Sri Lanka . . . 28 Q12
Foula, U.K. 10 A5
Foulness I., U.K. 9 F8
Foumban, Cameroon . . 36 C2
Fountain, U.S.A. 54 F2
Foúrnoi, Greece 17 F12
Fourth Cataract, Sudan 35 E12
Fouta Djalon, Guinea . 34 F3
Foux, Cap-à-, Haiti . . . 61 C5
Foveaux Str., N.Z. 39 M2
Fowey, U.K. 9 G3
Fowler, U.S.A. 54 F3
Fowlers B., Australia . . 41 F5
Fowman, Iran 31 B6
Fox →, Canada 51 B10
Fox Creek, Canada . . . 50 C5
Fox Lake, Canada 50 B6
Fox Valley, Canada . . . 51 C7
Foxe Basin, Canada . . 47 B12
Foxe Chan., Canada . . 47 B11
Foxe Pen., Canada . . . 47 B12
Foxton, N.Z. 39 J5
Foz do Iguaçu, Brazil . 64 B6
Franca, Brazil 63 H9
Francavilla Fontana,
Italy 17 D7
France ■, Europe 14 C5
Frances, Australia 43 F3
Frances →, Canada . . 50 A3
Frances L., Canada . . . 50 A3
Franceville, Gabon . . . 36 E2
Franche-Comté, France 14 C6
Francis Case, L., U.S.A. 54 D5
Francisco I. Madero,
Coahuila, Mexico . . 58 B4
Francisco I. Madero,
Durango, Mexico . . . 58 C4
Francistown, Botswana 37 J5
François, Canada 49 C8
François L., Canada . . 50 C3
Franeker, Neths. 11 A5
Frankfort, Ind., U.S.A. . 52 E2
Frankfort, Kans., U.S.A. 54 F6
Frankfort, Ky., U.S.A. . 52 F3
Frankfurt, Brandenburg,
Germany 12 B8
Frankfurt, Hessen,
Germany 12 C5

Fränkische Alb,
Germany 12 D6
Frankland →, Australia 41 G2
Franklin, Ky., U.S.A. . . 53 G2
Franklin, La., U.S.A. . . 55 L9
Franklin, N.H., U.S.A. . 52 D10
Franklin, Nebr., U.S.A. . 54 E5
Franklin, Pa., U.S.A. . . 52 E6
Franklin, Va., U.S.A. . . 53 G7
Franklin, W. Va., U.S.A. 52 F6
Franklin B., Canada . . 46 B7
Franklin D. Roosevelt L.,
U.S.A. 56 B4
Franklin I., Antarctica . 5 D11
Franklin L., U.S.A. . . . 56 F6
Franklin Mts., Canada . 46 B7
Franklin Str., Canada . 46 A10
Franklinton, U.S.A. . . . 55 K9
Franks Pk., U.S.A. . . . 56 E9
Frankston, Australia . . 43 F4
Frantsa Iosifa, Zemlya,
Russia 20 A6
Franz, Canada 48 C3
Franz Josef Land =
Frantsa Iosifa, Zemlya,
Russia 20 A6
Fraser →, B.C., Canada 50 D4
Fraser →, Nfld.,
Canada 49 A7
Fraser, Mt., Australia . . 41 E2
Fraser I., Australia . . . 43 D5
Fraser Lake, Canada . . 50 C4
Fraserburgh, U.K. 10 C5
Fraserdale, Canada . . . 48 C3
Fray Bentos, Uruguay . 64 C5
Fredericia, Denmark . . 7 J13
Frederick, Md., U.S.A. . 52 F7
Frederick, Okla., U.S.A. 55 H5
Frederick, S. Dak.,
U.S.A. 54 C5
Fredericksburg, Tex.,
U.S.A. 55 K5
Fredericksburg, Va.,
U.S.A. 52 F7
Fredericktown, U.S.A. . 55 G9
Frederico I. Madero,
Presa, Mexico 58 B3
Fredericton, Canada . . 49 C6
Fredericton Junction,
Canada 49 C6
Frederikshåb = Paamiut,
Greenland 4 C5
Frederikshavn, Denmark 7 H14
Frederiksted, Virgin Is. . 61 C7
Fredonia, Ariz., U.S.A. . 57 H7
Fredonia, Kans., U.S.A. 55 G7
Fredonia, N.Y., U.S.A. . 52 D6
Fredrikstad, Norway . . 7 G14
Free State □, S. Africa . 37 K5
Freels, C., Canada . . . 49 C9
Freeman, U.S.A. 54 D6
Freeport, Bahamas . . . 60 A4
Freeport, Ill., U.S.A. . . 54 D10
Freeport, N.Y., U.S.A. . 52 E9
Freeport, Tex., U.S.A. . 55 L7
Freetown, S. Leone . . . 34 G3
Frégate, L., Canada . . 48 B5
Fregenal de la Sierra,
Spain 15 C2
Freibourg = Fribourg,
Switz. 14 C7
Freiburg, Germany . . . 12 E4
Freire, Chile 64 D2
Freising, Germany . . . 12 D6
Freistadt, Austria 12 D8
Fréjus, France 14 E7
Fremantle, Australia . . 41 F2
Fremont, Calif., U.S.A. . 57 H2
Fremont, Mich., U.S.A. . 52 D3
Fremont, Nebr., U.S.A. . 54 E6
Fremont, Ohio, U.S.A. . 52 E4
Fremont →, U.S.A. . . 57 G8
French Guiana ■,
S. Amer. 63 C8
French Polynesia ■,
Pac. Oc. 45 K13
Frenchman Cr. →,
N. Amer. 56 B10
Frenchman Cr. →,
U.S.A. 54 E4
Fresco →, Brazil 63 E8
Freshfield, C., Antarctica 5 C10
Fresnillo, Mexico 58 C4
Fresno, U.S.A. 57 H4
Fresno Reservoir, U.S.A. 56 B9
Frew →, Australia . . . 42 C2
Freycinet Pen., Australia 42 G4
Fria, C., Namibia 37 H2
Frías, Argentina 64 B3
Fribourg, Switz. 14 C7
Friedrichshafen,
Germany 12 E5
Friendly Is. = Tonga ■,
Pac. Oc. 39 D11
Friesland □, Neths. . . . 11 A5
Frio →, U.S.A. 55 L5
Friona, U.S.A. 55 H3
Fritch, U.S.A. 55 H4
Frobisher B., Canada . 47 B13
Frobisher Bay = Iqaluit,
Canada 47 B13
Frobisher L., Canada . . 51 B7
Frohavet, Norway 6 E13
Frome, U.K. 9 F5
Frome →, U.K. 9 G5

Frome, L., Australia . . . 43 E2
Front Royal, U.S.A. . . . 52 F6
Frontera, Mexico 59 D6
Fronteras, Mexico 58 A3
Frosinone, Italy 16 D5
Frostburg, U.S.A. 52 F6
Frostisen, Norway 6 B17
Frøya, Norway 6 E13
Frunze = Bishkek,
Kyrgyzstan 20 E8
Frutal, Brazil 63 H9
Frýdek-Místek,
Czech Rep. 13 D10
Fuchou = Fuzhou, China 25 D6
Fuchū, Japan 23 G6
Fuengirola, Spain 15 D3
Fuentes de Oñoro,
Spain 15 B2
Fuerte →, Mexico . . . 58 B3
Fuerte Olimpo,
Paraguay 62 H7
Fuerteventura,
Canary Is. 34 C3
Fuhai, China 24 B3
Fuḥaymī, Iraq 30 C4
Fuji, Japan 23 G9
Fuji-San, Japan 23 G9
Fuji-Yoshida, Japan . . 23 G9
Fujian □, China 25 D6
Fujinomiya, Japan 23 G9
Fujisawa, Japan 23 G9
Fujiyama, Mt. = Fuji-
San, Japan 23 G9
Fukien = Fujian □,
China 25 D6
Fukuchiyama, Japan . . 23 G7
Fukue-Shima, Japan . . 23 H4
Fukui, Japan 23 F8
Fukui □, Japan 23 G8
Fukuoka, Japan 23 H5
Fukuoka □, Japan 23 H5
Fukushima, Japan 22 F10
Fukushima □, Japan . . 22 F10
Fukuyama, Japan 23 G6
Fulda, Germany 12 C5
Fulda →, Germany . . . 12 C5
Fullerton, U.S.A. 54 E6
Fulton, Mo., U.S.A. . . . 54 F9
Fulton, N.Y., U.S.A. . . . 52 D7
Funabashi, Japan 23 G10
Funafuti, Tuvalu 38 B10
Funchal, Madeira 34 B2
Fundación, Colombia . . 62 A4
Fundão, Portugal 15 B2
Fundy, B. of, Canada . 49 D6
Funtua, Nigeria 34 F7
Furano, Japan 22 C11
Furāt, Nahr al →, Asia 30 D5
Fürg, Iran 31 D7
Furneaux Group,
Australia 42 G4
Furqlus, Syria 33 A6
Fürstenwalde, Germany 12 B8
Fürth, Germany 12 D6
Furukawa, Japan 22 E10
Fury and Hecla Str.,
Canada 47 B11
Fusagasuga, Colombia 62 C4
Fushun, China 25 B7
Futuna, Wall. & F. Is. . 39 B8
Fuxin, China 25 B7
Fuzhou, China 25 D6
Fylde, U.K. 8 D5
Fyn, Denmark 7 J14

Gabela, Angola 36 G2
Gabès, Tunisia 35 B8
Gabès, G. de, Tunisia . 35 B8
Gabon ■, Africa 36 E2
Gaborone, Botswana . . 37 J5
Gabrovo, Bulgaria 17 C11
Gäbrīk, Iran 31 E8
Gāch Sār, Iran 31 B6
Gachsārān, Iran 31 D6
Gadag, India 28 M9
Gadarwara, India 28 H11
Gadhada, India 28 J7
Gadsden, U.S.A. 53 H3
Gadwal, India 28 L10
Gaffney, U.S.A. 53 H5
Gafsa, Tunisia 34 B7
Gagnoa, Ivory C. 34 G4
Gagnon, Canada 49 B6
Gagnon, L., Canada . . 51 A6
Gail →, U.S.A. 55 J4
Gaillimh = Galway,
Ireland 10 E2
Gainesville, Fla., U.S.A. 53 L4
Gainesville, Ga., U.S.A. 53 H4
Gainesville, Mo., U.S.A. 55 G8
Gainesville, Tex., U.S.A. 55 J6
Gainsborough, U.K. . . . 8 D7
Gairdner, L., Australia . 43 E2
Galápagos, Pac. Oc. . . 45 H18
Galashiels, U.K. 10 D5
Galați, Romania 13 F15
Galatina, Italy 17 D8
Galax, U.S.A. 53 G5
Galcaio, Somali Rep. . . 32 F4
Galdhøpiggen, Norway 7 F12
Galeana, Chihuahua,
Mexico 58 A3
Galeana, Nuevo León,
Mexico 58 A3

Galela, Indonesia 27 D7
Galena, U.S.A. 46 B4
Galera Point,
Trin. & Tob. 61 D7
Galesburg, U.S.A. 54 E9
Galich, Russia 18 C7
Galicia □, Spain 15 A2
Galilee = Hagalil, Israel 33 C4
Galilee, L., Australia . . 42 C4
Galilee, Sea of = Yam
Kinneret, Israel 33 C4
Galiuro Mts., U.S.A. . . 57 K8
Galiwinku, Australia . . 42 A2
Gallatin, U.S.A. 53 G2
Galle, Sri Lanka 28 R12
Gállego →, Spain 15 B5
Gallegos →, Argentina 64 G3
Gallinas, Pta., Colombia 62 A4
Gallipoli = Gelibolu,
Turkey 17 D12
Gallipoli, Italy 17 D8
Gallipolis, U.S.A. 52 F4
Gällivare, Sweden 6 C19
Galloway, Mull of, U.K. . 10 D4
Gallup, U.S.A. 57 J9
Galoya, Sri Lanka 28 Q12
Galva, U.S.A. 54 E9
Galveston, U.S.A. 55 L7
Galveston B., U.S.A. . . 55 L7
Gálvez, Argentina 64 C4
Galway, Ireland 10 E2
Galway B., Ireland . . . 10 E2
Gamagori, Japan 23 G8
Gambia ■, W. Afr. . . . 34 F2
Gambia →, W. Afr. . . . 34 F2
Gambier, C., Australia . 40 B5
Gambier Is., Australia . 43 F2
Gambo, Canada 49 C9
Gamboma, Congo 36 E3
Gamlakarleby =
Kokkola, Finland . . . 6 E20
Gammon →, Canada . 51 C9
Gan Jiang →, China . . 25 D6
Ganado, U.S.A. 57 J9
Gananoque, Canada . . 48 D4
Gananggi, India 28 E8
Gandak →, India 29 G14
Gandava, Pakistan . . . 28 E5
Gander, Canada 49 C9
Gander L., Canada . . . 49 C9
Gandhi Sagar, India . . 28 G9
Gandia, Spain 15 C5
Ganedidalem = Gani,
Indonesia 27 E7
Ganga →, India 29 H17
Ganganagar, India . . . 28 E8
Gangaw, Burma 29 H19
Gangdisê Shan, China . 29 D12
Ganges = Ganga →,
India 29 H17
Ganges, Canada 50 D4
Gangtok, India 29 F16
Gani, Indonesia 27 E7
Gannett Peak, U.S.A. . 56 E9
Gansu □, China 24 C5
Ganta, Liberia 34 G4
Gantheaume, C.,
Australia 43 F2
Gantheaume B.,
Australia 41 E1
Gantsevichi =
Hantsavichy, Belarus 13 B14
Ganyem = Genyem,
Indonesia 27 E10
Ganzhou, China 25 D6
Gao, Mali 34 E5
Gaoua, Burkina Faso . 34 F5
Gaoual, Guinea 34 F3
Gaoxiong = Kaohsiung,
Taiwan 25 D7
Gap, France 14 D7
Gapuwiyak, Australia . . 42 A2
Gar, China 24 C2
Garabogazköl Aylagy,
Turkmenistan 19 F9
Garachiné, Panama . . 60 E4
Garah, Australia 43 D4
Garanhuns, Brazil 63 E11
Garberville, U.S.A. . . . 56 F2
Garda, L. di, Italy 16 B4
Garde L., Canada 51 A7
Garden City, Ga., U.S.A. 53 J5
Garden City, Kans.,
U.S.A. 55 G4
Garden City, Tex.,
U.S.A. 55 K4
Gardez, Afghan. 28 C6
Gardiner, Maine, U.S.A. 53 C11
Gardiner, Mont., U.S.A. 56 D8
Gardner Canal, Canada 50 C3
Gardnerville, U.S.A. . . 56 G4
Gardo, Somali Rep. . . 32 F4
Garfield, U.S.A. 56 C5
Garforth, U.K. 8 D6
Gargano, Mte., Italy . . 16 D6
Garibaldi Prov. Park,
Canada 50 D4
Garigliano →, Italy . . . 16 D5
Garissa, Kenya 36 E7
Garland, Tex., U.S.A. . 55 J6

Garland, Utah, U.S.A. . 56 F7
Garm, Tajikistan 20 F8
Garmāb, Iran 31 C8
Garmisch-Partenkirchen,
Germany 12 E6
Garmsār, Iran 31 C7
Garner, U.S.A. 54 D8
Garnett, U.S.A. 54 F7
Garoe, Somali Rep. . . 32 F4
Garonne →, France . . 14 D3
Garoua, Cameroon . . . 35 G8
Garrison, Mont., U.S.A. 56 C7
Garrison, N. Dak., U.S.A. 54 B4
Garrison Res. =
Sakakawea, L., U.S.A. 54 B4
Garry, L., Canada 46 B9
Garson L., Canada . . . 51 B6
Garut, Indonesia 27 G12
Garvie Mts., N.Z. 39 L2
Garwa →, India 29 G10
Gary, U.S.A. 52 E2
Garzê, China 24 C5
Garzón, Colombia 62 C3
Gas-San, Japan 22 E10
Gasan Kuli = Esenguly,
Turkmenistan 20 F6
Gascogne, France . . . 14 E4
Gascogne, G. de,
Europe 14 D2
Gascony = Gascogne,
France 14 E4
Gascoyne →, Australia 41 D1
Gascoyne Junction,
Australia 41 E2
Gashaka, Nigeria 35 G8
Gashua, Nigeria 35 F8
Gaspé, Canada 49 C7
Gaspé, C. de, Canada . 49 C7
Gaspé, Pén. de, Canada 49 C6
Gaspésie, Parc de
Conservation de la,
Canada 49 C6
Gasteiz = Vitoria-
Gasteiz, Spain 15 A4
Gastonia, U.S.A. 53 H5
Gastre, Argentina 64 E3
Gata, C. de, Spain . . . 15 D4
Gata, Sierra de, Spain . 15 B2
Gataga →, Canada . . 50 B3
Gateshead, U.K. 8 C6
Gatesville, U.S.A. 55 K6
Gatineau →, Canada . 48 C4
Gatineau, Parc Nat. de
la, Canada 48 C4
Gatton, Australia 43 D5
Gatun, L., Panama . . . 60 E4
Gau, Fiji 39 D8
Gauer, L., Canada . . . 51 B9
Gauhati, India 29 F17
Gauja →, Latvia 7 H21
Gaula →, Norway 6 E14
Gausta, Norway 7 G13
Gāv Koshī, Iran 31 D8
Gävakān, Iran 31 D7
Gavāter, Iran 31 E9
Gāvbandī, Iran 31 E7
Gávdhos, Greece 17 G11
Gāvkhūnī, Bāṭlāq-e, Iran 31 C7
Gävle, Sweden 7 F17
Gawilgarh Hills, India . 28 J10
Gawler, Australia 43 E2
Gaxun Nur, China 24 B5
Gay, Russia 18 D10
Gaya, India 29 G14
Gaya, Niger 34 F6
Gaylord, U.S.A. 52 C3
Gayndah, Australia . . . 43 D5
Gaysin = Haysyn,
Ukraine 13 D15
Gayvoron = Hayvoron,
Ukraine 13 D15
Gaza, Gaza Strip 33 D3
Gaza Strip □, Asia . . . 33 D3
Gazanjyk, Turkmenistan 31 B8
Gāzbor, Iran 31 D8
Gaziantep, Turkey 19 G6
Gcuwa, S. Africa 37 L5
Gdańsk, Poland 13 A10
Gdańska, Zatoka, Poland 13 A10
Gdov, Russia 7 G22
Gdynia, Poland 13 A10
Gebe, Indonesia 27 D7
Gebze, Turkey 17 D13
Gedaref, Sudan 35 F13
Gediz →, Turkey 17 E12
Gedser, Denmark 7 J14
Geegully Cr. →,
Australia 40 C3
Geel, Belgium 11 C4
Geelong, Australia . . . 43 F3
Geesthacht, Germany . 12 B6
Geidam, Nigeria 35 F8
Geikie →, Canada . . . 51 B8
Gejiu, China 24 D5
Gel, Meydān-e, Iran . . 31 D7
Gela, Italy 16 F6
Gelderland □, Neths. . . 11 B6
Geldrop, Neths. 11 C5
Geleen, Neths. 11 D5

Gelibolu, Turkey 17 D12
Gelsenkirchen, Germany 12 C4
Gembloux, Belgium . . . 11 D4
Gemena, Dem. Rep. of
the Congo 36 D3
Gemerek, Turkey 30 B3
Gemlik, Turkey 17 D13
Genale →, Ethiopia . . 32 F2
General Acha, Argentina 64 D4
General Alvear,
Buenos Aires,
Argentina 64 D5
General Alvear,
Mendoza, Argentina . 64 D3
General Belgrano,
Argentina 64 D5
General Cepeda, Mexico 58 B4
General Juan
Madariaga, Argentina 64 D5
General La Madrid,
Argentina 64 D4
General MacArthur, Phil. 27 B7
General Pico, Argentina 64 D4
General Pinedo,
Argentina 64 B4
General Roca, Argentina 64 D3
General Santos, Phil. . . 27 C7
General Trevino, Mexico 59 B5
General Trías, Mexico . 58 B3
General Villegas,
Argentina 64 D4
Genesee, U.S.A. 56 C5
Genesee →, U.S.A. . . 52 D7
Geneseo, Ill., U.S.A. . . 54 E9
Geneseo, N.Y., U.S.A. . 52 D7
Geneva = Genève,
Switz. 14 C7
Geneva, Ala., U.S.A. . . 53 K3
Geneva, N.Y., U.S.A. . . 52 D7
Geneva, Nebr., U.S.A. . 54 E6
Geneva, Ohio, U.S.A. . 52 E5
Geneva, L. = Léman, L.,
Europe 14 C7
Geneva, L., U.S.A. . . . 52 D1
Genève, Switz. 14 C7
Genil →, Spain 15 D3
Genk, Belgium 11 D5
Gennargentu, Mti. del,
Italy 16 D3
Genoa = Génova, Italy 14 D8
Genoa, Australia 43 F4
Genoa, U.S.A. 54 E6
Génova, Italy 14 D8
Génova, G. di, Italy . . 16 C3
Genriyetty, Ostrov,
Russia 21 B16
Gent, Belgium 11 C3
Genteng, Indonesia . . . 27 G12
Genyem, Indonesia . . . 27 E10
Geographe B., Australia 41 F2
Geographe Chan.,
Australia 41 D1
Georga, Zemlya, Russia 20 A5
George →, Canada . . 49 A6
George, S. Africa 37 L4
George, L., N.S.W.,
Australia 43 F4
George, L., S. Austral.,
Australia 43 F3
George, L., W. Austral.,
Australia 40 D3
George, L., Fla., U.S.A. 53 L5
George, L., N.Y., U.S.A. 52 D9
George Gill Ra.,
Australia 40 D5
George River =
Kangiqsualujjuaq,
Canada 47 C13
George Sound, N.Z. . . 39 L1
George Town, Australia 42 G4
George Town, Bahamas 60 B4
George Town, Malaysia 26 C2
George V Land,
Antarctica 5 C10
George VI Sound,
Antarctica 5 D17
George West, U.S.A. . . 55 L5
Georgetown, Australia . 42 B3
Georgetown, Ont.,
Canada 48 D4
Georgetown, P.E.I.,
Canada 49 C7
Georgetown, Cayman Is. 60 C3
Georgetown, Gambia . 34 F3
Georgetown, Guyana . 62 B7
Georgetown, Colo.,
U.S.A. 56 G11
Georgetown, Ky., U.S.A. 52 F3
Georgetown, Ohio,
U.S.A. 52 F4
Georgetown, S.C.,
U.S.A. 53 J6
Georgetown, Tex.,
U.S.A. 55 K6
Georgia ■, Asia 19 F7
Georgia □, U.S.A. 53 K5
Georgia, Str. of, Canada 50 D4
Georgian B., Canada . . 48 C3
Georgina →, Australia 42 C2
Georgiu-Dezh = Liski,
Russia 19 D6
Georgiyevsk, Russia . . 19 F7
Gera, Germany 12 C7
Geraardsbergen,
Belgium 11 D3

Geral de Goiás, Serra

Geral de Goiás, Serra, *Brazil* 63 F9
Geraldine, *U.S.A.* 56 C8
Geraldton, *Australia* 41 E1
Geraldton, *Canada* 48 C2
Gereshk, *Afghan.* 28 D4
Gering, *U.S.A.* 54 E3
Gerlach, *U.S.A.* 56 F4
Germansen Landing, *Canada* 50 B4
Germantown, *U.S.A.* 55 M10
Germany ■, *Europe* 12 C6
Germī, *Iran* 31 B6
Germiston, *S. Africa* 37 K5
Gernika-Lumo, *Spain* 15 A4
Gero, *Japan* 23 G8
Gerona = Girona, *Spain* 15 B7
Gerrard, *Canada* 50 C5
Geser, *Indonesia* 27 E8
Getafe, *Spain* 15 B4
Gettysburg, *Pa., U.S.A.* 52 F7
Gettysburg, *S. Dak., U.S.A.* 54 C5
Getxo, *Spain* 15 A4
Getz Ice Shelf, *Antarctica* 5 D14
Geyser, *U.S.A.* 56 C8
Ghaghara →, *India* 29 G14
Ghana ■, *W. Afr.* 34 G5
Ghanzi, *Botswana* 37 J4
Ghardaïa, *Algeria* 34 B6
Gharyān, *Libya* 35 B8
Ghat, *Libya* 35 D8
Ghaţţī, *Si. Arabia* 30 D3
Ghawdex = Gozo, *Malta* 16 F6
Ghazal, Bahr el →, *Chad* 35 F9
Ghazâl, Bahr el →, *Sudan* 35 G12
Ghaziabad, *India* 28 E10
Ghazipur, *India* 29 G13
Ghaznī, *Afghan.* 28 C6
Ghaznī □, *Afghan.* 28 C6
Ghent = Gent, *Belgium* 11 C3
Gheorghe Gheorghiu-Dej = Oneşti, *Romania* 13 E14
Ghīnah, Wādī al →, *Si. Arabia* 30 D3
Ghizao, *Afghan.* 28 C4
Ghowr □, *Afghan.* 28 C4
Ghudaf, W. al →, *Iraq* 30 C4
Ghudāmis, *Libya* 35 B7
Ghugus, *India* 28 K11
Ghūriān, *Afghan.* 28 B2
Gia Lai = Plei Ku, *Vietnam* 26 B3
Giarabub = Al Jaghbūb, *Libya* 35 C10
Giarre, *Italy* 16 F6
Gibara, *Cuba* 60 B4
Gibb River, *Australia* 40 C4
Gibbon, *U.S.A.* 54 E5
Gibeon, *Namibia* 37 K3
Gibraltar ■, *Europe* 15 D3
Gibraltar, Str. of, *Medit. S.* 15 E3
Gibson Desert, *Australia* 40 D4
Gibsons, *Canada* 50 D4
Giddings, *U.S.A.* 55 K6
Giessen, *Germany* 12 C5
Gīfān, *Iran* 31 B8
Gift Lake, *Canada* 50 B5
Gifu, *Japan* 23 G8
Gifu □, *Japan* 23 G8
Giganta, Sa. de la, *Mexico* 58 B2
Giglio, *Italy* 16 C4
Gijón, *Spain* 15 A3
Gil I., *Canada* 50 C3
Gila →, *U.S.A.* 57 K6
Gila Bend, *U.S.A.* 57 K7
Gila Bend Mts., *U.S.A.* 57 K7
Gīlān □, *Iran* 31 B6
Gilbert →, *Australia* 42 B3
Gilbert Is., *Kiribati* 38 A10
Gilbert River, *Australia* 42 B3
Gilford I., *Canada* 50 C3
Gilgandra, *Australia* 43 E4
Gilgit, *India* 28 B9
Gilgunnia, *Australia* 43 E4
Gillam, *Canada* 51 B10
Gillen, L., *Australia* 41 E3
Gilles, L., *Australia* 43 E2
Gillette, *U.S.A.* 54 C2
Gilliat, *Australia* 42 C3
Gillingham, *U.K.* 9 F8
Gilmer, *U.S.A.* 55 J7
Gilmore, L., *Australia* 41 F3
Gilroy, *U.S.A.* 57 H3
Gimli, *Canada* 51 C9
Gin Gin, *Australia* 43 D5
Gingin, *Australia* 41 F2
Ginir, *Ethiopia* 32 F3
Gióna, Óros, *Greece* 17 E10
Gippsland, *Australia* 43 F4
Girâfi, W. →, *Egypt* 33 F3
Girard, *U.S.A.* 55 G7
Giresun, *Turkey* 19 F6
Girga, *Egypt* 35 C12
Giridih, *India* 29 G15
Girne = Kyrenia, *Cyprus* 30 C2
Girona, *Spain* 15 B7
Gironde →, *France* 14 D3
Giru, *Australia* 42 B4
Girvan, *U.K.* 10 D4
Gisborne, *N.Z.* 39 H7
Gisenyi, *Rwanda* 36 E5
Gislaved, *Sweden* 7 H15
Gitega, *Burundi* 36 E5
Giuba →, *Somali Rep.* 32 G3
Giurgiu, *Romania* 13 G13
Giza = El Gîza, *Egypt* 35 C12
Gizhiga, *Russia* 21 C17
Gizhiginskaya Guba, *Russia* 21 C16
Giżycko, *Poland* 13 A11
Gjirokastër, *Albania* 17 D9
Gjirokastra = Gjirokastër, *Albania* 17 D9
Gjoa Haven, *Canada* 46 B10
Gjøvik, *Norway* 7 F14
Glace Bay, *Canada* 49 C8
Glacier Bay National Park and Preserve, *U.S.A.* 50 B1
Glacier National Park, *Canada* 50 C5
Glacier National Park, *U.S.A.* 56 B7
Glacier Peak, *U.S.A.* 56 B3
Gladewater, *U.S.A.* 55 J7
Gladstone, *Queens., Australia* 42 C5
Gladstone, *S. Austral., Australia* 43 E2
Gladstone, *Canada* 51 C9
Gladstone, *U.S.A.* 52 C2
Gladwin, *U.S.A.* 52 D3
Glåma = Glomma →, *Norway* 7 G14
Gláma, *Iceland* 6 D2
Glasco, *U.S.A.* 54 F6
Glasgow, *U.K.* 10 D4
Glasgow, *Ky., U.S.A.* 52 G3
Glasgow, *Mont., U.S.A.* 56 B10
Glaslyn, *Canada* 51 C7
Glastonbury, *U.K.* 9 F5
Glazov, *Russia* 18 C9
Gleichen, *Canada* 50 C6
Gleiwitz = Gliwice, *Poland* 13 C10
Glen Canyon, *U.S.A.* 57 H8
Glen Canyon Dam, *U.S.A.* 57 H8
Glen Canyon National Recreation Area, *U.S.A.* 57 H8
Glen Innes, *Australia* 43 D5
Glen Ullin, *U.S.A.* 54 B4
Glencoe, *U.S.A.* 54 C7
Glendale, *Ariz., U.S.A.* 57 K7
Glendale, *Calif., U.S.A.* 57 J4
Glendive, *U.S.A.* 54 B2
Glendo, *U.S.A.* 54 D2
Glenelg →, *Australia* 43 F3
Glenmorgan, *Australia* 43 D4
Glennallen, *U.S.A.* 46 B5
Glenns Ferry, *U.S.A.* 56 E6
Glenore, *Australia* 42 B3
Glenreagh, *Australia* 43 E5
Glenrock, *U.S.A.* 56 E11
Glenrothes, *U.K.* 10 C5
Glens Falls, *U.S.A.* 52 D9
Glenville, *U.S.A.* 52 F5
Glenwood, *Canada* 49 C9
Glenwood, *Ark., U.S.A.* 55 H8
Glenwood, *Iowa, U.S.A.* 54 E7
Glenwood, *Minn., U.S.A.* 54 C7
Glenwood Springs, *U.S.A.* 56 G10
Glettinganes, *Iceland* 6 D7
Gliwice, *Poland* 13 C10
Globe, *U.S.A.* 57 K8
Głogów, *Poland* 12 C9
Glomma →, *Norway* 7 G14
Glorieuses, Is., *Ind. Oc.* 37 G9
Glossop, *U.K.* 8 D6
Gloucester, *Australia* 43 E5
Gloucester, *U.K.* 9 F5
Gloucester I., *Australia* 42 C4
Gloucester Point, *U.S.A.* 52 G7
Gloucestershire □, *U.K.* 9 F5
Glovertown, *Canada* 49 C9
Glusk, *Belarus* 13 B15
Gmünd, *Austria* 12 D8
Gmunden, *Austria* 12 E7
Gniezno, *Poland* 13 B9
Gnowangerup, *Australia* 41 F2
Gō-no-ura, *Japan* 23 H4
Goa, *India* 28 M8
Goa □, *India* 28 M8
Goalen Hd., *Australia* 43 F5
Goalpara, *India* 29 F17
Goba, *Ethiopia* 32 F2
Gobabis, *Namibia* 37 J3
Gobi, *Asia* 25 B5
Gobō, *Japan* 23 H7
Godavari →, *India* 29 L13
Godavari Pt., *India* 29 L13
Godbout, *Canada* 49 C6
Goderich, *Canada* 48 D3
Godfrey Ra., *Australia* 41 D2
Godhavn = Qeqertarsuaq, *Greenland* 4 C5
Godhra, *India* 28 H8
Godoy Cruz, *Argentina* 64 C3
Gods →, *Canada* 48 A1
Gods L., *Canada* 48 B1
Gods River, *Canada* 51 C10
Godthåb = Nuuk, *Greenland* 47 B14
Godwin Austen = K2, *Pakistan* 28 B10
Goeie Hoop, Kaap die = Good Hope, C. of, *S. Africa* 37 L3
Goéland, L. au, *Canada* 48 C4
Goeree, *Neths.* 11 C3
Goes, *Neths.* 11 C3
Gogama, *Canada* 48 C3
Gogebic, L., *U.S.A.* 54 B10
Gogra = Ghaghara →, *India* 29 G14
Gogriâl, *Sudan* 35 G11
Goiânia, *Brazil* 63 G9
Goiás, *Brazil* 63 G8
Goiás □, *Brazil* 63 F9
Goio-Ere, *Brazil* 64 A6
Gojō, *Japan* 23 G7
Gojra, *Pakistan* 28 D8
Gökçeada, *Turkey* 17 D11
Gökova Körfezi, *Turkey* 17 F12
Gokteik, *Burma* 29 H20
Gol Gol, *Australia* 43 E3
Golan Heights = Hagolan, *Syria* 33 C4
Golāshkerd, *Iran* 31 E8
Golchikha, *Russia* 4 B12
Golconda, *U.S.A.* 56 F5
Gold Beach, *U.S.A.* 56 E1
Gold Coast, *W. Afr.* 34 H5
Gold Hill, *U.S.A.* 56 E2
Gold River, *Canada* 50 D3
Golden, *Canada* 50 C5
Golden B., *N.Z.* 39 J4
Golden Gate, *U.S.A.* 56 H2
Golden Hinde, *Canada* 50 D3
Goldendale, *U.S.A.* 56 D3
Goldfield, *U.S.A.* 57 H5
Goldsand L., *Canada* 51 B8
Goldsboro, *U.S.A.* 53 H7
Goldsmith, *U.S.A.* 55 K3
Goldsworthy, *Australia* 40 D2
Goldthwaite, *U.S.A.* 55 K5
Goleniów, *Poland* 12 B8
Golestānak, *Iran* 31 D7
Golfito, *Costa Rica* 60 E3
Golfo Aranci, *Italy* 16 D3
Goliad, *U.S.A.* 55 L6
Golpāyegān, *Iran* 31 C6
Golspie, *U.K.* 10 C5
Goma, *Dem. Rep. of the Congo* 36 E5
Gombe, *Nigeria* 35 F8
Gomel = Homyel, *Belarus* 13 B16
Gomera, *Canary Is.* 34 C2
Gómez Palacio, *Mexico* 58 B4
Gomīshān, *Iran* 31 B7
Gomogomo, *Indonesia* 27 F8
Gomoh, *India* 29 H15
Gompa = Ganta, *Liberia* 34 G4
Gonābād, *Iran* 31 C8
Gonaïves, *Haiti* 61 C5
Gonâve, G. de la, *Haiti* 61 C5
Gonâve, I. de la, *Haiti* 61 C5
Gonbad-e Kāvūs, *Iran* 31 B7
Gonda, *India* 29 F12
Gonder, *Ethiopia* 32 E2
Gondia, *India* 28 J12
Gönen, *Turkey* 17 D12
Gonghe, *China* 24 C5
Gongolgon, *Australia* 43 E4
Gonzales, *Calif., U.S.A.* 57 H3
Gonzales, *Tex., U.S.A.* 55 L6
Good Hope, C. of, *S. Africa* 37 L3
Gooding, *U.S.A.* 56 E6
Goodland, *U.S.A.* 54 F4
Goodlow, *Canada* 50 B4
Goodooga, *Australia* 43 D4
Goole, *U.K.* 8 D7
Goolgowi, *Australia* 43 E4
Goolwa, *Australia* 43 F2
Goomalling, *Australia* 41 F2
Goomeri, *Australia* 43 D5
Goondiwindi, *Australia* 43 D5
Goongarrie, L., *Australia* 41 F3
Goonyella, *Australia* 42 C4
Goose →, *Canada* 49 B7
Goose Creek, *U.S.A.* 53 J5
Goose L., *U.S.A.* 56 F3
Gop, *India* 28 H6
Göppingen, *Germany* 12 D5
Gorakhpur, *India* 29 F13
Goražde, *Bos.-H.* 17 C8
Gorda, Pta., *Nic.* 60 D3
Gordan B., *Australia* 40 B5
Gordon, *U.S.A.* 54 D3
Gordon →, *Australia* 42 G4
Gordon L., *Alta., Canada* 51 B6
Gordon L., *N.W.T., Canada* 50 A6
Gordonvale, *Australia* 42 B4
Gore, *Ethiopia* 32 F2
Gore, *N.Z.* 39 M2
Gore Bay, *Canada* 48 C3
Gorg, *Iran* 31 D8
Gorgān, *Iran* 31 B7
Gorgona, I., *Colombia* 62 C3
Gorinchem, *Neths.* 11 C4
Goris, *Armenia* 19 G8
Gorízia, *Italy* 16 B5
Gorki = Nizhniy Novgorod, *Russia* 18 C7
Gorkiy = Nizhniy Novgorod, *Russia* 18 C7
Gorkovskoye Vdkhr., *Russia* 18 C7
Görlitz, *Germany* 12 C8
Gorlovka = Horlivka, *Ukraine* 19 E6
Gorna Dzhumayo = Blagoevgrad, *Bulgaria* 17 C10
Gorna Oryakhovitsa, *Bulgaria* 17 C11
Gorno-Altay □, *Russia* 20 D9
Gorno-Altaysk, *Russia* 20 D9
Gornyatski, *Russia* 18 A11
Gornyy, *Russia* 22 B6
Gorodenka = Horodenka, *Ukraine* 13 D13
Gorodok = Horodok, *Ukraine* 13 D12
Gorokhov = Horokhiv, *Ukraine* 13 C13
Gorong, Kepulauan, *Indonesia* 27 E8
Gorontalo, *Indonesia* 27 D6
Gorzów Wielkopolski, *Poland* 12 B8
Gosford, *Australia* 43 E5
Goshen, *U.S.A.* 52 E3
Goshogawara, *Japan* 22 D10
Goslar, *Germany* 12 C6
Gospič, *Croatia* 12 F8
Gosport, *U.K.* 9 G6
Gosse →, *Australia* 42 B1
Göta älv →, *Sweden* 7 H14
Göta kanal, *Sweden* 7 G16
Götaland, *Sweden* 7 G15
Göteborg, *Sweden* 7 H14
Gotha, *Germany* 12 C6
Gothenburg = Göteborg, *Sweden* 7 H14
Gothenburg, *U.S.A.* 54 E4
Gotland, *Sweden* 7 H18
Gotō-Rettō, *Japan* 23 H4
Gotska Sandön, *Sweden* 7 G18
Gōtsu, *Japan* 23 G6
Gott Pk., *Canada* 50 C4
Göttingen, *Germany* 12 C5
Gottwaldov = Zlín, *Czech Rep.* 13 D9
Gouda, *Neths.* 11 B4
Gough I., *Atl. Oc.* 2 G9
Gouin, Rés., *Canada* 48 C5
Goulburn, *Australia* 43 E4
Goulburn Is., *Australia* 42 A1
Goulimine, *Morocco* 34 C3
Gouverneur, *U.S.A.* 52 C8
Governador Valadares, *Brazil* 63 G10
Governor's Harbour, *Bahamas* 60 A4
Gowan Ra., *Australia* 42 D4
Gowanda, *U.S.A.* 52 D6
Gower, *U.K.* 9 F3
Goya, *Argentina* 64 B5
Goyder Lagoon, *Australia* 43 D2
Goyllarisquisga, *Peru* 62 F3
Goz Beïda, *Chad* 35 F10
Gozo, *Malta* 16 F6
Graaff-Reinet, *S. Africa* 37 L4
Gračac, *Croatia* 12 F8
Gracias a Dios, C., *Honduras* 60 D3
Grado, *Spain* 15 A2
Grady, *U.S.A.* 55 H3
Grafham Water, *U.K.* 9 E7
Grafton, *Australia* 43 D5
Grafton, *N. Dak., U.S.A.* 54 A6
Grafton, *W. Va., U.S.A.* 52 F5
Graham, *Canada* 48 C1
Graham, *U.S.A.* 55 J5
Graham, Mt., *U.S.A.* 57 K9
Graham Bell, Ostrov = Greem-Bell, Ostrov, *Russia* 20 A7
Graham I., *B.C., Canada* 50 C2
Graham I., *N.W.T., Canada* 46 C6
Graham Land, *Antarctica* 5 C17
Grahamstown, *S. Africa* 37 L5
Grain Coast, *W. Afr.* 34 H3
Grajaú, *Brazil* 63 E9
Grajaú →, *Brazil* 63 D10
Grampian Highlands = Grampian Mts., *U.K.* 10 C4
Grampian Mts., *U.K.* 10 C4
Grampians, The, *Australia* 43 F3
Gran Canaria, *Canary Is.* 34 C2
Gran Chaco, *S. Amer.* 64 B4
Gran Paradiso, *Italy* 14 D7
Gran Sasso d'Itália, *Italy* 16 C5
Granada, *Nic.* 60 D2
Granada, *Spain* 15 D4
Granada, *U.S.A.* 55 F3
Granbury, *U.S.A.* 55 J6
Granby, *Canada* 48 C5
Granby, *U.S.A.* 56 F11
Grand →, *Mo., U.S.A.* 54 F8
Grand →, *S. Dak., U.S.A.* 54 C4
Grand Bahama, *Bahamas* 60 A4
Grand Bank, *Canada* 49 C8
Grand Bassam, *Ivory C.* 34 G5
Grand-Bourg, *Guadeloupe* 61 C7
Grand Canyon, *U.S.A.* 57 H7
Grand Canyon National Park, *U.S.A.* 57 H7
Grand Cayman, *Cayman Is.* 60 C3
Grand Centre, *Canada* 51 C6
Grand Coulee, *U.S.A.* 56 C4
Grand Coulee Dam, *U.S.A.* 56 C4
Grand Erg du Bilma, *Niger* 35 E8
Grand Erg Occidental, *Algeria* 34 B6
Grand Erg Oriental, *Algeria* 34 B7
Grand Falls, *Canada* 49 C6
Grand Falls-Windsor, *Canada* 49 C8
Grand Forks, *Canada* 50 D5
Grand Forks, *U.S.A.* 54 B6
Grand Haven, *U.S.A.* 52 D2
Grand I., *U.S.A.* 52 B2
Grand Island, *U.S.A.* 54 E5
Grand Isle, *U.S.A.* 55 L9
Grand Junction, *U.S.A.* 57 G9
Grand L., *N.B., Canada* 49 C6
Grand L., *Nfld., Canada* 49 C8
Grand L., *Nfld., Canada* 49 B7
Grand L., *U.S.A.* 55 L8
Grand Lake, *U.S.A.* 56 F11
Grand Manan I., *Canada* 49 D6
Grand Marais, *Canada* 54 B9
Grand Marais, *U.S.A.* 52 B3
Grand-Mère, *Canada* 48 C5
Grand Portage, *U.S.A.* 54 B10
Grand Prairie, *U.S.A.* 55 J6
Grand Rapids, *Canada* 51 C9
Grand Rapids, *Mich., U.S.A.* 52 D2
Grand Rapids, *Minn., U.S.A.* 54 B8
Grand St-Bernard, Col du, *Europe* 14 D7
Grand Teton, *U.S.A.* 56 E8
Grand Teton National Park, *U.S.A.* 56 D8
Grand Union Canal, *U.K.* 9 E7
Grand View, *Canada* 51 C8
Grande →, *Bolivia* 62 G6
Grande →, *Bahia, Brazil* 63 F10
Grande →, *Minas Gerais, Brazil* 63 H8
Grande, B., *Argentina* 64 G3
Grande, Rio →, *U.S.A.* 55 N6
Grande Baleine, R. de la →, *Canada* 48 A4
Grande Cache, *Canada* 50 C5
Grande-Entrée, *Canada* 49 C7
Grande Prairie, *Canada* 50 B5
Grande-Rivière, *Canada* 49 C7
Grande-Vallée, *Canada* 49 C6
Grandfalls, *U.S.A.* 55 K3
Grandview, *U.S.A.* 56 C4
Granger, *U.S.A.* 56 F9
Grangeville, *U.S.A.* 56 D5
Granisle, *Canada* 50 C3
Granite City, *U.S.A.* 54 F9
Granite Falls, *U.S.A.* 54 C7
Granite L., *Canada* 49 C8
Granite Pk., *U.S.A.* 56 D9
Granity, *N.Z.* 39 J3
Granja, *Brazil* 63 D10
Granollers, *Spain* 15 B7
Grant, *U.S.A.* 54 E4
Grant, Mt., *U.S.A.* 56 G4
Grant City, *U.S.A.* 54 E7
Grant I., *Australia* 40 B5
Grant Range, *U.S.A.* 57 G6
Grantham, *U.K.* 8 E7
Grants, *U.S.A.* 57 J10
Grants Pass, *U.S.A.* 56 E2
Grantsville, *U.S.A.* 56 F7
Granville, *France* 14 B3
Granville, *N. Dak., U.S.A.* 54 A4
Granville, *N.Y., U.S.A.* 52 D9
Granville L., *Canada* 51 B8
Grass →, *Canada* 51 B9
Grass Range, *U.S.A.* 56 C9
Grass River Prov. Park, *Canada* 51 C8
Grass Valley, *Calif., U.S.A.* 56 G3
Grass Valley, *Oreg., U.S.A.* 56 D3
Grasse, *France* 14 E7
Grasslands Nat. Park, *Canada* 51 D7
Grassy, *Australia* 42 G3
Graulhet, *France* 14 E4
Gravelbourg, *Canada* 51 D7
's-Gravenhage, *Neths.* 11 B4
Gravenhurst, *Canada* 48 D4
Gravesend, *Australia* 43 D5
Gravesend, *U.K.* 9 F8
Gravois, Pointe-à-, *Haiti* 61 C5
Grayling, *U.S.A.* 52 C3
Grays Harbor, *U.S.A.* 56 C1
Grays L., *U.S.A.* 56 E8
Graz, *Austria* 12 E8
Greasy L., *Canada* 50 A4
Great Abaco I., *Bahamas* 60 A4
Great Artesian Basin, *Australia* 42 C3
Great Australian Bight, *Australia* 41 F5
Great Bahama Bank, *Bahamas* 60 B4
Great Barrier I., *N.Z.* 39 G5
Great Barrier Reef, *Australia* 42 B4
Great Basin, *U.S.A.* 56 G5
Great Basin Nat. Park, *U.S.A.* 56 G6
Great Bear →, *Canada* 46 B7
Great Bear L., *Canada* 46 B7
Great Belt = Store Bælt, *Denmark* 7 J14
Great Bend, *U.S.A.* 54 F5
Great Britain, *Europe* 10 D5
Great Britain, *Europe* 10 D5
Great Codroy, *Canada* 49 C8
Great Dividing Ra., *Australia* 42 C4
Great Driffield = Driffield, *U.K.* 8 C7
Great Exuma I., *Bahamas* 60 B4
Great Falls, *U.S.A.* 56 C8
Great Guana Cay, *Bahamas* 60 B4
Great Inagua I., *Bahamas* 61 B5
Great Indian Desert = Thar Desert, *India* 28 F8
Great Karoo, *S. Africa* 37 L4
Great Lake, *Australia* 42 G4
Great Malvern, *U.K.* 9 E5
Great Miami →, *U.S.A.* 52 F3
Great Ormes Head, *U.K.* 8 D4
Great Ouse →, *U.K.* 8 E8
Great Palm I., *Australia* 42 B4
Great Ruaha →, *Tanzania* 36 F7
Great Saint Bernard Pass = Grand St-Bernard, Col du, *Europe* 14 D7
Great Salt L., *U.S.A.* 56 F7
Great Salt Lake Desert, *U.S.A.* 56 F7
Great Salt Plains L., *U.S.A.* 55 G5
Great Sandy Desert, *Australia* 40 D3
Great Sangi = Sangihe, Pulau, *Indonesia* 27 D7
Great Slave L., *Canada* 50 A5
Great Smoky Mts. Nat. Park, *U.S.A.* 53 H4
Great Snow Mt., *Canada* 50 B4
Great Stour = Stour →, *U.K.* 9 F9
Great Victoria Desert, *Australia* 41 E4
Great Wall, *China* 25 C5
Great Whernside, *U.K.* 8 C6
Great Yarmouth, *U.K.* 9 E9
Greater Antilles, *W. Indies* 61 C5
Greater London □, *U.K.* 9 F7
Greater Manchester □, *U.K.* 8 D5
Greater Sunda Is., *Indonesia* 26 F4
Gredos, Sierra de, *Spain* 15 B3
Greece ■, *Europe* 17 E9
Greeley, *Colo., U.S.A.* 54 E2
Greeley, *Nebr., U.S.A.* 54 E5
Greem-Bell, Ostrov, *Russia* 20 A7
Green, *U.S.A.* 56 E2
Green →, *Ky., U.S.A.* 52 G2
Green →, *Utah, U.S.A.* 57 G9
Green B., *U.S.A.* 52 C2
Green Bay, *U.S.A.* 52 C2
Green C., *Australia* 43 F5
Green Cove Springs, *U.S.A.* 53 L5
Green Lake, *Canada* 51 C7
Green River, *Utah, U.S.A.* 57 G8
Green River, *Wyo., U.S.A.* 56 F9
Green Valley, *U.S.A.* 57 L8
Greenbush, *U.S.A.* 54 A6
Greencastle, *U.S.A.* 52 F2
Greenfield, *Ind., U.S.A.* 52 F3
Greenfield, *Iowa, U.S.A.* 54 E7
Greenfield, *Mass., U.S.A.* 52 D9
Greenfield, *Mo., U.S.A.* 55 G8
Greenland ■, *N. Amer.* 4 C5
Greenland Sea, *Arctic* 4 B7
Greenock, *U.K.* 10 D4
Greenough, *Australia* 41 E1
Greenough →, *Australia* 41 E1
Greensboro, *Ga., U.S.A.* 53 J4
Greensboro, *N.C., U.S.A.* 53 G6
Greensburg, *Ind., U.S.A.* 52 F3

Greensburg, Kans.,
U.S.A. 55 G5
Greensburg, Pa., U.S.A. 52 E6
Greenvale, Australia .. 42 B4
Greenville, Ala., U.S.A. 53 K2
Greenville, Calif., U.S.A. 56 F3
Greenville, Maine,
U.S.A. 53 C11
Greenville, Mich., U.S.A. 52 D3
Greenville, Miss., U.S.A. 55 J9
Greenville, Mo., U.S.A. 55 G9
Greenville, N.C., U.S.A. 53 H7
Greenville, Ohio, U.S.A. 52 E3
Greenville, Pa., U.S.A. 52 E5
Greenville, S.C., U.S.A. 53 H4
Greenville, Tenn., U.S.A. 53 G4
Greenville, Tex., U.S.A. 55 J6
Greenwater Lake Prov.
Park, Canada 51 C8
Greenwich □, U.K. 9 F8
Greenwood, Canada ... 50 D5
Greenwood, Ark., U.S.A. 55 H7
Greenwood, Ind., U.S.A. 52 F2
Greenwood, Miss.,
U.S.A. 55 J9
Greenwood, S.C., U.S.A. 53 H4
Greenwood, Mt.,
Australia 40 B5
Gregory, U.S.A. 54 D5
Gregory →, Australia . 42 B2
Gregory, L., S. Austral.,
Australia 43 D2
Gregory, L., W. Austral.,
Australia 41 E2
Gregory Downs,
Australia 42 B2
Gregory L., Australia .. 40 D4
Gregory Ra., Queens.,
Australia 42 B3
Gregory Ra.,
W. Austral., Australia 40 D3
Greifswald, Germany .. 12 A7
Greiz, Germany 12 C7
Gremikha, Russia 18 A6
Grenå, Denmark 7 H14
Grenada, U.S.A. 55 J10
Grenada ■, W. Indies . 62 A4
Grenadines, W. Indies . 61 D7
Grenen, Denmark 7 H14
Grenfell, Australia ... 43 E4
Grenfell, Canada 51 C8
Grenoble, France 14 D6
Grenville, C., Australia . 42 A3
Grenville Chan., Canada 50 C3
Gresham, U.S.A. 56 D2
Gresik, Indonesia 27 G15
Grevenmacher, Lux. .. 11 E6
Grey →, Canada 49 C8
Grey →, N.Z. 39 K3
Grey, C., Australia 42 A2
Grey Ra., Australia ... 43 D3
Greybull, U.S.A. 56 D9
Greymouth, N.Z. 39 K3
Greytown, N.Z. 39 J5
Gribbell I., Canada ... 50 C3
Gridley, U.S.A. 56 G3
Griffin, U.S.A. 53 J3
Griffith, Australia 43 E4
Grimari, C.A.R. 32
Grimaylov = Hrymayliv,
Ukraine 13 D14
Grimsby, U.K. 8 D7
Grimsey, Iceland 6 C5
Grimshaw, Canada ... 50 B5
Grimstad, Norway 7 G13
Grinnell, U.S.A. 54 E8
Gris-Nez, C., France .. 14 A4
Groais I., Canada 49 B8
Grodno = Hrodna,
Belarus 13 B12
Grodzyanka =
Hrodzyanka, Belarus 13 B15
Groesbeck, U.S.A. 55 K6
Grójec, Poland 13 C11
Grong, Norway 6 D15
Groningen, Neths. 11 A6
Groningen □, Neths. .. 11 A6
Groom, U.S.A. 55 H4
Groote Eylandt,
Australia 42 A2
Grootfontein, Namibia . 37 H3
Gros C., Canada 50 A6
Gros Morne Nat. Park,
Canada 49 C8
Grosser Arber, Germany 12 D7
Grosseto, Italy 16 C4
Grossglockner, Austria . 12 E7
Groswater B., Canada . 49 B8
Groton, U.S.A. 54 C5
Grouard Mission,
Canada 50 B5
Groundhog →, Canada 48 C3
Grouw, Neths. 11 A5
Grove Hill, U.S.A. 53 K2
Groves, U.S.A. 55 L8
Groveton, U.S.A. 52 C10
Groznyy, Russia 19 F8
Grudziądz, Poland ... 13 B10
Grundy Center, U.S.A. . 54 D8
Gruver, U.S.A. 55 G4
Gryazi, Russia 18 D5
Gryazovets, Russia ... 18 C7
Gua, India 29 H14
Guacanayabo, G. de,
Cuba 60 B4

Guadalajara, Mexico .. 58 C4
Guadalajara, Spain ... 15 B4
Guadalcanal,
Solomon Is. 38 B9
Guadalete →, Spain . 15 D2
Guadalquivir →, Spain 15 D2
Guadalupe =
Guadeloupe ■,
W. Indies 61 C7
Guadalupe, U.S.A. 57 J3
Guadalupe →, U.S.A. 55 L6
Guadalupe, Sierra de,
Spain 15 C3
Guadalupe Bravos,
Mexico 58 A3
Guadalupe Mts. Nat.
Park, U.S.A. 55 K2
Guadalupe Peak, U.S.A. 55 K2
Guadalupe y Calvo,
Mexico 58 B3
Guadarrama, Sierra de,
Spain 15 B4
Guadeloupe ■,
W. Indies 61 C7
Guadeloupe Passage,
W. Indies 61 C7
Guadiana →, Portugal 15 D2
Guadix, Spain 15 D4
Guafo, Boca del, Chile . 64 E2
Guainía □, Colombia .. 62 C5
Guaira, Brazil 64 A6
Guaitecas, Is., Chile .. 64 E2
Guajará-Mirim, Brazil . 62 F5
Guajira, Pen. de la,
Colombia 62 A4
Gualán, Guatemala ... 60 C2
Gualeguaychú,
Argentina 64 C5
Guam ■, Pac. Oc. 44 F6
Guamúchil, Mexico ... 58 B3
Guanabacoa, Cuba ... 60 B3
Guanacaste, Cordillera
del, Costa Rica 60 D2
Guanaceví, Mexico ... 58 B3
Guanahani = San
Salvador I., Bahamas 61 B5
Guanajay, Cuba 60 B3
Guanajuato, Mexico .. 58 C4
Guanajuato □, Mexico 58 C4
Guandacol, Argentina . 64 B3
Guane, Cuba 60 B3
Guangdong □, China .. 25 D6
Guangxi Zhuangzu
Zizhiqu □, China ... 25 D5
Guangzhou, China ... 25 D6
Guanipa →, Venezuela 62 B6
Guantánamo, Cuba ... 61 B4
Guápiles, Costa Rica .. 60 D3
Guaporé →, Brazil ... 62 F5
Guaqui, Bolivia 62 G5
Guarapuava, Brazil ... 64 B6
Guarda, Portugal 15 B2
Guardafui, C. = Asir,
Ras, Somali Rep. .. 32 E5
Guárico □, Venezuela . 62 B5
Guasave, Mexico 58 B3
Guasdualito, Venezuela 62 B4
Guatemala, Guatemala 60 D1
Guatemala ■,
Cent. Amer. 60 C1
Guaviare →, Colombia 62 C5
Guaxupé, Brazil 63 H9
Guayama, Puerto Rico . 61 C6
Guayaquil, Ecuador .. 62 D3
Guayaquil, G. de,
Ecuador 62 D2
Guaymas, Mexico 58 B2
Gubkin, Russia 19 D6
Gudbrandsdalen,
Norway 7 F14
Guddu Barrage,
Pakistan 28 E6
Gudur, India 28 M11
Guecho = Getxo, Spain 15 A4
Guelph, Canada 48 D3
Guéret, France 14 C4
Guernica = Gernika-
Lumo, Spain 15 A4
Guernsey, U.K. 9 H5
Guernsey, U.S.A. 54 D2
Guerrero □, Mexico .. 59 D5
Gügher, Iran 31 D8
Guhakolak, Tanjung,
Indonesia 27 G11
Guidónia-Montecélio,
Italy 16 C5
Guiją, Mozam. 37 J6
Guildford, U.K. 9 F7
Guilin, China 25 D6
Guillaume-Delisle L.,
Canada 48 A4
Guimarães, Portugal .. 15 B1
Guimaras □, Phil. 27 B6
Guinea ■, W. Afr. 34 F3
Guinea, Gulf of, Atl. Oc. 3 D10
Guinea, Gulf of, Atl. Oc. 3 D10
Guinea-Bissau ■, Africa 34 F3
Güines, Cuba 60 B3
Guingamp, France ... 14 B2
Güiria, Venezuela 62 A6
Guiuan, Phil. 27 B7
Guiyang, China 24 D5
Guizhou □, China 24 D5
Gujarat □, India 28 H7
Gujranwala, Pakistan . 28 C9

Gujrat, Pakistan 28 C9
Gulargambone,
Australia 43 E4
Gulbarga, India 28 L10
Gulbene, Latvia 7 H22
Gulf, The, Asia 31 E6
Gulfport, U.S.A. 55 K10
Gulgong, Australia ... 43 E4
Gull Lake, Canada ... 51 C7
Güllük, Turkey 17 F12
Gulshad, Kazakstan .. 20 E8
Gulu, Uganda 36 D6
Gumel, Nigeria 34 F7
Gumlu, Australia 42 B4
Gumma □, Japan 23 F9
Gumzai, Indonesia ... 27 F8
Guna, India 28 G10
Gunisao →, Canada . 51 C9
Gunisao L., Canada .. 51 C9
Gunnbjørn Fjeld,
Greenland 4 C6
Gunnedah, Australia .. 43 E5
Gunnewin, Australia .. 43 D4
Gunningbar Cr. →,
Australia 43 E4
Gunnison, Colo., U.S.A. 57 G10
Gunnison, Utah, U.S.A. 56 G8
Gunnison →, U.S.A. . 57 G9
Gunpowder, Australia . 42 B2
Guntakal, India 28 M10
Guntersville, U.S.A. .. 53 H2
Guntur, India 29 L12
Gunungapi, Indonesia . 27 F7
Gunungsitoli, Indonesia 26 D1
Gunza, Angola 36 G2
Gupis, Pakistan 28 A8
Gurdaspur, India 28 C9
Gurdon, U.S.A. 55 J8
Gurgueia →, Brazil .. 63 E10
Gurkha, Nepal 29 E14
Gurley, Australia 43 D4
Gürün, Turkey 19 G6
Gurupá, Brazil 63 D8
Gurupá, I. Grande de,
Brazil 63 D8
Gurupi, Brazil 63 F9
Gurupi →, Brazil 63 D9
Guryev = Atyraū,
Kazakstan 19 E9
Gusau, Nigeria 34 F7
Gusev, Russia 7 J20
Gushgy, Turkmenistan 20 F7
Gusinoozersk, Russia . 21 D11
Gustavus, U.S.A. 50 B1
Gustine, U.S.A. 57 H3
Güstrow, Germany ... 12 B7
Gütersloh, Germany .. 12 C5
Gutha, Australia 41 E2
Guthalungra, Australia 42 B4
Guthrie, Okla., U.S.A. . 55 H6
Guthrie, Tex., U.S.A. . 55 J4
Guttenberg, U.S.A. .. 54 D9
Guyana ■, S. Amer. .. 62 C7
Guyane française =
French Guiana ■,
S. Amer. 63 C8
Guyenne, France 14 D4
Guymon, U.S.A. 55 G4
Guyra, Australia 43 E5
Guzmán, L. de, Mexico 58 A3
Gvardeysk, Russia ... 7 J19
Gwa, Burma 29 L19
Gwabegar, Australia .. 43 E4
Gwädar, Pakistan 28 G3
Gwalior, India 28 F11
Gwanda, Zimbabwe .. 37 J5
Gweru, Zimbabwe ... 37 H5
Gwinn, U.S.A. 52 B2
Gwydir →, Australia . 43 D4
Gwynedd □, U.K. 8 E3
Gyandzha = Gäncä,
Azerbaijan 19 F8
Gyaring Hu, China ... 24 C4
Gydanskiy Poluostrov,
Russia 20 C8
Gympie, Australia ... 43 D5
Gyöngyös, Hungary .. 13 E10
Győr, Hungary 13 E9
Gypsum Pt., Canada .. 50 A6
Gypsumville, Canada . 51 C9
Gyula, Hungary 13 E11
Gyumri, Armenia 19 F7
Gyzylarbat,
Turkmenistan 20 F6
Gyzyletrek,
Turkmenistan 31 B7

Ha 'Arava →, Israel . 33 E4
Haaksbergen, Neths. . 11 B6
Haapsalu, Estonia ... 7 G20
Haarlem, Neths. 11 B4
Haast →, N.Z. 39 K2
Haast Bluff, Australia . 40 D5
Hab Nadi Chauki,
Pakistan 28 G5
Habay, Canada 50 B5
Habbānīyah, Iraq 30 C4
Haboro, Japan 22 B10
Ḥabshān, U.A.E. 31 F7
Hachijō-Jima, Japan .. 23 H9
Hachinohe, Japan ... 22 D10
Hachiōji, Japan 23 G9

Hadarba, Ras, Sudan . 35 D13
Hadarom □, Israel ... 33 E4
Hadd, Ra's al, Oman .. 32 C6
Hadejia, Nigeria 34 F7
Hadera, Israel 33 C3
Hadera, N. →, Israel . 33 C3
Haderslev, Denmark . 7 J13
Hadramawt = Yemen . 32 D4
Hadibu, Yemen 32 E5
Hadramawt, Yemen .. 32 D4
Ḥadrāniyah, Iraq 30 C4
Hadrian's Wall, U.K. .. 8 B5
Haeju, N. Korea 25 C7
Haerhpin = Harbin,
China 25 B7
Hafar al Bāţin, Si. Arabia 30 D5
Ḥafirat al 'Aydā,
Si. Arabia 30 E3
Hafit, Oman 31 F7
Ḥafit, Jabal, Oman ... 31 E7
Hafizabad, Pakistan .. 28 C8
Haflong, India 29 G18
Hafnarfjörður, Iceland . 6 D3
Haft Gel, Iran 31 D6
Hafun, Ras, Somali Rep. 32 E5
Hagalil, Israel 33 C4
Hagen, Germany 12 C4
Hagerman, U.S.A. ... 55 J2
Hagerstown, U.S.A. .. 52 F7
Hagfors, Sweden 7 F15
Hagi, Japan 23 G5
Hagolan, Syria 33 C4
Hagondange, France . 14 B7
Hague, C. de la, France 14 B3
Hague, The = 's-
Gravenhage, Neths. . 11 B4
Haguenau, France ... 14 B7
Haifa = Ḥefa, Israel .. 33 C4
Haikou, China 25 D6
Ḥā'il, Si. Arabia 30 E4
Hailar, China 25 B6
Hailey, U.S.A. 56 E6
Haileybury, Canada .. 48 C4
Hailuoto, Finland 6 D21
Hainan □, China 25 E5
Hainaut □, Belgium .. 11 D4
Haines, Alaska, U.S.A. . 50 B1
Haines, Oreg., U.S.A. . 56 D5
Haines City, U.S.A. ... 53 L5
Haines Junction,
Canada 50 A1
Haiphong, Vietnam .. 24 D5
Haiti ■, W. Indies 61 C5
Haiya, Sudan 35 E13
Hajdúböszörmény,
Hungary 13 E11
Hājji Muḥsin, Iraq ... 30 C5
Ḥājjiābād, Iran 31 D7
Ḥājjiābād-e Zarrīn, Iran 31 C7
Hajnówka, Poland ... 13 B12
Hakansson, Turkey .. 30 B4
Hakken-Zan, Japan .. 23 G7
Hakodate, Japan 22 D10
Haku-San, Japan 23 F8
Hakui, Japan 23 F8
Hala, Pakistan 28 G6
Ḥalab, Syria 30 B3
Ḥalabjah, Iraq 30 C5
Halaib, Sudan 35 D13
Hālat 'Ammār,
Si. Arabia 30 D3
Halbā, Lebanon 33 A5
Halberstadt, Germany . 12 C6
Halcombe, N.Z. 39 J5
Halcon, Phil. 27 B6
Halden, Norway 7 G14
Haldia, India 29 H16
Haldwani, India 28 E11
Hale →, Australia ... 42 C2
Halesowen, U.K. 9 E5
Haleyville, U.S.A. 53 H2
Halfmoon Bay, N.Z. .. 39 M2
Halfway →, Canada . 50 B4
Haliburton, Canada .. 48 C4
Halifax, Australia 42 B4
Halifax, Canada 49 D7
Halifax, U.K. 8 D6
Halifax B., Australia .. 42 B4
Halî'l →, Iran 31 E8
Hall Beach = Sanirajak,
Canada 47 B11
Hall Pen., Canada ... 47 B13
Hall Pt., Australia 40 C3
Halland, Sweden 7 H15
Halle, Belgium 11 D4
Halle, Germany 12 C6
Hällefors, Sweden ... 7 G16
Hallett, Australia 43 E2
Hallettsville, U.S.A. .. 55 L6
Hallingdalselvi →,
Norway 7 F13
Hallock, U.S.A. 54 A6
Halls Creek, Australia . 40 C4
Hallsberg, Sweden ... 7 G16
Halmahera, Indonesia . 27 D7
Halmstad, Sweden ... 7 H15
Hälsingborg =
Helsingborg, Sweden 7 H15
Häslsingland, Sweden . 7 F17
Halstead, U.K. 9 F8
Halti, Finland 6 B19
Halton □, U.K. 8 D5
Haltwhistle, U.K. 8 C5
Ḥalul, Qatar 31 E7

Ḥalvān, Iran 31 C8
Hamada, Japan 23 G6
Hamadān, Iran 31 C6
Hamadān □, Iran 31 C6
Hamāh, Syria 30 C3
Hamamatsu, Japan .. 23 G8
Hamar, Norway 7 F14
Hambantota, Sri Lanka 28 R12
Hamber Prov. Park,
Canada 50 C5
Hamburg, Germany .. 12 B5
Hamburg, Ark., U.S.A. 55 J9
Hamburg, N.Y., U.S.A. 52 D6
Ḥamd, W. al →,
Si. Arabia 30 E3
Häme, Finland 7 F20
Hämeenlinna, Finland . 7 F21
Hamelin Pool, Australia 41 E1
Hameln, Germany ... 12 B5
Hamerkaz □, Israel .. 33 C3
Hamersley Ra., Australia 40 D2
Hami, China 24 B4
Hamilton, Australia .. 43 F3
Hamilton, Canada ... 48 D4
Hamilton, N.Z. 39 G5
Hamilton, U.K. 10 D4
Hamilton, Ala., U.S.A. . 53 H1
Hamilton, Mont., U.S.A. 56 C6
Hamilton, N.Y., U.S.A. 52 D8
Hamilton, Ohio, U.S.A. 52 F3
Hamilton, Tex., U.S.A. 55 K5
Hamilton →, Australia 42 C2
Hamilton Inlet, Canada 49 B8
Hamina, Finland 7 F22
Hamlet, U.S.A. 53 H6
Hamley Bridge,
Australia 43 E2
Hamlin = Hameln,
Germany 12 B5
Hamlin, U.S.A. 55 J4
Hamm, Germany 12 C4
Hammār, Hawr al, Iraq 30 D5
Hammerfest, Norway . 6 A20
Hammond, Ind., U.S.A. 52 E2
Hammond, La., U.S.A. 55 K9
Hammonton, U.S.A. .. 52 F8
Hampden, N.Z. 39 L3
Hampshire □, U.K. ... 9 F6
Hampshire Downs, U.K. 9 F6
Hampton, Canada ... 49 C6
Hampton, Ark., U.S.A. 55 J8
Hampton, Iowa, U.S.A. 54 D8
Hampton, S.C., U.S.A. 53 J5
Hampton, Va., U.S.A. . 52 G7
Hampton Tableland,
Australia 41 F4
Han Pijesak, Bos.-H. . 17 B8
Hanak, Si. Arabia 30 E3
Hanamaki, Japan ... 22 E10
Hanau, Germany 12 C5
Hancock, U.S.A. 54 B10
Handa, Japan 23 G8
Handan, China 25 C6
Hanegev, Israel 33 E4
Hanford, U.S.A. 57 H4
Hangayn Nuruu,
Mongolia 24 B4
Hangchou = Hangzhou,
China 25 C7
Hangzhou, China 25 C7
Hangzhou Wan, China . 25 C7
Ḥanidh, Si. Arabia ... 31 E6
Ḥanish, Yemen 32 E3
Hankinson, U.S.A. ... 54 B6
Hanko, Finland 7 G20
Hanksville, U.S.A. ... 57 G8
Hanle, India 28 C11
Hanmer Springs, N.Z. . 39 K4
Hann →, Australia .. 40 C4
Hann, Mt., Australia .. 40 C4
Hanna, Canada 50 C6
Hannah B., Canada .. 48 B4
Hannibal, U.S.A. 54 F9
Hannover, Germany .. 12 B5
Hanoi, Vietnam 24 D5
Hanover = Hannover,
Germany 12 B5
Hanover, Canada 48 D3
Hanover, N.H., U.S.A. . 52 D9
Hanover, Pa., U.S.A. . 52 F7
Hanover, I., Chile 64 G2
Hansi, India 28 E9
Hanson, L., Australia . 43 E2
Hantsavichy, Belarus . 13 B14
Hanzhong, China 24 C5
Haora, India 29 H16
Haparanda, Sweden . 6 D21
Happy, U.S.A. 55 H4
Happy Camp, U.S.A. . 56 F2
Happy Valley-Goose
Bay, Canada 49 B7
Hapur, India 28 E10
Ḥaql, Si. Arabia 33 F3
Har, Indonesia 27 F8
Har Us Nuur, Mongolia 24 B4
Har Yehuda, Israel ... 33 D3
Ḥaraḍ, Si. Arabia 32 C4
Haranomachi, Japan . 22 F10
Harare, Zimbabwe ... 37 H6
Harbin, China 25 B7
Harbor Beach, U.S.A. . 52 D4
Harbour Breton, Canada 49 C8

Harbour Deep, Canada 49 B8
Hardangerfjorden,
Norway 7 F12
Hardangervidda,
Norway 7 F12
Hardenberg, Neths. .. 11 B6
Harderwijk, Neths. ... 11 B5
Hardey →, Australia . 40 D2
Hardin, U.S.A. 56 D10
Harding Ra., Australia . 40 C3
Hardisty, Canada 50 C6
Hardoi, India 28 F12
Hardwar = Haridwar,
India 28 E11
Hardy, Pen., Chile ... 64 H3
Hare B., Canada 49 B8
Hareid, Norway 7 E12
Harer, Ethiopia 32 F3
Hargeisa, Somali Rep. . 32 F3
Hari →, Indonesia ... 26 E2
Haridwar, India 28 E11
Harim, Jabal al, Oman 31 E8
Haringhata →, Bangla. 29 J16
Harīrūd →, Asia 28 A2
Härjedalen, Sweden .. 7 E15
Harlan, Iowa, U.S.A. .. 54 E7
Harlan, Ky., U.S.A. ... 53 G4
Harlech, U.K. 8 E3
Harlem, U.S.A. 56 B9
Harlingen, Neths. 11 A5
Harlingen, U.S.A. 55 M6
Harlow, U.K. 9 F8
Harlowton, U.S.A. ... 56 C9
Harney Basin, U.S.A. . 56 E4
Harney L., U.S.A. 56 E4
Harney Peak, U.S.A. . 54 D3
Härnösand, Sweden .. 7 E17
Harp L., Canada 49 A7
Harper, Liberia 34 H4
Harricana →, Canada 48 B4
Harriman, U.S.A. 53 H3
Harrington Harbour,
Canada 49 B8
Harris, U.K. 10 C3
Harris L., Australia ... 43 E2
Harrisburg, Ill., U.S.A. 55 G10
Harrisburg, Nebr.,
U.S.A. 54 E3
Harrisburg, Pa., U.S.A. 52 E7
Harrison, Ark., U.S.A. 55 G8
Harrison, Nebr., U.S.A. 54 D3
Harrison, C., Canada .. 49 B8
Harrison L., Canada .. 50 D4
Harrisonburg, U.S.A. . 52 F6
Harrisonville, U.S.A. . 54 F7
Harrisville, U.S.A. ... 52 C4
Harrodsburg, U.S.A. . 52 G3
Harrogate, U.K. 8 C6
Harrow →, Canada .. 9 F7
Harry S. Truman
Reservoir, U.S.A. ... 54 F7
Harsin, Iran 30 C5
Harstad, Norway 6 B17
Hart, U.S.A. 52 D2
Hart, L., Australia 43 E2
Hartford, Conn., U.S.A. 52 E9
Hartford, Ky., U.S.A. . 52 G2
Hartford, S. Dak., U.S.A. 54 D6
Hartford, Wis., U.S.A. 54 D10
Hartford City, U.S.A. . 52 E3
Hartland, Canada 49 C6
Hartland Pt., U.K. 9 F3
Hartlepool, U.K. 8 C6
Hartlepool □, U.K. ... 8 C6
Hartley Bay, Canada . 50 C3
Hartney, Canada 51 D8
Hartselle, U.S.A. 53 H2
Hartshorne, U.S.A. .. 55 H7
Hartsville, U.S.A. 53 H5
Hartwell, U.S.A. 53 H4
Harvand, Iran 31 D7
Harvey, Australia 41 F2
Harvey, Ill., U.S.A. ... 52 E2
Harvey, N. Dak., U.S.A. 54 B5
Harwich, U.K. 9 F9
Haryana □, India 28 E10
Haryn →, Belarus ... 13 B14
Harz, Germany 12 C6
Hasa □, Si. Arabia ... 31 E6
Ḥasanābād, Iran 31 C7
Hashimoto, Japan ... 23 G7
Hashtjerd, Iran 31 C6
Haskell, U.S.A. 55 J5
Haslemere, U.K. 9 F7
Hasselt, Belgium 11 D5
Hassi Messaoud, Algeria 34 B7
Hässleholm, Sweden . 7 H15
Hastings, N.Z. 39 H6
Hastings, U.K. 9 G8
Hastings, Mich., U.S.A. 52 D3
Hastings, Minn., U.S.A. 54 C8
Hastings, Nebr., U.S.A. 54 E5
Hastings Ra., Australia 43 E5
Hat Yai, Thailand 26 C2
Hatay = Antalya, Turkey 19 G5
Hatch, U.S.A. 57 K10
Hatchet L., Canada .. 51 B8
Hateruma-Shima, Japan 23 M1
Hatfield P.O., Australia 43 E3
Hatgal, Mongolia 24 A5
Hathras, India 28 F11
Hato Mayor, Dom. Rep. 61 C6
Hattah, Australia 43 E3
Hatteras, C., U.S.A. .. 53 H8

Hattiesburg, U.S.A. .. 55 K10
Hatvan, Hungary 13 E10
Hau Bon = Cheo Reo, Vietnam 26 B3
Haugesund, Norway .. 7 G11
Haukipudas, Finland .. 6 D21
Haultain →, Canada .. 51 B7
Hauraki G., N.Z. 39 G5
Haut Atlas, Morocco .. 34 B4
Hautes Fagnes = Hohe Venn, Belgium 11 D6
Havana = La Habana, Cuba 60 B3
Havana, U.S.A. 54 E9
Havant, U.K. 9 G7
Havasu, L., U.S.A. ... 57 J6
Havel →, Germany .. 12 B7
Havelock, Canada 48 D4
Havelock, N.Z. 39 J4
Havelock, U.S.A. 53 H7
Haverfordwest, U.K. .. 9 F3
Haverhill, U.S.A. 52 D10
Havířov, Czech. 13 D10
Havlíčkův Brod, Czech Rep. 12 D8
Havre, U.S.A. 56 B9
Havre-Aubert, Canada . 49 C7
Havre-St.-Pierre, Canada 49 B7
Haw →, U.S.A. 53 H6
Hawaiian Is., Pac. Oc. . 45 E12
Hawaiian Ridge, Pac. Oc. 45 E11
Hawarden, U.S.A. 54 D6
Hawea, L., N.Z. 39 L2
Hawera, N.Z. 39 H5
Hawick, U.K. 10 D5
Hawk Junction, Canada 48 C3
Hawke B., N.Z. 39 H6
Hawker, Australia 43 E2
Hawkesbury, Canada .. 48 C5
Hawkesbury →, Canada 50 C3
Hawkesbury Pt., Australia 42 A1
Hawkinsville, U.S.A. .. 53 J4
Hawley, U.S.A. 54 B6
Ḩawrān, W. →, Iraq .. 30 C4
Hawsh Mūssá, Lebanon 33 B4
Hawthorne, U.S.A. ... 56 G4
Hay, Australia 43 E3
Hay →, Australia 42 C2
Hay →, Canada 50 A5
Hay, C., Australia 40 B4
Hay L., Canada 50 B5
Hay-on-Wye, U.K. ... 9 E4
Hay River, Canada ... 50 A5
Hay Springs, U.S.A. .. 54 D3
Haya = Tehoru, Indonesia 27 E7
Hayachine-San, Japan . 22 E10
Hayden, U.S.A. 56 F10
Haydon, Australia 42 B3
Hayes →, U.S.A. 54 C4
Hayes →, Canada ... 48 A1
Hayes Creek, Australia 40 B5
Hayle, U.K. 9 G2
Hayling I., U.K. 9 G7
Hayrabolu, Turkey ... 17 D12
Hays, Canada 50 C6
Hays, U.S.A. 54 F5
Haysyn, Ukraine 13 D15
Hayvoron, Ukraine ... 13 D15
Hayward, Calif., U.S.A. 57 G2
Hayward, Wis., U.S.A. . 54 B9
Haywards Heath, U.K. . 9 G7
Ḩaẓafon □, Israel 33 C4
Hazārān, Kūh-e, Iran . 31 D8
Hazard, U.S.A. 52 G4
Hazaribag, India 29 H14
Hazelton, Canada 50 B3
Hazelton, U.S.A. 54 B4
Hazen, U.S.A. 54 B4
Hazlehurst, Ga., U.S.A. 53 K4
Hazlehurst, Miss., U.S.A. 55 K9
Hazleton, U.S.A. 52 E8
Hazlett, L., Australia .. 40 D4
Hazro, Turkey 30 B4
Head of Bight, Australia 41 F5
Healdsburg, U.S.A. ... 56 G2
Healdton, U.S.A. 55 H6
Healesville, Australia .. 43 F4
Heard I., Ind. Oc. 3 G13
Hearne, U.S.A. 55 K6
Hearst, Canada 48 C3
Heart →, U.S.A. 54 B4
Heart's Content, Canada 49 C9
Heath Pt., Canada ... 49 C7
Heavener, U.S.A. 55 H7
Hebbronville, U.S.A. .. 55 M5
Hebei □, China 25 C6
Hebel, Australia 43 D4
Heber City, U.S.A. ... 56 F8
Heber Springs, U.S.A. . 55 H9
Hebert, Canada 51 C7
Hebgen L., U.S.A. ... 56 D8
Hebron = Al Khalīl, West Bank 33 D4
Hebron, Canada 47 C13
Hebron, N. Dak., U.S.A. 54 B3
Hebron, Nebr., U.S.A. . 54 E6
Hecate Str., Canada .. 50 C2
Heceta I., U.S.A. 50 B2
Hechi, China 24 D5
Hechuan, China 24 C5
Hecla, U.S.A. 54 C5
Hecla I., Canada 51 C9

Hede, Sweden 7 E15
Hedemora, Sweden ... 7 F16
Heerde, Neths. 11 B6
Heerenveen, Neths. .. 11 B5
Heerhugowaard, Neths. 11 B4
Heerlen, Neths. 14 A6
Hefa, Israel 33 C4
Hefa □, Israel 33 C4
Hefei, China 25 C6
Hegang, China 25 B8
Heidelberg, Germany . 12 D5
Heilbronn, Germany . 12 D5
Heilongjiang □, China . 25 B7
Heilunkiang = Heilongjiang □, China 25 B7
Heimaey, Iceland 6 E3
Heinola, Finland 7 F22
Hejaz = Ḥijāz □, Si. Arabia 30 E3
Hekimhan, Turkey ... 30 B3
Hekla, Iceland 6 E4
Hekou, China 24 D5
Helen Atoll, Pac. Oc. . 27 D8
Helena, Ark., U.S.A. .. 55 H9
Helena, Mont., U.S.A. . 56 C7
Helensville, N.Z. 39 G5
Helenvale, Australia .. 42 B4
Helgeland, Norway .. 6 C15
Helgoland, Germany .. 12 A4
Heligoland = Helgoland, Germany 12 A4
Heligoland B. = Deutsche Bucht, Germany 12 A5
Hella, Iceland 6 E3
Hellespont = Çanakkale Boğazı, Turkey 17 D12
Hellevoetsluis, Neths. . 11 C4
Hellín, Spain 15 C5
Helmand □, Afghan. .. 28 D4
Helmand →, Afghan. . 28 D2
Helmond, Neths. 11 C5
Helmsdale, U.K. 10 C5
Helper, U.S.A. 56 G8
Helsingborg, Sweden . 7 H15
Helsingfors = Helsinki, Finland 7 F21
Helsingør, Denmark .. 7 H15
Helsinki, Finland 7 F21
Helston, U.K. 9 G2
Helvellyn, U.K. 8 C4
Helwân, Egypt 35 C12
Hemel Hempstead, U.K. 9 F7
Hemet, U.S.A. 57 K5
Hemingford, U.S.A. .. 54 D3
Hempstead, U.S.A. ... 55 K6
Hemse, Sweden 7 H18
Henan □, China 25 C6
Henares →, Spain ... 15 B4
Henashi-Misaki, Japan 22 D9
Henderson, Ky., U.S.A. 52 G2
Henderson, N.C., U.S.A. 53 G6
Henderson, Nev., U.S.A. 57 H6
Henderson, Tenn., U.S.A. 53 H1
Henderson, Tex., U.S.A. 55 J7
Hendersonville, N.C., U.S.A. 53 H4
Hendersonville, Tenn., U.S.A. 53 G2
Hendijān, Iran 31 D6
Hendorābī, Iran 31 E7
Hengelo, Neths. 11 B6
Hengyang, China 25 D6
Henlopen, C., U.S.A. . 52 F8
Hennessey, U.S.A. ... 55 G6
Henrietta, U.S.A. 55 J5
Henrietta, Ostrov = Genriyetty, Ostrov, Russia 21 B16
Henrietta Maria, C., Canada 48 A3
Henry, U.S.A. 54 E10
Henryetta, U.S.A. ... 55 H7
Hentiyn Nuruu, Mongolia 25 B5
Henty, Australia 43 F4
Henzada, Burma 29 L19
Heppner, U.S.A. 56 D4
Héraðsflói, Iceland .. 6 D6
Héraðsvötn →, Iceland 6 D4
Herald Cays, Australia . 42 B4
Herāt, Afghan. 28 B3
Herāt □, Afghan. 28 B3
Herbert →, Australia . 42 B4
Herberton, Australia .. 42 B4
Herceg-Novi, Montenegro, Yug. .. 17 C8
Herchmer, Canada ... 51 B10
Herðubreið, Iceland .. 6 D5
Hereford, U.K. 9 E5
Hereford, U.S.A. 55 H3
Herefordshire □, U.K. . 9 E5
Herentals, Belgium .. 11 C4
Herford, Germany ... 12 B5
Herington, U.S.A. ... 54 F6
Herkimer, U.S.A. 52 D8
Herm, U.K. 9 H5
Hermann, U.S.A. 54 F9
Hermannsburg, Australia 40 D5
Hermidale, Australia .. 43 E4
Hermiston, U.S.A. ... 56 D4
Hermite, I., Chile 64 H3

Hermon, Mt. = Shaykh, J. ash, Lebanon 33 B4
Hermosillo, Mexico ... 58 B2
Hernád →, Hungary . 13 D11
Hernando, U.S.A. 55 H10
Herne, Germany 11 C7
Herne Bay, U.K. 9 F9
Herning, Denmark ... 7 H13
Heroica = Caborca, Mexico 58 A2
Heroica Nogales = Nogales, Mexico 58 A2
Heron Bay, Canada .. 48 C2
Herreid, U.S.A. 54 C4
Herrin, U.S.A. 55 G10
Herstal, Belgium 11 D5
Hertford, U.K. 9 F7
Hertfordshire □, U.K. . 9 F7
's-Hertogenbosch, Neths. 11 C5
Hervey B., Australia .. 42 C5
Herzliyya, Israel 33 C3
Ḩeşār, Fārs, Iran 31 D6
Ḩeşār, Markazī, Iran .. 31 C6
Hesperia, U.S.A. 57 J5
Hesse = Hessen □, Germany 12 C5
Hessen □, Germany .. 12 C5
Hettinger, U.S.A. 54 C3
Hewitt, U.S.A. 55 K6
Hexham, U.K. 8 C5
Heydarābād, Iran 31 D7
Heysham, U.K. 8 C5
Heywood, Australia .. 43 F3
Hialeah, U.S.A. 53 N5
Hiawatha, U.S.A. 54 F7
Hibbing, U.S.A. 54 B8
Hibbs B., Australia ... 42 G4
Hibernia Reef, Australia 40 B3
Hickman, U.S.A. 55 G10
Hickory, U.S.A. 53 H5
Hicks, Pt., Australia .. 43 F4
Hicks L., Canada 51 A9
Hida-Gawa →, Japan 23 G8
Hida-Sammyaku, Japan 23 F8
Hidaka-Sammyaku, Japan 22 C11
Hidalgo, Mexico 59 C5
Hidalgo □, Mexico ... 59 C5
Hidalgo, Presa M., Mexico 58 B3
Hidalgo del Parral, Mexico 58 B3
Hierro, Canary Is. 34 C2
Higashiajima-San, Japan 22 F10
Higashiōsaka, Japan .. 23 G7
Higgins, U.S.A. 55 G4
High Atlas = Haut Atlas, Morocco 34 B4
High Level, Canada .. 50 B5
High Point, U.S.A. ... 53 H6
High Prairie, Canada .. 50 B5
High River, Canada ... 50 C6
High Tatra = Tatry, Slovak Rep. 13 D11
High Wycombe, U.K. . 9 F7
Highland Park, U.S.A. . 52 D2
Highmore, U.S.A. ... 54 C5
Highrock L., Man., Canada 51 B8
Highrock L., Sask., Canada 51 B7
Higüey, Dom. Rep. ... 61 C6
Hiiumaa, Estonia 7 G20
Ḩijāz □, Si. Arabia ... 30 E3
Hijo = Tagum, Phil. .. 27 C7
Hikari, Japan 23 H5
Hiko, U.S.A. 57 H6
Hikone, Japan 23 G8
Hikurangi, N.Z. 39 F5
Hikurangi, Mt., N.Z. .. 39 H6
Hildesheim, Germany . 12 B5
Hill →, Australia 41 F2
Hill City, Idaho, U.S.A. 56 E6
Hill City, Kans., U.S.A. 54 F5
Hill City, S. Dak., U.S.A. 54 D3
Hill Island L., Canada . 51 A7
Hillegom, Neths. 11 B4
Hillerød, Denmark ... 7 J15
Hillsboro, Kans., U.S.A. 54 F6
Hillsboro, N. Dak., U.S.A. 54 B6
Hillsboro, N.H., U.S.A. 52 D10
Hillsboro, Ohio, U.S.A. 52 F4
Hillsboro, Tex., U.S.A. 55 J6
Hillsborough, Grenada 61 D7
Hillsdale, U.S.A. 52 E3
Hillsport, Canada 48 C2
Hillston, Australia ... 43 E4
Hilton Head Island, U.S.A. 53 J5
Hilversum, Neths. ... 11 B5
Himachal Pradesh □, India 28 D10
Himalaya, Asia 29 E14
Himatnagar, India ... 28 H8
Himeji, Japan 23 G7
Himi, Japan 23 F8
Ḩimṣ, Syria 33 A5
Ḩimṣ □, Syria 33 A5
Hinche, Haiti 61 C5
Hinchinbrook I., Australia 42 B4

Hinckley, U.K. 9 E6
Hinckley, U.S.A. 54 B8
Hindmarsh, L., Australia 43 F3
Hindu Kush, Asia 28 B7
Hindubagh, Pakistan . 28 D5
Hindupur, India 28 N10
Hines Creek, Canada . 50 B5
Hinesville, U.S.A. ... 53 K5
Hinganghat, India ... 28 J11
Hingham, U.S.A. 56 B8
Hingoli, India 28 K10
Hinna = Imi, Ethiopia . 32 F3
Hinojosa del Duque, Spain 15 C3
Hinton, Canada 50 C5
Hinton, U.S.A. 52 G5
Hirado, Japan 23 H4
Hirakud Dam, India .. 29 J13
Hiratsuka, Japan 23 G9
Hiroo, Japan 22 C11
Hirosaki, Japan 22 D10
Hiroshima, Japan ... 23 G6
Hiroshima □, Japan .. 23 G6
Hisar, India 28 E9
Hisb →, Iraq 30 D5
Ḩismá, Si. Arabia 30 D3
Hispaniola, W. Indies . 61 C5
Ḩīt, Iraq 30 C4
Hita, Japan 23 H5
Hitachi, Japan 23 F10
Hitchin, U.K. 9 F7
Hitoyoshi, Japan 23 H5
Hitra, Norway 6 E13
Hixon, Canada 50 C4
Ḩiyyon, N. →, Israel . 33 E4
Hjalmar L., Canada .. 51 A7
Hjälmaren, Sweden .. 7 G16
Hjørring, Denmark ... 7 H13
Hkakabo Razi, Burma . 29 E20
Hlyboka, Ukraine 13 D13
Ho Chi Minh City = Thanh Pho Ho Chi Minh, Vietnam 26 B3
Hoai Nhon, Vietnam .. 26 B3
Hoare B., Canada ... 47 B13
Hobart, Australia 42 G4
Hobart, U.S.A. 55 H5
Hobbs, U.S.A. 55 J3
Hobbs Coast, Antarctica 5 D14
Hobe Sound, U.S.A. .. 53 M5
Hobro, Denmark 7 H13
Hoburgen, Sweden .. 7 H18
Hodaka-Dake, Japan . 23 F8
Hodgeville, Canada .. 51 C7
Hodgson, Canada ... 51 C9
Hódmezővásárhely, Hungary 13 E11
Hodna, Chott el, Algeria 34 A6
Hodonín, Czech Rep. . 13 D9
Hoek van Holland, Neths. 11 C4
Hof, Germany 12 C6
Höfn, Iceland 6 D6
Hofors, Sweden 7 F17
Hofsjökull, Iceland ... 6 D4
Hōfu, Japan 23 G5
Hogan Group, Australia 43 F4
Hogarth, Mt., Australia 42 C2
Hoggar = Ahaggar, Algeria 34 D7
Hogsty Reef, Bahamas 61 B5
Hohe Venn, Belgium . 11 D6
Hohenwald, U.S.A. .. 53 H2
Hoher Rhön = Rhön, Germany 12 C5
Hohhot, China 25 B6
Hoi An, Vietnam 26 A3
Hoisington, U.S.A. ... 54 F5
Hōjō, Japan 23 H6
Hokianga Harbour, N.Z. 39 F4
Hokitika, N.Z. 39 K3
Hokkaidō □, Japan .. 22 C11
Holbrook, Australia .. 43 F4
Holbrook, U.S.A. 57 J8
Holden, U.S.A. 56 G7
Holdenville, U.S.A. .. 55 H6
Holdrege, U.S.A. 54 E5
Holguín, Cuba 60 B4
Hollandale, U.S.A. ... 55 J9
Hollandia = Jayapura, Indonesia 27 E10
Hollidaysburg, U.S.A. . 52 E6
Hollis, U.S.A. 55 H5
Hollister, Calif., U.S.A. 57 H3
Hollister, Idaho, U.S.A. 56 E6
Holly Hill, U.S.A. 53 L5
Holly Springs, U.S.A. . 55 H10
Hollywood, U.S.A. ... 53 N5
Holman, Canada 46 A8
Hólmavík, Iceland ... 6 D3
Holmen, U.S.A. 54 D9
Holmes Reefs, Australia 42 B4
Holmsund, Sweden .. 6 E19
Holroyd →, Australia 42 A3
Holstebro, Denmark .. 7 H13
Holsworthy, U.K. 9 G3
Holton, Canada 49 B8
Holton, U.S.A. 54 F7
Holtville, U.S.A. 57 K6
Holwerd, Neths. 11 A5
Holy I., Angl., U.K. ... 8 D3
Holy I., Northumb., U.K. 8 B6
Holyhead, U.K. 8 D3

Holyoke, Colo., U.S.A. . 54 E3
Holyoke, Mass., U.S.A. 52 D9
Holyrood, Canada ... 49 C9
Homalin, Burma 29 G19
Homand, Iran 31 C8
Homathko →, Canada 50 C4
Hombori, Mali 34 E5
Home B., Canada ... 47 B13
Home Hill, Australia .. 42 B4
Homedale, U.S.A. ... 56 E5
Homer, Alaska, U.S.A. . 46 C4
Homer, La., U.S.A. ... 55 J8
Homestead, Australia . 42 C4
Homestead, U.S.A. .. 53 N5
Homs = Ḩimṣ, Syria . 33 A5
Homyel, Belarus 13 B16
Hon Chong, Vietnam . 26 B2
Honan = Henan □, China 25 C6
Honbetsu, Japan 22 C11
Hondo, Japan 23 H5
Hondo, U.S.A. 55 L5
Hondo →, Belize 59 D7
Honduras ■, Cent. Amer. 60 D2
Honduras, G. de, Caribbean 60 C2
Hønefoss, Norway .. 7 F14
Honey L., U.S.A. 56 F3
Honfleur, France 14 B4
Hong →, Vietnam .. 24 D5
Hong Kong □, China . 25 D6
Hongjiang, China ... 25 D5
Hongshui He →, China 25 D5
Honguedo, Détroit d', Canada 49 C7
Hongze Hu, China ... 25 C6
Honiara, Solomon Is. . 38 B8
Honiton, U.K. 9 G4
Honjō, Japan 22 E10
Honningsvåg, Norway . 6 A21
Honolulu, U.S.A. 45 E12
Honshū, Japan 25 C8
Honshū, Japan 25 C8
Hood, Mt., U.S.A. ... 56 D3
Hood, Pt., Australia .. 41 F2
Hood River, U.S.A. .. 56 D3
Hoodsport, U.S.A. ... 56 C2
Hoogeveen, Neths. .. 11 B6
Hoogezand-Sappemeer, Neths. 11 A6
Hooghly = Hugli →, India 29 J16
Hook I., Australia 42 C4
Hook of Holland = Hoek van Holland, Neths. . 11 C4
Hooker, U.S.A. 55 G4
Hooker Creek, Australia 40 C5
Hoonah, U.S.A. 50 B1
Hooper Bay, U.S.A. .. 46 B3
Hoopeston, U.S.A. .. 52 E2
Hoorn, Neths. 11 B5
Hoover, U.S.A. 53 J2
Hoover Dam, U.S.A. . 57 J6
Hope, Canada 50 D4
Hope, U.S.A. 55 J8
Hope, L., S. Austral., Australia 43 D2
Hope, L., W. Austral., Australia 41 F3
Hope Town, Bahamas 60 A4
Hopedale, Canada ... 49 A7
Hopei = Hebei □, China 25 C6
Hopelchén, Mexico .. 59 D7
Hopetoun, Vic., Australia 43 F3
Hopetoun, W. Austral., Australia 41 F3
Hopetown, S. Africa .. 37 K4
Hopevale, Australia .. 42 B4
Hopewell, U.S.A. ... 52 G7
Hopkins, L., Australia . 40 D4
Hopkinsville, U.S.A. .. 53 G2
Hopland, U.S.A. 56 G2
Hoquiam, U.S.A. 56 C2
Horden Hills, Australia 40 D5
Horlick Mts., Antarctica 5 E15
Horlivka, Ukraine 19 E6
Hormak, Iran 31 D9
Hormoz, Iran 31 E7
Hormoz, Jaz.-ye, Iran . 31 E8
Hormozgān □, Iran .. 31 E8
Hormuz, Kūh-e, Iran . 31 E7
Hormuz, Str. of, The Gulf 31 E8
Horn, Austria 12 D8
Horn, Iceland 6 C2
Horn →, Canada ... 50 A5
Horn, Cape = Hornos, C. de, Chile 64 H3
Horn I., Australia 42 A3
Horn Mts., Canada .. 50 A5
Hornavan, Sweden .. 6 C17
Hornbeck, U.S.A. ... 55 K8
Hornbrook, U.S.A. .. 56 F2
Horncastle, U.K. 8 D7
Hornell, U.S.A. 52 D7
Hornell L., Canada .. 50 A5
Hornepayne, Canada . 48 C3
Hornos, C. de, Chile .. 64 H3
Hornsea, U.K. 8 D7
Horobetsu, Japan ... 22 C10
Horodenka, Ukraine .. 13 D13
Horodok, Khmelnytskyy, Ukraine 13 D14

Horodok, Lviv, Ukraine 13 D12
Horokhiv, Ukraine ... 13 C13
Horqin Youyi Qianqi, China 25 B7
Horqueta, Paraguay .. 64 A5
Horse Creek, U.S.A. .. 54 E3
Horse Is., Canada ... 49 B8
Horsefly L., Canada .. 50 C4
Horsens, Denmark ... 7 J13
Horsham, Australia .. 43 F3
Horsham, U.K. 9 F7
Horten, Norway 7 G14
Horton, U.S.A. 54 F7
Horton →, Canada .. 46 B7
Horwood L., Canada . 48 C3
Hose, Gunung-Gunung, Malaysia 26 D4
Ḩoseynābād, Khuzestān, Iran 31 C6
Ḩoseynābād, Kordestān, Iran 30 C5
Hoshangabad, India .. 28 H10
Hoshiarpur, India ... 28 D9
Hospet, India 28 M10
Hoste, I., Chile 64 H3
Hot Creek Range, U.S.A. 56 G6
Hot Springs, Ark., U.S.A. 55 H8
Hot Springs, S. Dak., U.S.A. 54 D3
Hotagen, Sweden ... 6 E16
Hotan, China 24 C2
Hotazel, S. Africa 37 K4
Hotchkiss, U.S.A. ... 57 G10
Hotham, C., Australia . 40 B5
Hoting, Sweden 6 D17
Hotte, Massif de la, Haiti 61 C5
Houffalize, Belgium .. 11 D5
Houghton, U.S.A. ... 54 B10
Houghton L., U.S.A. . 52 C3
Houhora Heads, N.Z. . 39 F4
Houlton, U.S.A. 53 B12
Houma, U.S.A. 55 L9
Houston, Canada ... 50 C3
Houston, Mo., U.S.A. . 55 G9
Houston, Tex., U.S.A. . 55 L7
Houtman Abrolhos, Australia 41 E1
Hovd, Mongolia 24 B4
Hove, U.K. 9 G7
Hoveyzeh, Iran 31 D6
Hövsgöl Nuur, Mongolia 24 A5
Howard, Australia ... 43 D5
Howard, U.S.A. 54 C6
Howe, U.S.A. 56 E7
Howe, C., Australia .. 43 F5
Howell, U.S.A. 52 D4
Howick Group, Australia 42 A4
Howitt, L., Australia .. 43 D2
Howland I., Pac. Oc. .. 44 G10
Howrah = Haora, India 29 H16
Höxter, Germany 12 C5
Hoy, U.K. 10 B5
Høyanger, Norway ... 7 F12
Hoyerswerda, Germany 12 C8
Hoylake, U.K. 8 D4
Hpa-an = Pa-an, Burma 29 L20
Hpungan Pass, Burma . 29 F20
Hradec Králové, Czech Rep. 12 C8
Hrodna, Belarus 13 B12
Hrodzyanka, Belarus . 13 B15
Hron →, Slovak Rep. . 13 E10
Hrvatska = Croatia ■, Europe 12 F9
Hrymayliv, Ukraine .. 13 D14
Hsenwi, Burma 29 H20
Hsiamen = Xiamen, China 25 D6
Hsian = Xi'an, China .. 25 C5
Hsinchu, Taiwan 25 D7
Hsinhailien = Lianyungang, China . 25 C6
Hsüchou = Xuzhou, China 25 C6
Hua Hin, Thailand ... 26 B1
Huachinera, Mexico .. 58 A3
Huacho, Peru 62 F3
Huai He →, China ... 25 C6
Huainan, China 25 C6
Huaiyin, China 25 C6
Huajuapan de Leon, Mexico 59 D5
Hualapai Peak, U.S.A. . 57 J7
Hualgayoc, Peru 62 E3
Huallaga →, Peru ... 62 E3
Huambo, Angola 37 G3
Huancabamba, Peru . 62 E3
Huancane, Peru 62 G5
Huancavelica, Peru .. 62 F3
Huancayo, Peru 62 F3
Huanchaca, Bolivia .. 62 H5
Huang Hai = Yellow Sea, China 25 C7
Huang He →, China . 25 C6
Huangshan, China ... 25 D6
Huangshi, China 25 C6
Huánuco, Peru 62 E3
Huaraz, Peru 62 E3
Huarmey, Peru 62 F3
Huascarán, Peru 62 E3
Huasco, Chile 64 B2
Huatabampo, Mexico . 58 B3
Huauchinango, Mexico 59 C5
Huautla de Jiménez, Mexico 59 D5
Huay Namota, Mexico . 58 C4

Hubbard, *U.S.A.*	55	K6
Hubbart Pt., *Canada*	51	B10
Hubei □, *China*	25	C6
Hucknall, *U.K.*	8	D6
Huddersfield, *U.K.*	8	D6
Hudiksvall, *Sweden*	7	F17
Hudson, *Canada*	48	B1
Hudson, *N.Y., U.S.A.*	52	D9
Hudson, *Wis., U.S.A.*	54	C8
Hudson, *Wyo., U.S.A.*	56	E9
Hudson →, *U.S.A.*	52	E8
Hudson Bay, *N.W.T., Canada*	47	C11
Hudson Bay, *Sask., Canada*	51	C8
Hudson Falls, *U.S.A.*	52	D9
Hudson Mts., *Antarctica*	5	D16
Hudson Str., *Canada*	47	B13
Hudson's Hope, *Canada*	50	B4
Hue, *Vietnam*	26	A3
Huehuetenango, *Guatemala*	60	C1
Huejúcar, *Mexico*	58	C4
Huelva, *Spain*	15	D2
Huesca, *Spain*	15	A5
Huetamo, *Mexico*	58	D4
Hugh →, *Australia*	42	D1
Hughenden, *Australia*	42	C3
Hughes, *Australia*	41	F4
Hugli →, *India*	29	J16
Hugo, *Colo., U.S.A.*	54	F3
Hugo, *Okla., U.S.A.*	55	H7
Hugoton, *U.S.A.*	55	G4
Huichapán, *Mexico*	59	C5
Huila, Nevado del, *Colombia*	62	C3
Huinca Renancó, *Argentina*	64	C4
Huisache, *Mexico*	58	C4
Huixtla, *Mexico*	59	D6
Huize, *China*	24	D5
Hukawng Valley, *Burma*	29	F20
Ḥulayfā', *Si. Arabia*	30	E4
Huld = Ulaanjirem, *Mongolia*	24	B5
Hull = Kingston upon Hull, *U.K.*	8	D7
Hull, *Canada*	48	C4
Hull →, *U.K.*	8	D7
Hulst, *Neths.*	11	C4
Hulun Nur, *China*	25	B6
Humahuaca, *Argentina*	64	A3
Humaitá, *Brazil*	62	E6
Humber →, *U.K.*	8	D7
Humboldt, *Canada*	51	C7
Humboldt, *Iowa, U.S.A.*	54	D7
Humboldt, *Tenn., U.S.A.*	55	H10
Humboldt →, *U.S.A.*	56	F4
Humboldt Gletscher, *Greenland*	4	B4
Hume, L., *Australia*	43	F4
Humenné, *Slovak Rep.*	13	D11
Humphreys Peak, *U.S.A.*	57	J8
Hūn, *Libya*	35	C9
Húnaflói, *Iceland*	6	D3
Hunan □, *China*	25	D6
Hundred Mile House, *Canada*	50	C4
Hunedoara, *Romania*	13	F12
Hungary ■, *Europe*	13	E10
Hungerford, *Australia*	43	D3
Hüngnam, *N. Korea*	25	C7
Hunsrück, *Germany*	12	D4
Hunstanton, *U.K.*	8	E8
Hunter I., *Australia*	42	G3
Hunter I., *Canada*	50	C3
Hunter Ra., *Australia*	43	E5
Hunterville, *N.Z.*	39	H5
Huntingburg, *U.S.A.*	52	F2
Huntingdon, *Canada*	48	C5
Huntingdon, *U.K.*	9	E7
Huntingdon, *U.S.A.*	52	E7
Huntington, *Ind., U.S.A.*	52	E3
Huntington, *Oreg., U.S.A.*	56	D5
Huntington, *Utah, U.S.A.*	56	G8
Huntington, *W. Va., U.S.A.*	52	F4
Huntington Beach, *U.S.A.*	57	K5
Huntly, *N.Z.*	39	G5
Huntly, *U.K.*	10	C5
Huntsville, *Canada*	48	C4
Huntsville, *Ala., U.S.A.*	53	H2
Huntsville, *Tex., U.S.A.*	55	K7
Huonville, *Australia*	42	G4
Hupeh = Hubei □, *China*	25	C6
Ḥūr, *Iran*	31	D8
Hurghada, *Egypt*	35	C12
Hurley, *N. Mex., U.S.A.*	57	K9
Hurley, *Wis., U.S.A.*	54	B9
Huron, *U.S.A.*	54	C5
Huron, L., *U.S.A.*	52	C4
Hurricane, *U.S.A.*	57	H7
Hurunui →, *N.Z.*	39	K4
Húsavík, *Iceland*	6	C5
Huşi, *Romania*	13	E15
Huskvarna, *Sweden*	7	H16
Hustadvika, *Norway*	6	E12
Hutchinson, *Kans., U.S.A.*	55	F6
Hutchinson, *Minn., U.S.A.*	54	C7
Hutte Sauvage, L. de la, *Canada*	49	A7
Hutton, Mt., *Australia*	43	D4
Huy, *Belgium*	11	D5
Huzhou, *China*	25	C7
Hvammstangi, *Iceland*	6	D3
Hvar, *Croatia*	16	C7
Hvítá →, *Iceland*	6	D3
Hwang Ho = Huang He →, *China*	25	C6
Hwange, *Zimbabwe*	37	H5
Hyannis, *Mass., U.S.A.*	52	E10
Hyannis, *Nebr., U.S.A.*	54	E4
Hyargas Nuur, *Mongolia*	24	B4
Hydaburg, *U.S.A.*	50	B2
Hyden, *Australia*	41	F2
Hyder, *U.S.A.*	50	B2
Hyderabad, *India*	28	L11
Hyderabad, *Pakistan*	28	G6
Hyères, *France*	14	E7
Hyères, Îs. d', *France*	14	E7
Hyland →, *Canada*	50	B3
Hyndman Peak, *U.S.A.*	56	E6
Hyōgo □, *Japan*	23	G7
Hyrum, *U.S.A.*	56	F8
Hysham, *U.S.A.*	56	C10
Hythe, *U.K.*	9	F9
Hyūga, *Japan*	23	H5
Hyvinge = Hyvinkää, *Finland*	7	F21
Hyvinkää, *Finland*	7	F21
I-n-Gall, *Niger*	34	E7
Iaco →, *Brazil*	62	E5
Ialomiţa →, *Romania*	13	F14
Iaşi, *Romania*	13	E14
Iba, *Phil.*	27	A6
Ibadan, *Nigeria*	34	G6
Ibagué, *Colombia*	62	C3
Ibar →, *Serbia, Yug.*	17	C9
Ibaraki □, *Japan*	23	F10
Ibarra, *Ecuador*	62	C3
Iberville, *Canada*	48	C5
Iberville, Lac d', *Canada*	48	A5
Ibiá, *Brazil*	63	G9
Ibioapaba, Sa. da, *Brazil*	63	D10
Ibiza = Eivissa, *Spain*	15	C6
Ibonma, *Indonesia*	27	E8
Ibotirama, *Brazil*	63	F10
Ibrāhīm →, *Lebanon*	33	A4
'Ibrī, *Oman*	31	F8
Ibu, *Indonesia*	27	D7
Ibusuki, *Japan*	23	J5
Ica, *Peru*	62	F3
Içá →, *Brazil*	62	D5
Içana, *Brazil*	62	C5
Içana →, *Brazil*	62	C5
İçel = Mersin, *Turkey*	19	G5
Iceland ■, *Europe*	6	D4
Ich'ang = Yichang, *China*	25	C6
Ichchapuram, *India*	29	K14
Ichihara, *Japan*	23	G10
Ichikawa, *Japan*	23	G9
Ichilo →, *Bolivia*	62	G6
Ichinohe, *Japan*	22	D10
Ichinomiya, *Japan*	23	G8
Ichinoseki, *Japan*	22	E10
Ida Grove, *U.S.A.*	54	D7
Idabel, *U.S.A.*	55	J7
Idaho □, *U.S.A.*	56	D7
Idaho City, *U.S.A.*	56	E6
Idaho Falls, *U.S.A.*	56	E7
Idar-Oberstein, *Germany*	12	D4
Idfû, *Egypt*	35	D12
Ídhi Óros, *Greece*	17	G11
Ídhra, *Greece*	17	F10
Idi, *Indonesia*	26	C1
Idiofa, *Dem. Rep. of the Congo*	36	E3
Idlib, *Syria*	30	C3
Ieper, *Belgium*	11	D2
Ierápetra, *Greece*	17	G11
Iesi, *Italy*	16	C5
Ifakara, *Tanzania*	36	F7
'Ifāl, W. al →, *Si. Arabia*	30	D2
Ife, *Nigeria*	34	G6
Iférouâne, *Niger*	34	E7
Iffley, *Australia*	42	B3
Ifni, *Morocco*	34	C3
Iforas, Adrar des, *Mali*	34	E6
Ifould, L., *Australia*	41	F5
Igarapava, *Brazil*	63	H9
Igarka, *Russia*	20	C9
Iggesund, *Sweden*	7	F17
Iglésias, *Italy*	16	E3
Igloolik, *Canada*	47	B11
Igluligaarjuk, *Canada*	47	B10
Iglulik = Igloolik, *Canada*	47	B11
Ignace, *Canada*	48	C1
İğneada Burnu, *Turkey*	17	D13
Igoumenítsa, *Greece*	17	E9
Iguaçu →, *Brazil*	64	B6
Iguaçu, Cat. del, *Brazil*	64	B6
Iguaçu Falls = Iguaçu, Cat. del, *Brazil*	64	B6
Iguala, *Mexico*	59	D5
Igualada, *Spain*	15	B6
Iguassu = Iguaçu →, *Brazil*	64	B6
Iguatu, *Brazil*	63	E11
Iharana, *Madag.*	37	G10
Iheya-Shima, *Japan*	23	L3
Ihosy, *Madag.*	37	J9
Ii, *Finland*	6	D21
Ii-Shima, *Japan*	23	L3
Iida, *Japan*	23	G8
Iijoki →, *Finland*	6	D21
Iisalmi, *Finland*	6	E22
Iiyama, *Japan*	23	F9
Iizuka, *Japan*	23	H5
Ijebu-Ode, *Nigeria*	34	G6
IJmuiden, *Neths.*	11	B4
IJssel →, *Neths.*	11	B5
IJsselmeer, *Neths.*	11	B5
Ikaluktutiak, *Canada*	46	B9
Ikare, *Nigeria*	34	G7
Ikaría, *Greece*	17	F12
Ikeda, *Japan*	23	G6
Ikela, *Dem. Rep. of the Congo*	36	E4
Iki, *Japan*	23	H4
Ikopa →, *Madag.*	37	H9
Ilagan, *Phil.*	27	A6
Ilâm, *Iran*	30	C5
Ilam □, *Iran*	30	C5
Ilanskiy, *Russia*	21	D10
Iława, *Poland*	13	B10
Île-à-la-Crosse, *Canada*	51	B7
Île-à-la-Crosse, Lac, *Canada*	51	B7
Île-de-France □, *France*	14	B5
Ilebo, *Dem. Rep. of the Congo*	36	E4
Ilek, *Russia*	20	D6
Ilek →, *Russia*	18	D9
Ilesha, *Nigeria*	34	G6
Ilford, *Canada*	51	B9
Ilfracombe, *Australia*	42	C3
Ilfracombe, *U.K.*	9	F3
Ilhéus, *Brazil*	63	F11
Ili →, *Kazakstan*	20	E8
Iliamna L., *U.S.A.*	46	C4
Iligan, *Phil.*	27	C6
Ilkeston, *U.K.*	8	E6
Ilkley, *U.K.*	8	D6
Illampu = Ancohuma, Nevada, *Bolivia*	62	G5
Illana B., *Phil.*	27	C6
Illapel, *Chile*	64	C2
Iller →, *Germany*	12	D6
Illimani, Nevado, *Bolivia*	62	G5
Illinois □, *U.S.A.*	54	E10
Illium = Troy, *Turkey*	17	E12
Illizi, *Algeria*	34	C7
Illoqqortoormiit, *Greenland*	4	B6
Ilmajoki, *Finland*	7	E20
Ilmen, Ozero, *Russia*	18	C5
Ilo, *Peru*	62	G4
Iloilo, *Phil.*	27	B6
Ilorin, *Nigeria*	34	G6
Ilwaki, *Indonesia*	27	F7
Imabari, *Japan*	23	G6
Imandra, Ozero, *Russia*	18	A5
Imari, *Japan*	23	H4
Imatra, *Finland*	18	B4
Imbil, *Australia*	43	D5
imeni 26 Bakinskikh Komissarov = Neftçala, *Azerbaijan*	19	G8
imeni 26 Bakinskikh Komissarov, *Turkmenistan*	31	B7
Imeri, Serra, *Brazil*	62	C5
Imi, *Ethiopia*	32	F3
Imlay, *U.S.A.*	56	F4
Immingham, *U.K.*	8	D7
Immokalee, *U.S.A.*	53	M5
Ímola, *Italy*	16	B4
Imperatriz, *Brazil*	63	E9
Impéria, *Italy*	14	E8
Imperial, *Canada*	51	C7
Imperial, *U.S.A.*	54	E4
Imperial Dam, *U.S.A.*	57	K6
Imperieuse Reef, *Australia*	40	C2
Impfondo, *Congo*	36	D3
Imphal, *India*	29	G18
İmroz = Gökçeada, *Turkey*	17	D11
Imuris, *Mexico*	58	A2
Imuruan B., *Phil.*	27	B5
In Salah, *Algeria*	34	C6
Ina, *Japan*	23	G8
Inangahua Junction, *N.Z.*	39	J3
Inanwatan, *Indonesia*	27	E8
Iñapari, *Peru*	62	F5
Inari, *Finland*	6	B22
Inarijärvi, *Finland*	6	B22
Inawashiro-Ko, *Japan*	22	F10
Inca, *Spain*	15	C7
İnce Burun, *Turkey*	19	F5
İncesu, *Turkey*	30	B2
Inch'ŏn, *S. Korea*	25	C7
İncirliova, *Turkey*	17	F12
Incline Village, *U.S.A.*	56	G4
Incomáti →, *Mozam.*	37	K6
Indalsälven →, *Sweden*	7	E17
Indaw, *Burma*	29	G20
Independence, *Calif., U.S.A.*	57	H4
Independence, *Iowa, U.S.A.*	54	D9
Independence, *Kans., U.S.A.*	55	G7
Independence, *Ky., U.S.A.*	52	F3
Independence, *Mo., U.S.A.*	54	F7
Independence Fjord, *Greenland*	4	A6
Independence Mts., *U.S.A.*	56	F5
India ■, *Asia*	28	K11
Indian →, *U.S.A.*	53	M5
Indian Cabins, *Canada*	50	B5
Indian Harbour, *Canada*	49	B8
Indian Head, *Canada*	51	C8
Indian Ocean	3	E13
Indian Springs, *U.S.A.*	57	G6
Indiana, *U.S.A.*	52	E6
Indiana □, *U.S.A.*	52	F3
Indianapolis, *U.S.A.*	52	F2
Indianola, *Iowa, U.S.A.*	54	E8
Indianola, *Miss., U.S.A.*	55	J9
Indiga, *Russia*	18	A8
Indigirka →, *Russia*	21	B15
Indio, *U.S.A.*	57	K5
Indonesia ■, *Asia*	26	F5
Indore, *India*	28	H9
Indramayu, *Indonesia*	27	G13
Indravati →, *India*	29	K12
Indre □, *France*	14	C4
Indre →, *France*	14	C4
Indulkana, *Australia*	43	D1
Indus →, *Pakistan*	28	G5
İnebolu, *Turkey*	19	F5
Infiernillo, Presa del, *Mexico*	58	D4
Ingapirca, *Ecuador*	62	D3
Ingham, *Australia*	42	B4
Ingleborough, *U.K.*	8	C5
Inglewood, *Queens., Australia*	43	D5
Inglewood, *Vic., Australia*	43	F3
Inglewood, *N.Z.*	39	H5
Inglewood, *U.S.A.*	57	K4
Ingólfshöfði, *Iceland*	6	D5
Ingolstadt, *Germany*	12	D6
Ingomar, *U.S.A.*	56	C10
Ingonish, *Canada*	49	C7
Ingraj Bazar, *India*	29	G16
Ingrid Christensen Coast, *Antarctica*	5	C6
Ingulec = Inhulec, *Ukraine*	19	E5
Ingushetia □, *Russia*	19	F8
Ingwavuma, *S. Africa*	37	K6
Inhaca, *Mozam.*	37	K6
Inhafenga, *Mozam.*	37	J7
Inhambane, *Mozam.*	37	J7
Inharrime, *Mozam.*	37	J7
Inhulec, *Ukraine*	19	E5
Ining = Yining, *China*	20	E9
Inírida →, *Colombia*	62	C5
Injune, *Australia*	43	D4
Inklin →, *Canada*	50	B2
Inle L., *Burma*	29	J20
Inn →, *Austria*	12	D7
Innamincka, *Australia*	43	D3
Inner Hebrides, *U.K.*	10	C3
Inner Mongolia = Nei Monggol Zizhiqu □, *China*	25	B6
Innisfail, *Australia*	42	B4
Innisfail, *Canada*	50	C6
In'noshima, *Japan*	23	G6
Innsbruck, *Austria*	12	E6
Inongo, *Dem. Rep. of the Congo*	36	E3
Inoucdjouac = Inukjuak, *Canada*	47	C12
Inowrocław, *Poland*	13	B10
Inscription, C., *Australia*	41	E1
Insein, *Burma*	29	L20
Inta, *Russia*	18	A11
Interlaken, *Switz.*	14	C7
International Falls, *U.S.A.*	54	A8
Inukjuak, *Canada*	47	C12
Inútil, B., *Chile*	64	G2
Inuvik, *Canada*	46	B6
Invercargill, *N.Z.*	39	M2
Inverell, *Australia*	43	D5
Invergordon, *U.K.*	10	C4
Inverloch, *Australia*	43	F4
Invermere, *Canada*	50	C5
Inverness, *Canada*	49	C7
Inverness, *U.K.*	10	C4
Inverness, *U.S.A.*	53	L4
Inverurie, *U.K.*	10	C5
Investigator Group, *Australia*	43	E1
Investigator Str., *Australia*	43	F2
Inya, *Russia*	20	D9
Inyo Mts., *U.S.A.*	57	H5
Inyokern, *U.S.A.*	57	J5
Inza, *Russia*	18	D8
Iō-Jima, *Japan*	23	J5
Ioánnina, *Greece*	17	E9
Iola, *U.S.A.*	55	G7
Ione, *U.S.A.*	56	G3
Ionia, *U.S.A.*	52	D3
Ionian Is. = Iónioi Nísoi, *Greece*	17	E9
Ionian Sea, *Medit. S.*	17	E7
Iónioi Nísoi, *Greece*	17	E9
Íos, *Greece*	17	F11
Iowa, *U.S.A.*	54	D9
Iowa □, *U.S.A.*	54	D8
Iowa →, *U.S.A.*	54	E9
Iowa City, *U.S.A.*	54	E9
Iowa Falls, *U.S.A.*	54	D8
Iowa Park, *U.S.A.*	55	J5
Ipameri, *Brazil*	63	G9
Ipatinga, *Brazil*	63	G10
Ipiales, *Colombia*	62	C3
Ipin = Yibin, *China*	24	D5
Ipixuna, *Brazil*	62	E4
Ipoh, *Malaysia*	26	D2
Ippy, *C.A.R.*	36	C4
Ipsala, *Turkey*	17	D12
Ipswich, *Australia*	43	D5
Ipswich, *U.K.*	9	E9
Ipswich, *U.S.A.*	54	C5
Ipu, *Brazil*	63	D10
Iqaluit, *Canada*	47	B13
Iquique, *Chile*	62	H4
Iquitos, *Peru*	62	D4
Irabu-Jima, *Japan*	23	M2
Iracoubo, *Fr. Guiana*	63	B8
Irafshān, *Iran*	31	E9
Iráklion, *Greece*	17	G11
Iran ■, *Asia*	31	C7
Iran, Gunung-Gunung, *Malaysia*	26	D4
Iran Ra. = Iran, Gunung-Gunung, *Malaysia*	26	D4
Īrānshahr, *Iran*	31	E9
Irapuato, *Mexico*	58	C4
Iraq ■, *Asia*	30	C5
Irbid, *Jordan*	33	C4
Irbid □, *Jordan*	33	C5
Ireland ■, *Europe*	10	E2
Irian Jaya □, *Indonesia*	27	E9
Iringa, *Tanzania*	36	F7
Iriomote-Jima, *Japan*	23	M1
Iriona, *Honduras*	60	C2
Iriri →, *Brazil*	63	D8
Irish Republic ■, *Europe*	10	E3
Irish Republic ■, *Europe*	10	E3
Irish Sea, *U.K.*	8	D3
Irkutsk, *Russia*	21	D11
Irma, *Canada*	51	C6
Irō-Zaki, *Japan*	23	G9
Iron Baron, *Australia*	43	E2
Iron Gate = Portile de Fier, *Europe*	13	F12
Iron Knob, *Australia*	43	E2
Iron Mountain, *U.S.A.*	52	C1
Iron River, *U.S.A.*	54	B10
Ironton, *Mo., U.S.A.*	55	G9
Ironton, *Ohio, U.S.A.*	52	F4
Ironwood, *U.S.A.*	54	B9
Iroquois Falls, *Canada*	48	C3
Irpin, *Ukraine*	13	C16
Irrara Cr. →, *Australia*	43	D4
Irrawaddy □, *Burma*	29	L19
Irrawaddy →, *Burma*	29	M19
Irrawaddy, Mouths of the, *Burma*	29	M19
Irricana, *Canada*	50	C6
Irtysh →, *Russia*	20	C7
Irún, *Spain*	15	A5
Irunea = Pamplona, *Spain*	15	A5
Irvine, *Canada*	51	D6
Irvine, *U.K.*	10	D4
Irvine, *U.S.A.*	52	G4
Irving, *U.S.A.*	55	J6
Irwin →, *Australia*	41	E1
Irymple, *Australia*	43	E3
Isaac →, *Australia*	42	C4
Isabel, *U.S.A.*	54	C4
Isabela, *Phil.*	27	C6
Isabela, I., *Mexico*	58	C3
Isabelia, Cord., *Nic.*	60	D3
Isabella Ra., *Australia*	40	D3
Ísafjarðardjúp, *Iceland*	6	C2
Ísafjörður, *Iceland*	6	C2
Isahaya, *Japan*	23	H5
Isana = Içana →, *Brazil*	62	C5
Isar →, *Germany*	12	D7
Íschia, *Italy*	16	D5
Isdell →, *Australia*	40	C3
Ise, *Japan*	23	G8
Ise-Wan, *Japan*	23	G8
Isère □, *France*	14	D6
Isère →, *France*	14	D6
Isérnia, *Italy*	16	D6
Isfahan = Eşfahān, *Iran*	31	C6
Ishigaki-Shima, *Japan*	23	M2
Ishikari-Gawa →, *Japan*	22	C10
Ishikari-Sammyaku, *Japan*	22	C11
Ishikari-Wan, *Japan*	22	C10
Ishikawa □, *Japan*	23	F8
Ishim, *Russia*	20	D7
Ishim →, *Russia*	20	D8
Ishinomaki, *Japan*	22	E10
Ishioka, *Japan*	23	F10
Ishkuman, *Pakistan*	28	A8
Ishpeming, *U.S.A.*	52	B2
Isil Kul, *Russia*	20	D8
Isiro, *Dem. Rep. of the Congo*	36	D5
Isisford, *Australia*	42	C3
İskenderun, *Turkey*	19	G6
İskenderun Körfezi, *Turkey*	19	G6
Iskŭr →, *Bulgaria*	17	C11
Iskut →, *Canada*	50	B2
Islamabad, *Pakistan*	28	C8
Island L., *Canada*	51	C10
Island Lagoon, *Australia*	43	E2
Island Pond, *U.S.A.*	52	C10
Islands, B. of, *Canada*	49	C8
Islands, B. of, *N.Z.*	39	F5
Islay, *U.K.*	10	D3
Isle →, *France*	14	D3
Isle aux Morts, *Canada*	49	C8
Isle of Wight □, *U.K.*	9	G6
Isle Royale, *U.S.A.*	54	B10
Isle Royale National Park, *U.S.A.*	54	B10
Ismail = Izmayil, *Ukraine*	13	F15
Ismâ'ilîya, *Egypt*	35	B12
İsparta, *Turkey*	19	G5
İspica, *Italy*	16	F6
Israel ■, *Asia*	33	D3
Issoire, *France*	14	D5
Issyk-Kul, Ozero = Ysyk-Köl, Ozero, *Kyrgyzstan*	20	E8
İstanbul, *Turkey*	17	D13
İstanbul Boğazı, *Turkey*	17	D13
Istiaía, *Greece*	17	E10
Istokpoga, L., *U.S.A.*	53	M5
Istra, *Croatia*	12	F7
Istres, *France*	14	E6
Istria = Istra, *Croatia*	12	F7
Itaberaba, *Brazil*	63	F10
Itabira, *Brazil*	63	G10
Itabuna, *Brazil*	63	F11
Itacaunas →, *Brazil*	63	E9
Itacoatiara, *Brazil*	62	D7
Itaipú, Reprêsa de, *Brazil*	64	B6
Itaituba, *Brazil*	63	D7
Itajaí, *Brazil*	64	B7
Italy ■, *Europe*	16	C5
Itamaraju, *Brazil*	63	G11
Itampolo, *Madag.*	37	J8
Itapecuru-Mirim, *Brazil*	63	D10
Itaperuna, *Brazil*	63	H10
Itapicuru →, *Bahia, Brazil*	63	F11
Itapicuru →, *Maranhão, Brazil*	63	D10
Itapipoca, *Brazil*	63	D11
Itaquí, *Brazil*	64	B5
Itchen →, *U.K.*	9	G6
Ithaca = Itháki, *Greece*	17	E9
Itháki, *Greece*	17	E9
Ithaca, *U.S.A.*	52	D7
Itháki, *Greece*	17	E9
Itiquira →, *Brazil*	63	G7
Itō, *Japan*	23	G9
Ito Aba I., *S. China Sea*	26	B4
Itoigawa, *Japan*	23	F8
Itonamas →, *Bolivia*	62	F6
Ituiutaba, *Brazil*	63	G9
Itumbiara, *Brazil*	63	G9
Ituna, *Canada*	51	C8
Iturbe, *Argentina*	64	A3
Iturup, Ostrov, *Russia*	21	E15
Ituxi →, *Brazil*	62	E6
Itzehoe, *Germany*	12	B5
Ivaí →, *Brazil*	64	A6
Ivalo, *Finland*	6	B22
Ivalojoki →, *Finland*	6	B22
Ivanava, *Belarus*	13	B13
Ivanhoe, *Australia*	43	E3
Ivanhoe, *U.S.A.*	54	C6
Ivano-Frankivsk, *Ukraine*	13	D13
Ivano-Frankovsk = Ivano-Frankivsk, *Ukraine*	13	D13
Ivanovo = Ivanava, *Belarus*	13	B13
Ivanovo, *Russia*	18	C7
Ivatsevichy, *Belarus*	13	B13
Ivdel, *Russia*	18	B11
Ivory Coast, *W. Afr.*	34	H4
Ivory Coast ■, *Africa*	34	G4
Ivrea, *Italy*	14	D7
Ivujivik, *Canada*	47	B12
Ivybridge, *U.K.*	9	G4
Iwaizumi, *Japan*	22	E10
Iwaki, *Japan*	23	F10
Iwakuni, *Japan*	23	G6
Iwamizawa, *Japan*	22	C10
Iwanai, *Japan*	22	C10
Iwata, *Japan*	23	G8
Iwate □, *Japan*	22	E10
Iwate-San, *Japan*	22	E10
Iwo, *Nigeria*	34	G6
Ixiamas, *Bolivia*	62	F5
Ixtepec, *Mexico*	59	D5
Ixtlán del Río, *Mexico*	58	C4
Iyo, *Japan*	23	H6
Izabal, L. de, *Guatemala*	60	C2
Izamal, *Mexico*	59	C7
Izena-Shima, *Japan*	23	L3
Izhevsk, *Russia*	18	C9
Izhma →, *Russia*	18	A9
Izmayil, *Ukraine*	13	F15
İzmir, *Turkey*	17	E12
İzmit = Kocaeli, *Turkey*	19	F4
İznik Gölü, *Turkey*	17	D13
Izra, *Syria*	33	C5
Izu-Shotō, *Japan*	23	G10
Izúcar de Matamoros, *Mexico*	59	D5
Izumi-Sano, *Japan*	23	G7
Izumo, *Japan*	23	G6
Izyaslav, *Ukraine*	13	C14
Jabalpur, *India*	28	H11
Jabbūl, *Syria*	30	B3
Jabiru, *Australia*	40	B5
Jablah, *Syria*	30	C3

Jablonec nad Nisou,
Czech Rep. 12 C8
Jaboatão, Brazil 63 E11
Jaca, Spain 15 A5
Jacarei, Brazil 64 A7
Jackman, U.S.A. 53 C10
Jacksboro, U.S.A. 55 J5
Jackson, Ala., U.S.A. . . 53 K2
Jackson, Calif., U.S.A. . 56 G3
Jackson, Ky., U.S.A. . . 52 G4
Jackson, Mich., U.S.A. . 52 D3
Jackson, Minn., U.S.A. . 54 D7
Jackson, Miss., U.S.A. . 55 J9
Jackson, Mo., U.S.A. . . 55 G10
Jackson, Ohio, U.S.A. . 52 F4
Jackson, Tenn., U.S.A. . 53 H1
Jackson, Wyo., U.S.A. . 56 E8
Jackson B., N.Z. 39 K2
Jackson L., U.S.A. 56 E8
Jacksons, N.Z. 39 K3
Jackson's Arm, Canada 49 C8
Jacksonville, Ala.,
U.S.A. 53 J3
Jacksonville, Ark.,
U.S.A. 55 H8
Jacksonville, Fla., U.S.A. 53 K5
Jacksonville, Ill., U.S.A. 54 F9
Jacksonville, N.C.,
U.S.A. 53 H7
Jacksonville, Tex.,
U.S.A. 55 K7
Jacksonville Beach,
U.S.A. 53 K5
Jacmel, Haiti 61 C5
Jacob Lake, U.S.A. . . . 57 H7
Jacobabad, Pakistan . . 28 E6
Jacobina, Brazil 63 F10
Jacques Cartier, Dét. de,
Canada 49 C7
Jacques-Cartier, Mt.,
Canada 49 C6
Jacques Cartier, Parc
Prov., Canada 49 C5
Jacundá →, Brazil . . . 63 D8
Jadotville = Likasi,
Dem. Rep. of
the Congo 36 G5
Jaén, Peru 62 E3
Jaén, Spain 15 D4
Jaffa = Tel Aviv-Yafo,
Israel 33 C3
Jaffa, C., Australia . . . 43 F2
Jaffna, Sri Lanka 28 Q12
Jagadhri, India 28 D10
Jagdalpur, India 29 K13
Jaghīn →, Iran 31 E8
Jagodina, Serbia, Yug. 17 C9
Jagraon, India 28 D9
Jagtial, India 28 K11
Jaguariaíva, Brazil . . . 64 A7
Jaguaribe →, Brazil . . 63 D11
Jagüey Grande, Cuba . 60 B3
Jahrom, Iran 31 D7
Jailolo, Indonesia 27 D7
Jailolo, Selat, Indonesia 27 D7
Jaipur, India 28 F9
Jājarm, Iran 31 B8
Jakarta, Indonesia . . . 27 G12
Jakobstad = Pietarsaari,
Finland 6 E20
Jal, U.S.A. 55 J3
Jalālābād, Afghan. . . . 28 B7
Jalapa, Guatemala . . . 60 D2
Jalapa Enríquez, Mexico 59 D5
Jalasjärvi, Finland . . . 7 E20
Jalgaon, India 28 J9
Jalībah, Iraq 30 D5
Jalisco □, Mexico 58 D4
Jalna, India 28 K9
Jalón →, Spain 15 B5
Jalpa, Mexico 58 C4
Jalpaiguri, India 29 F16
Jaluit I., Marshall Is. . . 44 G8
Jalūlā, Iraq 30 C5
Jamaica ■, W. Indies . 60 C4
Jamalpur, Bangla. 29 G16
Jamalpur, India 29 G15
Jamanxim →, Brazil . . 63 D7
Jambi, Indonesia 26 E2
Jambi □, Indonesia . . . 26 E2
James →, S. Dak.,
U.S.A. 54 D6
James →, Va., U.S.A. . 52 G7
James B., Canada 48 B3
James Ranges, Australia 40 D5
James Ross I.,
Antarctica 5 C18
Jamestown, Australia . 43 E2
Jamestown, N. Dak.,
U.S.A. 54 B5
Jamestown, N.Y., U.S.A. 52 D6
Jamîlābād, Iran 31 C6
Jamiltepec, Mexico . . . 59 D5
Jamkhandi, India 28 L9
Jammu, India 28 C9
Jammu & Kashmir □,
India 28 B10
Jamnagar, India 28 H7
Jämsä, Finland 7 F21
Jamshedpur, India . . . 29 H15
Jämtland, Sweden . . . 6 E15
Jan L., Canada 51 C8
Jan Mayen, Arctic . . . 4 B7
Janakkala, Finland . . . 7 F21
Janaúba, Brazil 63 G10

Jand, Pakistan 28 C8
Jandaq, Iran 31 C7
Jandowae, Australia . . 43 D5
Janesville, U.S.A. 54 D10
Janīn, West Bank 33 C4
Janos, Mexico 58 A3
Januária, Brazil 63 G10
Jaora, India 28 H9
Japan ■, Asia 23 G8
Japan, Sea of, Asia . . 22 E7
Japan Trench, Pac. Oc. 44 D6
Japen = Yapen,
Indonesia 27 E9
Japurá →, Brazil 62 D5
Jaqué, Panama 60 E4
Jarābulus, Syria 30 B3
Jarama →, Spain 15 B4
Jarash, Jordan 33 C4
Jardines de la Reina,
Arch. de los, Cuba . . 60 B4
Jargalant = Hovd,
Mongolia 24 B4
Jari →, Brazil 63 D8
Jarīr, W. al →,
Si. Arabia 30 E4
Jarosław, Poland 13 C12
Jarrahdale, Australia . . 41 F2
Jarrahi →, Iran 31 D6
Järvenpää, Finland . . . 7 F21
Jarvis I., Pac. Oc. 45 H12
Jarwa, India 29 F13
Jāsimīyah, Iraq 30 C5
Jāsk, Iran 31 E8
Jasło, Poland 13 D11
Jasper, Canada 50 C5
Jasper, Ala., U.S.A. . . 53 J2
Jasper, Fla., U.S.A. . . . 53 K4
Jasper, Ind., U.S.A. . . 52 F2
Jasper, Tex., U.S.A. . . 55 K8
Jasper Nat. Park,
Canada 50 C5
Jászberény, Hungary . 13 E10
Jataí, Brazil 63 G8
Jatibarang, Indonesia . 27 G13
Jatinegara, Indonesia . 27 G12
Játiva = Xàtiva, Spain . 15 C5
Jaú, Brazil 63 H9
Jauja, Peru 62 F3
Jaunpur, India 29 G13
Java = Jawa, Indonesia 27 G14
Java Barat □, Indonesia 27 G12
Java Sea, Indonesia . . 26 E3
Java Tengah □,
Indonesia 27 G14
Java Timur □, Indonesia 27 G15
Java Trench, Ind. Oc. . 26 F3
Javhlant = Uliastay,
Mongolia 24 B4
Jawa, Indonesia 27 G14
Jaya, Puncak, Indonesia 27 E9
Jayanti, India 29 F16
Jayapura, Indonesia . . 27 E10
Jayawijaya,
Pegunungan,
Indonesia 27 E9
Jaynagar, India 29 F15
Jayrūd, Syria 30 C3
Jayton, U.S.A. 55 J4
Jāz Mūrīān, Hāmūn-e,
Iran 31 E8
Jazīreh-ye Shif, Iran . . 31 D6
Jazminal, Mexico 58 C4
Jazzīn, Lebanon 33 B4
Jean, U.S.A. 57 J6
Jean Marie River,
Canada 50 A4
Jean Rabel, Haiti 61 C5
Jeanerette, U.S.A. . . . 55 L9
Jeanette, Ostrov =
Zhannetty, Ostrov,
Russia 21 B16
Jebāl Bārez, Kūh-e, Iran 31 D8
Jebel, Bahr el →,
Sudan 35 G12
Jedburgh, U.K. 10 D5
Jedda = Jiddah,
Si. Arabia 32 C2
Jeddore L., Canada . . 49 C8
Jędrzejów, Poland . . . 13 C11
Jefferson, Iowa, U.S.A. 54 D7
Jefferson, Tex., U.S.A. 55 J7
Jefferson, Mt., Nev.,
U.S.A. 56 G5
Jefferson, Mt., Oreg.,
U.S.A. 56 D3
Jefferson City, Mo.,
U.S.A. 54 F8
Jefferson City, Tenn.,
U.S.A. 53 G4
Jeffersontown, U.S.A. . 52 F3
Jeffersonville, U.S.A. . . 52 F3
Jeffrey City, U.S.A. . . . 56 E10
Jega, Nigeria 34 F6
Jēkabpils, Latvia 7 H21
Jekyll I., U.S.A. 53 K5
Jelenia Góra, Poland . 12 C8
Jelgava, Latvia 7 H20
Jember, Indonesia . . . 27 H15
Jembongan, Malaysia . 26 C5
Jena, Germany 12 C6
Jena, U.S.A. 55 K8
Jenkins, U.S.A. 52 G4
Jennings, U.S.A. 55 K8
Jepara, Indonesia . . . 27 G14
Jeparit, Australia 43 F3

Jequié, Brazil 63 F10
Jequitinhonha, Brazil . 63 G10
Jequitinhonha →,
Brazil 63 G11
Jérémie, Haiti 61 C5
Jerez de García Salinas,
Mexico 58 C4
Jerez de la Frontera,
Spain 15 D2
Jerez de los Caballeros,
Spain 15 C2
Jericho = El Arīḥā,
West Bank 33 D4
Jericho, Australia 42 C4
Jerilderie, Australia . . 43 F4
Jerome, U.S.A. 56 E6
Jerramungup, Australia 41 F2
Jersey, U.K. 9 H5
Jersey City, U.S.A. . . . 52 E8
Jersey Shore, U.S.A. . . 52 E7
Jerseyville, U.S.A. . . . 54 F9
Jerusalem, Israel 33 D4
Jervis B., Australia . . . 43 F5
Jervis Inlet, Canada . . 50 C4
Jesselton = Kota
Kinabalu, Malaysia . . 26 C5
Jessore, Bangla. 29 H16
Jesup, U.S.A. 53 K5
Jesús Carranza, Mexico 59 D5
Jetmore, U.S.A. 55 F5
Jevnaker, Norway . . . 7 F14
Jeyḥūnābād, Iran 31 C6
Jeypore, India 29 K13
Jhal Jhao, Pakistan . . 28 F4
Jhalawar, India 28 G10
Jhang Maghiana,
Pakistan 28 D8
Jhansi, India 28 G11
Jharsuguda, India . . . 29 J14
Jhelum, Pakistan 28 C8
Jhelum →, Pakistan . . 28 D8
Jhunjhunu, India 28 E9
Ji-Paraná, Brazil 62 F6
Jiamusi, China 25 B8
Ji'an, China 25 D6
Jiangcheng, China . . . 24 D5
Jiangmen, China 25 D6
Jiangsu □, China 25 C7
Jiangxi □, China 25 D6
Jiaxing, China 25 C7
Jiayi = Chiai, Taiwan . 25 D7
Jiayu, China 25 D7
Jibuti = Djibouti ■,
Africa 32 E3
Jicarón, I., Panama . . . 60 E3
Jiddah, Si. Arabia 32 C2
Jido, India 29 E19
Jiggalong, Australia . . 40 D3
Jihlava, Czech Rep. . . 12 D8
Jihlava →, Czech Rep. 13 D9
Jijiga, Ethiopia 32 F3
Jilin, China 25 B7
Jilin □, China 25 B7
Jilong = Chilung,
Taiwan 25 D7
Jima, Ethiopia 32 F2
Jiménez, Mexico 58 B4
Jinan, China 25 C6
Jindabyne, Australia . . 43 F4
Jindřichův Hradec,
Czech Rep. 12 D8
Jingdezhen, China . . . 25 D6
Jinggu, China 24 D5
Jinhua, China 25 D6
Jining,
Nei Monggol Zizhiqu,
China 25 B6
Jining, Shandong, China 25 C6
Jinja, Uganda 36 D6
Jinnah Barrage,
Pakistan 28 C7
Jinotega, Nic. 60 D2
Jinotepe, Nic. 60 D2
Jinsha Jiang →, China 24 D5
Jinzhou, China 25 B7
Jiparaná →, Brazil . . . 62 E6
Jipijapa, Ecuador 62 D2
Jiquilpan, Mexico 58 D4
Jisr ash Shughūr, Syria 30 C3
Jitarning, Australia . . . 41 F2
Jiu →, Romania 13 F12
Jiujiang, China 25 D6
Jixi, China 25 B8
Jīzān, Si. Arabia 32 D3
Jizl, Wādī al, Si. Arabia 30 E3
Jizō-Zaki, Japan 23 G6
Jizzakh, Uzbekistan . . 20 E7
Joaçaba, Brazil 64 B6
João Pessoa, Brazil . . 63 E12
Joaquín V. González,
Argentina 64 B4
Jodhpur, India 28 F8
Joensuu, Finland 18 B4
Jōetsu, Japan 23 F9
Jõgeva, Estonia 7 G22
Jogjakarta =
Yogyakarta, Indonesia 27 G14
Johannesburg, S. Africa 37 K5
John Day, U.S.A. 56 D4
John Day →, U.S.A. . . 56 D3
John D'Or Prairie,
Canada 50 B5
John H. Kerr Reservoir,
U.S.A. 53 G6

John's Ra., Australia . . 42 C1
Johnson, U.S.A. 55 G4
Johnson City, Tenn.,
U.S.A. 53 G4
Johnson City, Tex.,
U.S.A. 55 K5
Johnson's Crossing,
Canada 50 A2
Johnston, L., Australia 41 F3
Johnston Falls =
Mambilima Falls,
Zambia 36 G5
Johnston I., Pac. Oc. . 45 F11
Johnstone Str., Canada 50 C3
Johnstown, N.Y., U.S.A. 52 D8
Johnstown, Pa., U.S.A. 52 E6
Johor Baharu, Malaysia 26 D2
Joinville, Brazil 64 B7
Joinville I., Antarctica . 5 C18
Jojutla, Mexico 59 D5
Jokkmokk, Sweden . . . 6 C18
Jökulsá á Bru →,
Iceland 6 D6
Jökulsá á Fjöllum →,
Iceland 6 C5
Jolfa,
Āzarbājān-e Sharqī,
Iran 30 B5
Jolfā, Eşfahan, Iran . . 31 C6
Joliet, U.S.A. 52 E1
Joliette, Canada 48 C5
Jolo, Phil. 27 C6
Jombang, Indonesia . . 27 G15
Jonava, Lithuania 7 J21
Jones Sound, Canada . 4 B3
Jonesboro, Ark., U.S.A. 55 H9
Jonesboro, La., U.S.A. 55 J8
Joniškis, Lithuania . . . 7 H20
Jönköping, Sweden . . 7 H16
Jonquière, Canada . . . 49 C5
Joplin, U.S.A. 55 G7
Jordan ■, Asia 33 E5
Jordan →, Asia 33 D4
Jordan Valley, U.S.A. . 56 E5
Jorhat, India 29 F19
Jörn, Sweden 6 D19
Jorong, Indonesia . . . 26 E4
Jørpeland, Norway . . . 7 G11
Jos, Nigeria 34 G7
Joseph, L., Canada . . 49 B6
Joseph Bonaparte G.,
Australia 40 B4
Joshua Tree National
Park, U.S.A. 57 K5
Jostedalsbreen, Norway 7 F12
Jotunheimen, Norway . 7 F13
Jourdanton, U.S.A. . . . 55 L5
Jovellanos, Cuba 60 B3
Juan Aldama, Mexico . 58 C4
Juan de Fuca Str., B.C.,
Canada 50 D4
Juan de Fuca Str., B.C.,
Canada 50 D4
Juan Fernández, Arch.
de, Pac. Oc. 45 L20
Juankoski, Finland . . . 6 E23
Juárez, Argentina . . . 64 D5
Juárez, Sierra de,
Mexico 58 A1
Juàzeiro, Brazil 63 E10
Juàzeiro do Norte, Brazil 63 E11
Juba, Sudan 35 H12
Jubayl, Lebanon 33 A4
Jubbah, Si. Arabia . . . 30 D4
Jubbulpore = Jabalpur,
India 28 H11
Jubilee L., Australia . . 41 E4
Juby, C., Morocco . . . 34 C3
Júcar = Xúquer →,
Spain 15 C5
Júcaro, Cuba 60 B4
Juchitán, Mexico 59 D5
Judaea = Har Yehuda,
Israel 33 D3
Judith →, U.S.A. 56 C9
Judith, Pt., U.S.A. . . . 52 E10
Judith Gap, U.S.A. . . . 56 C9
Jugoslavia =
Yugoslavia ■, Europe 17 B9
Juigalpa, Nic. 60 D2
Juiz de Fora, Brazil . . 63 H10
Julesburg, U.S.A. 54 E3
Juli, Peru 62 G5
Julia Cr. →, Australia . 42 C3
Julia Creek, Australia . 42 C3
Juliaca, Peru 62 G4
Julian, U.S.A. 57 K5
Julian L., Canada 48 B4
Julianatop, Surinam . . 63 C7
Julianehåb = Qaqortoq,
Greenland 4 C5
Julimes, Mexico 58 B3
Jullundur, India 28 D9
Jumentos Cays,
Bahamas 60 B4
Jumilla, Spain 15 C5
Jumla, Nepal 29 E13
Jumna = Yamuna →,
India 29 G12
Junagadh, India 28 J7
Junction, Tex., U.S.A. . 55 K5
Junction, Utah, U.S.A. . 57 G7
Junction B., Australia . 42 A1

Junction City, Kans.,
U.S.A. 54 F6
Junction City, Oreg.,
U.S.A. 56 D2
Junction Pt., Australia . 42 A1
Jundah, Australia 42 C3
Jundiai, Brazil 64 A7
Juneau, U.S.A. 50 B2
Junee, Australia 43 E4
Jungfrau, Switz. 14 C7
Junggar Pendi, China . 24 B3
Junin, Argentina 64 C4
Junin de los Andes,
Argentina 64 D2
Jūniyah, Lebanon 33 B4
Juntura, U.S.A. 56 E4
Jur, Nahr el →, Sudan 35 G11
Jura = Jura, Mts. du,
Europe 14 C7
Jura = Schwäbische
Alb, Germany 12 D5
Jura, U.K. 10 D4
Jura, Mts. du, Europe . 14 C7
Jurbarkas, Lithuania . . 7 J20
Jurien, Australia 41 F2
Jūrmala, Latvia 7 H20
Juruá →, Brazil 62 D5
Juruena, Brazil 62 F7
Juruena →, Brazil . . . 62 E7
Juruti, Brazil 63 D7
Justo Daract, Argentina 64 C3
Jutaí →, Brazil 62 D5
Juticalpa, Honduras . . 60 D2
Jutland = Jylland,
Denmark 7 H13
Juventud, I. de la, Cuba 60 B3
Jüy Zar, Iran 30 C5
Jwaneng, Botswana . . 37 J4
Jylland, Denmark 7 H13
Jyväskylä, Finland . . . 7 E21

K2, Pakistan 28 B10
Kaap Plateau, S. Africa 37 K4
Kaapstad = Cape Town,
S. Africa 37 L3
Kabaena, Indonesia . . 27 F6
Kabala, S. Leone 34 G3
Kabale, Uganda 36 E6
Kabalo, Dem. Rep. of
the Congo 36 F5
Kabanjahe, Indonesia . 26 D1
Kabardino-Balkar
Republic =
Kabardino-Balkaria □,
Russia 19 F7
Kabardino-Balkaria □,
Russia 19 F7
Kabarega Falls =
Murchison Falls,
Uganda 36 D6
Kabasalan, Phil. 27 C6
Kabetogama, U.S.A. . . 54 A8
Kabinakagami L.,
Canada 48 C3
Kabinda, Dem. Rep. of
the Congo 36 F4
Kabompo →, Zambia . 37 G4
Kabongo, Dem. Rep. of
the Congo 36 F5
Kabūd Gonbad, Iran . . 31 B8
Kābul, Afghan. 28 B6
Kābul □, Afghan. 28 B6
Kābul →, Pakistan . . . 28 C8
Kaburuang, Indonesia . 27 D7
Kabwe, Zambia 37 G5
Kachchh, Gulf of, India 28 H6
Kachchh, Rann of, India 28 H7
Kachin □, Burma 29 G20
Kachiry, Kazakstan . . . 20 D8
Kadan Kyun, Burma . . 26 B1
Kadina, Australia 43 E2
Kadirli, Turkey 30 B3
Kadiyevka = Stakhanov,
Ukraine 19 E6
Kadoka, U.S.A. 54 D4
Kadoma, Zimbabwe . . 37 H5
Kâdugli, Sudan 35 F11
Kaduna, Nigeria 34 F7
Kaédi, Mauritania 34 E3
Kaesŏng, N. Korea . . . 25 C7
Kāf, Si. Arabia 30 D3
Kafan = Kapan,
Armenia 19 G8
Kafanchan, Nigeria . . . 34 G7
Kafirévs, Ákra, Greece 17 E11
Kafue, Zambia 37 H5
Kafue →, Zambia 37 H5
Kaga Bandoro, C.A.R. . 36 C3
Kagan, Uzbekistan . . . 20 F7
Kagawa □, Japan 23 G7
Kağızman, Turkey . . . 30 B4
Kagoshima, Japan . . . 23 J5
Kagoshima □, Japan . . 23 J5
Kagul = Cahul, Moldova 13 F15
Kahak, Iran 31 B6
Kahama, Tanzania . . . 36 E6
Kahan, Pakistan 28 E3
Kahayan →, Indonesia 26 E4
Kahnūj, Iran 31 E8
Kahoka, U.S.A. 54 E9
Kahramanmaraş, Turkey 19 G6
Kai, Kepulauan,
Indonesia 27 F8
Kai Besar, Indonesia . 27 F8
Kai Is. = Kai,
Kepulauan, Indonesia 27 F8

Kai Kecil, Indonesia . . 27 F8
Kaiapoi, N.Z. 39 K4
Kaieteur Falls, Guyana 62 B7
Kaifeng, China 25 C6
Kaikohe, N.Z. 39 F4
Kaikoura, N.Z. 39 K4
Kaikoura Ra., N.Z. . . . 39 J4
Kaimana, Indonesia . . 27 E8
Kaimanawa Mts., N.Z. 39 H5
Kaingaroa Forest, N.Z. 39 H6
Kainji Res., Nigeria . . 34 F6
Kainuu, Finland 6 D23
Kaipara Harbour, N.Z. 39 G5
Kaipokok B., Canada . 49 B8
Kaironi, Indonesia . . . 27 E8
Kairouan, Tunisia 35 A7
Kaiserslautern, Germany 12 D4
Kaitaia, N.Z. 39 F4
Kaitangata, N.Z. 39 M2
Kajaani, Finland 6 D22
Kajabbi, Australia 42 C3
Kajana = Kajaani,
Finland 6 D22
Kajo Kaji, Sudan 35 H12
Kaka, Sudan 35 F12
Kakabeka Falls, Canada 48 C2
Kakadu Nat. Park,
Australia 40 B5
Kakamega, Kenya . . . 36 D6
Kakanui Mts., N.Z. . . . 39 L3
Kake, Japan 23 G6
Kake, U.S.A. 50 B2
Kakegawa, Japan . . . 23 G9
Kakeroma-Jima, Japan 23 K4
Kakhovka, Ukraine . . . 19 E5
Kakhovske Vdskh.,
Ukraine 19 E5
Kakinada, India 29 L13
Kakisa →, Canada . . . 50 A5
Kakisa L., Canada . . . 50 A5
Kakogawa, Japan . . . 23 G7
Kakwa →, Canada . . . 50 C5
Kāl Güsheh, Iran 31 D8
Kal Safid, Iran 30 C5
Kalaallit Nunaat =
Greenland ■,
N. Amer. 4 C5
Kalabagh, Pakistan . . 28 C7
Kalabahi, Indonesia . . 27 F6
Kalach, Russia 19 D7
Kaladan →, Burma . . . 29 J18
Kaladar, Canada 48 D4
Kalahari, Africa 37 J4
Kalajoki, Finland 6 D20
Kālak, Iran 31 E8
Kalakamati, Iran 21 D12
K'alak'unlun Shank'ou =
Karakoram Pass,
Pakistan 28 B10
Kalama, U.S.A. 56 D2
Kalámai, Greece 17 F10
Kalamata = Kalámai,
Greece 17 F10
Kalamazoo, U.S.A. . . . 52 D3
Kalamazoo →, U.S.A. . 52 D2
Kalan, Turkey 30 B3
Kalannie, Australia . . . 41 F2
Kalāntarī, Iran 31 C7
Kalao, Indonesia 27 F6
Kalaotoa, Indonesia . . 27 F6
Kalat, Pakistan 28 E5
Kalāteh, Iran 31 B7
Kalāteh-ye Ganj, Iran . 31 E8
Kalbarri, Australia . . . 41 E1
Kalce, Slovenia 12 F8
Kale, Turkey 17 F13
Kalegauk Kyun, Burma 29 M20
Kalemie, Dem. Rep. of
the Congo 36 F5
Kalewa, Burma 29 H19
Kaleybar, Iran 30 B5
Kalgan = Zhangjiakou,
China 25 B6
Kalgoorlie-Boulder,
Australia 41 F3
Kaliakra, Nos, Bulgaria 17 C13
Kalianda, Indonesia . . 26 F3
Kalibo, Phil. 27 B6
Kalima, Dem. Rep. of
the Congo 36 E5
Kalimantan □, Indonesia 26 E4
Kalimantan Barat □,
Indonesia 26 E4
Kalimantan Selatan □,
Indonesia 26 E4
Kalimantan Tengah □,
Indonesia 26 E4
Kalimantan Timur □,
Indonesia 26 D5
Kálimnos, Greece . . . 17 F12
Kalinin = Tver, Russia . 18 C6
Kaliningrad, Russia . . 7 J19
Kalinkavichy, Belarus . 13 B15
Kalinkovichi =
Kalinkavichy, Belarus 13 B15
Kalispell, U.S.A. 56 B6
Kalisz, Poland 13 C10
Kalix, Sweden 6 D20
Kalix →, Sweden 6 D20
Kalkarindji, Australia . 40 C5
Kalkaska, U.S.A. 52 C3
Kallavesi, Finland . . . 6 E22
Kallsjön, Sweden 6 E15
Kalmar, Sweden 7 H17
Kalmyk Republic =
Kalmykia □, Russia . 19 E8

Kalmykia □, *Russia* ... 19 E8
Kalmykovo, *Kazakstan* . 19 E9
Kalocsa, *Hungary* 13 E10
Kaluga, *Russia* 18 D6
Kalundborg, *Denmark* . 7 J14
Kalush, *Ukraine* 13 D13
Kalutara, *Sri Lanka* ... 28 R12
Kalya, *Russia* 18 B10
Kama →, *Russia* 18 C9
Kamaishi, *Japan* 22 E10
Kamaran, *Yemen* 32 D3
Kambalda, *Australia* .. 41 F3
Kambarka, *Russia* 18 C9
Kamchatka, Poluostrov,
  Russia 21 D16
Kamchatka Pen. =
  Kamchatka,
  Poluostrov, *Russia* . 21 D16
Kamchiya →, *Bulgaria* 17 C12
Kamen, *Russia* 20 D9
Kamen-Rybolov, *Russia* 22 B6
Kamenjak, Rt., *Croatia* . 12 F7
Kamenka, *Russia* 18 A7
Kamenka Bugskaya =
  Kamyanka-Buzka,
  Ukraine 13 C13
Kamensk Uralskiy,
  Russia 20 D7
Kamenskoye, *Russia* .. 21 C17
Kameoka, *Japan* 23 G7
Kamiah, *U.S.A.* 56 C5
Kamilukuak, L., *Canada* 51 A8
Kamin-Kashyrskyy,
  Ukraine 13 C13
Kamina, *Dem. Rep. of*
  the Congo 36 F5
Kaminak L., *Canada* .. 51 A10
Kaministiquia, *Canada* . 48 C1
Kaminoyama, *Japan* .. 22 E10
Kamloops, *Canada* ... 50 C4
Kamo, *Japan* 22 F9
Kampala, *Uganda* 36 D6
Kampang Chhnang,
  Cambodia 26 B2
Kampar, *Malaysia* ... 26 D2
Kampar →, *Indonesia* 26 D2
Kampen, *Neths.* 11 B5
Kampene, *Dem. Rep. of*
  the Congo 36 E5
Kampong Saom,
  Cambodia 26 B2
Kampong Saom, Chaak,
  Cambodia 26 B2
Kampot, *Cambodia* ... 26 B2
Kampuchea =
  Cambodia ■, *Asia* .. 26 B3
Kampungbaru =
  Tolitoli, *Indonesia* ... 27 D6
Kamrau, Teluk,
  Indonesia 27 E8
Kamsack, *Canada* 51 C8
Kamskoye Vdkhr.,
  Russia 18 C10
Kamuchawie L., *Canada* 51 B8
Kamui-Misaki, *Japan* .. 22 C10
Kamyanets-Podilskyy,
  Ukraine 13 D14
Kamyanka-Buzka,
  Ukraine 13 C13
Kāmyārān, *Iran* 30 C5
Kamyshin, *Russia* 19 D8
Kanaaupscow, *Canada* 48 B4
Kanaaupscow →,
  Canada 47 C12
Kanab, *U.S.A.* 57 H7
Kanab →, *U.S.A.* 57 H7
Kanagi, *Japan* 22 D10
Kanairiktok →, *Canada* 49 A7
Kananga, *Dem. Rep. of*
  the Congo 36 F4
Kanash, *Russia* 18 C8
Kanastraion, Ákra =
  Palioúrion, Ákra,
  Greece 17 E10
Kanawha →, *U.S.A.* .. 52 F4
Kanazawa, *Japan* ... 23 F8
Kanchanaburi, *Thailand* 26 B1
Kanchenjunga, *Nepal* . 29 F16
Kanchipuram, *India* .. 28 N11
Kandahar = Qandahār,
  Afghan. 28 D4
Kandalaksha, *Russia* .. 18 A5
Kandalakshskiy Zaliv,
  Russia 18 A6
Kandangan, *Indonesia* . 26 E5
Kandanghaur, *Indonesia* 27 G13
Kandavu, *Fiji* 39 D8
Kandi, *Benin* 34 F6
Kandla, *India* 28 H7
Kandos, *Australia* 43 E4
Kandy, *Sri Lanka* 28 R12
Kane, *U.S.A.* 52 E6
Kane Basin, *Greenland* . 4 B4
Kangān, *Fārs, Iran* ... 31 E7
Kangān, *Hormozgān,*
  Iran 31 E8
Kangaroo I., *Australia* . 43 F2
Kangaroo Mts.,
  Australia 42 C3
Kangasala, *Finland* ... 7 F21
Kangāvar, *Iran* 31 C6
Kangean, Kepulauan,
  Indonesia 26 F5
Kangean Is. = Kangean,
  Kepulauan, *Indonesia* 26 F5

Kangikajik, *Greenland* . 4 B6
Kangiqsliniq = Rankin
  Inlet, *Canada* 46 B10
Kangiqsualujjuaq,
  Canada 47 C13
Kangiqsujuaq, *Canada* . 47 B12
Kangiqtugaapik = Clyde
  River, *Canada* 47 A13
Kangirsuk, *Canada* ... 47 B13
Kangto, *India* 29 F18
Kaniapiskau =
  Caniapiscau →,
  Canada 49 A6
Kaniapiskau, Res. =
  Caniapiscau Rés. de,
  Canada 49 B6
Kanin, Poluostrov,
  Russia 18 A8
Kanin Nos, Mys, *Russia* 18 A7
Kanin Pen. = Kanin,
  Poluostrov, *Russia* . 18 A8
Kaniva, *Australia* 43 F3
Kankaanpää, *Finland* . 7 F20
Kankakee, *U.S.A.* 52 E2
Kankakee →, *U.S.A.* . 52 E1
Kankan, *Guinea* 34 F4
Kankendy = Xankändi,
  Azerbaijan 19 G8
Kanker, *India* 29 J12
Kannapolis, *U.S.A.* ... 53 H5
Kannauj, *India* 28 F11
Kannod, *India* 28 H10
Kano, *Nigeria* 34 F7
Kan'onji, *Japan* 23 G6
Kanowit, *Malaysia* ... 26 D4
Kanoya, *Japan* 23 J5
Kanpetlet, *Burma* ... 29 J18
Kanpur, *India* 28 F12
Kansas □, *U.S.A.* 54 F6
Kansas →, *U.S.A.* ... 54 F7
Kansas City, *Kans.,*
  U.S.A. 54 F7
Kansas City, *Mo., U.S.A.* 54 F7
Kansk, *Russia* 21 D10
Kansu = Gansu □,
  China 24 C5
Kantō □, *Japan* 23 F9
Kantō-Sanchi, *Japan* . 23 G9
Kanuma, *Japan* 23 F9
Kanye, *Botswana* ... 37 J5
Kaohsiung, *Taiwan* .. 25 D7
Kaolack, *Senegal* ... 34 F2
Kapan, *Armenia* 19 G8
Kapanga, *Dem. Rep. of*
  the Congo 36 F4
Kapchagai =
  Qapshaghay,
  Kazakstan 20 E8
Kapela = Velika Kapela,
  Croatia 12 F8
Kapfenberg, *Austria* .. 12 E8
Kapiri Mposhi, *Zambia* 37 G5
Kapiskau →, *Canada* . 48 B3
Kapit, *Malaysia* 26 D4
Kapiti I., *N.Z.* 39 J5
Kaplan, *U.S.A.* 55 K8
Kapoeta, *Sudan* 35 H12
Kaposvár, *Hungary* .. 13 E9
Kapsukas =
  Marijampolė,
  Lithuania 7 J20
Kapuas →, *Indonesia* 26 E3
Kapuas Hulu,
  Pegunungan,
  Malaysia 26 D4
Kapuas Hulu Ra. =
  Kapuas Hulu,
  Pegunungan,
  Malaysia 26 D4
Kapunda, *Australia* .. 43 E2
Kapuni, *N.Z.* 39 H5
Kapuskasing, *Canada* . 48 C3
Kapuskasing →,
  Canada 48 C3
Kaputar, *Australia* ... 43 E5
Kara, *Russia* 20 C7
Kara Bogaz Gol, Zaliv =
  Garabogazköl Aylagy,
  Turkmenistan 19 F9
Kara Kalpak Republic =
  Karakalpakstan □,
  Uzbekistan 20 E6
Kara Kum,
  Turkmenistan 20 F6
Kara Sea, *Russia* 20 B7
Karabiğa, *Turkey* 17 D12
Karabük, *Turkey* 19 F5
Karaburun, *Turkey* .. 17 E12
Karabutak = Qarabutaq,
  Kazakstan 20 E7
Karacabey, *Turkey* ... 17 D13
Karacasu, *Turkey* ... 17 F13
Karachey-Cherkessia □,
  Russia 19 F7
Karachi, *Pakistan* ... 28 G5
Karad, *India* 28 L9
Karaganda =
  Qaraghandy,
  Kazakstan 20 E8
Karagayly, *Kazakstan* . 20 E8
Karaginskiy, Ostrov,
  Russia 21 D17
Karagiye, Vpadina,
  Kazakstan 19 F9

Karagiye Depression =
  Karagiye, Vpadina,
  Kazakstan 19 F9
Karaikal, *India* 28 P11
Karaikkudi, *India* 28 P11
Karaj, *Iran* 31 C6
Karakalpakstan □,
  Uzbekistan 20 E6
Karakelong, *Indonesia* . 27 D7
Karakitang, *Indonesia* . 27 D7
Karaklis = Vanadzor,
  Armenia 19 F7
Karakoram Pass,
  Pakistan 28 B10
Karakoram Ra., *Pakistan* 28 B10
Karalon, *Russia* 21 D12
Karama, *Jordan* 33 D4
Karaman, *Turkey* ... 19 G5
Karamay, *China* 24 B3
Karambu, *Indonesia* . 26 E5
Karamea Bight, *N.Z.* . 39 J3
Karand, *Iran* 30 C5
Karanganyar, *Indonesia* 27 G13
Karasburg, *Namibia* .. 37 K3
Karasino, *Russia* 20 C9
Karasjok, *Norway* ... 6 B21
Karasuk, *Russia* 20 D8
Karasuyama, *Japan* .. 23 F10
Karatau = Qarataū,
  Kazakstan 20 E8
Karatau, Khrebet,
  Kazakstan 20 E7
Karatsu, *Japan* 23 H5
Karaul, *Russia* 20 B9
Karawang, *Indonesia* . 27 G12
Karawanken, *Europe* . 12 E8
Karayazı, *Turkey* ... 19 G7
Karazhal, *Kazakstan* . 20 E8
Karbalā', *Iraq* 30 C5
Karcag, *Hungary* ... 13 E11
Kardhitsa, *Greece* ... 17 E9
Kärdla, *Estonia* 7 G20
Kareima, *Sudan* 35 E12
Karelia □, *Russia* 18 A5
Karelian Republic =
  Karelia □, *Russia* .. 18 A5
Kārevāndar, *Iran* 31 E9
Kargasok, *Russia* 20 D9
Kargat, *Russia* 20 D9
Kargil, *India* 28 B10
Kargopol, *Russia* 18 B6
Kariān, *Iran* 31 E8
Kariba, L., *Zimbabwe* . 37 H5
Kariba Dam, *Zimbabwe* 37 H5
Kariba Gorge, *Zambia* . 37 H5
Karimata, Kepulauan,
  Indonesia 26 E3
Karimata, Selat,
  Indonesia 26 E3
Karimata Is. = Karimata,
  Kepulauan, *Indonesia* 26 E3
Karimnagar, *India* .. 28 K11
Karimunjawa,
  Kepulauan, *Indonesia* 26 F4
Karin, *Somali Rep.* .. 32 E4
Karīt, *Iran* 31 C8
Kariya, *Japan* 23 G8
Karkaralinsk =
  Qarqaraly, *Kazakstan* 20 E8
Karkheh →, *Iran* ... 30 D5
Karkinitska Zatoka,
  Ukraine 19 E5
Karkinitskiy Zaliv =
  Karkinitska Zatoka,
  Ukraine 19 E5
Karl-Marx-Stadt =
  Chemnitz, *Germany* . 12 C7
Karlovac, *Croatia* ... 12 F8
Karlovo, *Bulgaria* ... 17 C11
Karlovy Vary,
  Czech Rep. 12 C7
Karlsbad = Karlovy
  Vary, *Czech Rep.* .. 12 C7
Karlsborg, *Sweden* .. 7 G16
Karlshamn, *Sweden* . 7 H16
Karlskoga, *Sweden* .. 7 G16
Karlskrona, *Sweden* . 7 H16
Karlsruhe, *Germany* . 12 D5
Karlstad, *Sweden* ... 7 G15
Karlstad, *U.S.A.* 54 A6
Karmi'el, *Israel* 33 C4
Karnak, *Egypt* 35 C12
Karnal, *India* 28 E10
Karnali →, *Nepal* ... 29 E12
Karnaphuli Res., *Bangla.* 29 H18
Karnataka □, *India* .. 28 N10
Karnes City, *U.S.A.* .. 55 L6
Karnische Alpen, *Europe* 12 E7
Kärnten □, *Austria* .. 12 E8
Karonga, *Malawi* ... 36 F6
Karoonda, *Australia* . 43 F2
Karora, *Sudan* 35 E13
Kárpathos, *Greece* .. 17 G12
Karpinsk, *Russia* 18 C11
Karpogory, *Russia* ... 18 B7
Karpuz Burnu =
  Apostolos Andreas,
  C., *Cyprus* 30 C2
Karratha, *Australia* .. 40 D2
Kars, *Turkey* 19 F7
Karsakpay, *Kazakstan* . 20 E7
Karshi = Qarshi,
  Uzbekistan 20 F7
Kartaly, *Russia* 20 D7
Karufa, *Indonesia* ... 27 E8

Karumba, *Australia* .. 42 B3
Kārūn →, *Iran* 31 D6
Karungu, *Kenya* 36 E6
Karviná, *Czech Rep.* . 13 D10
Karwar, *India* 28 M9
Kasai →, *Dem. Rep. of*
  the Congo 36 E3
Kasama, *Zambia* 36 G6
Kasaragod, *India* ... 28 N9
Kasba L., *Canada* ... 51 A8
Käseh Garän, *Iran* .. 30 C5
Kasempa, *Zambia* ... 37 G5
Kasenga, *Dem. Rep. of*
  the Congo 36 G5
Kasese, *Uganda* 36 D6
Kashabowie, *Canada* . 48 C1
Kashaf, *Iran* 31 C9
Kāshān, *Iran* 31 C6
Kashechewan, *Canada* 48 B3
Kashi, *China* 24 C2
Kashiwazaki, *Japan* . 23 F9
Kashk-e Kohneh,
  Afghan. 28 B3
Kashkū'īyeh, *Iran* ... 31 D7
Kāshmar, *Iran* 31 C8
Kashmir, *Asia* 28 C10
Kashun Noerh = Gaxun
  Nur, *China* 24 B5
Kasimov, *Russia* 18 D7
Kasiruta, *Indonesia* .. 27 E7
Kaskaskia →, *U.S.A.* 54 G10
Kaskattama →, *Canada* 51 B10
Kaskinen, *Finland* ... 7 E19
Kaslo, *Canada* 50 D5
Kasmere L., *Canada* .. 51 B8
Kasongo, *Dem. Rep. of*
  the Congo 36 E5
Kasongo Lunda,
  Dem. Rep. of
  the Congo 36 F3
Kásos, *Greece* 17 G12
Kassalâ, *Sudan* 35 E13
Kassel, *Germany* 12 C5
Kasson, *U.S.A.* 54 C8
Kastamonu, *Turkey* . 19 F5
Kasterlee, *Belgium* .. 11 C4
Kastoria, *Greece* 17 D9
Kasumi, *Japan* 23 G7
Kasur, *Pakistan* 28 D9
Katahdin, Mt., *U.S.A.* 53 C11
Katanga □, *Dem. Rep.*
  of the Congo 36 F4
Katangi, *India* 28 J11
Katanning, *Australia* . 41 F2
Katerini, *Greece* 17 D10
Katha, *Burma* 29 G20
Katherîna, Gebel, *Egypt* 30 D2
Katherine, *Australia* . 40 B5
Katherine Gorge,
  Australia 40 B5
Kathiawar, *India* 28 H7
Kathikas, *India* 29 G15
Katima Mulilo, *Zambia* 37 H4
Katingan =
  Mendawai →,
  Indonesia 26 E4
Katiola, *Ivory C.* 34 G4
Katmandu, *Nepal* ... 29 F14
Katoomba, *Australia* . 43 E5
Katowice, *Poland* ... 13 C10
Katrineholm, *Sweden* . 7 G17
Katsina, *Nigeria* 34 F7
Katsumoto, *Japan* ... 23 H4
Katsuura, *Japan* ... 23 G10
Katsuyama, *Japan* .. 23 F8
Kattegat, *Denmark* .. 7 H14
Katwijk, *Neths.* 11 B4
Kaufman, *U.S.A.* 55 J6
Kauhajoki, *Finland* .. 7 E20
Kaukauna, *U.S.A.* ... 52 C1
Kaunas, *Lithuania* ... 7 J20
Kautokeino, *Norway* . 6 B20
Kavacha, *Russia* 21 C17
Kavalerovo, *Russia* .. 22 B7
Kavali, *India* 28 M12
Kaválla, *Greece* 17 D11
Kavār, *Iran* 31 D7
Kavir, Dasht-e, *Iran* . 31 C7
Kaw, *Fr. Guiana* 63 C8
Kawagoe, *Japan* 23 G9
Kawaguchi, *Japan* .. 23 G9
Kawanoe, *Japan* ... 23 G6
Kawardha, *India* 29 J12
Kawasaki, *Japan* ... 23 G9
Kawerau, *N.Z.* 39 H6
Kawhia Harbour, *N.Z.* 39 H5
Kawio, Kepulauan,
  Indonesia 27 D7
Kawnro, *Burma* 29 H21
Kawthoolei =
  Kawthule □, *Burma* . 29 L20
Kawthule □, *Burma* . 29 L20
Kaya, *Burkina Faso* .. 34 F5
Kayah □, *Burma* 29 K20
Kayan →, *Indonesia* . 26 D5
Kayeli, *Indonesia* ... 27 E7
Kayenta, *U.S.A.* 57 H8
Kayes, *Mali* 34 F3
Kayin = Kawthule □,
  Burma 29 L20
Kayoa, *Indonesia* ... 27 D7
Kayseri, *Turkey* 19 G6
Kaysville, *U.S.A.* 56 F8

Kazachye, *Russia* 21 B14
Kazakstan ■, *Asia* ... 20 E7
Kazan, *Russia* 18 C8
Kazan →, *Canada* ... 51 A9
Kazan-Rettō, *Pac. Oc.* 44 E6
Kazanlŭk, *Bulgaria* .. 17 C11
Kazatin = Kozyatyn,
  Ukraine 13 D15
Käzerün, *Iran* 31 D6
Kazi Magomed =
  Qazimämmäd,
  Azerbaijan 31 A6
Kazuno, *Japan* 22 D10
Kazym →, *Russia* ... 20 C7
Kéa, *Greece* 17 F11
Kearney, *U.S.A.* 54 E5
Kearny, *U.S.A.* 57 K8
Keban, *Turkey* 19 G6
Keban Baraji, *Turkey* . 19 G6
Kebnekaise, *Sweden* . 6 C18
Kebri Dehar, *Ethiopia* . 32 F3
Kebumen, *Indonesia* . 27 G13
Kechika →, *Canada* . 50 B3
Kecskemét, *Hungary* . 13 E10
Kédainiai, *Lithuania* . 7 J21
Kedgwick, *Canada* ... 49 C6
Kediri, *Indonesia* ... 27 G15
Keeley L., *Canada* ... 51 C7
Keeling Is. = Cocos Is.,
  Ind. Oc. 44 J1
Keelung = Chilung,
  Taiwan 25 D7
Keene, *U.S.A.* 52 D9
Keer-Weer, C., *Australia* 42 A3
Keetmanshoop, *Namibia* 37 K3
Keewatin, *Canada* ... 51 D10
Keewatin →, *Canada* . 51 B8
Kefallinía, *Greece* ... 17 E9
Kefamenanu, *Indonesia* 27 F6
Kefar Sava, *Israel* ... 33 C3
Keffi, *Nigeria* 34 G7
Keflavík, *Iceland* 6 D2
Keg River, *Canada* .. 50 B5
Kegaska, *Canada* ... 49 B7
Keighley, *U.K.* 8 D6
Keila, *Estonia* 7 G21
Keimoes, *S. Africa* ... 37 K4
Keitele, *Finland* 6 E22
Keith, *Australia* 43 F3
Keizer, *U.S.A.* 56 D2
Kejimkujik Nat. Park,
  Canada 49 D6
Kejser Franz Joseph Fd.,
  Greenland 4 B6
Kekri, *India* 28 G9
Kelang, *Malaysia* ... 26 D2
Kelkit →, *Turkey* ... 19 F6
Kellerberrin, *Australia* . 41 F2
Kellett, C., *Canada* .. 4 B1
Kellogg, *U.S.A.* 56 C5
Kells = Ceanannus Mor,
  Ireland 10 E3
Kelowna, *Canada* ... 50 D5
Kelseyville, *U.S.A.* .. 56 G2
Kelso, *N.Z.* 39 L2
Kelso, *U.S.A.* 56 C2
Keluang, *Malaysia* .. 26 D2
Kelvington, *Canada* . 51 C8
Kem, *Russia* 18 B5
Kem →, *Russia* 18 B5
Kema, *Indonesia* ... 27 D7
Kemah, *Turkey* 30 B3
Kemaman, *Malaysia* . 26 D2
Kemano, *Canada* ... 50 C3
Kemerovo, *Russia* .. 20 D9
Kemi, *Finland* 6 D21
Kemi älv =
  Kemijoki →, *Finland* 6 D21
Kemijärvi, *Finland* .. 6 C22
Kemijoki →, *Finland* . 6 D21
Kemmerer, *U.S.A.* .. 56 F8
Kemp, L., *U.S.A.* 55 J5
Kemp Land, *Antarctica* 5 C5
Kempsey, *Australia* .. 43 E5
Kempt, L., *Canada* .. 48 C5
Kempten, *Germany* .. 12 E6
Kempton, *Australia* .. 42 G4
Kemptville, *Canada* .. 48 B4
Kenai, *U.S.A.* 46 B4
Kendal, *Indonesia* ... 27 G14
Kendal, *U.K.* 8 C5
Kendall, *Australia* ... 43 E5
Kendall, *U.S.A.* 53 N5
Kendall →, *Australia* . 42 A3
Kendallville, *U.S.A.* .. 52 E3
Kendari, *Indonesia* .. 27 E6
Kendawangan,
  Indonesia 26 E4
Kendrapara, *India* ... 29 J15
Kenedy, *U.S.A.* 55 L6
Kenema, *S. Leone* ... 34 G3
Keng Tawng, *Burma* . 29 J21
Keng Tung, *Burma* .. 29 J21
Kenitra, *Morocco* ... 34 B4
Kenmare, *U.S.A.* 54 A3
Kenmare →, *Ireland* . 10 E2
Kennebec →, *U.S.A.* 53 D11
Kennedy Ra., *Australia* 41 D2
Kennedy Taungdeik,
  Burma 29 H18
Kenner, *U.S.A.* 55 L9
Kennet →, *U.K.* 9 F7
Kennett, *U.S.A.* 55 G9
Kennewick, *U.S.A.* .. 56 C4
Kenogami →, *Canada* 48 B3

Kenora, *Canada* 51 D10
Kenosha, *U.S.A.* 52 D2
Kensington, *Canada* . 49 C7
Kent, *U.S.A.* 55 K2
Kent □, *U.K.* 9 F8
Kent Group, *Australia* . 42 F4
Kent Pen., *Canada* .. 46 B9
Kentau, *Kazakstan* .. 20 E7
Kentland, *U.S.A.* 52 E2
Kenton, *U.S.A.* 52 E4
Kentucky □, *U.S.A.* .. 52 G3
Kentucky →, *U.S.A.* . 52 F3
Kentucky L., *U.S.A.* .. 53 G2
Kentville, *Canada* ... 49 C7
Kentwood, *U.S.A.* ... 55 K9
Kenya ■, *Africa* 36 D7
Kenya, Mt., *Kenya* ... 36 E7
Keokuk, *U.S.A.* 54 E9
Kepi, *Indonesia* 27 F9
Kerala □, *India* 28 P10
Kerama-Rettō, *Japan* . 23 L3
Kerang, *Australia* ... 43 F3
Keraudren, C., *Australia* 40 C2
Kerava, *Finland* 7 F21
Kerch, *Ukraine* 19 E6
Kerguelen, *Ind. Oc.* . 3 G13
Kericho, *Kenya* 36 E7
Kerinci, *Indonesia* ... 26 E2
Kerki, *Turkmenistan* . 20 F7
Kérkira, *Greece* 17 E8
Kerkrade, *Neths.* 11 D6
Kermadec Is., *Pac. Oc.* 38 E11
Kermadec Trench,
  Pac. Oc. 44 L10
Kerman, *Iran* 31 D8
Kermān □, *Iran* 31 D8
Kermān, Biābān-e, *Iran* 31 D8
Kermānshāh =
  Bākhtarān, *Iran* ... 30 C5
Kermit, *U.S.A.* 55 K3
Kern →, *U.S.A.* 57 J4
Kernow = Cornwall □,
  U.K. 9 G3
Kerrobert, *Canada* ... 51 C7
Kerrville, *U.S.A.* 55 K5
Kerulen →, *Asia* 25 B6
Kerzaz, *Algeria* 34 C5
Kesagami →, *Canada* 48 B4
Kesagami L., *Canada* . 48 B3
Keşan, *Turkey* 17 D12
Kesennuma, *Japan* .. 22 E10
Keshit, *Iran* 31 D8
Kestenga, *Russia* 18 A5
Keswick, *U.K.* 8 C4
Ket →, *Russia* 20 D9
Ketapang, *Indonesia* . 26 E4
Ketchikan, *U.S.A.* ... 50 B2
Ketchum, *U.S.A.* 56 E6
Ketef, Khalîg Umm el,
  Egypt 30 F2
Kętrzyn, *Poland* 13 A11
Kettering, *U.K.* 9 E7
Kettering, *U.S.A.* 52 F3
Kettle →, *Canada* ... 51 B11
Kettle Falls, *U.S.A.* .. 56 B4
Keuruu, *Finland* 7 E21
Kewanee, *U.S.A.* 54 E10
Kewaunee, *U.S.A.* ... 52 C2
Keweenaw B., *U.S.A.* . 52 B1
Keweenaw Pen., *U.S.A.* 52 B2
Keweenaw Pt., *U.S.A.* . 52 B2
Key Largo, *U.S.A.* ... 53 N5
Key West, *U.S.A.* 60 B3
Keynsham, *U.K.* 9 F5
Keyser, *U.S.A.* 52 F6
Kezhma, *Russia* 21 D11
Khabarovsk, *Russia* . 21 E14
Khabr, *Iran* 31 D8
Khābūr →, *Syria* 30 C4
Khachmas = Xaçmaz,
  Azerbaijan 19 F8
Khairpur, *Pakistan* .. 28 F6
Khakassia □, *Russia* . 20 D9
Khalafābād, *Iran* 31 D6
Khalīlī, *Iran* 31 E7
Khalkhāl, *Iran* 31 B6
Khalkís, *Greece* 17 E10
Khalmer-Sede =
  Tazovskiy, *Russia* .. 20 C8
Khalmer Yu, *Russia* . 20 C7
Khalturin, *Russia* ... 18 C8
Khalūf, *Oman* 32 C6
Khambhat, *India* 28 H8
Khambhat, G. of, *India* 28 J8
Khamir, *Iran* 31 E7
Khamir, *Yemen* 32 D3
Khamsa, *Egypt* 33 E1
Khān Abū Shāmat, *Syria* 33 B5
Khān Azād, *Iraq* 30 C5
Khān Mujiddah, *Iraq* . 30 C4
Khān Shaykhūn, *Syria* . 30 C3
Khān Yūnis, *Gaza Strip* 33 D3
Khānaqin, *Iraq* 30 C5
Khānbāghī, *Iran* 31 B7
Khandwa, *India* 28 J10
Khandyga, *Russia* .. 21 C14
Khaniá, *Greece* 17 G11
Khanion, Kólpos, *Greece* 17 G10
Khanka, L., *Asia* 21 E14
Khankendy = Xankändi,
  Azerbaijan 19 G8
Khanty-Mansiysk,
  Russia 20 C7

Khapcheranga, *Russia* . 21 E12
Kharagpur, *India* 29 H15
Kharan Kalat, *Pakistan* . 28 E4
Kharānaq, *Iran* 31 C7
Kharda, *India* 28 K9
Khârga, El Wâhât-el,
  Egypt 35 C12
Khargon, *India* 28 J9
Khārk, Jazīreh-ye, *Iran* . 31 D6
Kharkiv, *Ukraine* 19 E6
Kharkov = Kharkiv,
  Ukraine 19 E6
Kharovsk, *Russia* 18 C7
Kharta, *Turkey* 17 D13
Khartoum = El
  Khartûm, *Sudan* .. 35 E12
Khasan, *Russia* 22 C5
Khāsh, *Iran* 28 E2
Khashm el Girba, *Sudan* 35 F13
Khaskovo, *Bulgaria* .. 17 D11
Khatanga, *Russia* 21 B11
Khatanga →, *Russia* .. 21 B11
Khātūnābād, *Iran* 31 D7
Khatyrka, *Russia* 21 C18
Khaybar, Harrat,
  Si. Arabia 30 E4
Khayelitsha, *S. Africa* . 37 L3
Khāzimiyah, *Iraq* 30 C4
Khed Brahma, *India* .. 28 G8
Khemisset, *Morocco* .. 34 K4
Khemmarat, *Thailand* . 26 A3
Khenāmān, *Iran* 31 D8
Khenchela, *Algeria* ... 34 A7
Khersān →, *Iran* 31 D6
Kherson, *Ukraine* 19 E5
Kheta →, *Russia* 21 B11
Khilok, *Russia* 21 D12
Khíos, *Greece* 17 E12
Khiuma = Hiiumaa,
  Estonia 7 G20
Khiva, *Uzbekistan* 20 E7
Khīyāv, *Iran* 30 B5
Khmelnik, *Ukraine* ... 13 D14
Khmelnitskiy =
  Khmelnytskyy,
  Ukraine 13 D14
Khmelnytskyy, *Ukraine* 13 D14
Khmer Rep. =
  Cambodia ■, *Asia* . 26 B3
Khodoriv, *Ukraine* ... 13 D13
Khodzent = Khudzhand,
  Tajikistan 20 E7
Khojak Pass, *Afghan.* . 28 D5
Kholm, *Russia* 18 C5
Kholmsk, *Russia* 21 E15
Khomeyn, *Iran* 31 C6
Khomeyni Shahr, *Iran* . 31 C6
Khon Kaen, *Thailand* . 26 A2
Khong →, *Cambodia* . 26 B3
Khonuu, *Russia* 21 C15
Khopër →, *Russia* ... 19 D6
Khóra Sfakíon, *Greece* . 17 G11
Khorāsān □, *Iran* 31 C8
Khorat = Nakhon
  Ratchasima, *Thailand* 26 B2
Khorramābād,
  Khorāsān, Iran 31 C8
Khorramābād, *Lorestān,*
  Iran 31 C6
Khorrāmshahr, *Iran* .. 31 D6
Khorugh, *Tajikistan* .. 20 F8
Khosravī, *Iran* 31 D6
Khosrowābād,
  Khuzestān, Iran ... 31 D6
Khosrowābād,
  Kordestān, Iran ... 30 C5
Khosūyeh, *Iran* 31 D7
Khotyn, *Ukraine* 13 D14
Khouribga, *Morocco* .. 34 B4
Khowst, *Afghan.* 28 C6
Khoyniki, *Belarus* 13 C15
Khu Khan, *Thailand* .. 26 B2
Khudzhand, *Tajikistan* . 20 E7
Khuff, *Si. Arabia* 30 E5
Khūgīānī, *Afghan.* ... 28 D4
Khulna, *Bangla.* 29 H16
Khulna □, *Bangla.* .. 29 H16
Khūnsorkh, *Iran* 31 E8
Khūr, *Iran* 31 C8
Khurayş, *Si. Arabia* .. 31 E6
Khurīyā Murīyā, Jazā 'ir,
  Oman 32 D6
Khūrmāl, *Iraq* 30 C5
Khurr, Wādī al, *Iraq* .. 30 C4
Khūsf, *Iran* 31 C8
Khush, *Afghan.* 28 C3
Khushab, *Pakistan* ... 28 C5
Khust, *Ukraine* 13 D12
Khuzdar, *Pakistan* ... 28 F5
Khūzestān □, *Iran* ... 31 D6
Khvāf, *Iran* 31 C9
Khvājeh, *Iran* 30 B5
Khvānsār, *Iran* 31 D7
Khvor, *Iran* 31 C7
Khvorgū, *Iran* 31 E8
Khvormūj, *Iran* 31 D6
Khvoy, *Iran* 30 B5
Khyber Pass, *Afghan.* . 28 B7
Kiama, *Australia* 43 E5
Kiamba, *Phil.* 27 C6
Kiangsi = Jiangxi □,
  China 25 D6
Kiangsu = Jiangsu □,
  China 25 C7

Kibombo, *Dem. Rep. of*
  the Congo 36 E5
Kibre Mengist, *Ethiopia* 32 F2
Kibwezi, *Kenya* 36 E7
Kichmengskiy Gorodok,
  Russia 18 B8
Kicking Horse Pass,
  Canada 50 C5
Kidal, *Mali* 34 E6
Kidderminster, *U.K.* .. 9 E5
Kidnappers, C., *N.Z.* . 39 H6
Kidsgrove, *U.K.* 8 D5
Kidston, *Australia* ... 42 B3
Kiel, *Germany* 12 A6
Kiel Canal = Nord-
  Ostsee-Kanal,
  Germany 12 A5
Kielce, *Poland* 13 C11
Kielder Water, *U.K.* .. 8 B5
Kieler Bucht, *Germany* 12 A6
Kiev = Kyyiv, *Ukraine* . 13 C16
Kiffa, *Mauritania* 34 E3
Kifrī, *Iraq* 30 C5
Kigali, *Rwanda* 36 E6
Kigoma-Ujiji, *Tanzania* 36 E5
Kiğzı, *Turkey* 30 B4
Kihnu, *Estonia* 7 G21
Kii-Sanchi, *Japan* 23 G8
Kii-Suidō, *Japan* 23 H7
Kikaiga-Shima, *Japan* . 23 K4
Kikinda, *Serbia, Yug.* . 17 B9
Kikládhes, *Greece* ... 17 F11
Kikwit, *Dem. Rep. of*
  the Congo 36 E3
Kilcoy, *Australia* 43 D5
Kilgore, *U.S.A.* 55 J7
Kilimanjaro, *Tanzania* . 36 E7
Kilindini, *Tanzania* ... 36 E7
Kilis, *Turkey* 30 B3
Kiliya, *Ukraine* 13 F15
Kilkenny, *Ireland* 10 E3
Kilkis, *Greece* 17 D10
Killarney, *Australia* .. 43 D5
Killarney, *Canada* 51 D9
Killarney, *Ireland* 10 E2
Killdeer, *U.S.A.* 54 B3
Killeen, *U.S.A.* 55 K6
Killíni, *Greece* 17 F10
Kilmarnock, *U.K.* 10 D4
Kilmore, *Australia* ... 43 F3
Kilosa, *Tanzania* 36 F7
Kilrush, *Ireland* 10 E2
Kilwa Kivinje, *Tanzania* 36 F7
Kim, *U.S.A.* 55 G3
Kimaam, *Indonesia* .. 27 F9
Kimba, *Australia* 43 E2
Kimball, *Nebr., U.S.A.* 54 E3
Kimball, *S. Dak., U.S.A.* 54 D5
Kimberley, *Canada* ... 40 C4
Kimberley, *Canada* ... 50 D5
Kimberley, *S. Africa* .. 37 K4
Kimberly, *U.S.A.* 56 E6
Kimmirut, *Canada* ... 47 B13
Kimpese, *Dem. Rep. of*
  the Congo 36 F2
Kimry, *Russia* 18 C6
Kinabalu, Gunong,
  Malaysia 26 C5
Kinaskan L., *Canada* . 50 B2
Kinbasket L., *Canada* . 50 C5
Kincardine, *Canada* .. 48 D3
Kincolith, *Canada* ... 50 B2
Kinder Scout, *U.K.* ... 8 D6
Kindersley, *Canada* .. 51 C7
Kindia, *Guinea* 34 F3
Kindu, *Dem. Rep. of*
  the Congo 36 E5
Kineshma, *Russia* ... 18 C7
King, Mt., *Australia* .. 42 D4
King City, *U.S.A.* 57 H3
King Cr. →, *Australia* 42 C2
King Edward →,
  Australia 40 B4
King Frederick VI
  Land = Kong Frederik
  VI Kyst, *Greenland* . 4 C5
King George B., *Falk. Is.* 64 G4
King George I.,
  Antarctica 5 C18
King George Is., *Canada* 47 C11
King I. = Kadan Kyun,
  Burma 26 B1
King I., *Australia* 42 F3
King I., *Canada* 50 C3
King Leopold Ranges,
  Australia 40 C4
King Sd., *Australia* ... 40 C3
King William I., *Canada* 46 B10
Kingaok = Bathurst
  Inlet, *Canada* 46 B9
Kingaroy, *Australia* .. 43 D5
Kingfisher, *U.S.A.* ... 55 H6
Kingirbān, *Iraq* 30 C5
Kingisepp = Kuressaare,
  Estonia 7 G20
Kingman, *Ariz., U.S.A.* 57 J6
Kingman, *Kans., U.S.A.* 55 G5
Kingoonya, *Australia* . 43 E2
Kings →, *U.S.A.* 57 H4
Kings Canyon National
  Park, *U.S.A.* 57 H4
King's Lynn, *U.K.* 8 E8
Kings Mountain, *U.S.A.* 53 H5
King's Peak, *U.S.A.* .. 56 F8
Kingsbridge, *U.K.* ... 9 G4

Kingsburg, *U.S.A.* 57 H4
Kingscote, *Australia* . 43 F2
Kingsford, *U.S.A.* 52 C1
Kingsland, *U.S.A.* 53 K5
Kingsley, *U.S.A.* 54 D7
Kingsport, *U.S.A.* 53 G4
Kingston, *Canada* ... 48 D4
Kingston, *Jamaica* ... 60 C4
Kingston, *N.Z.* 39 L2
Kingston, *N.Y., U.S.A.* 52 E9
Kingston, *Pa., U.S.A.* . 52 E8
Kingston South East,
  Australia 43 F2
Kingston upon Hull,
  U.K. 8 D7
Kingston upon Hull □,
  U.K. 8 D7
Kingston-upon-
  Thames □, *U.K.* .. 9 F7
Kingstown, *St. Vincent* 61 D7
Kingstree, *U.S.A.* 53 J6
Kingsville, *Canada* ... 48 D3
Kingwood, *U.S.A.* ... 55 K7
Kınık, *Turkey* 17 E12
Kinistino, *Canada* ... 51 C7
Kinkala, *Congo* 36 E2
Kinki □, *Japan* 23 H8
Kinna, *Sweden* 7 H15
Kinngait = Cape Dorset,
  Canada 47 B12
Kino, *Mexico* 58 B2
Kinoje →, *Canada* .. 48 B3
Kinomoto, *Japan* ... 23 G8
Kinoosao, *Canada* ... 51 B8
Kinsale, *Ireland* 10 F2
Kinsha = Chang
  Jiang →, *China* ... 25 C7
Kinshasa, *Dem. Rep. of*
  the Congo 36 E3
Kinsley, *U.S.A.* 55 G5
Kinston, *U.S.A.* 53 H7
Kintore Ra., *Australia* . 40 D4
Kinushseo →, *Canada* 48 A3
Kinuso, *Canada* 50 B5
Kiosk, *Canada* 48 C4
Kiowa, *Kans., U.S.A.* . 55 G5
Kiowa, *Okla., U.S.A.* . 55 H7
Kipahigan L., *Canada* . 51 B8
Kiparissía, *Greece* ... 17 F9
Kiparissiakós Kólpos,
  Greece 17 F9
Kipawa, L., *Canada* .. 48 C4
Kipling, *Canada* 51 C8
Kipushi, *Dem. Rep. of*
  the Congo 37 G5
Kirensk, *Russia* 21 D11
Kirghizia =
  Kyrgyzstan ■, *Asia* . 20 E8
Kirghizstan =
  Kyrgyzstan ■, *Asia* . 20 E8
Kirgiziya Steppe,
  Eurasia 19 E10
Kiribati ■, *Pac. Oc.* .. 38 B10
Kırıkkale, *Turkey* 19 G5
Kirillov, *Russia* 18 C6
Kirin = Jilin, *China* ... 25 B7
Kiritimati, *Kiribati* ... 45 G12
Kirkby, *U.K.* 8 D5
Kirkby Lonsdale, *U.K.* . 8 C5
Kirkcaldy, *U.K.* 10 C5
Kirkcudbright, *U.K.* .. 10 D4
Kirkee, *India* 28 K8
Kirkenes, *Norway* ... 6 B23
Kirkjubæjarklaustur,
  Iceland 6 E4
Kirkkonummi, *Finland* 7 F21
Kirkland Lake, *Canada* . 48 C3
Kırklareli, *Turkey* .. 17 D12
Kirksville, *U.S.A.* 54 E8
Kirkūk, *Iraq* 30 C5
Kirkwall, *U.K.* 10 B5
Kirov, *Russia* 18 C8
Kirovabad = Gäncä,
  Azerbaijan 19 F8
Kirovakan = Vanadzor,
  Armenia 19 F7
Kirovograd =
  Kirovohrad, *Ukraine* . 19 E5
Kirovohrad, *Ukraine* . 19 E5
Kirovsk = Babadayhan,
  Turkmenistan 20 F7
Kirovsk, *Russia* 18 A5
Kirovskiy, *Kamchatka,*
  Russia 21 D16
Kirovskiy, *Primorsk,*
  Russia 22 B6
Kirsanov, *Russia* 18 D7
Kırşehir, *Turkey* 19 G5
Kirthar Range, *Pakistan* 28 F5
Kiruna, *Sweden* 6 C19
Kiryū, *Japan* 23 F9
Kisalaya, *Nic.* 60 D3
Kisangani, *Dem. Rep. of*
  the Congo 36 D5
Kisar, *Indonesia* 27 F7
Kisarazu, *Japan* 23 G9
Kishanganj, *India* ... 29 F16
Kishangarh, *India* ... 28 F7
Kishinev = Chişinău,
  Moldova 13 E15
Kishiwada, *Japan* ... 23 G7
Kishtwar, *India* 28 C9

Kisii, *Kenya* 36 E6
Kiskőrös, *Hungary* .. 13 E10
Kiskunfélegyháza,
  Hungary 13 E10
Kiskunhalas, *Hungary* . 13 E10
Kislovodsk, *Russia* .. 19 F7
Kiso-Gawa →, *Japan* . 23 G8
Kiso-Sammyaku, *Japan* 23 G8
Kisofukushima, *Japan* 23 G8
Kissidougou, *Guinea* . 34 G3
Kissimmee, *U.S.A.* .. 53 L5
Kissimmee →, *U.S.A.* 53 M5
Kississing L., *Canada* . 51 B8
Kisumu, *Kenya* 36 E6
Kit Carson, *U.S.A.* ... 54 F3
Kita, *Mali* 34 F4
Kitaibaraki, *Japan* .. 23 F10
Kitakami, *Japan* 22 E10
Kitakami-Gawa →,
  Japan 22 E10
Kitakami-Sammyaku,
  Japan 22 E10
Kitakata, *Japan* 22 F9
Kitakyūshū, *Japan* .. 23 H5
Kitale, *Kenya* 36 D7
Kitami, *Japan* 22 C11
Kitami-Sammyaku,
  Japan 22 B11
Kitchener, *Canada* .. 48 D3
Kitega = Gitega,
  Burundi 36 E5
Kíthira, *Greece* 17 F10
Kíthnos, *Greece* 17 F11
Kitimat, *Canada* 50 C3
Kitinen →, *Finland* .. 6 C22
Kitsuki, *Japan* 23 H5
Kittakittaooloo, L.,
  Australia 43 D2
Kittanning, *U.S.A.* ... 52 E6
Kittery, *U.S.A.* 53 D10
Kittilä, *Finland* 6 C21
Kitui, *Kenya* 36 E7
Kitwanga, *Canada* ... 50 B3
Kitwe, *Zambia* 37 G5
Kivarli, *India* 28 N11
Kivertsi, *Ukraine* ... 13 C13
Kivu, L., *Dem. Rep. of*
  the Congo 36 E5
Kiyev = Kyyiv, *Ukraine* 13 C16
Kiyevskoye Vdkhr. =
  Kyyivske Vdskh.,
  Ukraine 13 C16
Kizel, *Russia* 18 C10
Kızıl Irmak →, *Turkey* 19 F6
Kızıltepe, *Turkey* ... 30 B4
Kizlyar, *Russia* 19 F8
Kizyl-Arvat =
  Gyzylarbat,
  Turkmenistan 20 F6
Kjölur, *Iceland* 6 D4
Kladno, *Czech Rep.* .. 12 C8
Klagenfurt, *Austria* .. 12 E8
Klaipėda, *Lithuania* .. 7 J19
Klaksvík, *Færoe Is.* .. 6 E9
Klamath →, *U.S.A.* . 56 F1
Klamath Falls, *U.S.A.* . 56 E3
Klamath Mts., *U.S.A.* . 56 F2
Klamono, *Indonesia* . 27 E8
Klappan →, *Canada* . 50 B3
Klarälven →, *Sweden* 7 G15
Klatovy, *Czech Rep.* .. 12 D7
Klazienaveen, *Neths.* . 11 B6
Kleena Kleene, *Canada* 50 C4
Klerksdorp, *S. Africa* . 37 K5
Kletsk = Klyetsk,
  Belarus 13 B14
Kletskiy, *Russia* 19 E7
Klickitat, *U.S.A.* 56 D3
Klinaklini →, *Canada* . 50 C3
Klodzko, *Poland* 13 C9
Klouto, *Togo* 34 G6
Kluane L., *Canada* ... 46 B6
Kluane Nat. Park,
  Canada 50 A1
Kluczbork, *Poland* .. 13 C10
Klukwan, *U.S.A.* 50 B1
Klyetsk, *Belarus* 13 B14
Klyuchevskaya, Gora,
  Russia 21 D17
Knaresborough, *U.K.* . 8 C6
Knee L., *Man., Canada* 48 A1
Knee L., *Sask., Canada* 51 B7
Knight Inlet, *Canada* . 50 C3
Knighton, *U.K.* 9 E4
Knob, C., *Australia* .. 41 F2
Knokke-Heist, *Belgium* 11 C3
Knossós, *Greece* ... 17 G11
Knox, *U.S.A.* 52 E2
Knox Coast, *Antarctica* 5 C8
Knoxville, *Iowa, U.S.A.* 54 E8
Knoxville, *Tenn., U.S.A.* 53 H4
Koartac = Quaqtaq,
  Canada 47 B13
Koba, *Indonesia* 27 F8
Kobarid, *Slovenia* ... 12 E7
Kobayashi, *Japan* ... 23 J5
Kobdo = Hovd,
  Mongolia 24 B4
Kōbe, *Japan* 23 G7
Kōbi-Sho, *Japan* 23 M1
Koblenz, *Germany* .. 12 C4
Kobryn, *Belarus* 13 B13
Kocaeli, *Turkey* 19 F4
Kočani, *Macedonia* .. 17 D10
Koch Bihar, *India* ... 29 F16

Kisii, *Kenya* 36 E6
Kōchi, *Japan* 23 H6
Kōchi □, *Japan* 23 H6
Kochiu = Gejiu, *China* . 24 D5
Kodiak, *U.S.A.* 46 C4
Kodiak I., *U.S.A.* 46 C4
Kofiau, *Indonesia* ... 27 E7
Koforidua, *Ghana* ... 34 G5
Kōfu, *Japan* 23 G9
Koga, *Japan* 23 F9
Kogaluk →, *Canada* . 49 A7
Køge, *Denmark* 7 J15
Kohat, *Pakistan* 28 C7
Kohima, *India* 29 G19
Kohkīlūyeh va Būyer
  Aḥmadi □, *Iran* ... 31 D6
Kohler Ra., *Antarctica* . 5 D15
Kohtla-Järve, *Estonia* . 7 G22
Koillismaa, *Finland* .. 6 D23
Kojonup, *Australia* .. 41 F2
Kojūr, *Iran* 31 B6
Kokand = Qŭqon,
  Uzbekistan 20 E8
Kokas, *Indonesia* ... 27 E8
Kokchetav = Kökshetaū,
  Kazakstan 20 D7
Kokemäenjoki →,
  Finland 7 F19
Kokkola, *Finland* ... 6 E20
Koko Kyunzu, *Burma* . 29 M18
Kokomo, *U.S.A.* 52 E2
Kökshetaū, *Kazakstan* . 20 D7
Kōksu, *Japan* 23 F9
Kokstad, *S. Africa* ... 37 L5
Kokubu, *Japan* 23 J5
Kola, *Indonesia* 27 F8
Kola, *Russia* 18 A5
Kola Pen. = Kolskiy
  Poluostrov, *Russia* . 18 A6
Kolaka, *Indonesia* ... 27 E6
Kolar, *India* 28 N11
Kolar Gold Fields, *India* 28 N11
Kolari, *Finland* 6 C20
Kolayat, *India* 28 F8
Kolchugino = Leninsk-
  Kuznetskiy, *Russia* . 20 D9
Kolding, *Denmark* ... 7 J13
Kolepom = Dolak,
  Pulau, *Indonesia* .. 27 F9
Kolguyev, Ostrov,
  Russia 18 A8
Kolhapur, *India* 28 L9
Kolín, *Czech Rep.* ... 12 C8
Kolka, *Latvia* 7 H20
Kolkas rags, *Latvia* .. 7 H20
Kolkata, *India* 29 H16
Kollum, *Neths.* 11 A6
Köln, *Germany* 12 C4
Koło, *Poland* 13 B10
Kołobrzeg, *Poland* .. 12 A8
Kolomna, *Russia* 18 C6
Kolomyya, *Ukraine* .. 13 D13
Kolonodale, *Indonesia* . 27 E6
Kolosib, *India* 29 G18
Kolpashevo, *Russia* .. 20 D9
Kolpino, *Russia* 18 C5
Kolskiy Poluostrov,
  Russia 18 A6
Kolskiy Zaliv, *Russia* . 18 A5
Kolwezi, *Dem. Rep. of*
  the Congo 36 G5
Kolyma →, *Russia* .. 21 C17
Kolymskoye Nagorye,
  Russia 21 C16
Komandorskie Is. =
  Komandorskiye
  Ostrova, *Russia* .. 21 D17
Komandorskiye Ostrova,
  Russia 21 D17
Komárno, *Slovak Rep.* . 13 E10
Komatsu, *Japan* 23 F8
Komatsujima, *Japan* . 23 H7
Komi □, *Russia* 18 B10
Kommunarsk =
  Alchevsk, *Ukraine* . 19 E6
Kommunizma, Pik,
  Tajikistan 20 F8
Komodo, *Indonesia* . 27 F5
Komoran, Pulau,
  Indonesia 27 F9
Komoro, *Japan* 23 F9
Komotini, *Greece* ... 17 D11
Kompong Cham,
  Cambodia 26 B3
Kompong Chhnang =
  Kampang Chhnang,
  Cambodia 26 B2
Kompong Som =
  Kampong Saom,
  Cambodia 26 B2
Kompong Som,
  Chhung = Kampong
  Saom, Chaak,
  Cambodia 26 B2
Kompong Thom,
  Cambodia 26 B2
Komrat = Comrat,
  Moldova 13 E15
Komsomolets, Ostrov,
  Russia 21 A10
Komsomolsk, *Russia* . 21 D14
Kon Tum, *Vietnam* .. 26 B3
Konarhā □, *Afghan.* . 28 B7
Konch, *India* 28 G11
Kondinin, *Australia* .. 41 F2

Kondoa, *Tanzania* ... 36 E7
Kondopaga, *Russia* .. 18 B5
Kondratyevo, *Russia* . 21 D10
Köneürgench,
  Turkmenistan 20 E6
Konevo, *Russia* 18 B6
Kong = Khong →,
  Cambodia 26 B3
Kong, *Ivory C.* 34 G5
Kong, Koh, *Cambodia* . 26 B2
Kong Christian IX Land,
  Greenland 4 C6
Kong Christian X Land,
  Greenland 4 B6
Kong Frederik IX Land,
  Greenland 4 C5
Kong Frederik VI Kyst,
  Greenland 4 C5
Kong Frederik VIII Land,
  Greenland 4 B6
Kong Oscar Fjord,
  Greenland 4 B6
Konglu, *Burma* 29 F20
Kongolo, *Dem. Rep. of*
  the Congo 36 F5
Kongsberg, *Norway* .. 7 G13
Kongsvinger, *Norway* . 7 F15
Königsberg =
  Kaliningrad, *Russia* . 7 J19
Konin, *Poland* 13 B10
Konjic, *Bos.-H.* 17 C7
Konosha, *Russia* ... 18 B7
Kōnosu, *Japan* 23 F9
Konotop, *Ukraine* ... 19 D5
Końskie, *Poland* 13 C11
Konstanz, *Germany* . 12 E5
Kont, *Iran* 31 E9
Kontagora, *Nigeria* .. 34 F7
Konya, *Turkey* 19 G5
Koocanusa, L., *Canada* 56 B6
Kookynie, *Australia* .. 41 E3
Koolyanobbing,
  Australia 41 F2
Koonibba, *Australia* . 43 E1
Koorawatha, *Australia* . 43 E4
Koorda, *Australia* ... 41 F2
Kooskia, *U.S.A.* 56 C6
Kootenay →, *U.S.A.* . 50 D5
Kootenay L., *Canada* . 50 D5
Kootenay Nat. Park,
  Canada 50 C5
Kopaonik, *Yugoslavia* . 17 C9
Kópavogur, *Iceland* .. 6 D3
Koper, *Slovenia* 12 F7
Kopervik, *Norway* ... 7 G11
Kopet Dagh, *Asia* ... 31 B8
Kopi, *Australia* 43 E2
Köping, *Sweden* 7 G17
Koppeh Dāgh = Kopet
  Dagh, *Asia* 31 B8
Koprivnica, *Croatia* .. 16 A7
Kopychyntsi, *Ukraine* . 13 D13
Korab, *Macedonia* .. 17 D9
Korça = Korçë, *Albania* 17 D9
Korce = Korçë, *Albania* 17 D9
Korçë, *Albania* 17 D9
Korčula, *Croatia* 16 C7
Kord Küy, *Iran* 31 B7
Kord Sheykh, *Iran* ... 31 D7
Kordestān □, *Iran* ... 30 C5
Kordofân, *Sudan* ... 35 F11
Korea, North ■, *Asia* . 25 C7
Korea, South ■, *Asia* . 25 C7
Korea Bay, *Korea* ... 25 C7
Korea Strait, *Asia* ... 25 C7
Korets, *Ukraine* 13 C14
Korhogo, *Ivory C.* ... 34 G4
Korinthiakós Kólpos,
  Greece 17 E10
Kórinthos, *Greece* .. 17 F10
Kōriyama, *Japan* ... 22 F10
Korla, *China* 24 B3
Korneshty = Corneşti,
  Moldova 13 E15
Koro, *Fiji* 39 C8
Koro, *Ivory C.* 34 G4
Koro Sea, *Fiji* 39 C9
Korogwe, *Tanzania* .. 36 F7
Koronadal, *Phil.* 27 C6
Koror, *Palau* 27 C8
Körös →, *Hungary* .. 13 E11
Korosten, *Ukraine* .. 13 C15
Korostyshev, *Ukraine* . 13 C15
Korsakov, *Russia* ... 21 E15
Korshunovo, *Russia* . 21 D12
Korsør, *Denmark* ... 7 J14
Kortrijk, *Belgium* ... 11 D3
Koryakskoye Nagorye,
  Russia 21 C18
Kos, *Greece* 17 F12
Koschagyl, *Kazakstan* . 19 E9
Kościan, *Poland* 13 B9
Kosciusko, *U.S.A.* ... 55 J10
Kosciuszko, Mt.,
  Australia 43 F4
Kosha, *Sudan* 35 D12
K'oshih = Kashi, *China* 24 C2
Koshiki-Rettō, *Japan* . 23 J4
Košice, *Slovak Rep.* . 13 D11
Koslan, *Russia* 18 B8
Kosovo, Yug. 17 C9
Kosovska Mitrovica,
  Yugoslavia 17 C9
Kossou, L. de, *Ivory C.* 34 G3
Kôstî, *Sudan* 35 F12

Lakitusaki

Kostopil, *Ukraine* 13 C14
Kostroma, *Russia* 18 C7
Kostrzyn, *Poland* 12 B8
Koszalin, *Poland* 12 A9
Kota, *India* 28 G9
Kota Baharu, *Malaysia* 26 C2
Kota Belud, *Malaysia* 26 C5
Kota Kinabalu, *Malaysia* 26 C5
Kota Kubu Baharu, *Malaysia* 26 D2
Kota Tinggi, *Malaysia* 26 D2
Kotaagung, *Indonesia* 26 F2
Kotabaru, *Indonesia* 26 E5
Kotabumi, *Indonesia* 26 E2
Kotamobagu, *Indonesia* 27 D6
Kotcho L., *Canada* 50 B4
Kotelnich, *Russia* 18 C8
Kotelnikovo, *Russia* 19 E7
Kotelnyy, Ostrov, *Russia* 21 B14
Kotka, *Finland* 7 F22
Kotlas, *Russia* 18 B8
Kotor, *Montenegro, Yug.* 17 C8
Kotovsk, *Ukraine* 13 E15
Kotri, *Pakistan* 28 G6
Kotturu, *India* 28 M10
Kotuy —►, *Russia* 21 B11
Kotzebue, *U.S.A.* 46 B3
Koudougou, *Burkina Faso* 34 F5
Kouilou —►, *Congo* 36 E2
Koula Moutou, *Gabon* 36 E2
Koulen = Kulen, *Cambodia* 26 B2
Koumala, *Australia* 42 C4
Koumra, *Chad* 35 G9
Kounradskiy, *Kazakstan* 20 E8
Kountze, *U.S.A.* 55 K7
Kourou, *Fr. Guiana* 63 B8
Kousseri, *Cameroon* 35 F8
Kouvola, *Finland* 7 F22
Kovdor, *Russia* 18 A5
Kovel, *Ukraine* 13 C13
Kovrov, *Russia* 18 C7
Kowanyama, *Australia* 42 B3
Köyceğiz, *Turkey* 17 F13
Koza, *Japan* 23 L3
Kozan, *Turkey* 30 B2
Kozáni, *Greece* 17 D9
Kozhikode = Calicut, *India* 28 P9
Kozhva, *Russia* 18 A10
Kozyatyn, *Ukraine* 13 D15
Kra, Isthmus of = Kra, Kho Khot, *Thailand* 26 B1
Kra, Kho Khot, *Thailand* 26 B1
Kracheh, *Cambodia* 26 B3
Kragan, *Indonesia* 27 G14
Kragerø, *Norway* 7 G13
Kragujevac, *Serbia, Yug.* 17 B9
Krajina, *Bos.-H.* 16 B7
Krakatau = Rakata, Pulau, *Indonesia* 26 F3
Krakatoa = Rakata, Pulau, *Indonesia* 26 F3
Kraków, *Poland* 13 C10
Kraljevo, *Serbia, Yug.* 17 C9
Kramatorsk, *Ukraine* 19 E6
Kramfors, *Sweden* 7 E17
Kranj, *Slovenia* 12 E8
Krasavino, *Russia* 18 B8
Kraskino, *Russia* 21 E14
Kraśnik, *Poland* 13 C12
Krasnoarmeysk, *Russia* 20 D5
Krasnodar, *Russia* 19 E6
Krasnokamsk, *Russia* 18 C10
Krasnoperekopsk, *Ukraine* 19 E5
Krasnorechenskiy, *Russia* 22 B7
Krasnoselkup, *Russia* 20 C9
Krasnoturinsk, *Russia* 18 C11
Krasnoufimsk, *Russia* 18 C10
Krasnouralsk, *Russia* 18 C11
Krasnovishersk, *Russia* 18 B10
Krasnovodsk = Türkmenbashi, *Turkmenistan* 19 G9
Krasnoyarsk, *Russia* 21 D10
Krasnyy Kut, *Russia* 19 D8
Krasnýy Luch, *Ukraine* 19 E6
Krasnyy Yar, *Russia* 19 E8
Kratie = Kracheh, *Cambodia* 26 B3
Krau, *Indonesia* 27 E10
Krefeld, *Germany* 12 C4
Kremen, *Croatia* 12 F8
Kremenchug = Kremenchuk, *Ukraine* 19 E5
Kremenchuk, *Ukraine* 19 E5
Kremenchuksk Vdskh., *Ukraine* 19 E5
Kremenets, *Ukraine* 13 C13
Kremmling, *U.S.A.* 56 F10
Krems, *Austria* 12 D8
Kretinga, *Lithuania* 7 J19
Kribi, *Cameroon* 36 D1
Krichev = Krychaw, *Belarus* 13 B16
Krishna —►, *India* 29 M12
Krishnanagar, *India* 29 H16
Kristiansand, *Norway* 7 G13
Kristianstad, *Sweden* 7 H16
Kristiansund, *Norway* 6 E12
Kristiinankaupunki, *Finland* 7 E19
Kristinehamn, *Sweden* 7 G16
Kristinestad = Kristiinankaupunki, *Finland* 7 E19
Kríti, *Greece* 17 G11
Krivoy Rog = Kryvyy Rih, *Ukraine* 19 E5
Krk, *Croatia* 12 F8
Krong Kaoh Kong, *Cambodia* 26 B2
Kronprins Olav Kyst, *Antarctica* 5 C5
Kronshtadt, *Russia* 18 B4
Kroonstad, *S. Africa* 37 K5
Kropotkin, *Russia* 19 E7
Krosno, *Poland* 13 D11
Krotoszyn, *Poland* 13 C9
Krung Thep = Bangkok, *Thailand* 26 B2
Krupki, *Belarus* 13 A15
Kruševac, *Serbia, Yug.* 17 C9
Krychaw, *Belarus* 13 B16
Krymskiy Poluostrov = Krymskyy Pivostriv, *Ukraine* 19 F5
Krymskyy Pivostriv, *Ukraine* 19 F5
Kryvyy Rih, *Ukraine* 19 E5
Ksar el Kebir, *Morocco* 34 B4
Ksar es Souk = Ar Rachidiya, *Morocco* 34 B5
Kuala Belait, *Malaysia* 26 D4
Kuala Lipis, *Malaysia* 26 D2
Kuala Lumpur, *Malaysia* 26 D2
Kuala Sepetang, *Malaysia* 26 D2
Kuala Terengganu, *Malaysia* 26 C2
Kualajelai, *Indonesia* 26 E4
Kualakapuas, *Indonesia* 26 E4
Kualakurun, *Indonesia* 26 E4
Kualapembuang, *Indonesia* 26 E4
Kualasimpang, *Indonesia* 26 D1
Kuandang, *Indonesia* 27 D6
Kuangchou = Guangzhou, *China* 25 D6
Kuantan, *Malaysia* 26 D2
Kuba = Quba, *Azerbaijan* 19 F8
Kuban —►, *Russia* 19 E6
Kubokawa, *Japan* 23 H6
Kuching, *Malaysia* 26 D4
Kuchino-eruba-Jima, *Japan* 23 J5
Kuchino-Shima, *Japan* 23 K4
Kuchinotsu, *Japan* 23 H5
Kucing = Kuching, *Malaysia* 26 D4
Kuda, *India* 28 H7
Kudat, *Malaysia* 26 C5
Kudus, *Indonesia* 27 G14
Kudymkar, *Russia* 18 C9
Kueiyang = Guiyang, *China* 24 D5
Kufra Oasis = Al Kufrah, *Libya* 35 D10
Kufstein, *Austria* 12 E7
Kugluktuk, *Canada* 46 B8
Kugong I., *Canada* 48 A4
Kūhak, *Iran* 28 F3
Kūhbonān, *Iran* 31 D8
Kūhestak, *Iran* 31 E8
Kuhin, *Iran* 31 B6
Kūhīrī, *Iran* 31 E9
Kūhpāyeh, *Eşfahan, Iran* 31 C7
Kūhpāyeh, *Kermān, Iran* 31 D8
Kūhrān, Kūh-e, *Iran* 31 E8
Kuito, *Angola* 37 G3
Kuiu I., *U.S.A.* 50 B2
Kuji, *Japan* 22 D10
Kujū-San, *Japan* 23 H5
Kukës, *Albania* 17 C9
Kukësi = Kukës, *Albania* 17 C9
Kula, *Turkey* 17 E13
Kulasekarappattinam, *India* 28 Q11
Kuldīga, *Latvia* 7 H19
Kuldja = Yining, *China* 20 E9
Kulen, *Cambodia* 26 B2
Kulgera, *Australia* 42 D1
Kulin, *Australia* 41 F2
Kŭlob, *Tajikistan* 20 F7
Kulsary, *Kazakstan* 19 E9
Kulumbura, *Australia* 40 B4
Kulunda, *Russia* 20 D8
Kūlvand, *Iran* 31 D7
Kulwin, *Australia* 43 F3
Kulyab = Kŭlob, *Tajikistan* 20 F7
Kuma —►, *Russia* 19 F8
Kumagaya, *Japan* 23 F9
Kumai, *Indonesia* 26 E4
Kumamba, Kepulauan, *Indonesia* 27 E9
Kumamoto, *Japan* 23 H5
Kumamoto □, *Japan* 23 H5
Kumanovo, *Macedonia* 17 C9
Kumara, *N.Z.* 39 K3
Kumarina, *Australia* 41 D2
Kumasi, *Ghana* 34 G5
Kumayri = Gyumri, *Armenia* 19 F7
Kumba, *Cameroon* 36 D1
Kumbakonam, *India* 28 P11
Kumbarilla, *Australia* 43 D5
Kumbia, *Australia* 43 D5
Kume-Shima, *Japan* 23 L3
Kumertau, *Russia* 18 D10
Kumla, *Sweden* 7 G16
Kumo, *Nigeria* 35 F8
Kumon Bum, *Burma* 29 F20
Kunashir, Ostrov, *Russia* 21 E15
Kunda, *Estonia* 7 G22
Kunghit I., *Canada* 50 C2
Kungrad = Qŭnghirot, *Uzbekistan* 20 E6
Kungsbacka, *Sweden* 7 H15
Kungur, *Russia* 18 C10
Kuningan, *Indonesia* 27 G13
Kunlong, *Burma* 29 H21
Kunlun Shan, *Asia* 24 C3
Kunming, *China* 24 D5
Kununurra, *Australia* 40 C4
Kunya-Urgench = Köneürgench, *Turkmenistan* 20 E6
Kuopio, *Finland* 6 E22
Kupa —►, *Croatia* 12 F9
Kupang, *Indonesia* 27 F6
Kupreanof I., *U.S.A.* 50 B2
Kupyansk-Uzlovoi, *Ukraine* 19 E6
Kuqa, *China* 24 B3
Kür —►, *Azerbaijan* 19 G8
Kür Dili, *Azerbaijan* 31 B6
Kura = Kür —►, *Azerbaijan* 19 G8
Kuranda, *Australia* 42 B4
Kurashiki, *Japan* 23 G6
Kurayoshi, *Japan* 23 G6
Kŭrdzhali, *Bulgaria* 17 D11
Kure, *Japan* 23 G6
Kuressaare, *Estonia* 7 G20
Kurgan, *Russia* 20 D7
Kuria Maria Is. = Khurīyā Murīyā, Jazā 'ir, *Oman* 32 D6
Kuridala, *Australia* 42 C3
Kurigram, *Bangla.* 29 G16
Kurikka, *Finland* 7 E20
Kuril Is. = Kurilskiye Ostrova, *Russia* 21 E15
Kuril Trench, *Pac. Oc.* 44 C7
Kurilsk, *Russia* 21 E15
Kurilskiye Ostrova, *Russia* 21 E15
Kurino, *Japan* 23 J5
Kurinskaya Kosa = Kür Dili, *Azerbaijan* 31 B6
Kurnool, *India* 28 M11
Kuro-Shima, *Kagoshima, Japan* 23 J4
Kuro-Shima, *Okinawa, Japan* 23 M2
Kurow, *N.Z.* 39 L3
Kurri Kurri, *Australia* 43 E5
Kurrimine, *Australia* 42 B4
Kurshskiy Zaliv, *Russia* 7 J19
Kursk, *Russia* 18 D6
Kuruçay, *Turkey* 30 B3
Kuruktag, *China* 24 B3
Kuruman, *S. Africa* 37 K4
Kurume, *Japan* 23 H5
Kurunegala, *Sri Lanka* 28 R12
Kurya, *Russia* 18 B10
Kus Gölü, *Turkey* 17 D12
Kuşadası, *Turkey* 17 F12
Kusatsu, *Japan* 23 F9
Kusawa L., *Canada* 50 A1
Kushikino, *Japan* 23 J5
Kushima, *Japan* 23 J5
Kushimoto, *Japan* 23 H7
Kushiro, *Japan* 22 C12
Kushiro-Gawa —►, *Japan* 22 C12
Kūshk, *Iran* 31 D8
Kushka = Gushgy, *Turkmenistan* 20 F7
Kūshkī, *Iran* 30 C5
Kushtia, *Bangla.* 29 H16
Kushva, *Russia* 18 C10
Kuskokwim B., *U.S.A.* 46 C3
Kussharo-Ko, *Japan* 22 C12
Kustanay = Qostanay, *Kazakstan* 20 D7
Kut, Ko, *Thailand* 26 B2
Kütahya, *Turkey* 19 G5
Kutaisi, *Georgia* 19 F7
Kutaraja = Banda Aceh, *Indonesia* 26 C1
Kutch, Gulf of = Kachchh, Gulf of, *India* 28 H6
Kutch, Rann of = Kachchh, Rann of, *India* 28 H7
Kutno, *Poland* 13 B10
Kutu, *Dem. Rep. of the Congo* 36 E3
Kutum, *Sudan* 35 F10
Kuujjuaq, *Canada* 47 C13
Kuujjuarapik, *Canada* 48 A4
Kuusamo, *Finland* 6 D23
Kuusankoski, *Finland* 7 F22
Kuwait = Al Kuwayt, *Kuwait* 30 D5
Kuwait ■, *Asia* 30 D5
Kuwana, *Japan* 23 G8
Kuybyshev = Samara, *Russia* 18 D9
Kuybyshev, *Russia* 20 D8
Kuybyshevskoye Vdkhr., *Russia* 18 C8
Kūyeh, *Iran* 30 B5
Kūysanjaq, *Iraq* 30 B5
Kuyto, Ozero, *Russia* 18 B5
Kuyumba, *Russia* 21 C10
Kuzey Anadolu Dağları, *Turkey* 19 F6
Kuznetsk, *Russia* 18 D8
Kuzomen, *Russia* 18 A6
Kvænangen, *Norway* 6 A19
Kvaløy, *Norway* 6 B18
Kvarner, *Croatia* 12 F8
Kvarnerič, *Croatia* 12 F8
Kwa-Nobuhle, *S. Africa* 37 L5
Kwakoegron, *Surinam* 63 B7
KwaMashu, *S. Africa* 37 K6
Kwando —►, *Africa* 37 H4
Kwangju, *S. Korea* 25 C7
Kwangsi-Chuang = Guangxi Zhuangzu Zizhiqu □, *China* 25 D5
Kwangtung = Guangdong □, *China* 25 D6
Kwataboahegan —►, *Canada* 48 B3
Kwatisore, *Indonesia* 27 E8
Kweichow = Guizhou □, *China* 24 D5
Kwekwe, *Zimbabwe* 37 H5
Kwidzyn, *Poland* 13 B10
Kwinana New Town, *Australia* 41 F2
Kwoka, *Indonesia* 27 E8
Kyabra Cr. —►, *Australia* 43 D3
Kyabram, *Australia* 43 F4
Kyakhta, *Russia* 21 D11
Kyancutta, *Australia* 43 E2
Kyaukpadaung, *Burma* 29 J19
Kyaukpyu, *Burma* 29 K18
Kyaukse, *Burma* 29 J20
Kyle, *Canada* 51 C7
Kymijoki —►, *Finland* 7 F22
Kyneton, *Australia* 43 F3
Kynuna, *Australia* 42 C3
Kyō-ga-Saki, *Japan* 23 G7
Kyoga, L., *Uganda* 36 D6
Kyogle, *Australia* 43 D5
Kyongpyaw, *Burma* 29 L19
Kyōto, *Japan* 23 G7
Kyōto □, *Japan* 23 G7
Kyrenia, *Cyprus* 30 C2
Kyrgyzstan ■, *Asia* 20 E8
Kyrönjoki —►, *Finland* 6 E19
Kystatyam, *Russia* 21 C13
Kyunhla, *Burma* 29 H19
Kyuquot Sound, *Canada* 50 D3
Kyūshū, *Japan* 23 H5
Kyūshū □, *Japan* 23 H5
Kyūshū-Sanchi, *Japan* 23 H5
Kyustendil, *Bulgaria* 17 C10
Kyusyur, *Russia* 21 B13
Kyyiv, *Ukraine* 13 C16
Kyyivske Vdskh., *Ukraine* 13 C16
Kyzyl, *Russia* 21 D10
Kyzyl Kum, *Uzbekistan* 20 E7
Kyzyl-Kyya, *Kyrgyzstan* 20 E8
Kzyl-Orda = Qyzylorda, *Kazakstan* 20 E7

La Alcarria, *Spain* 15 B4
La Asunción, *Venezuela* 62 A6
La Baie, *Canada* 49 C5
La Banda, *Argentina* 64 B4
La Barca, *Mexico* 58 C4
La Barge, *U.S.A.* 56 E8
La Belle, *U.S.A.* 53 M5
La Biche —►, *Canada* 50 B4
La Biche, L., *Canada* 50 C6
La Bomba, *Mexico* 58 A1
La Carlota, *Argentina* 64 C4
La Ceiba, *Honduras* 60 C2
La Chaux-de-Fonds, *Switz.* 14 C7
La Chorrera, *Panama* 60 E4
La Cocha, *Argentina* 64 B3
La Concepción, *Panama* 60 E3
La Concordia, *Mexico* 59 D6
La Coruña = A Coruña, *Spain* 15 A1
La Crescent, *U.S.A.* 54 D9
La Crete, *Canada* 50 B5
La Crosse, *Kans., U.S.A.* 54 F5
La Crosse, *Wis., U.S.A.* 54 D9
La Cruz, *Costa Rica* 60 D2
La Cruz, *Mexico* 58 C3
La Désirade, *Guadeloupe* 61 C7
La Escondida, *Mexico* 58 C5
La Esperanza, *Cuba* 60 B3
La Esperanza, *Honduras* 60 D2
La Estrada = A Estrada, *Spain* 15 A1
La Fayette, *U.S.A.* 53 H3
La Fé, *Cuba* 60 B3
La Follette, *U.S.A.* 53 G3
La Grande, *U.S.A.* 56 D4
La Grande —►, *Canada* 48 B5
La Grande Deux, Rés., *Canada* 48 B4
La Grande Quatre, Rés., *Canada* 48 B5
La Grande Trois, Rés., *Canada* 48 B4
La Grange, *Ga., U.S.A.* 53 J3
La Grange, *Ky., U.S.A.* 52 F3
La Grange, *Tex., U.S.A.* 55 L6
La Guaira, *Venezuela* 62 A5
La Habana, *Cuba* 60 B3
La Independencia, *Mexico* 59 D6
La Isabela, *Dom. Rep.* 61 C5
La Junta, *U.S.A.* 55 F3
La Libertad, *Guatemala* 60 C1
La Libertad, *Mexico* 58 B2
La Línea de la Concepción, *Spain* 15 D3
La Loche, *Canada* 51 B7
La Louvière, *Belgium* 11 D4
La Malbaie, *Canada* 49 C5
La Mancha, *Spain* 15 C4
La Martre, L., *Canada* 50 A5
La Mesa, *U.S.A.* 57 K5
La Misión, *Mexico* 58 A1
La Moure, *U.S.A.* 54 B5
La Oroya, *Peru* 62
La Palma, *Canary Is.* 34 C2
La Palma, *Panama* 60 E4
La Palma del Condado, *Spain* 15 D2
La Paragua, *Venezuela* 62 B6
La Paz, *Entre Ríos, Argentina* 64 C5
La Paz, *San Luis, Argentina* 64 C3
La Paz, *Bolivia* 62 G5
La Paz, *Honduras* 60 D2
La Paz, *Mexico* 58 C2
La Paz Centro, *Nic.* 60 D2
La Pedrera, *Colombia* 62 D5
La Pérade, *Canada* 49 C5
La Perouse Str., *Asia* 22 B11
La Pesca, *Mexico* 59 C5
La Piedad, *Mexico* 58 C4
La Pine, *U.S.A.* 56 E3
La Plata, *Argentina* 64 D5
La Pocatière, *Canada* 49 C5
La Porte, *Ind., U.S.A.* 52 E2
La Porte, *Tex., U.S.A.* 55 L7
La Purísima, *Mexico* 58 B2
La Push, *U.S.A.* 56 C1
La Quiaca, *Argentina* 62 H5
La Rioja, *Argentina* 64 B3
La Rioja □, *Spain* 15 A4
La Robla, *Spain* 15 A3
La Roche-en-Ardenne, *Belgium* 11 D5
La Roche-sur-Yon, *France* 14 C3
La Rochelle, *France* 14 C3
La Roda, *Spain* 15 C4
La Romana, *Dom. Rep.* 61 C6
La Ronge, *Canada* 51 B7
La Salle, *U.S.A.* 54 E10
La Sarre, *Canada* 48 C4
La Scie, *Canada* 49 C8
La Serena, *Chile* 64 B2
La Seu d'Urgell, *Spain* 15 A6
La Seyne-sur-Mer, *France* 14 E6
La Soufrière, *St. Vincent* 61 D7
La Spézia, *Italy* 14 D8
La Tagua, *Colombia* 62 C4
La Tortuga, *Venezuela* 62 A5
La Tuque, *Canada* 48 C5
La Unión, *Chile* 64 E2
La Unión, *El Salv.* 60 D2
La Unión, *Mexico* 58 D4
La Urbana, *Venezuela* 62 B5
La Vall d'Uixó, *Spain* 15 C5
La Vega, *Dom. Rep.* 61 C5
La Vela de Coro, *Venezuela* 62 A5
La Venta, *Mexico* 59 D6
La Ventura, *Mexico* 58 C4
Labe = Elbe —►, *Europe* 12 B5
Labé, *Guinea* 34 F3
Laberge, L., *Canada* 50 A1
Labinsk, *Russia* 19 F7
Laboulaye, *Argentina* 64 C4
Labrador, *Canada* 49 B7
Labrador City, *Canada* 49 B6
Labrador Sea, *Atl. Oc.* 47 C14
Lábrea, *Brazil* 62 E6
Labuan, *Malaysia* 26 C5
Labuan, Pulau, *Malaysia* 26 C5
Labuha, *Indonesia* 27 E7
Labuhan, *Indonesia* 27 G11
Labuhanbajo, *Indonesia* 27 F6
Labuk, Telok, *Malaysia* 26 C5
Labyrinth, L., *Australia* 43 E2
Labytnangi, *Russia* 20 C7
Lac Bouchette, *Canada* 49 C5
Lac Édouard, *Canada* 48 C5
Lac La Biche, *Canada* 50 C6
Lac La Martre = Wha Ti, *Canada* 46 B8
Lac La Ronge Prov. Park, *Canada* 51 B7
Lac-Mégantic, *Canada* 49 C5
Lac Seul, Res., *Canada* 48 B1
Lacanau, *France* 14 D3
Lacantúm —►, *Mexico* 59 D6
Laccadive Is. = Lakshadweep Is., *Ind. Oc.* 3 D13
Lacepede B., *Australia* 43 F2
Lacepede Is., *Australia* 40 C3
Lachine, *Canada* 48 C5
Lachlan —►, *Australia* 43 E3
Lachute, *Canada* 48 C5
Lacombe, *Canada* 50 C6
Laconia, *U.S.A.* 52 D10
Ladakh Ra., *India* 28 C11
Lādīz, *Iran* 31 D9
Ladoga, L. = Ladozhskoye Ozero, *Russia* 18 B5
Ladozhskoye Ozero, *Russia* 18 B5
Lady Elliott I., *Australia* 42 C5
Ladysmith, *Canada* 50 D4
Ladysmith, *S. Africa* 37 K5
Ladysmith, *U.S.A.* 54 C9
Lae, *Papua N. G.* 38 B7
Læsø, *Denmark* 7 H14
Lafayette, *Colo., U.S.A.* 54 F2
Lafayette, *Ind., U.S.A.* 52 E2
Lafayette, *La., U.S.A.* 55 K9
Lafayette, *Tenn., U.S.A.* 53 G2
Laferte —►, *Canada* 50 A5
Lafia, *Nigeria* 34 G7
Lafleche, *Canada* 51 D7
Lagarfljót —►, *Iceland* 6 D6
Lågen —►, *Oppland, Norway* 7 F14
Lågen —►, *Vestfold, Norway* 7 G14
Laghouat, *Algeria* 34 B6
Lagonoy G., *Phil.* 27 B6
Lagos, *Nigeria* 34 G6
Lagos, *Portugal* 15 D1
Lagos de Moreno, *Mexico* 58 C4
Lagrange, *Australia* 40 C3
Lagrange B., *Australia* 40 C3
Laguna, *Brazil* 64 B7
Laguna, *U.S.A.* 57 J10
Lagunas, *Chile* 64 A3
Lagunas, *Peru* 62 E3
Lahad Datu, *Malaysia* 27 C5
Lahad Datu, Teluk, *Malaysia* 27 D5
Lahat, *Indonesia* 26 E2
Lahewa, *Indonesia* 26 D1
Lāhījān, *Iran* 31 B6
Lahn —►, *Germany* 12 C4
Laholm, *Sweden* 7 H15
Lahore, *Pakistan* 28 D9
Lahti, *Finland* 7 F21
Lahtis = Lahti, *Finland* 7 F21
Laï, *Chad* 35 G9
Laila = Laylá, *Si. Arabia* 32 C4
Lainio älv —►, *Sweden* 6 C20
Lairg, *U.K.* 10 B4
Laizhou, *China* 25 C6
Laja —►, *Mexico* 58 C4
Lajes, *Brazil* 64 B6
Lake Andes, *U.S.A.* 54 D5
Lake Arthur, *U.S.A.* 55 K8
Lake Cargelligo, *Australia* 43 E4
Lake Charles, *U.S.A.* 55 K8
Lake City, *Colo., U.S.A.* 57 G10
Lake City, *Fla., U.S.A.* 53 K4
Lake City, *Mich., U.S.A.* 52 C3
Lake City, *Minn., U.S.A.* 54 C8
Lake City, *S.C., U.S.A.* 53 J6
Lake Cowichan, *Canada* 50 D4
Lake District, *U.K.* 8 C4
Lake Grace, *Australia* 41 F2
Lake Harbour = Kimmirut, *Canada* 47 B13
Lake Havasu City, *U.S.A.* 57 J6
Lake Jackson, *U.S.A.* 55 L7
Lake Junction, *U.S.A.* 56 D8
Lake King, *Australia* 41 F2
Lake Lenore, *Canada* 51 C8
Lake Louise, *Canada* 50 C5
Lake Mead National Recreation Area, *U.S.A.* 57 J6
Lake Mills, *U.S.A.* 54 D8
Lake Providence, *U.S.A.* 55 J9
Lake Superior Prov. Park, *Canada* 48 C3
Lake Village, *U.S.A.* 55 J9
Lake Wales, *U.S.A.* 53 M5
Lake Worth, *U.S.A.* 53 M5
Lakefield, *Canada* 48 D4
Lakeland, *Australia* 42 B3
Lakeland, *U.S.A.* 53 M5
Lakemba, *Fiji* 39 D9
Lakeport, *U.S.A.* 56 G2
Lakes Entrance, *Australia* 43 F4
Lakeside, *Ariz., U.S.A.* 57 J9
Lakeside, *Nebr., U.S.A.* 54 D3
Lakeview, *U.S.A.* 56 E3
Lakeville, *U.S.A.* 54 C8
Lakewood, *Colo., U.S.A.* 54 F2
Lakewood, *Ohio, U.S.A.* 52 E5
Lakin, *U.S.A.* 55 G4
Lakitusaki —►, *Canada* 48 B3

Lakonikós Kólpos,
Greece 17 F10
Lakor, Indonesia 27 F7
Lakota, Ivory C. 34 G4
Lakota, U.S.A. 54 A5
Laksefjorden, Norway . 6 A22
Lakselv, Norway 6 A21
Lakshadweep Is.,
Ind. Oc. 3 D13
Lala Ghat, India .. 29 G18
L'Albufera, Spain ... 15 C5
Lāli, Iran 31 C6
Lalibela, Ethiopia .. 32 E2
Lalín, Spain 15 A1
Lamaing, Burma .. 29 M20
Lamar, Colo., U.S.A. .. 54 F3
Lamar, Mo., U.S.A. .. 55 G7
Lamas, Peru 62 E3
Lambaréné, Gabon ... 36 E2
Lambasa, Fiji 39 C8
Lambert Glacier,
Antarctica 5 D6
Lambi Kyun, Burma .. 26 B1
Lame Deer, U.S.A. .. 56 D10
Lamego, Portugal ... 15 B2
Lamèque, Canada ... 49 C7
Lameroo, Australia .. 43 F3
Lamesa, U.S.A. 55 J4
Lamía, Greece 17 E10
Lamon B., Phil. 27 B6
Lamont, Canada 50 C6
Lamont, U.S.A. ... 56 E10
Lampa, Peru 62 G4
Lampasas, U.S.A. ... 55 K5
Lampazos de Naranjo,
Mexico 58 B4
Lampedusa, Medit. S. .. 16 G5
Lampeter, U.K. 9 E3
Lampione, Medit. S. .. 16 G5
Lampman, Canada .. 51 D8
Lampung □, Indonesia 26 F2
Lamu, Kenya 36 E8
Lamy, U.S.A. 57 J11
Lanak La, India ... 28 B11
Lanak'o Shank'ou =
Lanak La, India .. 28 B11
Lancang Jiang →,
China 24 D5
Lancashire □, U.K. ... 8 D5
Lancaster, U.K. 8 C5
Lancaster, Calif., U.S.A. 57 J4
Lancaster, Ky., U.S.A. 52 G3
Lancaster, N.H., U.S.A. 52 C10
Lancaster, Ohio, U.S.A. 52 F4
Lancaster, Pa., U.S.A. . 52 E7
Lancaster, S.C., U.S.A. . 53 H5
Lancaster, Wis., U.S.A. 54 D9
Lancaster Sd., Canada 47 A11
Lancelin, Australia .. 41 F2
Lanchow = Lanzhou,
China 24 C5
Lanciano, Italy 16 C6
Landeck, Austria ... 12 E6
Lander, U.S.A. 56 E9
Lander →, Australia . 40 D5
Landes, France 14 D3
Landi Kotal, Pakistan .. 28 B7
Land's End, U.K. 9 G2
Landsborough Cr. →,
Australia 42 C3
Landshut, Germany .. 12 D7
Landskrona, Sweden .. 7 J15
Lanett, U.S.A. 53 J3
La'nga Co, China .. 29 D12
Langar, Iran 31 C9
Langara I., Canada .. 50 C2
Langdon, U.S.A. 54 A5
Langeland, Denmark .. 7 J14
Langenburg, Canada . 51 C8
Langjökull, Iceland 6 D3
Langkawi, Pulau,
Malaysia 26 C1
Langkon, Malaysia ... 26 C5
Langlade, St- P. & M. . 49 C8
Langøya, Norway 6 B16
Langreo, Spain 15 A3
Langres, France 14 C6
Langres, Plateau de,
France 14 C6
Langsa, Indonesia .. 26 D1
Langtry, U.S.A. 55 L4
Languedoc, France .. 14 E5
Lanigan, Canada ... 51 C7
Länkäran, Azerbaijan .. 19 G8
Lannion, France 14 B2
L'Annonciation, Canada 48 C5
Lansdowne, Australia . 43 E5
Lansdowne House,
Canada 48 B2
L'Anse, U.S.A. 52 B1
L'Anse au Loup, Canada 49 B8
L'Anse aux Meadows,
Canada 49 B8
Lansing, U.S.A. 52 D3
Lanusei, Italy 16 E3
Lanzarote, Canary Is. .. 34 C3
Lanzhou, China 24 C5
Laoag, Phil. 27 A6
Laoang, Phil. 27 B7
Laon, France 14 B5
Laona, U.S.A. 52 C1
Laos ■, Asia 26 A3
Lapeer, U.S.A. 52 D4
Lapland = Lappland,
Europe 6 B21

Lappeenranta, Finland . 7 F23
Lappland, Europe 6 B21
Lapseki, Turkey 17 D12
Laptev Sea, Russia .. 21 B13
Lapua, Finland 6 E20
L'Aquila, Italy 16 C5
Lār, Āzarbāijān-e Sharqī,
Iran 30 B5
Lār, Fārs, Iran 31 E7
Laramie, U.S.A. 54 E2
Laramie →, U.S.A. .. 56 F11
Laramie Mts., U.S.A. .. 54 E2
Laranjuka, Indonesia .. 27 F6
Larat, Indonesia 27 F8
Larder Lake, Canada .. 48 C4
Laredo, U.S.A. 55 M5
Laredo Sd., Canada .. 50 C3
Largo, U.S.A. 53 M4
Lariang, Indonesia .. 27 E5
Larimore, U.S.A. 54 B6
Lārīn, Iran 31 C7
Lárisa, Greece 17 E10
Larnaca, Cyprus ... 30 C2
Larne, U.K. 10 D4
Larose, U.S.A. 55 L9
Larrimah, Australia .. 40 C5
Larsen Ice Shelf,
Antarctica 5 C17
Larvik, Norway 7 G14
Las Animas, U.S.A. .. 54 F3
Las Anod, Somali Rep. . 32 F4
Las Aves, Is., W. Indies 61 C7
Las Cejas, Argentina .. 64 B4
Las Cruces, U.S.A. .. 57 K10
Las Flores, Argentina .. 64 D5
Las Lajas, Argentina .. 64 D2
Las Lomitas, Argentina 64 A4
Las Palmas, Canary Is. 34 C2
Las Plumas, Argentina 64 E3
Las Tablas, Panama ... 60 E3
Las Truchas, Mexico .. 58 D4
Las Varillas, Argentina 64 C4
Las Vegas, N. Mex.,
U.S.A. 57 J11
Las Vegas, Nev., U.S.A. 57 H6
Lash-e Joveyn, Afghan. .. 28 D2
Lashburn, Canada ... 51 C7
Lashio, Burma 29 H20
Lāsjerd, Iran 31 C7
Lassen Pk., U.S.A. .. 56 F3
Lassen Volcanic
National Park, U.S.A. 56 F3
Last Mountain L.,
Canada 51 C7
Lastoursville, Gabon .. 36 E2
Lastovo, Croatia ... 16 C7
Latacunga, Ecuador ... 62 D3
Latakia = Al Lādhiqīyah,
Syria 30 C2
Latchford, Canada .. 48 C4
Latham, Australia ... 41 E2
Latina, Italy 16 D5
Latium = Lazio □, Italy 16 C5
Latouche Treville, C.,
Australia 40 C3
Latrobe, Australia ... 42 G4
Latrobe, U.S.A. 52 E5
Latvia ■, Europe ... 7 H20
Lau Group, Fiji 39 C9
Lauchhammer,
Germany 12 D7
Laughlin, U.S.A. ... 57 J6
Laukaa, Finland 7 E21
Launceston, Australia . 42 G4
Launceston, U.K. ... 9 G3
Laura, Australia 42 B3
Laurel, Miss., U.S.A. . 55 K10
Laurel, Mont., U.S.A. . 56 D9
Laurens, U.S.A. 53 H4
Laurentian Plateau,
Canada 49 B6
Lauria, Italy 16 E6
Laurie L., Canada .. 51 B8
Laurinburg, U.S.A. .. 53 H6
Laurium, U.S.A. 52 B1
Lausanne, Switz. ... 14 C7
Laut, Indonesia 26 D3
Laut, Pulau, Indonesia . 26 E5
Laut Kecil, Kepulauan,
Indonesia 26 E5
Lautoka, Fiji 39 C7
Laval, France 14 B3
Lāvar Meydān, Iran .. 31 D7
Laverton, Australia .. 41 E3
Lávrion, Greece ... 17 F11
Lawas, Malaysia ... 26 D5
Lawele, Indonesia .. 27 F6
Lawng Pit, Burma .. 29 G20
Lawqah, Si. Arabia .. 30 D4
Lawrence, N.Z. 39 L2
Lawrence, Kans., U.S.A. 54 F7
Lawrence, Mass., U.S.A. 52 D10
Lawrenceburg, Ind.,
U.S.A. 52 F3
Lawrenceburg, Tenn.,
U.S.A. 53 H2
Lawrenceville, U.S.A. .. 53 J4
Lawton, U.S.A. 55 H5
Lawu, Indonesia .. 27 G14
Laylá, Si. Arabia ... 32 C4
Laylān, Iraq 30 C5
Layton, U.S.A. 56 F7
Laytonville, U.S.A. .. 56 G2
Lazio □, Italy 16 C5
Lazo, Russia 22 C6

Le Creusot, France 14 C6
Le François, Martinique 61 D7
Le Havre, France 14 B4
Le Mans, France 14 C4
Le Mars, U.S.A. 54 D6
Le Mont-St-Michel,
France 14 B3
Le Moule, Guadeloupe 61 C7
Le Puy-en-Velay, France 14 D5
Le Sueur, U.S.A. ... 54 C8
Le Touquet-Paris-Plage,
France 14 A4
Le Tréport, France ... 14 A4
Le Verdon-sur-Mer,
France 14 D3
Lea →, U.K. 9 F8
Lead, U.S.A. 54 C3
Leader, Canada 51 C7
Leadville, U.S.A. ... 57 G10
Leaf →, U.S.A. 55 K10
Leaf Rapids, Canada .. 51 B9
Leamington, Canada .. 48 D3
Leamington, U.S.A. .. 56 G7
Leamington Spa =
Royal Leamington
Spa, U.K. 9 E6
Learmonth, Australia .. 40 D1
Leask, Canada 51 C7
Leatherhead, U.K. ... 9 F7
Leavenworth, Kans.,
U.S.A. 54 F7
Leavenworth, Wash.,
U.S.A. 56 C3
Lebak, Phil. 27 C6
Lebanon, Ind., U.S.A. .. 52 E2
Lebanon, Kans., U.S.A. 54 F5
Lebanon, Ky., U.S.A. .. 52 G3
Lebanon, Mo., U.S.A. .. 55 G8
Lebanon, N.H., U.S.A. .. 52 D9
Lebanon, Oreg., U.S.A. 56 D2
Lebanon, Pa., U.S.A. .. 52 E7
Lebanon, Tenn., U.S.A. 53 G2
Lebanon ■, Asia ... 33 B5
Lebel-sur-Quévillon,
Canada 48 C4
Lębork, Poland 13 A9
Lebrija, Spain 15 D2
Lebu, Chile 64 D2
Lecce, Italy 17 D8
Lecco, Italy 14 D8
Lech →, Germany .. 12 D6
Łęczyca, Poland ... 13 B10
Leduc, Canada 50 C6
Leech L., U.S.A. 54 B7
Leeds, U.K. 8 D6
Leeds, U.S.A. 53 J2
Leek, Neths. 11 A6
Leek, U.K. 8 D5
Leeman, Australia ... 41 E1
Leer, Germany 12 B4
Leesburg, U.S.A. ... 53 L5
Leesville, U.S.A. ... 55 K8
Leeton, Australia ... 43 E4
Leeuwarden, Neths. .. 11 A5
Leeuwin, C., Australia .. 41 F2
Leeward Is., Atl. Oc. .. 61 C7
Lefroy, L., Australia .. 41 F3
Leganés, Spain 15 B4
Legazpi, Phil. 27 B6
Legendre I., Australia .. 40 D2
Leghorn = Livorno, Italy 16 C4
Legionowo, Poland .. 13 B11
Legnago, Italy 16 B4
Legnica, Poland 12 C9
Leh, India 28 B10
Lehigh Acres, U.S.A. .. 53 M5
Leicester, U.K. 9 E6
Leicester City □, U.K. .. 9 E6
Leicestershire □, U.K. .. 9 E6
Leichhardt →,
Australia 42 B2
Leichhardt Ra., Australia 42 C4
Leiden, Neths. 11 B4
Leie →, Belgium ... 11 C3
Leigh Creek, Australia . 43 E2
Leine →, Germany .. 12 B5
Leinster, Australia .. 41 E3
Leinster □, Ireland ... 10 E3
Leipzig, Germany ... 12 C7
Leiria, Portugal 15 C1
Leirvik, Norway 7 G11
Leisler, Mt., Australia .. 40 D4
Leith Hill, U.K. 9 F7
Leitrim, Ireland 10 D3
Leizhou Bandao, China 25 D6
Lek →, Neths. 11 C4
Leka, Norway 6 D14
Lékva Óros, Greece .. 17 G11
Leland, Mich., U.S.A. .. 52 C3
Leland, Miss., U.S.A. .. 55 J9
Leleque, Argentina .. 64 E2
Lelystad, Neths. 11 B5
Léman, L., Europe .. 14 C7
Lemhi Ra., U.S.A. .. 56 D7
Lemmer, Neths. 11 B5
Lemmon, U.S.A. 54 C3
Lemoore, U.S.A. 57 H4
Lemvig, Denmark ... 7 H13
Lena →, Russia ... 21 B13
Lendeh, Iran 31 D6
Leninabad =
Khudzhand, Tajikistan 20 E7
Leninakan = Gyumri,
Armenia 19 F7

Leningrad = Sankt-
Peterburg, Russia .. 18 C5
Leninogorsk, Kazakstan 20 D9
Leninsk, Russia 19 E8
Leninsk-Kuznetskiy,
Russia 20 D9
Lenkoran = Länkäran,
Azerbaijan 19 G8
Lenmalu, Indonesia .. 27 E8
Lennox, U.S.A. 54 D6
Lenoir, U.S.A. 53 H5
Lenoir City, U.S.A. .. 53 H3
Lenore L., Canada ... 51 C8
Lens, France 14 A5
Lensk, Russia 21 C12
Lentini, Italy 16 F6
Lenya, Burma 26 B1
Leoben, Austria 12 E8
Leodhas = Lewis, U.K. 10 B3
Leola, U.S.A. 54 C5
Leominster, U.K. ... 9 E5
Leominster, U.S.A. .. 52 D10
León, Mexico 58 C4
León, Nic. 60 D2
León, Spain 15 A3
Leon, U.S.A. 54 E8
León, Montes de, Spain 15 A2
Leonardtown, U.S.A. . 52 F7
Leongatha, Australia . 43 F4
Leonora, Australia .. 41 E3
Léopold II, Lac = Mai-
Ndombe, L.,
Dem. Rep. of
the Congo 36 E3
Leopoldsburg, Belgium 11 C5
Léopoldville =
Kinshasa, Dem. Rep.
of the Congo 36 E3
Leoti, U.S.A. 54 F4
Leova, Moldova 13 E15
Leoville, Canada ... 51 C7
Lepel = Lyepyel,
Belarus 18 D4
Leppävirta, Finland ... 7 E22
Lerdo, Mexico 58 B4
Lérida = Lleida, Spain .. 15 B6
Lerwick, U.K. 10 A6
Les Cayes, Haiti ... 61 C5
Les Sables-d'Olonne,
France 14 C3
Lesbos = Lésvos,
Greece 17 E12
Leshan, China 24 D5
Leshukonskoye, Russia 18 B8
Leskov I., Antarctica .. 5 B1
Leskovac, Serbia, Yug. 17 C9
Lesopilnoye, Russia .. 22 A7
Lesotho ■, Africa ... 37 K5
Lesozavodsk, Russia .. 21 E14
Lesse →, Belgium .. 11 D4
Lesser Antilles,
W. Indies 61 D7
Lesser Slave L., Canada 50 B5
Lesser Sunda Is.,
Indonesia 27 F6
Lessines, Belgium .. 11 D3
Lestock, Canada ... 51 C8
Lesuer I., Australia .. 40 B4
Lésvos, Greece ... 17 E12
Leszno, Poland 12 C9
Letchworth, U.K. ... 9 F7
Lethbridge, Canada .. 50 D6
Lethem, Guyana ... 62 C7
Leti, Kepulauan,
Indonesia 27 F7
Leti Is. = Leti,
Kepulauan, Indonesia 27 F7
Leticia, Colombia ... 62 D5
Letong, Indonesia .. 26 D3
Letpadan, Burma .. 29 L19
Letpan, Burma 29 K19
Letsôk-aw Kyun, Burma 26 B1
Letterkenny, Ireland .. 10 D3
Leuser, G., Indonesia .. 26 D1
Leuven, Belgium ... 11 D4
Leuze-en-Hainaut,
Belgium 11 D3
Levádhia, Greece .. 17 E10
Levanger, Norway .. 6 E14
Levelland, U.S.A. ... 55 J3
Leveque C., Australia . 40 C3
Levice, Slovak Rep. .. 13 D10
Levin, N.Z. 39 J5
Lévis, Canada 49 C5
Levis, L., Canada .. 50 A5
Levittown, U.S.A. ... 52 E9
Levkás, Greece ... 17 E9
Levkôsia = Nicosia,
Cyprus 30 C2
Levskigrad = Karlovo,
Bulgaria 17 C11
Levuka, Fiji 39 C8
Lewes, U.K. 9 G8
Lewes, U.S.A. 52 F8
Lewis, U.K. 10 B3
Lewis Ra., Australia .. 40 D4
Lewis Range, U.S.A. .. 56 C7
Lewisburg, Tenn.,
U.S.A. 53 H2
Lewisburg, W. Va.,
U.S.A. 52 G5
Lewisporte, Canada .. 49 C8
Lewiston, Idaho, U.S.A. 56 C5
Lewiston, Maine, U.S.A. 53 C11

Lewistown, Mont.,
U.S.A. 56 C9
Lewistown, Pa., U.S.A. 52 E7
Lexington, Ill., U.S.A. .. 54 E10
Lexington, Ky., U.S.A. .. 52 F3
Lexington, Mo., U.S.A. 54 F8
Lexington, N.C., U.S.A. 53 H5
Lexington, Nebr., U.S.A. 54 E5
Lexington, Tenn., U.S.A. 53 H1
Lexington, Va., U.S.A. .. 52 G6
Lexington Park, U.S.A. 52 F7
Leyburn, U.K. 8 C6
Leyland, U.K. 8 D5
Leyte □, Phil. 27 B6
Lezha = Lezhë, Albania 17 D8
Lezhë, Albania 17 D8
Lhasa, China 24 D4
Lhazê, China 24 D3
Lhokkruet, Indonesia .. 26 D1
Lhokseumawe,
Indonesia 26 C1
Lhokseumawe,
Indonesia 26 C1
L'Hospitalet de
Llobregat, Spain .. 15 B7
Lianga, Phil. 27 C7
Liangpran, Indonesia .. 26 D4
Lianyungang, China .. 25 C6
Liaoning □, China ... 25 B7
Liaoyang, China 25 B7
Liaoyuan, China 25 B7
Liard →, Canada ... 50 A4
Liard River, Canada .. 50 B3
Libau = Liepāja, Latvia 7 H19
Libby, U.S.A. 56 B6
Libenge, Dem. Rep. of
the Congo 36 D3
Liberal, U.S.A. 55 G4
Liberec, Czech Rep. .. 12 C8
Liberia, Costa Rica .. 60 D2
Liberia ■, W. Afr. .. 34 G4
Liberty, Mo., U.S.A. .. 54 F7
Liberty, N.Y., U.S.A. .. 52 E8
Liberty, Tex., U.S.A. .. 55 K7
Lîbîya, Sahrâ', Africa .. 35 C10
Libobo, Tanjung,
Indonesia 27 E7
Libode, Dem. Rep. of
the Congo 36 G5
Libourne, France 14 D3
Libramont, Belgium .. 11 E5
Libreville, Gabon 36 D1
Libya ■, N. Afr. ... 35 C9
Libyan Desert = Lîbîya,
Sahrâ', Africa 35 C10
Licantén, Chile 64 D2
Licata, Italy 16 F5
Lichfield, U.K. 9 E6
Lichinga, Mozam. ... 37 G7
Licking →, U.S.A. .. 52 F3
Lida, Belarus 7 K21
Lidköping, Sweden .. 7 G15
Liebig, Mt., Australia .. 40 D5
Liechtenstein ■, Europe 14 C8
Liège, Belgium 11 D5
Liège □, Belgium ... 11 D5
Liegnitz = Legnica,
Poland 12 C9
Lienyünchiangshih =
Lianyungang, China .. 25 C6
Lienz, Austria 12 E7
Liepāja, Latvia 7 H19
Lier, Belgium 11 C4
Lièvre →, Canada .. 48 C4
Liffey →, Ireland .. 10 E5
Lifford, Ireland 10 B4
Lifudzin, Russia 22 B7
Lightning Ridge,
Australia 43 D4
Liguria □, Italy 14 D8
Ligurian Sea, Medit. S. 16 C3
Lihou Reefs and Cays,
Australia 42 B5
Lijiang, China 24 D5
Likasi, Dem. Rep. of
the Congo 36 G5
Lille, France 14 A5
Lille Bælt, Denmark .. 7 J13
Lillehammer, Norway . 7 F14
Lillesand, Norway ... 7 G13
Lillian Pt., Australia .. 41 E4
Lillooet, Canada ... 50 C4
Lillooet →, Canada .. 50 D4
Lilongwe, Malawi ... 37 G6
Liloy, Phil. 27 C6
Lim →, Bos.-H. 17 C8
Lima, Indonesia 27 E7
Lima, Mont., U.S.A. .. 56 D7
Lima, Ohio, U.S.A. .. 52 E3
Lima, Peru 62 F3
Lima →, Portugal .. 15 B1
Liman, Indonesia .. 27 G14
Limay →, Argentina . 64 D3
Limay Mahuida,
Argentina 64 D3
Limbang, Brunei ... 26 D5
Limbaži, Latvia 7 H21
Limbe, Cameroon .. 36 D1
Limburg, Germany .. 12 C5
Limburg □, Belgium .. 11 C5
Limburg □, Neths. .. 11 C5
Limeira, Brazil 63 H9
Limerick, Ireland .. 10 D2
Limestone →, Canada 51 B10
Limfjorden, Denmark . 7 H13
Limia = Lima →,
Portugal 15 B1
Limingen, Norway .. 6 D15

Limmen Bight, Australia 42 A2
Limmen Bight →,
Australia 42 B2
Límnos, Greece ... 17 E11
Limoges, France ... 14 D4
Limón, Costa Rica .. 60 E3
Limon, U.S.A. 54 F3
Limousin, France ... 14 D4
Limoux, France 14 E5
Limpopo →, Africa .. 37 K6
Limuru, Kenya 36 E7
Linares, Chile 64 D2
Linares, Mexico 59 C5
Linares, Spain 15 C4
Lincoln, Argentina .. 64 C4
Lincoln, N.Z. 39 K4
Lincoln, U.K. 8 D7
Lincoln, Ill., U.S.A. .. 54 E10
Lincoln, Kans., U.S.A. 54 F5
Lincoln, Maine, U.S.A. 53 C11
Lincoln, N. Mex., U.S.A. 57 K11
Lincoln, Nebr., U.S.A. .. 54 E6
Lincoln City, U.S.A. .. 56 D1
Lincoln Hav = Lincoln
Sea, Arctic 4 A5
Lincoln Sea, Arctic .. 4 A5
Lincolnshire □, U.K. .. 8 D7
Lincolnshire Wolds, U.K. 8 D7
Lincolnton, U.S.A. .. 53 H5
Lind, U.S.A. 56 C4
Linden, Guyana ... 62 B7
Linden, Ala., U.S.A. .. 53 J2
Linden, Tex., U.S.A. .. 55 J7
Lindesnes, Norway .. 7 H12
Líndhos, Greece ... 17 F13
Lindi, Tanzania 36 F7
Lindsay, Canada ... 48 D4
Lindsay, Calif., U.S.A. .. 57 H4
Lindsay, Okla., U.S.A. .. 55 H6
Lindsborg, U.S.A. .. 54 F6
Lingayen, Phil. 27 A6
Lingayen G., Phil. ... 27 A6
Lingen, Germany ... 12 B4
Lingga, Indonesia .. 26 E2
Lingga, Kepulauan,
Indonesia 26 E2
Lingga Arch. = Lingga,
Kepulauan, Indonesia 26 E2
Lingle, U.S.A. 54 D2
Linguère, Senegal .. 34 E2
Linhai, China 25 D7
Linhares, Brazil 63 G10
Linköping, Sweden .. 7 G16
Linosa, I., Medit. S. .. 16 G5
Lins, Brazil 63 H9
Linton, Ind., U.S.A. .. 52 F2
Linton, N. Dak., U.S.A. 54 B4
Linxia, China 24 C5
Linz, Austria 12 D8
Lion, G. du, France .. 14 E6
Lions, G. of = Lion, G.
du, France 14 E6
Lipa, Phil. 27 B6
Lípari, Italy 16 E6
Lípari, Is. = Éolie, Ís.,
Italy 16 E6
Lipcani, Moldova ... 13 D14
Lipetsk, Russia 18 D6
Lipkany = Lipcani,
Moldova 13 D14
Lipovcy Manzovka,
Russia 22 B6
Lipovets, Ukraine .. 13 D15
Lippe →, Germany .. 12 C4
Lipscomb, U.S.A. ... 55 G4
Liptrap C., Australia .. 43 F4
Lira, Uganda 36 D6
Liria = Lliria, Spain .. 15 C5
Lisala, Dem. Rep. of
the Congo 36 D4
Lisboa, Portugal ... 15 C1
Lisbon = Lisboa,
Portugal 15 C1
Lisbon, U.S.A. 54 B6
Lisbon Falls, U.S.A. .. 53 D10
Lisburn, U.K. 10 D3
Lisianski I., Pac. Oc. .. 44 E10
Lisichansk =
Lysychansk, Ukraine 19 E6
Lisieux, France 14 B4
Liski, Russia 19 D6
Lismore, Australia .. 43 D5
Lista, Norway 7 G12
Lister, Mt., Antarctica .. 5 D11
Liston, Australia ... 43 D5
Listowel, Canada ... 48 D3
Listowel, Ireland ... 10 D2
Litani →, Lebanon .. 33 B4
Litchfield, Ill., U.S.A. .. 54 F10
Litchfield, Minn., U.S.A. 54 C7
Lithgow, Australia .. 43 E5
Líthinon, Ákra, Greece 17 G11
Lithuania ■, Europe .. 7 J20
Litoměřice, Czech Rep. 12 C8
Little Abaco I., Bahamas 60 A4
Little Barrier I., N.Z. .. 39 G5
Little Belt Mts., U.S.A. 56 C8
Little Blue →, U.S.A. 54 F6
Little Buffalo →,
Canada 50 A6
Little Cayman,
Cayman Is. 60 C3
Little Churchill →,
Canada 51 B9

Little Colorado →, U.S.A. ... 57 H8
Little Current, Canada . 48 C3
Little Current →, Canada ... 48 B3
Little Falls, Minn., U.S.A. 54 C7
Little Falls, N.Y., U.S.A. 52 D8
Little Fork →, U.S.A. .. 54 A8
Little Grand Rapids, Canada ... 51 C9
Little Humboldt →, U.S.A. ... 56 F5
Little Inagua I., Bahamas 61 B5
Little Laut Is. = Laut Kecil, Kepulauan, Indonesia ... 26 E5
Little Mecatina = Petit-Mécatina →, Canada 49 B8
Little Missouri →, U.S.A. ... 54 B3
Little Ouse →, U.K. .. 9 E9
Little Red →, U.S.A. . 55 H9
Little River, N.Z. ... 39 K4
Little Rock, U.S.A. ... 55 H8
Little Sable Pt., U.S.A. . 52 D2
Little Sioux →, U.S.A. 54 E6
Little Smoky →, Canada ... 50 C5
Little Snake →, U.S.A. 56 F9
Little Wabash →, U.S.A. ... 52 G1
Little White →, U.S.A. 54 D4
Littlefield, U.S.A. ... 55 J3
Littlehampton, U.K. .. 9 G7
Littleton, U.S.A. ... 52 C10
Liukang Tenggaja = Sabalana, Kepulauan, Indonesia ... 27 F5
Liuwa Plain, Zambia . 37 G4
Liuzhou, China ... 25 D5
Live Oak, U.S.A. ... 53 K4
Livermore, Mt., U.S.A. . 55 K2
Livermore Falls, U.S.A. 53 C11
Liverpool, Canada ... 49 D7
Liverpool, U.K. ... 8 D4
Liverpool Bay, U.K. .. 8 D4
Liverpool Plains, Australia ... 43 E5
Liverpool Ra., Australia 43 E5
Livingston, Guatemala 60 C2
Livingston, Ala., U.S.A. 53 J1
Livingston, Mont., U.S.A. ... 56 D8
Livingston, S.C., U.S.A. 53 J5
Livingston, Tenn., U.S.A. ... 53 G3
Livingston, Tex., U.S.A. 55 K7
Livingston, L., U.S.A. . 55 K7
Livingstone, Zambia . 37 H5
Livny, Russia ... 18 D6
Livonia, U.S.A. ... 52 D4
Livorno, Italy ... 16 C4
Lizard I., Australia ... 42 A4
Lizard Pt., U.K. ... 9 H2
Ljubljana, Slovenia ... 12 E8
Ljungan →, Sweden . 7 E17
Ljungby, Sweden ... 7 H15
Ljusdal, Sweden ... 7 F17
Ljusnan →, Sweden . 7 F17
Ljusne, Sweden ... 7 F17
Llancanelo, Salina, Argentina ... 64 D3
Llandeilo, U.K. ... 9 F4
Llandovery, U.K. ... 9 F4
Llandrindod Wells, U.K. 9 E4
Llandudno, U.K. ... 8 D4
Llanelli, U.K. ... 9 F3
Llanes, Spain ... 15 A3
Llangollen, U.K. ... 8 E4
Llanidloes, U.K. ... 9 E4
Llano, U.S.A. ... 55 K5
Llano →, U.S.A. ... 55 K5
Llano Estacado, U.S.A. 55 J3
Llanos, S. Amer. ... 62 C4
Llanquihue, L., Chile . 64 E1
Llanwrtyd Wells, U.K. . 9 E4
Lleida, Spain ... 15 B6
Llera, Mexico ... 59 C5
Lleyn Peninsula, U.K. . 8 E3
Lliria, Spain ... 15 C5
Llobregat →, Spain .. 15 B7
Lloret de Mar, Spain . 15 B7
Lloyd B., Australia ... 42 A3
Lloyd L., Canada ... 51 B7
Lloydminster, Canada . 51 C7
Llucmajor, Spain ... 15 C7
Llullaillaco, Volcán, S. Amer. ... 64 A3
Loa, U.S.A. ... 57 G8
Loa →, Chile ... 62 H4
Loaita I., S. China Sea . 26 B4
Loange →, Dem. Rep. of the Congo ... 36 E4
Lobatse, Botswana ... 37 K5
Lobería, Argentina ... 64 D5
Lobito, Angola ... 37 G2
Lobos, I., Mexico ... 58 B2
Locarno, Switz. ... 14 C8
Loch Garman = Wexford, Ireland ... 10 D5
Loche, L. La, Canada . 51 B7
Lochem, Neths. ... 11 B6
Loches, France ... 14 C4
Lochnagar, Australia . 42 C4
Lock, Australia ... 43 E2

Lock Haven, U.S.A. ... 52 E7
Lockeport, Canada ... 49 D6
Lockhart, Australia ... 43 F4
Lockhart, U.S.A. ... 55 L6
Lockhart, L., Australia . 41 F2
Lockhart River, Australia 42 A3
Lockney, U.S.A. ... 55 H4
Lockport, U.S.A. ... 52 D6
Lod, Israel ... 33 D3
Lodeinoye Pole, Russia 18 B5
Lodge Bay, Canada ... 49 B8
Lodge Grass, U.S.A. .. 56 D10
Lodgepole Cr. →, U.S.A. ... 54 E2
Lodhran, Pakistan ... 28 E7
Lodi, Italy ... 14 D8
Lodi, U.S.A. ... 56 G3
Lodja, Dem. Rep. of the Congo ... 36 E4
Lodwar, Kenya ... 36 D7
Łódź, Poland ... 13 C10
Loei, Thailand ... 26 A2
Lofoten, Norway ... 6 B15
Logan, Iowa, U.S.A. .. 54 E7
Logan, Ohio, U.S.A. .. 52 F4
Logan, Utah, U.S.A. .. 56 F8
Logan, W. Va., U.S.A. . 52 G5
Logan, Mt., Canada .. 46 B5
Logansport, Ind., U.S.A. 52 E2
Logansport, La., U.S.A. 55 K8
Logone →, Chad ... 35 F9
Logroño, Spain ... 15 A4
Lohardaga, India ... 29 H14
Lohja, Finland ... 7 F21
Loi-kaw, Burma ... 29 K20
Loimaa, Finland ... 7 F20
Loir →, France ... 14 C3
Loire →, France ... 14 C2
Loja, Ecuador ... 62 D3
Loja, Spain ... 15 D3
Loji = Kawasi, Indonesia ... 27 E7
Lokeren, Belgium ... 11 C3
Lokitaung, Kenya ... 36 D7
Lokkan tekojärvi, Finland ... 6 C22
Lokoja, Nigeria ... 34 G7
Lolland, Denmark ... 7 J14
Lolo, U.S.A. ... 56 C6
Lom, Bulgaria ... 17 C10
Lomami →, Dem. Rep. of the Congo ... 36 D4
Lombadina, Australia . 40 C3
Lombárdia □, Italy ... 14 D8
Lombardy = Lombárdia □, Italy . 14 D8
Lomblen, Indonesia .. 27 F6
Lombok, Indonesia ... 26 F5
Lomé, Togo ... 34 G6
Lomela, Dem. Rep. of the Congo ... 36 E4
Lomela →, Dem. Rep. of the Congo ... 36 E4
Lommel, Belgium ... 11 C5
Lomond, Canada ... 50 C6
Lomond, L., U.K. ... 10 C4
Lompobatang, Indonesia ... 27 F5
Lompoc, U.S.A. ... 57 J3
Łomża, Poland ... 13 B12
Loncoche, Chile ... 64 D2
Londa, India ... 28 M9
London, Canada ... 48 D3
London, U.K. ... 9 F7
London, Ky., U.S.A. .. 52 G3
London, Ohio, U.S.A. . 52 F4
London, Greater □, U.K. 9 F7
Londonderry, U.K. ... 10 D3
Londonderry, C., Australia ... 40 B4
Londonderry, I., Chile . 64 H2
Londres, Argentina ... 64 B3
Londrina, Brazil ... 64 A6
Lone Pine, U.S.A. ... 57 H4
Long B., U.S.A. ... 53 J6
Long Beach, Calif., U.S.A. ... 57 K4
Long Beach, Wash., U.S.A. ... 56 C1
Long Branch, U.S.A. .. 52 E9
Long Creek, U.S.A. ... 56 D4
Long Eaton, U.K. ... 8 E6
Long I., Australia ... 42 C4
Long I., Bahamas ... 61 B4
Long I., Canada ... 48 B4
Long I., U.S.A. ... 52 E9
Long Island Sd., U.S.A. 52 E9
Long L., Canada ... 48 C2
Long Lake, U.S.A. ... 52 D8
Long Prairie →, U.S.A. 54 C7
Long Range Mts., Canada ... 49 C8
Long Reef, Australia . 40 B4
Long Spruce, Canada . 51 B10
Long Str. = Longa, Proliv, Russia ... 4 C16
Long Xuyen, Vietnam . 26 B3
Longa, Proliv, Russia . 4 C16
Longbenton, U.K. ... 8 B6
Longboat Key, U.S.A. . 53 M4
Longford, Australia ... 42 G4
Longford, Ireland ... 10 E3
Longiram, Indonesia .. 26 E5
Longlac, Canada ... 48 C2

Longmont, U.S.A. ... 54 E2
Longnawan, Indonesia 26 D4
Longreach, Australia . 42 C3
Longview, Tex., U.S.A. 55 J7
Longview, Wash., U.S.A. 56 C2
Lonoke, U.S.A. ... 55 H9
Lonquimay, Chile ... 64 D2
Lons-le-Saunier, France 14 C6
Looe, U.K. ... 9 G3
Lookout, C., Canada .. 48 A3
Lookout, C., U.S.A. ... 53 H7
Loon →, Alta., Canada 50 B5
Loon →, Man., Canada 51 B8
Loon Lake, Canada ... 51 C7
Loongana, Australia ... 41 F4
Lop Nor = Lop Nur, China ... 24 B4
Lop Nur, China ... 24 B4
Lopatina, Gora, Russia 21 D15
Lopez, C., Gabon ... 36 E1
Lopphavet, Norway ... 6 A19
Lora →, Afghan. ... 28 D4
Lora, Hämün-i-, Pakistan 28 E4
Lora Cr. →, Australia . 43 D2
Lora del Río, Spain ... 15 D3
Lorain, U.S.A. ... 52 E4
Loralai, Pakistan ... 28 D6
Lorca, Spain ... 15 D5
Lord Howe I., Pac. Oc. 38 E8
Lord Howe Ridge, Pac. Oc. ... 44 L8
Lordsburg, U.S.A. ... 57 K9
Loreto, Brazil ... 63 E9
Loreto, Mexico ... 58 B2
Lorient, France ... 14 C2
Lorne, Australia ... 43 F3
Lorraine □, France ... 14 B7
Los Alamos, U.S.A. ... 57 J10
Los Andes, Chile ... 64 C2
Los Angeles, Chile ... 64 D2
Los Angeles, U.S.A. .. 57 K4
Los Angeles, Bahia de, Mexico ... 58 B2
Los Angeles Aqueduct, U.S.A. ... 57 J5
Los Banos, U.S.A. ... 57 H3
Los Blancos, Argentina 64 A4
Los Chiles, Costa Rica . 60 D3
Los Hermanos Is., Venezuela ... 62 A6
Los Lunas, U.S.A. ... 57 J10
Los Mochis, Mexico .. 58 B3
Los Palacios, Cuba ... 60 B3
Los Reyes, Mexico ... 58 D4
Los Roques Is., Venezuela ... 62 A5
Los Teques, Venezuela 62 A5
Los Testigos, Is., Venezuela ... 62 A6
Los Vilos, Chile ... 64 C2
Lošinj, Croatia ... 12 F8
Lostwithiel, U.K. ... 9 G3
Lot →, France ... 14 D4
Lota, Chile ... 64 D2
Lotfābād, Iran ... 31 B8
Loubomo, Congo ... 36 E2
Louga, Senegal ... 34 E2
Loughborough, U.K. .. 8 E6
Louis Trichardt, S. Africa ... 37 J5
Louis XIV, Pte., Canada 48 B4
Louisa, U.S.A. ... 52 F4
Louisburg, Canada ... 49 C8
Louise I., Canada ... 50 C2
Louiseville, Canada ... 48 C5
Louisiade Arch., Papua N. G. ... 38 C8
Louisiana, U.S.A. ... 54 F9
Louisiana □, U.S.A. .. 55 K9
Louisville, Ky., U.S.A. . 52 F3
Louisville, Miss., U.S.A. 55 J10
Loulé, Portugal ... 15 D1
Loup City, U.S.A. ... 54 E5
Loups Marins, Lacs des, Canada ... 48 A5
Lourdes, France ... 14 E3
Lourenço-Marques = Maputo, Mozam. . 37 K6
Louth, Australia ... 43 E4
Louth, U.K. ... 8 D7
Louvain = Leuven, Belgium ... 11 D4
Lovech, Bulgaria ... 17 C11
Loveland, U.S.A. ... 54 E2
Lovell, U.S.A. ... 56 D9
Lovelock, U.S.A. ... 56 F4
Loviisa, Finland ... 7 F22
Loving, U.S.A. ... 55 J2
Lovington, U.S.A. ... 55 J3
Lovisa = Loviisa, Finland ... 7 F22
Low, L., Canada ... 48 B4
Low Pt., Australia ... 41 F4
Low Tatra = Nízké Tatry, Slovak Rep. . 13 D10
Lowell, U.S.A. ... 52 D10
Lower Alkali L., U.S.A. . 56 F3
Lower Arrow L., Canada 50 D5
Lower California = Baja California, Mexico . 58 A1
Lower Hutt, N.Z. ... 39 J5
Lower Manitou L., Canada ... 51 D10
Lower Post, Canada ... 50 B3

Lower Red L., U.S.A. .. 54 B7
Lower Saxony = Niedersachsen □, Germany ... 12 B5
Lower Tunguska = Tunguska, Nizhnyaya →, Russia 21 C9
Lowestoft, U.K. ... 9 E9
Łowicz, Poland ... 13 B10
Lowville, U.S.A. ... 52 D8
Loxton, Australia ... 43 E3
Loyalty Is. = Loyauté, Is., N. Cal. ... 38 D9
Loyang = Luoyang, China ... 25 C6
Loyauté, Is., N. Cal. .. 38 D9
Loyev, Belarus ... 13 C16
Loyew, Belarus ... 13 C16
Luachimo, Angola ... 36 F4
Lualaba →, Dem. Rep. of the Congo ... 36 D5
Luanda, Angola ... 36 F2
Luang, Thale, Thailand 26 C2
Luangwa →, Zambia . 37 G6
Luanshya, Zambia ... 37 G5
Luapula →, Africa ... 36 F5
Luarca, Spain ... 15 A2
Luau, Angola ... 36 G4
Lubana, Ozero = Lubānas Ezers, Latvia 7 H22
Lubānas Ezers, Latvia 7 H22
Lubang Is., Phil. ... 27 B6
Lubbock, U.S.A. ... 55 J4
Lübeck, Germany ... 12 B6
Lubero = Luofu, Dem. Rep. of the Congo ... 36 E5
Lubicon L., Canada ... 50 B5
Lubilash →, Dem. Rep. of the Congo ... 36 F4
Lubin, Poland ... 12 C9
Lublin, Poland ... 13 C12
Lubnān, Jabal, Lebanon 33 B4
Lubny, Ukraine ... 20 D4
Lubudi, Dem. Rep. of the Congo ... 36 F5
Lubuklinggau, Indonesia 26 E2
Lubuksikaping, Indonesia ... 26 D2
Lubumbashi, Dem. Rep. of the Congo ... 37 G5
Lubutu, Dem. Rep. of the Congo ... 36 E5
Lucania, Mt., Canada .. 46 B5
Lucca, Italy ... 16 C4
Lucea, Jamaica ... 60 C4
Lucedale, U.S.A. ... 53 K1
Lucena, Phil. ... 27 B6
Lucena, Spain ... 15 D3
Lučenec, Slovak Rep. . 13 D10
Lucerne = Luzern, Switz. ... 14 C8
Lucero, Mexico ... 58 A3
Lucinda, Australia ... 42 B4
Lucindale, Australia ... 43 F3
Luckenwalde, Germany 12 B7
Lucknow, India ... 29 F12
Lüda = Dalian, China . 25 C7
Lüderitz, Namibia ... 37 K3
Ludhiana, India ... 28 D9
Ludington, U.S.A. ... 52 D2
Ludlow, U.K. ... 9 E5
Ludlow, U.S.A. ... 57 J5
Ludvika, Sweden ... 7 F16
Ludwigsburg, Germany 14 D5
Ludwigshafen, Germany 12 D5
Lufira →, Dem. Rep. of the Congo ... 36 F5
Lufkin, U.S.A. ... 55 K7
Luga, Russia ... 18 C4
Lugano, Switz. ... 14 C8
Lugansk = Luhansk, Ukraine ... 19 E6
Lugenda →, Mozam. . 37 G7
Lugh Ganana, Somali Rep. ... 32 G3
Lugo, Italy ... 16 B4
Lugo, Spain ... 15 A2
Lugoj, Romania ... 13 F11
Lugovoy, Kazakstan ... 20 E8
Luhansk, Ukraine ... 19 E6
Luimneach = Limerick, Ireland ... 10 E2
Luis Correia, Brazil ... 63 D10
Luitpold Coast, Antarctica ... 5 D1
Luiza, Dem. Rep. of the Congo ... 36 F4
Lukanga Swamp, Zambia ... 37 G5
Lukenie →, Dem. Rep. of the Congo ... 36 E3
Łuków, Poland ... 13 C12
Lule älv →, Sweden . 6 D19
Luleå, Sweden ... 6 D20
Lüleburgaz, Turkey ... 17 D12
Luling, U.S.A. ... 55 L6
Lulonga →, Dem. Rep. of the Congo ... 36 D3
Lulua →, Dem. Rep. of the Congo ... 36 E4
Luluabourg = Kananga, Dem. Rep. of the Congo ... 36 F4
Lumajang, Indonesia . 27 H15

Lumbala N'guimbo, Angola ... 37 G4
Lumberton, U.S.A. ... 53 H6
Lumsden, Canada ... 51 C8
Lumsden, N.Z. ... 39 L2
Lumut, Tanjung, Indonesia ... 26 E3
Lund, Sweden ... 7 J15
Lundazi, Zambia ... 37 G6
Lundu, Malaysia ... 26 D3
Lundy, U.K. ... 9 F3
Lune →, U.K. ... 8 C5
Lüneburg, Germany .. 12 B6
Lüneburg Heath = Lüneburger Heide, Germany ... 12 B6
Lüneburger Heide, Germany ... 12 B6
Lunel, France ... 14 E6
Lunéville, France ... 14 B7
Lunglei, India ... 29 H18
Luni, India ... 28 G8
Luni →, India ... 28 G7
Luninets = Luninyets, Belarus ... 13 B14
Luning, U.S.A. ... 56 G4
Luninyets, Belarus ... 13 B14
Luofu, Dem. Rep. of the Congo ... 36 E5
Luoyang, China ... 25 C6
Lupanshui, China ... 24 D5
Luray, U.S.A. ... 52 F6
Lurgan, U.K. ... 10 D3
Lusaka, Zambia ... 37 H5
Lusambo, Dem. Rep. of the Congo ... 36 E4
Luseland, Canada ... 51 C7
Lushnja = Lushnjë, Albania ... 17 D8
Lushnjë, Albania ... 17 D8
Lusk, U.S.A. ... 54 D2
Lüt, Dasht-e, Iran ... 31 D8
Luta = Dalian, China . 25 C7
Lutherstadt Wittenberg, Germany ... 12 C7
Luton, U.K. ... 9 F7
Luton □, U.K. ... 9 F7
Lutselke, Canada ... 51 A6
Lutsk, Ukraine ... 13 C13
Lützow Holmbukta, Antarctica ... 5 C4
Luverne, Ala., U.S.A. .. 53 K2
Luverne, Minn., U.S.A. 54 D6
Luwuk, Indonesia ... 27 E6
Luxembourg, Lux. ... 14 B7
Luxembourg □, Belgium 11 E5
Luxembourg ■, Europe 14 B7
Luxi, China ... 24 D4
Luxor = El Uqsur, Egypt 35 C12
Luza, Russia ... 18 B8
Luzern, Switz. ... 14 C8
Luzhou, China ... 24 D5
Luziânia, Brazil ... 63 G9
Luzon, Phil. ... 27 A6
Lviv, Ukraine ... 13 D13
Lvov = Lviv, Ukraine . 13 D13
Lyakhavichy, Belarus . 13 B14
Lyakhovskiye, Ostrova, Russia ... 21 B15
Lyallpur = Faisalabad, Pakistan ... 28 D8
Lycksele, Sweden ... 6 D18
Lydda = Lod, Israel ... 33 D3
Lydenburg, S. Africa .. 37 K6
Lydia, Turkey ... 17 E13
Lyell, N.Z. ... 39 J4
Lyell I., Canada ... 50 C2
Lyepyel, Belarus ... 18 D4
Lyman, U.S.A. ... 56 F8
Lyme B., U.K. ... 9 G4
Lyme Regis, U.K. ... 9 G5
Lymington, U.K. ... 9 G6
Łyna →, Poland ... 7 J19
Lynchburg, U.S.A. ... 52 G6
Lynd →, Australia ... 42 B3
Lynd Ra., Australia ... 43 D4
Lynden, U.S.A. ... 56 B2
Lyndhurst, Australia .. 43 E2
Lyndon →, Australia . 41 D1
Lyndonville, U.S.A. ... 52 C9
Lyngen, Norway ... 6 B19
Lynher Reef, Australia . 40 C3
Lynn, U.S.A. ... 52 D10
Lynn Lake, Canada ... 51 B8
Lynton, U.K. ... 9 F4
Lynx L., Canada ... 51 A7
Lyon, France ... 14 D6
Lyonnais, France ... 14 D6
Lyons = Lyon, France . 14 D6
Lyons, Ga., U.S.A. ... 53 J4
Lyons, Kans., U.S.A. .. 54 F5
Lyons →, Australia ... 41 E2
Lys = Leie →, Belgium 11 C3
Lysva, Russia ... 18 C10
Lysychansk, Ukraine .. 19 E6
Lytham St. Anne's, U.K. 8 D4
Lyttelton, N.Z. ... 39 K4
Lytton, Canada ... 50 C4
Lyubertsy, Russia ... 18 C6
Lyuboml, Ukraine ... 13 C13

M.R. Gomez, Presa, Mexico ... 59 B5

Ma'adaba, Jordan ... 33 E4
Ma'ān, Jordan ... 33 E4
Ma'ān □, Jordan ... 33 F5
Maanselkä, Finland ... 6 C23
Ma'anshan, China ... 25 C6
Maarianhamina, Finland 7 F18
Ma'arrat an Nu'mān, Syria ... 30 C3
Maas →, Neths. ... 11 C4
Maaseik, Belgium ... 11 C5
Maasin, Phil. ... 27 B6
Maastricht, Neths. ... 14 A6
Mabel L., Canada ... 50 C5
Mablethorpe, U.K. ... 8 D8
McAlester, U.S.A. ... 55 H7
McAllen, U.S.A. ... 55 M5
MacAlpine L., Canada . 46 B9
Macamic, Canada ... 48 C4
Macao = Macau □, China ... 25 D6
Macapá, Brazil ... 63 C8
McArthur →, Australia 42 B2
McArthur, Port, Australia ... 42 B2
Macau, Brazil ... 63 E11
Macau □, China ... 25 D6
McBride, Canada ... 50 C4
McCall, U.S.A. ... 56 D5
McCamey, U.S.A. ... 55 K3
McCammon, U.S.A. ... 56 E7
McCauley I., Canada .. 50 C2
Macclenny, U.S.A. ... 53 K4
Macclesfield, U.K. ... 8 D5
M'Clintock Chan., Canada ... 46 A9
McClintock Ra., Australia ... 40 C4
McCloud, U.S.A. ... 56 F2
M'Clure Str., Canada . 4 B2
McClusky, U.S.A. ... 54 B4
McComb, U.S.A. ... 55 K9
McConaughy, L., U.S.A. 54 E4
McCook, U.S.A. ... 54 E4
McCreary, Canada ... 51 C9
McCusker →, Canada 51 B7
McDame, Canada ... 50 B3
McDermitt, U.S.A. ... 56 F5
Macdonald, L., Australia 40 D4
McDonald Is., Ind. Oc. . 3 G13
MacDonnell Ranges, Australia ... 40 D5
MacDowell L., Canada 48 B1
Macedonia = Makedhonía □, Greece ... 17 D10
Macedonia ■, Europe . 17 D9
Maceió, Brazil ... 63 E11
Macerata, Italy ... 16 C5
McFarlane →, Canada 51 B7
Macfarlane, L., Australia 43 E2
McGehee, U.S.A. ... 55 J9
McGill, U.S.A. ... 56 G6
Macgillycuddy's Reeks, Ireland ... 10 E2
McGregor, U.S.A. ... 54 D9
McGregor Ra., Australia 43 D3
Mach, Pakistan ... 28 E5
Mäch Kowr, Iran ... 31 E9
Machado = Jiparaná →, Brazil 62 E6
Machakos, Kenya ... 36 E7
Machala, Ecuador ... 62 D3
Machattie, L., Australia 42 C2
Machias, U.S.A. ... 53 C12
Machichi →, Canada . 51 B10
Machilipatnam, India .. 29 L12
Machiques, Venezuela 62 A4
Machupicchu, Peru ... 62 F4
Machynlleth, U.K. ... 9 E4
McIlwraith Ra., Australia 42 A3
McInnes L., Canada ... 51 C10
McIntosh, U.S.A. ... 54 C4
McIntosh L., Canada .. 51 B8
Macintosh Ra., Australia 41 E4
Macintyre →, Australia 43 D5
Mackay, Australia ... 42 C4
Mackay, U.S.A. ... 56 E7
MacKay →, Canada .. 50 B6
Mackay, L., Australia . 40 D4
McKay Ra., Australia . 40 D3
McKeesport, U.S.A. ... 52 E6
Mackenzie, Canada ... 50 B4
McKenzie, U.S.A. ... 53 G1
Mackenzie →, Australia ... 42 C4
Mackenzie →, Canada 46 B6
McKenzie →, U.S.A. . 56 D2
Mackenzie Bay, Canada 4 B1
Mackenzie City = Linden, Guyana ... 62 B7
Mackenzie Mts., Canada 46 B6
Mackinaw City, U.S.A. . 52 C3
McKinlay, Australia ... 42 C3
McKinlay →, Australia 42 C3
McKinley, Mt., U.S.A. . 46 B4
McKinley Sea, Arctic . 4 A7
McKinney, U.S.A. ... 55 J6
Macklin, Canada ... 51 C7
Macksville, Australia .. 43 E5
McLaughlin, U.S.A. ... 54 C4
Maclean, Australia ... 43 D5
McLean, U.S.A. ... 55 H4
McLeansboro, U.S.A. . 54 F10
Maclear, S. Africa ... 37 L5

Macleay →, Australia 43 E5
McLennan, Canada . . . 50 B5
McLeod →, Canada . . 50 C5
McLeod, B., Canada . . 51 A7
McLeod, L., Australia . . 41 D1
McLeod Lake, Canada . . 50 C4
McLoughlin, Mt., U.S.A. 56 E2
McMinnville, Oreg.,
  U.S.A. 56 D2
McMinnville, Tenn.,
  U.S.A. 53 H3
McMurdo Sd.,
  Antarctica 5 D11
McMurray = Fort
  McMurray, Canada . . 50 B6
Macomb, U.S.A. 54 E9
Mâcon, France 14 C6
Macon, Ga., U.S.A. . . 53 J4
Macon, Miss., U.S.A. . . 53 J1
Macon, Mo., U.S.A. . . 54 F8
Macoun L., Canada . . 51 B8
McPherson, U.S.A. 54 F6
McPherson Ra.,
  Australia 43 D5
Macquarie →,
  Australia 43 E4
Macquarie Harbour,
  Australia 42 G4
Macquarie Is., Pac. Oc. 44 N7
MacRobertson Land,
  Antarctica 5 D6
Macusani, Peru 62 F4
Macuspana, Mexico . . 59 D6
Madadeni, S. Africa . . 37 K6
Madagascar ■, Africa . . 37 J9
Madā'in Sālih,
  Si. Arabia 30 E3
Madama, Niger 35 D8
Madame I., Canada . . 49 C7
Madang, Papua N. G. . . 38 B7
Madaripur, Bangla. . . 29 H17
Madauk, Burma 29 L20
Madawaska →,
  Canada 48 C4
Madaya, Burma 29 H20
Maddalena, Italy 16 D3
Madeira, Atl. Oc. 34 B2
Madeira →, Brazil . . 62 D7
Madeleine, Îs. de la,
  Canada 49 C7
Madera, Mexico 58 B3
Madera, U.S.A. 57 H3
Madha, India 28 L9
Madhya Pradesh □,
  India 28 J11
Madidi →, Bolivia . . 62 F5
Madikeri, India 28 N9
Madill, U.S.A. 55 H6
Madimba, Dem. Rep. of
  the Congo 36 E3
Ma'din, Syria 30 C3
Madingou, Congo 36 E2
Madison, Fla., U.S.A. . . 53 K4
Madison, Ind., U.S.A. . . 52 F3
Madison, Nebr., U.S.A. . . 54 E6
Madison, S. Dak., U.S.A. 54 D6
Madison, Wis., U.S.A. . . 54 D10
Madison →, U.S.A. . . 56 D8
Madison Heights, U.S.A. 52 G6
Madisonville, Ky., U.S.A. 52 G2
Madisonville, Tex.,
  U.S.A. 55 K7
Madiun, Indonesia . . 27 G14
Madona, Latvia 7 H22
Madrakah, Ra's al,
  Oman 32 D6
Madras = Chennai,
  India 28 N12
Madras = Tamil
  Nadu □, India 28 P10
Madras, U.S.A. 56 D3
Madre, Laguna, U.S.A. 55 M6
Madre, Sierra, Phil. . . 27 A6
Madre de Dios →,
  Bolivia 62 F5
Madre de Dios, I., Chile 64 G1
Madre del Sur, Sierra,
  Mexico 59 D5
Madre Occidental,
  Sierra, Mexico 58 B3
Madre Oriental, Sierra,
  Mexico 58 C5
Madrid, Spain 15 B4
Madura, Australia 41 F4
Madura, Indonesia . . 27 G15
Madura, Selat,
  Indonesia 27 G15
Madurai, India 28 Q11
Madurantakam, India . . 28 N11
Mae Sot, Thailand . . 26 A1
Maebashi, Japan 23 F9
Maesteg, U.K. 9 F4
Maestra, Sierra, Cuba 60 B4
Maevatanana, Madag. . . 37 H9
Mafeking, Canada 51 C8
Mafeteng, Lesotho . . 37 K13
Maffra, Australia 43 F4
Mafia I., Tanzania . . 36 F7
Mafra, Brazil 64 B7
Mafra, Portugal 15 C1
Magadan, Russia 21 D16
Magallanes, Estrecho
  de, Chile 64 G2
Magangué, Colombia . 62 B4

Magdalen Is. =
  Madeleine, Îs. de la,
  Canada 49 C7
Magdalena, Argentina . . 64 D5
Magdalena, Bolivia . . 62 F6
Magdalena, Mexico . . 58 A2
Magdalena, U.S.A. . . 57 J10
Magdalena →,
  Colombia 62 A4
Magdalena →, Mexico 58 A2
Magdalena, B., Mexico 58 C2
Magdalena, Llano de la,
  Mexico 58 C2
Magdeburg, Germany . . 12 B6
Magdelaine Cays,
  Australia 42 B5
Magee, U.S.A. 55 K10
Magelang, Indonesia . . 27 G14
Magellan's Str. =
  Magallanes, Estrecho
  de, Chile 64 G2
Magenta, L., Australia . 41 F2
Magerøya, Norway . . 6 A21
Maggiore, Lago, Italy . . 14 D8
Maghâgha, Egypt . . . 35 C12
Maghreb, N. Afr. . . . 34 B5
Magistralnyy, Russia . . 21 D11
Magnetic Pole (North) =
  North Magnetic Pole,
  Canada 4 B2
Magnetic Pole (South) =
  South Magnetic Pole,
  Antarctica 5 C9
Magnitogorsk, Russia . 18 D10
Magnolia, Ark., U.S.A. 55 J8
Magnolia, Miss., U.S.A. 55 K9
Magog, Canada 49 C5
Magosa = Famagusta,
  Cyprus 30 C2
Magozal, Mexico 59 C5
Magpie, L., Canada . . 49 B7
Magrath, Canada 50 D6
Maguarinho, C., Brazil . 63 D9
Magūsa = Famagusta,
  Cyprus 30 C2
Maguse L., Canada . . 51 A9
Maguse Pt., Canada . . 51 A10
Magwe, Burma 29 J19
Mahābād, Iran 30 B5
Mahabo, Madag. 37 J8
Mahajanga, Madag. . . 37 H9
Mahakam →,
  Indonesia 26 E5
Mahalapye, Botswana . 37 J5
Maḥallāt, Iran 31 C6
Mahān, Iran 31 D8
Mahanadi →, India . . 29 J15
Maharashtra □, India . . 28 J9
Mahasham, W. →,
  Egypt 33 E3
Mahattat ash Shidīyah,
  Jordan 33 F4
Mahattat 'Unayzah,
  Jordan 33 E4
Mahbubnagar, India . . 28 L10
Maḥdah, Oman 31 E7
Mahdia, Tunisia 35 A8
Mahenge, Tanzania . . 36 F7
Mahesana, India 28 H8
Mahia Pen., N.Z. . . . 39 H6
Mahilyow, Belarus . . 13 B16
Mahnomen, U.S.A. . . 54 B7
Mahón = Maó, Spain . 15 C8
Mahone Bay, Canada . 49 D7
Mai-Ndombe, L.,
  Dem. Rep. of
  the Congo 36 E3
Maicurú →, Brazil . . 63 D8
Maidenhead, U.K. . . . 9 F7
Maidstone, Canada . . 51 C7
Maidstone, U.K. 9 F8
Maiduguri, Nigeria . . 35 F8
Maijdi, Bangla. 29 H17
Maikala Ra., India . . 29 J12
Main →, Germany . . 12 C5
Maine, France 14 C3
Maine □, U.S.A. . . . 53 C11
Maingkwan, Burma . . 29 F20
Mainit, L., Phil. 27 C7
Mainland, Orkney, U.K. 10 B5
Mainland, Shet., U.K. . . 10 A6
Mainoru, Australia 42 A1
Mainz, Germany 12 C5
Maipú, Argentina 64 D5
Maiquetía, Venezuela . 62 A5
Mairabari, India 29 F18
Maisí, Cuba 61 B5
Maisí, Pta. de, Cuba . . 61 B5
Maitland, N.S.W.,
  Australia 43 E5
Maitland, S. Austral.,
  Australia 43 E2
Maiz, Is. del, Nic. . . . 60 D3
Maizuru, Japan 23 G7
Majalengka, Indonesia . 27 G13
Majene, Indonesia . . 27 E5
Majorca = Mallorca,
  Spain 15 C7
Makale, Indonesia . . 27 E5
Makarikari =
  Makgadikgadi Salt
  Pans, Botswana . . . 37 J5
Makarovo, Russia 21 D11

Makasar = Ujung
  Pandang, Indonesia . 27 F5
Makasar, Selat,
  Indonesia 27 E5
Makasar, Str. of =
  Makasar, Selat,
  Indonesia 27 E5
Makat, Kazakstan . . . 19 E9
Makedhonía □, Greece 17 D10
Makedonija =
  Macedonia ■, Europe 17 D9
Makeyevka = Makiyivka,
  Ukraine 19 E6
Makgadikgadi Salt Pans,
  Botswana 37 J5
Makhachkala, Russia . . 19 F8
Makhmūr, Iraq 30 C4
Makian, Indonesia . . 27 D7
Makinsk, Kazakstan . . 20 D8
Makiyivka, Ukraine . . 19 E6
Makkah, Si. Arabia . . 32 C2
Makkovik, Canada . . . 49 A8
Makó, Hungary 13 E11
Makokou, Gabon 36 D2
Makrai, India 28 H10
Makran Coast Range,
  Pakistan 28 G4
Mākū, Iran 30 B5
Makurazaki, Japan . . 23 J5
Makurdi, Nigeria 34 G7
Makūyeh, Iran 31 D7
Mala, Pta., Panama . . 60 E3
Malabar Coast, India . . 28 P9
Malabo = Rey Malabo,
  Eq. Guin. 36 D1
Malacca, Str. of,
  Indonesia 26 D2
Malad City, U.S.A. . . 56 E7
Maladzyechna, Belarus 13 A14
Málaga, Spain 15 D3
Malagasy Rep. =
  Madagascar ■, Africa 37 J9
Malaita, Solomon Is. . . 38 B9
Malakâl, Sudan 35 G12
Malakand, Pakistan . . 28 B7
Malakula, Vanuatu . . 38 C9
Malamala, Indonesia . 27 E6
Malanda, Australia 42 B4
Malang, Indonesia . . 27 G15
Malangen, Norway . . 6 B18
Malanje, Angola 36 F3
Mälaren, Sweden . . . 7 G17
Malargüe, Argentina . . 64 D3
Malartic, Canada 48 C4
Malaryta, Belarus . . . 13 C13
Malatya, Turkey 19 G6
Malawi ■, Africa . . . 37 G6
Malawi, L. = Nyasa, L.,
  Africa 37 G6
Malay Pen., Asia . . . 26 D2
Malay Pen., Asia . . . 26 D2
Malaya Vishera, Russia 18 C5
Malaybalay, Phil. . . . 27 C7
Malāyer, Iran 31 C6
Malaysia ■, Asia . . . 26 D4
Malazgirt, Turkey . . . 19 G7
Malbon, Australia 42 C3
Malbooma, Australia . . 43 E1
Malbork, Poland 13 B10
Malcolm, Australia 41 E3
Malcolm, Pt., Australia 41 F3
Maldegem, Belgium . . 11 C3
Malden, U.S.A. 55 G10
Malden I., Kiribati . . 45 H12
Maldives ■, Ind. Oc. . . 3 D13
Maldonado, Uruguay . . 64 C6
Maldonado, Punta,
  Mexico 59 D5
Malé Karpaty,
  Slovak Rep. 13 D9
Maléa, Ákra, Greece . . 17 F10
Malegaon, India 28 J9
Malek Kandī, Iran . . 30 B5
Malema, Mozam. 37 G7
Maleny, Australia 43 D5
Malgomaj, Sweden . . . 6 D17
Malha, Sudan 35 E11
Malheur →, U.S.A. . . 56 D5
Malheur L., U.S.A. . . 56 E4
Mali ■, Africa 34 E5
Mali →, Burma 29 G20
Mali Kyun, Burma . . . 26 B1
Maliku, Indonesia . . 27 E6
Malili, Indonesia . . . 27 E6
Malimba, Mts.,
  Dem. Rep. of
  the Congo 36 F5
Malin Hd., Ireland . . 10 D3
Malindi, Kenya 36 E8
Malines = Mechelen,
  Belgium 11 C4
Malino, Indonesia . . 27 D6
Malita, Phil. 27 C7
Maliwun, Burma 26 B1
Malkara, Turkey 17 D12
Mallacoota Inlet,
  Australia 43 F4
Mallaig, U.K. 10 C4
Mallawi, Egypt 35 C12
Mallicolo = Malakula,
  Vanuatu 38 C9
Mallorca, Spain 15 C7
Mallow, Ireland 10 E2
Malmberget, Sweden . 6 C19
Malmédy, Belgium . . 11 D6

Malmö, Sweden 7 J15
Malolos, Phil. 27 B6
Malone, U.S.A. 52 C8
Måløy, Norway 7 F11
Malpelo, I. de, Colombia 62 C2
Malta, Idaho, U.S.A. . . 56 E7
Malta, Mont., U.S.A. . . 56 B10
Malta ■, Europe 16 G6
Maltahöhe, Namibia . . 37 J3
Malton, U.K. 8 C7
Maluku, Indonesia . . 27 E7
Maluku □, Indonesia . 27 E7
Maluku Sea = Molucca
  Sea, Indonesia 27 E6
Malvan, India 28 L8
Malvern, U.S.A. 55 H8
Malvern Hills, U.K. . . 9 E5
Malvinas, Is. = Falkland
  Is. □, Atl. Oc. 64 G5
Malyn, Ukraine 13 C15
Malyy Lyakhovskiy,
  Ostrov, Russia 21 B15
Mama, Russia 21 D12
Mamanguape, Brazil . . 63 E11
Mamarr Mitlā, Egypt . . 33 E1
Mamasa, Indonesia . . 27 E5
Mamberamo →,
  Indonesia 27 E9
Mambilima Falls,
  Zambia 36 G5
Mamburao, Phil. 27 B6
Mameigwess L., Canada 48 B2
Mammoth, U.S.A. . . . 57 K8
Mammoth Cave
  National Park, U.S.A. 52 G3
Mamoré →, Bolivia . . 62 F5
Mamou, Guinea 34 F3
Mamuju, Indonesia . . 27 E5
Man, Ivory C. 34 G4
Man, I. of, U.K. 8 C3
Man Na, Burma 29 H20
Manaar, G. of =
  Mannar, G. of, Asia . 28 Q11
Manacapuru, Brazil . . 62 D6
Manacor, Spain 15 C7
Manado, Indonesia . . 27 D6
Managua, Nic. 60 D2
Managua, L. de, Nic. . . 60 D2
Manakara, Madag. . . . 37 J9
Manama = Al
  Manāmah, Bahrain . . 31 E6
Mananjary, Madag. . . 37 J9
Manaos = Manaus,
  Brazil 62 D7
Manapire →,
  Venezuela 62 B5
Manapouri, N.Z. 39 L1
Manapouri, L., N.Z. . . 39 L1
Manār, Jabal, Yemen . . 32 E3
Manas, China 24 B3
Manas →, India 29 F17
Manassa, U.S.A. 57 H11
Manaung, Burma 29 K18
Manaus, Brazil 62 D7
Manawan L., Canada . 51 B8
Manbij, Syria 30 B3
Manchegorsk, Russia . 20 C4
Manchester, U.K. 8 D5
Manchester, Ga., U.S.A. 53 J3
Manchester, Iowa,
  U.S.A. 54 D9
Manchester, Ky., U.S.A. 52 G4
Manchester, N.H.,
  U.S.A. 52 D10
Manchester, Tenn.,
  U.S.A. 53 H2
Manchester L., Canada 51 A7
Manchuria = Dongbei,
  China 25 B7
Mand →, Iran 31 D7
Mandal, Norway 7 G12
Mandala, Puncak,
  Indonesia 27 E10
Mandalay, Burma . . . 29 J20
Mandale = Mandalay,
  Burma 29 J20
Mandalī, Iraq 30 C5
Mandan, U.S.A. 54 B4
Mandar, Teluk,
  Indonesia 27 E5
Mandaue, Phil. 27 B6
Mandi, India 28 D10
Mandimba, Mozam. . . 37 G7
Mandioli, Indonesia . . 27 E7
Mandla, India 29 H12
Mandorah, Australia . . 40 B5
Mandritsara, Madag. . . 37 H9
Mandsaur, India 28 G9
Mandurah, Australia . . 41 F2
Mandvi, India 28 H6
Mandya, India 28 N10
Maneh, Iran 31 B8
Maneroo Cr. →,
  Australia 42 C3
Manfalût, Egypt 35 C12
Manfredónia, Italy . . 16 D6
Mangaung, S. Africa . . 37 K5
Mangawan, N.Z. 39 H5
Manggar, Indonesia . . 26 E3
Manggawitu, Indonesia 27 E8

Mangkalihat, Tanjung,
  Indonesia 27 D5
Mangla Dam, Pakistan 28 C8
Mangnai, China 24 C4
Mango, Togo 34 F6
Mangoche, Malawi . . . 37 G7
Mangoky →, Madag. . . 37 J8
Mangole, Indonesia . . 27 E6
Mangonui, N.Z. 39 F4
Mangueira, L. da, Brazil 64 C6
Mangum, U.S.A. 55 H5
Mangyshlak Poluostrov,
  Kazakstan 20 E6
Manhattan, U.S.A. . . . 54 F6
Manica, Mozam. 37 H6
Manicoré, Brazil 62 E6
Manicouagan →,
  Canada 49 C6
Manicouagan, Rés.,
  Canada 49 B6
Manifah, Si. Arabia . . 31 E6
Manifold, C., Australia 42 C5
Manigotagan, Canada . 51 C9
Manigotagan →,
  Canada 51 C9
Manihiki, Cook Is. . . . 45 J11
Manila, Phil. 27 B6
Manila, U.S.A. 56 F9
Manila B., Phil. 27 B6
Manilla, Australia 43 E5
Maningrida, Australia . 42 A1
Manipur □, India . . . 29 G19
Manipur →, Burma . . 29 H19
Manisa, Turkey 17 E12
Manistee, U.S.A. 52 C2
Manistee →, U.S.A. . . 52 C2
Manistique, U.S.A. . . 52 C2
Manito L., Canada . . 51 C7
Manitoba □, Canada . 51 B9
Manitoba, L., Canada . 51 C9
Manitou, Canada 51 D9
Manitou, L., Canada . . 49 B6
Manitou Is., U.S.A. . . 52 C3
Manitou Springs, U.S.A. 54 F2
Manitoulin I., Canada . 48 C3
Manitouwadge, Canada 48 C2
Manitowoc, U.S.A. . . 52 C2
Manizales, Colombia . 62 B3
Manjhand, Pakistan . . 28 G6
Manjil, Iran 31 B6
Manjimup, Australia . . 41 F2
Manjra →, India . . . 28 K10
Mankato, Kans., U.S.A. 54 F5
Mankato, Minn., U.S.A. 54 C8
Mankota, Canada . . . 51 D7
Manmad, India 28 J9
Mann Ranges, Australia 41 E5
Manna, Indonesia . . 26 E2
Mannahill, Australia . . 43 E3
Mannar, Sri Lanka . . 28 Q11
Mannar, G. of, Asia . . 28 Q11
Mannar, I., Sri Lanka . 28 Q11
Mannheim, Germany . . 12 D5
Manning, Canada . . . 50 B5
Manning, U.S.A. 53 J5
Manning Prov. Park,
  Canada 50 D4
Mannum, Australia 43 E2
Manono, Dem. Rep. of
  the Congo 36 F5
Manosque, France . . . 14 E6
Manouane →, Canada 49 C5
Manouane, L., Canada 49 B5
Manresa, Spain 15 B6
Mansa, Zambia 36 G5
Mansel I., Canada . . . 47 B11
Mansfield, Australia . . 43 F4
Mansfield, U.K. 8 D6
Mansfield, La., U.S.A. . 55 J8
Mansfield, Ohio, U.S.A. 52 E4
Manson Creek, Canada 50 B4
Manta, Ecuador 62 D2
Mantalingajan, Mt., Phil. 27 C5
Manteca, U.S.A. 57 H3
Manteo, U.S.A. 53 H8
Mantes-la-Jolie, France 14 B4
Manthani, India 28 K11
Manti, U.S.A. 56 G8
Mántova, Italy 16 B4
Manton, U.S.A. 52 C3
Mántova, Italy 16 B4
Mänttä, Finland 7 E21
Mantua = Mántova,
  Italy 16 B4
Manu, Peru 62 F4
Manu →, Peru 62 F4
Manua Is.,
  Amer. Samoa 39 B14
Manuel Alves →, Brazil 63 F9
Manui, Indonesia . . . 27 E6
Manukau, N.Z. 39 G5
Manuripi →, Bolivia . . 62 F5
Many, U.S.A. 55 K8
Manych-Gudilo, Ozero,
  Russia 19 E7
Manzai, Pakistan . . . 28 C7
Manzanares, Spain . . 15 C4
Manzanillo, Cuba . . . 60 B4
Manzanillo, Mexico . . 58 D4
Manzanillo, Pta.,
  Panama 60 E4
Manzano Mts., U.S.A. 57 J10
Manzariyeh, Iran . . . 31 C6
Manzhouli, China . . . 25 B6
Mao, Chad 35 F9

Maó, Spain 15 C8
Maoke, Pegunungan,
  Indonesia 27 E9
Maoming, China 25 D6
Mapam Yumco, China . 24 C3
Mapastepec, Mexico . . 59 D6
Mapia, Kepulauan,
  Indonesia 27 D8
Mapimí, Mexico 58 B4
Mapimí, Bolsón de,
  Mexico 58 B4
Maple Creek, Canada . 51 D7
Mapleton, U.S.A. . . . 56 D2
Mapuera →, Brazil . . 62 D7
Maputo, Mozam. 37 K6
Maqnā, Si. Arabia . . . 30 D2
Maquela do Zombo,
  Angola 36 F3
Maquinchao, Argentina 64 E3
Maquoketa, U.S.A. . . 54 D9
Mar Chiquita, L.,
  Argentina 64 C4
Mar del Plata, Argentina 64 D5
Mar Menor, Spain . . . 15 D5
Maraã, Brazil 62 D5
Marabá, Brazil 63 E9
Maracá, I. de, Brazil . . 63 C8
Maracaibo, Venezuela . 62 A4
Maracaibo, L. de,
  Venezuela 62 B4
Maracay, Venezuela . . 62 A5
Maradi, Niger 34 F7
Marāgheh, Iran 30 B5
Marāh, Si. Arabia . . . 30 E5
Marajó, I. de, Brazil . . 63 D9
Marākand, Iran 30 B5
Maralinga, Australia . . 41 F5
Marana, U.S.A. 57 K8
Maranboy, Australia . . 40 B5
Marand, Iran 30 B5
Maranguape, Brazil . . 63 D11
Maranhão = São Luís,
  Brazil 63 D10
Maranhão □, Brazil . . 63 E9
Maranoa →, Australia 43 D4
Marañón →, Peru . . . 62 D4
Marão, Mozam. 37 J6
Maraş =
  Kahramanmaraş,
  Turkey 19 G6
Marathon, Australia . . 42 C3
Marathon, Canada . . . 48 C2
Marathon, U.S.A. . . . 55 K3
Maratua, Indonesia . . 27 D5
Maravatío, Mexico . . . 58 D4
Marāwih, U.A.E. 31 E7
Marbella, Spain 15 D3
Marble Bar, Australia . 40 D2
Marble Falls, U.S.A. . . 55 K5
Marburg, Germany . . . 12 C5
March, U.K. 9 E8
Marche, France 14 C4
Marche-en-Famenne,
  Belgium 11 D5
Marchena, Spain . . . 15 D3
Marco, U.S.A. 53 N5
Marcus I. = Minami-
  Tori-Shima, Pac. Oc. 44 E7
Marcus Necker Ridge,
  Pac. Oc. 44 F9
Mardan, Pakistan . . . 28 B8
Mardin, Turkey 19 G7
Mareeba, Australia . . 42 B4
Marek = Stanke
  Dimitrov, Bulgaria . . 17 C10
Marengo, U.S.A. 54 E8
Marfa, U.S.A. 55 K2
Margaret →, Australia 40 C4
Margaret Bay, Canada 50 C3
Margaret L., Canada . 50 B5
Margaret River,
  Australia 41 F2
Margarita, I. de,
  Venezuela 62 A6
Margaritovo, Russia . . 22 C7
Margate, U.K. 9 F9
Mārgow, Dasht-e,
  Afghan. 28 D3
Marguerite, Canada . . 50 C4
Mari El □, Russia . . . 18 C8
Mari Republic = Mari
  El □, Russia 18 C8
Maria I., N. Terr.,
  Australia 42 A2
Maria I., Tas., Australia 42 G4
Maria van Diemen, C.,
  N.Z. 39 F4
Marian, Australia 42 C4
Marian L., Canada . . . 50 A5
Mariana Trench,
  Pac. Oc. 44 F6
Marianao, Cuba 60 B3
Marianna, Ark., U.S.A. 55 H9
Marianna, Fla., U.S.A. 53 K3
Marías, Is., Mexico . . 58 C3
Mariato, Punta, Panama 60 E3
Maribor, Slovenia . . . 9 E8
Maricopa, Ariz., U.S.A. 57 K7
Maricopa, Calif., U.S.A. 57 J4
Marié →, Brazil 62 D5
Marie Byrd Land,
  Antarctica 5 D14
Marie-Galante,
  Guadeloupe 61 C7

Mariecourt =
Kangiqsujuaq, Canada 47 B12
Mariembourg, Belgium 11 D4
Mariental, Namibia . . 37 J3
Mariestad, Sweden . . 7 G15
Marietta, Ga., U.S.A. . 53 J3
Marietta, Ohio, U.S.A. . 52 F5
Mariinsk, Russia . . . 20 D9
Marijampolė, Lithuania 7 J20
Marília, Brazil 63 H9
Marín, Spain 15 A1
Marinduque, Phil. . . . 27 B6
Marinette, U.S.A. . . . 52 C2
Maringá, Brazil 64 A6
Marion, Ala., U.S.A. . 53 J2
Marion, Ill., U.S.A. . . 55 G10
Marion, Ind., U.S.A. . . 52 E3
Marion, Iowa, U.S.A. . 54 D9
Marion, Kans., U.S.A. . 54 F6
Marion, N.C., U.S.A. . 53 H5
Marion, Ohio, U.S.A. . 52 E4
Marion, S.C., U.S.A. . 53 H6
Marion, Va., U.S.A. . . 53 G5
Marion, L., U.S.A. . . . 53 J5
Mariposa, U.S.A. 57 H4
Mariscal Estigarribia,
Paraguay 62 H6
Maritime Alps =
Maritimes, Alpes,
Europe 14 D7
Maritimes, Alpes,
Europe 14 D7
Maritsa = Évros →,
Bulgaria 17 D12
Mariupol, Ukraine . . 19 E6
Marīvān, Iran 30 C5
Marj 'Uyūn, Lebanon . . 33 B4
Markazī □, Iran 31 C6
Marked Tree, U.S.A. . 55 H9
Market Drayton, U.K. . . 8 E5
Market Harborough,
U.K. 9 E7
Market Rasen, U.K. . . . 8 D7
Markham, Mt.,
Antarctica 5 E11
Markovo, Russia 21 C17
Marks, Russia 18 D8
Marksville, U.S.A. . . . 55 K8
Marla, Australia 43 D1
Marlborough, Australia 42 C4
Marlborough, U.K. 9 F6
Marlborough Downs,
U.K. 9 F6
Marlin, U.S.A. 55 K6
Marlow, U.S.A. 55 H6
Marmagao, India . . . 28 M8
Marmara, Turkey . . . 17 D12
Marmara, Sea of =
Marmara Denizi,
Turkey 17 D13
Marmara Denizi, Turkey 17 D13
Marmaris, Turkey . . . 17 F13
Marmion, Mt., Australia 41 E2
Marmion L., Canada . . 48 C1
Marmolada, Mte., Italy 16 A4
Marmora, Canada 48 D4
Marne →, France . . . 14 B5
Maroantsetra, Madag. . 37 H9
Marondera, Zimbabwe 37 H6
Maroni →, Fr. Guiana 63 B8
Maroochydore, Australia 43 D5
Maroona, Australia . . 43 F3
Maroua, Cameroon . . 35 F8
Marovoay, Madag. . . . 37 H9
Marquesas Is. =
Marquises, Is.,
Pac. Oc. 45 H14
Marquette, U.S.A. . . . 52 B2
Marquises, Is., Pac. Oc. 45 H14
Marra, Djebel, Sudan . 35 F10
Marrakech, Morocco . . 34 B4
Marrawah, Australia . . 42 G3
Marree, Australia 43 D2
Marrero, U.S.A. 55 L9
Marrowie Cr. →,
Australia 43 E4
Marrupa, Mozam. . . . 37 G7
Mars Hill, U.S.A. . . . 53 B12
Marsá Matrûh, Egypt . 35 B11
Marsabit, Kenya 36 D7
Marsala, Italy 16 F5
Marsden, Australia . . 43 E4
Marseille, France . . . 14 E6
Marseilles = Marseille,
France 14 E6
Marsh I., U.S.A. 55 L9
Marshall, Ark., U.S.A. . 55 H8
Marshall, Mich., U.S.A. 52 D3
Marshall, Minn., U.S.A. 54 C7
Marshall, Mo., U.S.A. . 54 F8
Marshall, Tex., U.S.A. . 55 J7
Marshall →, Australia 42 C2
Marshall Is. ■, Pac. Oc. 38 A10
Marshalltown, U.S.A. . 54 D8
Marshfield, Mo., U.S.A. 55 G8
Marshfield, Wis., U.S.A. 54 C9
Marshün, Iran 31 B6
Märsta, Sweden 7 G17
Mart, U.S.A. 55 K6
Martaban, Burma . . . 29 L20
Martaban, G. of, Burma 29 L20
Martapura, Kalimantan,
Indonesia 26 E4
Martapura, Sumatera,
Indonesia 26 E2

Martelange, Belgium . . 11 E5
Martha's Vineyard,
U.S.A. 52 E10
Martigny, Switz. 14 C7
Martigues, France . . . 14 E6
Martin, Slovak Rep. . . 13 D10
Martin, S. Dak., U.S.A. . 54 D4
Martin, Tenn., U.S.A. . 55 G10
Martin, L., U.S.A. . . . 53 J3
Martina Franca, Italy . 16 D7
Martinborough, N.Z. . 39 J5
Martinez, U.S.A. 53 J4
Martinique ■, W. Indies 61 D7
Martinique Passage,
W. Indies 61 C7
Martins Ferry, U.S.A. . 52 E5
Martinsburg, U.S.A. . . 52 F7
Martinsville, Ind., U.S.A. 52 F2
Martinsville, Va., U.S.A. 53 G6
Marton, N.Z. 39 J5
Martos, Spain 15 D4
Marudi, Malaysia . . . 26 D4
Ma'ruf, Afghan. 28 D5
Marugame, Japan . . . 23 G6
Marv Dasht, Iran . . . 31 D7
Marvast, Iran 31 D7
Marvel Loch, Australia 41 F2
Marwar, India 28 G8
Mary, Turkmenistan . . 20 F7
Maryborough = Port
Laoise, Ireland . . . 10 E3
Maryborough, Queens.,
Australia 43 D5
Maryborough, Vic.,
Australia 43 F3
Maryfield, Canada . . . 51 D8
Maryland □, U.S.A. . . 52 F7
Maryport, U.K. 8 C4
Mary's Harbour, Canada 49 B8
Marystown, Canada . . 49 C8
Marysville, Canada . . 50 D5
Marysville, Calif., U.S.A. 56 G3
Marysville, Kans., U.S.A. 54 F6
Marysville, Ohio, U.S.A. 52 E4
Maryville, Mo., U.S.A. . 54 E7
Maryville, Tenn., U.S.A. 53 H4
Marzūq, Libya 35 C8
Masaka, Uganda 36 E6
Masalembo, Kepulauan,
Indonesia 26 F4
Masalima, Kepulauan,
Indonesia 26 F5
Masamba, Indonesia . . 27 E6
Masan, S. Korea 25 C7
Masandam, Ra's, Oman 31 E8
Masasi, Tanzania 36 G7
Masaya, Nic. 60 D2
Masbate, Phil. 27 B6
Mascara, Algeria 34 A4
Mascota, Mexico 58 C4
Masela, Indonesia . . . 27 F7
Maseru, Lesotho 37 K5
Mashābih, Si. Arabia . . 30 E3
Mashhad, Iran 31 B8
Mashiz, Iran 31 D8
Māshkel, Hāmūn-i-,
Pakistan 28 E3
Mashki Chāh, Pakistan 28 E3
Mashonaland,
Zimbabwe 37 H6
Masindi, Uganda 36 D6
Maşīrah, Oman 32 C6
Maşīrah, Khalīj, Oman 32 C6
Masjed Soleyman, Iran 31 D6
Mask, L., Ireland 10 E2
Maskin, Oman 31 F8
Masoala, Tanjon' i,
Madag. 37 H10
Masohi = Amahai,
Indonesia 27 E7
Mason, U.S.A. 55 K5
Mason City, U.S.A. . . . 54 D8
Masqat, Oman 32 C6
Massa, Italy 14 D9
Massachusetts □, U.S.A. 52 D10
Massakory, Chad 35 F9
Massangena, Mozam. . 37 J6
Massango, Angola . . . 36 F3
Massawa = Mitsiwa,
Eritrea 32 D2
Massena, U.S.A. 52 C8
Massénya, Chad 35 F9
Masset, Canada 50 C2
Massif Central, France . 14 D5
Massillon, U.S.A. 52 E5
Massinga, Mozam. . . . 37 J7
Masson I., Antarctica . 5 C7
Mastanli =
Momchilgrad,
Bulgaria 17 D11
Masterton, N.Z. 39 J5
Mastuj, Pakistan 28 A8
Mastung, Pakistan . . . 28 E2
Masty, Belarus 13 B13
Masuda, Japan 23 G5
Masvingo, Zimbabwe . 37 J6
Maşyāf, Syria 30 C3
Matabeleland,
Zimbabwe 37 H5
Matachewan, Canada . 48 C3
Matadi, Dem. Rep. of
the Congo 36 F2
Matagalpa, Nic. 60 D2
Matagami, Canada . . 48 C4
Matagami, L., Canada . 48 C4

Matagorda B., U.S.A. . 55 L6
Matagorda I., U.S.A. . . 55 L6
Matak, Indonesia . . . 26 D3
Matam, Senegal 34 E3
Matamoros, Campeche,
Mexico 59 D6
Matamoros, Coahuila,
Mexico 58 B4
Matamoros,
Tamaulipas, Mexico . 59 B5
Ma'tan as Sarra, Libya 35 D10
Matane, Canada 49 C6
Matanzas, Cuba 60 B3
Matapan, C. = Taínaron,
Ákra, Greece 17 F10
Matapédia, Canada . . 49 C6
Matara, Sri Lanka . . . 28 S12
Mataram, Indonesia . . 26 F5
Matarani, Peru 62 G4
Mataranka, Australia . 40 B5
Matarma, Râs, Egypt . 33 E1
Mataró, Spain 15 B7
Mataura, N.Z. 39 M2
Matehuala, Mexico . . 58 C4
Matera, Italy 16 D7
Mathráki, Greece . . . 17 E8
Mathura, India 28 F10
Mati, Phil. 27 C7
Matías Romero, Mexico 59 D5
Matiri Ra., N.Z. 39 J4
Matlock, U.K. 8 D6
Mato Grosso □, Brazil 63 F8
Mato Grosso, Planalto
do, Brazil 63 G8
Mato Grosso do Sul □,
Brazil 63 G8
Matochkin Shar, Russia 20 B6
Matosinhos, Portugal . 15 B1
Matruḥ, Oman 32 C6
Matsue, Japan 23 G6
Matsumae, Japan . . . 22 D10
Matsumoto, Japan . . . 23 F9
Matsusaka, Japan . . . 23 G8
Matsuura, Japan 23 H4
Matsuyama, Japan . . . 23 H6
Mattagami →, Canada 48 B3
Mattancheri, India . . . 28 Q10
Mattawa, Canada . . . 48 C4
Matterhorn, Switz. . . . 14 D7
Matthew Town,
Bahamas 61 B5
Matthew's Ridge,
Guyana 62 B6
Mattice, Canada 48 C3
Mattō, Japan 23 F8
Mattoon, U.S.A. 52 F1
Matucana, Peru 62 F3
Matun = Khowst,
Afghan. 28 C6
Maturín, Venezuela . . 62 B6
Mau Ranipur, India . . 28 G11
Maubeuge, France . . . 14 A6
Maud, Pt., Australia . . 40 D1
Maude, Australia 43 E3
Maudin Sun, Burma . . 29 M19
Maués, Brazil 62 D7
Mauganj, India 29 G12
Maughold Hd., U.K. . . . 8 C3
Maulamyaing =
Moulmein, Burma . 29 L20
Maumee, U.S.A. 52 E4
Maumee →, U.S.A. . . 52 E4
Maumere, Indonesia . 27 F6
Maun, Botswana 37 H4
Maungmagan Kyunzu,
Burma 26 B1
Maupin, U.S.A. 56 D3
Maurepas, L., U.S.A. . 55 K9
Maurice, L., Australia . 41 E5
Mauricie, Parc Nat. de
la, Canada 48 C5
Mauritania ■, Africa . 34 E3
Mauritius ■, Ind. Oc. . 3 F12
Mauston, U.S.A. 54 D9
Mawk Mai, Burma . . . 29 J20
Mawlaik, Burma 29 H19
Mawlamyine =
Moulmein, Burma . 29 L20
Mawqaq, Si. Arabia . . 30 E4
Mawson Coast,
Antarctica 5 C6
Max, U.S.A. 54 B4
Maxcanú, Mexico . . . 59 C6
Maxhamish L., Canada 50 B4
Maxwelton, Australia . 42 C3
May, C., U.S.A. 52 F8
May Pen, Jamaica . . . 60 a
Maya →, Russia . . . 21 D14
Maya Mts., Belize . . . 59 D7
Mayaguana, Bahamas . 61 B5
Mayagüez, Puerto Rico 61 C6
Mayamey, Iran 31 B7
Mayanup, Australia . . 41 F2
Mayapan, Mexico . . . 59 C7
Mayari, Cuba 61 B4
Maybell, U.S.A. 56 F9
Maydan, Iraq 30 C5
Maydena, Australia . . 42 G4
Mayenne →, France . 14 C3
Mayer, U.S.A. 57 J7
Mayerthorpe, Canada . 50 C5
Mayfield, U.S.A. 53 G1
Mayhill, U.S.A. 57 K11
Maykop, Russia 19 F7

Maynard Hills, Australia 41 E2
Mayne →, Australia . . 42 C3
Mayo, Canada 46 B6
Mayon Volcano, Phil. . . 27 B6
Mayor I., N.Z. 39 G6
Mayotte, Ind. Oc. . . . 37 G9
Maysville, U.S.A. 52 F4
Mayu, Indonesia 27 D7
Mayville, U.S.A. 54 B6
Mayya, Russia 21 C14
Mazabuka, Zambia . . 37 H5
Mazagán = El Jadida,
Morocco 34 B4
Mazagão, Brazil 63 D8
Mazán, Peru 62 D4
Māzandarān □, Iran . . 31 B7
Mazapil, Mexico 58 C4
Mazara del Vallo, Italy . 16 F5
Mazarrón, Spain 15 D5
Mazaruni →, Guyana 62 B7
Mazatán, Mexico . . . 58 B2
Mazatenango,
Guatemala 60 D1
Mazatlán, Mexico . . . 58 C3
Mažeikiai, Lithuania . . 7 H20
Māzhān, Iran 31 C8
Mazinān, Iran 31 B8
Mazoe →, Mozam. . . 37 H6
Mazurian Lakes =
Mazurski, Pojezierze,
Poland 13 B11
Mazurski, Pojezierze,
Poland 13 B11
Mazyr, Belarus 13 B15
Mbabane, Swaziland . 37 K6
Mbaïki, C.A.R. 36 D3
Mbala, Zambia 36 F6
Mbale, Uganda 36 D6
Mbalmayo, Cameroon . 36 D2
Mbandaka, Dem. Rep. of
the Congo 36 D3
Mbanza Congo, Angola 36 F2
Mbanza Ngungu,
Dem. Rep. of
the Congo 36 F2
Mbarara, Uganda . . . 36 E6
Mbeya, Tanzania 36 F6
Mbini □, Eq. Guin. . . 36 D2
Mbour, Senegal 34 F2
Mbuji-Mayi, Dem. Rep.
of the Congo 36 F4
Mdantsane, S. Africa . 37 L5
Mead, L., U.S.A. 57 H6
Meade, U.S.A. 55 G4
Meadow Lake, Canada 51 C7
Meadow Lake Prov.
Park, Canada 51 C7
Meadow Valley
Wash →, U.S.A. . . 57 H6
Meadville, U.S.A. . . . 52 E5
Meaford, Canada . . . 48 D3
Mealy Mts., Canada . . 49 B8
Meander River, Canada 50 B5
Meares, C., U.S.A. . . . 56 D2
Mearim →, Brazil . . . 63 D10
Meath □, Ireland . . . 10 E3
Meath Park, Canada . . 51 C7
Meaux, France 14 B5
Mebechi-Gawa →,
Japan 22 D10
Mecca = Makkah,
Si. Arabia 32 C2
Mechelen, Belgium . . 11 C4
Mecheria, Algeria . . . 34 B5
Mecklenburg, Germany 12 B7
Mecklenburger Bucht,
Germany 12 A6
Medan, Indonesia . . . 26 D1
Medanosa, Pta.,
Argentina 64 F3
Médéa, Algeria 34 A6
Medellín, Colombia . . 62 B3
Medelpad, Sweden . . 7 E17
Medemblik, Neths. . . 11 B5
Medford, Oreg., U.S.A. 56 E2
Medford, Wis., U.S.A. . 54 C9
Medgidia, Romania . . 13 F15
Mediaş, Romania . . . 13 E13
Medicine Bow, U.S.A. . 56 F10
Medicine Bow Pk.,
U.S.A. 56 F10
Medicine Bow Ra.,
U.S.A. 56 F10
Medicine Hat, Canada . 51 D6
Medicine Lake, U.S.A. . 54 A2
Medicine Lodge, U.S.A. 55 G5
Medina = Al Madīnah,
Si. Arabia 30 E3
Medina, N. Dak., U.S.A. 54 B5
Medina, N.Y., U.S.A. . 52 D6
Medina, Ohio, U.S.A. . 52 E5
Medina →, U.S.A. . . 55 L5
Medina del Campo,
Spain 15 B3
Medina L., U.S.A. . . . 55 L5
Medina Sidonia, Spain 15 D3
Medinipur, India 29 H15
Mediterranean Sea,
Europe 3 C10
Mediterranean Sea,
Europe 3 C10
Médoc, France 14 D3
Medveditsa →, Russia 19 E7
Medvezhi, Ostrava,
Russia 21 B17
Medvezhyegorsk, Russia 18 B5

Medway □, U.K. 9 F8
Medway →, U.K. 9 F8
Meekatharra, Australia 41 E2
Meeker, U.S.A. 56 F10
Meerut, India 28 E10
Meeteetse, U.S.A. . . . 56 D9
Mega, Ethiopia 32 G2
Mégara, Greece 17 F10
Meghalaya □, India . . 29 G17
Mégiscane, L., Canada 48 C4
Meharry, Mt., Australia 40 D2
Mehlville, U.S.A. 54 F9
Mehr Jān, Iran 31 C7
Mehrābād, Iran 30 B5
Mehrān, Iran 30 C5
Mehrīz, Iran 31 D7
Meiktila, Burma 29 J19
Meissen, Germany . . 12 C7
Meizhou, China 25 D6
Mejillones, Chile 64 A2
Mekele, Ethiopia 32 E2
Mekhtar, Pakistan . . . 28 D6
Meknès, Morocco . . . 34 B4
Mekong →, Asia 26 C3
Mekongga, Indonesia . 27 E6
Mekvari = Kür →,
Azerbaijan 19 G8
Melagiri Hills, India . . 28 N10
Melaka, Malaysia . . . 26 D2
Melalap, Malaysia . . . 26 C5
Melanesia, Pac. Oc. . . 44 H7
Melbourne, Australia . 43 F4
Melbourne, U.S.A. . . . 53 L5
Melchor Múzquiz,
Mexico 58 B4
Melchor Ocampo,
Mexico 58 C4
Mélèzes →, Qué.,
Canada 47 C12
Mélèzes →, Qué.,
Canada 48 A5
Melfort, Canada 51 C8
Melhus, Norway 6 E14
Melilla, N. Afr. 15 E4
Melita, Canada 51 D8
Melitopol, Ukraine . . 19 E6
Melk, Austria 12 D8
Mellansel, Sweden . . 6 E18
Mellen, U.S.A. 54 B9
Mellerud, Sweden . . . 7 G15
Mellette, U.S.A. 54 C5
Melo, Uruguay 64 C6
Melolo, Indonesia . . . 27 F6
Melrose, Australia . . . 43 E4
Melrose, Minn., U.S.A. 54 C7
Melrose, N. Mex., U.S.A. 55 H3
Melstone, U.S.A. 56 C10
Melton Mowbray, U.K. . 9 E7
Melun, France 14 B5
Melville, Canada 51 C8
Melville, C., Australia . 42 A3
Melville, L., Canada . . 49 B8
Melville B., Australia . 42 A2
Melville I., Australia . . 40 B5
Melville I., Canada . . . 4 B2
Melville Pen., Canada . 47 B11
Memboro, Indonesia . 27 F5
Memel = Klaipėda,
Lithuania 7 J19
Memmingen, Germany 12 E6
Mempawah, Indonesia 26 D3
Memphis, Tenn., U.S.A. 55 H10
Memphis, Tex., U.S.A. . 55 H4
Mena, U.S.A. 55 H7
Menai Strait, U.K. 8 D3
Ménaka, Mali 34 E6
Menan = Chao
Phraya →, Thailand 26 B2
Menard, U.S.A. 55 K5
Mendawai →,
Indonesia 26 E4
Mende, France 14 D5
Mendez, Mexico 59 B5
Mendip Hills, U.K. . . . 9 F5
Mendocino, U.S.A. . . 56 G2
Mendocino, C., U.S.A. 56 F1
Mendooran, Australia . 43 E4
Mendota, Calif., U.S.A. 57 H3
Mendota, Ill., U.S.A. . 54 E10
Mendoza, Argentina . 64 C3
Mene Grande,
Venezuela 62 B4
Menemen, Turkey . . . 17 E12
Menen, Belgium 11 D3
Menggala, Indonesia . 26 E3
Mengzi, China 24 D5
Menihek, Canada . . . 49 B6
Menihek L., Canada . . 49 B6
Menin = Menen,
Belgium 11 D3
Menindee, Australia . . 43 E3
Menindee L., Australia 43 E3
Meningie, Australia . . 43 F2
Menominee, U.S.A. . . 52 C2
Menominee →, U.S.A. 52 C2
Menomonie, U.S.A. . . 54 C9
Menongue, Angola . . 37 G3
Menorca, Spain 15 C8
Mentawai, Kepulauan,
Indonesia 26 E1
Menton, France 14 E7
Mentor, U.S.A. 52 E5
Menzelinsk, Russia . . 18 C9
Menzies, Australia . . 41 E3

Me'ona, Israel 33 B4
Meoqui, Mexico 58 B3
Meppel, Neths. 11 B6
Merabéllou, Kólpos,
Greece 17 G11
Merak, Indonesia . . . 27 F12
Meramangye, L.,
Australia 41 E5
Meran = Merano, Italy 16 A4
Merano, Italy 16 A4
Merauke, Indonesia . . 27 F10
Merbein, Australia . . . 43 E3
Merca, Somali Rep. . . 32 G3
Merced, U.S.A. 57 H3
Mercedes,
Buenos Aires,
Argentina 64 C5
Mercedes, Corrientes,
Argentina 64 B5
Mercedes, San Luis,
Argentina 64 C3
Mercedes, Uruguay . . 64 C5
Mercedes, U.S.A. . . . 55 M6
Mercer, N.Z. 39 G5
Mercy, C., Canada . . . 47 B13
Mere, U.K. 9 F5
Meredith, C., Falk. Is. . 64 G4
Meredith, L., U.S.A. . . 55 H4
Mergui, Burma 26 B1
Mergui Arch. = Myeik
Kyunzu, Burma . . . 26 B1
Mérida, Mexico 59 C7
Mérida, Spain 15 C2
Mérida, Venezuela . . 62 B4
Mérida, Cord. de,
Venezuela 62 B4
Mérida, Cord. de,
Venezuela 62 B4
Meriden, U.K. 9 E6
Meriden, U.S.A. 52 E9
Meridian, Idaho, U.S.A. 56 E5
Meridian, Miss., U.S.A. 53 J1
Merimbula, Australia . 43 F4
Merinda, Australia . . 42 C4
Meringur, Australia . . 43 E3
Merir, Pac. Oc. 27 D8
Meriruma, Brazil 63 C8
Merkel, U.S.A. 55 J5
Mermaid Reef, Australia 40 C2
Merredin, Australia . . 41 F2
Merrill, Oreg., U.S.A. . 56 E3
Merrill, Wis., U.S.A. . . 54 C10
Merriman, U.S.A. . . . 54 D4
Merritt, Canada 50 C4
Merritt Island, U.S.A. . 53 L5
Merriwa, Australia . . . 43 E5
Merry I., Canada 48 A4
Merryville, U.S.A. . . . 55 K8
Mersch, Lux. 11 E6
Mersea I., U.K. 9 F8
Merseburg, Germany . 12 C6
Mersey →, U.K. 8 D4
Merseyside □, U.K. . . . 8 D4
Mersin, Turkey 19 G5
Mersing, Malaysia . . . 26 D2
Merthyr Tydfil, U.K. . . . 9 F4
Merthyr Tydfil □, U.K. . 9 F4
Mértola, Portugal . . . 15 D2
Mertzon, U.S.A. 55 K4
Meru, Kenya 36 D7
Meru, Tanzania 36 E7
Mesa, U.S.A. 57 K8
Mesa Verde National
Park, U.S.A. 57 H9
Mesgouez, L., Canada 48 B5
Meshed = Mashhad,
Iran 31 B8
Mesilinka →, Canada 50 B4
Mesilla, U.S.A. 57 K10
Mesolóngion, Greece . 17 E9
Mesopotamia = Al
Jazirah, Iraq 30 C5
Mesquite, U.S.A. 57 H6
Messad, Algeria 34 B6
Messina, Italy 16 E6
Messina, S. Africa . . . 37 J6
Messina, Str. di, Italy . 16 F6
Messíni, Greece 17 F10
Messiniakós Kólpos,
Greece 17 F10
Mesta →, Bulgaria . . 17 D11
Meta →, S. Amer. . . 62 B5
Meta Incognita
Peninsula, Canada . 47 B13
Metabetchouan, Canada 49 C5
Metairie, U.S.A. 55 L9
Metaline Falls, U.S.A. . 56 B5
Metán, Argentina . . . 64 B3
Methven, N.Z. 39 K3
Metlakatla, U.S.A. . . . 46 C6
Metropolis, U.S.A. . . . 55 G10
Metu, Ethiopia 32 F2
Metz, France 14 B7
Meulaboh, Indonesia . 26 D1
Meureudu, Indonesia . 26 C1
Meuse →, Europe . . 14 A6
Mexia, U.S.A. 55 K6
Mexiana, I., Brazil . . . 63 D9
Mexicali, Mexico . . . 58 A1
Mexican Water, U.S.A. 57 H9
México, Mexico 59 D5
México, U.S.A. 54 F9
México □, Mexico . . . 59 D5
Mexico ■, Cent. Amer. 58 C4

Mexico, G. of

Mexico, G. of, Cent. Amer. 59 C7
Meydān-e Naftūn, Iran 31 D6
Meydani, Ra's-e, Iran 31 E8
Meymaneh, Afghan. 28 B4
Mezen, Russia 18 A7
Mezen →, Russia 18 A7
Mézenc, Mt., France 14 D6
Mezhdurechenskiy, Russia 20 D7
Mezőkövesd, Hungary 13 E11
Mezőtúr, Hungary 13 E11
Mezquital, Mexico 58 C4
Mhow, India 28 H9
Miahuatlán, Mexico 59 D5
Miami, Fla., U.S.A. 53 N5
Miami, Okla., U.S.A. 55 G7
Miami, Tex., U.S.A. 55 H4
Miami Beach, U.S.A. 53 N5
Miāndarreh, Iran 31 C7
Miāndowāb, Iran 30 B5
Miandrivazo, Madag. 37 H9
Miāneh, Iran 30 B5
Mianwali, Pakistan 28 C7
Miass, Russia 18 D11
Michalovce, Slovak Rep. 13 D11
Michigan □, U.S.A. 52 C3
Michigan, L., U.S.A. 52 D2
Michigan City, U.S.A. 52 E2
Michipicoten I., Canada 48 C2
Michoacan □, Mexico 58 D4
Michurin, Bulgaria 17 C12
Michurinsk, Russia 18 D7
Mico, Pta., Nic. 60 D3
Micronesia, Pac. Oc. 44 G7
Micronesia, Federated States of ■, Pac. Oc. 38 A8
Midai, Indonesia 26 D3
Midale, Canada 51 D8
Middelburg, Neths. 11 C3
Middelburg, S. Africa 37 L5
Middle Alkali L., U.S.A. 56 F3
Middle I., Australia 41 F3
Middle Loup →, U.S.A. 54 E5
Middle Sackville, Canada 49 D7
Middleburg, U.S.A. 53 K5
Middlebury, U.S.A. 52 C9
Middlemount, Australia 42 C4
Middleport, U.S.A. 52 F4
Middlesboro, U.S.A. 53 G4
Middlesbrough, U.K. 8 C6
Middlesbrough □, U.K. 8 C6
Middlesex, Belize 60 C2
Middleton, Australia 42 C3
Middleton, Canada 49 D6
Middleton Cr. →, Australia 42 C3
Middletown, N.Y., U.S.A. 52 E8
Middletown, Ohio, U.S.A. 52 F3
Midhurst, U.K. 9 G7
Midi, Canal du →, France 14 E4
Midland, Canada 48 D4
Midland, Mich., U.S.A. 52 D3
Midland, Tex., U.S.A. 55 K3
Midlothian, U.S.A. 55 J6
Midway Is., Pac. Oc. 44 E10
Midwest, U.S.A. 56 E10
Midwest City, U.S.A. 55 H6
Midyat, Turkey 30 B4
Midzŏr, Bulgaria 17 C10
Mie □, Japan 23 G8
Międzychód, Poland 12 B8
Międzyrzec Podlaski, Poland 13 C12
Mielec, Poland 13 C11
Miercurea-Ciuc, Romania 13 E13
Mieres, Spain 15 A3
Mifraz Hefa, Israel 33 C4
Miguel Alemán, Presa, Mexico 59 D5
Mihara, Japan 23 G6
Mikhaylovgrad = Montana, Bulgaria 17 C10
Mikhaylovka, Russia 19 D7
Mikkeli, Finland 7 F22
Mikkwa →, Canada 50 B6
Mikonos, Greece 17 F11
Mikun, Russia 18 B9
Milaca, U.S.A. 54 C8
Milagro, Ecuador 62 D3
Milan = Milano, Italy 14 D8
Milan, Mo., U.S.A. 54 E8
Milan, Tenn., U.S.A. 53 H1
Milang, Australia 43 F2
Milano, Italy 14 D8
Milâs, Turkey 17 F12
Milazzo, Italy 16 E6
Milbank, U.S.A. 54 C6
Milbanke Sd., Canada 50 C3
Milden, Canada 51 C7
Mildenhall, U.K. 9 E8
Mildura, Australia 43 E3
Miles, Australia 43 D5
Miles City, U.S.A. 54 B2
Milestone, Canada 51 D8
Miletus, Turkey 17 F12
Milford, Del., U.S.A. 52 F8
Milford, Utah, U.S.A. 57 G7
Milford Haven, U.K. 9 F2
Milford Sd., N.Z. 39 L1
Milḩ, Baḩr al, Iraq 30 C4
Milikapiti, Australia 40 B5
Miling, Australia 41 F2
Milk →, U.S.A. 56 B10
Milk River, Canada 50 D6
Mill I., Antarctica 5 C8
Millau, France 14 D5
Mille Lacs, L. des, Canada 48 C1
Mille Lacs L., U.S.A. 54 B8
Milledgeville, U.S.A. 53 J4
Millen, U.S.A. 53 J5
Miller, U.S.A. 54 C5
Millicent, Australia 43 F3
Millington, U.S.A. 55 H10
Millinocket, U.S.A. 53 C11
Millmerran, Australia 43 D5
Millom, U.K. 8 C4
Mills L., Canada 50 A5
Millville, U.S.A. 52 F8
Millwood L., U.S.A. 55 J8
Milne →, Australia 42 C2
Milo, U.S.A. 53 C11
Milos, Greece 17 F11
Milparinka, Australia 43 D3
Milton, Canada 49 D7
Milton, N.Z. 39 M2
Milton, Fla., U.S.A. 53 K2
Milton, Pa., U.S.A. 52 E7
Milton-Freewater, U.S.A. 56 D4
Milton Keynes, U.K. 9 E7
Milton Keynes □, U.K. 9 E7
Milwaukee, U.S.A. 52 D2
Milwaukee Deep, Atl. Oc. 61 C6
Milwaukie, U.S.A. 56 D2
Min Jiang →, Fujian, China 25 D6
Min Jiang →, Sichuan, China 24 D5
Mīnā Su'ud, Si. Arabia 31 D6
Mīnā'al Aḩmadī, Kuwait 31 D6
Minago →, Canada 51 C9
Minaki, Canada 51 D10
Minamata, Japan 23 H5
Minami-Tori-Shima, Pac. Oc. 44 E7
Minas, Uruguay 64 C5
Minas, Sierra de las, Guatemala 60 C2
Minas Basin, Canada 49 C7
Minas Gerais □, Brazil 63 G9
Minatitlán, Mexico 59 D6
Minbu, Burma 29 J19
Mindanao, Phil. 27 C6
Mindanao Sea = Bohol Sea, Phil. 27 C6
Mindanao Trench, Pac. Oc. 27 B7
Minden, Germany 12 B5
Minden, La., U.S.A. 55 J8
Minden, Nev., U.S.A. 56 G4
Mindiptana, Indonesia 27 F10
Mindoro, Phil. 27 B6
Mindoro Str., Phil. 27 B6
Mine, Japan 23 G5
Minehead, U.K. 9 F4
Mineola, U.S.A. 55 J7
Mineral Wells, U.S.A. 55 J5
Mingäçevir Su Anbarı, Azerbaijan 19 F8
Mingan, Canada 49 B7
Mingechaurskoye Vdkhr. = Mingäçevir Su Anbarı, Azerbaijan 19 F8
Mingela, Australia 42 B4
Mingenew, Australia 41 E2
Mingera Cr. →, Australia 42 C2
Mingin, Burma 29 H19
Minho = Miño →, Spain 15 A2
Minho, Portugal 15 B1
Minidoka, U.S.A. 56 E7
Minigwal, L., Australia 41 E3
Minilya →, Australia 41 D1
Minilya Roadhouse, Australia 41 D1
Minipi L., Canada 49 B7
Mink L., Canada 50 A5
Minna, Nigeria 34 G7
Minneapolis, Kans., U.S.A. 54 F6
Minneapolis, Minn., U.S.A. 54 C8
Minnedosa, Canada 51 C9
Minnesota □, U.S.A. 54 B8
Minnesota →, U.S.A. 54 C8
Minnewaukan, U.S.A. 54 A5
Minnipa, Australia 43 E2
Minnitaki L., Canada 48 C1
Mino, Japan 23 G8
Miño →, Spain 15 A2
Minorca = Menorca, Spain 15 C8
Minot, U.S.A. 54 A4
Minsk, Belarus 13 B14
Mińsk Mazowiecki, Poland 13 B11
Mintabie, Australia 43 D1
Minto, Canada 49 C6
Minto, L., Canada 48 A5
Minton, Canada 51 D8
Minturn, U.S.A. 56 G10
Minusinsk, Russia 21 D10
Minutang, India 29 E20
Miquelon, Canada 48 C4
Miquelon, St- P. & M. 49 C8
Mīr Kūh, Iran 31 E8
Mīr Shahdād, Iran 31 E8
Mira, Italy 16 B5
Mira por vos Cay, Bahamas 61 B5
Miraj, India 28 L9
Miram Shah, Pakistan 28 C7
Miramichi, Canada 49 C6
Miramichi B., Canada 49 C7
Miranda, Brazil 63 H7
Miranda →, Brazil 62 G7
Miranda de Ebro, Spain 15 A4
Miranda do Douro, Portugal 15 B2
Mirbāţ, Oman 32 D5
Miri, Malaysia 26 D4
Miriam Vale, Australia 42 C5
Mirim, L., S. Amer. 64 C6
Mirnyy, Russia 21 C12
Mirond L., Canada 51 B8
Mirpur Khas, Pakistan 28 G6
Mirtağ, Turkey 30 B4
Mirzapur, India 29 G13
Mirzapur-cum-Vindhyachal = Mirzapur, India 29 G13
Misantla, Mexico 59 D5
Misawa, Japan 22 D10
Miscou I., Canada 49 C7
Mish'āb, Ra's al, Si. Arabia 31 D6
Mishan, China 25 B8
Mishawaka, U.S.A. 52 E2
Mishima, Japan 23 G9
Miskah, Si. Arabia 30 E4
Miskitos, Cayos, Nic. 60 D3
Miskolc, Hungary 13 D11
Misool, Indonesia 27 E8
Misrātah, Libya 35 B9
Missanabie, Canada 48 C3
Missinaibi →, Canada 48 B3
Missinaibi L., Canada 48 C3
Mission, Canada 50 D4
Mission, S. Dak., U.S.A. 54 D4
Mission, Tex., U.S.A. 55 M5
Mission Beach, Australia 42 B4
Mission Viejo, U.S.A. 57 K5
Missisa L., Canada 48 B2
Missisicabi →, Canada 48 B4
Mississagi →, Canada 48 C3
Mississippi □, U.S.A. 55 J10
Mississippi →, U.S.A. 55 L10
Mississippi River Delta, U.S.A. 55 L9
Mississippi Sd., U.S.A. 55 K10
Missoula, U.S.A. 56 C7
Missouri □, U.S.A. 54 F8
Missouri →, U.S.A. 54 F9
Missouri City, U.S.A. 55 L7
Missouri Valley, U.S.A. 54 E7
Mistassibi →, Canada 49 B5
Mistassini, Canada 49 C5
Mistassini →, Canada 49 C5
Mistassini, L., Canada 48 B5
Mistastin L., Canada 49 A7
Mistinibi, L., Canada 49 A7
Misty L., Canada 51 B8
Misurata = Misrātah, Libya 35 B9
Mitchell, Australia 43 D4
Mitchell, Nebr., U.S.A. 54 E3
Mitchell, Oreg., U.S.A. 56 D3
Mitchell, S. Dak., U.S.A. 54 D6
Mitchell →, Australia 42 B3
Mitchell, Mt., U.S.A. 53 H4
Mitchell Ranges, Australia 42 A2
Mitilíni, Greece 17 E12
Mito, Japan 23 F10
Mitrovica = Kosovska Mitrovica, Kosovo, Yug. 17 C9
Mitsiwa, Eritrea 32 D2
Mitsukaidō, Japan 23 F9
Mittagong, Australia 43 E5
Mittimatalik = Pond Inlet, Canada 47 A12
Mitú, Colombia 62 C4
Mitumba, Mts., Dem. Rep. of the Congo 36 F5
Mitwaba, Dem. Rep. of the Congo 36 F5
Mixteco →, Mexico 59 D5
Miyagi □, Japan 22 E10
Miyāh, W. el →, Syria 30 C3
Miyake-Jima, Japan 23 G9
Miyako, Japan 22 E10
Miyako-Jima, Japan 23 M2
Miyako-Rettō, Japan 23 M2
Miyakonojō, Japan 23 J5
Miyanoura-Dake, Japan 23 J5
Miyazaki, Japan 23 J5
Miyazaki □, Japan 23 H5
Miyazu, Japan 23 G7
Miyet, Bahr el = Dead Sea, Asia 33 D4
Miyoshi, Japan 23 G6
Mizdah, Libya 35 B8
Mizoram □, India 29 H18
Mizpe Ramon, Israel 33 E3
Mizusawa, Japan 22 E10
Mjölby, Sweden 7 G16
Mjøsa, Norway 7 F14
Mladá Boleslav, Czech Rep. 12 C8
Mlanje, Pic, Malawi 37 H7
Mława, Poland 13 B11
Mljet, Croatia 16 C7
Mmabatho, S. Africa 37 K5
Mo i Rana, Norway 6 C16
Moa, Cuba 61 B4
Moa, Indonesia 27 F7
Moab, U.S.A. 57 G9
Moala, Fiji 39 D8
Moama, Australia 43 F3
Mobārakābād, Iran 31 D7
Mobaye, C.A.R. 36 D4
Mobayi, Dem. Rep. of the Congo 36 D4
Moberley Lake, Canada 50 B4
Moberly, U.S.A. 54 F8
Mobile, U.S.A. 53 K1
Mobile B., U.S.A. 53 K2
Mobridge, U.S.A. 54 C4
Mobutu Sese Seko, L. = Albert L., Africa 36 D6
Moçambique, Mozam. 37 H8
Moçâmedes = Namibe, Angola 37 H2
Mochudi, Botswana 37 J5
Mocimboa da Praia, Mozam. 36 G8
Moclips, U.S.A. 56 C1
Mocoa, Colombia 62 C3
Mocorito, Mexico 58 B3
Moctezuma, Mexico 58 B3
Moctezuma →, Mexico 59 C5
Mocuba, Mozam. 37 H7
Mocúzari, Presa, Mexico 58 B3
Modane, France 14 D7
Módena, Italy 16 B4
Modena, U.S.A. 57 H7
Modesto, U.S.A. 57 H3
Módica, Italy 16 F6
Moe, Australia 43 F4
Moengo, Surinam 63 B8
Mogadishu = Muqdisho, Somali Rep. 32 G4
Mogador = Essaouira, Morocco 34 B4
Mogami-Gawa →, Japan 22 E10
Mogaung, Burma 29 G20
Mogi das Cruzes, Brazil 64 A7
Mogi-Mirim, Brazil 63 H9
Mogilev = Mahilyow, Belarus 13 B16
Mogilev-Podolskiy = Mohyliv-Podilskyy, Ukraine 13 D14
Mogocha, Russia 21 D12
Mogok, Burma 29 H20
Mogollon Rim, U.S.A. 57 J8
Mogumber, Australia 41 F2
Mohács, Hungary 13 F10
Mohall, U.S.A. 54 A4
Moḩammadābād, Iran 31 B8
Mohammedia, Morocco 34 B4
Mohave, L., U.S.A. 57 J6
Mohyliv-Podilskyy, Ukraine 13 D14
Moisaküla, Estonia 7 G21
Moisie, Canada 49 B6
Moisie →, Canada 49 B6
Mojave, U.S.A. 57 J4
Mojave Desert, U.S.A. 57 J5
Mojokerto, Indonesia 27 G15
Mokai, N.Z. 39 H5
Mokau, N.Z. 39 H5
Mokokchung, India 29 F19
Mokra Gora, Yugoslavia 17 C9
Mol, Belgium 11 C5
Molchanovo, Russia 20 D9
Mold, U.K. 8 D4
Moldavia = Moldova ■, Europe 13 E15
Molde, Norway 6 E12
Moldova ■, Europe 13 E15
Moldoveanu, Vf., Romania 13 F13
Mole →, U.K. 9 F7
Mole Creek, Australia 42 G4
Molepolole, Botswana 37 J5
Molfetta, Italy 16 D7
Moline, U.S.A. 54 E9
Mollendo, Peru 62 G4
Mollerin, L., Australia 41 F2
Molodechno = Maladzyechna, Belarus 13 A14
Molong, Australia 43 E4
Molopo →, Africa 37 K4
Molotov = Perm, Russia 18 C10
Molson L., Canada 51 C9
Molu, Indonesia 27 F8
Molucca Sea, Indonesia 27 E6
Moluccas = Maluku, Indonesia 27 E7
Moma, Mozam. 37 H7
Mombasa, Kenya 36 E7
Mombetsu, Japan 22 B11
Momchilgrad, Bulgaria 17 D11
Mompós, Colombia 62 B4
Møn, Denmark 7 J15
Mona, Canal de la, W. Indies 61 C6
Mona, Isla, Puerto Rico 61 C6
Mona, Pta., Costa Rica 60 E3
Monaco ■, Europe 14 E7
Monahans, U.S.A. 55 K3
Monarch Mt., Canada 50 C3
Monashee Mts., Canada 50 C5
Monastir = Bitola, Macedonia 17 D9
Moncayo, Sierra del, Spain 15 B5
Monchegorsk, Russia 18 A5
Mönchengladbach, Germany 12 C4
Monchique, Portugal 15 D1
Moncks Corner, U.S.A. 53 J5
Monclova, Mexico 58 B4
Moncton, Canada 49 C7
Mondego →, Portugal 15 B1
Mondeodo, Indonesia 27 E6
Mondovì, Italy 14 D7
Mondrain I., Australia 41 F3
Monessen, U.S.A. 52 E6
Monett, U.S.A. 55 G8
Monforte de Lemos, Spain 15 A2
Mong Hsu, Burma 29 J21
Mong Kung, Burma 29 J20
Mong Nai, Burma 29 J20
Mong Pawk, Burma 29 H21
Mong Ton, Burma 29 J21
Mong Wa, Burma 29 J22
Mong Yai, Burma 29 H21
Mongalla, Sudan 35 G12
Mongers, L., Australia 41 E2
Monghyr = Munger, India 29 G15
Mongibello = Etna, Italy 16 F6
Mongo, Chad 35 F9
Mongolia ■, Asia 21 E10
Mongu, Zambia 37 H4
Monkey Mia, Australia 41 E1
Monkey River, Belize 59 D7
Monkoto, Dem. Rep. of the Congo 36 E4
Monmouth, U.K. 9 F5
Monmouth, Ill., U.S.A. 54 E9
Monmouth, Oreg., U.S.A. 56 D2
Monmouthshire □, U.K. 9 F5
Mono L., U.S.A. 57 H4
Monópoli, Italy 16 D7
Monroe, Ga., U.S.A. 53 J4
Monroe, La., U.S.A. 55 J8
Monroe, Mich., U.S.A. 52 E4
Monroe, N.C., U.S.A. 53 H5
Monroe, Utah, U.S.A. 57 G7
Monroe, Wis., U.S.A. 54 D10
Monroe City, U.S.A. 54 F9
Monroeville, U.S.A. 53 K2
Monrovia, Liberia 34 G3
Mons, Belgium 11 D3
Monse, Indonesia 27 E6
Mont-de-Marsan, France 14 E3
Mont-Joli, Canada 49 C6
Mont-Laurier, Canada 48 C4
Mont-Louis, Canada 49 C6
Mont-St-Michel, Le = Le Mont-St-Michel, France 14 B3
Mont Tremblant, Parc Recr. du, Canada 48 C5
Montagu I., Antarctica 5 B1
Montague, Canada 49 C7
Montague, I., Mexico 58 A2
Montague Ra., Australia 41 E2
Montague Sd., Australia 40 B4
Montalbán, Spain 15 B5
Montana, Bulgaria 17 C10
Montaña, Peru 62 E4
Montana □, U.S.A. 56 C9
Montargis, France 14 C5
Montauban, France 14 D4
Montauk Pt., U.S.A. 52 E10
Montbéliard, France 14 C7
Montceau-les-Mines, France 14 C6
Monte Albán, Mexico 59 D5
Monte Alegre, Brazil 63 D8
Monte Azul, Brazil 63 G10
Monte Bello Is., Australia 40 D2
Monte-Carlo, Monaco 14 E7
Monte Caseros, Argentina 64 C5
Monte Comán, Argentina 64 C3
Monte Cristi, Dom. Rep. 61 C5
Monte Quemado, Argentina 64 B4
Monte Santu, C. di, Italy 16 D3
Monte Vista, U.S.A. 57 H10
Montebello, Canada 48 C5
Montecristo, Italy 16 C4
Montego Bay, Jamaica 60 C4
Montélimar, France 14 D6
Montello, U.S.A. 54 D10
Montemorelos, Mexico 59 B5
Montenegro □, Yugoslavia 17 C8
Montepuez, Mozam. 37 G7
Monterey, U.S.A. 57 H3
Montería, Colombia 62 B3
Monterrey, Mexico 58 B4
Montes Claros, Brazil 63 G10
Montesano, U.S.A. 56 C2
Montesilvano, Italy 16 C6
Montevideo, Uruguay 64 C5
Montevideo, U.S.A. 54 C7
Montezuma, U.S.A. 54 E8
Montgomery = Sahiwal, Pakistan 28 D8
Montgomery, U.K. 9 E4
Montgomery, Ala., U.S.A. 53 J2
Montgomery, W. Va., U.S.A. 52 F5
Montgomery City, U.S.A. 54 F9
Monticello, Ark., U.S.A. 55 J9
Monticello, Fla., U.S.A. 53 K4
Monticello, Ind., U.S.A. 52 E2
Monticello, Iowa, U.S.A. 54 D9
Monticello, Ky., U.S.A. 53 G3
Monticello, Minn., U.S.A. 54 C8
Monticello, Miss., U.S.A. 55 K9
Monticello, Utah, U.S.A. 57 H9
Montijo, Portugal 15 C1
Montilla, Spain 15 D3
Montluçon, France 14 C5
Montmagny, Canada 49 C5
Montmartre, Canada 51 C8
Montmorillon, France 14 C4
Monto, Australia 42 C5
Montoro, Spain 15 C3
Montpelier, Idaho, U.S.A. 56 E8
Montpelier, Vt., U.S.A. 52 C9
Montpellier, France 14 E5
Montréal, Canada 48 C5
Montreal →, Canada 48 C3
Montreal L., Canada 51 C7
Montreal Lake, Canada 51 C7
Montreux, Switz. 14 C7
Montrose, U.K. 10 C5
Montrose, U.S.A. 57 G10
Monts, Pte. des, Canada 49 C6
Montserrat ■, W. Indies 61 C7
Monywa, Burma 29 H19
Monza, Italy 14 D8
Monze, Zambia 37 H5
Monze, C., Pakistan 28 G5
Monzón, Spain 15 B6
Moonah →, Australia 42 C2
Moonda, L., Australia 42 D3
Moonie, Australia 43 D5
Moonie →, Australia 43 D4
Moonta, Australia 43 E2
Moora, Australia 41 F2
Moorcroft, U.S.A. 54 C2
Moore →, Australia 41 F2
Moore, L., Australia 41 E2
Moore Park, Australia 42 C5
Moore Reefs, Australia 42 B4
Moorefield, U.S.A. 52 F6
Moorhead, U.S.A. 54 B6
Moose →, Canada 48 B3
Moose Factory, Canada 48 B3
Moose Jaw, Canada 51 C7
Moose Jaw →, Canada 51 C7
Moose Lake, Canada 51 C8
Moose Lake, U.S.A. 54 B8
Moose Mountain Prov. Park, Canada 51 D8
Moosehead L., U.S.A. 53 C11
Mooselookmeguntic L., U.S.A. 53 C10
Moosomin, Canada 51 C8
Moosonee, Canada 48 B3
Mopti, Mali 34 F5
Moquegua, Peru 62 G4
Mora, Sweden 7 F16
Mora, Minn., U.S.A. 54 C8
Mora, N. Mex., U.S.A. 57 J11
Mora →, U.S.A. 55 H2
Moradabad, India 28 E11
Morafenobe, Madag. 37 H8
Moramanga, Madag. 37 H9
Moran, Kans., U.S.A. 55 G7
Moran, Wyo., U.S.A. 56 E8
Moranbah, Australia 42 C4
Morant Cays, Jamaica 60 C4
Morant Pt., Jamaica 60 C4
Moratuwa, Sri Lanka 28 R11
Morava →, Serbia, Yug. 17 B9
Morava →, Slovak Rep. 13 D9
Moravian Hts. = Českomoravská Vrchovina, Czech Rep. 12 D8
Morawa, Australia 41 E2
Morawhanna, Guyana 62 B7
Moray Firth, U.K. 10 C5
Morden, Canada 51 D9
Mordovian Republic = Mordvinia □, Russia 18 D7
Mordvinia □, Russia 18 D7
Moreau →, U.S.A. 54 C4
Morecambe, U.K. 8 C5
Morecambe B., U.K. 8 C5
Moree, Australia 43 D4
Morehead, U.S.A. 52 F4
Morehead City, U.S.A. 53 H7
Morelia, Mexico 58 D4
Morella, Australia 42 C3
Morella, Spain 15 B5
Morelos, Mexico 58 B3

Morelos □, Mexico . . . 59 D5
Morena, Sierra, Spain . . 15 C3
Moresby I., Canada . . 50 C2
Moreton I., Australia . . 43 D5
Morgan, U.S.A. 56 F8
Morgan City, U.S.A. . . 55 L9
Morganfield, U.S.A. . . 52 G2
Morganton, U.S.A. . . . 53 H5
Morgantown, U.S.A. . . 52 F6
Morghak, Iran 31 D8
Moriarty, U.S.A. 57 J10
Morice L., Canada . . . 50 C3
Morinville, Canada 50 C6
Morioka, Japan 22 E10
Moris, Mexico 58 B3
Morlaix, France 14 B2
Mornington, Australia . . 43 F4
Mornington, I., Chile . . 64 F1
Mornington I., Australia 42 B2
Moro G., Phil. 27 C6
Morocco ■, N. Afr. . . . 34 B4
Morogoro, Tanzania . . 36 F7
Moroleón, Mexico . . . 58 C4
Morombe, Madag. . . . 37 J8
Morón, Cuba 60 B4
Morón de la Frontera,
  Spain 15 D3
Morona →, Peru 62 D3
Morondava, Madag. . . 37 J8
Moroni, U.S.A. 56 G8
Morotai, Indonesia . . . 27 D7
Moroto, Uganda 36 D6
Morpeth, U.K. 8 B6
Morphou, Cyprus . . . 30 C2
Morrilton, U.S.A. 55 H8
Morrinhos, Brazil . . . 63 G9
Morrinsville, N.Z. . . . 39 G5
Morris, Canada 51 D9
Morris, Ill., U.S.A. . . . 54 E10
Morris, Minn., U.S.A. . 54 C7
Morris, Mt., Australia . 41 E5
Morristown, Ariz.,
  U.S.A. 57 K7
Morristown, Tenn.,
  U.S.A. 53 G4
Morro Bay, U.S.A. . . . 57 J3
Morrosquillo, G. de,
  Colombia 60 E4
Morshansk, Russia . . . 18 D7
Morteros, Argentina . . 64 C4
Mortlach, Canada . . . 51 C7
Mortlake, Australia . . . 43 F3
Morton, Tex., U.S.A. . . 55 J3
Morton, Wash., U.S.A. 56 C2
Morundah, Australia . . 43 E4
Moruya, Australia . . . 43 F5
Morvan, France 14 C6
Morven, Australia . . . 43 D4
Morwell, Australia . . . 43 F4
Morzhovets, Ostrov,
  Russia 18 A7
Moscos Is., Burma . . . 26 B1
Moscow = Moskva,
  Russia 18 C6
Moscow, U.S.A. 56 C5
Mosel →, Europe . . . 14 A7
Moselle = Mosel →,
  Europe 14 A7
Moses Lake, U.S.A. . . 56 C4
Mosgiel, N.Z. 39 L3
Moshi, Tanzania 36 E7
Mosjøen, Norway 6 D15
Moskenesøya, Norway . 6 C15
Moskenstraumen,
  Norway 6 C15
Moskva, Russia 18 C6
Moson-magyaróvár,
  Hungary 13 E9
Mosquera, Colombia . . 62 C3
Mosquero, U.S.A. . . . 55 H3
Mosquitia, Honduras . . 60 C3
Mosquito Coast =
  Mosquitia, Honduras 60 C3
Mosquito L., Canada . . 51 A8
Mosquitos, G. de los,
  Panama 60 E3
Moss, Norway 7 G14
Moss Vale, Australia . . 43 E5
Mossbank, Canada . . . 51 D7
Mossburn, N.Z. 39 L2
Mosselbaai, S. Africa . 37 L4
Mossendjo, Congo . . . 36 E2
Mossgiel, Australia . . . 43 E3
Mossman, Australia . . 42 B4
Mossoró, Brazil 63 E11
Most, Czech Rep. 12 C7
Mostaganem, Algeria . 34 A6
Mostar, Bos.-H. 17 C7
Mostardas, Brazil 64 C6
Mostiska = Mostyska,
  Ukraine 13 D12
Mosty = Masty, Belarus 13 B13
Mostyska, Ukraine . . . 13 D12
Mosul = Al Mawṣil, Iraq 30 B4
Motagua →,
  Guatemala 60 C2
Motala, Sweden 7 G16
Motihari, India 29 F14
Motozintla de Mendoza,
  Mexico 59 D6
Motril, Spain 15 D4
Mott, U.S.A. 54 B3
Motueka, N.Z. 39 J4
Motueka →, N.Z. 39 J4
Motul, Mexico 59 C7

Mouchalagane →,
  Canada 49 B6
Moúdhros, Greece . . . 17 E11
Mouila, Gabon 36 E2
Moulamein, Australia . . 43 F3
Moulins, France 14 C5
Moulmein, Burma . . . 29 L20
Moulouya, O. →,
  Morocco 34 B5
Moultrie, U.S.A. 53 K4
Moultrie, L., U.S.A. . . . 53 J5
Mound City, Mo., U.S.A. 54 E7
Mound City, S. Dak.,
  U.S.A. 54 C4
Moundou, Chad 35 G9
Moundsville, U.S.A. . . 52 F5
Mount Airy, U.S.A. . . . 53 G5
Mount Barker,
  S. Austral., Australia 43 F2
Mount Barker,
  W. Austral., Australia 41 F2
Mount Beauty, Australia 43 F4
Mount Burr, Australia . 43 F3
Mount Carmel, U.S.A. . 52 F2
Mount Coolon, Australia 42 C4
Mount Desert I., U.S.A. 53 D6
Mount Dora, U.S.A. . . 53 L5
Mount Edziza Prov.
  Park, Canada 50 B2
Mount Forest, Canada . 48 D3
Mount Gambier,
  Australia 43 F3
Mount Garnet, Australia 42 B4
Mount Hope, N.S.W.,
  Australia 43 E4
Mount Hope, S. Austral.,
  Australia 43 E2
Mount Isa, Australia . . 42 C2
Mount Larcom,
  Australia 42 C5
Mount Lofty Ra.,
  Australia 43 E2
Mount Magnet,
  Australia 41 E2
Mount Maunganui, N.Z. 39 G6
Mount Molloy, Australia 42 B4
Mount Morgan,
  Australia 42 C5
Mount Pearl, Canada . 49 C9
Mount Perry, Australia 43 D5
Mount Pleasant, Iowa,
  U.S.A. 54 E9
Mount Pleasant, Mich.,
  U.S.A. 52 D3
Mount Pleasant, S.C.,
  U.S.A. 53 J6
Mount Pleasant, Tenn.,
  U.S.A. 53 H2
Mount Pleasant, Tex.,
  U.S.A. 55 J7
Mount Pleasant, Utah,
  U.S.A. 56 G8
Mount Rainier Nat. Park,
  U.S.A. 56 C3
Mount Revelstoke Nat.
  Park, Canada 50 C5
Mount Robson Prov.
  Park, Canada 50 C5
Mount Shasta, U.S.A. . 56 F2
Mount Sterling, Ill.,
  U.S.A. 54 F9
Mount Sterling, Ky.,
  U.S.A. 52 F4
Mount Surprise,
  Australia 42 B3
Mount Vernon, Ill.,
  U.S.A. 52 F1
Mount Vernon, Ind.,
  U.S.A. 54 F10
Mount Vernon, Ohio,
  U.S.A. 52 E4
Mount Vernon, Wash.,
  U.S.A. 56 B2
Mountain Ash, U.K. . . . 9 F4
Mountain City, Nev.,
  U.S.A. 56 F6
Mountain City, Tenn.,
  U.S.A. 53 G5
Mountain Grove, U.S.A. 55 G8
Mountain Home, Ark.,
  U.S.A. 55 G8
Mountain Home, Idaho,
  U.S.A. 56 E6
Mountain Iron, U.S.A. . 54 B8
Mountain View, U.S.A. . 55 H9
Mountainair, U.S.A. . . 57 J10
Moura, Australia 42 C4
Moura, Brazil 62 D6
Moura, Portugal 15 C2
Mourdi, Dépression du,
  Chad 35 E10
Mourilyan, Australia . . 42 B4
Mouscron, Belgium . . 11 D3
Moussoro, Chad 35 F9
Moutong, Indonesia . . 27 D6
Movas, Mexico 58 B3
Moville, Ireland 10 D3
Moy →, Ireland 10 B2
Moyale, Kenya 36 D7
Moyen Atlas, Morocco . 34 B4
Moyne, L. le, Canada . 49 A6
Moyo, Indonesia 26 F5
Moyobamba, Peru . . . 62 E3
Moyyero →, Russia . . 21 C11
Moyynty, Kazakhstan . 20 E8

Mozambique =
  Moçambique, Mozam. 37 H8
Mozambique ■, Africa 37 H7
Mozambique Chan.,
  Africa 3 F11
Mozambique Chan.,
  Africa 3 F11
Mozdok, Russia 19 F7
Mozdūrān, Iran 31 B9
Mozhnābād, Iran 31 C9
Mozyr = Mazyr, Belarus 13 B15
Mpanda, Tanzania . . . 36 F6
Mpika, Zambia 37 G6
Mpwapwa, Tanzania . . 36 F7
M'sila →, Algeria 34 A6
Mstislavl = Mstsislaw,
  Belarus 13 A16
Mstsislaw, Belarus . . . 13 A16
Mtwara-Mikindani,
  Tanzania 36 G8
Mu Us Shamo, China . 25 C5
Muang Khong, Laos . . 26 B3
Muar, Malaysia 26 D2
Muarabungo, Indonesia 26 E2
Muaraenim, Indonesia . 26 E2
Muarajuloi, Indonesia . 26 E4
Muarakaman, Indonesia 26 E5
Muaratebo, Indonesia . 26 E2
Muaratembesi,
  Indonesia 26 E2
Muaratewe, Indonesia . 26 E4
Mubarraz = Al
  Mubarraz, Si. Arabia 31 E6
Mubi, Nigeria 35 F8
Mucajaí →, Brazil . . . 62 C6
Muckadilla, Australia . . 43 D4
Mucuri, Brazil 63 G11
Mudanjiang, China . . . 25 B7
Mudanya, Turkey 17 D13
Muddy Cr. →, U.S.A. . 57 H8
Mudgee, Australia . . . 43 E4
Mudjatik →, Canada . . 51 B7
Mueller Ra., Australia . 40 C4
Muerto, Mar, Mexico . . 59 D6
Mufulira, Zambia 37 G5
Mughayrā', Si. Arabia . 30 D3
Mugi, Japan 23 H7
Muğla, Turkey 17 F13
Mugu, Nepal 29 E13
Muhammad, Ras, Egypt 30 E2
Muhammad Qol, Sudan 35 D13
Mühlhausen, Germany . 12 C6
Mühlig Hofmann fjell,
  Antarctica 5 D3
Muhos, Finland 6 D22
Muhu, Estonia 7 G20
Muir, L., Australia . . . 41 F2
Mujnak, Uzbekistan . . 20 E6
Mukacheve, Ukraine . . 13 D12
Mukachevo =
  Mukacheve, Ukraine 13 D12
Mukah, Malaysia 26 D4
Mukden = Shenyang,
  China 25 B7
Mukhtuya = Lensk,
  Russia 21 C12
Mukinbudin, Australia . 41 F2
Mukomuko, Indonesia . 26 E2
Muktsar, India 28 D9
Mukutawa →, Canada . 51 C9
Mula, Spain 15 C5
Mulchén, Chile 64 D2
Mulde →, Germany . . 12 C7
Mule Creek Junction,
  U.S.A. 54 D2
Mulejé, Mexico 58 B2
Muleshoe, U.S.A. 55 H3
Mulgrave, Canada . . . 49 C7
Mulhacén, Spain 15 D4
Mülheim, Germany . . . 25 C4
Mulhouse, France . . . 14 C7
Mull, U.K. 10 C4
Mullaittivu, Sri Lanka . 28 Q12
Mullen, U.S.A. 54 D4
Mullens, U.S.A. 52 G5
Muller, Pegunungan,
  Indonesia 26 D4
Mullewa, Australia . . . 41 E2
Mulligan →, Australia . 42 D2
Mullingar, Ireland 10 E3
Mullins, U.S.A. 53 H6
Mullumbimby, Australia 43 D5
Multan, Pakistan 28 D7
Mulvane, U.S.A. 55 G6
Mumbai, India 28 K8
Mun →, Thailand 26 A2
Muna, Indonesia 27 F6
Munamagi, Estonia . . . 7 H22
München, Germany . . 12 D6
Munchen-Gladbach =
  Mönchengladbach,
  Germany 12 C4
Muncho Lake, Canada . 50 B3
Muncie, U.S.A. 52 E3
Muncoonie, L., Australia 42 D2
Mundabbera, Australia 43 D5
Munday, U.S.A. 55 J5
Münden, Germany . . . 12 C5
Mundiwindi, Australia . 40 D3
Mundo Novo, Brazil . . 63 F10
Mundrabilla, Australia . 41 F4
Mungallala, Australia . 43 D4
Mungallala Cr. →,
  Australia 43 D4
Mungana, Australia . . 42 B3

Mungbere, Dem. Rep. of
  the Congo 36 D5
Munger, India 29 G15
Munich = München,
  Germany 12 D6
Munising, U.S.A. 52 B2
Munku-Sardyk, Russia . 21 D11
Muñoz Gamero, Pen.,
  Chile 64 G2
Munroe L., Canada . . . 51 B9
Munster □, Ireland . . . 10 E2
Muntadgin, Australia . . 41 F2
Muntok, Indonesia . . . 26 E3
Muonio, Finland 6 C20
Muonionjoki →,
  Finland 6 C20
Muqdisho, Somali Rep. 32 G4
Mur →, Austria 13 E9
Murakami, Japan 22 E9
Murallón, Cerro, Chile . 64 F2
Murang'a, Kenya 36 E7
Murashi, Russia 18 C8
Murat →, Turkey 19 G7
Muratlı, Turkey 17 D12
Murayama, Japan . . . 22 E10
Murban, U.A.E. 31 F7
Murchison →,
  Australia 41 E1
Murchison, Mt.,
  Antarctica 5 D11
Murchison Falls,
  Uganda 36 D6
Murchison Ra., Australia 42 C1
Murcia, Spain 15 D5
Murcia □, Spain 15 D5
Murdo, U.S.A. 54 D4
Murdoch Pt., Australia . 42 A3
Mureş →, Romania . . 13 E11
Mureşul = Mureş →,
  Romania 13 E11
Murfreesboro, N.C.,
  U.S.A. 53 G7
Murfreesboro, Tenn.,
  U.S.A. 53 H2
Murgab = Murghob,
  Tajikistan 20 F8
Murgab →,
  Turkmenistan 31 B9
Murgenella, Australia . 40 B5
Murghob, Tajikistan . . 20 F8
Murgon, Australia . . . 43 D5
Muria, Indonesia 27 G14
Müritz, Germany 12 B7
Murmansk, Russia . . . 18 A5
Murom, Russia 18 C7
Muroran, Japan 22 C10
Muroto, Japan 23 H7
Muroto-Misaki, Japan . 23 H7
Murphy, U.S.A. 56 E5
Murray, Ky., U.S.A. . . 53 G1
Murray, Utah, U.S.A. . . 56 F8
Murray →, Australia . . 43 F2
Murray →, U.S.A. . . . 53 H5
Murray Bridge, Australia 43 F2
Murray Harbour,
  Canada 49 C7
Murrumbidgee →,
  Australia 43 E3
Murrumburrah,
  Australia 43 E4
Murrurundi, Australia . 43 E5
Murtle L., Canada . . . 50 C5
Murtoa, Australia 43 F3
Mururoa, Pac. Oc. . . . 45 K14
Murwara, India 29 H12
Murwillumbah, Australia 43 D5
Mürzzuschlag, Austria . 12 E8
Muş, Turkey 19 G7
Mûsa, Gebel, Egypt . . 30 D2
Musa Khel, Pakistan . . 28 D6
Mûsa Qal'eh, Afghan. . 28 C4
Musaffargarh, Pakistan 28 D7
Musala, Bulgaria 17 C10
Musala, Indonesia . . . 26 D1
Musay'id, Qatar 31 E6
Muscat = Masqat,
  Oman 32 C6
Muscat & Oman =
  Oman ■, Asia 32 C6
Muscatine, U.S.A. . . . 54 E9
Musgrave Harbour,
  Canada 49 C9
Musgrave Ranges,
  Australia 41 E5
Mushie, Dem. Rep. of
  the Congo 36 E3
Musi →, Indonesia . . . 26 E2
Muskeg →, Canada . . 50 A4
Muskegon, U.S.A. . . . 52 D2
Muskegon →, U.S.A. . 52 D2
Muskegon Heights,
  U.S.A. 52 D2
Muskogee, U.S.A. . . . 55 H7
Muskwa →, Canada . . 50 B4
Muslīmiyah, Syria . . . 30 B3
Musoma, Tanzania . . . 36 E6
Musquaro, L., Canada . 49 B7
Musquodoboit Harbour,
  Canada 49 D7
Musselshell →, U.S.A. 56 C10
Mussoorie, India 28 D11
Mustafakemalpaşa,
  Turkey 17 D13
Mustang, Nepal 29 E13

Musters, L., Argentina . 64 F3
Muswellbrook, Australia 43 E5
Mût, Egypt 35 C11
Mut, Turkey 30 B2
Mutare, Zimbabwe . . . 37 H6
Muting, Indonesia . . . 27 F10
Mutoray, Russia 21 C11
Mutsu, Japan 22 D10
Mutsu-Wan, Japan . . . 22 D10
Muttaburra, Australia . 42 C3
Muweilih, Egypt 33 E3
Muy Muy, Nic. 60 D2
Muzaffarabad, Pakistan 28 B8
Muzaffargarh, Pakistan 28 D7
Muzaffarnagar, India . . 28 E10
Muzaffarpur, India . . . 29 F14
Muzhi, Russia 18 A11
Mvuma, Zimbabwe . . . 37 H6
Mwanza, Dem. Rep. of
  the Congo 36 F5
Mwanza, Tanzania . . . 36 E6
Mweka, Dem. Rep. of
  the Congo 36 E4
Mweru, L., Zambia . . . 36 F5
Mwinilunga, Zambia . . 37 G4
My Tho, Vietnam 26 B3
Myanaung, Burma . . . 29 K19
Myanmar = Burma ■,
  Asia 29 J20
Myaungmya, Burma . . 29 L19
Mycenæ, Greece 17 F10
Myeik Kyunzu, Burma . 26 B1
Myers Chuck, U.S.A. . . 50 B2
Myingyan, Burma 29 J19
Myitkyina, Burma 29 G20
Mykines, Færoe Is. . . . 6 E9
Mykolayiv, Ukraine . . . 19 E5
Mymensingh, Bangla. . 29 G17
Mynydd Du, U.K. 9 F4
Mýrdalsjökull, Iceland . 6 E4
Myrtle Beach, U.S.A. . . 53 J6
Myrtle Creek, U.S.A. . . 56 E2
Myrtle Point, U.S.A. . . 56 E1
Mysia, Turkey 17 E12
Mysore = Karnataka □,
  India 28 N10
Mysore, India 28 N10
Myszków, Poland 13 C10
Mytishchi, Russia 18 C6
Mývatn, Iceland 6 D5
Mzuzu, Malawi 36 G6

Na Hearadh = Harris,
  U.K. 10 C3
Naab →, Germany . . . 12 D6
Naantali, Finland 7 F19
Nababeep, S. Africa . . 37 K3
Nabari, Japan 23 G8
Nabawa, Australia . . . 41 E1
Nabberu, L., Australia . 41 E3
Naberezhnyye Chelny,
  Russia 18 C9
Nabeul, Tunisia 35 A8
Nabīd, Iran 31 D8
Nabire, Indonesia . . . 27 E9
Nabisipi →, Canada . . 49 B7
Nablus = Nābulus,
  West Bank 33 C4
Nābulus, West Bank . . 33 C4
Nacala, Mozam. 37 G8
Nacaome, Honduras . . 60 D2
Naches, U.S.A. 56 C3
Nachicapau, L., Canada 49 A6
Nachingwea, Tanzania 36 G7
Nacimiento L., U.S.A. . 57 J3
Naco, Mexico 58 A3
Nacogdoches, U.S.A. . 55 K7
Nácori Chico, Mexico . 58 B3
Nacozari, Mexico 58 A3
Nadiad, India 28 H8
Nador, Morocco 34 B5
Nadūshan, Iran 31 C7
Nadvirna, Ukraine . . . 13 D13
Nadvoitsy, Russia . . . 18 B5
Nadvornaya =
  Nadvirna, Ukraine . 13 D13
Nadym, Russia 20 C8
Nadym →, Russia . . . 20 C8
Nærbø, Norway 7 G11
Næstved, Denmark . . . 7 J14
Naft-e Safīd, Iran 31 D6
Naftshahr, Iran 30 C5
Nafud Desert = An
  Nafūd, Si. Arabia . . 30 D4
Naga, Phil. 27 B6
Nagahama, Japan . . . 22 E10
Nagaland □, India . . . 29 G19
Nagano, Japan 23 F9
Nagano □, Japan 23 F9
Nagaoka, Japan 23 F9
Nagappattinam, India . 28 P11
Nagar Parkar, Pakistan 28 G7
Nagasaki, Japan 23 H4
Nagasaki □, Japan . . . 23 H4
Nagaur, India 28 F8
Nagercoil, India 28 Q10
Nagina, India 28 E11
Nagineh, Iran 31 C8
Nagir, Pakistan 28 A9
Nagornyy, Russia 21 D13
Nagorno-Karabakh,
  Azerbaijan 19 F8
Nagoya, Japan 23 G8
Nagpur, India 28 J11

Nagua, Dom. Rep. . . . 61 C6
Nagykanizsa, Hungary . 13 E9
Nagykőrös, Hungary . . 13 E10
Naha, Japan 23 L3
Nahanni Butte, Canada 50 A4
Nahanni Nat. Park,
  Canada 50 A4
Nahariyya, Israel 30 C2
Nahāvand, Iran 31 C6
Naicá, Mexico 58 B3
Naicam, Canada 51 C8
Naikoon Prov. Park,
  Canada 50 C2
Nain, Canada 49 A7
Nā'īn, Iran 31 C7
Nainpur, India 28 H12
Nairn, U.K. 10 C5
Nairobi, Kenya 36 E7
Naissaar, Estonia 7 G21
Najafābād, Iran 31 C6
Najd, Si. Arabia 32 B3
Najibabad, India 28 E11
Najmah, Si. Arabia . . . 31 E6
Nakadōri-Shima, Japan 23 H4
Nakaminato, Japan . . 23 F10
Nakamura, Japan . . . 23 H6
Nakano, Japan 23 F9
Nakano-Shima, Japan . 23 K4
Nakashibetsu, Japan . 22 C12
Nakfa, Eritrea 32 D2
Nakhfar al Buşayyah,
  Iraq 30 D5
Nakhichevan =
  Naxçıvan, Azerbaijan 19 G8
Nakhichevan Republic =
  Naxçıvan □,
  Azerbaijan 19 G8
Nakhl, Egypt 33 F2
Nakhl-e Taqī, Iran . . . 31 E7
Nakhodka, Russia . . . 21 E14
Nakhon Phanom,
  Thailand 26 A2
Nakhon Ratchasima,
  Thailand 26 B2
Nakhon Sawan,
  Thailand 26 A2
Nakhon Si Thammarat,
  Thailand 26 C2
Nakina, Canada 48 B2
Nakskov, Denmark . . . 7 J14
Nakuru, Kenya 36 E7
Nakusp, Canada 50 C5
Nal →, Pakistan 28 G4
Nalchik, Russia 19 F7
Nalgonda, India 28 L11
Nallamalai Hills, India . 28 M11
Nam Co, China 24 C4
Nam-Phan, Vietnam . . 26 B3
Nam Tok, Thailand . . . 26 B1
Namak, Daryācheh-ye,
  Iran 31 C7
Namak, Kavir-e, Iran . . 31 C8
Namakzar, Daryācheh-
  ye, Iran 31 C9
Namaland, Namibia . . 37 K3
Namangan, Uzbekistan 20 E8
Namapa, Mozam. . . . 37 G7
Namber, Indonesia . . . 27 E8
Nambour, Australia . . 43 D5
Nambucca Heads,
  Australia 43 E5
Namcha Barwa, China . 24 D4
Namew L., Canada . . . 51 C8
Namib Desert =
  Namibwoestyn,
  Namibia 37 J3
Namibe, Angola 37 H2
Namibia ■, Africa . . . 37 J3
Namibwoestyn, Namibia 37 J3
Namlea, Indonesia . . . 27 E7
Namoi →, Australia . . 43 E4
Nampa, U.S.A. 56 E5
Namp'o, N. Korea . . . 25 C7
Nampō-Shotō, Japan . 23 J10
Nampula, Mozam. . . . 37 H7
Namrole, Indonesia . . 27 E7
Namse Shankou, China 29 E13
Namsen →, Norway . . 6 D14
Namsos, Norway 6 D14
Namtsy, Russia 21 C13
Namtu, Burma 29 H20
Namu, Canada 50 C3
Namur, Belgium 11 D4
Namur □, Belgium . . . 11 D4
Nan-ch'ang =
  Nanchang, China . . 25 D6
Nanaimo, Canada . . . 50 D4
Nanango, Australia . . . 43 D5
Nanao, Japan 23 F8
Nanchang, China 25 D6
Nanching = Nanjing,
  China 25 C6
Nanchong, China 24 C5
Nancy, France 14 B7
Nanda Devi, India . . . 28 D11
Nandan, Japan 23 G7
Nanded, India 28 K10
Nandewar Ra., Australia 43 E5
Nandi, Fiji 39 C7
Nandurbar, India 28 J9
Nandyal, India 28 M11
Nanga-Eboko,
  Cameroon 36 D2
Nanga Parbat, Pakistan 28 B9
Nangapinoh, Indonesia 26 E4

93

Name	Page	Grid
Nangarhār □, *Afghan.*	28	B7
Nangatayap, *Indonesia*	26	E4
Nanjing, *China*	25	C6
Nanking = Nanjing, *China*	25	C6
Nankoku, *Japan*	23	H6
Nanning, *China*	24	D5
Nannup, *Australia*	41	F2
Nanping, *China*	25	D6
Nansei-Shotō = Ryūkyū-rettō, *Japan*	23	M3
Nansen Sd., *Canada*	4	A3
Nanshan I., *S. China Sea*	26	B5
Nantes, *France*	14	C3
Nanticoke, *U.S.A.*	52	E7
Nanton, *Canada*	50	C6
Nantong, *China*	25	C7
Nantucket I., *U.S.A.*	52	E10
Nantwich, *U.K.*	8	D5
Nanuque, *Brazil*	63	G10
Nanusa, Kepulauan, *Indonesia*	27	D7
Nanutarra Roadhouse, *Australia*	40	D2
Nanyang, *China*	25	C6
Nanyuki, *Kenya*	36	D7
Nao, C. de la, *Spain*	15	C5
Naococane, L., *Canada*	49	B5
Napa, *U.S.A.*	56	G2
Napanee, *Canada*	48	D4
Napier, *N.Z.*	39	H6
Napier Broome B., *Australia*	40	B4
Napier Pen., *Australia*	42	A2
Naples = Nápoli, *Italy*	16	D6
Naples, *U.S.A.*	53	M5
Napo →, *Peru*	62	D4
Napoleon, *N. Dak., U.S.A.*	54	B5
Napoleon, *Ohio, U.S.A.*	52	E3
Nápoli, *Italy*	16	D6
Naqb, Ra's an, *Jordan*	33	F4
Naqqāsh, *Iran*	31	C6
Nara, *Japan*	23	G7
Nara, *Mali*	34	E4
Nara →, *Japan*	23	G8
Nara Visa, *U.S.A.*	55	H3
Naracoorte, *Australia*	43	F3
Naradhan, *Australia*	43	E4
Narasapur, *India*	29	L12
Narathiwat, *Thailand*	26	C2
Narayanganj, *Bangla.*	29	H17
Narayanpet, *India*	28	L10
Narbonne, *France*	14	E5
Nardīn, *Iran*	31	B7
Nardò, *Italy*	17	D8
Narembeen, *Australia*	41	F2
Naretha, *Australia*	41	F3
Narew →, *Poland*	13	B11
Narin, *Afghan.*	28	A6
Narita, *Japan*	23	G10
Narmada →, *India*	28	J8
Narmland, *Sweden*	7	F15
Narodnaya, *Russia*	18	A10
Narooma, *Australia*	43	F5
Narrabri, *Australia*	43	E4
Narran →, *Australia*	43	D4
Narrandera, *Australia*	43	E4
Narrogin, *Australia*	41	F2
Narromine, *Australia*	43	E4
Narrow Hills Prov. Park, *Canada*	51	C8
Narsimhapur, *India*	28	H11
Naruto, *Japan*	23	G7
Narva, *Estonia*	18	C4
Narva →, *Russia*	7	G22
Narvik, *Norway*	6	B17
Naryan-Mar, *Russia*	18	A9
Narym, *Russia*	20	D9
Naryn, *Kyrgyzstan*	20	E8
Nasa, *Norway*	6	C16
Naseby, *N.Z.*	39	L3
Naser, Buheirat en, *Egypt*	35	D12
Nashua, *Mont., U.S.A.*	56	B10
Nashua, *N.H., U.S.A.*	52	D10
Nashville, *Ark., U.S.A.*	55	J8
Nashville, *Ga., U.S.A.*	53	K4
Nashville, *Tenn., U.S.A.*	53	G2
Nasik, *India*	28	K8
Nasirabad, *India*	28	F9
Naskaupi →, *Canada*	49	B7
Naṣrābād, *Iran*	31	C6
Naṣriān-e Pā'īn, *Iran*	30	C5
Nass →, *Canada*	50	C3
Nassau, *Bahamas*	60	A4
Nassau, B., *Chile*	64	H3
Nasser, L. = Naser, Buheirat en, *Egypt*	35	D12
Nasser City = Kôm Ombo, *Egypt*	35	D12
Nässjö, *Sweden*	7	H16
Nastapoka →, *Canada*	48	A4
Nastapoka, Is., *Canada*	48	A4
Natal, *Brazil*	63	E11
Natal, *Indonesia*	26	D1
Natal, *S. Africa*	37	K6
Naţanz, *Iran*	31	C6
Natashquan, *Canada*	49	B7
Natashquan →, *Canada*	49	B7
Natchez, *U.S.A.*	55	K9
Natchitoches, *U.S.A.*	55	K8
Nathalia, *Australia*	43	F4

Name	Page	Grid
Nathdwara, *India*	28	G8
Natimuk, *Australia*	43	F3
Nation →, *Canada*	50	B4
Natitingou, *Benin*	34	F5
Natividad, I., *Mexico*	58	B1
Natkyizin, *Burma*	26	B1
Natron, L., *Tanzania*	36	E7
Natuna Besar, Kepulauan, *Indonesia*	26	D3
Natuna Is. = Natuna Besar, Kepulauan, *Indonesia*	26	D3
Natuna Selatan, Kepulauan, *Indonesia*	26	D3
Naturaliste, C., *Tas., Australia*	42	G4
Naturaliste, C., *W. Austral., Australia*	38	E4
Naujaat = Repulse Bay, *Canada*	47	B11
Naumburg, *Germany*	12	C6
Nā'ūr at Tunayb, *Jordan*	33	D4
Nauru ■, *Pac. Oc.*	38	B9
Naushahra = Nowshera, *Pakistan*	28	C8
Nauta, *Peru*	62	D4
Nautanwa, *India*	29	F13
Nautla, *Mexico*	59	C5
Nava, *Mexico*	58	B4
Navahrudak, *Belarus*	13	B13
Navajo Reservoir, *U.S.A.*	57	H10
Navalmoral de la Mata, *Spain*	15	C3
Navarino, I., *Chile*	64	H3
Navarra □, *Spain*	15	A5
Navasota, *U.S.A.*	55	K6
Navassa I., *W. Indies*	61	C5
Năvodari, *Romania*	13	F15
Navoi = Nawoiy, *Uzbekistan*	20	E7
Navojoa, *Mexico*	58	B3
Navolato, *Mexico*	58	C3
Návpaktos, *Greece*	17	E9
Návplion, *Greece*	17	F10
Navsari, *India*	28	J8
Nawabshah, *Pakistan*	28	F6
Nawakot, *Nepal*	29	F14
Nawalgarh, *India*	28	F9
Nawoiy, *Uzbekistan*	20	E7
Naxçivan, *Azerbaijan*	19	G8
Naxçivan □, *Azerbaijan*	19	G8
Náxos, *Greece*	17	F11
Nay, Mui, *Vietnam*	26	B3
Nāy Band, *Būshehr, Iran*	31	E7
Nāy Band, *Khorāsān, Iran*	31	C8
Nayakhan, *Russia*	21	C16
Nayarit □, *Mexico*	58	C4
Nayoro, *Japan*	22	B11
Nayyāl, W. →, *Si. Arabia*	30	D3
Nazaré, *Brazil*	63	F11
Nazareth = Naẕerat, *Israel*	33	C4
Nazas, *Mexico*	58	B4
Nazas →, *Mexico*	58	B4
Nazca, *Peru*	62	F4
Naze, The, *U.K.*	9	F9
Naẕerat, *Israel*	33	C4
Nāzik, *Iran*	30	B5
Nazilli, *Turkey*	17	F13
Nazko, *Canada*	50	C4
Nazko →, *Canada*	50	C4
Nazret, *Ethiopia*	32	F2
Nazwá, *Oman*	32	C6
Ndalatando, *Angola*	36	F2
Ndélé, *C.A.R.*	36	C4
Ndjamena, *Chad*	35	F8
Ndola, *Zambia*	37	G5
Neagh, Lough, *U.K.*	10	D3
Neah Bay, *U.S.A.*	56	B1
Neale, L., *Australia*	40	D5
Near Is., *U.S.A.*	46	C1
Neath, *U.K.*	9	F4
Neath Port Talbot □, *U.K.*	9	F4
Nebine Cr. →, *Australia*	43	D4
Nebitdag, *Turkmenistan*	19	G9
Nebo, *Australia*	42	C4
Nebraska □, *U.S.A.*	54	E5
Nebraska City, *U.S.A.*	54	E7
Nébrodi, Monti, *Italy*	16	F6
Necedah, *U.S.A.*	54	C9
Nechako →, *Canada*	50	C4
Neches →, *U.S.A.*	55	L8
Neckar →, *Germany*	12	D5
Necochea, *Argentina*	64	D5
Needles, *Canada*	50	D5
Needles, *U.S.A.*	57	J6
Needles, The, *U.K.*	9	G6
Neemuch = Nimach, *India*	28	G9
Neenah, *U.S.A.*	52	C1
Neepawa, *Canada*	51	C9
Neftçala, *Azerbaijan*	19	G8
Neftekumsk, *Russia*	19	F7
Nefyn, *U.K.*	8	E3
Negapatam = Nagappattinam, *India*	28	P11
Negaunee, *U.S.A.*	52	B2
Negele, *Ethiopia*	32	F2
Negombo, *Sri Lanka*	28	R11

Name	Page	Grid
Negotin, *Serbia, Yug.*	17	B10
Negra, Pta., *Peru*	62	E2
Negrais, C. = Maudin Sun, *Burma*	29	M19
Negril, *Jamaica*	60	C4
Negro →, *Argentina*	64	E4
Negro →, *Brazil*	62	D7
Negro →, *Uruguay*	64	C5
Negros, *Phil.*	27	C6
Neguac, *Canada*	49	C6
Nehāvand, *Iran*	31	C6
Nehbandān, *Iran*	31	D9
Nei Monggol Zizhiqu □, *China*	25	B6
Neijiang, *China*	24	D5
Neillsville, *U.S.A.*	54	C9
Neilton, *U.S.A.*	56	C2
Neiva, *Colombia*	62	C3
Nejanilini L., *Canada*	51	B9
Nejd = Najd, *Si. Arabia*	32	B3
Nekā, *Iran*	31	B7
Nekemte, *Ethiopia*	32	F2
Neksø, *Denmark*	7	J16
Nelia, *Australia*	42	C3
Neligh, *U.S.A.*	54	D5
Nelkan, *Russia*	21	D14
Nellore, *India*	28	M11
Nelson, *Canada*	50	D5
Nelson, *N.Z.*	39	J4
Nelson, *U.K.*	8	D5
Nelson, *U.S.A.*	57	J7
Nelson →, *Canada*	51	C9
Nelson, C., *Australia*	43	F3
Nelson, Estrecho, *Chile*	64	G2
Nelson Bay, *Australia*	43	E5
Nelson Forks, *Canada*	50	B4
Nelson House, *Canada*	51	B9
Nelson L., *Canada*	51	B8
Nelspruit, *S. Africa*	37	K6
Néma, *Mauritania*	34	E4
Neman, *Russia*	7	J20
Neman →, *Lithuania*	7	J19
Nemeiben L., *Canada*	51	B7
Némiscau, *Canada*	48	B4
Némiscau, L., *Canada*	48	B4
Nemunas = Neman →, *Lithuania*	7	J19
Nemuro, *Japan*	22	C12
Nemuro-Kaikyō, *Japan*	22	C12
Nen Jiang →, *China*	25	B7
Nenagh, *Ireland*	10	E2
Nene →, *U.K.*	9	E8
Nenjiang, *China*	25	B7
Neodesha, *U.S.A.*	55	G7
Neosho, *U.S.A.*	55	G7
Neosho →, *U.S.A.*	55	H7
Nepal ■, *Asia*	29	F14
Nepalganj, *Nepal*	29	E12
Nephi, *U.S.A.*	56	G8
Nerang, *Australia*	43	D5
Nerchinsk, *Russia*	21	D12
Néret, L., *Canada*	49	B5
Neretva →, *Croatia*	17	C7
Neringa, *Lithuania*	7	J19
Neryungri, *Russia*	21	D13
Ness, L., *U.K.*	10	C4
Ness City, *U.S.A.*	54	F5
Nesterov, *Poland*	13	C12
Nesvizh = Nyasvizh, *Belarus*	13	B14
Netanya, *Israel*	33	C3
Nete →, *Belgium*	11	C4
Netherdale, *Australia*	42	C4
Netherlands ■, *Europe*	11	C5
Netherlands Antilles ■, *W. Indies*	62	A5
Nettilling L., *Canada*	47	B12
Netzahualcoyotl, Presa, *Mexico*	59	D6
Neubrandenburg, *Germany*	12	B7
Neuchâtel, *Switz.*	14	C7
Neuchâtel, Lac de, *Switz.*	14	C7
Neufchâteau, *Belgium*	11	E5
Neumünster, *Germany*	12	A5
Neunkirchen, *Germany*	12	D4
Neuquén, *Argentina*	64	D3
Neuruppin, *Germany*	12	B7
Neuse →, *U.S.A.*	53	H7
Neusiedler See, *Austria*	13	E9
Neustrelitz, *Germany*	12	B7
Neva →, *Russia*	18	C5
Nevada, *Iowa, U.S.A.*	54	D8
Nevada, *Mo., U.S.A.*	55	G7
Nevada □, *U.S.A.*	56	G5
Nevada, Sierra, *Spain*	15	D4
Nevada, Sierra, *U.S.A.*	56	G3
Nevada City, *U.S.A.*	56	G3
Nevel, *Russia*	18	C4
Nevers, *France*	14	C5
Nevertire, *Australia*	43	E4
Neville, *Canada*	51	D7
Nevinnomyssk, *Russia*	19	F7
Nevis, *W. Indies*	61	C7
Nevşehir, *Turkey*	30	B2
Nevyansk, *Russia*	18	C11
New →, *U.S.A.*	52	F5
New Aiyansh, *Canada*	50	B3
New Albany, *Ind., U.S.A.*	52	F3
New Albany, *Miss., U.S.A.*	55	H10
New Amsterdam, *Guyana*	62	B7

Name	Page	Grid
New Angledool, *Australia*	43	D4
New Baltimore, *U.S.A.*	52	D4
New Bedford, *U.S.A.*	52	E10
New Bern, *U.S.A.*	53	H7
New Boston, *U.S.A.*	55	J7
New Braunfels, *U.S.A.*	55	L5
New Brighton, *N.Z.*	39	K4
New Britain, *Papua N. G.*	38	B8
New Britain, *U.S.A.*	52	E9
New Brunswick, *U.S.A.*	52	E8
New Brunswick □, *Canada*	49	C6
New Caledonia ■, *Pac. Oc.*	38	D9
New Castile = Castilla-La Mancha □, *Spain*	15	C4
New Castle, *Ind., U.S.A.*	52	F3
New Castle, *Pa., U.S.A.*	52	E5
New Delhi, *India*	28	E10
New Denver, *Canada*	50	D5
New England, *U.S.A.*	54	B3
New England Ra., *Australia*	43	E5
New Forest, *U.K.*	9	G6
New Glasgow, *Canada*	49	C7
New Guinea, *Oceania*	38	B6
New Hampshire □, *U.S.A.*	52	D10
New Hampton, *U.S.A.*	54	D8
New Haven, *U.S.A.*	52	E9
New Hazelton, *Canada*	50	B3
New Hebrides = Vanuatu ■, *Pac. Oc.*	38	C9
New Iberia, *U.S.A.*	55	K9
New Ireland, *Papua N. G.*	38	B8
New Jersey □, *U.S.A.*	52	E8
New Lexington, *U.S.A.*	52	F4
New Liskeard, *Canada*	48	C4
New London, *Conn., U.S.A.*	52	E9
New London, *Wis., U.S.A.*	54	C10
New Madrid, *U.S.A.*	55	G10
New Martinsville, *U.S.A.*	52	F5
New Meadows, *U.S.A.*	56	D5
New Mexico □, *U.S.A.*	57	J10
New Norcia, *Australia*	41	F2
New Norfolk, *Australia*	42	G4
New Orleans, *U.S.A.*	55	L9
New Philadelphia, *U.S.A.*	52	E5
New Plymouth, *N.Z.*	39	H5
New Plymouth, *U.S.A.*	56	E5
New Port Richey, *U.S.A.*	53	L4
New Providence, *Bahamas*	60	A4
New Quay, *U.K.*	9	E3
New Radnor, *U.K.*	9	E4
New Richmond, *Canada*	49	C6
New Richmond, *U.S.A.*	54	C8
New Roads, *U.S.A.*	55	K9
New Rockford, *U.S.A.*	54	B5
New Romney, *U.K.*	9	G8
New Salem, *U.S.A.*	54	B4
New Siberian I. = Novaya Sibir, Ostrov, *Russia*	21	B16
New Siberian Is. = Novosibirskiye Ostrova, *Russia*	21	B15
New Smyrna Beach, *U.S.A.*	53	L5
New South Wales □, *Australia*	43	E4
New Town, *U.S.A.*	54	B3
New Tredegar, *U.K.*	9	F4
New Ulm, *U.S.A.*	54	C7
New Waterford, *Canada*	49	C7
New York, *U.S.A.*	52	E9
New York □, *U.S.A.*	52	D8
New York Mts., *U.S.A.*	57	J6
New Zealand ■, *Oceania*	39	J6
Newark, *Del., U.S.A.*	52	F8
Newark, *N.J., U.S.A.*	52	E8
Newark, *N.Y., U.S.A.*	52	D7
Newark, *Ohio, U.S.A.*	52	E4
Newark-on-Trent, *U.K.*	8	D7
Newberg, *U.S.A.*	56	D2
Newberry, *Mich., U.S.A.*	52	B3
Newberry, *S.C., U.S.A.*	53	H5
Newburgh, *U.S.A.*	52	E8
Newbury, *U.K.*	9	F6
Newburyport, *U.S.A.*	53	D10
Newcastle, *Australia*	43	E5
Newcastle, *N.B., Canada*	49	C6
Newcastle, *Ont., Canada*	48	D4
Newcastle, *U.K.*	10	D4
Newcastle, *U.S.A.*	54	D2
Newcastle Emlyn, *U.K.*	9	E3
Newcastle Ra., *Australia*	40	C5
Newcastle-under-Lyme, *U.K.*	8	D5
Newcastle-upon-Tyne, *U.K.*	8	C6
Newcastle Waters, *Australia*	42	B1
Newdegate, *Australia*	41	F2
Newell, *Australia*	42	B4
Newell, *U.S.A.*	54	C3
Newfoundland □, *Canada*	49	B8
Newhaven, *U.K.*	9	G8

Name	Page	Grid
Newkirk, *U.S.A.*	55	G6
Newlyn, *U.K.*	9	G2
Newman, *Australia*	40	D2
Newmarket, *U.K.*	9	E8
Newnan, *U.S.A.*	53	J3
Newport, *I. of W., U.K.*	9	G6
Newport, *Newp., U.K.*	9	F5
Newport, *Ark., U.S.A.*	55	H9
Newport, *Ky., U.S.A.*	52	F3
Newport, *N.H., U.S.A.*	52	D9
Newport, *Oreg., U.S.A.*	56	D1
Newport, *R.I., U.S.A.*	52	E10
Newport, *Tenn., U.S.A.*	53	H4
Newport, *Vt., U.S.A.*	52	C9
Newport, *Wash., U.S.A.*	56	B5
Newport □, *U.K.*	9	F4
Newport Beach, *U.S.A.*	57	K5
Newport News, *U.S.A.*	52	G7
Newport Pagnell, *U.K.*	9	E7
Newquay, *U.K.*	9	G2
Newry, *U.K.*	10	D3
Newton, *Ill., U.S.A.*	54	F10
Newton, *Iowa, U.S.A.*	54	E8
Newton, *Kans., U.S.A.*	55	F6
Newton, *Mass., U.S.A.*	52	D10
Newton, *Miss., U.S.A.*	55	J10
Newton, *N.C., U.S.A.*	53	H5
Newton, *N.J., U.S.A.*	52	E8
Newton, *Tex., U.S.A.*	55	K8
Newton Abbot, *U.K.*	9	G4
Newton Aycliffe, *U.K.*	8	C6
Newtown, *U.K.*	9	E4
Neya, *Russia*	18	C7
Neyrīz, *Iran*	31	D7
Neyshābūr, *Iran*	31	B8
Nezhin = Nizhyn, *Ukraine*	19	D5
Nezperce, *U.S.A.*	56	C5
Ngabang, *Indonesia*	26	D3
Ngabordamlu, Tanjung, *Indonesia*	27	F8
N'Gage, *Angola*	36	F3
Nganglong Kangri, *China*	29	C12
Ngaoundéré, *Cameroon*	36	C2
Ngapara, *N.Z.*	39	L3
Ngawi, *Indonesia*	27	G14
Ngoring Hu, *China*	24	C4
Nguigmi, *Niger*	35	F8
Nguiu, *Australia*	40	B5
Ngukurr, *Australia*	42	A1
Ngulu Atoll, *Pac. Oc.*	27	C9
Nguru, *Nigeria*	35	F8
Nha Trang, *Vietnam*	26	B3
Nhamundá →, *Brazil*	63	D7
Nhill, *Australia*	43	F3
Nhulunbuy, *Australia*	42	A2
Niagara Falls, *Canada*	48	D4
Niagara Falls, *U.S.A.*	52	D6
Niah, *Malaysia*	26	D4
Niamey, *Niger*	34	F6
Nias, *Indonesia*	26	D1
Nibāk, *Si. Arabia*	31	E7
Nicaragua ■, *Cent. Amer.*	60	D2
Nicaragua, L. de, *Nic.*	60	D2
Nicastro, *Italy*	16	E7
Nice, *France*	14	E7
Niceville, *U.S.A.*	53	K2
Nichicun, L., *Canada*	49	B5
Nichinan, *Japan*	23	J5
Nicholás, Canal, *W. Indies*	60	B3
Nicholasville, *U.S.A.*	52	G3
Nicholson, *Australia*	40	C4
Nicholson →, *Australia*	42	B2
Nicholson L., *Canada*	51	A8
Nicholson Ra., *Australia*	41	E2
Nicobar Is., *Ind. Oc.*	3	D14
Nicola, *Canada*	50	C4
Nicolls Town, *Bahamas*	60	A4
Nicosia, *Cyprus*	30	C2
Nicoya, *Costa Rica*	60	D2
Nicoya, G. de, *Costa Rica*	60	E3
Nicoya, Pen. de, *Costa Rica*	60	E2
Nidd →, *U.K.*	8	D6
Niedersachsen □, *Germany*	12	B5
Niemen = Neman →, *Lithuania*	7	J19
Nienburg, *Germany*	12	B5
Nieuw Amsterdam, *Surinam*	63	B7
Nieuw Nickerie, *Surinam*	63	B7
Nieuwpoort, *Belgium*	11	C2
Niğde, *Turkey*	19	G5
Niger ■, *W. Afr.*	34	E7
Niger →, *W. Afr.*	34	G7
Nigeria ■, *W. Afr.*	34	G7
Nightcaps, *N.Z.*	39	L2
Nii-Jima, *Japan*	23	G9
Niigata, *Japan*	22	F9
Niigata □, *Japan*	23	F9
Niihama, *Japan*	23	H6
Niimi, *Japan*	23	G6
Niitsu, *Japan*	22	F9
Nijil, *Jordan*	33	E4
Nijkerk, *Neths.*	11	B5
Nijmegen, *Neths.*	11	C5
Nijverdal, *Neths.*	11	B6
Nīk Pey, *Iran*	31	B6

Name	Page	Grid
Nikiniki, *Indonesia*	27	F6
Nikkō, *Japan*	23	F9
Nikolayev = Mykolayiv, *Ukraine*	19	E5
Nikolayevsk, *Russia*	19	E8
Nikolayevsk-na-Amur, *Russia*	21	D15
Nikolskoye, *Russia*	21	D17
Nikopol, *Ukraine*	19	E5
Nikshahr, *Iran*	31	E9
Nikšić, *Montenegro, Yug.*	17	C8
Nîl, Nahr en →, *Africa*	35	B12
Nîl el Abyad →, *Sudan*	35	E12
Nîl el Azraq →, *Sudan*	35	E12
Nila, *Indonesia*	27	F7
Nile = Nîl, Nahr en →, *Africa*	35	B12
Niles, *U.S.A.*	52	E2
Nîmes, *France*	14	E6
Nimfaíon, Ákra = Pínnes, Ákra, *Greece*	17	D11
Nimmitabel, *Australia*	43	F4
Nindigully, *Australia*	43	D4
Nineveh = Nīnawā, *Iraq*	30	B4
Ningbo, *China*	25	D7
Ningjing Shan, *China*	24	D4
Ningpo = Ningbo, *China*	25	D7
Ningsia Hui A.R. = Ningxia Huizu Zizhiqu □, *China*	24	C5
Ningxia Huizu Zizhiqu □, *China*	24	C5
Ninove, *Belgium*	11	D4
Niobrara, *U.S.A.*	54	D6
Niobrara →, *U.S.A.*	54	D6
Nioro du Sahel, *Mali*	34	E4
Niort, *France*	14	C3
Nipawin, *Canada*	51	C8
Nipigon, *Canada*	48	C2
Nipigon, L., *Canada*	48	C2
Nipishish L., *Canada*	49	B7
Nipissing, L., *Canada*	48	C4
Nipomo, *U.S.A.*	57	J3
Niquelândia, *Brazil*	63	F9
Nīr, *Iran*	30	B5
Nirasaki, *Japan*	23	G9
Nirmal, *India*	28	K11
Nirmali, *India*	29	F15
Niš, *Serbia, Yug.*	17	C9
Niṣāb, *Si. Arabia*	30	D5
Niṣāb, *Yemen*	32	E4
Nishinomiya, *Japan*	23	G7
Nishino'omote, *Japan*	23	J5
Nishiwaki, *Japan*	23	G7
Niskibi →, *Canada*	48	A2
Nissum Bredning, *Denmark*	7	H13
Nistru = Dnister →, *Europe*	13	E16
Nisutlin →, *Canada*	50	A2
Nitchequon, *Canada*	49	B5
Niterói, *Brazil*	63	H10
Nitra, *Slovak Rep.*	13	D10
Nitra →, *Slovak Rep.*	13	E10
Niuafo'ou, *Tonga*	39	B11
Niue, *Cook Is.*	45	J11
Niut, *Indonesia*	26	D4
Nivala, *Finland*	6	E21
Nivelles, *Belgium*	11	D4
Nivernais, *France*	14	C5
Nixon, *U.S.A.*	55	L6
Nizamabad, *India*	28	K11
Nizamghat, *India*	29	E19
Nizhne Kolymsk, *Russia*	21	C17
Nizhnekamsk, *Russia*	18	C9
Nizhneudinsk, *Russia*	21	D10
Nizhnevartovsk, *Russia*	20	C8
Nizhniy Novgorod, *Russia*	18	C7
Nizhniy Tagil, *Russia*	18	C10
Nizhyn, *Ukraine*	19	D5
Nizip, *Turkey*	30	B3
Nízké Tatry, *Slovak Rep.*	13	D10
Nkhotakota, *Malawi*	37	G6
Nkongsamba, *Cameroon*	36	D1
Nmai →, *Burma*	29	G20
Noakhali = Maijdi, *Bangla.*	29	H17
Nobeoka, *Japan*	23	H5
Noblesville, *U.S.A.*	52	E3
Nocera Inferiore, *Italy*	16	D6
Nocona, *U.S.A.*	55	J6
Noda, *Japan*	23	G9
Nogales, *Mexico*	58	A2
Nogales, *U.S.A.*	57	L8
Nōgata, *Japan*	23	H5
Noggerup, *Australia*	41	F2
Noginsk, *Russia*	21	C10
Nogoa →, *Australia*	42	C4
Noire, Mts., *France*	14	E5
Noirmoutier, Î. de, *France*	14	C2
Nojima-Zaki, *Japan*	23	G9
Nok Kundi, *Pakistan*	28	E3
Nokia, *Finland*	7	F20
Nokomis, *Canada*	51	C8
Nokomis L., *Canada*	51	B8
Nola, *C.A.R.*	36	D3
Nombre de Dios, *Panama*	60	E4

Nome, U.S.A. 46 B3
Nomo-Zaki, Japan . . . 23 H4
Nonacho L., Canada . . 51 A8
Nonda, Australia 42 C3
Nong Khai, Thailand . 26 A2
Nonoava, Mexico 58 B3
Nonoava →, Mexico . 58 B3
Noonamah, Australia . 40 B5
Noord Brabant □, Neths. 11 C5
Noord Holland □, Neths. 11 B4
Noordbeveland, Neths. 11 C3
Noordoostpolder, Neths. 11 B5
Noordwijk, Neths. . . . 11 B4
Nootka I., Canada . . . 50 D3
Nopiming Prov. Park, Canada 51 C9
Noralee, Canada 50 C3
Noranda = Rouyn-Noranda, Canada . . 48 C4
Nord-Ostsee-Kanal, Germany 12 A5
Nordaustlandet, Svalbard 4 B9
Nordegg, Canada 50 C5
Norderney, Germany . . 12 B4
Norderstedt, Germany . 12 B5
Nordfjord, Norway . . . 7 F11
Nordfriesische Inseln, Germany 12 A5
Nordhausen, Germany 12 C6
Norðoyar, Færoe Is. . . 6 E9
Nordkapp, Norway 6 A21
Nordkapp, Svalbard . . 4 A9
Nordkinn-halvøya, Norway 6 A22
Nordrhein-Westfalen □, Germany 12 C4
Nordvik, Russia 21 B12
Norfolk, Nebr., U.S.A. . 54 D6
Norfolk, Va., U.S.A. . . 52 G7
Norfolk □, U.K. 9 E8
Norfolk I., Pac. Oc. . . 38 D9
Norfork L., U.S.A. . . . 55 G8
Norilsk, Russia 21 C9
Norma, Mt., Australia . 42 C3
Normal, U.S.A. 54 E10
Norman, U.S.A. 55 H6
Norman →, Australia . 42 B3
Norman Wells, Canada 46 B7
Normanby →, Australia 42 A3
Normandie, France . . 14 B4
Normandin, Canada . . 48 C5
Normandy = Normandie, France . 14 B4
Normanhurst, Mt., Australia 41 E3
Normanton, Australia . 42 B3
Normétal, Canada . . . 48 C4
Norquay, Canada 51 C8
Norquinco, Argentina . 64 E2
Norrbotten □, Sweden . 6 C19
Norris Point, Canada . 49 C8
Norristown, U.S.A. . . . 52 E8
Norrköping, Sweden . . 7 G17
Norrland, Sweden 7 E16
Norrtälje, Sweden . . . 7 G18
Norseman, Australia . 41 F3
Norsk, Russia 21 D14
Norte, Serra do, Brazil . 62
North, C., Canada 49 C7
North Adams, U.S.A. . 52 D9
North Arm, Canada . . 50 A5
North Augusta, U.S.A. . 53 J5
North Battleford, Canada 51 C7
North Bay, Canada . . . 48 C4
North Belcher Is., Canada 48 A4
North Bend, U.S.A. . . 56 E1
North C., Canada 49 C7
North C., N.Z. 39 F4
North Canadian →, U.S.A. 55 H7
North Cape = Nordkapp, Norway . 6 A21
North Cape = Nordkapp, Svalbard . 4 A9
North Caribou L., Canada 48 B1
North Carolina □, U.S.A. 53 H6
North Cascades National Park, U.S.A. 56 B3
North Channel, Canada 48 C3
North Channel, U.K. . . . 10 D4
North Charleston, U.S.A. 53 J6
North Chicago, U.S.A. . 52 D2
North Dakota □, U.S.A. 54 B5
North Downs, U.K. . . . 9 F8
North East Frontier Agency = Arunachal Pradesh □, India 29 F19
North East Lincolnshire □, U.K. . 8 D7
North Foreland, U.K. . . 9 F9
North Fork Grand →, U.S.A. 54 C3
North Fork Red →, U.S.A. 55 H5
North Frisian Is. = Nordfriesische Inseln, Germany 12 A5
North Hd., Australia . . 41 F1

North Henik L., Canada 51 A9
North I., N.Z. 39 H5
North Knife →, Canada 51 B10
North Korea ■, Asia . 25 C7
North Lakhimpur, India 29 F19
North Las Vegas, U.S.A. 57 H6
North Lincolnshire □, U.K. 8 D7
North Little Rock, U.S.A. 55 H8
North Loup →, U.S.A. 54 E5
North Magnetic Pole, Canada 4 B2
North Minch, U.K. . . . 10 B4
North Moose L., Canada 51 C8
North Myrtle Beach, U.S.A. 53 J6
North Nahanni →, Canada 50 A4
North Ossetia □, Russia 19 F7
North Pagai, I. = Pagai Utara, Pulau, Indonesia 26 E2
North Palisade, U.S.A. . 57 H4
North Platte, U.S.A. . . 54 E4
North Platte →, U.S.A. 54 E4
North Pole, Arctic . . . . 4 A
North Portal, Canada . 51 D8
North Powder, U.S.A. . 56 D5
North Rhine Westphalia = Nordrhein-Westfalen □, Germany 12 C4
North River, Canada . . 49 B8
North Saskatchewan →, Canada 51 C7
North Sea, Europe 10 C7
North Seal →, Canada 51 B9
North Somerset □, U.K. 9 F5
North Sporades = Vóriai Sporádhes, Greece 17 E10
North Sydney, Canada 49 C7
North Taranaki Bight, N.Z. 39 H5
North Thompson →, Canada 50 C4
North Tonawanda, U.S.A. 52 D6
North Truchas Pk., U.S.A. 57 J11
North Twin I., Canada . 48 B4
North Tyne →, U.K. . . 8 B5
North Uist, U.K. 10 C3
North Vancouver, Canada 50 D4
North Vernon, U.S.A. . 52 F3
North Wabasca L., Canada 50 B6
North Walsham, U.K. . 8 E9
North West C., Australia 40 D1
North West Christmas I. Ridge, Pac. Oc. . . 45 G11
North West Frontier □, Pakistan 28 C7
North West Highlands, U.K. 10 C4
North West River, Canada 49 B7
North Wildwood, U.S.A. 52 F8
North York Moors, U.K. 8 C7
North Yorkshire □, U.K. 8 C6
Northallerton, U.K. . . . 8 C6
Northam, Australia . . . 41 F2
Northampton, Australia 41 E1
Northampton, U.K. . . . 9 E7
Northampton, U.S.A. . 52 D9
Northamptonshire □, U.K. 9 E7
Northcliffe, Australia . 41 F2
Northeast Providence Chan., W. Indies . . . 60 A4
Northern Circars, India 29 L13
Northern Indian L., Canada 51 B9
Northern Ireland □, U.K. 10 D3
Northern Light L., Canada 48 C1
Northern Marianas ■, Pac. Oc. 44 F6
Northern Territory □, Australia 40 D5
Northfield, U.S.A. 54 C8
Northland □, N.Z. . . . 39 F4
Northome, U.S.A. 54 B7
Northport, Ala., U.S.A. 53 J2
Northport, Wash., U.S.A. 56 B5
Northumberland □, U.K. 8 B6
Northumberland, C., Australia 43 F3
Northumberland Is., Australia 42 C4
Northumberland Str., Canada 49 C7
Northwest Providence Channel, W. Indies . 60 A4
Northwest Territories □, Canada 46 B9
Northwood, Iowa, U.S.A. 54 D8
Northwood, N. Dak., U.S.A. 54 B6
Norton, U.S.A. 54 F5

Norton Sd., U.S.A. 46 B3
Norwalk, Conn., U.S.A. 52 E9
Norwalk, Iowa, U.S.A. . 54 E8
Norwalk, Ohio, U.S.A. . 52 E4
Norway, Maine, U.S.A. 53 C10
Norway, Mich., U.S.A. . 52 C2
Norway ■, Europe 6 E14
Norway House, Canada 51 C9
Norwegian Sea, Atl. Oc. 4 C8
Norwich, U.K. 9 E9
Norwich, Conn., U.S.A. 52 E9
Norwich, N.Y., U.S.A. . 52 D8
Noshiro, Japan 22 D10
Noşratābād, Iran 31 D8
Nossob →, S. Africa . 37 K4
Nosy Barren, Madag. . . 37 H8
Nosy Be, Madag. 37 G9
Nosy Boraha, Madag. . 37 H9
Nosy Varika, Madag. . 37 J9
Noteć →, Poland 12 B8
Notikewin →, Canada 50 B5
Notodden, Norway . . . 7 G13
Notre Dame B., Canada 49 C8
Notre Dame de Koartac = Quaqtaq, Canada 47 B13
Notre Dame d'Ivugivic = Ivujivik, Canada 47 B12
Notre-Dame-du-Nord, Canada 48 C4
Nottaway →, Canada 48 B4
Nottingham, U.K. 8 E6
Nottingham, City of □, U.K. 8 E6
Nottingham I., Canada 47 B12
Nottinghamshire □, U.K. 8 D6
Nottoway →, U.S.A. . 52 G7
Nouâdhibou, Mauritania 34 D2
Nouâdhibou, Ras, Mauritania 34 D2
Nouakchott, Mauritania 34 E1
Nouméa, N. Cal. 38 D9
Nouveau Comptoir = Wemindji, Canada . . 48 B4
Nouvelle-Amsterdam, I., Ind. Oc. 3 F13
Nouvelle-Calédonie = New Caledonia ■, Pac. Oc. 38 D9
Nova Casa Nova, Brazil 63 E10
Nova Friburgo, Brazil . 63 H10
Nova Gaia = Cambundi-Catembo, Angola . . 36 G3
Nova Iguaçu, Brazil . . 64 A8
Nova Iorque, Brazil . . 63 E10
Nova Lima, Brazil 63 G10
Nova Lisboa = Huambo, Angola 37 G3
Nova Scotia □, Canada 49 C7
Nova Venécia, Brazil . 63 G10
Nova Zagora, Bulgaria 17 C11
Novara, Italy 14 D8
Novaya Ladoga, Russia 18 B5
Novaya Lyalya, Russia 18 C11
Novaya Sibir, Ostrov, Russia 21 B16
Novaya Zemlya, Russia 20 B6
Nové Zámky, Slovak Rep. 13 D10
Novgorod, Russia 18 C5
Novgorod-Severskiy = Novhorod-Siverskyy, Ukraine 18 D5
Novhorod-Siverskyy, Ukraine 18 D5
Novi Ligure, Italy 14 D8
Novi Pazar, Serbia, Yug. 17 C9
Novi Sad, Serbia, Yug. 17 B8
Nôvo Hamburgo, Brazil 64 B6
Novo Mesto, Slovenia . 16 B8
Novo Remanso, Brazil . 63 E10
Novoataysk, Russia . . 20 D9
Novocherkassk, Russia 19 E7
Novogrudok = Navahrudak, Belarus 13 B13
Novohrad-Volynskyy, Ukraine 13 C14
Novokachalinsk, Russia 22 B6
Novokazalinsk = Zhangaqazaly, Kazakstan 20 E7
Novokuybyshevsk, Russia 18 D8
Novokuznetsk, Russia . 20 D9
Novomoskovsk, Russia 18 D6
Novorossiysk, Russia . 19 F6
Novorybnoye, Russia . 21 B11
Novoselytsya, Ukraine 13 D14
Novoshakhtinsk, Russia 19 E6
Novosibirsk, Russia . . 20 D9
Novosibirskiye Ostrova, Russia 21 B15
Novotroitsk, Russia . . 18 D10
Novouzensk, Russia . . 19 D8
Novovolynsk, Ukraine . 13 C13
Novska, Croatia 16 B7
Novvy Urengoy, Russia 20 C8
Novyy Bor, Russia . . . 18 A9
Novyy Port, Russia . . . 20 C8
Now Shahr, Iran 31 B6
Nowa Sól, Poland . . . 12 C8
Nowata, U.S.A. 55 G7
Nowbarān, Iran 31 C6
Nowghāb, Iran 31 C8

Nowgong, India 29 F18
Nowra-Bomaderry, Australia 43 E5
Nowshera, Pakistan . . 28 C8
Nowy Sącz, Poland . . . 13 D11
Nowy Targ, Poland . . . 13 D11
Nowy Tomyśl, Poland . 12 B9
Noxon, U.S.A. 56 C6
Noyabr'sk, Russia 20 C8
Noyon, France 14 B5
Nsanje, Malawi 37 H7
Nu Jiang →, China . . 24 D4
Nu Shan, China 24 D4
Nubian Desert = Nûbîya, Es Sahrâ en, Sudan 35 D12
Nûbîya, Es Sahrâ en, Sudan 35 D12
Nuboai, Indonesia . . . 27 E9
Nueces →, U.S.A. . . . 55 M6
Nueltin L., Canada . . . 51 A9
Nueva Gerona, Cuba . 60 B3
Nueva Rosita, Mexico . 58 B4
Nueva San Salvador, El Salv. 60 D2
Nuéve de Julio, Argentina 64 D4
Nuevitas, Cuba 60 B4
Nuevo, G., Argentina . 64 E4
Nuevo Casas Grandes, Mexico 58 A3
Nuevo Guerrero, Mexico 59 B5
Nuevo Laredo, Mexico 59 B5
Nuevo León □, Mexico 58 C5
Nuevo Rocafuerte, Ecuador 62 D3
Nugget Pt., N.Z. 39 M2
Nuhaka, N.Z. 39 H6
Nukey Bluff, Australia . 43 E2
Nukhuyb, Iraq 30 C4
Nuku'alofa, Tonga . . . 39 E12
Nukus, Uzbekistan . . . 20 E6
Nullagine, Australia . . 40 D3
Nullagine →, Australia 40 D3
Nullarbor, Australia . . 41 F5
Nullarbor Plain, Australia 41 F4
Numalla, L., Australia . 43 D3
Numan, Nigeria 35 G8
Numata, Japan 23 F9
Numazu, Japan 23 G9
Numbulwar, Australia . 42 A2
Numfoor, Indonesia . . 27 E8
Numurkah, Australia . 43 F4
Nunaksaluk I., Canada 49 A7
Nunap Isua, Greenland 4 D5
Nunavut □, Canada . . 47 B11
Nuneaton, U.K. 10 E6
Nungarin, Australia . . 41 F2
Nunivak I., U.S.A. . . . 46 B3
Nunkun, India 28 C10
Núoro, Italy 16 D3
Nūrābād, Iran 31 E8
Nuremberg = Nürnberg, Germany 12 D6
Nuri, Mexico 58 B3
Nuriootpa, Australia . 43 E2
Nürnberg, Germany . . 12 D6
Nurran, L. = Terewah, L., Australia 43 D4
Nurrari Lakes, Australia 41 E5
Nusa Barung, Indonesia 27 H15
Nusa Kambangan, Indonesia 27 G13
Nusa Tenggara Barat □, Indonesia 26 F5
Nusa Tenggara Timur □, Indonesia . 27 F6
Nusaybin, Turkey 19 G7
Nushki, Pakistan 28 E5
Nuuk, Greenland 47 B14
Nuwakot, Nepal 29 E13
Nuweiba', Egypt 30 D2
Nuweveldberge, S. Africa 37 L4
Nuyts, C., Australia . . . 41 F5
Nuyts, Pt., Australia . . 41 G2
Nuyts Arch., Australia . 43 E1
Nyabing, Australia . . . 41 F2
Nyagan, Russia 20 C7
Nyahururu, Kenya . . . 36 D7
Nyaingentanglha Shan, China 24 D4
Nyâlâ, Sudan 35 F10
Nyandoma, Russia . . . 18 B7
Nyasa, L., Africa 37 G6
Nyasvizh, Belarus . . . 13 B14
Nyazepetrovsk, Russia 18 C10
Nybro, Sweden 7 H16
Nyda, Russia 20 C8
Nyíregyháza, Hungary 13 E11
Nykøbing, Storstrøm, Denmark 7 J14
Nykøbing, Vestsjælland, Denmark 7 J14
Nykøbing, Viborg, Denmark 7 H13
Nyköping, Sweden . . . 7 G17
Nylstroom, S. Africa . 37 J5
Nymagee, Australia . . 43 E4
Nynäshamn, Sweden . 7 G17
Nyngan, Australia . . . 43 E4
Nyoman = Neman →, Lithuania 7 J19

Nysa, Poland 13 C9
Nysa →, Europe 12 B8
Nyssa, U.S.A. 56 E5
Nyunzu, Dem. Rep. of the Congo 36 F5
Nyurba, Russia 21 C12
Nzega, Tanzania 36 E6
Nzérékoré, Guinea . . . 34 G4
Nzeto, Angola 36 F2
Ô-Shima, Japan 23 G9
Oacoma, U.S.A. 54 D5
Oahe, L., U.S.A. 54 C4
Oahe Dam, U.S.A. . . . 54 C4
Oak Harbor, U.S.A. . . 56 B2
Oak Hill, U.S.A. 52 G5
Oak Ridge, U.S.A. . . . 53 G3
Oakan-Dake, Japan . . 22 C12
Oakdale, U.S.A. 55 K8
Oakes, U.S.A. 54 B5
Oakesdale, U.S.A. . . . 56 C5
Oakey, Australia 43 D5
Oakham, U.K. 9 E7
Oakland, U.S.A. 57 H2
Oakley, Idaho, U.S.A. . 56 E7
Oakley, Kans., U.S.A. . 54 F4
Oakover →, Australia 40 D3
Oakridge, U.S.A. 56 E2
Oakville, U.S.A. 56 C1
Oamaru, N.Z. 39 L3
Oates Land, Antarctica 5 C11
Oatlands, Australia . . 42 G4
Oaxaca, Mexico 59 D5
Oaxaca □, Mexico . . . 59 D5
Ob →, Russia 20 C7
Oba, Canada 48 C3
Obama, Japan 23 G7
Oban, U.K. 10 C4
Obbia, Somali Rep. . . 32 F4
Oberhausen, Germany 12 C4
Oberlin, Kans., U.S.A. . 54 F4
Oberlin, La., U.S.A. . . 55 K8
Oberon, Australia . . . 43 E4
Obi, Kepulauan, Indonesia 27 E7
Obi Is. = Obi, Kepulauan, Indonesia 27 E7
Óbidos, Brazil 63 D7
Obihiro, Japan 22 C11
Obilatu, Indonesia . . . 27 E7
Obluchye, Russia 21 E14
Obo, C.A.R. 36 C5
Oboyan, Russia 20 D4
Obozerskaya = Obozerskiy, Russia . . 18 B7
Obozerskiy, Russia . . 18 B7
Observatory Inlet, Canada 50 B3
Obskaya Guba, Russia 20 C8
Obuasi, Ghana 34 G5
Ocala, U.S.A. 53 L4
Ocampo, Chihuahua, Mexico 58 B3
Ocampo, Tamaulipas, Mexico 59 C5
Ocaña, Spain 15 C4
Ocanomowoc, U.S.A. . 54 D10
Occidental, Cordillera, Colombia 62 C3
Ocean City, Md., U.S.A. 52 F8
Ocean City, N.J., U.S.A. 52 F8
Ocean Falls, Canada . 50 C3
Ocean I. = Banaba, Kiribati 44 H8
Ocean Park, U.S.A. . . 56 C1
Oceanside, U.S.A. . . . 57 K5
Ocilla, U.S.A. 53 K4
Ocmulgee →, U.S.A. . 53 K4
Ocniţa, Moldova 13 D14
Oconee →, U.S.A. . . . 53 K4
Oconto, U.S.A. 52 C2
Oconto Falls, U.S.A. . . 52 C1
Ocosingo, Mexico . . . 59 D6
Ocotal, Nic. 60 D2
Ocotlán, Mexico 58 C4
Ocotlán de Morelos, Mexico 59 D5
Ôda, Japan 23 G6
Óðáðahraun, Iceland . 6 D5
Odate, Japan 22 D10
Odawara, Japan 23 G9
Odda, Norway 7 F12
Odei →, Canada 51 B9
Ödemiş, Turkey 17 E13
Odense, Denmark . . . 7 J14
Oder →, Europe 12 B8
Odesa, Ukraine 19 E5
Odessa = Odesa, Ukraine 19 E5
Odessa, Tex., U.S.A. . . 55 K3
Odessa, Wash., U.S.A. 56 C4
Odienné, Ivory C. . . . 34 G4
Odintsovo, Russia . . . 18 C6
Odorheiu Secuiesc, Romania 13 E13
Odra = Oder →, Europe 12 B8
Odzi, Zimbabwe 37 H6
Oeiras, Brazil 63 E10
Oelrichs, U.S.A. 54 D3
Oelwein, U.S.A. 54 D9
Oenpelli, Australia . . . 40 B5
Ofanto →, Italy 16 D7
Offa, Nigeria 34 G6

Offenbach, Germany . 12 C5
Offenburg, Germany . 12 D4
Ofotfjorden, Norway . 6 B17
Ôfunato, Japan 22 E10
Oga, Japan 22 E9
Oga-Hantō, Japan . . . 22 E9
Ogaden, Ethiopia 32 F3
Ôgaki, Japan 23 G8
Ogallala, U.S.A. 54 E4
Ogasawara Gunto, Pac. Oc. 44 E6
Ogbomosho, Nigeria . 34 G6
Ogden, U.S.A. 56 F7
Ogdensburg, U.S.A. . 52 C8
Ogeechee →, U.S.A. 53 K5
Oglio →, Italy 16 B4
Ogmore, Australia . . . 42 C4
Ogoki, Canada 48 B2
Ogoki →, Canada . . . 48 B2
Ogoki L., Canada . . . 48 B2
Ogoki Res., Canada . 48 B2
Ogooué →, Gabon . . 36 E1
Ogowe = Ogooué →, Gabon 36 E1
Ogre, Latvia 7 H21
Ogurchinskiy, Ostrov, Turkmenistan 31 B7
Ohai, N.Z. 39 L2
Ohakune, N.Z. 39 H5
Ohata, Japan 22 D10
Ohau, L., N.Z. 39 L2
Ohio □, U.S.A. 52 E3
Ohio →, U.S.A. 52 G1
Ohře →, Czech Rep. . 12 C8
Ohrid, Macedonia . . . 17 D9
Ohridsko Jezero, Macedonia 17 D9
Oiapoque, Brazil 63
Oil City, U.S.A. 52 E6
Oise →, France 14 B5
Ôita, Japan 23 H5
Ôita □, Japan 23 H5
Oiticica, Brazil 63 E10
Ojacaliente, Mexico . 58 C4
Ojai, U.S.A. 57 J4
Ojinaga, Mexico 58 B4
Ojiya, Japan 23 F9
Ojos del Salado, Cerro, Argentina 64 B3
Oka →, Russia 18 C7
Okaba, Indonesia . . . 27 F9
Okahandja, Namibia . 37 J3
Okanagan L., Canada . 50 D5
Okanogan, U.S.A. . . . 56 B4
Okanogan →, U.S.A. 56 B4
Okara, Pakistan 28 D8
Okavango Swamps, Botswana 37 H4
Okaya, Japan 23 F9
Okayama, Japan 23 G6
Okayama □, Japan . . 23 G6
Okazaki, Japan 23 G8
Okeechobee, U.S.A. . 53 M5
Okeechobee, L., U.S.A. 53 M5
Okefenokee Swamp, U.S.A. 53 K4
Okehampton, U.K. . . . 9 G4
Okha, Russia 21 D15
Okhotsk, Russia 21 D15
Okhotsk, Sea of, Asia . 21 D15
Okhotskiy Perevoz, Russia 21 C14
Okhtyrka, Ukraine . . . 19 D5
Oki-Shotō, Japan . . . 23 F6
Okinawa □, Japan . . 23 L4
Okinawa-Guntō, Japan 23 L4
Okinawa-Jima, Japan 23 L4
Okino-erabu-Shima, Japan 23 L4
Oklahoma □, U.S.A. . 55 H6
Oklahoma City, U.S.A. 55 H6
Okmulgee, U.S.A. . . . 55 H7
Oknitsa = Ocniţa, Moldova 13 D14
Okolona, U.S.A. 55 J10
Okotoks, Canada . . . 50 C6
Oksibil, Indonesia . . . 27 E10
Oksovskiy, Russia . . . 18 B6
Oktabrsk = Oktyabrsk, Kazakstan 19 E10
Oktyabrsk, Kazakstan 19 E10
Oktyabrskiy = Aktsyabrski, Belarus 13 B15
Oktyabrskiy, Russia . . 18 D9
Oktyabrskoy Revolyutsii, Ostrov, Russia 21 B10
Okuru, N.Z. 39 K2
Okushiri-Tō, Japan . . 22 C9
Ola, U.S.A. 55 H8
Ólafsfjörður, Iceland . 6 C4
Ólafsvík, Iceland 6 D2
Olancha, U.S.A. 57 H4
Olanchito, Honduras . 60 C2
Öland, Sweden 7 H17
Olary, Australia 43 E3
Olathe, U.S.A. 54 F7
Olavarría, Argentina . 64 D4
Oława, Poland 13 C9
Ólbia, Italy 16 D3
Old Bahama Chan. = Bahama, Canal Viejo de, W. Indies 60 B4
Old Castile = Castilla y Leon □, Spain . . . 15 B3
Old Crow, Canada . . . 46 B6

Old Perlican

Old Perlican, Canada 49 C9
Old Town, U.S.A. 53 C11
Old Wives L., Canada 51 C7
Oldbury, U.K. 9 F5
Oldenburg, Germany 12 B5
Oldenzaal, Neths. 11 B6
Oldham, U.K. 8 D5
Oldman →, Canada 50 D6
Olds, Canada 50 C6
Olean, U.S.A. 52 D6
Olekma →, Russia 21 C13
Olekminsk, Russia 21 C13
Oleksandriya, Ukraine 13 C14
Olenegorsk, Russia 18 A5
Olenek, Russia 21 C12
Olenek →, Russia 21 B13
Oléron, Î. d', France 14 D3
Oleśnica, Poland 13 C9
Olevsk, Ukraine 13 C14
Olga, Russia 21 E14
Olga, L., Canada 48 C4
Olga, Mt., Australia 41 E5
Olhão, Portugal 15 D2
Olifants →, Africa 37 J6
Ólimbos, Óros, Greece 17 D10
Olinda, Brazil 63 E12
Olivenza, Spain 15 C2
Oliver, Canada 50 D5
Oliver L., Canada 51 B8
Ollagüe, Chile 62 H5
Olney, Ill., U.S.A. 52 F1
Olney, Tex., U.S.A. 55 J5
Olomane →, Canada 49 B7
Olomouc, Czech Rep. 13 D9
Olonets, Russia 18 B5
Olongapo, Phil. 27 B6
Olot, Spain 15 A7
Olovyannaya, Russia 21 D12
Oloy →, Russia 21 C16
Olsztyn, Poland 13 B11
Olt →, Romania 13 G13
Olteniţa, Romania 13 F14
Olton, U.S.A. 55 H3
Olympia, Greece 17 F9
Olympia, U.S.A. 56 C2
Olympic Dam, Australia 43 E2
Olympic Mts., U.S.A. 56 C2
Olympic Nat. Park, U.S.A. 56 C2
Olympus, Cyprus 30 C2
Olympus, Mt. = Ólimbos, Óros, Greece 17 D10
Olympus, Mt. = Uludağ, Turkey 17 D13
Olympus, Mt., U.S.A. 56 C2
Om →, Russia 20 D8
Ōma, Japan 22 D10
Ōmachi, Japan 23 F8
Omae-Zaki, Japan 23 G9
Ōmagari, Japan 22 E10
Omagh, U.K. 10 D3
Omaha, U.S.A. 54 E7
Omak, U.S.A. 56 B4
Oman ■, Asia 32 C6
Oman, G. of, Asia 31 E8
Omaruru, Namibia 37 J3
Omate, Peru 62 G4
Ombai, Selat, Indonesia 27 F6
Omboué, Gabon 36 E1
Ombrone →, Italy 16 C4
Omdurmân, Sudan 35 E12
Omeo, Australia 43 F4
Ometepe, I. de, Nic. 60 D2
Ometepec, Mexico 59 D5
Ominato, Japan 22 D10
Omineca →, Canada 50 B4
Ōmiya, Japan 23 G9
Ommen, Neths. 11 B6
Omo →, Ethiopia 32 F2
Omolon →, Russia 21 C16
Omono-Gawa →, Japan 22 E10
Omsk, Russia 20 D8
Omsukchan, Russia 21 C16
Ōmu, Japan 22 B11
Omul, Vf., Romania 13 F13
Ōmura, Japan 23 H4
Omuramba Omatako →, Namibia 37 H4
Ōmuta, Japan 23 H5
Onaga, U.S.A. 54 F6
Onalaska, U.S.A. 54 D9
Onancock, U.S.A. 52 G8
Onang, Indonesia 27 E5
Onaping L., Canada 48 C3
Onavas, Mexico 58 B3
Onawa, U.S.A. 54 D6
Onda, Spain 15 C5
Ondangua, Namibia 37 H3
Öndverðarnes, Iceland 6 D1
One Tree, Australia 43 E3
Onega, Russia 18 B6
Onega →, Russia 18 B6
Onega, G. of = Onezhskaya Guba, Russia 18 B6
Onega, L. = Onezhskoye Ozero, Russia 18 B6
Oneida, U.S.A. 52 D8
Oneida L., U.S.A. 52 D8
O'Neill, U.S.A. 54 D5
Onekotan, Ostrov, Russia 21 E16
Oneonta, U.S.A. 52 D8
Oneşti, Romania 13 E14
Onezhskaya Guba, Russia 18 B6
Onezhskoye Ozero, Russia 18 B6
Ongarue, N.Z. 39 H5
Ongerup, Australia 41 F2
Ongole, India 28 M12
Onida, U.S.A. 54 C4
Onilahy →, Madag. 37 J8
Onitsha, Nigeria 34 G7
Onoda, Japan 23 G5
Onslow, Australia 40 D2
Onslow B., U.S.A. 53 H7
Ontake-San, Japan 23 G8
Ontario, Calif., U.S.A. 57 J5
Ontario, Oreg., U.S.A. 56 D5
Ontario □, Canada 48 B2
Ontario, L., N. Amer. 48 D4
Ontonagon, U.S.A. 54 B10
Oodnadatta, Australia 43 D2
Ooldea, Australia 41 F5
Oombulgurri, Australia 40 C4
Oorindi, Australia 42 C3
Oost-Vlaanderen □, Belgium 11 C3
Oostende, Belgium 11 C2
Oosterhout, Neths. 11 C4
Oosterschelde →, Neths. 11 C4
Oosterwolde, Neths. 11 B6
Ootacamund = Udagamandalam, India 28 P10
Ootsa L., Canada 50 C3
Opala, Dem. Rep. of the Congo 36 E4
Opanake, Sri Lanka 28 R12
Opasatika, Canada 48 C3
Opasquia Prov. Park, Canada 48 B1
Opava, Czech Rep. 13 D9
Opelika, U.S.A. 53 J3
Opelousas, U.S.A. 55 K8
Opémisca, L., Canada 48 C5
Opheim, U.S.A. 56 B10
Ophthalmia Ra., Australia 40 D2
Opinaca →, Canada 48 B4
Opinaca, Rés., Canada 48 B4
Opinnagau →, Canada 48 B3
Opiscoteo, L., Canada 49 B6
Opole, Poland 13 C9
Oporto = Porto, Portugal 15 B1
Opotiki, N.Z. 39 H6
Opp, U.S.A. 53 K2
Oppdal, Norway 7 E13
Opportunity, U.S.A. 56 C5
Opua, N.Z. 39 F5
Opunake, N.Z. 39 H4
Oracle, U.S.A. 57 K8
Oradea, Romania 13 E11
Öræfajökull, Iceland 6 D5
Orai, India 28 G11
Oral = Zhayyq →, Kazakstan 19 E9
Oral, Kazakstan 19 D9
Oran, Algeria 34 A5
Orange, Australia 43 E4
Orange, France 14 D6
Orange, Tex., U.S.A. 55 K8
Orange, Va., U.S.A. 52 F6
Orange →, S. Africa 37 K3
Orange, C., Brazil 63 C8
Orange Free State = Free State □, S. Africa 37 K5
Orange Grove, U.S.A. 55 M6
Orange Walk, Belize 59 D7
Orangeburg, U.S.A. 53 J5
Orangeville, Canada 48 D3
Oranienburg, Germany 12 B7
Oranje = Orange →, S. Africa 37 K3
Oranje Vrystaat = Free State □, S. Africa 37 K5
Orapa, Botswana 37 J5
Oras, Phil. 27 B7
Oraşul Stalin = Braşov, Romania 13 F13
Orbetello, Italy 16 C4
Orbost, Australia 43 F4
Orchard City, U.S.A. 57 G10
Orchila, I., Venezuela 62 A5
Ord, U.S.A. 54 E5
Ord →, Australia 40 C4
Ord, Mt., Australia 40 C4
Orderville, U.S.A. 57 H7
Ordos = Mu Us Shamo, China 25 C5
Ordu, Turkey 19 F6
Ordway, U.S.A. 54 F3
Ordzhonikidze = Vladikavkaz, Russia 19 F7
Ore Mts. = Erzgebirge, Germany 12 C7
Örebro, Sweden 7 G16
Oregon, U.S.A. 54 D10
Oregon □, U.S.A. 56 E3
Oregon City, U.S.A. 56 D2
Orekhovo-Zuyevo, Russia 18 C6
Orel, Russia 18 D6
Orem, U.S.A. 56 F8
Ören, Turkey 17 F12
Orenburg, Russia 18 D10
Orense = Ourense, Spain 15 A2
Orepuki, N.Z. 39 M1
Orestiás, Greece 17 D12
Orestos Pereyra, Mexico 58 B3
Orford Ness, U.K. 9 E9
Orgaz, Spain 15 C4
Orgeyev = Orhei, Moldova 13 E15
Orhaneli, Turkey 17 E13
Orhangazi, Turkey 17 D13
Orhei, Moldova 13 E15
Orhon Gol →, Mongolia 24 A5
Oriental, Cordillera, Colombia 62 B4
Orihuela, Spain 15 C5
Orillia, Canada 48 D4
Orinoco →, Venezuela 62 B6
Orion, Canada 51 D6
Orissa □, India 29 K14
Orissaare, Estonia 7 G20
Oristano, Italy 16 E3
Oristano, G. di, Italy 16 E3
Orizaba, Mexico 59 D5
Orkanger, Norway 6 E13
Orkla →, Norway 6 E13
Orkney Is., U.K. 10 B5
Orland, U.S.A. 56 G2
Orlando, U.S.A. 53 L5
Orléanais, France 14 C5
Orléans, France 14 C4
Orléans, I. d', Canada 49 C5
Ormara, Pakistan 28 G4
Ormoc, Phil. 27 B6
Ormond, N.Z. 39 H6
Ormond Beach, U.S.A. 53 L5
Ormskirk, U.K. 8 D5
Örnsköldsvik, Sweden 6 E18
Oro →, Mexico 58 B3
Oro Valley, U.S.A. 57 K8
Orocué, Colombia 62 C4
Orofino, U.S.A. 56 C5
Orol Dengizi = Aral Sea, Asia 20 E7
Oromocto, Canada 49 C6
Orono, U.S.A. 53 C11
Oroqen Zizhiqi, China 25 A7
Oroquieta, Phil. 27 C6
Orosháza, Hungary 13 E11
Orotukan, Russia 21 C16
Oroville, Calif., U.S.A. 56 G3
Oroville, Wash., U.S.A. 56 B4
Orroroo, Australia 43 E2
Orsha, Belarus 18 D5
Orsk, Russia 20 D6
Orşova, Romania 13 F12
Ortaca, Turkey 17 F13
Ortegal, C., Spain 15 A2
Orthez, France 14 E3
Ortigueira, Spain 15 A2
Ortles, Italy 14 C9
Ortón →, Bolivia 62 F5
Ortonville, U.S.A. 54 C6
Orūmīyeh, Iran 30 B5
Orūmīyeh, Daryācheh-ye, Iran 30 B5
Oruro, Bolivia 62 G5
Orust, Sweden 7 G14
Oruzgān □, Afghan. 28 C5
Orvieto, Italy 16 C5
Orwell →, U.K. 9 F9
Oryakhovo, Bulgaria 17 C10
Osa, Russia 18 C10
Osa, Pen. de, Costa Rica 60 E3
Osage, U.S.A. 54 D8
Osage →, U.S.A. 54 F9
Osage City, U.S.A. 54 F7
Ōsaka, Japan 23 G7
Osawatomie, U.S.A. 54 F7
Osborne, U.S.A. 54 F5
Osceola, Ark., U.S.A. 55 H10
Osceola, Iowa, U.S.A. 54 E8
Oscoda, U.S.A. 52 C4
Ösel = Saaremaa, Estonia 7 G20
Osh, Kyrgyzstan 20 E8
Oshakati, Namibia 37 H3
Oshawa, Canada 48 D4
Oshkosh, Nebr., U.S.A. 54 E3
Oshkosh, Wis., U.S.A. 54 C10
Oshmyany = Ashmyany, Belarus 7 J21
Oshnovīyeh, Iran 30 B5
Oshogbo, Nigeria 34 G6
Oshtorīnān, Iran 31 C6
Oshwe, Dem. Rep. of the Congo 36 E3
Osijek, Croatia 17 B8
Osipenko = Berdyansk, Ukraine 19 E6
Osipovichi = Asipovichy, Belarus 13 B15
Osizweni, S. Africa 37 K6
Oskaloosa, U.S.A. 54 E8
Oskarshamn, Sweden 7 H17
Oskélanéo, Canada 48 C4
Öskemen, Kazakstan 20 E9
Oslo, Norway 7 G14
Oslofjorden, Norway 7 G14
Osmanabad, India 28 K10
Osmaniye, Turkey 19 G6
Osnabrück, Germany 12 B5
Osorno, Chile 64 E2
Osoyoos, Canada 50 D5
Osøyro, Norway 7 F11
Ospika →, Canada 50 B4
Osprey Reef, Australia 42 A4
Oss, Neths. 11 C5
Ossa, Mt., Australia 42 G4
Óssa, Óros, Greece 17 E10
Ossabaw I., U.S.A. 53 K5
Ossokmanuan L., Canada 49 B7
Ossora, Russia 21 D17
Ostend = Oostende, Belgium 11 C2
Oster, Ukraine 13 C16
Österdalälven, Sweden 7 F16
Østerdalen, Norway 7 F14
Östersund, Sweden 6 E16
Ostfriesische Inseln, Germany 12 B4
Ostrava, Czech Rep. 13 D10
Ostróda, Poland 13 B10
Ostroh, Ukraine 13 C14
Ostrołęka, Poland 13 B11
Ostrów Mazowiecka, Poland 13 B11
Ostrów Wielkopolski, Poland 13 C9
Ostrowiec-Świętokrzyski, Poland 13 C11
Ostuni, Italy 17 D7
Ōsumi-Kaikyō, Japan 23 J5
Ōsumi-Shotō, Japan 23 J5
Osuna, Spain 15 D3
Oswego, U.S.A. 52 D7
Oswestry, U.K. 8 E4
Oświęcim, Poland 13 C10
Otago □, N.Z. 39 L2
Otago Harbour, N.Z. 39 L3
Ōtake, Japan 23 G6
Otaki, N.Z. 39 J5
Otaru, Japan 22 C10
Otaru-Wan = Ishikari-Wan, Japan 22 C10
Otavalo, Ecuador 62 C3
Otelnuk L., Canada 49 A6
Othello, U.S.A. 56 C4
Otjiwarongo, Namibia 37 J3
Otoineppu, Japan 22 B11
Otorohanga, N.Z. 39 H5
Otoskwin →, Canada 48 B2
Otra →, Norway 7 G13
Otranto, Italy 17 D8
Otranto, C. d', Italy 17 D8
Otranto, Str. of, Italy 17 D8
Ōtsu, Japan 23 G7
Ōtsuki, Japan 23 G9
Ottawa = Outaouais →, Canada 48 C5
Ottawa, Canada 48 C4
Ottawa, Ill., U.S.A. 54 E10
Ottawa, Kans., U.S.A. 54 F7
Ottawa Is., Canada 47 C11
Otter L., Canada 51 B8
Ottery St. Mary, U.K. 9 G4
Ottumwa, U.S.A. 54 E8
Oturkpo, Nigeria 34 G7
Otway, B., Chile 64 G2
Otway, C., Australia 43 F3
Otwock, Poland 13 B11
Ou-Sammyaku, Japan 22 E10
Ouachita →, U.S.A. 55 K9
Ouachita, L., U.S.A. 55 H8
Ouachita Mts., U.S.A. 55 H7
Ouadda, C.A.R. 32
Ouagadougou, Burkina Faso 34 F5
Ouahran = Oran, Algeria 34 A5
Ouallene, Algeria 34 D6
Ouanda Djallé, C.A.R. 32
Ouargla, Algeria 34 B7
Ouarzazate, Morocco 34 B4
Oubangi →, Dem. Rep. of the Congo 36 E3
Ouddorp, Neths. 11 C3
Oude Rijn →, Neths. 11 B4
Oudenaarde, Belgium 11 D3
Oudtshoorn, S. Africa 37 L4
Ouessant, Î. d', France 14 B1
Ouesso, Congo 36 D3
Ouest, Pte. de l', Canada 49 C7
Ouezzane, Morocco 34 B4
Oujda, Morocco 34 B5
Oulainen, Finland 6 D21
Oulu, Finland 6 D21
Oulujärvi, Finland 6 D22
Oulujoki →, Finland 6 D21
Oum Chalouba, Chad 35 E10
Oum Hadjer, Chad 35 F9
Ounasjoki →, Finland 6 C21
Ounianga Sérir, Chad 35 E10
Our →, Lux. 11 E6
Ouray, U.S.A. 57 G10
Ourense, Spain 15 A2
Ouricuri, Brazil 63 E10
Ourinhos, Brazil 64 A7
Ouro Prêto, Brazil 63 H10
Ourthe →, Belgium 11 D5
Ouse →, E. Susx., U.K. 9 G8
Ouse →, N. Yorks., U.K. 8 D7
Outaouais →, Canada 48 C5
Outardes →, Canada 49 C6
Outer Hebrides, U.K. 10 C3
Outjo, Namibia 37 J3
Outlook, Canada 51 C7
Outokumpu, Finland 6 E23
Ouyen, Australia 43 F3
Ovalau, Fiji 39 C8
Ovalle, Chile 64 C2
Ovamboland, Namibia 37 H3
Overflakkee, Neths. 11 C4
Overijssel □, Neths. 11 B6
Overland Park, U.S.A. 54 F7
Overton, U.S.A. 57 H6
Övertorneå, Sweden 6 C20
Oviedo, Spain 15 A3
Oviši, Latvia 7 H19
Øvre Årdal, Norway 7 F12
Ovruch, Ukraine 13 C15
Owaka, N.Z. 39 M2
Owambo = Ovamboland, Namibia 37 H3
Owase, Japan 23 G8
Owatonna, U.S.A. 54 C8
Owbeh, Afghan. 28 B3
Owen Sound, Canada 48 D3
Owen Stanley Ra., Papua N. G. 38 B7
Owens L., U.S.A. 57 H5
Owensboro, U.S.A. 52 G2
Owl →, Canada 51 B10
Owo, Nigeria 34 G7
Owosso, U.S.A. 52 D3
Owyhee, U.S.A. 56 F5
Owyhee →, U.S.A. 56 E5
Owyhee, L., U.S.A. 56 E5
Öxarfjörður, Iceland 6 C5
Oxbow, Canada 51 D8
Oxelösund, Sweden 7 G17
Oxford, N.Z. 39 K4
Oxford, U.K. 9 F6
Oxford, Miss., U.S.A. 55 H10
Oxford, N.C., U.S.A. 53 G6
Oxford, Ohio, U.S.A. 52 F3
Oxford L., Canada 51 C9
Oxfordshire □, U.K. 9 F6
Oxnard, U.S.A. 57 J4
Oxus = Amudarya →, Uzbekistan 20 E6
Oya, Malaysia 26 D4
Oyama, Japan 23 F9
Oyem, Gabon 36 D2
Oyen, Canada 51 C6
Oymyakon, Russia 21 C15
Oyo, Nigeria 34 G6
Öyübari, Japan 22 C11
Ozamiz, Phil. 27 C6
Ozark, Ala., U.S.A. 53 K3
Ozark, Ark., U.S.A. 55 H8
Ozark, Mo., U.S.A. 55 G8
Ozark Plateau, U.S.A. 55 G9
Ozarks, L. of the, U.S.A. 54 F8
Ózd, Hungary 13 D11
Ozona, U.S.A. 55 K4
Ozuluama, Mexico 59 C5

Pa-an, Burma 29 L20
Pa Sak →, Thailand 26 B2
Paamiut, Greenland 4 C5
Paarl, S. Africa 37 L3
Pab Hills, Pakistan 28 F5
Pabianice, Poland 13 C10
Pabna, Bangla. 29 G16
Pacaja →, Brazil 63 D8
Pacaraima, Sa., S. Amer. 62 C6
Pacasmayo, Peru 62 E3
Pachitea →, Peru 62 E4
Pachpadra, India 28 G8
Pachuca, Mexico 59 C5
Pacific, Canada 50 C3
Pacific-Antarctic Ridge, Pac. Oc. 45 M16
Pacific Grove, U.S.A. 57 H3
Pacific Ocean, Pac. Oc. 45 G14
Pacitan, Indonesia 27 H14
Padaido, Kepulauan, Indonesia 27 E9
Padang, Indonesia 26 E2
Padangpanjang, Indonesia 26 E2
Padangsidempuan, Indonesia 26 D1
Paddle Prairie, Canada 50 B5
Paddockwood, Canada 51 C7
Paderborn, Germany 12 C5
Pádova, Italy 16 B4
Padre I., U.S.A. 55 M6
Padstow, U.K. 9 G3
Padua = Pádova, Italy 16 B4
Paducah, Ky., U.S.A. 52 G1
Paducah, Tex., U.S.A. 55 H4
Paeroa, N.Z. 39 G5
Pag, Croatia 12 F8
Pagadian, Phil. 27 C6
Pagai Selatan, Pulau, Indonesia 26 E2
Pagai Utara, Pulau, Indonesia 26 E2
Pagastikós Kólpos, Greece 17 E10
Pagatan, Indonesia 26 E5
Page, U.S.A. 57 H8
Pago Pago, Amer. Samoa 39 B13
Pagosa Springs, U.S.A. 57 H10
Pagwa River, Canada 48 B2
Pahiatua, N.Z. 39 J5
Pahokee, U.S.A. 53 M5
Pahrump, U.S.A. 57 H6
Paide, Estonia 7 G21
Paignton, U.K. 9 G4
Päijänne, Finland 7 F21
Painan, Indonesia 26 E2
Paint Hills = Wemindji, Canada 48 B4
Paint L., Canada 51 B9
Painted Desert, U.S.A. 57 J8
Paintsville, U.S.A. 52 G4
País Vasco □, Spain 15 A4
Paisley, U.K. 10 D4
Paisley, U.S.A. 56 E3
Paita, Peru 62 E2
Pajares, Puerto de, Spain 15 A3
Pak Phanang, Thailand 26 C2
Pakistan ■, Asia 28 E7
Pakokku, Burma 29 J19
Pakowki L., Canada 51 D6
Paktīā □, Afghan. 28 C6
Pakwach, Uganda 36 D6
Pakxe, Laos 26 A3
Pala, Chad 35 G9
Palacios, U.S.A. 55 L6
Palagruža, Croatia 16 C7
Palam, India 28 K10
Palampur, India 28 C10
Palana, Australia 42 F4
Palana, Russia 21 D16
Palanan, Phil. 27 A6
Palanan Pt., Phil. 27 A6
Palanga, Lithuania 7 J19
Palangkaraya, Indonesia 26 E4
Palani Hills, India 28 P10
Palanpur, India 28 G8
Palapye, Botswana 37 J5
Palatka, Russia 21 C16
Palatka, U.S.A. 53 L5
Palau ■, Pac. Oc. 38 A6
Palawan, Phil. 26 C5
Palayankottai, India 28 Q10
Paldiski, Estonia 7 G21
Paleleh, Indonesia 27 D6
Palembang, Indonesia 26 E2
Palencia, Spain 15 A3
Palenque, Mexico 59 D6
Palermo, Italy 16 E5
Palermo, U.S.A. 56 G3
Palestina, Chile 64 A3
Palestine, Asia 33 D4
Palestine, U.S.A. 55 K7
Paletwa, Burma 29 J18
Palghat, India 28 P10
Palgrave, Mt., Australia 40 D2
Pali, India 28 G8
Palikir, Micronesia 44 G7
Paliouríon, Ákra, Greece 17 E10
Palisades Reservoir, U.S.A. 56 E8
Paliseul, Belgium 11 E5
Palitana, India 28 J7
Palizada, Mexico 59 D6
Palk Bay, Asia 28 Q11
Palk Strait, Asia 28 Q11
Palkānah, Iraq 30 C5
Pallanza = Verbánia, Italy 14 D8
Pallarenda, Australia 42 B4
Pallinup →, Australia 41 F2
Palm Bay, U.S.A. 53 L5
Palm Beach, U.S.A. 53 M6
Palm Coast, U.S.A. 53 L5
Palm Is., Australia 42 B4
Palm Springs, U.S.A. 57 K5
Palma, B. de, Spain 15 C7
Palma de Mallorca, Spain 15 C7
Palma Soriano, Cuba 60 B4
Palmares, Brazil 63 E11
Palmas, Brazil 64 B6
Palmas, C., Liberia 34 H4
Pálmas, G. di, Italy 16 E3
Palmdale, U.S.A. 57 J4
Palmeira dos Índios, Brazil 63 E11
Palmer, U.S.A. 46 B5
Palmer →, Australia 42 B3
Palmer Arch., Antarctica 5 C17
Palmer Lake, U.S.A. 54 F2
Palmer Land, Antarctica 5 D18
Palmerston, N.Z. 39 L3
Palmerston North, N.Z. 39 J5
Palmetto, U.S.A. 53 M4
Palmi, Italy 16 E6
Palmira, Colombia 62 C3
Palmyra = Tudmur, Syria 30 C3
Palmyra, U.S.A. 54 F9
Palmyra Is., Pac. Oc. 45 G11
Palopo, Indonesia 27 E6
Palos, C. de, Spain 15 D5
Palu, Indonesia 27 E5
Palu, Turkey 19 G7
Pamanukan, Indonesia 27 G12
Pamiers, France 14 E4
Pamir, Tajikistan 20 F8
Pamlico →, U.S.A. 53 H7
Pamlico Sd., U.S.A. 53 H8
Pampa, U.S.A. 55 H4

Pampanua, Indonesia . 27 E6
Pampas, Argentina .. 64 D4
Pampas, Peru 62 F4
Pamplona, Colombia .. 62 B4
Pamplona, Spain 15 A5
Pana, U.S.A. 54 F10
Panaca, U.S.A. 57 H6
Panaitan, Indonesia .. 27 G11
Panaji, India 28 M8
Panamá, Panama 60 E4
Panama ■, Cent. Amer. 60 E4
Panamá, G. de, Panama 60 E4
Panama Canal, Panama 60 E4
Panama City, U.S.A. .. 53 K3
Panamint Range, U.S.A. 57 H5
Panão, Peru 62 E3
Panay, G., Phil. 27 B6
Panay, Phil. 27 B6
Pančevo, Serbia, Yug. . 17 B9
Pandan, Phil. 27 B6
Pandegelang, Indonesia 27 G12
Pandharpur, India ... 28 L9
Pando, L. = Hope, L.,
    Australia 43 D2
Pandora, Costa Rica .. 60 E3
Panevėžys, Lithuania . 7 J21
Panfilov, Kazakstan .. 20 E8
Pang-Long, Burma ... 29 H21
Pang-Yang, Burma ... 29 H21
Pangani, Tanzania ... 36 F7
Pangfou = Bengbu,
    China 25 C6
Pangkah, Tanjung,
    Indonesia 27 G15
Pangkajene, Indonesia . 27 E5
Pangkalanbrandan,
    Indonesia 26 D1
Pangkalanbuun,
    Indonesia 26 E4
Pangkalpinang,
    Indonesia 26 E3
Pangnirtung, Canada . 47 B13
Panguitch, U.S.A. 57 H7
Pangutaran Group, Phil. 27 C6
Panhandle, U.S.A. ... 55 H4
Panjgur, Pakistan ... 28 F4
Panjim = Panaji, India 28 M8
Panjinad Barrage,
    Pakistan 28 E7
Panna, India 28 G12
Pannawonica, Australia 40 D2
Pannirtuuq =
    Pangnirtung, Canada 47 B13
Panorama, Brazil 63 H8
Pantanal, Brazil 62 H7
Pantar, Indonesia ... 27 F6
Pante Macassar,
    Indonesia 27 F6
Pantelleria, Italy ... 16 F4
Pánuco, Mexico 59 C5
Paola, U.S.A. 54 F7
Paonia, U.S.A. 57 G10
Paoting = Baoding,
    China 25 C6
Paot'ou = Baotou,
    China 25 B6
Paoua, C.A.R. 36 C3
Pápa, Hungary 13 E9
Papagayo →, Mexico 59 D5
Papagayo, G. de,
    Costa Rica 60 D2
Papakura, N.Z. 39 G5
Papantla, Mexico ... 59 C5
Papar, Malaysia 26 C5
Papeete, Tahiti 45 J13
Papigochic →, Mexico 58 B3
Papua, G. of,
    Papua N. G. 38 B7
Papua New Guinea ■,
    Oceania 38 B7
Papudo, Chile 64 C2
Papun, Burma 29 K20
Papunya, Australia .. 40 D5
Pará = Belém, Brazil . 63 D9
Pará □, Brazil 63 D8
Paraburdoo, Australia . 40 D2
Paracatu, Brazil 63 G9
Paracel Is., S. China Sea 26 A4
Parachilna, Australia . 43 E2
Paradip, India 29 J15
Paradise, U.S.A. 56 G3
Paradise →, Canada . 49 B8
Paradise Hill, Canada . 51 C7
Paradise River, Canada 49 B8
Paradise Valley, U.S.A. 56 F5
Parado, Indonesia ... 27 F5
Paragould, U.S.A. ... 55 G9
Paragua →, Venezuela 62 B6
Paraguaçu →, Brazil . 63 F11
Paraguaná, Pen. de,
    Venezuela 62 A5
Paraguari, Paraguay .. 64 B5
Paraguay ■, S. Amer. . 62 H7
Paraguay →, Paraguay 64 B5
Paraíba = João Pessoa,
    Brazil 63 E12
Paraíba □, Brazil 63 E11

Paran →, Israel 33 E4
Paraná, Argentina ... 64 C4
Paraná, Brazil 63 F9
Paraná □, Brazil 64 A6
Paraná →, Argentina . 64 C5
Paranaguá, Brazil ... 64 B7
Paranaíba, Brazil 63 G8
Paranaíba →, Brazil . 63 H8
Paranapanema →,
    Brazil 63 H8
Parang, Maguindanao,
    Phil. 27 C6
Parang, Sulu, Phil. .. 27 C6
Parângul Mare, Vf.,
    Romania 13 F12
Paraparaumu, N.Z. .. 39 J5
Parbhani, India 28 K10
Parchim, Germany .. 12 B6
Pardes Hanna-Karkur,
    Israel 33 C3
Pardo →, Bahia, Brazil 63 G11
Pardo →,
    Mato Grosso, Brazil . 63 H8
Pardubice, Czech Rep. . 12 C8
Pare, Indonesia 27 G15
Parecis, Serra dos,
    Brazil 62 F7
Paren, Russia 21 C17
Parent, Canada 48 C5
Parent, L., Canada .. 48 C4
Parepare, Indonesia .. 27 E5
Párga, Greece 17 E9
Pariaguán, Venezuela . 62 B6
Paricutín, Cerro, Mexico 58 D4
Parigi, Indonesia ... 27 E6
Parika, Guyana 62 B7
Parima, Serra, Brazil . 62 C6
Parinari, Peru 62 D4
Parintins, Brazil 63 D7
Pariparit Kyun, Burma . 29 M18
Paris, France 14 B5
Paris, Idaho, U.S.A. .. 56 E8
Paris, Ky., U.S.A. ... 52 F3
Paris, Tenn., U.S.A. . 53 G1
Paris, Tex., U.S.A. .. 55 J7
Park City, U.S.A. ... 55 G6
Park Falls, U.S.A. ... 54 C9
Park Hills, U.S.A. ... 55 G9
Park Range, U.S.A. .. 56 G10
Park Rapids, U.S.A. .. 54 B7
Park River, U.S.A. .. 54 A6
Parkā Bandar, Iran .. 31 E8
Parkano, Finland ... 7 E20
Parker, U.S.A. 57 J6
Parker Dam, U.S.A. . 57 J6
Parkersburg, U.S.A. . 52 F5
Parkes, Australia ... 43 E4
Parkston, U.S.A. ... 54 D6
Parksville, Canada .. 50 D4
Parla, Spain 15 B4
Parma, Italy 14 D9
Parma, Idaho, U.S.A. . 56 E5
Parma, Ohio, U.S.A. . 52 E5
Parnaguá, Brazil ... 63 F10
Parnaíba, Brazil 63 D10
Parnaíba →, Brazil . 63 D10
Parnassós, Greece .. 17 E10
Pärnu, Estonia 7 G21
Paroo →, Australia .. 43 E3
Páros, Greece 17 F11
Parowan, U.S.A. ... 57 H7
Parral, Chile 64 D2
Parras, Mexico 58 B4
Parrett →, U.K. 9 F4
Parris I., U.S.A. 53 J5
Parrsboro, Canada .. 49 C7
Parry Is., Canada ... 4 B2
Parry Sound, Canada . 48 C4
Parsnip →, Canada . 50 B4
Parsons, U.S.A. 55 G7
Parsons Ra., Australia . 42 A2
Partinico, Italy 16 E5
Partridge I., Canada . 48 A2
Paru →, Brazil 63 D8
Parvān □, Afghan. .. 28 B6
Parvatipuram, India . 29 K13
Pasadena, Canada .. 49 C8
Pasadena, Calif., U.S.A. 57 J4
Pasadena, Tex., U.S.A. 55 L8
Pascagoula, U.S.A. . 55 K10
Pascagoula →, U.S.A. 55 K10
Pascani, Romania .. 13 E14
Pasco, U.S.A. 56 C4
Pasco, Cerro de, Peru . 62 F3
Pasco I., Australia .. 40 D2
Pascua, I. de, Pac. Oc. . 45 K17
Pasfield L., Canada . 51 B7
Pashmakli = Smolyan,
    Bulgaria 17 D11
Pasir Mas, Malaysia . 26 C2
Pasirian, Indonesia .. 27 H15
Pasirkuning, Indonesia 26 E2
Paskūh, Iran 31 E9
Pasley, C., Australia . 41 F3
Pašman, Croatia ... 12 G8
Pasni, Pakistan 28 G3
Paso de Indios,
    Argentina 64 E3
Paso Robles, U.S.A. . 57 J3
Paspébiac, Canada .. 49 C6
Passau, Germany .. 12 D7
Passero, C., Italy ... 16 F6
Passo Fundo, Brazil .. 64 B6
Passos, Brazil 63 H9

Pastavy, Belarus 7 J22
Pastaza →, Peru ... 62 D3
Pasto, Colombia 62 C3
Pasuruan, Indonesia . 27 G15
Patagonia, Argentina . 64 F3
Patagonia, U.S.A. ... 57 L8
Patambar, Iran 31 D9
Patan, India 28 H8
Patani, Indonesia .. 27 D7
Patchewollock, Australia 43 F3
Patchogue, U.S.A. .. 52 E9
Patea, N.Z. 39 H5
Paternò, Italy 16 F6
Pateros, U.S.A. 56 B4
Paterson, U.S.A. ... 52 E8
Paterson Ra., Australia 40 D3
Pathankot, India .. 28 C9
Pathfinder Reservoir,
    U.S.A. 56 E10
Pati, Indonesia 27 G14
Patía →, Colombia .. 62 C3
Patiala, India 28 D10
Patkai Bum, India .. 29 F19
Pátmos, Greece ... 17 F12
Patna, India 29 G14
Pato Branco, Brazil .. 64 B6
Patos, Brazil 63 E11
Patos, L. dos, Brazil . 64 C6
Patos de Minas, Brazil . 63 G9
Patquía, Argentina .. 64 C3
Pátrai, Greece 17 E9
Pátraikós Kólpos,
    Greece 17 E9
Patras = Pátrai, Greece 17 E9
Patrocínio, Brazil ... 63 G9
Pattani, Thailand ... 26 C2
Pattaya, Thailand .. 26 B2
Patten, U.S.A. 53 C11
Patterson, Calif., U.S.A. 57 H3
Patterson, La., U.S.A. . 55 L9
Patuakhali, Bangla. .. 29 H17
Patuanak, Canada .. 51 B7
Patuca →, Honduras . 60 C3
Patuca, Punta, Honduras 60 C3
Pátzcuaro, Mexico .. 58 D4
Pau, France 14 E3
Pauk, Burma 29 J19
Paul I., Canada 49 A7
Paulis = Isiro,
    Dem. Rep. of
    the Congo 36 D5
Paulistana, Brazil ... 63 E10
Paulo Afonso, Brazil . 63 E11
Pauls Valley, U.S.A. . 55 H6
Pāveh, Iran 30 C5
Pavia, Italy 14 D8
Pāvilosta, Latvia ... 7 H19
Pavlodar, Kazakstan . 20 D8
Pavlograd = Pavlohrad,
    Ukraine 19 E6
Pavlohrad, Ukraine .. 19 E6
Pavlovo, Russia 18 C7
Pavlovsk, Russia ... 19 D7
Pavlovskaya, Russia . 19 E6
Pawhuska, U.S.A. .. 55 G6
Pawnee, U.S.A. 55 G6
Pawnee City, U.S.A. . 54 E6
Pawtucket, U.S.A. .. 52 E10
Paxoí, Greece 17 E9
Paxton, Ill., U.S.A. .. 52 E1
Paxton, Nebr., U.S.A. . 54 E4
Payakumbuh, Indonesia 26 E2
Payette, U.S.A. 56 D5
Payne Bay = Kangirsuk,
    Canada 47 B13
Payne L., Canada .. 47 C12
Paynes Find, Australia . 41 E2
Paynesville, U.S.A. . 54 C7
Paysandú, Uruguay .. 64 C5
Payson, U.S.A. 57 J8
Paz →, Guatemala .. 60 D1
Paz, B. la, Mexico .. 58 C2
Pāzanān, Iran 31 D6
Pazardzhik, Bulgaria . 17 C11
Peace →, Canada ... 50 B6
Peace Point, Canada . 50 B6
Peace River, Canada . 50 B5
Peach Springs, U.S.A. . 57 J7
Peachland, Canada .. 50 D5
Peachtree City, U.S.A. . 53 J3
Peak, The = Kinder
    Scout, U.K. 8 D6
Peak District, U.K. .. 8 D6
Peak Hill, N.S.W.,
    Australia 43 E4
Peak Hill, W. Austral.,
    Australia 41 E2
Peak Ra., Australia .. 42 C4
Peake Cr. →, Australia 43 D2
Peale, Mt., U.S.A. .. 57 G9
Pearl →, U.S.A. ... 55 K10
Pearsall, U.S.A. 55 L5
Peary Land, Greenland 4 A6
Pease →, U.S.A. ... 55 H5
Peawanuck, Canada . 47 C11
Pebane, Mozam. ... 37 H7
Pebas, Peru 62 D4
Peć, Kosovo, Yug. .. 17 C9
Pechenga, Russia ... 18 A5
Pechenizhyn, Ukraine . 13 D13
Pechora, Russia 18 A10
Pechora →, Russia . 18 A9
Pechorskaya Guba,
    Russia 18 A9

Pečory, Russia 7 H22
Pecos, U.S.A. 55 K3
Pecos →, U.S.A. ... 55 L3
Pécs, Hungary 13 E10
Pedder, L., Australia . 42 G4
Pédernales, Dom. Rep. . 61 C5
Pedirka, Australia .. 43 D2
Pedra Azul, Brazil ... 63 G10
Pedreiras, Brazil ... 63 D10
Pedro Afonso, Brazil . 63 E9
Pedro Cays, Jamaica . 60 C4
Pedro Juan Caballero,
    Paraguay 63 H7
Pee Dee →, U.S.A. . 53 J6
Peebinga, Australia . 43 E3
Peekskill, U.S.A. ... 52 E9
Peel, U.K. 8 C3
Peel →, Australia .. 43 E5
Peel →, Canada ... 46 B6
Peel Sound, Canada . 46 A10
Peera Peera Poolanna
    L., Australia 43 D2
Peerless Lake, Canada . 50 B6
Peers, Canada 50 C5
Pegasus Bay, N.Z. .. 39 K4
Pegu, Burma 29 L20
Pegu Yoma, Burma . 29 K20
Pehuajó, Argentina .. 64 D4
Peine, Germany ... 12 B6
Peip'ing = Beijing,
    China 25 C6
Peipus, L. = Chudskoye,
    Ozero, Russia 7 G22
Peixe, Brazil 63 F9
Peixe →, Brazil 63 H8
Pekalongan, Indonesia 27 G13
Pekanbaru, Indonesia . 26 D2
Pekin, U.S.A. 54 E10
Peking = Beijing, China 25 C6
Pelabuhan Kelang,
    Malaysia 26 D2
Pelabuhan Ratu, Teluk,
    Indonesia 27 G12
Pelabuhanratu,
    Indonesia 27 G12
Pelagie, Is., Italy ... 16 G5
Pelaihari, Indonesia . 26 E4
Peleaga, Vf., Romania . 13 F12
Pelée, Mt., Martinique . 61 D7
Pelée, Pt., Canada .. 48 D3
Pelee I., Canada ... 48 D3
Peleng, Indonesia .. 27 E6
Pelican, U.S.A. 50 B1
Pelican L., Canada .. 51 C8
Pelican Narrows,
    Canada 51 B8
Peljesac, Croatia ... 16 C7
Pelkosenniemi, Finland 6 C22
Pella, U.S.A. 54 E8
Pello, Finland 6 C21
Pelly →, Canada ... 46 B6
Pelly Bay, Canada .. 47 B11
Peloponnese =
    Pelopónnisos □,
    Greece 17 F10
Pelopónnisos □, Greece 17 F10
Pelorus Sd., N.Z. ... 39 J4
Pelotas, Brazil 64 C6
Pelvoux, Massif du,
    France 14 D7
Pemalang, Indonesia . 27 G13
Pematangsiantar,
    Indonesia 26 D1
Pemba, Mozam. ... 37 G8
Pemba I., Tanzania .. 36 F7
Pemberton, Australia . 41 F2
Pemberton, Canada . 50 C4
Pembina, U.S.A. ... 54 A6
Pembroke, Canada .. 48 C4
Pembroke, U.K. 9 F3
Pembrokeshire □, U.K. 9 F3
Pen-y-Ghent, U.K. .. 8 C5
Penang = Pinang,
    Malaysia 26 C2
Penápolis, Brazil ... 63 H8
Peñarroya-Pueblonuevo,
    Spain 15 C3
Penarth, U.K. 9 F4
Peñas, C. de, Spain .. 15 A3
Peñas, G. de, Chile .. 64 F2
Pench'i = Benxi, China 25 B7
Pend Oreille →, U.S.A. 56 B5
Pend Oreille, L., U.S.A. 56 C5
Pender B., Australia . 40 C3
Pendleton, U.S.A. .. 56 D4
Pendra, Brazil 63 F11
Penedo, Brazil 63 F11
Penetanguishene,
    Canada 48 D4
Pengalengan, Indonesia 27 G12
Penguin, Australia .. 42 G4
Peniche, Portugal .. 15 C1
Penida, Indonesia .. 26 F5
Peninsular Malaysia □,
    Malaysia 26 D2
Penitente, Serra do,
    Brazil 63 E9
Penkridge, U.K. ... 8 E5
Penmarch, Pte. de,
    France 14 C1
Penn Hills, U.S.A. .. 52 E6
Penn Yan, U.S.A. .. 52 D7
Pennant, Canada ... 51 C7
Penner →, India ... 28 M12

Pennines, U.K. 8 C5
Pennsylvania □, U.S.A. 52 E7
Penny, Canada 50 C4
Penobscot →, U.S.A. . 53 C11
Penobscot B., U.S.A. . 53 C11
Penola, Australia ... 43 F3
Penong, Australia .. 41 F5
Penonomé, Panama .. 60 E3
Penrith, Australia .. 43 E5
Penrith, U.K. 8 C5
Penryn, U.K. 9 G2
Pensacola, U.S.A. .. 53 K2
Pensacola Mts.,
    Antarctica 5 E1
Pense, Canada 51 C8
Penshurst, Australia . 43 F3
Penticton, Canada .. 50 D5
Pentland, Australia . 42 C4
Pentland Firth, U.K. . 10 B5
Penza, Russia 18 D8
Penzance, U.K. 9 G2
Penzhino, Russia ... 21 C17
Penzhinskaya Guba,
    Russia 21 C17
Peoria, Ariz., U.S.A. . 57 K7
Peoria, Ill., U.S.A. .. 54 E10
Pera Hd., Australia .. 42 A3
Perabumulih, Indonesia 26 E2
Peräpohjola, Finland . 6 C22
Percé, Canada 49 C7
Perche, Collines du,
    France 14 B4
Percival Lakes, Australia 40 D4
Percy Is., Australia .. 42 C5
Perdido, Mte., Spain . 15 A6
Perdu, Mt. = Perdido,
    Mte., Spain 15 A6
Pereira, Colombia .. 62 C3
Perenjori, Australia .. 41 E2
Pereslav-
    Khmelnytskyy,
    Ukraine 19 D5
Pérez, I., Mexico ... 59 C7
Pergamino, Argentina . 64 C4
Perham, U.S.A. 54 B7
Perhentian, Kepulauan,
    Malaysia 26 C2
Péribonca →, Canada 49 C5
Péribonca, L., Canada . 49 B5
Perico, Argentina ... 64 A3
Pericos, Mexico 58 B3
Périgueux, France .. 14 D4
Perijá, Sierra de,
    Colombia 62 B4
Perito Moreno,
    Argentina 64 F2
Perlas, Arch. de las,
    Panama 60 E4
Perlas, Punta de, Nic. . 60 D3
Perm, Russia 18 C10
Pernambuco = Recife,
    Brazil 63 E12
Pernambuco □, Brazil . 63 E11
Pernatty Lagoon,
    Australia 43 E2
Pernik, Bulgaria ... 17 C10
Peron Is., Australia .. 40 B5
Peron Pen., Australia . 41 E1
Perow, Canada 50 C3
Perpendicular Pt.,
    Australia 43 E5
Perpignan, France .. 14 E5
Perry, Fla., U.S.A. .. 53 K4
Perry, Ga., U.S.A. .. 53 J4
Perry, Iowa, U.S.A. . 54 E7
Perry, Okla., U.S.A. . 55 G6
Perryton, U.S.A. ... 55 G4
Perryville, U.S.A. ... 55 G10
Persepolis, Iran 31 D7
Pershotravensk, Ukraine 13 C14
Persia = Iran ■, Asia . 31 C7
Persian Gulf = Gulf,
    The, Asia 31 E6
Perth, Australia 41 F2
Perth, Canada 48 D4
Perth, U.K. 10 C5
Perth Amboy, U.S.A. . 52 E8
Perth-Andover, Canada 49 C6
Peru, U.S.A. 54 C9
Peru ■, S. Amer. ... 62 D4
Peru-Chile Trench,
    Pac. Oc. 62 G3
Perúgia, Italy 16 C5
Pervomaysk, Ukraine . 19 E5
Pervouralsk, Russia .. 18 C10
Pésaro, Italy 16 C5
Pescara, Italy 16 C6
Peshawar, Pakistan . 28 B7
Peshkopi, Albania .. 17 D9
Peshtigo, U.S.A. ... 52 C2
Pesqueira, Brazil ... 63 E11
Petah Tiqwa, Israel . 33 C3
Petaluma, U.S.A. ... 56 G2
Pétange, Lux. 11 E5
Petatlán, Mexico ... 58 D4
Petauke, Zambia ... 37 G6
Petawawa, Canada .. 48 C4
Petén Itzá, L.,
    Guatemala 60 C2
Peter I.s Øy, Antarctica . 5 C16
Peter Pond L., Canada . 51 B7
Peterbell, Canada .. 48 C3
Peterborough, Australia 43 E2
Peterborough, Canada . 48 D4

Peterborough, U.K. .. 9 E7
Peterborough □, U.K. . 9 E7
Peterhead, U.K. 10 C6
Peterlee, U.K. 8 C6
Petermann Ranges,
    Australia 40 E5
Petersburg, Alaska,
    U.S.A. 46 C6
Petersburg, Va., U.S.A. 52 G7
Petersburg, W. Va.,
    U.S.A. 52 F6
Petersfield, U.K. ... 9 F7
Petit Goâve, Haiti .. 61 C5
Petit Jardin, Canada . 49 C8
Petit Lac Manicouagan,
    Canada 49 B6
Petit-Mécatina →,
    Canada 49 B8
Petit-Mécatina, I. du,
    Canada 49 B8
Petitcodiac, Canada . 49 C6
Petite Baleine →,
    Canada 48 A4
Petite Saguenay,
    Canada 49 C5
Petitot →, Canada .. 50 A4
Petitsikapau L., Canada 49 B6
Petlad, India 28 H8
Peto, Mexico 59 C7
Petone, N.Z. 39 J5
Petoskey, U.S.A. ... 52 C3
Petra, Jordan 33 E4
Petra, Ostrova, Russia . 4 B13
Petra Velikogo, Zaliv,
    Russia 22 C6
Petrich, Bulgaria ... 17 D10
Petrified Forest National
    Park, U.S.A. 57 J9
Petrikov = Pyetrikaw,
    Belarus 13 B15
Petrograd = Sankt-
    Peterburg, Russia . 18 C5
Petrolândia, Brazil .. 63 E11
Petrolia, Canada ... 48 D3
Petrolina, Brazil ... 63 E10
Petropavl, Kazakstan . 20 D7
Petropavlovsk =
    Petropavl, Kazakstan 20 D7
Petropavlovsk-
    Kamchatskiy, Russia . 21 D16
Petrópolis, Brazil ... 63 H10
Petroşani, Romania . 13 F12
Petrovaradin,
    Serbia, Yug. 17 B8
Petrovsk, Russia ... 18 D8
Petrovsk-Zabaykalskiy,
    Russia 21 D11
Petrozavodsk, Russia . 18 B5
Peureulak, Indonesia . 26 D1
Pevek, Russia 21 C18
Pforzheim, Germany . 12 D5
Phagwara, India ... 28 D9
Phalodi, India 28 F8
Phan Rang, Vietnam . 26 B3
Phan Thiet, Vietnam . 26 B3
Phangan, Ko, Thailand 26 C2
Phangnga, Thailand . 26 C1
Pharr, U.S.A. 55 M5
Phatthalung, Thailand . 26 C2
Phelps, Canada 51 B8
Phenix City, U.S.A. . 53 J3
Phet Buri, Thailand .. 26 B1
Phetchabun, Thailand . 26 A2
Phetchaburi = Phet
    Buri, Thailand ... 26 B1
Philadelphia, Miss.,
    U.S.A. 55 J10
Philadelphia, Pa., U.S.A. 52 F8
Philip, U.S.A. 54 C4
Philip I., Australia .. 43 F4
Philippeville, Belgium . 11 D4
Philippi, U.S.A. 52 F5
Philippi L., Australia . 42 C2
Philippines ■, Asia .. 27 B6
Philippopolis = Plovdiv,
    Bulgaria 17 C11
Philipsburg, U.S.A. . 56 C7
Phillip I., Australia .. 43 F4
Phillips, U.S.A. 54 C9
Phillipsburg, U.S.A. . 54 F5
Philomath, U.S.A. .. 56 D2
Phitsanulok, Thailand . 26 A2
Phnom Dangrek,
    Thailand 26 B2
Phnom Penh, Cambodia 26 B2
Phnum Penh = Phnom
    Penh, Cambodia .. 26 B2
Phoenix, U.S.A. 57 K7
Phoenix Is., Kiribati . 44 H10
Phong →, Thailand . 26 A2
Phosphate Hill, Australia 42 C2
Phra Nakhon Si
    Ayutthaya, Thailand . 26 B2
Phu Quoc, Dao, Vietnam 26 B2
Phuket, Thailand ... 26 C1
Piacenza, Italy 14 D8
Pian Cr. →, Australia . 43 E4
Pianosa, Italy 16 C4
Piapot, Canada 51 D7
Piatra Neamţ, Romania 13 E14
Piauí □, Brazil 63 E10
Piauí →, Brazil 63 E10
Piave →, Italy 16 B5
Pibor Post, Sudan .. 35 G12
Picardie, France ... 14 B5

Picardy = Picardie, France ... 14 B5
Picayune, U.S.A. ... 55 K10
Pichilemu, Chile ... 64 C2
Pickerel L., Canada ... 48 C1
Pickering, U.K. ... 8 C7
Pickering, Vale of, U.K. ... 8 C7
Pickle Lake, Canada ... 48 B1
Pickwick L., U.S.A. ... 53 H1
Pico Truncado, Argentina ... 64 F3
Picos, Brazil ... 63 E10
Picton, Australia ... 43 E5
Picton, Canada ... 48 D4
Picton, N.Z. ... 39 J5
Pictou, Canada ... 49 C7
Picture Butte, Canada ... 50 D6
Picún Leufú, Argentina 64 D3
Pidurutalagala, Sri Lanka ... 28 R12
Piedmont = Piemonte □, Italy ... 14 D7
Piedmont, U.S.A. ... 53 J3
Piedras Negras, Mexico 58 B4
Pieksämäki, Finland ... 7 E22
Piemonte □, Italy ... 14 D7
Pierceland, Canada ... 51 C7
Pierre, U.S.A. ... 54 C4
Piet Retief, S. Africa ... 37 K6
Pietarsaari, Finland ... 6 E20
Pietermaritzburg, S. Africa ... 37 K6
Pietersburg, S. Africa ... 37 J5
Pietrosul, Vf., Maramureş, Romania 13 E13
Pietrosul, Vf., Suceava, Romania ... 13 E13
Piggott, U.S.A. ... 55 G9
Pigüe, Argentina ... 64 D4
Pihlajavesi, Finland ... 7 F23
Pijijiapan, Mexico ... 59 D6
Pikangikum Berens, Canada ... 51 C10
Pikes Peak, U.S.A. ... 54 F2
Pikeville, U.S.A. ... 52 G4
Pikwitonei, Canada ... 51 B9
Piła, Poland ... 13 B9
Pilar, Paraguay ... 64 B5
Pilaya →, Bolivia ... 62 H1
Pilbara, Australia ... 40 D2
Pilcomayo →, Paraguay ... 64 B5
Pilibhit, India ... 28 E11
Pilica →, Poland ... 13 C11
Pilliga, Australia ... 43 E4
Pílos, Greece ... 17 F9
Pilot Mound, Canada ... 51 D9
Pilot Point, U.S.A. ... 55 J6
Pilot Rock, U.S.A. ... 56 D4
Pilsen = Plzeň, Czech Rep. ... 12 D7
Pima, U.S.A. ... 57 K9
Pimba, Australia ... 43 E2
Pimenta Bueno, Brazil ... 62 F6
Pimentel, Peru ... 62 E3
Pinang, India ... 26 C2
Pinar del Río, Cuba ... 60 B3
Pınarhisar, Turkey ... 17 D12
Pinatubo, Mt., Phil. ... 27 A6
Pincher Creek, Canada 50 D6
Pinchi L., Canada ... 50 C4
Pinckneyville, U.S.A. 54 F10
Pińczów, Poland ... 13 C11
Pindar, Australia ... 41 E2
Pindos Óros, Greece ... 17 E9
Pindus Mts. = Pindos Óros, Greece ... 17 E9
Pine →, B.C., Canada 50 B4
Pine →, Sask., Canada 51 B7
Pine, C., Canada ... 49 C9
Pine Bluff, U.S.A. ... 55 H9
Pine Bluffs, U.S.A. ... 54 E2
Pine City, U.S.A. ... 54 C8
Pine Creek, Australia 40 B5
Pine Falls, Canada ... 51 C9
Pine Pass, Canada ... 50 B4
Pine Point, Canada ... 50 A6
Pine Ridge, U.S.A. ... 54 D3
Pine River, Canada ... 51 C8
Pine River, U.S.A. ... 54 B7
Pinedale, U.S.A. ... 56 E9
Pinega →, Russia ... 18 B8
Pinehill, Australia ... 42 C4
Pinehouse L., Canada 51 B7
Pineimuta →, Canada 48 B1
Pinerolo, Italy ... 14 D7
Pinetop, U.S.A. ... 57 J9
Pineville, U.S.A. ... 55 K8
Ping →, Thailand ... 26 A2
Pingaring, Australia ... 41 F2
Pingdingshan, China ... 25 C6
Pingdong, Taiwan ... 25 D7
Pingelly, Australia ... 41 F2
Pingliang, China ... 24 C5
Pingrup, Australia ... 41 F2
P'ingtung, Taiwan ... 25 D7
Pingxiang, China ... 24 D5
Pinheiro, Brazil ... 63 D9
Pinhel, Portugal ... 15 B2
Pini, Indonesia ... 26 D1
Piniós →, Greece ... 17 E10
Pinjarra, Australia ... 41 F2
Pink Mountain, Canada 50 B4
Pinnaroo, Australia ... 43 F3

Pínnes, Ákra, Greece ... 17 D11
Pinos, Mexico ... 58 C4
Pinos, Mt., U.S.A. ... 57 J4
Pinos Pt., U.S.A. ... 57 H3
Pinotepa Nacional, Mexico ... 59 D5
Pinrang, Indonesia ... 27 E5
Pinsk, Belarus ... 13 B14
Pintados, Chile ... 62 H5
Pinyug, Russia ... 18 B8
Pioche, U.S.A. ... 57 H6
Piombino, Italy ... 16 C4
Pioner, Ostrov, Russia 21 B10
Piorini, L., Brazil ... 62 D6
Piotrków Trybunalski, Poland ... 13 C10
Pip, Iran ... 31 E9
Pipestone, U.S.A. ... 54 D6
Pipestone →, Canada 48 B2
Pipestone Cr. →, Canada ... 51 D8
Pipmuacan, Rés., Canada ... 49 C5
Pippingarra, Australia 40 D2
Piqua, U.S.A. ... 52 E3
Piquiri →, Brazil ... 64 A6
Pir Sohrāb, Iran ... 31 E9
Piracanjuba, Brazil ... 63 H9
Piracicaba, Brazil ... 64 A6
Piracuruca, Brazil ... 63 D10
Piræus = Piraiévs, Greece ... 17 F10
Piraiévs, Greece ... 17 F10
Pirané, Argentina ... 64 B5
Pirapora, Brazil ... 63 G10
Pírgos, Greece ... 17 F9
Pirimapun, Indonesia 27 F10
Pirin Planina, Bulgaria 17 D10
Pirineos = Pyrénées, Europe ... 14 E4
Piripiri, Brazil ... 63 D10
Pirmasens, Germany ... 12 D4
Pirot, Serbia, Yug. ... 17 C10
Piru, Indonesia ... 27 E7
Pisa, Italy ... 16 C4
Pisagua, Chile ... 62 G4
Pisco, Peru ... 62 F3
Písek, Czech Rep. ... 12 D8
Pishan, China ... 24 C2
Pīshīn, Iran ... 31 E9
Pising, Indonesia ... 27 F6
Pistóia, Italy ... 16 C4
Pistol B., Canada ... 51 A10
Pisuerga →, Spain ... 15 B3
Pit →, U.S.A. ... 56 F2
Pitarpunga, L., Australia 43 E3
Pitcairn I., Pac. Oc. ... 45 K14
Pite älv →, Sweden ... 6 D19
Piteå, Sweden ... 6 D19
Piteşti, Romania ... 13 F13
Pithapuram, India ... 29 L13
Pithara, Australia ... 41 F2
Pitt I., Canada ... 50 C3
Pittsburg, Kans., U.S.A. 55 G7
Pittsburg, Tex., U.S.A. 55 J7
Pittsburgh, U.S.A. ... 52 E6
Pittsfield, Ill., U.S.A. 54 F9
Pittsfield, Maine, U.S.A. 53 C11
Pittsfield, Mass., U.S.A. 52 D9
Pittsworth, Australia ... 43 D5
Pituri →, Australia ... 42 C2
Piura, Peru ... 62 E2
Placentia, Canada ... 49 C9
Placentia B., Canada ... 49 C9
Placerville, U.S.A. ... 56 G3
Placetas, Cuba ... 60 B4
Plainfield, U.S.A. ... 52 E8
Plains, Mont., U.S.A. ... 56 C6
Plains, Tex., U.S.A. ... 55 J3
Plainview, Nebr., U.S.A. 54 D6
Plainview, Tex., U.S.A. 55 H4
Plainwell, U.S.A. ... 52 D3
Pláka, Ákra, Greece ... 17 G12
Plana Cays, Bahamas 61 B5
Plano, U.S.A. ... 55 J6
Plant City, U.S.A. ... 53 M4
Plaquemine, U.S.A. ... 55 K9
Plasencia, Spain ... 15 B2
Plaster Rock, Canada 49 C6
Plastun, Russia ... 22 B8
Plata, Río de la, S. Amer. ... 64 C5
Plátani →, Italy ... 16 F5
Platte, U.S.A. ... 54 D5
Platte →, Mo., U.S.A. 54 F7
Platte →, Nebr., U.S.A. 54 E7
Platteville, U.S.A. ... 54 D9
Plattsburgh, U.S.A. ... 52 C9
Plattsmouth, U.S.A. ... 54 E7
Plauen, Germany ... 12 C7
Plavinas, Latvia ... 7 H21
Playgreen L., Canada 51 C9
Pleasant Bay, Canada 49 C7
Pleasanton, U.S.A. ... 55 L5
Pleasantville, U.S.A. ... 52 F8
Plei Ku, Vietnam ... 26 B3
Plenty →, Australia ... 42 C2
Plenty, B. of, N.Z. ... 39 G6
Plentywood, U.S.A. ... 54 A2
Plesetsk, Russia ... 18 B7
Plessisville, Canada ... 49 C5
Plétipi, L., Canada ... 49 B5
Pleven, Bulgaria ... 17 C11
Plevlja, Montenegro, Yug. ... 17 C8
Płock, Poland ... 13 B10

Plöckenstein, Germany 12 D7
Ploiești, Romania ... 13 F14
Plonge, Lac la, Canada 51 B7
Plovdiv, Bulgaria ... 17 C11
Plummer, U.S.A. ... 56 C5
Plumtree, Zimbabwe ... 37 J5
Plunge, Lithuania ... 7 J19
Plymouth, U.K. ... 9 G3
Plymouth, Ind., U.S.A. 52 E2
Plymouth, N.C., U.S.A. 53 H7
Plymouth, Wis., U.S.A. 52 D2
Plynlimon = Pumlumon Fawr, U.K. ... 9 E4
Plzeň, Czech Rep. ... 12 D7
Po →, Italy ... 16 B5
Po Hai = Bo Hai, China 25 C6
Pobeda, Russia ... 21 C15
Pobedy, Pik, Kyrgyzstan 20 E8
Pocahontas, Ark., U.S.A. 55 G9
Pocahontas, Iowa, U.S.A. ... 54 D7
Pocatello, U.S.A. ... 56 E7
Pochutla, Mexico ... 59 D5
Pocito Casas, Mexico ... 58 B2
Pocomoke City, U.S.A. 52 F8
Poços de Caldas, Brazil 63 H9
Podgorica, Montenegro, Yug. ... 17 C8
Podilska Vysochyna, Ukraine ... 13 D14
Podolsk, Russia ... 18 C6
Podporozhye, Russia ... 18 B5
Pogranitšnyi, Russia ... 22 B5
Poh, Indonesia ... 27 E6
Pohjanmaa, Finland ... 6 E20
Pohnpei, Micronesia ... 44 G7
Poinsett, C., Antarctica 5 C8
Point Baker, U.S.A. ... 50 B2
Point Edward, Canada 48 D3
Point Hope, U.S.A. ... 46 B3
Point L., Canada ... 46 B8
Point Pedro, Sri Lanka 28 Q12
Point Pleasant, U.S.A. 52 F4
Pointe-à-Pitre, Guadeloupe ... 61 C7
Pointe-Noire, Congo ... 36 E2
Poisonbush Ra., Australia ... 40 D3
Poissonnier Pt., Australia ... 40 C2
Poitiers, France ... 14 C4
Poitou, France ... 14 C3
Pojoaque, U.S.A. ... 57 J11
Pokataroo, Australia ... 43 D4
Poko, Dem. Rep. of the Congo ... 36 D5
Pokrovsk = Engels, Russia ... 19 D8
Pokrovsk, Russia ... 21 C13
Pola = Pula, Croatia ... 12 F7
Polacca, U.S.A. ... 57 J8
Polan, Iran ... 31 E9
Poland ■, Europe ... 13 C10
Polar Bear Prov. Park, Canada ... 48 A2
Polatsk, Belarus ... 18 C4
Polessk, Russia ... 7 J19
Polesye = Pripet Marshes, Europe ... 13 B15
Polevskoy, Russia ... 18 C11
Police, Poland ... 12 B8
Polillo Is., Phil. ... 27 B6
Políyiros, Greece ... 17 D10
Polnovat, Russia ... 20 C7
Polonne, Ukraine ... 13 C14
Polonnoye = Polonne, Ukraine ... 13 C14
Polson, U.S.A. ... 56 C6
Poltava, Ukraine ... 19 E5
Põltsamaa, Estonia ... 7 G21
Polunochnoye, Russia 20 C7
Põlva, Estonia ... 7 G22
Polyarny, Russia ... 18 A5
Polynesia, Pac. Oc. ... 45 J11
Polynésie française = French Polynesia ■, Pac. Oc. ... 45 K13
Pomarão, Mexico ... 58 D4
Pombal, Portugal ... 15 C1
Pomeroy, Ohio, U.S.A. 52 F4
Pomeroy, Wash., U.S.A. 56 C5
Pomézia, Italy ... 16 D5
Pomona, Australia ... 43 D5
Pomona, U.S.A. ... 57 J5
Pomorskie, Pojezierze, Poland ... 13 B9
Pompano Beach, U.S.A. 53 M5
Pompeys Pillar, U.S.A. 56 D10
Ponape = Pohnpei, Micronesia ... 44 G7
Ponask L., Canada ... 48 B1
Ponca, U.S.A. ... 54 D6
Ponca City, U.S.A. ... 55 G6
Ponce, Puerto Rico ... 61 C6
Ponchatoula, U.S.A. ... 55 K9
Poncheville, L., Canada 48 B4
Pond Inlet, Canada ... 47 A12
Pondicherry, India ... 28 P11
Ponds, I. of, Canada ... 49 B8
Ponferrada, Spain ... 15 A2
Ponnani, India ... 28 P9
Ponoka, Canada ... 50 C6

Ponorogo, Indonesia ... 27 G14
Ponoy, Russia ... 18 A7
Ponoy →, Russia ... 18 A7
Ponta Grossa, Brazil ... 64 B6
Ponta Pora, Brazil ... 63 H7
Pontarlier, France ... 14 C7
Pontchartrain L., U.S.A. 55 K10
Ponte Nova, Brazil ... 63 H10
Ponteix, Canada ... 51 D7
Pontevedra, Spain ... 15 A1
Pontiac, Ill., U.S.A. ... 54 E10
Pontiac, Mich., U.S.A. 52 D4
Pontianak, Indonesia ... 26 E3
Pontine Is. = Ponziane, Ísole, Italy ... 16 D5
Pontine Mts. = Kuzey Anadolu Dağları, Turkey ... 19 F6
Pontivy, France ... 14 B2
Pontoise, France ... 14 B5
Ponton →, Canada ... 50 B5
Pontypool, U.K. ... 9 F4
Pontypridd, U.K. ... 9 F4
Poochera, Australia ... 43 E1
Poole, U.K. ... 9 G6
Poole □, U.K. ... 9 G6
Poona = Pune, India ... 28 K8
Pooncarie, Australia ... 43 E3
Poopelloe L., Australia 43 E3
Poopó, L. de, Bolivia ... 62 G5
Popayán, Colombia ... 62 C3
Poperinge, Belgium ... 11 D2
Popilta, L., Australia ... 43 E3
Popio L., Australia ... 43 E3
Poplar →, Canada ... 51 C9
Poplar Bluff, U.S.A. ... 55 G9
Poplarville, U.S.A. ... 55 K10
Popocatépetl, Volcán, Mexico ... 59 D5
Popokabaka, Dem. Rep. of the Congo ... 36 F3
Poprad, Slovak Rep. ... 13 D11
Porbandar, India ... 28 J6
Porcher I., Canada ... 50 C2
Porcupine →, Canada 51 B8
Porcupine →, U.S.A. 46 B5
Pordenone, Italy ... 16 B5
Pori, Finland ... 7 F19
Porlamar, Venezuela ... 62 A6
Poronaysk, Russia ... 21 E15
Poroshiri-Dake, Japan 22 C11
Poroszló, Hungary ... —
Porcupine B., Antarctica 5 C8
Porsangen, Norway ... 6 A21
Porsgrunn, Norway ... 7 G13
Port Alberni, Canada ... 50 D4
Port Alice, Canada ... 50 C3
Port Allegany, U.S.A. 52 E6
Port Allen, U.S.A. ... 55 K9
Port Alma, Australia ... 42 C5
Port Angeles, U.S.A. ... 56 B2
Port Antonio, Jamaica 60 C4
Port Aransas, U.S.A. ... 55 M6
Port Arthur, Australia 42 G4
Port Arthur, U.S.A. ... 55 L8
Port au Choix, Canada 49 B8
Port au Port B., Canada 49 C8
Port-au-Prince, Haiti ... 61 C5
Port Augusta, Australia 43 E2
Port Austin, U.S.A. ... 52 C4
Port Blandford, Canada 49 C9
Port Bradshaw, Australia ... 42 A2
Port Broughton, Australia ... 43 E2
Port Campbell, Australia 43 F3
Port-Cartier, Canada ... 49 B6
Port Chalmers, N.Z. ... 39 L3
Port Charlotte, U.S.A. 53 M4
Port Chester, U.S.A. ... 52 E9
Port Clements, Canada 50 C2
Port Clinton, U.S.A. ... 52 E4
Port Colborne, Canada 48 D4
Port Coquitlam, Canada 50 D4
Port Curtis, Australia ... 42 C5
Port Darwin, Australia 40 B5
Port Darwin, Falk. Is. ... 64 G5
Port Davey, Australia ... 42 G4
Port-de-Paix, Haiti ... 61 C5
Port Dickson, Malaysia 26 D2
Port Douglas, Australia 42 B4
Port Edward, Canada ... 50 C2
Port Elgin, Canada ... 48 D3
Port Elizabeth, S. Africa 37 L5
Port Erin, U.K. ... 8 C3
Port Essington, Australia 40 B5
Port Etienne = Nouâdhibou, Mauritania ... 34 D2
Port Fairy, Australia ... 43 F3
Port-Gentil, Gabon ... 36 E1
Port Germein, Australia 43 E2
Port Gibson, U.S.A. ... 55 K9
Port Harcourt, Nigeria 34 H7
Port Hardy, Canada ... 50 C3
Port Harrison = Inukjuak, Canada ... 47 C12
Port Hawkesbury, Canada ... 49 C7
Port Hedland, Australia 40 D2
Port Henry, U.S.A. ... 52 C9
Port Hood, Canada ... 49 C7
Port Hope, Canada ... 48 D4

Port Hope Simpson, Canada ... 49 B8
Port Huron, U.S.A. ... 52 D4
Port Jefferson, U.S.A. 52 E9
Port Kelang = Pelabuhan Kelang, Malaysia ... 26 D2
Port Kenny, Australia 43 E1
Port Laoise, Ireland ... 10 E3
Port Lavaca, U.S.A. ... 55 L6
Port Lincoln, Australia 43 E2
Port Loko, S. Leone ... 34 G3
Port Lyautey = Kenitra, Morocco ... 34 B4
Port MacDonnell, Australia ... 43 F3
Port McNeill, Canada 50 C3
Port Macquarie, Australia ... 43 E5
Port Maria, Jamaica ... 60 C4
Port Mellon, Canada ... 50 D4
Port-Menier, Canada ... 49 C7
Port Morant, Jamaica 60 C4
Port Moresby, Papua N. G. ... 38 B7
Port Musgrave, Australia ... 42 A3
Port Neches, U.S.A. ... 55 L8
Port Nolloth, S. Africa 37 K3
Port Nouveau-Québec = Kangiqsualujjuaq, Canada ... 47 C13
Port of Spain, Trin. & Tob. ... 62 A6
Port Orange, U.S.A. ... 53 L5
Port Orford, U.S.A. ... 56 E1
Port Pegasus, N.Z. ... 39 M1
Port Perry, Canada ... 48 D4
Port Phillip B., Australia 43 F3
Port Pirie, Australia ... 43 E2
Port Radium = Echo Bay, Canada ... 46 B8
Port Renfrew, Canada 50 D4
Port Roper, Australia 42 A2
Port Safaga = Būr Safâga, Egypt ... 30 E2
Port Said = Būr Sa'îd, Egypt ... 35 B12
Port St. Joe, U.S.A. ... 53 L3
Port St. Johns = Umzimvubu, S. Africa 37 L5
Port St. Lucie, U.S.A. 53 M5
Port Shepstone, S. Africa ... 37 L6
Port Simpson, Canada 50 C2
Port Stanley = Stanley, Falk. Is. ... 64 G5
Port Stanley, Canada 48 D3
Port Sudan = Būr Sûdân, Sudan ... 35 E13
Port Sulphur, U.S.A. 55 L10
Port Talbot, U.K. ... 9 F4
Port Townsend, U.S.A. 56 B2
Port-Vendres, France 14 E5
Port Vila, Vanuatu ... 38 C9
Port Vladimir, Russia 18 A5
Port Wakefield, Australia 43 E2
Port Washington, U.S.A. 52 D2
Port Weld = Kuala Sepetang, Malaysia 26 D2
Porta Orientalis, Romania ... 13 F12
Portadown, U.K. ... 10 D3
Portage, U.S.A. ... 54 D10
Portage La Prairie, Canada ... 51 D9
Portageville, U.S.A. 55 G10
Portalegre, Portugal 15 C2
Portales, U.S.A. ... 55 H3
Portbou, Spain ... 15 A7
Porter L., N.W.T., Canada ... 51 A7
Porter L., Sask., Canada 51 B7
Porterville, U.S.A. ... 57 H4
Porthcawl, U.K. ... 9 F4
Porthill, U.S.A. ... 56 B5
Porthmadog, U.K. ... 8 E3
Portile de Fier, Europe 13 F12
Portimão, Portugal ... 15 D1
Portishead, U.K. ... 9 F5
Portland, N.S.W., Australia ... 43 E5
Portland, Vic., Australia 43 F3
Portland, Maine, U.S.A. 47 D12
Portland, Mich., U.S.A. 52 D3
Portland, Oreg., U.S.A. 56 D2
Portland, Tex., U.S.A. 55 M6
Portland, I. of, U.K. ... 9 G5
Portland B., Australia 43 F3
Portland Bill, U.K. ... 9 G5
Portland Canal, U.S.A. 50 B2
Portmadoc = Porthmadog, U.K. ... 8 E3
Porto, Portugal ... 15 B1
Pôrto Alegre, Brazil ... 64 C6
Porto Amboim = Gunza, Angola ... 36 G2
Pôrto de Móz, Brazil ... 63 D8
Porto Empédocle, Italy 16 F5
Pôrto Esperança, Brazil 62 G7
Pôrto Franco, Brazil ... 63 E9
Porto Mendes, Brazil ... 64 A6

Pôrto Murtinho, Brazil . 62 H7
Pôrto Nacional, Brazil . 63 F9
Porto-Novo, Benin ... 34 G6
Porto Santo, Madeira ... 34 B2
Pôrto Seguro, Brazil ... 63 G11
Pôrto Tôrres, Italy ... 16 D3
Pôrto União, Brazil ... 64 B6
Pôrto Válter, Brazil ... 62 E4
Porto-Vecchio, France 14 F8
Pôrto Velho, Brazil ... 62 E6
Portobelo, Panama ... 60 E4
Portoferráio, Italy ... 16 C4
Portola, U.S.A. ... 56 G3
Portoscuso, Italy ... 16 E3
Portoviejo, Ecuador ... 62 D2
Portree, U.K. ... 10 C3
Portsmouth, Domin. ... 61 C7
Portsmouth, U.K. ... 9 G6
Portsmouth, N.H., U.S.A. ... 53 D10
Portsmouth, Ohio, U.S.A. ... 52 F4
Portsmouth, Va., U.S.A. 52 G7
Portsmouth □, U.K. ... 9 G6
Porttipahtan tekojärvi, Finland ... 6 B22
Portugal ■, Europe ... 15 C1
Porvenir, Chile ... 64 G2
Porvoo, Finland ... 7 F21
Posadas, Argentina ... 64 B5
Posht-e-Badam, Iran . 31 C7
Poso, Indonesia ... 27 E6
Posse, Brazil ... 63 F9
Possession I., Antarctica 5 D11
Possum Kingdom L., U.S.A. ... 55 J5
Post, U.S.A. ... 55 J4
Post Falls, U.S.A. ... 56 C5
Postavy = Pastavy, Belarus ... 7 J22
Poste-de-la-Baleine = Kuujjuarapik, Canada 48 A4
Postmasburg, S. Africa 37 K4
Postojna, Slovenia ... 12 F8
Postville, Canada ... 49 B8
Potchefstroom, S. Africa 37 K5
Poteau, U.S.A. ... 55 H7
Poteet, U.S.A. ... 55 L5
Potenza, Italy ... 16 D6
Poteriteri, L., N.Z. ... 39 M1
Potgietersrus, S. Africa 37 J5
Poti, Georgia ... 19 F7
Potiskum, Nigeria ... 35 F8
Potomac →, U.S.A. ... 52 G7
Potosí, Bolivia ... 62 G5
Pototan, Phil. ... 27 B6
Potrerillos, Chile ... 64 B3
Potsdam, Germany ... 12 B7
Potsdam, U.S.A. ... 52 C8
Pottstown, U.S.A. ... 52 E8
Pottsville, U.S.A. ... 52 E7
Pottuvil, Sri Lanka ... 28 R12
Pouce Coupé, Canada 50 B4
Poughkeepsie, U.S.A. 52 E9
Poulsbo, U.S.A. ... 56 C2
Pouthisat, Cambodia ... 26 B2
Považská Bystrica, Slovak Rep. ... 13 D10
Povenets, Russia ... 18 B5
Poverty B., N.Z. ... 39 H7
Póvoa de Varzim, Portugal ... 15 B1
Povungnituk = Puvirnituq, Canada ... 47 B12
Powassan, Canada ... 48 C4
Powder →, U.S.A. ... 54 B2
Powder River, U.S.A. 56 E10
Powell, U.S.A. ... 56 D9
Powell, L., U.S.A. ... 57 H8
Powell River, Canada 50 D4
Powers, U.S.A. ... 52 C2
Powys □, U.K. ... 9 E4
Poyang Hu, China ... 25 D6
Poyarkovo, Russia ... 21 E13
Poza Rica, Mexico ... 59 C5
Požarevac, Serbia, Yug. 17 B9
Poznań, Poland ... 13 B9
Pozo Almonte, Chile ... 62 H5
Pozoblanco, Spain ... 15 C3
Pozzuoli, Italy ... 16 D6
Prachuap Khiri Khan, Thailand ... 26 B1
Prado, Brazil ... 63 G11
Prague = Praha, Czech Rep. ... 12 C8
Praha, Czech Rep. ... 12 C8
Prainha, Amazonas, Brazil ... 62 E6
Prainha, Pará, Brazil ... 63 D8
Prairie, Australia ... 42 C3
Prairie City, U.S.A. ... 56 D4
Prairie Dog Town Fork →, U.S.A. ... 55 H5
Prairie du Chien, U.S.A. 54 D9
Prairies, L. of the, Canada ... 51 C8
Prapat, Indonesia ... 26 D1
Prata, Brazil ... 63 G9
Prato, Italy ... 16 C4
Pratt, U.S.A. ... 55 G5
Prattville, U.S.A. ... 53 J2
Pravia, Spain ... 15 A2
Praya, Indonesia ... 26 F5

Preeceville, Canada . . . 51 C8
Preiļi, Latvia 7 H22
Premont, U.S.A. 55 M5
Prentice, U.S.A. 54 C9
Preobrazheniye, Russia 22 C6
Preparis North Channel,
    Ind. Oc. 29 M18
Preparis South Channel,
    Ind. Oc. 29 M18
Přerov, Czech Rep. 13 D9
Prescott, Canada 48 D4
Prescott, Ariz., U.S.A. . 57 J7
Prescott, Ark., U.S.A. . . 55 J8
Prescott Valley, U.S.A. . 57 J7
Preservation Inlet, N.Z. 39 M1
Presho, U.S.A. 54 D4
Presidencia Roque
    Saenz Peña, Argentina 64 B4
Presidente Epitácio,
    Brazil 63 H8
Presidente Prudente,
    Brazil 63 H8
Presidio, Mexico 58 B4
Presidio, U.S.A. 55 L2
Prešov, Slovak Rep. . . . 13 D11
Prespa, L. = Prespansko
    Jezero, Macedonia . 17 D9
Prespansko Jezero,
    Macedonia 17 D9
Presque Isle, U.S.A. . . 53 B12
Prestatyn, U.K. 8 D4
Presteigne, U.K. 9 E5
Preston, U.K. 8 D5
Preston, Idaho, U.S.A. . . 56 E8
Preston, Minn., U.S.A. . 54 D8
Preston, C., Australia . . 40 D2
Prestonburg, U.S.A. . . 52 G4
Pretoria, S. Africa . . . 37 K5
Préveza, Greece 17 E9
Prey Veng, Cambodia . 26 B3
Pribilof Is., U.S.A. 46 C2
Příbram, Czech Rep. . . 12 D8
Price, U.S.A. 56 G8
Price I., Canada 50 C3
Prichard, U.S.A. 53 K1
Priekule, Latvia 7 H19
Prienai, Lithuania 7 J20
Prieska, S. Africa 37 K4
Priest L., U.S.A. 56 B5
Priest River, U.S.A. . . . 56 B5
Prievidza, Slovak Rep. . 13 D10
Prikaspiyskaya
    Nizmennost =
    Caspian Depression,
    Eurasia 19 E8
Prilep, Macedonia 17 D9
Priluki = Pryluky,
    Ukraine 19 D5
Prime Seal I., Australia 42 G4
Primrose L., Canada . . 51 C7
Prince Albert, Canada . 51 C7
Prince Albert Mts.,
    Antarctica 5 D11
Prince Albert Nat. Park,
    Canada 51 C7
Prince Albert Pen.,
    Canada 46 A8
Prince Albert Sd.,
    Canada 46 A8
Prince Alfred, C.,
    Canada 4 B1
Prince Charles I.,
    Canada 47 B12
Prince Charles Mts.,
    Antarctica 5 D6
Prince Edward I. □,
    Canada 49 C7
Prince Edward Is.,
    Ind. Oc. 3 G11
Prince George, Canada 50 C4
Prince of Wales I.,
    Australia 42 A3
Prince of Wales I.,
    Canada 46 A10
Prince of Wales I.,
    U.S.A. 46 C6
Prince Patrick I., Canada 4 B2
Prince Regent Inlet,
    Canada 4 B3
Prince Rupert, Canada . 50 C2
Princess Charlotte B.,
    Australia 42 A3
Princess May Ranges,
    Australia 40 C4
Princess Royal I.,
    Canada 50 C3
Princeton, Canada . . . 50 D4
Princeton, Ill., U.S.A. . 54 E10
Princeton, Ind., U.S.A. . 52 F2
Princeton, Ky., U.S.A. . 52 G2
Princeton, Mo., U.S.A. . 54 E8
Princeton, N.J., U.S.A. . 52 E8
Princeton, W. Va.,
    U.S.A. 52 G5
Principe, I. de, Atl. Oc. . 3 D10
Principe, I. de, Atl. Oc. . 3 D10
Principe da Beira, Brazil 62 F6
Prineville, U.S.A. 56 D3
Prins Harald Kyst,
    Antarctica 5 D4
Prinsesse Astrid Kyst,
    Antarctica 5 D3
Prinsesse Ragnhild Kyst,
    Antarctica 5 D4

Prinzapolca, Nic. 60 D3
Priozersk, Russia 18 B5
Pripet = Prypyat →,
    Europe 13 C16
Pripet Marshes, Europe 13 B15
Pripyat Marshes =
    Pripet Marshes,
    Europe 13 B15
Pripyats = Prypyat →,
    Europe 13 C16
Priština, Kosovo, Yug. . 17 C9
Privas, France 14 D6
Privolzhskaya
    Vozvyshennost,
    Russia 19 D8
Prizren, Kosovo, Yug. . 17 C9
Probolinggo, Indonesia 27 G15
Proddatur, India 28 M11
Profondeville, Belgium 11 D4
Progreso, Coahuila,
    Mexico 58 B4
Progreso, Yucatán,
    Mexico 59 C7
Prokopyevsk, Russia . . 20 D9
Prokuplje, Serbia, Yug. . 17 C9
Prome = Pyè, Burma . . 29 K19
Prophet →, Canada . . 50 B4
Prophet River, Canada . 50 B4
Propriá, Brazil 63 F11
Proserpine, Australia . . 42 C4
Prosna →, Poland . . . 13 B9
Prosser, U.S.A. 56 C4
Prostějov, Czech Rep. . 13 D9
Proston, Australia . . . 43 D5
Provence, France 14 E6
Providence, Ky., U.S.A. . 52 G2
Providence, R.I., U.S.A. . 52 E10
Providence Bay, Canada 48 C3
Providencia, I. de,
    Colombia 60 D3
Provideniya, Russia . . 21 C19
Provins, France 14 B5
Provo, U.S.A. 56 F8
Provost, Canada 51 C6
Prudhoe Bay, U.S.A. . . 46 A5
Prudhoe I., Australia . . 42 C4
Prud'homme, Canada . 51 C7
Pruszków, Poland . . . 13 B11
Prut →, Romania . . . 13 F15
Pruzhany, Belarus . . . 13 B13
Prydz B., Antarctica . . 5 C6
Pryluky, Ukraine 19 D5
Pryor, U.S.A. 55 G7
Prypyat →, Europe . . . 13 C16
Przemyśl, Poland . . . 13 D12
Przhevalsk, Kyrgyzstan 20 E8
Psará, Greece 17 E11
Pskov, Russia 18 C4
Ptich = Ptsich →,
    Belarus 13 B15
Ptolemais, Greece . . . 17 D9
Ptsich →, Belarus . . . 13 B15
Puán, Argentina 64 D4
Pucallpa, Peru 62 E4
Pudasjärvi, Finland . . . 6 D22
Pudozh, Russia 18 B6
Pudukkottai, India . . . 28 P11
Puebla, Mexico 59 D5
Puebla □, Mexico . . . 59 D5
Pueblo, U.S.A. 54 F2
Puelches, Argentina . . 64 D3
Puente Alto, Chile . . . 64 C2
Puente-Genil, Spain . . 15 D3
Puerco →, U.S.A. 57 J10
Puerto Aisén, Chile . . 64 F2
Puerto Ángel, Mexico . 59 D5
Puerto Arista, Mexico . 59 D6
Puerto Armuelles,
    Panama 60 E3
Puerto Ayacucho,
    Venezuela 62 B5
Puerto Barrios,
    Guatemala 60 C2
Puerto Bermúdez, Peru 62 F4
Puerto Bolívar, Ecuador 62 D3
Puerto Cabello,
    Venezuela 62 A5
Puerto Cabezas, Nic. . 60 D3
Puerto Cabo Gracias á
    Dios, Nic. 60 D3
Puerto Carreño,
    Colombia 62 B5
Puerto Castilla,
    Honduras 60 C2
Puerto Chicama, Peru . 62 E3
Puerto Coig, Argentina 64 G3
Puerto Cortés,
    Costa Rica 60 E3
Puerto Cortés, Honduras 60 C2
Puerto Cumarebo,
    Venezuela 62 A5
Puerto Deseado,
    Argentina 64 F3
Puerto Escondido,
    Mexico 59 D5
Puerto Heath, Bolivia . 62 F5
Puerto Inírida, Colombia 62 C5
Puerto Juárez, Mexico . 59 C7
Puerto La Cruz,
    Venezuela 62 A6
Puerto Leguízamo,
    Colombia 62 D4
Puerto Limón, Colombia 62 C4
Puerto Lobos, Argentina 64 E3

Puerto Madryn,
    Argentina 64 E3
Puerto Maldonado, Peru 62 F5
Puerto Manotí, Cuba . 60 B4
Puerto Montt, Chile . . 64 E2
Puerto Morazán, Nic. . 60 D2
Puerto Morelos, Mexico 59 C7
Puerto Natales, Chile . 64 G2
Puerto Padre, Cuba . . 60 B4
Puerto Páez, Venezuela 62 B5
Puerto Peñasco, Mexico 58 A2
Puerto Pinasco,
    Paraguay 62 H7
Puerto Plata, Dom. Rep. 61 C5
Puerto Princesa, Phil. . . 27 C5
Puerto Quepos,
    Costa Rica 60 E3
Puerto Rico ■, W. Indies 61 C6
Puerto Rico Trench,
    Atl. Oc. 61 C6
Puerto San Julián,
    Argentina 64 F3
Puerto Sastre, Paraguay 62 H7
Puerto Suárez, Bolivia . 62 G7
Puerto Vallarta, Mexico 58 C3
Puerto Wilches,
    Colombia 62 B4
Puertollano, Spain . . . 15 C3
Pueyrredón, L.,
    Argentina 64 F2
Pugachev, Russia 18 D8
Puget Sound, U.S.A. . . 56 C2
Pūgūnzi, Iran 31 E8
Puigcerdà, Spain 15 A6
Pukaki L., N.Z. 39 L3
Pukapuka, Cook Is. . . 45 J11
Pukaskwa Nat. Park,
    Canada 48 C2
Pukatawagan, Canada . 51 B8
Pukekohe, N.Z. 39 G5
Pula, Croatia 12 F7
Pulacayo, Bolivia 62 H5
Pularumpi, Australia . . 40 B5
Pulaski, N.Y., U.S.A. . . 52 D7
Pulaski, Tenn., U.S.A. . 53 H2
Pulaski, Va., U.S.A. . . 52 G5
Pulau →, Indonesia . . 27 F9
Puławy, Poland 13 C11
Pulicat L., India 28 N12
Pullman, U.S.A. 56 C5
Pulo-Anna, Pac. Oc. . . 27 D8
Pulog, Mt., Phil. 27 A4
Pułtusk, Poland 13 B11
Pumlumon Fawr, U.K. . 9 E4
Puná, I., Ecuador 62 D2
Punakha, Bhutan 29 F16
Punata, Bolivia 62 G5
Punch, India 28 C9
Pune, India 28 K8
Punjab □, India 28 D10
Punjab □, Pakistan . . 28 E9
Puno, Peru 62 G4
Punta Alta, Argentina . 64 D4
Punta Arenas, Chile . . 64 G2
Punta de Diaz, Chile . . 64 B2
Punta Gorda, Belize . . 59 D7
Punta Gorda, U.S.A. . . 53 M5
Punta Prieta, Mexico . 58 B2
Puntarenas, Costa Rica 60 E3
Punto Fijo, Venezuela . 62 A4
Punxsatawney, U.S.A. . 52 E6
Puquio, Peru 62 F4
Pur →, Russia 20 C8
Purace, Vol., Colombia 62 C3
Puralia = Puruliya, India 29 H15
Purbeck, Isle of, U.K. . 9 G6
Purcell, U.S.A. 55 H6
Purcell Mts., Canada . 50 D5
Puri, India 29 K14
Purmerend, Neths. . . 11 B4
Purnia, India 29 G15
Pursat = Pouthisat,
    Cambodia 26 B2
Purukcahu, Indonesia . 26 E4
Puruliya, India 29 H15
Purus →, Brazil 62 D6
Purvis, U.S.A. 55 K10
Purwakarta, Indonesia . 27 G12
Purwodadi, Indonesia . 27 G14
Purwokerto, Indonesia . 27 G13
Pusan, S. Korea 25 C7
Pushkino, Russia 19 D8
Putahow L., Canada . . 51 B8
Putao, Burma 29 F20
Putaruru, N.Z. 39 H5
Putignano, Italy 16 D7
Puting, Tanjung,
    Indonesia 26 E4
Putorana, Gory, Russia 21 C10
Puttalam, Sri Lanka . . 28 Q11
Puttgarden, Germany . 12 A6
Putumayo →, S. Amer. 62 D5
Putussibau, Indonesia . 26 D4
Puvirnituq, Canada . . 47 B12
Puy-de-Dôme, France . 14 D5
Puyallup, U.S.A. 56 C2
Pūzeh Rīg, Iran 31 E8
Pwllheli, U.K. 8 E3
Pya-ozero, Russia . . . 18 A5
Pyasina →, Russia . . . 21 B9
Pyatigorsk, Russia . . . 19 F7
Pyapon, Burma 29 L19
Pyè, Burma 29 K19
Pyetrikaw, Belarus . . . 13 B15

Pyhäjoki, Finland 6 D21
Pyinmana, Burma . . . 29 K20
P'yŏngyang, N. Korea . 25 C7
Pyote, U.S.A. 55 K3
Pyramid L., U.S.A. . . . 56 G4
Pyrénées, Europe . . . 14 E4
Pyu, Burma 29 K20

Qaanaaq, Greenland . . 4 B4
Qa'el Jafr, Jordan . . . 33 E5
Qa'emābād, Iran 31 D9
Qā'emshahr, Iran . . . 31 B7
Qahremānshahr =
    Bākhtarān, Iran . . 30 C5
Qaidam Pendi, China . 24 C4
Qajarīyeh, Iran 31 D6
Qal'at al Akhḍar,
    Si. Arabia 30 E3
Qal'at Dizah, Iraq . . . 30 B5
Qal'at Şāliḥ, Iraq . . . 30 D5
Qal'at Sukkar, Iraq . . 30 D5
Qamani'tuaq = Baker
    Lake, Canada 46 B10
Qamdo, China 24 C4
Qamruddin Karez,
    Pakistan 28 D6
Qandahār, Afghan. . . 28 D4
Qandahār □, Afghan. . 28 D4
Qapān, Iran 31 B7
Qapshaghay, Kazakstan 20 E8
Qaqortoq, Greenland . 4 C5
Qarabutaq, Kazakstan . 20 E7
Qārah, Si. Arabia . . . 30 D4
Qarataū, Kazakstan . . 20 E8
Qareh →, Iran 30 B5
Qareh Tekān, Iran . . . 31 B6
Qarqan He →, China . 24 C3
Qarqaraly, Kazakstan . 20 E8
Qarshi, Uzbekistan . . 20 F7
Qartabā, Lebanon . . . 33 A4
Qaryat al Gharab, Iraq 30 D5
Qaryat al 'Ulyā,
    Si. Arabia 30 E5
Qasr 'Amra, Jordan . . 30 D3
Qaşr-e Qand, Iran . . . 31 E9
Qasr Farāfra, Egypt . . 35 C11
Qatanā, Syria 33 B5
Qatar ■, Asia 31 E6
Qatlish, Iran 31 B8
Qattāra, Munkhafed el,
    Egypt 35 C11
Qattâra Depression =
    Qattâra, Munkhafed
    el, Egypt 35 C11
Qawām al Ḥamzah, Iraq 30 D5
Qāyen, Iran 31 C8
Qazaqstan =
    Kazakstan ■, Asia . 20 E7
Qāzimāmmād,
    Azerbaijan 31 A6
Qazvin, Iran 31 B6
Qena, Egypt 35 C12
Qeqertarsuaq,
    Greenland 4 C5
Qeqertarsuaq,
    Greenland 4 C5
Qeshlāq, Iran 30 C5
Qeshm, Iran 31 E8
Qeys, Iran 31 E7
Qezel Owzen →, Iran . 31 B6
Qezi'ot, Israel 33 E3
Qikiqtarjuaq, Canada . 47 B13
Qila Safed, Pakistan . . 28 E2
Qila Saifullāh, Pakistan 28 D6
Qilian Shan, China . . 24 C4
Qingdao, China 25 C7
Qinghai □, China . . . 24 C4
Qinghai Hu, China . . 24 C5
Qingjiang = Huaiyin,
    China 25 C6
Qinhuangdao, China . 25 C6
Qinzhou, China 24 D5
Qiqihar, China 21 E13
Qiraîya, W. →, Egypt . 33 E3
Qiryat Ata, Israel . . . 33 C4
Qiryat Gat, Israel . . . 33 D3
Qiryat Mal'akhi, Israel . 33 D3
Qiryat Shemona, Israel 33 B4
Qiryat Yam, Israel . . . 33 C4
Qitai, China 24 B3
Qīzlağac Körfāzi,
    Azerbaijan 31 B6
Qojūr, Iran 30 B5
Qom, Iran 31 C6
Qomolangma Feng =
    Everest, Mt., Nepal . 29 E15
Qomsheh, Iran 31 D6
Qostanay, Kazakstan . 20 D7
Quairading, Australia . 41 F2
Qualicum Beach,
    Canada 50 D4
Quambatook, Australia 43 F3
Quambone, Australia . 43 E4
Quamby, Australia . . 42 C3
Quan Long = Ca Mau,
    Vietnam 26 C3
Quanah, U.S.A. 55 H5
Quang Tri, Vietnam . . 26 A3
Quantock Hills, U.K. . 9 F4
Quanzhou, China . . . 25 D6

Qu'Appelle, Canada . . 51 C8
Quartu Sant'Elena, Italy 16 E3
Quartzsite, U.S.A. . . . 57 K6
Quatsino Sd., Canada . 50 C3
Quba, Azerbaijan . . . 19 F8
Qūchān, Iran 31 B8
Queanbeyan, Australia 43 F4
Québec, Canada 49 C5
Québec □, Canada . . 49 C6
Queen Alexandra Ra.,
    Antarctica 5 E11
Queen Charlotte City,
    Canada 50 C2
Queen Charlotte Is.,
    Canada 50 C2
Queen Charlotte Sd.,
    Canada 50 C3
Queen Charlotte Strait,
    Canada 50 C3
Queen Elizabeth Is.,
    Canada 2 A5
Queen Mary Land,
    Antarctica 5 D7
Queen Maud G., Canada 46 B9
Queen Maud Land,
    Antarctica 5 D3
Queen Maud Mts.,
    Antarctica 5 E13
Queens Chan., Australia 40 C4
Queenscliff, Australia . 43 F3
Queensland □, Australia 42 C3
Queenstown, Australia 42 G4
Queenstown, N.Z. . . . 39 L2
Queenstown, S. Africa . 37 L5
Queimadas, Brazil . . . 63 F11
Quelimane, Mozam. . . 37 H7
Quellón, Chile 64 E2
Quelpart = Cheju do,
    S. Korea 25 C7
Quemado, N. Mex.,
    U.S.A. 57 J9
Quemado, Tex., U.S.A. 55 L4
Querétaro, Mexico . . 58 C4
Querétaro □, Mexico . 58 C5
Quesnel, Canada . . . 50 C4
Quesnel →, Canada . 50 C4
Quesnel L., Canada . . 50 C4
Questa, U.S.A. 57 H11
Quetico Prov. Park,
    Canada 48 C1
Quetta, Pakistan . . . 28 D5
Quezaltenango,
    Guatemala 60 D1
Quezon City, Phil. . . . 27 B6
Qufār, Si. Arabia . . . 30 E4
Qui Nhon, Vietnam . . 26 B3
Quibaxe, Angola . . . 36 F2
Quibdo, Colombia . . 62 B3
Quiberon, France . . . 14 C2
Quiet L., Canada . . . 50 A2
Quila, Mexico 58 C3
Quilán, C., Chile 64 E2
Quill Lakes, Canada . . 51 C8
Quillabamba, Peru . . 62 F4
Quillagua, Chile 62 H5
Quillota, Chile 64 C2
Quilon, India 28 Q10
Quilpie, Australia . . . 43 D3
Quimilí, Argentina . . 64 B4
Quimper, France 14 B1
Quimperlé, France . . 14 C2
Quincy, Calif., U.S.A. . 56 G3
Quincy, Fla., U.S.A. . . 53 K3
Quincy, Ill., U.S.A. . . 54 F9
Quincy, Mass., U.S.A. . 52 D10
Quincy, Wash., U.S.A. . 56 C4
Quines, Argentina . . 64 C3
Quinns Rocks, Australia 41 F2
Quintana Roo □, Mexico 59 D7
Quintanar de la Orden,
    Spain 15 C4
Quirindi, Australia . . . 43 E5
Quirinópolis, Brazil . . 63 G8
Quissanga, Mozam. . . 37 G8
Quitman, U.S.A. 53 K4
Quito, Ecuador 62 D3
Quixadá, Brazil 63 D11
Qul'an, Jazā'ir, Egypt . 30 E2
Qŭnghirot, Uzbekistan 20 E6
Quoin I., Australia . . . 40 B4
Quorn, Australia 43 E2
Qŭqon, Uzbekistan . . 20 E8
Qurnat as Sawdā',
    Lebanon 33 A5
Quşaybā', Si. Arabia . . 30 E4
Qusaybah, Iraq 30 C4
Quseir, Egypt 35 C12
Qūshchī, Iran 30 B5
Qūţīābād, Iran 31 C6
Quzhou, China 25 D6
Qyzylorda, Kazakstan . 20 E7

Ra, Ko, Thailand 26 A1
Råbor, Iran 31 D8
Race, C., Canada 49 C9
Rach Gia, Vietnam . . 26 B3
Rachid, Mauritania . . 34 E3
Raciborz, Poland . . . 13 C10
Racine, U.S.A. 52 D2
Rădăuți, Romania . . . 13 E13
Radcliff, U.S.A. 52 G3
Radekhiv, Ukraine . . . 13 C13
Radekhov = Radekhiv,
    Ukraine 13 C13
Radford, U.S.A. 52 G5
Radhwa, Jabal,
    Si. Arabia 30 E3
Radisson, Qué., Canada 48 B4
Radisson, Sask., Canada 51 C7
Radium Hot Springs,
    Canada 50 C5
Radnor Forest, U.K. . . 9 E4
Radom, Poland 13 C11
Radomsko, Poland . . 13 C10
Radomyshl, Ukraine . 13 C15
Radstock, C., Australia 43 E1
Radviliškis, Lithuania . 7 J20
Radville, Canada . . . 51 D8
Rae Bareli, India . . . 29 F12
Rae, Canada 50 A5
Rae Isthmus, Canada . 47 B11
Raeren, Belgium . . . 11 D6
Raeside, L., Australia . 41 E3
Raetihi, N.Z. 39 H5
Rafaela, Argentina . . 64 C4
Rafah, Gaza Strip . . . 33 D3
Rafḥā, Si. Arabia . . . 30 D4
Rafsanjān, Iran 31 D8
Raft Pt., Australia . . . 40 C3
Râgâ, Sudan 35 G11
Ragachow, Belarus . . 13 B16
Ragama, Sri Lanka . . 28 R11
Ragged, Mt., Australia 41 F3
Raglan, N.Z. 39 G5
Ragusa, Italy 16 F6
Raha, Indonesia 27 E6
Rahaeng = Tak,
    Thailand 26 A1
Raḥīmah, Si. Arabia . . 31 E6
Rahimyar Khan,
    Pakistan 28 E7
Rāhjerd, Iran 31 C6
Raichur, India 28 L10
Raigarh, India 29 J13
Raijua, Indonesia . . . 27 F6
Railton, Australia . . . 42 G4
Rainbow Lake, Canada 50 B5
Rainier, U.S.A. 56 C2
Rainier, Mt., U.S.A. . . 56 C3
Rainy L., Canada . . . 51 D10
Rainy River, Canada . 51 D10
Raippaluoto, Finland . 6 E19
Raipur, India 29 J12
Raisio, Finland 7 F20
Raj Nandgaon, India . 29 J12
Raja, Ujung, Indonesia 26 D1
Raja Ampat, Kepulauan,
    Indonesia 27 E7
Rajahmundry, India . . 29 L12
Rajang →, Malaysia . . 26 D4
Rajapalaiyam, India . . 28 Q10
Rajasthan □, India . . 28 F8
Rajasthan Canal, India 28 F8
Rajgarh, India 28 G10
Rajkot, India 28 H7
Rajpipla, India 28 J8
Rajshahi, Bangla. . . . 29 G16
Rajshahi □, Bangla. . 29 G16
Rakaia, N.Z. 39 K4
Rakaia →, N.Z. 39 K4
Rakan, Ra's, Qatar . . 31 E6
Rakaposhi, Pakistan . 28 A9
Rakata, Pulau, Indonesia 26 F3
Rakhiv, Ukraine 13 D13
Rakitnoye, Russia . . . 22 B7
Rakvere, Estonia 7 G22
Raleigh, U.S.A. 53 H6
Ralls, U.S.A. 55 J4
Ram →, Canada 50 A4
Rām Allāh, West Bank . 33 D4
Ram Hd., Australia . . 43 F4
Rama, Nic. 60 D3
Ramanathapuram, India 28 Q11
Ramat Gan, Israel . . . 33 C3
Rambipuji, Indonesia . 27 H15
Ramechhap, Nepal . . 29 F15
Ramgarh, Bihar, India . 29 H14
Ramgarh, Raj., India . 28 F7
Rāmhormoz, Iran . . . 31 D6
Ramían, Iran 31 B7
Ramingining, Australia 42 A2
Ramla, Israel 33 D3
Ramnad =
    Ramanathapuram,
    India 28 Q11
Râmnicu Sărat,
    Romania 13 F14
Râmnicu Vâlcea,
    Romania 13 F13
Ramona, U.S.A. 57 K5
Ramore, Canada . . . 48 C3
Rampur, India 28 E11
Rampur Hat, India . . 29 G15
Ramree I., Burma . . . 29 K19
Rāmsar, Iran 31 B6
Ramsey, U.K. 8 C3
Ramsey L., Canada . . 48 C3

Ramsgate, *U.K.* 9 F9
Ramtek, *India* 28 J11
Ranaghat, *India* 29 H16
Ranau, *Malaysia* 26 C5
Rancagua, *Chile* 64 C2
Rancheria →, *Canada* 50 A3
Ranchester, *U.S.A.* . . . 56 D10
Ranchi, *India* 29 H14
Randers, *Denmark* 7 H14
Randolph, *Utah, U.S.A.* 56 F8
Randolph, *Vt., U.S.A.* . 52 D9
Râne älv →, *Sweden* . 6 D20
Rangaunu B., *N.Z.* . . . 39 F4
Rangeley, *U.S.A.* 52 C10
Rangely, *U.S.A.* 56 F9
Ranger, *U.S.A.* 55 J5
Rangia, *India* 29 F17
Rangiora, *N.Z.* 39 K4
Rangitaiki →, *N.Z.* . . . 39 G6
Rangitata →, *N.Z.* . . . 39 K3
Rangkasbitung,
  Indonesia 27 G12
Rangon →, *Burma* . . . 29 L20
Rangoon, *Burma* 29 L20
Rangpur, *Bangla.* 29 G16
Ranibennur, *India* 28 M9
Raniganj, *India* 29 H15
Raniwara, *India* 28 G8
Rānīyah, *Iraq* 30 B5
Ranken →, *Australia* . 42 C2
Rankin, *U.S.A.* 55 K4
Rankin Inlet, *Canada* . 46 B10
Rankins Springs,
  Australia 43 E4
Ranohira, *Madag.* . . . 37 J9
Ranong, *Thailand* . . . 26 C1
Ränsa, *Iran* 31 C6
Ransiki, *Indonesia* . . . 27 E8
Rantauprapat, *Indonesia* 26 D1
Rantemario, *Indonesia* 27 E5
Rantoul, *U.S.A.* 52 E1
Rapa, *Pac. Oc.* 45 K13
Rapallo, *Italy* 14 D8
Räpch, *Iran* 31 E8
Raper, C., *Canada* . . . 47 B13
Rapid City, *U.S.A.* . . . 54 D3
Rapid River, *U.S.A.* . . 52 C2
Rapla, *Estonia* 7 G21
Rarotonga, *Cook Is.* . . 45 K12
Ra's al 'Ayn, *Syria* . . . 30 B4
Ra's al Khaymah, *U.A.E.* 31 E7
Raseiniai, *Lithuania* . . 7 J20
Rasht, *Iran* 31 B6
Rason L., *Australia* . . 41 E3
Rat Islands, *U.S.A.* . . 46 C1
Rat L., *Canada* 51 B9
Ratangarh, *India* 28 E9
Raţāwī, *Iraq* 30 D5
Ratcatchers L., *Australia* 43 E3
Rathenow, *Germany* . . 12 B7
Ratibor = Racibórz,
  Poland 13 C10
Ratlam, *India* 28 H9
Ratnagiri, *India* 28 L8
Raton, *U.S.A.* 55 G2
Ratz, Mt., *Canada* . . . 50 B2
Raudales de Malpaso,
  Mexico 59 D6
Raufarhöfn, *Iceland* . . 6 C6
Raufoss, *Norway* 7 F14
Raukumara Ra., *N.Z.* . 39 H6
Rauma, *Finland* 7 F19
Raurkela, *India* 29 H14
Rausu-Dake, *Japan* . . 22 B12
Rava-Ruska, *Poland* . . 13 C12
Rava Russkaya = Rava-
  Ruska, *Poland* 13 C12
Ravalli, *U.S.A.* 56 C6
Rāvānsar, *Iran* 30 C5
Rāvar, *Iran* 31 D8
Ravenna, *Italy* 16 B5
Ravenna, *U.S.A.* 54 E5
Ravensburg, *Germany* . 12 E5
Ravenshoe, *Australia* . 42 B4
Ravensthorpe, *Australia* 41 F3
Ravenswood, *Australia* 42 C4
Ravenswood, *U.S.A.* . . 52 F5
Ravi →, *Pakistan* . . . 28 D7
Rawalpindi, *Pakistan* . 28 C8
Rawāndūz, *Iraq* 30 B5
Rawene, *N.Z.* 39 F4
Rawlinna, *Australia* . . 41 F4
Rawlins, *U.S.A.* 56 F10
Rawlinson Ra., *Australia* 41 D4
Rawson, *Argentina* . . . 64 E3
Ray, *U.S.A.* 54 A3
Ray, C., *Canada* 49 C8
Rayadurg, *India* 28 M10
Rayagada, *India* 29 K13
Raychikhinsk, *Russia* . 21 E13
Räyen, *Iran* 31 D8
Rayleigh, *U.K.* 9 F8
Raymond, *Canada* . . . 50 D6
Raymond, *U.S.A.* 56 C2
Raymond Terrace,
  Australia 43 E5
Raymondville, *U.S.A.* . 55 M6
Raymore, *Canada* . . . 51 C8
Rayón, *Mexico* 58 B2
Rayong, *Thailand* . . . 26 B2
Rayville, *U.S.A.* 55 J9
Raz, Pte. du, *France* . . 14 C1
Razan, *Iran* 31 C6
Razdel'naya = Rozdilna,
  Ukraine 13 E16

Razdolnoye, *Russia* . . . 22 C5
Razeh, *Iran* 31 C6
Razgrad, *Bulgaria* . . . 17 C12
Razim, Lacul, *Romania* 13 F15
Ré, Î. de, *France* 14 C3
Reading, *U.K.* 9 F7
Reading, *U.S.A.* 52 E8
Reading □, *U.K.* 9 F7
Realicó, *Argentina* . . . 64 D4
Reata, *Mexico* 58 B4
Rebi, *Indonesia* 27 F8
Rebiana, *Libya* 35 D10
Rebun-Tō, *Japan* 22 B10
Recherche, Arch. of the,
  Australia 41 F3
Rechytsa, *Belarus* . . . 13 B16
Recife, *Brazil* 63 E12
Recklinghausen,
  Germany 11 C7
Reconquista, *Argentina* 64 B5
Recreo, *Argentina* . . . 64 B3
Red →, *La., U.S.A.* . . 55 K9
Red →, *N. Dak., U.S.A.* 46 C10
Red Bay, *Canada* 49 B8
Red Bluff, *U.S.A.* 56 F2
Red Bluff L., *U.S.A.* . . 55 K3
Red Cliffs, *Australia* . . 43 E3
Red Cloud, *U.S.A.* . . . 54 E5
Red Deer, *Canada* . . . 50 C6
Red Deer →, *Alta.,*
  Canada 51 C7
Red Deer →, *Man.,*
  Canada 51 C8
Red Deer L., *Canada* . . 51 C8
Red Indian L., *Canada* . 49 C8
Red L., *Canada* 51 C10
Red Lake, *Canada* . . . 51 C10
Red Lake Falls, *U.S.A.* 54 B6
Red Lake Road, *Canada* 51 C10
Red Lodge, *U.S.A.* . . . 56 D9
Red Oak, *U.S.A.* 54 E7
Red Rock, *Canada* . . . 48 C2
Red Rock, L., *U.S.A.* . . 54 E8
Red Rocks Pt., *Australia* 41 F4
Red Sea, *Asia* 32 C2
Red Sucker L., *Canada* 48 B1
Red Tower Pass =
  Turnu Roşu, P.,
  Romania 13 F13
Red Wing, *U.S.A.* 54 C8
Redang, *Malaysia* . . . 26 C2
Redange, *Lux.* 11 E5
Redcar, *U.K.* 8 C6
Redcar & Cleveland □,
  U.K. 8 C7
Redcliff, *Canada* 51 C6
Redcliffe, *Australia* . . 43 D5
Redcliffe, Mt., *Australia* 41 E3
Redding, *U.S.A.* 56 F2
Redditch, *U.K.* 9 E6
Redfield, *U.S.A.* 54 C5
Redmond, *U.S.A.* 56 D3
Redon, *France* 14 C2
Redonda, *Antigua* . . . 61 C7
Redondela, *Spain* . . . 15 A1
Redruth, *U.K.* 9 G2
Redvers, *Canada* 51 D8
Redwater, *Canada* . . . 50 C6
Redwood City, *U.S.A.* . 57 H2
Redwood Falls, *U.S.A.* 54 C7
Redwood National Park,
  U.S.A. 56 F1
Ree, L., *Ireland* 10 E3
Reed, L., *Canada* 51 C8
Reed City, *U.S.A.* 52 D3
Reedley, *U.S.A.* 57 H4
Reedsburg, *U.S.A.* . . . 54 D9
Reedsport, *U.S.A.* . . . 56 E1
Reefton, *N.Z.* 39 K3
Reese →, *U.S.A.* 56 F5
Refugio, *U.S.A.* 55 L6
Regensburg, *Germany* 12 D7
Réggio di Calábria, *Italy* 16 E6
Réggio nell'Emília, *Italy* 16 B4
Reghin, *Romania* 13 E13
Regina, *Canada* 51 C8
Regina Beach, *Canada* 51 C8
Registro, *Brazil* 64 A7
Rehoboth, *Namibia* . . 37 J3
Rehovot, *Israel* 33 D3
Reichenbach, *Germany* 12 C7
Reid, *Australia* 41 F4
Reidsville, *U.S.A.* 53 G6
Reigate, *U.K.* 9 F7
Reims, *France* 14 B6
Reina Adelaida, Arch.,
  Chile 64 G2
Reindeer →, *Canada* . 51 B8
Reindeer I., *Canada* . . 51 C9
Reindeer L., *Canada* . . 51 B8
Reinga, C., *N.Z.* 39 F4
Reinosa, *Spain* 15 A3
Reliance, *Canada* . . . 51 A7
Remarkable, Mt.,
  Australia 43 E2
Rembang, *Indonesia* . 27 G14
Remedios, *Panama* . . 60 E3
Remeshk, *Iran* 31 E8
Remich, *Lux.* 11 E6
Remscheid, *Germany* . 11 C7
Rendsburg, *Germany* . 12 A5
Renfrew, *Canada* 48 C4
Rengat, *Indonesia* . . . 26 E2
Reni, *Ukraine* 13 F15

Renmark, *Australia* . . . 43 E3
Rennell Sd., *Canada* . . 50 C2
Renner Springs,
  Australia 42 B1
Rennes, *France* 14 B3
Rennie L., *Canada* . . . 51 A7
Reno, *U.S.A.* 56 G4
Reno →, *Italy* 16 B5
Rensselaer, *U.S.A.* . . . 52 E2
Rentería, *Spain* 15 A5
Renton, *U.S.A.* 56 C2
Republic, *Mo., U.S.A.* . 55 G8
Republic, *Wash., U.S.A.* 56 B4
Republican →, *U.S.A.* 54 F6
Repulse Bay, *Canada* . 47 B11
Requena, *Peru* 62 E4
Requena, *Spain* 15 C5
Reşadiye = Datça,
  Turkey 17 F12
Reserve, *U.S.A.* 57 K9
Resht = Rasht, *Iran* . . 31 B6
Resistencia, *Argentina* . 64 B5
Reşiţa, *Romania* 13 F11
Resolution I., *Canada* . 47 B13
Resolution I., *N.Z.* . . . 39 L1
Reston, *Canada* 51 D8
Retalhuleu, *Guatemala* 60 D1
Retford, *U.K.* 8 D7
Réthímnon, *Greece* . . . 17 G11
Réunion ■, *Ind. Oc.* . . 3 E12
Reus, *Spain* 15 B6
Reutlingen, *Germany* . 12 D5
Reval = Tallinn, *Estonia* 7 G21
Revda, *Russia* 18 C10
Revelstoke, *Canada* . . 50 C5
Reventazón, *Peru* 62 E2
Revillagigedo, Is. de,
  Pac. Oc. 58 D2
Rewa, *India* 29 G12
Rewari, *India* 28 E10
Rexburg, *U.S.A.* 56 E8
Rey, *Iran* 31 C6
Rey, I. del, *Panama* . . 60 E4
Rey Malabo, *Eq. Guin.* 36 D1
Reyðarfjörður, *Iceland* . 6 D6
Reykjahlíð, *Iceland* . . . 6 D5
Reykjanes, *Iceland* . . . 6 E2
Reykjavík, *Iceland* . . . 6 D3
Reynolds Ra., *Australia* 40 D5
Reynosa, *Mexico* 59 B5
Rēzekne, *Latvia* 7 H22
Rezvān, *Iran* 31 E8
Rhayader, *U.K.* 9 E4
Rhein →, *Europe* 11 C6
Rhein-Main-Donau-
  Kanal, *Germany* 12 D6
Rheine, *Germany* 11 B4
Rheinland-Pfalz □,
  Germany 12 C4
Rhin = Rhein →,
  Europe 11 C6
Rhine = Rhein →,
  Europe 11 C6
Rhineland-Palatinate =
  Rheinland-Pfalz □,
  Germany 12 C4
Rhinelander, *U.S.A.* . . 54 C10
Rhir, Cap, *Morocco* . . 34 B4
Rhode Island □, *U.S.A.* 52 E10
Rhodes = Ródhos,
  Greece 17 F13
Rhodesia =
  Zimbabwe ■, *Africa* . 37 H5
Rhodope Mts. =
  Rhodopi Planina,
  Bulgaria 17 D11
Rhodopi Planina,
  Bulgaria 17 D11
Rhön, *Germany* 12 C5
Rhondda, *U.K.* 9 F4
Rhondda Cynon Taff □,
  U.K. 9 F4
Rhône →, *France* 14 E6
Rhum, *U.K.* 10 C3
Rhyl, *U.K.* 8 D4
Riachão, *Brazil* 63 E9
Riasi, *India* 28 C9
Riau □, *Indonesia* . . . 26 D2
Riau, Kepulauan,
  Indonesia 26 D2
Riau Arch. = Riau,
  Kepulauan, *Indonesia* 26 D2
Ribadeo, *Spain* 15 A2
Ribas do Rio Pardo,
  Brazil 63 H8
Ribble →, *U.K.* 8 D5
Ribe, *Denmark* 7 J13
Ribeirão Prêto, *Brazil* . 63 H9
Riberalta, *Bolivia* 62 F5
Riccarton, *N.Z.* 39 K4
Rice Lake, *U.S.A.* 54 C9
Richards Bay, *S. Africa* 37 K6
Richardson →, *Canada* 51 B6
Richardson Lakes,
  U.S.A. 52 C10
Riche, C., *Australia* . . 41 F2
Richey, *U.S.A.* 54 B2
Richfield, *U.S.A.* 57 G8
Richibucto, *Canada* . . 49 C7
Richland, *Ga., U.S.A.* . 53 J3
Richland, *Wash., U.S.A.* 56 C4
Richland Center, *U.S.A.* 54 D9
Richlands, *U.S.A.* 52 G5
Richmond, *Australia* . . 42 C3

Richmond, *N.Z.* 39 J4
Richmond, *U.K.* 8 C6
Richmond, *Calif., U.S.A.* 56 H2
Richmond, *Ind., U.S.A.* 52 F3
Richmond, *Ky., U.S.A.* 52 G3
Richmond, *Mo., U.S.A.* 54 F8
Richmond, *Tex., U.S.A.* 55 L7
Richmond, *Utah, U.S.A.* 56 F8
Richmond, *Va., U.S.A.* 52 G7
Richmond Ra., *Australia* 43 D5
Richwood, *U.S.A.* 52 F5
Ridder = Leninogorsk,
  Kazakstan 20 D9
Ridgecrest, *U.S.A.* . . . 57 J5
Ridgeland, *U.S.A.* 53 J5
Ridgetown, *Canada* . . 48 D3
Ridgway, *U.S.A.* 52 E6
Riding Mountain Nat.
  Park, *Canada* 51 C9
Ridley, Mt., *Australia* . 41 F3
Ried, *Austria* 12 D7
Riesa, *Germany* 12 C7
Rieti, *Italy* 16 C5
Rifle, *U.S.A.* 56 G10
Rīga, *Latvia* 7 H21
Riga, G. of, *Latvia* . . . 7 H20
Rīgān, *Iran* 31 D8
Rīgas Jūras Līcis =
  Riga, G. of, *Latvia* . . 7 H20
Rigby, *U.S.A.* 56 E8
Rigestān, *Afghan.* . . . 28 D4
Riggins, *U.S.A.* 56 D5
Rigolet, *Canada* 49 B8
Riihimäki, *Finland* . . . 7 F21
Riiser-Larsen-halvøya,
  Antarctica 5 C4
Rijeka, *Croatia* 12 F8
Rijssen, *Neths.* 11 B6
Rikuzentakada, *Japan* . 22 E10
Riley, *U.S.A.* 56 E4
Rimah, Wadi ar →,
  Si. Arabia 30 E4
Rimbey, *Canada* 50 C6
Rímini, *Italy* 16 B5
Rimouski, *Canada* . . . 49 C6
Rinca, *Indonesia* 27 F5
Rincón de Romos,
  Mexico 58 C4
Rinconada, *Argentina* . 62 H5
Ringkøbing, *Denmark* . 7 H13
Ringvassøy, *Norway* . . 6 B18
Rinjani, *Indonesia* . . . 26 F5
Rio Branco, *Brazil* . . . 62 E5
Río Branco, *Uruguay* . 64 C6
Río Bravo del Norte →,
  Mexico 59 B5
Rio Claro, *Brazil* 64 A7
Rio Claro, *Trin. & Tob.* 61 D7
Río Colorado, *Argentina* 64 D4
Río Cuarto, *Argentina* . 64 C4
Rio de Janeiro, *Brazil* . 63 H10
Rio de Janeiro □, *Brazil* 63 H10
Río Gallegos, *Argentina* 64 G3
Rio Grande = Grande,
  Rio →, *U.S.A.* 55 N6
Río Grande, *Argentina* 64 G3
Rio Grande, *Brazil* . . . 64 C6
Río Grande, *Mexico* . . 58 C4
Río Grande, *Nic.* 60 D3
Río Grande City, *U.S.A.* 55 M5
Río Grande de
  Santiago →, *Mexico* 58 C3
Rio Grande do Norte □,
  Brazil 63 E11
Rio Grande do Sul □,
  Brazil 64 C6
Río Hato, *Panama* . . . 60 E3
Rio Largo, *Brazil* 63 E11
Río Mulatos, *Bolivia* . . 62 G5
Río Muni = Mbini □,
  Eq. Guin. 36 D2
Rio Negro, *Brazil* 64 B7
Rio Rancho, *U.S.A.* . . 57 J10
Rio Verde, *Brazil* 63 G8
Río Verde, *Mexico* . . . 59 C5
Ríobamba, *Ecuador* . . 62 D3
Ríohacha, *Colombia* . . 62 A4
Ríosucio, *Colombia* . . 62 B3
Riou L., *Canada* 51 B7
Ripley, *Tenn., U.S.A.* . 55 H10
Ripley, *W. Va., U.S.A.* 52 F5
Ripon, *U.K.* 8 C6
Ripon, *U.S.A.* 52 D1
Rishā', W. ar →,
  Si. Arabia 30 E5
Rishiri-Tō, *Japan* 22 B10
Rishon le Ziyyon, *Israel* 33 D3
Rison, *U.S.A.* 55 J8
Risør, *Norway* 7 G13
Rita Blanca Cr. →,
  U.S.A. 55 H3
Ritzville, *U.S.A.* 56 C4
Riva del Garda, *Italy* . 16 B4
Rivadavia, *Chile* 64 B2
Rivas, *Nic.* 60 D2
River Cess, *Liberia* . . 34 G4
Rivera, *Argentina* 64 D4
Rivera, *Uruguay* 64 C5
Riverhead, *U.S.A.* 52 E9
Riverhurst, *Canada* . . 51 C7
Rivers, *Canada* 51 C8
Rivers Inlet, *Canada* . . 50 C3

Riverside, *U.S.A.* 57 K5
Riverton, *Australia* . . . 43 E2
Riverton, *Canada* 51 C9
Riverton, *N.Z.* 39 M2
Riverton, *U.S.A.* 56 E9
Riviera di Levante, *Italy* 14 D8
Riviera di Ponente, *Italy* 14 D8
Rivière-au-Renard,
  Canada 49 C7
Rivière-du-Loup, *Canada* 49 C6
Rivière-Pentecôte,
  Canada 49 C6
Rivière-Pilote,
  Martinique 61 D7
Rivière St. Paul, *Canada* 49 B8
Rivne, *Ukraine* 13 C14
Rívoli, *Italy* 14 D7
Rivoli B., *Australia* . . . 43 F3
Riyadh = Ar Riyāḍ,
  Si. Arabia 30 E5
Rize, *Turkey* 19 F7
Rizzuto, C., *Italy* 16 E7
Rjukan, *Norway* 7 G13
Road Town, *Virgin Is.* . 61 C7
Roan Plateau, *U.S.A.* . 56 G9
Roanne, *France* 14 C6
Roanoke, *Ala., U.S.A.* 53 J3
Roanoke, *Va., U.S.A.* . 52 G6
Roanoke →, *U.S.A.* . . 53 H7
Roanoke I., *U.S.A.* . . . 53 H8
Roanoke Rapids, *U.S.A.* 53 G7
Roatán, *Honduras* . . . 60 C2
Robāt Sang, *Iran* 31 C8
Robbins I., *Australia* . . 42 G4
Robe →, *Australia* . . . 40 D2
Robe, *Australia* 43 F2
Robert Lee, *U.S.A.* . . . 55 K4
Robertson I., *Antarctica* 5 C18
Robertson Ra., *Australia* 40 D3
Robertstown, *Australia* 43 E2
Roberval, *Canada* . . . 49 C5
Robeson Chan.,
  Greenland 4 A4
Robinson, *U.S.A.* 52 F2
Robinson →, *Australia* 42 B2
Robinson Ra., *Australia* 41 E2
Robinvale, *Australia* . . 43 E3
Roblin, *Canada* 51 C8
Roboré, *Bolivia* 62 G7
Robson, Mt., *Canada* . 50 C5
Robstown, *U.S.A.* 55 M6
Roca, C. da, *Portugal* . 15 C1
Roca Partida, I., *Mexico* 58 D2
Rocas, I., *Brazil* 63 D12
Rocha, *Uruguay* 64 C6
Rochdale, *U.K.* 8 D5
Rochefort, *Belgium* . . 11 D5
Rochefort, *France* . . . 14 D3
Rocher River, *Canada* . 50 A6
Rochester, *U.K.* 9 F8
Rochester, *Ind., U.S.A.* 52 E2
Rochester, *Minn., U.S.A.* 54 C8
Rochester, *N.H., U.S.A.* 52 D10
Rochester, *N.Y., U.S.A.* 52 D7
Rock →, *Canada* 50 B3
Rock Falls, *U.S.A.* . . . 54 E10
Rock Hill, *U.S.A.* 53 H5
Rock Island, *U.S.A.* . . 54 E9
Rock Rapids, *U.S.A.* . . 54 D6
Rock Sound, *Bahamas* 60 B4
Rock Springs, *Mont.,*
  U.S.A. 56 C10
Rock Springs, *Wyo.,*
  U.S.A. 56 F9
Rock Valley, *U.S.A.* . . 54 D6
Rockdale, *U.S.A.* 55 K6
Rockefeller Plateau,
  Antarctica 5 E14
Rockford, *U.S.A.* 54 D10
Rockglen, *Canada* . . . 51 D7
Rockhampton, *Australia* 42 C5
Rockingham, *Australia* 41 F2
Rockingham, *U.S.A.* . . 53 H6
Rockingham B.,
  Australia 42 B4
Rocklake, *U.S.A.* 54 A5
Rockland, *Idaho, U.S.A.* 56 E7
Rockland, *Maine, U.S.A.* 53 C11
Rockland, *Mich., U.S.A.* 54 B10
Rockmart, *U.S.A.* 53 H3
Rockport, *Mo., U.S.A.* 54 E7
Rockport, *Tex., U.S.A.* 55 L6
Rockville, *U.S.A.* 52 F7
Rockwall, *U.S.A.* 55 J6
Rockwell City, *U.S.A.* . 54 D7
Rockwood, *Maine,*
  U.S.A. 53 C11
Rockwood, *Tenn.,*
  U.S.A. 53 H3
Rocky Ford, *U.S.A.* . . 54 F3
Rocky Gully, *Australia* . 41 F2
Rocky Harbour, *Canada* 49 C8
Rocky Island L., *Canada* 48 C3
Rocky Lane, *Canada* . . 50 B5
Rocky Mount, *U.S.A.* . 53 H7
Rocky Mountain House,
  Canada 50 C6
Rocky Mountain
  National Park, *U.S.A.* 56 F11
Rocky Mts., *N. Amer.* . 56 G10
Rod, *Pakistan* 28 E3

Rødbyhavn, *Denmark* . 7 J14
Roddickton, *Canada* . . 49 B8
Rodez, *France* 14 D5
Ródhos, *Greece* 17 F13
Rodney, C., *N.Z.* 39 G5
Rodriguez, *Ind. Oc.* . . 3 E13
Roebourne, *Australia* . 40 D2
Roebuck B., *Australia* . 40 C3
Roermond, *Neths.* . . . 11 C6
Roes Welcome Sd.,
  Canada 47 B11
Roeselare, *Belgium* . . 11 D3
Rogachev = Ragachow,
  Belarus 13 B16
Rogagua, L., *Bolivia* . . 62 F5
Rogatyn, *Ukraine* 13 D13
Rogers, *U.S.A.* 55 G7
Rogers City, *U.S.A.* . . 52 C4
Rogersville, *Canada* . . 49 C6
Roggan →, *Canada* . . 48 B4
Roggan L., *Canada* . . 48 B4
Rogoaguado, L., *Bolivia* 62 F5
Rogue →, *U.S.A.* 56 E1
Rohri, *Pakistan* 28 F6
Rohtak, *India* 28 E10
Roi Et, *Thailand* 26 A2
Roja, *Latvia* 7 H20
Rojo, C., *Mexico* 59 C5
Rokan →, *Indonesia* . 26 D2
Rokiškis, *Lithuania* . . . 7 J21
Rolândia, *Brazil* 64 A6
Rolla, *U.S.A.* 55 G9
Rolleston, *Australia* . . 42 C4
Rollingstone, *Australia* 42 B4
Roma, *Australia* 43 D4
Roma, *Italy* 16 D5
Roma, *Sweden* 7 H18
Roma, *U.S.A.* 55 M5
Romain C., *U.S.A.* . . . 53 J6
Romaine, *Canada* . . . 49 B7
Romaine →, *Canada* . 49 B7
Roman, *Romania* 13 E14
Romang, *Indonesia* . . 27 F7
Români, *Egypt* 33 E1
Romania ■, *Europe* . . 13 F12
Romano, Cayo, *Cuba* . 60 B4
Romanovka =
  Basarabeasca,
  Moldova 13 E15
Romans-sur-Isère,
  France 14 D6
Romblon, *Phil.* 27 B6
Rome = Roma, *Italy* . . 16 D5
Rome, *Ga., U.S.A.* . . . 53 H3
Rome, *N.Y., U.S.A.* . . 52 D8
Romney, *U.S.A.* 52 F6
Romney Marsh, *U.K.* . 9 F8
Rømø, *Denmark* 7 J13
Romorantin-Lanthenay,
  France 14 C4
Romsdalen, *Norway* . . 7 E12
Romsey, *U.K.* 9 G6
Ronan, *U.S.A.* 56 C6
Roncador, Cayos,
  Caribbean 60 D3
Roncador, Serra do,
  Brazil 63 F8
Ronda, *Spain* 15 D3
Rondane, *Norway* 7 F13
Rondônia □, *Brazil* . . . 62 F6
Rondonópolis, *Brazil* . . 63 G8
Ronge, L. la, *Canada* . 51 B7
Rønne, *Denmark* 7 J16
Ronne Ice Shelf,
  Antarctica 5 D18
Ronsard, C., *Australia* . 41 D1
Ronse, *Belgium* 11 D3
Roof Butte, *U.S.A.* . . . 57 H9
Roorkee, *India* 28 E10
Roosendaal, *Neths.* . . 11 C4
Roosevelt, *U.S.A.* 56 F8
Roosevelt →, *Brazil* . . 62 E6
Roosevelt, Mt., *Canada* 50 B3
Roosevelt I., *Antarctica* 5 D12
Roper →, *Australia* . . 42 A2
Roper Bar, *Australia* . . 42 A1
Roquetas de Mar, *Spain* 15 D4
Roraima □, *Brazil* . . . 62 C6
Roraima, Mt., *Venezuela* 62 B6
Røros, *Norway* 7 E14
Rosa, L., *Bahamas* . . . 61 B5
Rosa, Monte, *Europe* . 14 D7
Rosalia, *U.S.A.* 56 C5
Rosario, *Argentina* . . . 64 C4
Rosário, *Brazil* 63 D10
Rosario, *Baja Calif.,*
  Mexico 58 B1
Rosario, *Sinaloa,*
  Mexico 58 C3
Rosario, *Paraguay* . . . 64 A5
Rosario de la Frontera,
  Argentina 64 B4
Rosário do Sul, *Brazil* . 64 C6
Roscommon, *Ireland* . 10 E2
Rose →, *Australia* . . . 42 A2
Rose Blanche, *Canada* 49 C8
Rose Pt., *Canada* 50 C2
Rose Valley, *Canada* . . 51 C8
Roseau, *Domin.* 61 C7
Roseau, *U.S.A.* 54 A7
Rosebud, *S. Dak., U.S.A.* 54 D4
Rosebud, *Tex., U.S.A.* 55 K6
Roseburg, *U.S.A.* 56 E2

Rosedale, U.S.A. 55 J9
Rosemary, Canada .. 50 C6
Rosenberg, U.S.A. ... 55 L7
Rosenheim, Germany . 12 E7
Roses, G. de, Spain ... 15 A7
Rosetown, Canada ... 51 C7
Roseville, U.S.A. 56 G3
Rosewood, Australia .. 43 D5
Roshkhvār, Iran 31 C8
Rosignano Marittimo,
  Italy 16 C4
Rosignol, Guyana .. 62 B7
Roşiori de Vede,
  Romania 13 F13
Roskilde, Denmark .. 7 J15
Roslavl, Russia 18 D5
Ross, Australia 42 G4
Ross, N.Z. 39 K3
Ross I., Antarctica ... 5 D11
Ross Ice Shelf,
  Antarctica 5 E12
Ross L., U.S.A. 56 B3
Ross-on-Wye, U.K. ... 9 F5
Ross River, Australia . 42 C1
Ross River, Canada .. 50 A2
Ross Sea, Antarctica . 5 D11
Rossall Pt., U.K. 8 D4
Rossano, Italy 16 E7
Rossburn, Canada ... 51 C8
Rossignol, L., Canada . 48 B5
Rossignol Res., Canada 49 D6
Rossland, Canada 50 D5
Rosslare, Ireland 10 E5
Rosso, Mauritania ... 34 E2
Rossosh, Russia 19 D6
Røssvatnet, Norway .. 6 D16
Røst, Norway 6 C15
Rosthern, Canada ... 51 C7
Rostock, Germany ... 12 A7
Rostov, Don, Russia .. 19 E6
Rostov, Yaroslavl,
  Russia 18 C6
Roswell, Ga., U.S.A. .. 53 H3
Roswell, N. Mex., U.S.A. 55 J2
Rotan, U.S.A. 55 J4
Rother →, U.K. 9 G8
Rotherham, U.K. 8 D6
Rothesay, Canada ... 49 C6
Roti, Indonesia 27 F6
Roto, Australia 43 E4
Rotondo Mte., France . 14 E8
Rotoroa, L., N.Z. 39 J4
Rotorua, N.Z. 39 H6
Rotorua, L., N.Z. 39 H6
Rotterdam, Neths. ... 11 C4
Rottnest I., Australia . 41 F2
Rottumeroog, Neths. . 11 A6
Rottweil, Germany ... 12 D5
Rotuma, Fiji 38 C10
Roubaix, France 14 A5
Rouen, France 14 B4
Rouleau, Canada 51 C8
Round Mountain, U.S.A. 56 G5
Round Mt., Australia . 43 E5
Round Rock, U.S.A. .. 55 K6
Roundup, U.S.A. 56 C9
Roussillon, France ... 14 E5
Rouyn-Noranda, Canada 48 C4
Rovaniemi, Finland .. 6 C21
Rovereto, Italy 16 B4
Rovigo, Italy 16 B4
Rovinj, Croatia 12 F7
Rovno = Rivne, Ukraine 13 C14
Rovuma = Ruvuma →,
  Tanzania 36 G8
Row'ān, Iran 31 C6
Rowena, Australia ... 43 D4
Rowley Shoals,
  Australia 40 C2
Roxas, Phil. 27 B6
Roxboro, U.S.A. 53 G6
Roxburgh, N.Z. 39 L2
Roy, Mont., U.S.A. ... 56 C9
Roy, N. Mex., U.S.A. .. 55 H2
Roy, Utah, U.S.A. 56 F7
Royal Leamington Spa,
  U.K. 9 E6
Royal Tunbridge Wells,
  U.K. 9 F8
Royan, France 14 D3
Royston, U.K. 9 E7
Rozdilna, Ukraine ... 13 E16
Rozhyshche, Ukraine . 13 C13
Rtishchevo, Russia ... 18 D7
Ruahine Ra., N.Z. 39 H6
Ruapehu, N.Z. 39 H5
Ruapuke I., N.Z. 39 M2
Ruâq, W. →, Egypt .. 33 F2
Rub' al Khālī, Si. Arabia 32 D4
Rubio, Venezuela 62 B4
Rubtsovsk, Russia ... 20 D9
Ruby, L., U.S.A. 56 F6
Ruby Mts., U.S.A. 56 F6
Rubyvale, Australia .. 42 C4
Rūd Sar, Iran 31 B6
Rudall, Australia 43 E2
Rudall →, Australia .. 40 D3
Rudnyy, Kazakstan ... 20 D7
Rudolfa, Ostrov, Russia 20 A6
Rudyard, U.S.A. 52 B3
Rufiji →, Tanzania ... 36 F7
Rufino, Argentina ... 64 C4

Rügen, Germany 12 A7
Ruhnu, Estonia 7 H20
Ruhr →, Germany ... 12 C4
Ruidoso, U.S.A. 57 K11
Rujm Tal'at al Jamā'ah,
  Jordan 33 E4
Ruki →, Dem. Rep. of
  the Congo 36 E3
Rukwa, L., Tanzania .. 36 F6
Rulhieres, C., Australia 27 F5
Rum = Rhum, U.K. ... 10 C3
Rum Cay, Bahamas ... 61 B5
Rum Jungle, Australia . 40 B5
Rumāh, Si. Arabia ... 30 E5
Rumania = Romania ■,
  Europe 13 F12
Rumaylah, Iraq 30 D5
Rumbek, Sudan 35 G11
Rumford, U.S.A. 53 C10
Rumia, Poland 13 A10
Rumoi, Japan 22 C10
Runanga, N.Z. 39 K3
Runaway, C., N.Z. ... 39 G6
Runcorn, U.K. 8 D5
Rundu, Namibia 37 H3
Rungwe, Mt., Tanzania 36 F6
Runton Ra., Australia . 40 D3
Ruoqiang, China 24 C3
Rupa, India 29 F18
Rupat, Indonesia 26 D2
Rupert →, Canada .. 56 E7
Rupert →, Canada .. 48 B4
Rupert B., Canada ... 48 B4
Rupert House =
  Waskaganish, Canada 48 B4
Rurrenabaque, Bolivia . 62 F5
Ruschuk = Ruse,
  Bulgaria 17 C12
Ruse, Bulgaria 17 C12
Rushden, U.K. 9 E7
Rushmore, Mt., U.S.A. 54 D3
Rushville, Ill., U.S.A. .. 54 E9
Rushville, Ind., U.S.A. . 52 F3
Rushville, Nebr., U.S.A. 54 D3
Russas, Brazil 63 D11
Russell, Canada 51 C8
Russell, U.S.A. 54 F5
Russell, Man., Canada 51 B8
Russell L., N.W.T.,
  Canada 50 A5
Russellkonda, India .. 29 K14
Russellville, Ala., U.S.A. 53 H2
Russellville, Ark., U.S.A. 55 H8
Russellville, Ky., U.S.A. 53 G2
Russia ■, Eurasia ... 21 C11
Russkoye Ustie, Russia 4 B15
Rustavi, Georgia 19 F8
Rustenburg, S. Africa . 37 K5
Ruston, U.S.A. 55 J8
Ruteng, Indonesia ... 27 F6
Rutland, U.S.A. 52 D9
Rutland □, U.K. 9 E7
Rutland Water, U.K. .. 9 E7
Rutledge →, Canada . 51 A6
Rutledge L., Canada .. 51 A6
Ruvuma →, Tanzania 36 G8
Ruwais, U.A.E. 31 E7
Ruwenzori, Africa ... 36 D5
Ružomberok,
  Slovak Rep. 13 D10
Rwanda ■, Africa ... 36 E5
Ryazan, Russia 18 D6
Ryazhsk, Russia 18 D7
Rybache = Rybachye,
  Kazakstan 20 E9
Rybachiy Poluostrov,
  Russia 18 A5
Rybachye, Kazakstan . 20 E9
Rybinsk, Russia 18 C6
Rybinskoye Vdkhr.,
  Russia 18 C6
Rybnitsa = Râbniţa,
  Moldova 13 E15
Rycroft, Canada 50 B5
Ryde, U.K. 9 G6
Rye, U.K. 9 G8
Rye →, U.K. 8 C7
Rye Bay, U.K. 9 G8
Rye Patch Reservoir,
  U.S.A. 56 F4
Ryegate, U.S.A. 56 C9
Ryley, Canada 50 C6
Rylstone, Australia ... 43 E4
Ryōtsu, Japan 22 E9
Rypin, Poland 13 B10
Ryūgasaki, Japan 23 G10
Ryūkyū Is. = Ryūkyū-
  rettō, Japan 23 M3
Ryūkyū-rettō, Japan .. 23 M3
Rzeszów, Poland 13 C11
Rzhev, Russia 18 C5

Sa Dec, Vietnam 26 B3
Sa'ādatābād, Fārs, Iran 31 D7
Sa'ādatābād,
  Hormozgān, Iran .. 31 D7
Sa'ādatābād, Kermān,
  Iran 31 D7
Saale →, Germany .. 12 C6
Saalfeld, Germany ... 12 C6
Saar →, Europe 14 B7
Saarbrücken, Germany 12 D4
Saaremaa, Estonia ... 7 G20

Saarijärvi, Finland 7 E21
Saariselkä, Finland ... 6 B23
Sab 'Ābar, Syria 30 C3
Šabac, Serbia, Yug. ... 17 B8
Sabadell, Spain 15 B7
Sabah □, Malaysia ... 26 C5
Sabalān, Kūhhā-ye, Iran 30 B5
Sabalana, Kepulauan,
  Indonesia 27 F5
Sábana de la Mar,
  Dom. Rep. 61 C6
Sábanalarga, Colombia 62 A4
Sabang, Indonesia ... 26 C1
Sabará, Brazil 63 G10
Saberania, Indonesia . 27 E9
Sabhah, Libya 35 C8
Sabinal, Mexico 58 A3
Sabinal, U.S.A. 55 L5
Sabinas, Mexico 58 B4
Sabinas →, Mexico .. 58 B4
Sabinas Hidalgo,
  Mexico 58 B4
Sabine →, U.S.A. 55 L8
Sabine L., U.S.A. 55 L8
Sabine Pass, U.S.A. .. 55 L8
Sabkhet el Bardawîl,
  Egypt 33 D2
Sablayan, Phil. 27 B6
Sable, Canada 49 A6
Sable, C., Canada 49 D6
Sable, C., U.S.A. 60 A3
Sable I., Canada 49 D8
Sabrina Coast,
  Antarctica 5 C9
Sabulubbek, Indonesia 26 E1
Sabzevār, Iran 31 B8
Sabzvārān, Iran 31 D8
Sac City, U.S.A. 54 D7
Săcele, Romania 13 F13
Sachigo →, Canada .. 48 A2
Sachigo, L., Canada .. 48 B1
Sachsen □, Germany . 12 C7
Sachsen-Anhalt □,
  Germany 12 C7
Sackville, Canada 49 C7
Saco, Maine, U.S.A. .. 53 D10
Saco, Mont., U.S.A. .. 56 B10
Sacramento, U.S.A. .. 56 G3
Sacramento →, U.S.A. 56 G3
Sacramento Mts., U.S.A. 57 K11
Sada-Misaki, Japan .. 23 H6
Sadd el Aali, Egypt .. 35 D12
Sado, Japan 22 F9
Sadon, Burma 29 G20
Sæby, Denmark 7 H14
Şafājah, Si. Arabia ... 30 E3
Säffle, Sweden 7 G15
Safford, U.S.A. 57 K9
Saffron Walden, U.K. . 9 E8
Safi, Morocco 34 B4
Şafiābād, Iran 31 B8
Safid Dasht, Iran 31 C6
Safid Kūh, Afghan. ... 28 B3
Safid Rūd →, Iran ... 31 B6
Safwān, Iraq 30 D5
Saga, Japan 23 H5
Saga □, Japan 23 H5
Sagae, Japan 22 E10
Sagar, India 28 M9
Saginaw, U.S.A. 52 D4
Saginaw →, U.S.A. .. 52 D4
Saginaw B., U.S.A. ... 52 D4
Saglouc = Salluit,
  Canada 47 B12
Sagua la Grande, Cuba 60 B3
Saguache, U.S.A. 57 G10
Saguaro Nat. Park,
  U.S.A. 57 K8
Saguenay →, Canada 49 C5
Sagunt, Spain 15 C5
Sagunto = Sagunt,
  Spain 15 C5
Sahagún, Spain 15 A3
Şaham al Jawlān, Syria 33 C4
Sahand, Kūh-e, Iran .. 30 B5
Sahara, Africa 34 D6
Saharan Atlas =
  Saharien, Atlas,
  Algeria 34 B6
Saharanpur, India ... 28 E10
Saharien, Atlas, Algeria 34 B6
Sahel, Africa 34 E5
Sāhīlīyah, Iraq 30 C4
Sahiwal, Pakistan ... 28 D8
Şahneh, Iran 30 C5
Sahuaripa, Mexico ... 58 B3
Sahuarita, U.S.A. 57 L8
Sahuayo, Mexico 58 C4
Sa'id Bundâs, Sudan . 35 G10
Sa'īdābād, Kermān, Iran 31 D7
Sa'īdābād, Semnān, Iran 31 B7
Sa'īdīyeh, Iran 31 B6
Saidpur, Bangla. 29 G16
Saidu, Pakistan 28 B7
Saigon = Thanh Pho Ho
  Chi Minh, Vietnam .. 26 B3
Saijō, Japan 23 H6
Saikhoa Ghat, India .. 29 F19
Saiki, Japan 23 H5
Sailolof, Indonesia ... 27 E8
Saimaa, Finland 7 F23
Sa'in Dezh, Iran 30 B5
St. Alban's, Canada .. 49 C8

St. Albans, U.K. 9 F7
St. Albans, Vt., U.S.A. . 52 C9
St. Albans, W. Va.,
  U.S.A. 52 F5
St. Alban's Head, U.K. . 9 G5
St. Albert, Canada ... 50 C6
St. Andrew's, Canada . 49 C8
St. Andrews, U.K. ... 10 C5
St. Ann B., Canada ... 49 C7
St. Ann's Bay, Jamaica 60 C4
St. Anthony, Canada .. 49 B8
St. Anthony, U.S.A. .. 56 E8
St. Antoine, Canada .. 49 C7
St. Arnaud, Australia . 43 F3
St-Augustin →,
  Canada 49 B8
St-Augustin-Saguenay,
  Canada 49 B8
St. Augustine, U.S.A. . 53 L5
St. Austell, U.K. 9 G3
St. Barbe, Canada ... 49 B8
St-Barthélemy,
  W. Indies 61 C7
St. Bees Hd., U.K. ... 8 C4
St. Bride's, Canada ... 49 C9
St. Brides B., U.K. ... 9 F2
St-Brieuc, France 14 B2
St. Catharines, Canada 48 D4
St. Catherines I., U.S.A. 53 K5
St. Catherine's Pt., U.K. 9 G6
St-Chamond, France . 14 D6
St. Charles, Ill., U.S.A. . 52 E1
St. Charles, Mo., U.S.A. 54 F9
St. Charles, Va., U.S.A. 52 F7
St. Christopher-Nevis =
  St. Kitts & Nevis ■,
  W. Indies 61 C7
St. Clair, L., Canada .. 48 D3
St. Claude, Canada ... 51 D9
St. Cloud, Fla., U.S.A. . 53 L5
St. Cloud, Minn., U.S.A. 54 C7
St. Cricq, C., Australia . 41 E1
St. Croix, Virgin Is. ... 61 C7
St. Croix →, U.S.A. .. 54 C8
St. Croix Falls, U.S.A. . 54 C8
St. David's, Canada .. 49 C8
St. David's, U.K. 9 F2
St. David's Head, U.K. . 9 F2
St-Denis, France 14 B5
St-Dizier, France 14 B6
St. Elias, Mt., U.S.A. .. 46 B5
St. Elias Mts., Canada . 50 A1
St. Elias Mts., U.S.A. . 46 C6
St-Étienne, France ... 14 D6
St. Eustatius, W. Indies 61 C7
St-Félicien, Canada .. 48 C5
St-Flour, France 14 D5
St. Francis, U.S.A. ... 54 F4
St. Francis →, U.S.A. . 55 H9
St. Francisville, U.S.A. 55 K9
St-Gabriel, Canada ... 48 C5
St. Gallen = Sankt
  Gallen, Switz. 14 C8
St-Gaudens, France .. 14 E4
St. George, Australia .. 43 D4
St. George, Canada ... 49 C6
St. George, S.C., U.S.A. 53 J5
St. George, Utah, U.S.A. 57 H7
St. George, C., Canada 49 C8
St. George, C., U.S.A. .. 53 L3
St. George Ra., Australia 40 C4
St. George's, Canada .. 49 C8
St. George's, Grenada . 62 A6
St. George's B., Canada 49 C8
St. Georges Basin,
  N.S.W., Australia ... 43 F5
St. Georges Basin,
  W. Austral., Australia 40 C4
St. George's Channel,
  Europe 10 F3
St. Georges Hd.,
  Australia 43 F5
St. Gotthard P. = San
  Gottardo, P. del,
  Switz. 14 C8
St. Helena, U.S.A. ... 56 G2
St. Helena ■, Atl. Oc. . 2 G9
St. Helena B., S. Africa 37 L3
St. Helens, Australia .. 42 G4
St. Helens, U.K. 8 D5
St. Helens, Mt., U.S.A. 56 C2
St. Helier, U.K. 9 H5
St-Hubert, Belgium ... 11 D5
St-Hyacinthe, Canada . 48 C5
St. Ignace, Canada ... 52 C3
St. Ignace I., Canada . 48 C2
St. Ignatius, U.S.A. .. 56 C6
St. Ives, U.K. 9 G2
St. James, U.S.A. 54 D7
St-Jean →, Canada .. 49 B7
St-Jean, L., Canada .. 49 C5
St-Jean-Port-Joli,
  Canada 49 C5
St-Jean-sur-Richelieu,
  Canada 48 C5
St-Jérôme, Canada ... 49 C5
St. John, Canada 49 C6
St. John, U.S.A. 55 G5
St. John →, U.S.A. .. 53 C12
St. John, C., Canada .. 49 C8
St. John's, Antigua ... 61 C7
St. John's, Canada ... 49 C9

St. Johns, Ariz., U.S.A. 57 J9
St. Johns, Mich., U.S.A. 52 D3
St. Johns →, U.S.A. . 53 K5
St. Johnsbury, U.S.A. . 52 C9
St. Joseph, La., U.S.A. 55 K9
St. Joseph, Mo., U.S.A. 54 F7
St. Joseph →, U.S.A. 52 D2
St. Joseph, I., Canada . 48 C3
St. Joseph, L., Canada 48 B1
St-Jovite, Canada ... 48 C5
St. Kilda, U.K. 10 C2
St. Kitts & Nevis ■,
  W. Indies 61 C7
St. Laurent, Canada .. 51 C9
St. Lawrence, Australia 42 C4
St. Lawrence, Canada . 49 C8
St. Lawrence →,
  Canada 49 C6
St. Lawrence, Gulf of,
  Canada 49 C7
St. Lawrence I., U.S.A. 46 B3
St. Leonard, Canada .. 49 C6
St. Lewis →, Canada . 49 B8
St-Lô, France 14 B3
St. Louis, Senegal ... 34 E2
St. Louis, U.S.A. 54 F9
St. Louis →, U.S.A. .. 54 B8
St. Lucia ■, W. Indies . 61 D7
St. Lucia Channel,
  W. Indies 61 D7
St. Maarten, W. Indies . 61 C7
St-Malo, France 14 B2
St-Marc, Haiti 61 C5
St. Maries, U.S.A. ... 56 C5
St-Martin, W. Indies .. 61 C7
St. Martin, L., Canada . 51 C9
St. Mary Pk., Australia 43 E2
St. Marys, Australia .. 42 G4
St. Mary's, U.K. 9 H1
St. Marys, Ga., U.S.A. 53 K5
St. Marys, Pa., U.S.A. . 52 E6
St. Mary's, Canada .. 49 C9
St. Marys B., Canada . 49 C9
St. Marys Bay, Canada 49 D6
St-Mathieu, Pte., France 14 B1
St. Matthew I., U.S.A. 46 B2
St. Matthews, I. =
  Zadetkyi Kyun, Burma 26 C1
St-Maurice →, Canada 48 C5
St-Nazaire, France ... 14 C2
St. Neots, U.K. 9 E7
St-Niklaas, Belgium .. 11 C4
St-Omer, France 14 A5
St-Pamphile, Canada . 49 C6
St. Pascal, Canada ... 49 C6
St. Paul, Canada 50 C6
St. Paul, Minn., U.S.A. 54 C8
St. Paul, Nebr., U.S.A. 54 E5
St-Paul →, Canada .. 49 B8
St. Paul, I., Ind. Oc. .. 3 F13
St. Paul I., Canada ... 49 C7
St. Peter, U.S.A. 54 C8
St. Peter Port, U.K. .. 9 H5
St. Peters, N.S., Canada 49 C7
St. Peters, P.E.I., Canada 49 C7
St. Petersburg = Sankt-
  Peterburg, Russia .. 18 C5
St. Petersburg, U.S.A. 53 M4
St-Pierre, St- P. & M. . 49 C8
St-Pierre, L., Canada .. 48 C5
St-Pierre et Miquelon □,
  St- P. & M. 49 C8
St. Quentin, Canada .. 49 C6
St-Quentin, France ... 14 B5
St. Regis, U.S.A. 56 C6
St-Siméon, Canada ... 49 C6
St. Simons I., U.S.A. .. 53 K5
St. Simons Island,
  U.S.A. 53 K5
St. Stephen, Canada .. 49 C6
St. Thomas, Canada .. 48 D3
St. Thomas I., Virgin Is. 61 C7
St-Tite, Canada 48 C5
St-Tropez, France ... 14 E7
St. Troud = St. Truiden,
  Belgium 11 D5
St. Truiden, Belgium . 11 D5
St. Vincent, G., Australia 43 F2
St. Vincent & the
  Grenadines ■,
  W. Indies 61 D7
St. Vincent Passage,
  W. Indies 61 D7
St-Vith, Belgium 11 D6
St. Walburg, Canada . 51 C7
Ste-Agathe-des-Monts,
  Canada 48 C5
Ste-Anne, L., Canada . 49 B6
Ste-Anne-des-Monts,
  Canada 49 C6
Ste. Genevieve, U.S.A. 54 G9
Ste-Marguerite →,
  Canada 49 B6
Ste-Marie, Martinique . 61 D7
Ste-Marie de la
  Madeleine, Canada . 49 C5
Ste-Rose, Guadeloupe . 61 C7
Ste. Rose du Lac,
  Canada 51 C9
Saintes, France 14 D3
Saintes, I. des,
  Guadeloupe 61 C7
Saintonge, France ... 14 D3
Saipan, Pac. Oc. 44 F6

Sairang, India 29 H18
Saitama □, Japan ... 23 F9
Sajama, Bolivia 62 G5
Sajószentpéter, Hungary 13 D11
Sakai, Japan 23 G7
Sakaide, Japan 23 G6
Sakaiminato, Japan .. 23 G6
Sakākah, Si. Arabia .. 30 D4
Sakakawea, L., U.S.A. 54 B4
Sakami, Canada 48 B4
Sakami, L., Canada .. 48 B4
Sakarya, Turkey 19 F5
Sakashima-Guntō,
  Japan 23 M2
Sakata, Japan 22 E9
Sakha □, Russia 21 C13
Sakhalin, Russia 21 D15
Sakhalinskiy Zaliv,
  Russia 21 D15
Šakiai, Lithuania 7 J20
Sakon Nakhon, Thailand 26 A2
Sakuma, Japan 23 G8
Sakurai, Japan 23 G7
Sala, Sweden 9 G17
Sala Consilina, Italy .. 16 D6
Sala-y-Gómez, Pac. Oc. 45 K17
Salaberry-de-Valleyfield,
  Canada 48 C5
Saladillo, Argentina .. 64 D5
Salado →,
  Buenos Aires,
  Argentina 64 D5
Salado →, La Pampa,
  Argentina 64 D3
Salado →, Santa Fe,
  Argentina 64 C4
Salado →, Mexico ... 55 M5
Salaga, Ghana 34 G5
Sālah, Syria 33 C5
Salālah, Oman 32 D5
Salamanca, Chile 64 C2
Salamanca, Spain ... 15 B3
Salamanca, U.S.A. .. 52 D6
Salāmatābād, Iran ... 30 C5
Salamís, Greece 17 F10
Salar de Uyuni, Bolivia 62 H5
Salatiga, Indonesia .. 27 G14
Salavat, Russia 18 D10
Salaverry, Peru 62 E3
Salawati, Indonesia .. 27 E8
Salayar, Indonesia ... 27 F6
Salcombe, U.K. 9 G4
Saldanha, S. Africa .. 37 L3
Saldus, Latvia 7 H20
Sale, Australia 43 F4
Salé, Morocco 34 B4
Sale, U.K. 8 D5
Salekhard, Russia ... 20 C7
Salem, India 28 P11
Salem, Ill., U.S.A. ... 52 F1
Salem, Ind., U.S.A. .. 52 F2
Salem, Mass., U.S.A. . 52 D10
Salem, Mo., U.S.A. .. 55 G9
Salem, N.J., U.S.A. .. 52 F8
Salem, Ohio, U.S.A. .. 52 E5
Salem, Oreg., U.S.A. . 56 D2
Salem, S. Dak., U.S.A. 54 D6
Salem, Va., U.S.A. ... 52 G5
Salerno, Italy 16 D6
Salford, U.K. 8 D5
Salgótarján, Hungary . 13 D10
Salgueiro, Brazil 63 E11
Salibabu, Indonesia .. 27 D7
Salihli, Turkey 17 E13
Salihorsk, Belarus ... 13 B14
Salima, Malawi 37 G6
Salina, Italy 16 E6
Salina, Kans., U.S.A. . 54 F6
Salina, Utah, U.S.A. .. 57 G8
Salina Cruz, Mexico .. 59 D5
Salinas, Brazil 63 G10
Salinas, Ecuador 62 D2
Salinas, U.S.A. 57 H3
Salinas →, Guatemala 59 D6
Salinas →, U.S.A. ... 57 H3
Salinas, B. de, Nic. ... 60 D2
Salinas de Hidalgo,
  Mexico 58 C4
Salinas Grandes,
  Argentina 64 C4
Saline →, Ark., U.S.A. 55 J8
Saline →, Kans.,
  U.S.A. 54 F6
Salinópolis, Brazil ... 63 D9
Salisbury = Harare,
  Zimbabwe 37 H6
Salisbury, U.K. 9 F6
Salisbury, Md., U.S.A. 52 F8
Salisbury, N.C., U.S.A. 53 H5
Salisbury I., Canada .. 47 B12
Salisbury Plain, U.K. . 9 F6
Şalkhad, Syria 33 C5
Salla, Finland 6 C23
Salliq, Canada 47 B11
Salluit, Canada 47 B12
Salmās, Iran 30 B5
Salmo, Canada 50 D5
Salmon, U.S.A. 56 D7
Salmon →, Canada .. 50 C4
Salmon →, U.S.A. ... 56 D5
Salmon Arm, Canada . 50 C5
Salmon Gums, Australia 41 F3
Salmon River Mts.,
  U.S.A. 56 D6

Salo, Finland 7 F20
Salome, U.S.A. 57 K7
Salon-de-Provence, France 14 E6
Salonica = Thessaloníki, Greece 17 D10
Salonta, Romania 13 E11
Salpausselkä, Finland . 7 F22
Salsk, Russia 19 E7
Salso →, Italy 16 F5
Salt →, Canada 50 B6
Salt →, U.S.A. 57 K7
Salt Lake City, U.S.A. . 56 F8
Salta, Argentina 64 A3
Saltash, U.K. 9 G3
Saltburn by the Sea, U.K. 8 C7
Saltfjellet, Norway .. 6 C16
Saltfjorden, Norway ... 6 C16
Saltillo, Mexico 58 B4
Salto →, Italy 16 C5
Salto del Guaíra, Paraguay 64 A6
Salton Sea, U.S.A. 57 K6
Saluda →, U.S.A. 53 J5
Salûm, Egypt 35 B11
Salur, India 29 K13
Salvador, Brazil 63 F11
Salvador, Canada 51 C7
Salvador, L., U.S.A. ... 55 L9
Salween →, Burma 29 L20
Salyan, Azerbaijan 19 G8
Salzach →, Austria ... 12 D7
Salzburg, Austria 12 E7
Salzgitter, Germany ... 12 B6
Salzwedel, Germany ... 12 B6
Sam Rayburn Reservoir, U.S.A. 55 K7
Sama de Langreo = Langreo, Spain 15 A3
Samagaltay, Russia .. 21 D10
Samales Group, Phil. .. 27 C6
Samana □, Dom. Rep. . 61 C6
Samaná, Dom. Rep. ... 61 C6
Samana Cay, Bahamas 61 B5
Samani, Japan 22 C11
Samar, Phil. 27 B7
Samara, Russia 18 D9
Samaria = Shōmrōn, West Bank 33 C4
Samarinda, Indonesia . 26 E5
Samarkand = Samarqand, Uzbekistan 20 F7
Samarqand, Uzbekistan 20 F7
Sāmarrā, Iraq 30 C4
Sambalpur, India 29 J14
Sambar, Tanjung, Indonesia 26 E4
Sambas, Indonesia ... 26 D3
Sambhal, India 28 E11
Sambhar, India 28 F9
Sambiase, Italy 16 E7
Sambir, Ukraine 13 D12
Samnah, Si. Arabia ... 30 E3
Samoa ■, Pac. Oc. ... 39 B13
Samokov, Bulgaria ... 17 C10
Sámos, Greece 17 F12
Samothráki = Mathráki, Greece 17 E8
Samothráki, Greece ... 17 D11
Sampang, Indonesia .. 27 G15
Sampit, Indonesia ... 26 E4
Sampit, Teluk, Indonesia 26 E4
Samsø, Denmark 7 J14
Samsun, Turkey 19 F6
Samui, Ko, Thailand .. 26 C2
Samut Prakan, Thailand 26 B2
Samut Songkhram →, Thailand 26 B1
San, Mali 34 F5
San →, Cambodia ... 26 B3
San →, Poland 13 C11
San Agustin, C., Phil. . 27 C7
San Ambrosio, Pac. Oc. 45 K20
San Andreas, U.S.A. .. 56 G3
San Andrés, I. de, Caribbean 60 D3
San Andres Mts., U.S.A. 57 K10
San Andrés Tuxtla, Mexico 59 D5
San Angelo, U.S.A. ... 55 K4
San Antonio, Belize .. 59 D7
San Antonio, Chile ... 64 C2
San Antonio, N. Mex., U.S.A. 57 K10
San Antonio, Tex., U.S.A. 55 L5
San Antonio →, U.S.A. 55 L6
San Antonio, C., Argentina 64 D5
San Antonio, C., Cuba . 60 B3
San Antonio de los Baños, Cuba 60 B3
San Antonio de los Cobres, Argentina .. 64 A3
San Antonio Oeste, Argentina 64 E4
San Benedetto del Tronto, Italy 16 C5
San Benedicto, I., Mexico 58 D2
San Benito, U.S.A. ... 55 M6
San Bernardino, U.S.A. 57 J5

San Bernardino Str., Phil. 27 B6
San Bernardo, Chile .. 64 C2
San Bernardo, I. de, Colombia 62 B3
San Blas, Mexico 58 B3
San Blas, Arch. de, Panama 60 E4
San Blas, C., U.S.A. .. 53 L3
San Borja, Bolivia 62 F5
San Buenaventura, Mexico 58 B4
San Carlos, Argentina . 64 C3
San Carlos, Chile 64 D2
San Carlos, Baja Calif. S., Mexico 58 C2
San Carlos, Coahuila, Mexico 58 B4
San Carlos, Nic. 60 D3
San Carlos, Phil. 27 B6
San Carlos, Uruguay .. 64 C6
San Carlos, U.S.A. ... 57 K8
San Carlos, Venezuela . 62 B5
San Carlos de Bariloche, Argentina 64 E2
San Carlos de Bolívar, Argentina 64 D4
San Carlos del Zulia, Venezuela 62 B4
San Carlos L., U.S.A. .. 57 K8
San Clemente, U.S.A. . 57 K5
San Clemente I., U.S.A. 57 K4
San Cristóbal, Argentina 64 C4
San Cristóbal, Dom. Rep. 61 C5
San Cristóbal, Solomon Is. 38 C9
San Cristóbal, Venezuela 62 B4
San Cristóbal de la Casas, Mexico 59 D6
San Diego, Calif., U.S.A. 57 K5
San Diego, Tex., U.S.A. 55 M5
San Diego, C., Argentina 64 G3
San Diego de la Unión, Mexico 58 C4
San Felipe, Chile 64 C2
San Felipe, Mexico ... 58 A2
San Felipe, Venezuela . 62 A5
San Félix, Pac. Oc. ... 45 K20
San Fernando, Chile .. 64 C2
San Fernando, Baja Calif., Mexico . 58 B1
San Fernando, Tamaulipas, Mexico . 59 C5
San Fernando, La Union, Phil. 27 A6
San Fernando, Pampanga, Phil. ... 27 A6
San Fernando, Spain .. 15 D2
San Fernando, Trin. & Tob. 62 A6
San Fernando de Apure, Venezuela 62 B5
San Fernando de Atabapo, Venezuela . 62 C5
San Francisco, Argentina 64 C4
San Francisco, U.S.A. . 57 H2
San Francisco →, U.S.A. 57 K9
San Francisco de Macorís, Dom. Rep. . 61 C5
San Francisco del Oro, Mexico 58 B3
San Gottardo, P. del, Switz. 14 C8
San Ignacio, Belize ... 59 D7
San Ignacio, Bolivia .. 62 G6
San Ignacio, Mexico .. 58 B2
San Ignacio, Paraguay . 64 B5
San Ignacio, L., Mexico 58 B2
San Ildefonso, C., Phil. 27 A6
San Javier, Bolivia ... 62 G6
San Jeronimo Taviche, Mexico 59 D5
San Joaquin →, U.S.A. 57 G3
San Jon, U.S.A. 55 H3
San Jorge, Argentina . 64 C4
San Jorge, B. de, Mexico 58 A2
San Jorge, G., Argentina 64 F3
San José, Costa Rica .. 60 E3
San José, Guatemala . 60 D1
San José, Mexico 58 C2
San Jose, Mind. Occ., Phil. 27 B6
San Jose, Nueva Ecija, Phil. 27 A6
San Jose, U.S.A. 57 H3
San Jose →, U.S.A. .. 57 J10
San Jose de Buenavista, Phil. 27 B6
San José de Chiquitos, Bolivia 62 G6
San José de Jáchal, Argentina 64 C3
San José de Mayo, Uruguay 64 C5
San José del Cabo, Mexico 58 C3
San José del Guaviare, Colombia 62 C4

San Juan, Argentina .. 64 C3
San Juan, Mexico 58 C4
San Juan, Puerto Rico . 61 C6
San Juan □, Dom. Rep. 61 C5
San Juan →, Nic. 60 D3
San Juan →, U.S.A. .. 57 H8
San Juan Bautista Valle Nacional, Mexico ... 59 D5
San Juan de Guadalupe, Mexico 58 C4
San Juan de la Costa, Mexico 58 C2
San Juan de los Morros, Venezuela 62 B5
San Juan del Norte, Nic. 60 D3
San Juan del Norte, B. de, Nic. 60 D3
San Juan del Río, Mexico 59 C5
San Juan del Sur, Nic. . 60 D2
San Juan Mts., U.S.A. . 57 H10
San Justo, Argentina .. 64 C4
San Lázaro, C., Mexico 58 C2
San Lázaro, Sa., Mexico 58 C3
San Lorenzo, Ecuador . 62 C3
San Lorenzo →, Mexico 58 C4
San Lorenzo, I., Mexico 58 B2
San Lorenzo, Mte., Argentina 64 F2
San Lucas, Bolivia 62 H5
San Lucas, Baja Calif. S., Mexico 58 C3
San Lucas, Baja Calif. S., Mexico 58 B2
San Lucas, C., Mexico . 58 C3
San Luis, Argentina .. 64 C3
San Luis, Cuba 60 B3
San Luis, Guatemala .. 60 C2
San Luis, Ariz., U.S.A. . 57 K6
San Luis, Colo., U.S.A. 57 H11
San Luis □, Argentina 64 C3
San Luis de la Paz, Mexico 58 C4
San Luis Obispo, U.S.A. 57 J3
San Luis Potosí, Mexico 58 C4
San Luis Potosí □, Mexico 58 C4
San Luis Río Colorado, Mexico 58 A2
San Manuel, U.S.A. .. 57 K8
San Marcos, Guatemala 60 D1
San Marcos, Mexico .. 58 B2
San Marcos, U.S.A. .. 55 L6
San Marino, San Marino 12 G7
San Marino ■, Europe 16 C5
San Martín →, Bolivia 62 F6
San Martín, L., Argentina 64 F2
San Martin de los Andes, Argentina .. 64 E2
San Mateo, U.S.A. ... 57 H2
San Matías, Bolivia ... 62 G7
San Matías, G., Argentina 64 E4
San Miguel, El Salv. .. 60 D2
San Miguel, Panama .. 60 E4
San Miguel, U.S.A. ... 57 J3
San Miguel →, Bolivia 62 F6
San Miguel de Tucumán, Argentina 64 B3
San Miguel I., U.S.A. . 57 J3
San Nicolás de los Arroyas, Argentina . 64 C4
San Nicolas I., U.S.A. . 57 K4
San Pédro, Ivory C. .. 34 H4
San Pedro, Mexico ... 58 C2
San Pedro →, Chihuahua, Mexico . 58 B3
San Pedro →, Nayarit, Mexico 58 C3
San Pedro →, U.S.A. . 57 K8
San Pedro de las Colonias, Mexico ... 58 B4
San Pedro de Macorís, Dom. Rep. 61 C6
San Pedro del Norte, Nic. 60 D3
San Pedro del Paraná, Paraguay 64 B5
San Pedro Mártir, Sierra, Mexico 58 A1
San Pedro Mixtepec, Mexico 59 D5
San Pedro Ocampo = Melchor Ocampo, Mexico 58 C4
San Pedro Sula, Honduras 60 C2
San Pietro, Italy 16 E3
San Quintín, Mexico .. 58 A1
San Rafael, Argentina . 64 C3
San Rafael, Calif., U.S.A. 56 H2
San Rafael, N. Mex., U.S.A. 57 J10
San Remo, Italy 14 E7
San Roque, Argentina . 64 B4
San Roque, Spain 15 D3
San Rosendo, Chile ... 64 D2
San Saba, U.S.A. 55 K5
San Salvador, El Salv. . 60 D2
San Salvador de Jujuy, Argentina 64 A4
San Salvador I., Bahamas 61 B5

San Sebastián = Donostia-San Sebastián, Spain 15 A5
San Sebastián, Argentina 64 G3
San Severo, Italy 16 D6
San Simon, U.S.A. ... 57 K9
San Telmo, Mexico ... 58 A1
San Tiburcio, Mexico . 58 C4
San Valentin, Mte., Chile 64 F2
San Vicente de la Barquera, Spain 15 A3
San Vito, Costa Rica .. 60 E3
Sana', Yemen 32 D3
Sana →, Bos.-H. 12 F9
Sanaga →, Cameroon 36 D1
Sanaloa, Presa, Mexico 58 C3
Sanana, Indonesia ... 27 E7
Sanandaj, Iran 30 C5
Sánchez, Dom. Rep. .. 61 C6
Sancti Spíritus, Cuba .. 60 B4
Sancy, Puy de, France . 14 D5
Sand Hills, U.S.A. 54 D4
Sand Springs, U.S.A. . 55 G6
Sanda, Japan 23 G7
Sandakan, Malaysia .. 26 C5
Sandanski, Bulgaria .. 17 D10
Sanday, U.K. 10 B5
Sandefjord, Norway .. 7 G14
Sanders, U.S.A. 57 J9
Sanderson, U.S.A. ... 55 K3
Sandersville, U.S.A. .. 53 J4
Sandfire Roadhouse, Australia 40 C3
Sandfly L., Canada ... 51 B7
Sandía, Peru 62 F5
Sandnes, Norway 7 G11
Sandnessjøen, Norway 6 C15
Sandoa, Dem. Rep. of the Congo 36 F4
Sandomierz, Poland ... 13 C11
Sandover →, Australia 42 C2
Sandoway, Burma 29 K19
Sandoy, Færoe Is. 6 F9
Sandpoint, U.S.A. 56 B5
Sandringham, U.K. ... 8 E8
Sandstone, Australia .. 41 E2
Sandusky, Mich., U.S.A. 52 D4
Sandusky, Ohio, U.S.A. 52 E4
Sandviken, Sweden ... 7 F17
Sandwich, C., Australia 42 B4
Sandwich B., Canada .. 49 B8
Sandy →, U.S.A. 56 F8
Sandy Bight, Australia . 41 F3
Sandy C., Queens., Australia 42 C5
Sandy C., Tas., Australia 42 G3
Sandy Cay, Bahamas .. 61 B4
Sandy Cr. →, U.S.A. .. 56 F9
Sandy L., Canada 48 B1
Sandy Lake, Canada .. 48 B1
Sanford, Fla., U.S.A. .. 53 L5
Sanford, Maine, U.S.A. 53 D10
Sanford, N.C., U.S.A. . 53 H6
Sanford →, Australia . 41 E2
Sanford, Mt., U.S.A. .. 46 B5
Sanga →, Congo 36 E3
Sangamner, India 28 K9
Sangar, Russia 21 C13
Sangay, Ecuador 62 D3
Sangeang, Indonesia . 27 F5
Sanger, U.S.A. 57 H4
Sangerhausen, Germany 12 C6
Sanggau, Indonesia .. 26 D4
Sanghe, Kepulauan, Indonesia 27 D7
Sanghe, Pulau, Indonesia 27 D7
Sangkapura, Indonesia 26 F4
Sangkulirang, Indonesia 26 D5
Sangli, India 28 L9
Sangmélima, Cameroon 36 D2
Sangre de Cristo Mts., U.S.A. 55 G2
Sangudo, Canada 50 C6
Sangue →, Brazil ... 62 F7
Sanibel, U.S.A. 53 M4
Sanirajak, Canada ... 47 B11
Sanjo, Japan 22 F9
Sankt Gallen, Switz. .. 14 C8
Sankt Moritz, Switz. .. 14 C8
Sankt-Peterburg, Russia 18 C5
Sankt Pölten, Austria . 12 D8
Sankuru →, Dem. Rep. of the Congo 36 E4
Sanliurfa, Turkey 19 G6
Sanlúcar de Barrameda, Spain 15 D2
Sanmenxia, China ... 25 C6
Sanming, China 25 D6
Sannicandro Gargánico, Italy 16 D6
Sânnicolau Mare, Romania 13 E11
Sannin, J., Lebanon .. 33 B4
Sanniquellie, Liberia . 34 G4
Sanok, Poland 13 D12
Sanquhar, U.K. 10 F5
Sant Antoni Abat, Spain 15 C6
Sant Feliu de Guíxols, Spain 15 B7
Sant Jordi, G. de, Spain 15 B6
Santa Ana, Bolivia ... 62 F5

Santa Ana, El Salv. ... 60 D2
Santa Ana, Mexico ... 58 A2
Santa Ana, U.S.A. ... 57 K5
Sant' Antíoco, Italy ... 16 E3
Santa Barbara, Honduras 60 D2
Santa Bárbara, Mexico 58 B3
Santa Barbara, U.S.A. . 57 J4
Santa Catalina, Gulf of, U.S.A. 57 K5
Santa Catalina, I., Mexico 58 B2
Santa Catalina I., U.S.A. 57 K4
Santa Catarina □, Brazil 64 B7
Santa Clara, Cuba 60 B4
Santa Clara, El Golfo de, Mexico 58 A2
Santa Clara, El Salv. .. 60 D2
Santa Clotilde, Peru .. 62 D4
Santa Coloma de Gramenet, Spain ... 15 B7
Santa Cruz, Argentina . 64 G3
Santa Cruz, Bolivia ... 62 G6
Santa Cruz, Costa Rica 60 D2
Santa Cruz, Phil. 27 B6
Santa Cruz →, Argentina 64 G3
Santa Cruz de Tenerife, Canary Is. 34 C2
Santa Cruz del Norte, Cuba 60 B3
Santa Cruz del Sur, Cuba 60 B4
Santa Cruz do Sul, Brazil 64 B6
Santa Cruz I., U.S.A. .. 57 K4
Santa Cruz Is., Solomon Is. 38 C9
Santa Domingo, Cay, Bahamas 60 B4
Santa Elena, C., Costa Rica 60 D2
Santa Fe, Argentina .. 64 C4
Santa Fé, U.S.A. 57 J11
Santa Fé do Sul, Brazil 63 H8
Santa Filomena, Brazil . 63 E9
Santa Inês, Brazil 63 F11
Santa Inês, I., Chile ... 64 G2
Santa Isabel = Rey Malabo, Eq. Guin. .. 36 D1
Santa Isabel, Argentina 64 D3
Santa Isabel do Morro, Brazil 63 F8
Santa Lucia Range, U.S.A. 57 J3
Santa Magdalena, I., Mexico 58 C2
Santa Margarita, I., Mexico 58 C2
Santa Maria, Brazil ... 64 B6
Santa Maria, U.S.A. .. 57 J3
Santa María →, Mexico 58 A3
Santa María, B. de, Mexico 58 B3
Santa Maria da Vitória, Brazil 63 F10
Santa Maria di Léuca, C., Italy 17 E8
Santa Marta, Colombia 62 A4
Santa Marta, Sierra Nevada de, Colombia 62 A4
Santa Maura = Levkás, Greece 17 E9
Santa Monica, U.S.A. . 57 K4
Santa Rita, U.S.A. ... 57 K10
Santa Rosa, La Pampa, Argentina 64 D4
Santa Rosa, San Luis, Argentina 64 C3
Santa Rosa, Calif., U.S.A. 56 G2
Santa Rosa, N. Mex., U.S.A. 55 H2
Santa Rosa de Copán, Honduras 60 D2
Santa Rosa del Sara, Bolivia 62 G6
Santa Rosa I., Calif., U.S.A. 57 K3
Santa Rosa I., Fla., U.S.A. 53 K2
Santa Rosa Range, U.S.A. 56 F5
Santa Rosalía, Mexico . 58 B2
Santa Tecla = Nueva San Salvador, El Salv. 60 D2
Santa Teresa, Australia 42 C1
Santa Teresa, Mexico . 59 B5
Santa Vitória do Palmar, Brazil 64 C6
Santai, China 24 C5
Santana, Coxilha de, Brazil 64 C5
Santana do Livramento, Brazil 64 C5
Santander, Spain 15 A4
Santander Jiménez, Mexico 59 C5
Santaquin, U.S.A. ... 56 G8
Santarém, Brazil 63 D8
Santarém, Portugal .. 15 C1

Santaren Channel, W. Indies 60 B4
Santee →, U.S.A. ... 53 J6
Santiago, Brazil 64 B6
Santiago, Chile 64 C2
Santiago, Panama 60 E3
Santiago →, Peru ... 62 D3
Santiago de Compostela, Spain .. 15 A1
Santiago de Cuba, Cuba 60 C4
Santiago de los Cabelleros, Dom. Rep. 61 C5
Santiago del Estero, Argentina 64 B4
Santiago Ixcuintla, Mexico 58 C3
Santiago Papasquiaro, Mexico 58 C3
Santiaguillo, L. de, Mexico 58 C4
Santo Amaro, Brazil .. 63 F11
Santo Ângelo, Brazil . 64 B6
Santo Antônio do Içá, Brazil 62 D5
Santo Antônio do Leverger, Brazil 63 G7
Santo Domingo, Dom. Rep. 61 C6
Santo Domingo, Baja Calif., Mexico . 58 A1
Santo Domingo, Baja Calif. S., Mexico 58 B2
Santo Domingo, Nic. . 60 D3
Santo Domingo de los Colorados, Ecuador . 62 D3
Santo Domingo Pueblo, U.S.A. 57 J10
Santo Tomás, Mexico . 58 A1
Santo Tomás, Peru ... 62 F4
Santo Tomé, Argentina 64 B5
Santo Tomé de Guayana = Ciudad Guayana, Venezuela . 62 B6
Santoña, Spain 15 A4
Santoríni = Thíra, Greece 17 F11
Santos, Brazil 64 A7
São Bernardo do Campo, Brazil 64 A7
São Borja, Brazil 64 B5
São Carlos, Brazil ... 63 H9
São Cristóvão, Brazil . 63 F11
São Domingos, Brazil . 63 F9
São Francisco, Brazil . 63 G10
São Francisco →, Brazil 63 F11
São Francisco do Sul, Brazil 64 B7
São Gabriel, Brazil ... 64 C6
São João da Madeira, Portugal 15 B1
São João del Rei, Brazil 63 H10
São João do Araguaia, Brazil 63 E9
São João do Piauí, Brazil 63 E10
São José do Rio Prêto, Brazil 63 H9
São Leopoldo, Brazil . 64 B6
São Lourenço, Brazil . 63 H9
São Lourenço →, Brazil 63 G7
São Luís, Brazil 63 D10
São Marcos →, Brazil 63 G9
São Marcos, B. de, Brazil 63 D10
São Mateus, Brazil ... 63 G11
São Paulo, Brazil 64 A7
São Paulo □, Brazil .. 63 H9
São Paulo, I., Atl. Oc. . 2 D8
São Paulo de Olivença, Brazil 62 D5
São Roque, C. de, Brazil 63 E11
São Sebastião, I. de, Brazil 64 A7
São Tomé & Príncipe ■, Africa 3 D10
São Vicente, C. de, Portugal 15 D1
Saona, I., Dom. Rep. .. 61 C6
Saône →, France ... 14 D6
Saonek, Indonesia ... 27 E8
Saparua, Indonesia .. 27 E7
Sapele, Nigeria 34 G7
Sapelo I., U.S.A. 53 K5
Saposoa, Peru 62 E3
Sapphire, Australia .. 42 C4
Sapporo, Japan 22 C10
Sapulpa, U.S.A. 55 H6
Saqqez, Iran 30 B5
Sar Dasht, Iran 31 D6
Sar Gachineh, Iran ... 31 D6
Sar Planina, Macedonia 17 C9
Sara Buri = Saraburi, Thailand 26 B2
Saráb, Iran 30 B5
Sarabadi, Iraq 30 C5
Saraburi, Thailand ... 26 B2
Saragossa = Zaragoza, Spain 15 B5
Saraguro, Ecuador ... 62 D3
Sarajevo, Bos.-H. 17 C8
Sarakhs, Turkmenistan 31 B9
Saran, Gunung, Indonesia 26 E4

Shijiazhuang

Saranac Lake, U.S.A. 52 C8
Sarangani B., Phil. 27 C7
Sarangani Is., Phil. 27 C7
Sarangarh, India 29 J13
Saransk, Russia 18 D8
Sarapul, Russia 18 C9
Sarasota, U.S.A. 53 M4
Saratoga, U.S.A. 56 F10
Saratoga Springs, U.S.A. 52 D9
Saratok, Malaysia 26 D4
Saratov, Russia 19 D8
Saravane, Laos 26 A3
Sarawak □, Malaysia 26 D4
Saray, Turkey 17 D12
Sarayköy, Turkey 17 F13
Sarbāz, Iran 31 E9
Sarbīsheh, Iran 31 C8
Sarda →, India 29 F12
Sardarshahr, India 28 E9
Sardegna □, Italy 16 D3
Sardinia = Sardegna □, Italy 16 D3
Sardis, Turkey 17 E12
Sārdūīyeh = Dar Mazār, Iran 31 D8
Sarera, G. of, Indonesia 38 B6
Sargasso Sea, Atl. Oc. 45 D20
Sargodha, Pakistan 28 C8
Sarh, Chad 35 G9
Sārī, Iran 31 B7
Sarıgöl, Turkey 17 E13
Sarikei, Malaysia 26 D4
Sarina, Australia 42 C4
Sarita, U.S.A. 55 M6
Sark, U.K. 9 H5
Şarköy, Turkey 17 D12
Sarlat-la-Canéda, France 14 D4
Sarmi, Indonesia 27 E9
Sarmiento, Argentina 64 F3
Särna, Sweden 7 F15
Sarnia, Canada 48 D3
Sarolangun, Indonesia 26 E2
Saronikós Kólpos, Greece 17 F10
Saros Körfezi, Turkey 17 D12
Sarpsborg, Norway 7 G14
Sarre = Saar →, Europe 14 B7
Sarreguemines, France 14 B7
Sarthe →, France 14 C3
Sarvestān, Iran 31 D7
Sary-Tash, Kyrgyzstan 20 F8
Saryshagan, Kazakstan 20 E8
Sasaram, India 29 G14
Sasebo, Japan 23 H4
Saser, India 28 B10
Saskatchewan □, Canada 51 C7
Saskatchewan →, Canada 51 C8
Saskatoon, Canada 51 C7
Saskylakh, Russia 21 B12
Sasovo, Russia 18 D7
Sassandra, Ivory C. 34 H4
Sassandra →, Ivory C. 34 H4
Sássari, Italy 16 D3
Sassnitz, Germany 12 A7
Sassuolo, Italy 16 B4
Sasyk, Ozero, Ukraine 13 F15
Sata-Misaki, Japan 23 J5
Satadougou, Mali 34 F3
Satakunta, Finland 7 F20
Satara, India 28 L8
Satevó, Mexico 58 B3
Satilla →, U.S.A. 53 K5
Satka, Russia 18 C10
Satmala Hills, India 28 J9
Satna, India 29 G12
Sátoraljaújhely, Hungary 13 D11
Satpura Ra., India 28 J10
Satsuna-Shotō, Japan 23 K5
Sattahip, Thailand 26 B2
Satu Mare, Romania 13 E12
Satui, Indonesia 26 E5
Satun, Thailand 26 C2
Saturnina →, Brazil 62 F7
Sauceda, Mexico 58 B4
Saucillo, Mexico 58 B3
Sauda, Norway 7 G12
Sauðarkrókur, Iceland 6 D4
Saudi Arabia ■, Asia 30 B3
Sauerland, Germany 12 C4
Saugerties, U.S.A. 52 D9
Sauk Centre, U.S.A. 54 C7
Sauk Rapids, U.S.A. 54 C7
Sault Ste. Marie, Canada 48 C3
Sault Ste. Marie, U.S.A. 47 D11
Saumlaki, Indonesia 27 F8
Saumur, France 14 C3
Saunders C., N.Z. 39 L3
Saunders I., Antarctica 5 B1
Saunders Point, Australia 41 E4
Saurimo, Angola 36 F4
Savá, Honduras 60 C2
Sava →, Serbia, Yug. 17 B9
Savage, U.S.A. 54 B2
Savage I. = Niue, Cook Is. 45 J11
Savage River, Australia 42 G4
Savai'i, Samoa 39 A12
Savalou, Benin 34 G6
Savanna, U.S.A. 54 D9
Savanna-la-Mar, Jamaica 60 C4
Savannah, Ga., U.S.A. 53 J5
Savannah, Mo., U.S.A. 54 F7
Savannah, Tenn., U.S.A. 53 H1
Savannah →, U.S.A. 53 J5
Savannakhet, Laos 26 A2
Savant L., Canada 48 B1
Savant Lake, Canada 48 B1
Save →, Mozam. 37 J6
Sāveh, Iran 31 C6
Savelugu, Ghana 34 G5
Savo, Finland 6 E22
Savoie □, France 14 D7
Savona, Italy 14 D8
Savonlinna, Finland 18 B4
Savoy = Savoie □, France 14 D7
Savur, Turkey 30 B4
Sawahlunto, Indonesia 26 E2
Sawai, Indonesia 27 E7
Sawai Madhopur, India 28 G10
Sawankhalok, Thailand 26 A1
Sawara, Japan 23 G10
Sawatch Range, U.S.A. 57 G10
Sawtooth Range, U.S.A. 56 E6
Sawu, Indonesia 27 F6
Sawu Sea, Indonesia 27 F6
Saxby →, Australia 42 B3
Saxmundham, U.K. 9 E9
Saxony = Sachsen □, Germany 12 C7
Saxony, Lower = Niedersachsen □, Germany 12 B5
Sayabec, Canada 49 C6
Sayán, Peru 62 F3
Sayan, Vostochnyy, Russia 21 D10
Sayan, Zapadnyy, Russia 21 D10
Saydā, Lebanon 33 B4
Sayḥūt, Yemen 32 D5
Saynshand, Mongolia 25 B6
Sayre, Okla., U.S.A. 55 H5
Sayre, Pa., U.S.A. 52 E7
Sayula, Mexico 58 D4
Sayward, Canada 50 C3
Sazanit, Albania 17 D8
Sázava →, Czech Rep. 12 D8
Sazin, Pakistan 28 B8
Scafell Pike, U.K. 8 C4
Scandia, Canada 50 C6
Scandicci, Italy 16 C4
Scandinavia, Europe 6 E16
Scandinavia, Europe 6 E16
Scarborough, Trin. & Tob. 62 A6
Scarborough, U.K. 8 C7
Scebeli, Wabi →, Somali Rep. 32 G3
Schaffhausen, Switz. 14 C8
Schagen, Neths. 11 B4
Schefferville, Canada 49 B6
Schelde →, Belgium 11 C4
Schell Creek Ra., U.S.A. 56 G6
Schenectady, U.S.A. 52 D9
Schiedam, Neths. 11 C4
Schiermonnikoog, Neths. 11 A6
Schio, Italy 16 B4
Schleswig, Germany 12 A5
Schleswig-Holstein □, Germany 12 A5
Schouten I., Australia 42 G4
Schouten Is. = Supiori, Indonesia 27 E9
Schouwen, Neths. 11 C3
Schreiber, Canada 48 C2
Schuler, Canada 51 C6
Schumacher, Canada 48 C3
Schurz, U.S.A. 56 G4
Schuyler, U.S.A. 54 E6
Schwäbische Alb, Germany 12 D5
Schwaner, Pegunungan, Indonesia 26 E4
Schwarzwald, Germany 12 D5
Schwedt, Germany 12 B8
Schweinfurt, Germany 12 C6
Schwenningen = Villingen-Schwenningen, Germany 12 D5
Schwerin, Germany 12 B6
Schwyz, Switz. 14 C8
Sciacca, Italy 16 F5
Scilla, Italy 16 E6
Scilly, Isles of, U.K. 9 H1
Scioto →, U.S.A. 52 F4
Scobey, U.S.A. 54 A2
Scone, Australia 43 E5
Scoresbysund = Illoqqortoormiit, Greenland 4 B6
Scotia, U.S.A. 56 F1
Scotia Sea, Antarctica 5 B18
Scotland □, U.K. 10 C5
Scott, C., Australia 40 B4
Scott City, U.S.A. 54 F4
Scott Glacier, Antarctica 5 C8
Scott I., Antarctica 5 C11
Scott Is., Canada 50 C3
Scott L., Canada 51 B7
Scott Reef, Australia 40 B3
Scottsbluff, U.S.A. 54 E3
Scottsboro, U.S.A. 53 H3
Scottsburg, U.S.A. 52 F3
Scottsdale, Australia 42 G4
Scottsdale, U.S.A. 57 K7
Scottsville, Ky., U.S.A. 53 G2
Scottville, U.S.A. 52 D2
Scranton, U.S.A. 52 E8
Scunthorpe, U.K. 8 D7
Seabrook, L., Australia 41 F2
Seaford, U.K. 9 G8
Seaford, U.S.A. 52 F8
Seaforth, Australia 42 C4
Seagraves, U.S.A. 55 J3
Seaham, U.K. 8 C6
Seal →, Canada 51 B10
Seal L., Canada 49 B7
Sealy, U.S.A. 55 L6
Searchlight, U.S.A. 57 J6
Searcy, U.S.A. 55 H9
Searles L., U.S.A. 57 J5
Seascale, U.K. 8 C4
Seaside, Calif., U.S.A. 57 G3
Seaside, Oreg., U.S.A. 56 D2
Seaspray, Australia 43 F4
Seattle, U.S.A. 56 C2
Seaview Ra., Australia 42 B4
Sebastián Vizcaíno, B., Mexico 58 B2
Sebastopol = Sevastopol, Ukraine 19 F5
Sebewaing, U.S.A. 52 D4
Sebha = Sabhah, Libya 35 C8
Şebinkarahisar, Turkey 19 F6
Sebring, U.S.A. 53 M5
Sebta = Ceuta, N. Afr. 15 E3
Sebuku, Indonesia 26 E5
Sebuku, Teluk, Malaysia 26 D5
Sechelt, Canada 50 D4
Sechura, Desierto de, Peru 62 E2
Secretary I., N.Z. 39 L1
Secunderabad, India 28 L11
Security-Widefield, U.S.A. 54 F2
Sedalia, U.S.A. 54 F8
Sedan, France 14 B6
Sedan, U.S.A. 55 G6
Seddon, N.Z. 39 J5
Seddonville, N.Z. 39 J4
Sedé Boqér, Israel 33 E3
Sedeh, Fārs, Iran 31 D7
Sedeh, Khorāsān, Iran 31 C8
Sederot, Israel 33 D3
Sédhiou, Senegal 34 F2
Sedley, Canada 51 C8
Sedona, U.S.A. 57 J8
Sedova, Pik, Russia 20 B6
Sedro Woolley, U.S.A. 56 B2
Seferihisar, Turkey 17 E12
Seg-ozero, Russia 18 B5
Segamat, Malaysia 26 D2
Segesta, Italy 16 F5
Seget, Indonesia 27 E8
Segezha, Russia 18 B5
Ségou, Mali 34 F4
Segovia = Coco →, Cent. Amer. 60 D3
Segovia, Spain 15 B3
Segre →, Spain 15 B6
Séguéla, Ivory C. 34 G4
Seguin, U.S.A. 55 L6
Segura →, Spain 15 C5
Seh Konj, Kūh-e, Iran 31 D8
Seh Qal'eh, Iran 31 C8
Sehore, India 28 H10
Seiland, Norway 6 A20
Seiling, U.S.A. 55 G5
Seinäjoki, Finland 7 E20
Seine →, France 14 B4
Seistan = Sīstān, Asia 31 D9
Seistan, Daryācheh-ye = Sīstān, Daryācheh-ye, Iran 31 D9
Sekayu, Indonesia 26 E2
Sekondi-Takoradi, Ghana 34 H5
Selah, U.S.A. 56 C3
Selaru, Indonesia 27 F8
Selby, U.K. 8 D6
Selby, U.S.A. 54 C4
Selçuk, Turkey 17 F12
Selden, U.S.A. 54 F4
Sele →, Italy 16 D6
Selebi-Pikwe, Botswana 37 J5
Selemdzha →, Russia 21 D13
Selenga = Selenge Mörön →, Asia 24 A5
Selenge Mörön →, Asia 24 A5
Seletan, Tanjung, Indonesia 26 E4
Sélibabi, Mauritania 34 E3
Seligman, U.S.A. 57 J7
Selîma, El Wâhât el, Sudan 35 D11
Selkirk, Canada 51 C9
Selkirk I., Canada 51 C9
Selkirk Mts., Canada 46 C8
Sells, U.S.A. 57 L8
Selma, Ala., U.S.A. 53 J2
Selma, Calif., U.S.A. 57 H4
Selma, N.C., U.S.A. 53 H6
Selmer, U.S.A. 53 H1
Selpele, Indonesia 27 E8
Selsey Bill, U.K. 9 G7
Seltso, Russia 18 D5
Selu, Indonesia 27 F8
Selva, Argentina 64 B4
Selvas, Brazil 62 E5
Selwyn L., Canada 51 B8
Selwyn Mts., Canada 46 B6
Selwyn Ra., Australia 42 C3
Seman →, Albania 17 D8
Semani → = Seman →, Albania 17 D8
Semarang, Indonesia 27 G14
Semeru, Indonesia 27 H15
Semey, Kazakstan 20 D9
Seminoe Reservoir, U.S.A. 56 F10
Seminole, Okla., U.S.A. 55 H6
Seminole, Tex., U.S.A. 55 J3
Seminole Draw →, U.S.A. 55 J3
Semipalatinsk = Semey, Kazakstan 20 D9
Semirara Is., Phil. 27 B6
Semitau, Indonesia 26 D4
Semiyarka, Kazakstan 20 D8
Semiyarskoye = Semiyarka, Kazakstan 20 D8
Semmering P., Austria 12 E8
Semnān, Iran 31 C7
Semnān □, Iran 31 C7
Semporna, Malaysia 27 D5
Semuda, Indonesia 26 E4
Sen →, Cambodia 26 B3
Senā, Iran 31 D6
Sena Madureira, Brazil 62 E5
Senador Pompeu, Brazil 63 E11
Senanga, Zambia 37 H4
Senatobia, U.S.A. 55 H10
Sendai, Kagoshima, Japan 23 J5
Sendai, Miyagi, Japan 22 E10
Sendai-Wan, Japan 22 E10
Seneca, U.S.A. 53 H4
Seneca Falls, U.S.A. 52 D7
Seneca L., U.S.A. 52 D7
Senegal ■, W. Afr. 34 F3
Sénégal →, W. Afr. 34 E2
Senge Khambab = Indus →, Pakistan 28 G5
Senhor-do-Bonfim, Brazil 63 F10
Senigállia, Italy 16 C5
Senj, Croatia 12 F8
Senja, Norway 6 B17
Senkaku-Shotō, Japan 23 L1
Senlis, France 14 B5
Senmonorom, Cambodia 26 B3
Senneterre, Canada 48 C4
Sens, France 14 B5
Senta, Serbia, Yug. 17 B9
Sentani, Indonesia 27 E10
Sentinel, U.S.A. 57 K7
Seo de Urgel = La Seu d'Urgell, Spain 15 A6
Seoul = Sŏul, S. Korea 25 C7
Sepīdān, Iran 31 D7
Sept-Îles, Canada 49 B6
Sequim, U.S.A. 56 B2
Sequoia National Park, U.S.A. 57 H4
Seraing, Belgium 11 D5
Seram, Indonesia 27 E7
Seram Sea, Indonesia 27 E7
Serang, Indonesia 27 G12
Serasan, Indonesia 26 D3
Serbia □, Yugoslavia 17 C9
Serdobsk, Russia 18 D7
Seremban, Malaysia 26 D2
Sereth = Siret →, Romania 13 F14
Sergino, Russia 20 C7
Sergipe □, Brazil 63 F11
Sergiyev Posad, Russia 18 C6
Seria, Brunei 26 D4
Serian, Malaysia 26 D4
Seribu, Kepulauan, Indonesia 26 F3
Sérifos, Greece 17 F11
Sérigny →, Canada 49 A6
Seringapatam Reef, Australia 40 B3
Sermata, Indonesia 27 F7
Serov, Russia 18 C11
Serowe, Botswana 37 J5
Serpentine Lakes, Australia 41 E4
Serpukhov, Russia 18 D6
Serra do Navio, Brazil 63 C8
Sérrai, Greece 17 D10
Serrinha, Brazil 63 F11
Serua, Indonesia 27 F8
Serui, Indonesia 27 E9
Sesepe, Indonesia 27 E7
Setana, Japan 22 C9
Sète, France 14 E5
Sete Lagôas, Brazil 63 G10
Sétif, Algeria 34 A7
Seto, Japan 23 G8
Setonaikai, Japan 23 G6
Settat, Morocco 34 B4
Setting L., Canada 51 C9
Settle, U.K. 8 C5
Settlement Pt., Bahamas 53 M6
Setúbal, Portugal 15 C1
Setúbal, B. de, Portugal 15 C1
Seul, Lac, Canada 46 C10
Sevan, Ozero = Sevana Lich, Armenia 19 F8
Sevana Lich, Armenia 19 F8
Sevastopol, Ukraine 19 F5
Seven Sisters, Canada 50 C3
Severn →, Canada 48 A2
Severn →, U.K. 9 F5
Severn L., Canada 48 B1
Severnaya Zemlya, Russia 21 B10
Severnyye Uvaly, Russia 18 C8
Severo-Kurilsk, Russia 21 D16
Severo-Yeniseyskiy, Russia 21 C10
Severodvinsk, Russia 18 B6
Severomorsk, Russia 18 A5
Severouralsk, Russia 18 B10
Sevier, U.S.A. 57 G7
Sevier →, U.S.A. 57 G7
Sevier Desert, U.S.A. 56 G7
Sevier L., U.S.A. 56 G7
Sevilla, Spain 15 D2
Seville = Sevilla, Spain 15 D2
Sevlievo, Bulgaria 17 C11
Seward, Alaska, U.S.A. 46 B5
Seward, Nebr., U.S.A. 54 E6
Seward Peninsula, U.S.A. 46 B3
Sewer, Indonesia 27 F8
Sexsmith, Canada 50 B5
Seychelles ■, Ind. Oc. 3 E12
Seyðisfjörður, Iceland 6 D6
Seydişehir, Turkey 19 G5
Seydvān, Iran 30 B5
Seyhan →, Turkey 30 B2
Seym →, Ukraine 19 D5
Seymour, Australia 43 F4
Seymour, Ind., U.S.A. 52 F3
Seymour, Tex., U.S.A. 55 J5
Sfântu Gheorghe, Romania 13 F13
Sfax, Tunisia 35 B8
Shaanxi □, China 25 C5
Shaba = Katanga □, Dem. Rep. of the Congo 36 F4
Shabogamo L., Canada 49 B6
Shache, China 24 C2
Shackleton Ice Shelf, Antarctica 5 C8
Shackleton Inlet, Antarctica 5 E11
Shādegān, Iran 31 D6
Shadrinsk, Russia 20 D7
Shafter, U.S.A. 57 J4
Shaftesbury, U.K. 9 F5
Shahba, Syria 33 C5
Shahdād, Iran 31 D8
Shahdād, Namakzār-e, Iran 31 D8
Shahdadkot, Pakistan 28 F5
Shahgarh, India 28 F6
Shahjahanpur, India 28 F11
Shahr-e Bābak, Iran 31 D7
Shahr-e Kord, Iran 31 C6
Shāhrakht, Iran 31 C9
Shahrig, Pakistan 28 D5
Shajapur, India 28 H10
Shakhty, Russia 19 E7
Shakhunya, Russia 18 C8
Shaki, Nigeria 34 G6
Shalqar, Kazakstan 20 E6
Shaluli Shan, China 24 C4
Shām, Iran 31 E8
Shām, Bādiyat ash, Asia 30 C3
Shamattawa, Canada 48 A1
Shamattawa →, Canada 48 A2
Shamīl, Iran 31 E8
Shāmkūh, Iran 31 C8
Shammar, Jabal, Si. Arabia 30 E4
Shamo = Gobi, Asia 25 B5
Shamo, L., Ethiopia 32 F2
Shamokin, U.S.A. 52 E7
Shamrock, U.S.A. 55 H4
Shan □, Burma 29 J21
Shāndak, Iran 31 D9
Shandong □, China 25 C6
Shanga, Nigeria 34 F6
Shangani →, Zimbabwe 37 H5
Shanghai, China 25 C7
Shangqiu, China 25 C6
Shangrao, China 25 D6
Shangshui, China 25 C6
Shannon, N.Z. 39 J5
Shannon →, Ireland 10 E2
Shansi = Shanxi □, China 25 C6
Shantar, Ostrov Bolshoy, Russia 21 D14
Shantou, China 25 D6
Shantung = Shandong □, China 25 C6
Shanxi □, China 25 C6
Shaoguan, China 25 D6
Shaoxing, China 25 D7
Shaoyang, China 25 D6
Shap, U.K. 8 C5
Shaqra', Si. Arabia 30 E5
Shaqrā', Yemen 32 E4
Sharafkhāneh, Iran 30 B5
Shari, Japan 22 C12
Sharjah = Ash Shāriqah, U.A.E. 31 E7
Shark B., Australia 41 E1
Sharon, U.S.A. 52 E5
Sharon Springs, U.S.A. 54 F4
Sharp Pt., Australia 42 A3
Sharpe L., Canada 48 B1
Sharya, Russia 18 C8
Shashemene, Ethiopia 32 F2
Shashi, China 25 C6
Shasta, Mt., U.S.A. 56 F2
Shasta L., U.S.A. 56 F2
Shatt al Arab = Arab, Shatt al →, Asia 31 D6
Shaunavon, Canada 51 D7
Shaw →, Australia 40 D2
Shaw I., Australia 42 C4
Shawano, U.S.A. 52 C1
Shawinigan, Canada 48 C5
Shawnee, U.S.A. 55 H6
Shay Gap, Australia 40 D3
Shaybārā, Si. Arabia 30 E3
Shaykh, J. ash, Lebanon 33 B4
Shaykh Miskīn, Syria 33 C5
Shaykh Sa'īd, Iraq 30 C5
Shcherbakov = Rybinsk, Russia 18 C6
Shchuchinsk, Kazakstan 20 D8
Shebele = Scebeli, Wabi →, Somali Rep. 32 G3
Sheboygan, U.S.A. 52 D2
Shediac, Canada 49 C7
Sheerness, U.K. 9 F8
Sheet Harbour, Canada 49 D7
Sheffield, U.K. 8 D6
Sheffield, U.S.A. 53 H2
Shekhupura, Pakistan 28 D8
Shelburne, N.S., Canada 49 D6
Shelburne, Ont., Canada 48 D3
Shelburne B., Australia 42 A3
Shelby, Mich., U.S.A. 52 D2
Shelby, Miss., U.S.A. 55 J9
Shelby, Mont., U.S.A. 56 B8
Shelby, N.C., U.S.A. 53 H5
Shelbyville, Ill., U.S.A. 54 F10
Shelbyville, Ind., U.S.A. 52 F3
Shelbyville, Ky., U.S.A. 52 F3
Shelbyville, Tenn., U.S.A. 53 H2
Sheldon, U.S.A. 54 D7
Sheldrake, Canada 49 B7
Shelikhova, Zaliv, Russia 21 D16
Shell Lakes, Australia 41 E4
Shellbrook, Canada 51 C7
Shellharbour, Australia 43 E5
Shelton, U.S.A. 56 C2
Shenandoah, Iowa, U.S.A. 54 E7
Shenandoah, Pa., U.S.A. 52 E7
Shenandoah, Va., U.S.A. 52 F6
Shenandoah →, U.S.A. 52 F7
Shenandoah National Park, U.S.A. 52 F6
Shendam, Nigeria 34 G7
Shendî, Sudan 35 E12
Shensi = Shaanxi □, China 25 C5
Shenyang, China 25 B7
Sheopur Kalan, India 28 G10
Shepetivka, Ukraine 13 C14
Shepetovka = Shepetivka, Ukraine 13 C14
Shepparton, Australia 43 F4
Sheppey, I. of, U.K. 9 F8
Shepton Mallet, U.K. 9 F5
Sherborne, U.K. 9 G5
Sherbro I., S. Leone 34 G3
Sherbrooke, N.S., Canada 49 C7
Sherbrooke, Qué., Canada 49 C5
Sheridan, Ark., U.S.A. 55 H8
Sheridan, Wyo., U.S.A. 56 D10
Sheringham, U.K. 8 E9
Sherman, U.S.A. 55 J6
Sherridon, Canada 51 B8
Sherwood Forest, U.K. 8 D6
Sherwood Park, Canada 50 C6
Sheslay →, Canada 50 B2
Shethanei L., Canada 51 B9
Shetland Is., U.K. 10 A6
Sheyenne →, U.S.A. 54 B6
Shibām, Yemen 32 D4
Shibata, Japan 22 F9
Shibecha, Japan 22 C12
Shibetsu, Japan 22 B11
Shibogama L., Canada 48 B2
Shibushi, Japan 23 J5
Shickshock Mts. = Chic-Chocs, Mts., Canada 49 C6
Shido, Japan 23 G7
Shield, C., Australia 42 A2
Shiga □, Japan 23 G8
Shihchiachuangi = Shijiazhuang, China 25 C6
Shijiazhuang, China 25 C6

Shikarpur, *Pakistan* . . . **28 F6**
Shikoku □, *Japan* **23 H6**
Shikoku-Sanchi, *Japan* **23 H6**
Shiliguri, *India* **29 F16**
Shilka, *Russia* **21 D12**
Shilka →, *Russia* **21 D13**
Shillong, *India* **29 G17**
Shilo, *West Bank* **33 C4**
Shimabara, *Japan* **23 H5**
Shimada, *Japan* **23 G9**
Shimane □, *Japan* **23 G6**
Shimanovsk, *Russia* . . **21 D13**
Shimizu, *Japan* **23 G9**
Shimodate, *Japan* **23 F9**
Shimoga, *India* **28 N9**
Shimonoseki, *Japan* . . **23 H5**
Shinano-Gawa →,
  Japan **23 F9**
Shināṣ, *Oman* **31 E8**
Shīndand, *Afghan.* **28 C3**
Shingū, *Japan* **23 H7**
Shinjō, *Japan* **22 E10**
Shinshār, *Syria* **33 A5**
Shinyanga, *Tanzania* . . **36 E6**
Shio-no-Misaki, *Japan* . **23 H7**
Shiogama, *Japan* **22 E10**
Shiojiri, *Japan* **23 F8**
Shipchenski Prokhod,
  Bulgaria **17 C11**
Shiping, *China* **24 D5**
Shippegan, *Canada* . . . **49 C7**
Shippensburg, *U.S.A.* . . **52 F7**
Shiprock, *U.S.A.* **57 H9**
Shiqma, N. →, *Israel* . **33 D3**
Shiquan He =
  Indus →, *Pakistan* . **28 G5**
Shīr Kūh, *Iran* **31 D7**
Shiragami-Misaki, *Japan* **22 D10**
Shirakawa, *Fukushima*,
  Japan **23 F10**
Shirakawa, *Gifu*, *Japan* **23 F8**
Shirane-San, *Gumma*,
  Japan **23 F9**
Shirane-San,
  Yamanashi, *Japan* . **23 G9**
Shiraoi, *Japan* **22 C10**
Shīrāz, *Iran* **31 D7**
Shire →, *Africa* **37 H7**
Shiretoko-Misaki, *Japan* **23 B12**
Shiriya-Zaki, *Japan* . . **22 D10**
Shiroishi, *Japan* **22 F10**
Shīrvān, *Iran* **31 B8**
Shirwa, L. = Chilwa, L.,
  Malawi **37 H7**
Shivpuri, *India* **28 G10**
Shizuoka, *Japan* **23 G9**
Shizuoka □, *Japan* . . . **23 G9**
Shklov = Shklow,
  Belarus **13 A16**
Shklow, *Belarus* **13 A16**
Shkoder = Shkodër,
  Albania **17 C8**
Shkodër, *Albania* **17 C8**
Shkodra = Shkodër,
  Albania **17 C8**
Shkumbini →, *Albania* **17 D8**
Shmidta, Ostrov, *Russia* **21 A10**
Shō-Gawa →, *Japan* . **23 F8**
Shoal L., *Canada* **51 D9**
Shoal Lake, *Canada* . . . **51 C8**
Shōdo-Shima, *Japan* . . **23 G7**
Sholapur = Solapur,
  India **28 L9**
Shologontsy, *Russia* . . **21 C12**
Shōmrōn, *West Bank* . . **33 C4**
Shoreham by Sea, *U.K.* **9 G7**
Shoshone, *U.S.A.* **56 E6**
Shoshone L., *U.S.A.* . . . **56 D8**
Shoshone Mts., *U.S.A.* . **56 G5**
Shoshoni, *U.S.A.* **56 E9**
Show Low, *U.S.A.* **57 J9**
Shreveport, *U.S.A.* **55 J8**
Shrewsbury, *U.K.* **9 E5**
Shrirampur, *India* **29 H16**
Shropshire □, *U.K.* . . . **9 E5**
Shu, *Kazakstan* **20 E8**
Shuangliao, *China* **25 B7**
Shuangyashan, *China* . **25 B8**
Shule, *China* **24 C2**
Shumagin Is., *U.S.A.* . . **46 C4**
Shumen, *Bulgaria* . . . **17 C12**
Shumikha, *Russia* **20 D7**
Shūr →, *Fārs*, *Iran* . . **31 D7**
Shūr →, *Kermān*, *Iran* **31 D8**
Shūr →, *Yazd*, *Iran* . . **31 D7**
Shūr Āb, *Iran* **31 C6**
Shūr Gaz, *Iran* **31 D8**
Shūrāb, *Iran* **31 C6**
Shūrjestān, *Iran* **31 D7**
Shurugwi, *Zimbabwe* . . **37 H6**
Shūsf, *Iran* **31 D9**
Shūshtar, *Iran* **31 D6**
Shuswap L., *Canada* . . **50 C5**
Shūzū, *Iran* **31 D7**
Shwebo, *Burma* **29 H19**
Shwegu, *Burma* **29 G20**
Shweli →, *Burma* . . . **29 H20**
Shymkent, *Kazakstan* . . **20 E7**
Shyok, *India* **28 B11**
Shyok →, *India* **28 B8**
Si Kiang = Xi Jiang →,
  China **25 D6**

Siaksriindrapura,
  Indonesia **26 D2**
Sialkot, *Pakistan* **28 C9**
Siam = Thailand ■,
  Asia **26 A2**
Sian = Xi'an, *China* . . . **25 C5**
Siantan, *Indonesia* **26 D3**
Siāreh, *Iran* **31 D9**
Siargao I., *Phil.* **27 C7**
Siasi, *Phil.* **27 C6**
Siau, *Indonesia* **27 D7**
Šiauliai, *Lithuania* **7 J20**
Sibâi, Gebel el, *Egypt* . **30 E2**
Sibay, *Russia* **18 D10**
Šibenik, *Croatia* **16 C6**
Siberia, *Russia* **4 D13**
Siberut, *Indonesia* **26 E1**
Sibi, *Pakistan* **28 E5**
Sibil = Oksibil,
  Indonesia **27 E10**
Sibiti, *Congo* **36 E2**
Sibiu, *Romania* **13 F13**
Sibolga, *Indonesia* **26 D1**
Sibsagar, *India* **29 F19**
Sibu, *Malaysia* **26 D4**
Sibuco, *Phil.* **27 C6**
Sibuguey B., *Phil.* **27 C6**
Sibut, *C.A.R.* **36 C3**
Sibutu, *Phil.* **27 D5**
Sibutu Passage,
  E. Indies **27 D5**
Sibuyan I., *Phil.* **27 B6**
Sibuyan Sea, *Phil.* **27 B6**
Sicamous, *Canada* **50 C5**
Sichuan □, *China* **24 C5**
Sicilia, *Italy* **16 F6**
Sicily = Sicilia, *Italy* . . **16 F6**
Sicuani, *Peru* **62 F4**
Siddipet, *India* **28 K11**
Sidi-bel-Abbès, *Algeria* . **34 A5**
Sidley, Mt., *Antarctica* . **5 D14**
Sidmouth, *U.K.* **9 G4**
Sidmouth, C., *Australia* **42 A3**
Sidney, *Canada* **50 D4**
Sidney, *Mont.*, *U.S.A.* . **54 B2**
Sidney, *N.Y.*, *U.S.A.* . . **52 D8**
Sidney, *Nebr.*, *U.S.A.* . **54 E3**
Sidney, *Ohio*, *U.S.A.* . . **52 E3**
Sidney Lanier, L., *U.S.A.* **53 H4**
Sidoarjo, *Indonesia* . . **27 G15**
Sidon = Saydā,
  Lebanon **33 B4**
Sidra, G. of = Surt,
  Khalīj, *Libya* **35 B9**
Siedlce, *Poland* **13 B12**
Sieg →, *Germany* **12 C4**
Siegen, *Germany* **12 C5**
Siem Reap = Siemreab,
  Cambodia **26 B2**
Siemreab, *Cambodia* . . **26 B2**
Siena, *Italy* **16 C4**
Sieradz, *Poland* **13 C10**
Sierra Blanca, *U.S.A.* . . **57 L11**
Sierra Blanca Peak,
  U.S.A. **57 K11**
Sierra Colorada,
  Argentina **64 E3**
Sierra Gorda, *Chile* . . . **62 H5**
Sierra Leone ■, *W. Afr.* **34 G3**
Sierra Madre, *Mexico* . **59 D6**
Sierra Mojada, *Mexico* . **58 B4**
Sierra Vista, *U.S.A.* . . . **57 L8**
Sifnos, *Greece* **17 F11**
Sifton, *Canada* **51 C8**
Sifton Pass, *Canada* . . **50 B3**
Sighetu-Marmaţiei,
  Romania **13 E12**
Sighişoara, *Romania* . . **13 E13**
Sigli, *Indonesia* **26 C1**
Siglufjörður, *Iceland* . . **6 C4**
Sigsig, *Ecuador* **62 D3**
Sigüenza, *Spain* **15 B4**
Siguiri, *Guinea* **34 F4**
Sigulda, *Latvia* **7 H21**
Sihanoukville =
  Kampong Saom,
  Cambodia **26 B2**
Siikajoki →, *Finland* . . **6 D21**
Siilinjärvi, *Finland* **6 E22**
Sikar, *India* **28 F9**
Sikasso, *Mali* **34 F4**
Sikeston, *U.S.A.* **55 G10**
Sikhote Alin, Khrebet,
  Russia **21 E14**
Sikhote Alin Ra. =
  Sikhote Alin, Khrebet,
  Russia **21 E14**
Sikinos, *Greece* **17 F11**
Sikkani Chief →,
  Canada **50 B4**
Sikkim □, *India* **29 F16**
Sikotu-Ko, *Japan* **22 C10**
Sil →, *Spain* **15 A2**
Silacayoapan, *Mexico* . **59 D5**
Silchar, *India* **29 G18**
Siler City, *U.S.A.* **53 H6**
Silesia = Śląsk, *Poland* **12 C9**
Silgarhi Doti, *Nepal* . . **29 E12**
Silghat, *India* **29 F18**
Silifke, *Turkey* **19 G5**
Siliguri = Shiliguri,
  India **29 F16**

Siling Co, *China* **24 C3**
Silistra, *Bulgaria* **17 B12**
Silivri, *Turkey* **17 D13**
Siljan, *Sweden* **7 F16**
Silkeborg, *Denmark* . . . **7 H13**
Silkwood, *Australia* . . . **42 B4**
Sillajhuay, Cordillera,
  Chile **62 G5**
Sillamäe, *Estonia* **7 G22**
Silloth, *U.K.* **8 C4**
Siloam Springs, *U.S.A.* **55 G7**
Silsbee, *U.S.A.* **55 K7**
Šilutė, *Lithuania* **7 J19**
Silva Porto = Kuito,
  Angola **37 G3**
Silver City, *U.S.A.* **57 K9**
Silver Cr. →, *U.S.A.* . . **56 E4**
Silver Lake, *U.S.A.* . . . **56 E3**
Silverton, *Colo.*, *U.S.A.* **57 H10**
Silverton, *Tex.*, *U.S.A.* . **55 H4**
Silvies →, *U.S.A.* **56 E4**
Simanggang = Bandar
  Sri Aman, *Malaysia* . **26 D4**
Simard, L., *Canada* . . . **48 C4**
Simav, *Turkey* **17 E13**
Simbirsk, *Russia* **18 D8**
Simcoe, *Canada* **48 D3**
Simcoe, L., *Canada* . . . **48 D4**
Simeria, *Romania* **13 F12**
Simeulue, *Indonesia* . . **26 D1**
Simferopol, *Ukraine* . . **19 F5**
Sími, *Greece* **17 F12**
Simi Valley, *U.S.A.* **57 J4**
Simikot, *Nepal* **29 E12**
Simla, *India* **28 D10**
Simmie, *Canada* **51 D7**
Simojoki →, *Finland* . . **6 D21**
Simojovel, *Mexico* . . . **59 D6**
Simonette →, *Canada* . **50 B5**
Simplonpass, *Switz.* . . **14 C8**
Simpson Desert,
  Australia **42 D2**
Simpson Pen., *Canada* **47 B11**
Simrishamn, *Sweden* . . **7 J16**
Simushir, Ostrov, *Russia* **21 E16**
Sin Cowe I.,
  S. China Sea **26 C4**
Sinabang, *Indonesia* . . **26 D1**
Sinadogo, *Somali Rep.* **32 F4**
Sinai = Es Sînâ', *Egypt* **33 F3**
Sinai, Mt. = Mûsa,
  Gebel, *Egypt* **30 D2**
Sinai Peninsula, *Egypt* . **33 F3**
Sinaloa □, *Mexico* . . . **58 C3**
Sinaloa de Leyva,
  Mexico **58 B3**
Sincelejo, *Colombia* . . **62 B3**
Sinclair, *U.S.A.* **56 F10**
Sinclair Mills, *Canada* . **50 C4**
Sincorá, Serra do, *Brazil* **63 F10**
Sind □, *Pakistan* **28 G6**
Sind Sagar Doab,
  Pakistan **28 D7**
Sindangan, *Phil.* **27 C6**
Sindangbarang,
  Indonesia **27 G12**
Sines, *Portugal* **15 D1**
Sines, C. de, *Portugal* . **15 D1**
Singa, *Sudan* **35 F12**
Singapore ■, *Asia* **26 D2**
Singaraja, *Indonesia* . . **26 F5**
Singida, *Tanzania* **36 E6**
Singitikós Kólpos,
  Greece **17 D11**
Singkaling Hkamti,
  Burma **29 G19**
Singkang, *Indonesia* . . **27 E6**
Singkawang, *Indonesia* **26 D3**
Singkep, *Indonesia* . . . **26 E2**
Singleton, *Australia* . . . **43 E5**
Singleton, Mt., *N. Terr.*,
  Australia **40 D5**
Singleton, Mt.,
  W. Austral., *Australia* **41 E2**
Singora = Songkhla,
  Thailand **26 C2**
Sînî □, *Egypt* **33 F3**
Sinjai, *Indonesia* **27 F6**
Sinjār, *Iraq* **30 B4**
Sinkat, *Sudan* **35 E13**
Sinkiang Uighur =
  Xinjiang Uygur
  Zizhiqu □, *China* . . **24 C3**
Sinnamary, *Fr. Guiana* **63 B8**
Sinni →, *Italy* **16 D7**
Sinop, *Turkey* **19 F6**
Sinsk, *Russia* **21 C13**
Sintang, *Indonesia* . . . **26 D4**
Sinton, *U.S.A.* **55 L6**
Sintra, *Portugal* **15 C1**
Siocon, *Phil.* **27 C6**
Siófok, *Hungary* **13 E10**
Sion, *Switz.* **14 C7**
Sioux City, *U.S.A.* **54 D6**
Sioux Falls, *U.S.A.* **54 D6**
Sioux Lookout, *Canada* **48 B1**
Sioux Narrows, *Canada* **51 D10**
Siping, *China* **25 B7**
Sipiwesk L., *Canada* . . **51 B9**
Sipura, *Indonesia* **26 E1**
Siquia →, *Nic.* **60 D3**
Siquijor, *Phil.* **27 C6**
Siquirres, *Costa Rica* . . **60 D3**
Şīr Banī Yās, *U.A.E.* . . **31 E7**

Sir Edward Pellew
  Group, *Australia* **42 B2**
Sir Graham Moore Is.,
  Australia **40 B4**
Sir James MacBrien,
  Mt., *Canada* **46 B7**
Sira →, *Norway* **7 G12**
Siracusa, *Italy* **16 F6**
Sirajganj, *Bangla.* **29 G16**
Sīrdān, *Iran* **31 B6**
Sirdaryo =
  Syrdarya →,
  Kazakstan **20 E7**
Siren, *U.S.A.* **54 C8**
Siret →, *Romania* **13 F14**
Sirghāyā, *Syria* **33 B5**
Sirohi, *India* **28 G8**
Sironj, *India* **28 G10**
Síros, *Greece* **17 F11**
Sirsa, *India* **28 E9**
Sisak, *Croatia* **12 F9**
Sisaket, *Thailand* **26 A2**
Sisipuk L., *Canada* . . . **51 B8**
Sisophon, *Cambodia* . . **26 B2**
Sisseton, *U.S.A.* **54 C6**
Sīstān, *Asia* **31 D9**
Sīstān, Daryācheh-ye,
  Iran **31 D9**
Sīstān va
  Balūchestān □, *Iran* . **31 E9**
Sitapur, *India* **29 F12**
Sitges, *Spain* **15 B6**
Sitía, *Greece* **17 G12**
Sitka, *U.S.A.* **50 B1**
Sittang Myit →, *Burma* **29 L20**
Sittard, *Neths.* **11 C5**
Sittingbourne, *U.K.* . . . **9 F8**
Sittoung = Sittang
  Myit →, *Burma* **29 L20**
Sittwe, *Burma* **29 J18**
Siuna, *Nic.* **60 D3**
Siuri, *India* **29 H15**
Sīvand, *Iran* **31 D7**
Sivas, *Turkey* **19 G6**
Siverek, *Turkey* **30 B3**
Sivomaskinskiy, *Russia* **18 A11**
Sivrihisar, *Turkey* **19 G5**
Sîwa, *Egypt* **35 C11**
Siwalik Range, *Nepal* . . **29 F13**
Siwan, *India* **29 F14**
Sixth Cataract, *Sudan* . **35 E12**
Sjælland, *Denmark* . . . **7 J14**
Sjumen = Shumen,
  Bulgaria **17 C12**
Skadarsko Jezero,
  Montenegro, *Yug.* . . **17 C8**
Skaftafell, *Iceland* **6 D5**
Skagafjörður, *Iceland* . . **6 D4**
Skagastølstindane,
  Norway **7 F12**
Skagaströnd, *Iceland* . . **6 D3**
Skagen, *Denmark* **7 H14**
Skagerrak, *Denmark* . . **7 H13**
Skagway, *U.S.A.* **46 C6**
Skala-Podilska, *Ukraine* **13 D14**
Skala Podolskaya =
  Skala-Podilska,
  Ukraine **13 D14**
Skalat, *Ukraine* **13 D13**
Skåne, *Sweden* **7 J15**
Skara, *Sweden* **7 G15**
Skardu, *Pakistan* **28 B9**
Skarżysko-Kamienna,
  Poland **13 C11**
Skeena →, *Canada* . . **50 C2**
Skeena Mts., *Canada* . **50 B3**
Skegness, *U.K.* **8 D8**
Skeldon, *Guyana* **62 B7**
Skellefte älv →,
  Sweden **6 D19**
Skellefteå, *Sweden* . . . **6 D19**
Skelleftehamn, *Sweden* **6 D19**
Skerries, The, *U.K.* . . . **8 D3**
Ski, *Norway* **7 G14**
Skíathos, *Greece* **17 E10**
Skiddaw, *U.K.* **8 C4**
Skidegate, *Canada* . . . **50 C2**
Skien, *Norway* **7 G13**
Skierniewice, *Poland* . . **13 C11**
Skikda, *Algeria* **34 A7**
Skilloura, *U.K.* . . . . . . [missing]
Skipton, *U.K.* **8 D5**
Skirmish Pt., *Australia* . **42 A1**
Skíros, *Greece* **17 E11**
Skive, *Denmark* **7 H13**
Skjálfandafljót →,
  Iceland **6 D5**
Skjálfandi, *Iceland* **6 C5**
Skoghall, *Sweden* **7 G15**
Skole, *Ukraine* **13 D12**
Skópelos, *Greece* **17 E10**
Skopje, *Macedonia* . . . **17 C9**
Skövde, *Sweden* **7 G15**
Skovorodino, *Russia* . . **21 D13**
Skowhegan, *U.S.A.* . . . **53 C11**
Skull →, *Canada* **50 B6**
Skuodas, *Lithuania* . . . **7 H19**
Skvyra, *Ukraine* **13 D15**
Skye, *U.K.* **10 C3**
Skykomish, *U.S.A.* **56 C3**
Skyros = Skíros, *Greece* **17 E11**

Slagelse, *Denmark* . . . **7 J14**
Slamet, *Indonesia* **27 G13**
Śląsk, *Poland* **12 C9**
Slate Is., *Canada* **48 C2**
Slatina, *Romania* **13 F13**
Slaton, *U.S.A.* **55 J4**
Slave →, *Canada* **50 A6**
Slave Coast, *W. Afr.* . . **34 G6**
Slave Lake, *Canada* . . . **50 B6**
Slave Pt., *Canada* **50 A5**
Slavgorod, *Russia* **20 D8**
Slavonski Brod, *Croatia* **17 B8**
Slavuta, *Ukraine* **13 C14**
Slavyanka, *Russia* **22 C5**
Slavyansk = Slovyansk,
  Ukraine **19 E6**
Slawharad, *Belarus* . . . **13 B16**
Sleaford, *U.K.* **8 D7**
Sleaford B., *Australia* . . **43 E2**
Sleeper Is., *Canada* . . . **47 C11**
Sleepy Eye, *U.S.A.* . . . **54 C7**
Slemon L., *Canada* . . . **50 A5**
Slidell, *U.S.A.* **55 K10**
Sligeach = Sligo,
  Ireland **10 D2**
Sligo, *Ireland* **10 D2**
Slite, *Sweden* **7 H18**
Sliven, *Bulgaria* **17 C12**
Slobodskoy, *Russia* . . . **18 C9**
Slobozia, *Romania* . . . **13 F14**
Slocan, *Canada* **50 D5**
Slonim, *Belarus* **13 B13**
Slough, *U.K.* **9 F7**
Slough □, *U.K.* **9 F7**
Slovak Rep. ■, *Europe* **13 D10**
Slovakia = Slovak
  Rep. ■, *Europe* **13 D10**
Slovakian Ore Mts. =
  Slovenské Rudohorie,
  Slovak Rep. **13 D10**
Slovenia ■, *Europe* . . **12 F8**
Slovenija = Slovenia ■,
  Europe **12 F8**
Slovenské Rudohorie,
  Slovak Rep. **13 D10**
Slovyansk, *Ukraine* . . . **19 E6**
Sluch →, *Ukraine* . . . **13 C14**
Sluis, *Neths.* **11 C3**
Słupsk, *Poland* **13 A9**
Slutsk, *Belarus* **13 B14**
Slyudyanka, *Russia* . . . **21 D11**
Småland, *Sweden* . . . **7 H16**
Smalltree L., *Canada* . . **51 A8**
Smallwood Res.,
  Canada **49 B7**
Smara, *Morocco* **34 B4**
Smarhon, *Belarus* **13 A14**
Smeaton, *Canada* **51 C8**
Smederevo,
  Serbia, *Yug.* **17 B9**
Smidovich, *Russia* **21 E14**
Smith, *Canada* **50 B6**
Smith Center, *U.S.A.* . . **54 F5**
Smith Sund, *Greenland* **4 B4**
Smithburne →,
  Australia **42 B3**
Smithers, *Canada* **50 C3**
Smithfield, *N.C.*, *U.S.A.* **53 H6**
Smithfield, *Utah*, *U.S.A.* **56 F8**
Smiths Falls, *Canada* . . **48 D4**
Smithton, *Australia* . . . **42 G4**
Smithville, *U.S.A.* **55 K6**
Smoky →, *Canada* . . . **50 B5**
Smoky Bay, *Australia* . . **43 E1**
Smoky Hill →, *U.S.A.* . **54 F6**
Smoky Hills, *U.S.A.* . . . **54 F5**
Smoky Lake, *Canada* . . **50 C6**
Smøla, *Norway* **6 E13**
Smolensk, *Russia* **18 D5**
Smolikas, Óros, *Greece* **17 D9**
Smolyan, *Bulgaria* **17 D11**
Smooth Rock Falls,
  Canada **48 C3**
Smoothstone L., *Canada* **51 C7**
Smorgon = Smarhon,
  Belarus **13 A14**
Smyrna = İzmir, *Turkey* **17 E12**
Smyrna, *U.S.A.* **52 F8**
Snæfell, *Iceland* **6 D6**
Snaefell, *U.K.* **8 C3**
Snæfellsjökull, *Iceland* . **6 D2**
Snake →, *U.S.A.* **56 C4**
Snake I., *Australia* **43 F4**
Snake Range, *U.S.A.* . . **56 G6**
Snake River Plain,
  U.S.A. **56 E7**
Snåsavatnet, *Norway* . **6 D14**
Sneek, *Neths.* **11 A5**
Snežka, *Europe* **12 C8**
Snøhetta, *Norway* **7 E13**
Snohomish, *U.S.A.* . . . **56 C2**
Snow Hill, *U.S.A.* **52 F8**
Snow Lake, *Canada* . . . **51 C8**
Snowbird L., *Canada* . . **51 A8**
Snowdon, *U.K.* **8 D3**
Snowdrift →, *Canada* . **51 A6**
Snowflake, *U.S.A.* **57 J8**
Snowshoe Pk., *U.S.A.* . **56 B6**
Snowtown, *Australia* . . **43 E2**
Snowville, *U.S.A.* **56 F7**
Snowy →, *Australia* . . **43 F4**
Snowy Mts., *Australia* . **43 F4**
Snug Corner, *Bahamas* **61 B5**
Snyatyn, *Ukraine* **13 D13**

Snyder, *Okla.*, *U.S.A.* . . **55 H5**
Snyder, *Tex.*, *U.S.A.* . . **55 J4**
Sobat, Nahr →, *Sudan* **35 G12**
Sobradinho, Reprêsa de,
  Brazil **63 E10**
Sobral, *Brazil* **63 D10**
Soc Trang, *Vietnam* . . . **26 C3**
Socastee, *U.S.A.* **53 J6**
Soch'e = Shache, *China* **24 C2**
Sochi, *Russia* **19 F6**
Société, Is. de la,
  Pac. Oc. **45 J12**
Society Is. = Société, Is.
  de la, *Pac. Oc.* **45 J12**
Socompa, Portezuelo
  de, *Chile* **64 A3**
Socorro, *N. Mex.*, *U.S.A.* **57 J10**
Socorro, *Tex.*, *U.S.A.* . . **57 L10**
Socorro, I., *Mexico* . . . **58 D2**
Socotra, *Ind. Oc.* **32 E5**
Soda L., *U.S.A.* **57 J5**
Soda Springs, *U.S.A.* . . **56 E8**
Sodankylä, *Finland* . . . **6 C22**
Soddy-Daisy, *U.S.A.* . . **53 H3**
Söderhamn, *Sweden* . . **7 F17**
Söderköping, *Sweden* . **7 G17**
Södermanland, *Sweden* **7 G17**
Södertälje, *Sweden* . . . **7 G17**
Sodiri, *Sudan* **35 F11**
Soest, *Neths.* **11 B5**
Sofia = Sofiya, *Bulgaria* **17 C10**
Sofia →, *Madag.* **37 H9**
Sofiya, *Bulgaria* **17 C10**
Sōfu-Gan, *Japan* **23 K10**
Sogamoso, *Colombia* . **62 B4**
Sogār, *Iran* **31 E8**
Sogndalsfjøra, *Norway* **7 F12**
Søgne, *Norway* **7 G12**
Sognefjorden, *Norway* . **7 F11**
Soh, *Iran* **31 C6**
Sohâg, *Egypt* **35 C12**
Soignies, *Belgium* **11 D4**
Soissons, *France* **14 B5**
Sōja, *Japan* **23 G6**
Sokal, *Ukraine* **13 C13**
Söke, *Turkey* **17 F12**
Sokhumi, *Georgia* **19 F7**
Sokodé, *Togo* **34 G6**
Sokol, *Russia* **18 C7**
Sokółka, *Poland* **13 B12**
Sokołów Podlaski,
  Poland **13 B12**
Sokoto, *Nigeria* **34 F7**
Sol Iletsk, *Russia* **18 D10**
Solano, *Phil.* **27 A6**
Solapur, *India* **28 L9**
Soldotna, *U.S.A.* **46 B4**
Soledad, *Colombia* . . . **62 A4**
Soledad, *U.S.A.* **57 H3**
Soledad, *Venezuela* . . . **62 B6**
Solent, The, *U.K.* **9 G6**
Solfonn, *Norway* **7 F12**
Solhan, *Turkey* **30 B4**
Soligalich, *Russia* **18 C7**
Soligorsk = Salihorsk,
  Belarus **13 B14**
Solihull, *U.K.* **9 E6**
Solikamsk, *Russia* **18 C10**
Solimões =
  Amazonas →,
  S. Amer. **63 D9**
Solingen, *Germany* . . . **12 C4**
Sollefteå, *Sweden* **6 E17**
Sóller, *Spain* **15 C7**
Solo →, *Indonesia* . . . **27 G15**
Sologne, *France* **14 C4**
Solok, *Indonesia* **26 E2**
Sololá, *Guatemala* **60 D1**
Solomon, N. Fork →,
  U.S.A. **54 F5**
Solomon, S. Fork →,
  U.S.A. **54 F5**
Solomon Is. ■, *Pac. Oc.* **38 B8**
Solon, *China* **25 B7**
Solon Springs, *U.S.A.* . **54 B9**
Solor, *Indonesia* **27 F6**
Solothurn, *Switz.* **14 C7**
Šolta, *Croatia* **16 C7**
Solṭānābād, *Khorāsān*,
  Iran **31 C8**
Solṭānābād, *Khorāsān*,
  Iran **31 B8**
Solunska Glava,
  Macedonia **17 D9**
Solvang, *U.S.A.* **57 J3**
Solvay, *U.S.A.* **52 D7**
Sölvesborg, *Sweden* . . **7 H16**
Solvychegodsk, *Russia* . **18 B8**
Solway Firth, *U.K.* **8 C4**
Solwezi, *Zambia* **37 G5**
Sōma, *Japan* **22 F10**
Soma, *Turkey* **17 E12**
Somali Rep. ■, *Africa* . **32 F4**
Somalia = Somali
  Rep. ■, *Africa* **32 F4**
Sombor, *Serbia*, *Yug.* . **17 B8**
Sombrerete, *Mexico* . . **58 C4**
Sombrero, *Anguilla* . . . **61 C7**
Somers, *U.S.A.* **56 B6**
Somerset, *Ky.*, *U.S.A.* . **52 G3**
Somerset, *Pa.*, *U.S.A.* . **52 E6**
Somerset □, *U.K.* **9 F5**
Somerset I., *Canada* . . **46 A10**
Somerton, *U.S.A.* **57 K6**

Someş →, Romania . 13 D12
Somme →, France ... 14 A4
Somosierra, Puerto de, Spain ... 15 B4
Somoto, Nic. 60 D2
Somport, Puerto de, Spain 14 E3
Soná, Panama 60 E3
Sóndrio, Italy 14 C8
Sonepur, India ... 29 J13
Sønderborg, Denmark . 7 J13
Sóndrio, Italy 14 C8
Sonepur, India ... 29 J13
Song Cau, Vietnam ... 26 B3
Songea, Tanzania ... 36 G7
Songhua Jiang →, China 25 B8
Songkhla, Thailand ... 26 C2
Songo, Mozam. 37 H6
Songo, Sudan 35 G10
Songpan, China ... 24 C5
Sonipat, India 28 E10
Sonmiani, Pakistan ... 28 G5
Sono →, Brazil 63 E9
Sonora, Calif., U.S.A. . 57 H3
Sonora, Tex., U.S.A. . 55 K4
Sonora □, Mexico 58 B2
Sonora →, Mexico ... 58 B2
Sonoran Desert, U.S.A. 57 K6
Sonoyta, Mexico 58 A2
Sonsonate, El Salv. ... 60 D2
Sonsorol Is., Pac. Oc. . 27 C8
Soochow = Suzhou, China 25 C7
Sopi, Indonesia 27 D7
Sopot, Poland 13 A10
Sopron, Hungary ... 13 E9
Sør-Rondane, Antarctica 5 D4
Sorel, Canada 48 C5
Sórgono, Italy 16 D3
Soria, Spain 15 B4
Sorkh, Kuh-e, Iran ... 31 C8
Soroca, Moldova 13 D15
Sorocaba, Brazil 64 A7
Sorochinsk, Russia ... 18 D9
Soroki = Soroca, Moldova 13 D15
Sorong, Indonesia ... 27 E8
Soroti, Uganda 36 D6
Sørøya, Norway 6 A20
Sørøysundet, Norway . 6 A20
Sorrell, Australia ... 42 G4
Sorsele, Sweden 6 D17
Sorsogon, Phil. 27 B6
Sortavala, Russia ... 18 B5
Sortland, Norway ... 6 B16
Soscumica, L., Canada 48 B4
Sosnogorsk, Russia ... 18 B9
Sosnowiec, Poland ... 13 C10
Sotkamo, Finland ... 6 D23
Soto la Marina →, Mexico 59 C5
Sotuta, Mexico 59 C7
Souanké, Congo 36 D2
Soúdhas, Kólpos, Greece 17 G11
Soufrière, St. Lucia . 61 D7
Sóul, S. Korea 25 C7
Sound, The, U.K. 9 G3
Sources, Mt. aux, Lesotho 37 K5
Soure, Brazil 63 D9
Souris, Man., Canada . 51 D8
Souris, P.E.I., Canada . 49 C7
Souris →, Canada ... 51 D9
Sousa, Brazil 63 E11
Sousse, Tunisia 35 A8
South Africa ■, Africa . 37 L4
South Aulatsivik I., Canada 49 A7
South Australia □, Australia 43 E2
South Baldy, U.S.A. . 57 J10
South Bend, U.S.A. . 52 E2
South Boston, U.S.A. . 53 G6
South Branch, Canada . 49 C8
South Brook, Canada . 49 C8
South C., Australia ... 38 F7
South Carolina □, U.S.A. 53 J5
South Charleston, U.S.A. 52 F5
South China Sea, Asia . 26 C4
South Dakota □, U.S.A. 54 C5
South Downs, U.K. ... 9 G7
South East C., Australia 42 G4
South East Is., Australia 41 F3
South Foreland, U.K. . 9 F9
South Fork Grand →, U.S.A. 54 C3
South Fork Republican →, U.S.A. 54 E4
South Georgia, Antarctica 64 G9
South Gloucestershire □, U.K. 9 F5
South Haven, U.S.A. . 52 D2
South Henik, L., Canada 51 A9
South Honshu Ridge, Pac. Oc. 44 E6
South Horr, Kenya ... 36 D7
South I., N.Z. 39 L3
South Indian Lake, Canada 51 B9

South Invercargill, N.Z. 39 M2
South Knife →, Canada 51 B10
South Korea ■, Asia . 25 C7
South Lake Tahoe, U.S.A. 56 G3
South Loup →, U.S.A. 54 E5
South Magnetic Pole, Antarctica 5 C9
South Milwaukee, U.S.A. 52 D2
South Molton, U.K. ... 9 F4
South Moose L., Canada 51 C8
South Nahanni →, Canada 50 A4
South Natuna Is. = Natuna Selatan, Kepulauan, Indonesia 26 D3
South Negril Pt., Jamaica 60 C4
South Orkney Is., Antarctica 5 C18
South Ossetia □, Georgia 19 F7
South Pagai, I. = Pagai Selatan, Pulau, Indonesia 26 E2
South Pittsburg, U.S.A. 53 H3
South Platte →, U.S.A. 54 E4
South Pole, Antarctica . 5 E
South Porcupine, Canada 48 C3
South Portland, U.S.A. 53 D10
South River, Canada . 48 C4
South Ronaldsay, U.K. 10 B5
South Sandwich Is., Antarctica 5 B1
South Saskatchewan →, Canada 51 C7
South Seal →, Canada 51 B9
South Shetland Is., Antarctica 5 C18
South Shields, U.K. . 8 C6
South Sioux City, U.S.A. 54 D6
South Taranaki Bight, N.Z. 39 H5
South Thompson →, Canada 50 C4
South Twin I., Canada . 48 B4
South Tyne →, U.K. . 8 C5
South Uist, U.K. 10 C3
South West Africa = Namibia ■, Africa . 37 J3
South West C., Australia 42 G4
South West Rocks, Australia 43 E5
South Yorkshire □, U.K. 8 D6
Southampton, Canada . 48 D3
Southampton, U.K. .. 9 G6
Southampton, U.S.A. . 52 E9
Southampton □, U.K. . 9 G6
Southampton I., Canada 47 B11
Southaven, U.S.A. ... 55 H9
Southbank, Canada .. 50 C3
Southbridge, N.Z. 39 K4
Southend, Canada ... 51 B8
Southend-on-Sea, U.K. 9 F8
Southend-on-Sea □, U.K. 9 F8
Southern Alps, N.Z. . 39 K3
Southern Cross, Australia 41 F2
Southern Indian L., Canada 51 B9
Southern Ocean, Antarctica 5 C6
Southern Pines, U.S.A. 53 H6
Southern Uplands, U.K. 10 D5
Southland □, N.Z. ... 39 L1
Southport, Australia .. 43 D5
Southport, U.K. 8 D4
Southport, U.S.A. ... 53 K3
Southwest C., N.Z. ... 39 M1
Southwold, U.K. 9 E9
Sovetsk, Kaliningd., Russia 7 J19
Sovetsk, Kirov, Russia . 18 C8
Sovetskaya Gavan = Vanino, Russia ... 21 E15
Soweto, S. Africa ... 37 K5
Sōya-Kaikyō = La Perouse Str., Asia . 22 B11
Sōya-Misaki, Japan .. 22 B10
Sozh →, Belarus ... 13 B16
Spa, Belgium 11 D5
Spain ■, Europe ... 15 B4
Spalding, Australia .. 43 E2
Spalding, U.K. 8 E7
Spanish, Canada ... 48 C3
Spanish Fork, U.S.A. . 56 F8
Spanish Town, Jamaica 60 C4
Sparks, U.S.A. 56 G4
Sparta = Spárti, Greece 17 F10
Sparta, Mich., U.S.A. . 52 D3
Sparta, Wis., U.S.A. . 54 D9
Spartanburg, U.S.A. . 53 H5
Spárti, Greece 17 F10
Spartivento, C., Calabria, Italy 16 F7
Spartivento, C., Sard., Italy 16 E3
Sparwood, Canada .. 50 D6
Spassk Dalniy, Russia . 21 E14

Spátha, Ákra, Greece .. 17 G10
Spatsizi →, Canada .. 50 B3
Spatsizi Plateau Wilderness Park, Canada 50 B3
Spearfish, U.S.A. 54 C3
Spearman, U.S.A. ... 55 G4
Speightstown, Barbados 61 D8
Spencer, Idaho, U.S.A. 56 D7
Spencer, Iowa, U.S.A. 54 D7
Spencer, Nebr., U.S.A. 54 D5
Spencer, C., Australia . 43 F2
Spencer G., Australia . 43 E2
Spences Bridge, Canada 50 C4
Spennymoor, U.K. ... 8 C6
Spenser Mts., N.Z. ... 39 K4
Spey →, U.K. 10 C5
Speyer, Germany ... 12 D5
Spirit River, Canada .. 50 B5
Spiritwood, Canada .. 51 C7
Spithead, U.K. 9 G6
Spitzbergen = Svalbard, Arctic 4 B8
Spjelkavik, Norway ... 7 E12
Split, Croatia 16 C7
Split L., Canada 51 B9
Split Lake, Canada ... 51 B9
Spofford, U.S.A. 55 L4
Spokane, U.S.A. 56 C5
Spoleto, Italy 16 C5
Spooner, U.S.A. 54 C9
Sporyy Navolok, Mys, Russia 20 B7
Sprague, U.S.A. 56 C5
Spratly I., S. China Sea 26 C4
Spratly Is., S. China Sea 26 C4
Spray, U.S.A. 56 D4
Spree →, Germany .. 12 B7
Sprengisandur, Iceland 6 D5
Spring Creek, U.S.A. . 56 F6
Spring Hill, U.S.A. ... 53 L4
Spring Mts., U.S.A. ... 57 H6
Springdale, Canada .. 49 C8
Springdale, U.S.A. ... 55 G7
Springer, U.S.A. 55 G2
Springerville, U.S.A. . 57 J9
Springfield, Canada .. 48 D4
Springfield, Colo., U.S.A. 55 G3
Springfield, Ill., U.S.A. 54 F10
Springfield, Mass., U.S.A. 52 D9
Springfield, Mo., U.S.A. 55 G8
Springfield, Ohio, U.S.A. 52 F4
Springfield, Oreg., U.S.A. 56 D2
Springfield, Tenn., U.S.A. 53 G2
Springfield, Vt., U.S.A. 52 D9
Springhill, Canada .. 49 C7
Springhill, U.S.A. ... 55 J8
Springhouse, Canada . 50 C4
Springs, S. Africa ... 37 K5
Springsure, Australia . 42 C4
Springville, U.S.A. ... 56 F8
Spur, U.S.A. 55 J4
Spurn Hd., U.K. 8 D8
Spuzzum, Canada ... 50 D4
Squamish, Canada ... 50 D4
Square Islands, Canada 49 B8
Squires, Mt., Australia 41 E4
Srbija = Serbia □, Yugoslavia 17 C9
Sre Ambel, Cambodia . 26 B2
Sre Umbell = Sre Ambel, Cambodia .. 26 B2
Srebrenica, Bos.-H. .. 17 B8
Sredinny Ra. = Sredinnyy Khrebet, Russia 21 D16
Sredinnyy Khrebet, Russia 21 D16
Srednekolymsk, Russia 21 C16
Śrem, Poland 13 B9
Sremska Mitrovica, Serbia, Yug. 17 B8
Srepok →, Cambodia 26 B3
Sretensk, Russia ... 21 D12
Sri Lanka ■, Asia ... 28 R12
Srikakulam, India ... 29 K13
Srinagar, India 28 B9
Staaten →, Australia . 42 B3
Stade, Germany ... 12 B5
Stadskanaal, Neths. .. 11 A6
Stafford, U.K. 8 E5
Stafford, U.S.A. 55 G5
Staffordshire □, U.K. . 8 E5
Staines, U.K. 9 F7
Stakhanov, Ukraine .. 19 E6
Stalingrad = Volgograd, Russia 19 E7
Staliniri = Tskhinvali, Georgia 19 F7
Stalino = Donetsk, Ukraine 19 E6
Stalinogorsk = Novomoskovsk, Russia 18 D6
Stalowa Wola, Poland . 13 C12
Stalybridge, U.K. ... 8 D5
Stamford, Australia .. 42 C3
Stamford, U.K. 9 E7
Stamford, Conn., U.S.A. 52 E9
Stamford, Tex., U.S.A. 55 J5

Stamps, U.S.A. 55 J8
Standish, U.S.A. 52 D4
Stanford, U.S.A. 56 C8
Stanislav = Ivano-Frankivsk, Ukraine .. 13 D13
Stanke Dimitrov, Bulgaria 17 C10
Stanley, Canada 51 B8
Stanley, Falk. Is. 64 G5
Stanley, U.K. 8 C6
Stanley, Idaho, U.S.A. 56 D6
Stanley, N. Dak., U.S.A. 54 A3
Stanovoy Khrebet, Russia 21 D13
Stanovoy Ra. = Stanovoy Khrebet, Russia 21 D13
Stansmore Ra., Australia 40 D4
Stanthorpe, Australia . 43 D5
Stanton, U.S.A. 55 J4
Staples, U.S.A. 54 B7
Star City, Canada ... 51 C8
Stara Planina, Bulgaria 17 C10
Stara Zagora, Bulgaria 17 C11
Starachowice, Poland . 13 C11
Staraya Russa, Russia . 18 C5
Staraya Russa, Russia . 18 C5
Starbuck I., Kiribati .. 45 H12
Stargard Szczeciński, Poland 12 B8
Staritsa, Russia 18 C5
Starke, U.S.A. 53 L4
Starogard Gdański, Poland 13 B10
Starokonstantinov = Starokonstyantyniv, Ukraine 13 D14
Starokonstyantyniv, Ukraine 13 D14
Start Pt., U.K. 9 G4
Staryy Chartoriysk, Ukraine 13 C13
Staryy Oskol, Russia . 19 D6
State College, U.S.A. . 52 E7
Staten, I. = Estados, I. de Los, Argentina . 64 G4
Statesboro, U.S.A. ... 53 J5
Statesville, U.S.A. ... 53 H5
Staunton, Ill., U.S.A. . 54 F10
Staunton, Va., U.S.A. . 52 F6
Stavanger, Norway .. 7 G11
Staveley, N.Z. 39 K3
Stavelot, Belgium ... 11 D5
Stavern, Norway ... 7 G14
Stavoren, Neths. 11 B5
Stavropol, Russia ... 19 E7
Stawell, Australia ... 43 F3
Stawell →, Australia . 42 C3
Stayton, U.S.A. 56 D2
Steamboat Springs, U.S.A. 56 F10
Steele, U.S.A. 54 B5
Steelton, U.S.A. 52 E7
Steen River, Canada . 50 B5
Steenkool = Bintuni, Indonesia 27 E8
Steens Mt., U.S.A. ... 56 E4
Steenwijk, Neths. ... 11 B6
Steep Pt., Australia .. 41 E1
Steep Rock, Canada . 51 C9
Stefanie L. = Chew Bahir, Ethiopia 32 G2
Stefansson Bay, Antarctica 5 C5
Steiermark □, Austria . 12 E8
Steinbach, Canada ... 51 D9
Steinkjer, Norway ... 6 D14
Stellarton, Canada ... 49 C7
Stendal, Germany ... 12 B6
Steornabhaigh = Stornoway, U.K. ... 10 B3
Stepanakert = Xankändi, Azerbaijan 19 G8
Stephens Creek, Australia 43 E3
Stephens I., Canada .. 50 C2
Stephens L., Canada . 51 B9
Stephenville, Canada . 49 C8
Stephenville, U.S.A. . 55 J5
Stepnoi = Elista, Russia 19 E7
Sterling, Colo., U.S.A. 54 E3
Sterling, Ill., U.S.A. . 54 E10
Sterling, Kans., U.S.A. 54 F5
Sterling City, U.S.A. . 55 K4
Sterling Heights, U.S.A. 52 D4
Sterlitamak, Russia .. 18 D10
Stettin = Szczecin, Poland 12 B8
Stettiner Haff, Germany 12 B8
Stettler, Canada 50 C6
Steubenville, U.S.A. . 52 E5
Stevenage, U.K. 9 F7
Stevens Point, U.S.A. . 54 C10
Stevenson L., Canada . 51 C9
Stewart, B.C., Canada . 50 B3
Stewart, C., Australia . 42 A1
Stewart, I., Chile ... 64 G2
Stewart I., N.Z. 39 M1
Stewartville, U.S.A. .. 54 D8
Stewiacke, Canada .. 49 C7
Steyr, Austria 12 D8

Stigler, U.S.A. 55 H7
Stikine →, Canada .. 50 B2
Stillwater, N.Z. 39 K3
Stillwater, Minn., U.S.A. 54 C8
Stillwater, Okla., U.S.A. 55 G6
Stillwater Range, U.S.A. 56 G4
Stilwell, U.S.A. 55 H7
Stirling, U.K. 10 C5
Stirling Ra., Australia . 41 F2
Stjernøya, Norway ... 6 A20
Stjørdalshalsen, Norway 6 E14
Stockerau, Austria ... 12 D9
Stockholm, Sweden .. 7 G18
Stockport, U.K. 8 D5
Stocksbridge, U.K. .. 8 D6
Stockton, Calif., U.S.A. 57 H3
Stockton, Kans., U.S.A. 54 F5
Stockton, Mo., U.S.A. . 55 G8
Stockton-on-Tees, U.K. 8 C6
Stockton-on-Tees □, U.K. 8 C6
Stockton Plateau, U.S.A. 55 K3
Stoeng Treng, Cambodia 26 B3
Stoke-on-Trent, U.K. . 8 D5
Stoke-on-Trent □, U.K. 8 D5
Stokes Pt., Australia .. 42 G3
Stokes Ra., Australia . 40 C5
Stokksnes, Iceland .. 6 D6
Stokmarknes, Norway . 6 B16
Stolac, Bos.-H. 17 C7
Stolbovoy, Ostrov, Russia 21 B14
Stolbtsy = Stowbtsy, Belarus 13 B14
Stolin, Belarus 13 C14
Stone, U.K. 8 E5
Stonehaven, U.K. ... 10 C5
Stonehenge, Australia . 42 C3
Stonehenge, U.K. ... 9 F6
Stonewall, Canada ... 51 C9
Stony L., Canada ... 51 B9
Stony Rapids, Canada . 51 B7
Stony Tunguska = Tunguska, Podkamennaya →, Russia 21 C10
Stora Lulevatten, Sweden 6 C18
Storavan, Sweden ... 6 D18
Stord, Norway 7 G11
Store Bælt, Denmark . 7 J14
Storm B., Australia ... 42 G4
Storm Lake, U.S.A. .. 54 D7
Stormberge, S. Africa . 37 L5
Stornoway, U.K. 10 B3
Storozhinets = Storozhynets, Ukraine 13 D13
Storozhynets, Ukraine . 13 D13
Storsjön, Sweden ... 6 E16
Storuman, Sweden ... 6 D17
Storuman, sjö, Sweden 6 D17
Stoughton, Canada .. 51 D8
Stour →, Dorset, U.K. 9 G6
Stour →, Kent, U.K. . 9 F9
Stour →, Suffolk, U.K. 9 F9
Stourbridge, U.K. ... 9 E5
Stout L., Canada ... 51 C10
Stowbtsy, Belarus ... 13 B14
Stowmarket, U.K. ... 9 E9
Strahan, Australia ... 42 G4
Stralsund, Germany .. 12 A7
Stranda, Møre og Romsdal, Norway 7 E12
Stranda, Nord-Trøndelag, Norway 6 E14
Stranraer, U.K. 10 D4
Strasbourg, Canada .. 51 C8
Strasbourg, France .. 14 B7
Stratford, Canada ... 48 D3
Stratford, N.Z. 39 H5
Stratford, U.S.A. 55 G3
Stratford-upon-Avon, U.K. 9 E6
Strathalbyn, Australia . 43 F2
Strathcona Prov. Park, Canada 50 D3
Strathmore, Canada . 50 C6
Strathnaver, Canada . 50 C4
Strathroy, Canada ... 48 D3
Straubing, Germany . 12 D7
Straumnes, Iceland .. 6 C2
Strawberry →, U.S.A. 56 F8
Streaky B., Australia . 43 E1
Streaky Bay, Australia . 43 E1
Streator, U.S.A. 54 E10
Strelka, Russia 21 D10
Streymoy, Færoe Is. . 6 E9
Strezhevoy, Russia .. 20 C8
Strimón →, Greece .. 17 D10
Strimonikós Kólpos, Greece 17 D11
Strómboli, Italy 16 E6
Stromsburg, U.S.A. .. 54 E6
Strömstad, Sweden .. 7 G14
Strömsund, Sweden . 6 E16
Stronsay, U.K. 10 B5
Stroud, U.K. 9 F5
Stroud Road, Australia 43 E5
Struer, Denmark ... 7 H13
Strumica, Macedonia . 17 D10

Struthers, Canada 48 C2
Stryker, U.S.A. 56 B6
Stryy, Ukraine 13 D12
Stuart, Fla., U.S.A. .. 53 M5
Stuart, Nebr., U.S.A. . 54 D5
Stuart →, Canada .. 50 C4
Stuart Bluff Ra., Australia 40 D5
Stuart L., Canada ... 50 C4
Stuart Ra., Australia . 43 D1
Stull L., Canada ... 48 B1
Stung Treng = Stoeng Treng, Cambodia .. 26 B3
Stupart →, Canada .. 48 A1
Sturgeon B., Canada . 51 C9
Sturgeon Bay, U.S.A. . 52 C2
Sturgeon Falls, Canada 48 C4
Sturgeon L., Alta., Canada 50 B5
Sturgeon L., Ont., Canada 48 C1
Sturgis, Canada 51 C8
Sturgis, Mich., U.S.A. . 52 E3
Sturgis, S. Dak., U.S.A. 54 C3
Sturt Cr. →, Australia 40 C4
Stuttgart, Germany .. 12 D5
Stuttgart, U.S.A. 55 H9
Stykkishólmur, Iceland 6 D2
Styria = Steiermark □, Austria 12 E8
Suakin, Sudan 35 E13
Suaqui, Mexico 58 B3
Subang, Indonesia ... 27 G12
Subansiri →, India .. 29 F18
Subayhah, Si. Arabia . 30 D3
Subi, Indonesia 26 D3
Subotica, Serbia, Yug. . 17 A8
Suceava, Romania ... 13 E14
Suchan, Russia 22 C6
Suchitoto, El Salv. ... 60 D2
Suchou = Suzhou, China 25 C7
Süchow = Xuzhou, China 25 C6
Sucre, Bolivia 62 G5
Sucuriú →, Brazil ... 63 H8
Sud, Pte. du, Canada . 49 C7
Sud-Ouest, Pte. du, Canada 49 C7
Sudan, U.S.A. 55 H3
Sudan ■, Africa ... 35 E11
Sudbury, Canada ... 48 C3
Sudbury, U.K. 9 E8
Sûdd, Sudan 35 G12
Sudeten Mts. = Sudety, Europe 13 C9
Sudety, Europe 13 C9
Suðuroy, Færoe Is. . 6 F9
Sudirman, Pegunungan, Indonesia 27 E9
Sueca, Spain 15 C5
Suemez I., U.S.A. ... 50 B2
Suez = El Suweis, Egypt 35 C12
Suez, G. of = Suweis, Khalîg el, Egypt ... 35 C12
Suez Canal = Suweis, Qanâ es, Egypt ... 35 B12
Suffield, Canada ... 50 C6
Suffolk, U.S.A. 52 G7
Suffolk □, U.K. ... 9 E9
Sugluk = Salluit, Canada 47 B12
Şuḥār, Oman 31 E8
Suhl, Germany 12 C6
Suihua, China 25 B7
Sukabumi, Indonesia . 27 G12
Sukadana, Indonesia . 26 E3
Sukagawa, Japan ... 23 F10
Sukaraja, Indonesia . 26 E4
Sukarnapura = Jayapura, Indonesia . 27 E10
Sukhona →, Russia .. 18 C6
Sukhumi = Sokhumi, Georgia 19 F7
Sukkur, Pakistan ... 28 F6
Sukkur Barrage, Pakistan 28 F6
Sukumo, Japan 23 H6
Sukunka →, Canada . 50 B4
Sula, Kepulauan, Indonesia 27 E6
Sulaco →, Honduras . 60 C2
Sulaiman Range, Pakistan 28 D6
Sülär, Iran 31 D6
Sulawesi, Indonesia . 27 E6
Sulawesi □, Indonesia 27 E6
Sulawesi Sea = Celebes Sea, Indonesia ... 27 D6
Sulawesi Selatan □, Indonesia 27 E6
Sulawesi Utara □, Indonesia 27 D6
Sulima, S. Leone ... 34 G3
Sulina, Romania ... 13 F15
Sulitjelma, Norway .. 6 C17
Sullana, Peru 62 D2
Sullivan, Ill., U.S.A. . 54 F10
Sullivan, Ind., U.S.A. . 52 F2
Sullivan, Mo., U.S.A. . 54 F9
Sullivan Bay, Canada . 50 C3
Sullivan I. = Lambi Kyun, Burma 26 B1

Sulphur, La., U.S.A. ... 55 K8
Sulphur, Okla., U.S.A. ... 55 H6
Sulphur Pt., Canada . 50 A6
Sulphur Springs, U.S.A. 55 J7
Sultan, Canada 48 C3
Sultanpur, India 29 F13
Sulu Arch., Phil. 27 C6
Sulu Sea, E. Indies ... 27 C6
Suluq, Libya 35 B10
Sulzberger Ice Shelf, Antarctica 5 D10
Sumalata, Indonesia .. 27 D6
Sumatera □, Indonesia 26 D2
Sumatera Barat □, Indonesia 26 E2
Sumatera Utara □, Indonesia 26 D1
Sumatra = Sumatera □, Indonesia 26 D2
Sumba, Indonesia 27 F5
Sumba, Selat, Indonesia 27 F5
Sumbawa, Indonesia .. 26 F5
Sumbawa Besar, Indonesia 26 F5
Sumbawanga □, Tanzania 36 F6
Sumbe, Angola 36 G2
Sumedang, Indonesia . 27 G12
Sumen = Shumen, Bulgaria 17 C12
Sumenep, Indonesia .. 27 G15
Sumgait = Sumqayıt, Azerbaijan 19 F8
Summer L., U.S.A. ... 56 E3
Summerland, Canada . 50 D5
Summerside, Canada . 49 C7
Summersville, U.S.A. . 52 F5
Summerville, Ga., U.S.A. 53 H3
Summerville, S.C., U.S.A. 53 J5
Summit Lake, Canada . 50 C4
Summit Peak, U.S.A. . 57 H10
Sumner, U.S.A. 54 D8
Sumoto, Japan 23 G7
Šumperk, Czech Rep. . 13 D9
Sumqayıt, Azerbaijan . 19 F8
Sumter, U.S.A. 53 J5
Sumy, Ukraine 19 D5
Sun City, U.S.A. 57 K7
Sun City Center, U.S.A. 53 M4
Sun Lakes, U.S.A. 57 K8
Sun Valley, U.S.A. ... 56 E6
Sunagawa, Japan 22 C10
Sunburst, U.S.A. 56 B8
Sunbury, Australia ... 43 F3
Sunbury, U.S.A. 52 E7
Sunda, Selat, Indonesia 26 F3
Sunda Is., Indonesia .. 44 H2
Sunda Str. = Sunda, Selat, Indonesia .. 26 F3
Sundance, Canada ... 51 B10
Sundance, U.S.A. 54 C2
Sundarbans, The, Asia 29 J16
Sundargarh, India ... 29 H14
Sunderland, U.K. 8 C6
Sundre, Canada 50 C6
Sundsvall, Sweden ... 7 E17
Sungai Patani, Malaysia 26 C2
Sungaigerong, Indonesia 26 E2
Sungailiat, Indonesia . 26 E3
Sungaipenuh, Indonesia 26 E2
Sungari = Songhua Jiang →, China 25 B8
Sunghua Chiang = Songhua Jiang →, China 25 B8
Sunland Park, U.S.A. . 57 L10
Sunndalsøra, Norway . 7 E13
Sunnyside, U.S.A. 56 C3
Sunnyvale, U.S.A. ... 57 H2
Suntar, Russia 21 C12
Suomenselkä, Finland . 6 E21
Suomussalmi, Finland . 6 D23
Suoyarvi, Russia 18 B5
Supai, U.S.A. 57 H7
Supaul, India 29 F15
Superior, Ariz., U.S.A. 57 K8
Superior, Mont., U.S.A. 56 C6
Superior, Nebr., U.S.A. 54 E5
Superior, Wis., U.S.A. 54 B8
Superior, L., N. Amer. . 48 C2
Suphan Dağı, Turkey . 30 B4
Supiori, Indonesia ... 27 E9
Süq Suwayq, Si. Arabia 30 E3
Sür, Lebanon 33 B4
Sür, Oman 32 C6
Sur, Pt., U.S.A. 57 H3
Sura →, Russia 18 C8
Surabaja = Surabaya, Indonesia 27 G15
Surabaya, Indonesia .. 27 G15
Surakarta, Indonesia . 27 G14
Surat, Australia 43 D4
Surat, India 28 J8
Suratgarh, India 28 E8
Surat Thani, Thailand . 26 C1
Surgut, Russia 20 C8
Suriapet, India 28 L11
Surigao, Phil. 27 C7
Surinam ■, S. Amer. . 63 C7
Suriname = Surinam ■, S. Amer. 63 C7

Suriname →, Surinam 63 B7
Sürmaq, Iran 31 D7
Surrey □, U.K. 9 F7
Surt, Libya 35 B9
Surt, Khalīj, Libya ... 35 B9
Surtsey, Iceland 6 E3
Suruga-Wan, Japan .. 23 G9
Susaki, Japan 23 H6
Süsangerd, Iran 31 D6
Susanville, U.S.A. ... 56 F3
Susquehanna →, U.S.A. 52 F7
Susques, Argentina .. 64 A3
Sussex, Canada 49 C6
Sussex, E. □, U.K. ... 9 G8
Sussex, W. □, U.K. ... 9 G7
Sustut →, Canada ... 50 B3
Susuman, Russia 21 C15
Susunu, Indonesia ... 27 E8
Susurluk, Turkey 17 E13
Sutherland, S. Africa . 37 L4
Sutherland, U.S.A. ... 54 E4
Sutherland Falls, N.Z. . 39 L1
Sutherlin, U.S.A. 56 E2
Sutlej →, Pakistan .. 28 E7
Sutton, Nebr., U.S.A. . 54 E6
Sutton, W. Va., U.S.A. 52 F5
Sutton →, Canada ... 48 A3
Sutton Coldfield, U.K. . 9 E6
Sutton in Ashfield, U.K. 8 D6
Sutton L., Canada ... 48 B3
Suttor →, Australia .. 42 C4
Suttsu, Japan 22 C10
Suva, Fiji 39 D8
Suva Planina, Serbia, Yug. 17 C10
Suvorov Is. = Suwarrow Is., Cook Is. 45 J11
Suwałki, Poland 13 A12
Suwannee →, U.S.A. . 53 L4
Suwarrow Is., Cook Is. 45 J11
Suwayq aş Şuqban, Iraq 30 D5
Suweis, Khalīg el, Egypt 35 C12
Suweis, Qanâ es, Egypt 35 B12
Suzdal, Russia 18 C7
Suzhou, China 25 C7
Suzu, Japan 23 F8
Suzu-Misaki, Japan .. 23 F8
Suzuka, Japan 23 G8
Svalbard, Arctic 4 B8
Svappavaara, Sweden . 6 C19
Svartisen, Norway ... 6 C15
Svay Rieng, Cambodia 26 B3
Svealand □, Sweden . 7 G16
Sveg, Sweden 7 E16
Svendborg, Denmark . 7 J14
Sverdlovsk = Yekaterinburg, Russia 20 D7
Sverdrup Is., Canada . 4 B3
Svetlaya, Russia 22 A9
Svetlogorsk = Svyetlahorsk, Belarus 13 B15
Svir →, Russia 18 B5
Svishtov, Bulgaria ... 17 C11
Svislach, Belarus 13 B13
Svobodnyy, Russia .. 21 D13
Svolvær, Norway 6 B16
Svyetlahorsk, Belarus . 13 B15
Swabian Alps = Schwäbische Alb, Germany 12 D5
Swainsboro, U.S.A. .. 53 J4
Swakopmund, Namibia 37 J2
Swale →, U.K. 8 C6
Swan →, Australia ... 41 F2
Swan →, Canada 51 C8
Swan Hill, Australia .. 43 F3
Swan Hills, Canada .. 50 C5
Swan Is., W. Indies .. 60 C3
Swan L., Canada 51 C8
Swan Peak, U.S.A. ... 56 C7
Swan Ra., U.S.A. 56 C7
Swan Reach, Australia 43 E2
Swan River, Canada .. 51 C8
Swanage, U.K. 9 G6
Swansea, Australia .. 42 G4
Swansea, U.K. 9 F4
Swansea □, U.K. 9 F3
Swastika, Canada ... 48 C3
Swatow = Shantou, China 25 D6
Swaziland ■, Africa . 37 K6
Sweden ■, Europe .. 7 G16
Sweet Home, U.S.A. . 56 D2
Sweetgrass, U.S.A. .. 56 B8
Sweetwater, Tenn., U.S.A. 53 H3
Sweetwater, Tex., U.S.A. 55 J4
Sweetwater →, U.S.A. 56 E10
Swellendam, S. Africa . 37 L4
Świdnica, Poland ... 13 C9
Świdnik, Poland 13 C12
Świebodzin, Poland .. 12 B8
Świecie, Poland 13 B10
Swift Current, Canada . 51 C7
Swiftcurrent →, Canada 51 C7
Swindon, U.K. 9 F6
Swindon □, U.K. 9 F6
Swinemünde = Świnoujście, Poland . 12 B8
Świnoujście, Poland .. 12 B8

Switzerland ■, Europe 14 C8
Sydney, Australia 43 E5
Sydney, Canada 49 C7
Sydney L., Canada ... 51 C10
Sydney Mines, Canada 49 C7
Sydprøven = Alluitsup Paa, Greenland 4 C5
Sydra, G. of = Surt, Khalīj, Libya 35 B9
Syktyvkar, Russia ... 18 B9
Sylacauga, U.S.A. ... 53 J2
Sylarna, Sweden 6 E15
Sylhet, Bangla. 29 G17
Sylt, Germany 12 A5
Sylvan Lake, Canada . 50 C6
Sylvania, U.S.A. 53 J5
Sylvester, U.S.A. 53 K4
Sym, Russia 20 C9
Symón, Mexico 58 C4
Synnott Ra., Australia . 40 C4
Syracuse, Kans., U.S.A. 55 G4
Syracuse, N.Y., U.S.A. 52 D7
Syracuse, Nebr., U.S.A. 54 E6
Syrdarya →, Kazakstan 20 E7
Syria ■, Asia 30 C3
Syrian Desert = Shām, Bādiyat ash, Asia .. 30 C3
Syzran, Russia 18 D8
Szczecin, Poland 12 B8
Szczecinek, Poland .. 13 B9
Szczeciński, Zalew = Stettiner Haff, Germany 12 B8
Szczytno, Poland 13 B11
Szechwan = Sichuan □, China 24 C5
Szeged, Hungary 13 E11
Székesfehérvár, Hungary 13 E10
Szekszárd, Hungary . 13 E10
Szentes, Hungary ... 13 E11
Szolnok, Hungary ... 13 E11
Szombathely, Hungary 13 E9

Tabacal, Argentina ... 64 A4
Tabaco, Phil. 27 B6
Ţābah, Si. Arabia 30 E4
Ţabas, Khorāsān, Iran . 31 C9
Ţabas, Khorāsān, Iran . 31 C8
Tabasará, Serrania de, Panama 60 E3
Tabasco □, Mexico .. 59 D6
Tābāsīn, Iran 31 D8
Tabatinga, Serra da, Brazil 63 F10
Taber, Canada 50 D6
Tablas I., Phil. 27 B6
Table B. = Tafelbaai, S. Africa 37 L3
Table B., Canada 49 B8
Table Mt., S. Africa .. 37 L3
Table Rock L., U.S.A. . 55 G8
Tabletop, Mt., Australia 42 C4
Tábor, Czech Rep. ... 12 D8
Tabora, Tanzania 36 F6
Tabou, Ivory C. 34 H4
Tabrīz, Iran 30 B5
Tabuaeran, Pac. Oc. . 45 G12
Tabūk, Si. Arabia 30 D3
Tacámbaro de Codallos, Mexico 58 D4
Tacheng, China 24 B3
Tacloban, Phil. 27 B6
Tacna, Peru 62 G4
Tacoma, U.S.A. 56 C2
Tacuarembó, Uruguay . 64 C5
Tademaït, Plateau du, Algeria 34 C6
Tadjoura, Djibouti ... 32 E3
Tadmor, Syria 30 C3
Tadoule, L., Canada .. 51 B9
Tadoussac, Canada .. 49 C6
Tadzhikistan = Tajikistan ■, Asia ... 20 F8
Taegu, S. Korea 25 C7
Taejon, S. Korea 25 C7
Tafalla, Spain 15 A5
Tafelbaai, S. Africa ... 37 L3
Tafermaar, Indonesia . 27 F8
Tafīhān, Iran 31 D7
Tafresh, Iran 31 C6
Taft, Iran 31 D7
Taft, Phil. 27 B7
Taft, U.S.A. 57 J4
Taftān, Kūh-e, Iran .. 31 D9
Taga Dzong, Bhutan . 29 F16
Taganrog, Russia ... 19 E6
Tagbilaran, Phil. 27 C6
Tagish, Canada 50 A2
Tagish L., Canada ... 50 A2
Tagliamento →, Italy . 16 B5
Taguatinga, Brazil ... 63 F10
Tagum, Phil. 27 C7
Tagus = Tejo →, Europe 15 C1
Tahakopa, N.Z. 39 M2
Tahan, Gunong, Malaysia 26 D2
Tahat, Algeria 34 D7
Tāherī, Iran 31 E7
Tahiti, Pac. Oc. 45 J13
Tahlequah, U.S.A. ... 55 H7
Tahoe, L., U.S.A. 56 G3

Tahoe City, U.S.A. ... 56 G3
Tahoka, U.S.A. 55 J4
Tahoua, Niger 34 F7
Tahrūd, Iran 31 D8
Tahsis, Canada 50 D3
Tahta, Egypt 35 C12
Tahulandang, Indonesia 27 D7
Tahuna, Indonesia ... 27 D7
Taibei = T'aipei, Taiwan 25 D7
T'aichung, Taiwan ... 25 D7
Taieri →, N.Z. 39 M3
Taihape, N.Z. 39 H5
Tailem Bend, Australia 43 F2
Taimyr Peninsula = Taymyr, Poluostrov, Russia 21 B11
Tain, U.K. 10 C4
T'ainan, Taiwan 25 D7
Tainaron, Ákra, Greece 17 F10
T'aipei, Taiwan 25 D7
Taiping, Malaysia ... 26 D2
Taitao, Pen. de, Chile . 64 F2
T'aitung, Taiwan 25 D7
Taivalkoski, Finland .. 6 D23
Taiwan ■, Asia 25 D7
Taïyetos Óros, Greece . 17 F10
Taiyiba, Israel 33 C4
Taiyuan, China 25 C6
Taizhong = T'aichung, Taiwan 25 D7
Ta'izz, Yemen 32 E3
Tājābād, Iran 31 D7
Tajikistan ■, Asia ... 20 F8
Tajima, Japan 23 F9
Tajo →, Europe 15 C1
Tajrīsh, Iran 31 C6
Tak, Thailand 26 A1
Takāb, Iran 30 B5
Takachiho, Japan ... 23 H5
Takada, Japan 23 F9
Takahagi, Japan 23 F10
Takaka, N.Z. 39 J4
Takamatsu, Japan ... 23 G7
Takaoka, Japan 23 F8
Takapuna, N.Z. 39 G5
Takasaki, Japan 23 F9
Takatsuki, Japan 23 G7
Takayama, Japan ... 23 F8
Take-Shima, Japan .. 23 J5
Takefu, Japan 23 G8
Takengon, Indonesia . 26 D1
Takeo, Japan 23 H5
Tākestān, Iran 31 C6
Taketa, Japan 23 H5
Takev, Cambodia ... 26 B2
Takikawa, Japan 22 C10
Takla L., Canada 50 B3
Takla Landing, Canada 50 B3
Takla Makan = Taklamakan Shamo, China 24 C3
Taklamakan Shamo, China 24 C3
Taku →, Canada 50 B2
Tal Halāl, Iran 31 D7
Talamanca, Cordillera de, Cent. Amer. 60 E3
Talara, Peru 62 D2
Talas, Kyrgyzstan ... 20 E8
Talâta, Egypt 33 E1
Talaud, Kepulauan, Indonesia 27 D7
Talaud Is. = Talaud, Kepulauan, Indonesia 27 D7
Talavera de la Reina, Spain 15 C3
Talayan, Phil. 27 C6
Talbot, C., Australia .. 40 B4
Talbragar →, Australia 43 E4
Talca, Chile 64 D2
Talcahuano, Chile ... 64 D2
Talcher, India 29 J14
Taldy Kurgan = Taldyqorghan, Kazakstan 20 E8
Taldyqorghan, Kazakstan 20 E8
Tālesh, Iran 31 B6
Tālesh, Kūhhā-ye, Iran . 31 B6
Tali Post, Sudan 35 G12
Taliabu, Indonesia ... 27 E6
Talibon, Phil. 27 B6
Talihina, U.S.A. 55 H7
Taliwang, Indonesia . 26 F5
Tall 'Afar, Iraq 30 B4
Tall Kalakh, Syria ... 33 A5
Talladega, U.S.A. ... 53 J2
Tallahassee, U.S.A. .. 53 K3
Tallangatta, Australia . 43 F4
Tallering Pk., Australia 41 E2
Tallinn, Estonia 7 G21
Tallulah, U.S.A. 55 J9
Taloyoak, Canada ... 46 B10
Talpa de Allende, Mexico 58 C4
Talsi, Latvia 7 H20
Taltal, Chile 64 B2
Taltson →, Canada .. 50 A6
Talurqjuak = Taloyoak, Canada 46 B10
Talwood, Australia .. 43 D4
Talyawalka →, Australia 43 E3
Tama, U.S.A. 54 E8

Tamale, Ghana 34 G5
Tamano, Japan 23 G6
Tamanrasset, Algeria . 34 D7
Tamar →, U.K. 9 G3
Tamashima, Japan .. 23 G6
Tamaulipas □, Mexico 59 C5
Tamaulipas, Sierra de, Mexico 59 C5
Tamazula, Mexico ... 58 C3
Tamazunchale, Mexico 59 C5
Tambacounda, Senegal 34 F3
Tambelan, Kepulauan, Indonesia 26 D3
Tambellup, Australia . 41 F2
Tambo, Australia 42 C4
Tambo de Mora, Peru 62 F3
Tambora, Indonesia .. 26 F5
Tambov, Russia 18 D7
Tambuku, Indonesia . 27 G15
Tâmega →, Portugal . 15 B1
Tamenglong, India .. 29 G18
Tamiahua, L. de, Mexico 59 C5
Tamil Nadu □, India . 28 P10
Tammerfors = Tampere, Finland ... 7 F20
Tammisaari, Finland . 7 F20
Tamo Abu, Pegunungan, Malaysia 26 D5
Tampa, U.S.A. 53 M4
Tampa B., U.S.A. 53 M4
Tampere, Finland ... 7 F20
Tampico, Mexico ... 59 C5
Tamu, Burma 29 G19
Tamworth, Australia . 43 E5
Tamworth, U.K. 9 E6
Tan-Tan, Morocco ... 34 C3
Tana →, Kenya 36 E8
Tana →, Norway 6 A23
Tana, L., Ethiopia ... 32 E2
Tanabe, Japan 23 H7
Tanafjorden, Norway . 6 A23
Tanahbala, Indonesia . 26 E1
Tanahgrogot, Indonesia 26 E5
Tanahjampea, Indonesia 27 F6
Tanahmasa, Indonesia 26 E1
Tanahmerah, Indonesia 27 F10
Tanakura, Japan 23 F10
Tanami, Australia ... 40 C4
Tanami Desert, Australia 40 C5
Tanana, U.S.A. 46 B4
Tananarive = Antananarivo, Madag. 37 H9
Tánaro →, Italy 14 D8
Tandag, Phil. 27 C7
Tandil, Argentina ... 64 D5
Tando Adam, Pakistan 28 G3
Tandou L., Australia . 43 E3
Tane-ga-Shima, Japan 23 J5
Taneatua, N.Z. 39 H6
Tanen Tong Dan, Burma 29 L21
Tanezrouft, Algeria .. 34 D6
Tang, Ra's-e, Iran ... 31 E8
Tanga, Tanzania 36 F7
Tanganyika, L., Africa . 36 F6
Tanger = Tangier, Morocco 34 A4
Tangerang, Indonesia 27 G12
Tanggula Shan, China . 24 C4
Tangier, Morocco ... 34 A4
Tangorin, Australia .. 42 C3
Tangshan, China 25 C6
Tanimbar, Kepulauan, Indonesia 27 F8
Tanimbar Is. = Tanimbar, Kepulauan, Indonesia 27 F8
Tanjay, Phil. 27 C6
Tanjore = Thanjavur, India 28 P11
Tanjung, Indonesia .. 26 E5
Tanjungbalai, Indonesia 26 D1
Tanjungbatu, Indonesia 26 D5
Tanjungkarang Telukbetung, Indonesia 26 F3
Tanjungpandan, Indonesia 26 E3
Tanjungpinang, Indonesia 26 D2
Tanjungredeb, Indonesia 26 D5
Tanjungselor, Indonesia 26 D5
Tannu-Ola, Russia ... 21 D10
Tannum Sands, Australia 42 C5
Tanout, Niger 34 F7
Tanta, Egypt 35 B12
Tantoyuca, Mexico .. 59 C5
Tantung = Dandong, China 25 B7
Tanunda, Australia .. 43 E2
Tanzania ■, Africa .. 36 F6
Tanzilla →, Canada .. 50 B2
Taolanaro, Madag. .. 37 K9
Taos, U.S.A. 57 H11
Taoudenni, Mali 34 D5
Tapa, Estonia 7 G21
Tapa Shan = Daba Shan, China 25 C5
Tapachula, Mexico .. 59 E6
Tapajós →, Brazil ... 63 D8
Tapaktuan, Indonesia 26 D1
Tapanahoni →, Surinam 63 C8

Tapanui, N.Z. 39 L2
Tapauá →, Brazil ... 62 E6
Tapeta, Liberia 34 G4
Tapi →, India 28 J8
Tapirapecó, Serra, Venezuela 62 C6
Tapuaenuku, Mt., N.Z. 39 K4
Tapul Group, Phil. ... 27 C6
Tapurucuará, Brazil .. 62 D5
Taqtaq, Iraq 30 C5
Taquari →, Brazil ... 62 G7
Tara, Australia 43 D5
Tara, Russia 20 D8
Tara →, Montenegro, Yug. 17 C8
Tarabagatay, Khrebet, Kazakstan 20 E9
Tarābulus, Lebanon .. 33 A4
Tarābulus, Libya 35 B8
Tarakan, Indonesia .. 26 D5
Tarama-Jima, Japan . 23 M2
Taran, Mys, Russia .. 7 J18
Taranaki □, N.Z. 39 H5
Taranaki, Mt., N.Z. .. 39 H5
Tarancón, Spain 15 B4
Táranto, Italy 16 D7
Táranto, G. di, Italy .. 16 D7
Tarapacá, Colombia .. 62 D5
Tarapoto, Peru 62 E3
Tararua Ra., N.Z. 39 J5
Tarashcha, Ukraine .. 13 D16
Tarauacá, Brazil 62 E4
Tarauacá →, Brazil .. 62 E5
Tarawa, Kiribati 44 G9
Tarawera, N.Z. 39 H6
Tarawera L., N.Z. ... 39 H6
Tarazona, Spain 15 B5
Tarbela Dam, Pakistan 28 B8
Tarboro, U.S.A. 53 H7
Tarcoola, Australia .. 43 E1
Tarcoon, Australia .. 43 E4
Taree, Australia 43 E5
Tarfaya, Morocco ... 34 C3
Târgoviște, Romania . 13 F13
Târgu-Jiu, Romania . 13 F12
Târgu Mureș, Romania 13 E13
Tarif, U.A.E. 31 E7
Tarifa, Spain 15 D3
Tarija, Bolivia 62 H6
Tariku →, Indonesia . 27 E9
Tarim Basin = Tarim Pendi, China 24 B3
Tarim He →, China .. 24 C3
Tarim Pendi, China .. 24 B3
Taritatu →, Indonesia 27 E9
Tarkhankut, Mys, Ukraine 19 E5
Tarko Sale, Russia ... 20 C8
Tarkwa, Ghana 34 G5
Tarlac, Phil. 27 A6
Tarma, Peru 62 F3
Tarn →, France 14 E4
Târnăveni, Romania . 13 E13
Tarnobrzeg, Poland . 13 C11
Tarnów, Poland 13 C11
Tarnowskie Góry, Poland 13 C10
Ţārom, Iran 31 D7
Taroom, Australia .. 43 D4
Taroudannt, Morocco 34 B4
Tarpon Springs, U.S.A. 53 L4
Tarragona, Spain ... 15 B6
Tarraleah, Australia . 42 G4
Tarrasa = Terrassa, Spain 15 B7
Tarshiha = Me'ona, Israel 33 B4
Tarso Emissi, Chad .. 35 D9
Tarsus, Turkey 19 G5
Tartagal, Argentina .. 62 H6
Tartu, Estonia 7 G22
Ţarţūs, Syria 30 C2
Tarumizu, Japan 23 J5
Tarutao, Ko, Thailand 26 C1
Tarutung, Indonesia . 26 D1
Taseko →, Canada .. 50 C4
Tash-Kömür, Kyrgyzstan 20 E8
Tash-Kumyr = Tash-Kömür, Kyrgyzstan . 20 E8
Tashauz = Dashhowuz, Turkmenistan ... 20 E6
Tashi Chho Dzong = Thimphu, Bhutan . 29 F16
Tashk, Daryācheh-ye, Iran 31 D7
Tashkent = Toshkent, Uzbekistan 20 E7
Tashtagol, Russia ... 20 D9
Tasiilaq, Greenland .. 4 C6
Tasikmalaya, Indonesia 27 G13
Tåsjön, Sweden 6 D16
Taskan, Russia 21 C16
Tasman B., N.Z. 39 J4
Tasman Mts., N.Z. .. 39 J4
Tasman Pen., Australia 42 G4
Tasman Sea, Pac. Oc. 38 E9
Tasmania □, Australia . 42 G4
Tassili n'Ajjer, Algeria . 34 C7
Tatabánya, Hungary . 13 E10
Tataouine, Tunisia ... 35 B8
Tatar Republic = Tatarstan □, Russia . 18 C9
Tatarbunary, Ukraine . 13 F15

Tobyl

Tatarsk, *Russia* 20 D8
Tatarstan □, *Russia* 18 C9
Tateyama, *Japan* 23 G9
Tathlina L., *Canada* 50 A5
Tathra, *Australia* 43 F4
Tatinnai L., *Canada* 51 A9
Tatla L., *Canada* 50 C4
Tatnam, C., *Canada* 51 B10
Tatra = Tatry, *Slovak Rep.* 13 D11
Tatry, *Slovak Rep.* 13 D11
Tatshenshini →, *Canada* 50 B1
Tatsuno, *Japan* 23 G7
Tatta, *Pakistan* 28 G5
Tatum, *U.S.A.* 55 J3
Tat'ung = Datong, *China* 25 B6
Tatvan, *Turkey* 19 G7
Taubaté, *Brazil* 64 A7
Tauern, *Austria* 12 E7
Taumarunui, *N.Z.* 39 H5
Taumaturgo, *Brazil* 62 E4
Taungdwingyi, *Burma* 29 J19
Taunggyi, *Burma* 29 J20
Taungup, *Burma* 29 K19
Taungup Taunggya, *Burma* 29 K18
Taunton, *U.K.* 9 F4
Taunton, *U.S.A.* 52 E10
Taunus, *Germany* 12 C5
Taupo, *N.Z.* 39 H6
Taupo, L., *N.Z.* 39 H5
Tauragė, *Lithuania* 7 J20
Tauranga, *N.Z.* 39 G6
Tauranga Harb., *N.Z.* 39 G6
Taureau, Rés., *Canada* 48 C5
Taurianova, *Italy* 16 E7
Taurus Mts. = Toros Dağları, *Turkey* 19 G5
Tavda, *Russia* 20 D7
Tavda →, *Russia* 20 D7
Taveuni, *Fiji* 39 C9
Tavira, *Portugal* 15 D2
Tavistock, *U.K.* 9 G3
Tavoy = Dawei, *Burma* 26 B1
Taw →, *U.K.* 9 F3
Tawas City, *U.S.A.* 52 C4
Tawau, *Malaysia* 26 D5
Tawitawi, *Phil.* 27 B6
Taxco de Alarcón, *Mexico* 59 D5
Tay →, *U.K.* 10 C5
Tay, L., *Australia* 41 F3
Tayabamba, *Peru* 62 E3
Taylakova, *Russia* 20 D8
Taylakovy = Taylakova, *Russia* 20 D8
Taylor, *Canada* 50 B4
Taylor, *Nebr., U.S.A.* 54 E5
Taylor, *Tex., U.S.A.* 55 K6
Taylor, Mt., *U.S.A.* 57 J10
Taylorville, *U.S.A.* 54 F10
Taymā, *Si. Arabia* 30 E3
Taymyr, Oz., *Russia* 21 B11
Taymyr, Poluostrov, *Russia* 21 B11
Tayshet, *Russia* 21 D10
Taytay, *Phil.* 27 B5
Taz →, *Russia* 20 C8
Taza, *Morocco* 34 B5
Tāzah Khurmātū, *Iraq* 30 C5
Tazawa-Ko, *Japan* 22 E10
Tazin, *Canada* 51 B7
Tazin L., *Canada* 51 B7
Tazovskiy, *Russia* 20 C8
Tbilisi, *Georgia* 19 F7
Tchad = Chad ■, *Africa* 35 E9
Tchad, L., *Chad* 35 F8
Tch'eng-tou = Chengdu, *China* 24 C5
Tchentlo L., *Canada* 50 B4
Tchibanga, *Gabon* 36 E2
Tch'ong-k'ing = Chongqing, *China* 24 D5
Tczew, *Poland* 13 A10
Te Anau, *N.Z.* 39 L1
Te Anau, L., *N.Z.* 39 L1
Te Aroha, *N.Z.* 39 G5
Te Awamutu, *N.Z.* 39 H5
Te Kuiti, *N.Z.* 39 H5
Te Puke, *N.Z.* 39 G6
Te Waewae B., *N.Z.* 39 M1
Teague, *U.S.A.* 55 K6
Teapa, *Mexico* 59 D6
Tebakang, *Malaysia* 26 D4
Tébessa, *Algeria* 34 A7
Tebicuary →, *Paraguay* 64 B5
Tebingtinggi, *Indonesia* 26 D1
Tebintingii, *Indonesia* 26 E2
Tecate, *Mexico* 58 A1
Tecka, *Argentina* 64 E2
Tecomán, *Mexico* 58 D4
Tecoripa, *Mexico* 58 B3
Tecuala, *Mexico* 58 C3
Tecuci, *Romania* 13 F14
Tecumseh, *Mich., U.S.A.* 52 D4
Tecumseh, *Okla., U.S.A.* 55 H6
Tedzhen = Tejen, *Turkmenistan* 20 F7
Tees →, *U.K.* 8 C6
Tees B., *U.K.* 8 C6
Tefé, *Brazil* 62 D6
Tegal, *Indonesia* 27 G13
Tegid, L. = Bala, L., *U.K.* 8 E4
Tegucigalpa, *Honduras* 60 D2
Tehachapi, *U.S.A.* 57 J4
Tehachapi Mts., *U.S.A.* 57 J4
Tehoru, *Indonesia* 27 E7
Tehrān, *Iran* 31 C6
Tehuacán, *Mexico* 59 D5
Tehuantepec, *Mexico* 59 D5
Tehuantepec, G. de, *Mexico* 59 D5
Tehuantepec, Istmo de, *Mexico* 59 D6
Teifi →, *U.K.* 9 E3
Teign →, *U.K.* 9 G4
Teignmouth, *U.K.* 9 G4
Tejen, *Turkmenistan* 20 F7
Tejen →, *Turkmenistan* 31 B9
Tejo →, *Europe* 15 C1
Tekamah, *U.S.A.* 54 E6
Tekapo, L., *N.Z.* 39 K3
Tekax, *Mexico* 59 C7
Tekeli, *Kazakstan* 20 E8
Tekirdağ, *Turkey* 17 D12
Tekkali, *India* 29 K14
Tekoa, *U.S.A.* 56 C5
Tel Aviv-Yafo, *Israel* 33 C3
Tel Lakhish, *Israel* 33 D3
Tel Megiddo, *Israel* 33 C4
Tela, *Honduras* 60 C2
Telanaipura = Jambi, *Indonesia* 26 E2
Telavi, *Georgia* 19 F8
Telegraph Creek, *Canada* 50 B2
Telekhany = Tsyelyakhany, *Belarus* 13 B13
Telemark, *Norway* 7 G12
Teleng, *Iran* 31 E9
Teles Pires →, *Brazil* 62 E7
Telescope Pk., *U.S.A.* 57 H5
Telfer Mine, *Australia* 40 C3
Telford, *U.K.* 9 E5
Telford and Wrekin □, *U.K.* 8 E5
Telkwa, *Canada* 50 C3
Tell City, *U.S.A.* 52 G2
Tellicherry, *India* 28 P9
Telluride, *U.S.A.* 57 H10
Teloloapán, *Mexico* 59 D5
Telpos Iz, *Russia* 18 B10
Telsen, *Argentina* 64 E3
Telšiai, *Lithuania* 7 H20
Teluk Anson = Teluk Intan, *Malaysia* 26 D2
Teluk Betung = Tanjungkarang Telukbetung, *Indonesia* 26 F3
Teluk Intan, *Malaysia* 26 D2
Telukbutun, *Indonesia* 26 D3
Telukdalem, *Indonesia* 26 D1
Tema, *Ghana* 34 G5
Temax, *Mexico* 59 C7
Tembagapura, *Indonesia* 27 E9
Teme →, *U.K.* 9 E5
Temecula, *U.S.A.* 57 K5
Temerloh, *Malaysia* 26 D2
Teminabuan, *Indonesia* 27 E8
Temir, *Kazakstan* 19 E10
Temirtau, *Kazakstan* 20 D8
Temirtau, *Russia* 20 D9
Temiscamie →, *Canada* 49 B5
Témiscaming, *Canada* 48 C4
Témiscamingue, L., *Canada* 48 C4
Temosachic, *Mexico* 58 B3
Tempe, *U.S.A.* 57 K8
Temple, *U.S.A.* 55 K6
Temple B., *Australia* 42 A3
Templeton →, *Australia* 42 C2
Tempoal, *Mexico* 59 C5
Temuco, *Chile* 64 D2
Temuka, *N.Z.* 39 L3
Tenabo, *Mexico* 59 C6
Tenaha, *U.S.A.* 55 K7
Tenakee Springs, *U.S.A.* 50 B1
Tenali, *India* 29 L12
Tenancingo, *Mexico* 59 D5
Tenango, *Mexico* 59 D5
Tenasserim, *Burma* 26 B1
Tenby, *U.K.* 9 F3
Tenda, Colle di, *France* 14 D7
Tendaho, *Ethiopia* 32 E3
Ténéré, *Niger* 34 E7
Tenerife, *Canary Is.* 34 C2
Tengah □, *Indonesia* 27 E6
Tengah, Kepulauan, *Indonesia* 26 F5
Tengchong, *China* 24 D4
Tenggara □, *Indonesia* 27 E6
Tenggarong, *Indonesia* 26 E5
Tenggol, Pulau, *Malaysia* 26 D2
Tengiz, Ozero, *Kazakstan* 20 D7
Tenkasi, *India* 28 Q10
Tennant Creek, *Australia* 42 B1
Tennessee □, *U.S.A.* 53 H2
Tennessee →, *U.S.A.* 52 G1
Tenom, *Malaysia* 26 C5
Tenosique, *Mexico* 59 D6
Tenryū-Gawa →, *Japan* 23 G8
Tenterden, *U.K.* 9 F8
Tenterfield, *Australia* 43 D5
Teófilo Otoni, *Brazil* 63 G10
Tepa, *Indonesia* 27 F7
Tepalcatepec →, *Mexico* 58 D4
Tepehuanes, *Mexico* 58 B3
Tepetongo, *Mexico* 58 C4
Tepic, *Mexico* 58 C4
Teplice, *Czech Rep.* 12 C7
Tepoca, C., *Mexico* 58 A2
Tequila, *Mexico* 58 C4
Ter →, *Spain* 15 A7
Ter Apel, *Neths.* 11 B7
Teraina, *Kiribati* 45 G11
Téramo, *Italy* 16 C5
Terang, *Australia* 43 F3
Terebovlya, *Ukraine* 13 D13
Terek →, *Russia* 19 F8
Teresina, *Brazil* 63 E10
Terewah, L., *Australia* 43 D4
Teridgerie Cr. →, *Australia* 43 E4
Termez = Termiz, *Uzbekistan* 20 F7
Términi Imerese, *Italy* 16 F5
Términos, L. de, *Mexico* 59 D6
Termiz, *Uzbekistan* 20 F7
Térmoli, *Italy* 16 C6
Ternate, *Indonesia* 27 D7
Terneuzen, *Neths.* 11 C3
Terney, *Russia* 21 E14
Terni, *Italy* 16 C5
Ternopil, *Ukraine* 13 D13
Ternopol = Ternopil, *Ukraine* 13 D13
Terowie, *Australia* 43 E2
Terra Nova Nat. Park, *Canada* 49 C9
Terrace, *Canada* 50 C3
Terrace Bay, *Canada* 48 C2
Terracina, *Italy* 16 D5
Terralba, *Italy* 16 E3
Terranova = Ólbia, *Italy* 16 D3
Terrassa, *Spain* 15 B7
Terre Haute, *U.S.A.* 52 F2
Terrebonne B., *U.S.A.* 55 L9
Terrell, *U.S.A.* 55 J6
Terrenceville, *Canada* 49 C9
Terry, *U.S.A.* 54 B2
Terschelling, *Neths.* 11 A5
Teruel, *Spain* 15 B5
Tervola, *Finland* 6 C21
Teryaweyna L., *Australia* 43 E3
Teshio, *Japan* 22 B10
Teshio-Gawa →, *Japan* 22 B10
Tesiyn Gol →, *Mongolia* 24 A4
Teslin, *Canada* 50 A2
Teslin →, *Canada* 50 A2
Teslin L., *Canada* 50 A2
Tessalit, *Mali* 34 D6
Test →, *U.K.* 9 G6
Testigos, Is. Las, *Venezuela* 61 D7
Tetachuck L., *Canada* 50 C3
Tetas, Pta., *Chile* 64 A2
Tete, *Mozam.* 37 H6
Teterev →, *Ukraine* 13 C16
Teteven, *Bulgaria* 17 C11
Tethul →, *Canada* 50 A6
Tetiyev, *Ukraine* 13 D15
Teton →, *U.S.A.* 56 C8
Tétouan, *Morocco* 34 A4
Tetovo, *Macedonia* 17 C9
Teuco →, *Argentina* 64 B4
Teulon, *Canada* 51 C9
Teun, *Indonesia* 27 F7
Teutoburger Wald, *Germany* 12 B5
Tevere →, *Italy* 16 D5
Teverya, *Israel* 33 C4
Tewantin, *Australia* 43 D5
Tewkesbury, *U.K.* 9 F5
Texada I., *Canada* 50 D4
Texarkana, *Ark., U.S.A.* 55 J8
Texarkana, *Tex., U.S.A.* 55 J7
Texas, *Australia* 43 D5
Texas □, *U.S.A.* 55 K5
Texas City, *U.S.A.* 55 L7
Texel, *Neths.* 11 A4
Texline, *U.S.A.* 55 G3
Texoma, L., *U.S.A.* 55 J6
Teziutlán, *Mexico* 59 D5
Tezpur, *India* 29 F18
Tezzeron L., *Canada* 50 C4
Tha-anne →, *Canada* 51 A10
Thabana Ntlenyana, *Lesotho* 37 K5
Thabazimbi, *S. Africa* 37 J5
Thādiq, *Si. Arabia* 30 E5
Thailand ■, *Asia* 26 A2
Thailand, G. of, *Asia* 26 B2
Thakhek, *Laos* 26 A2
Thal, *Pakistan* 28 C7
Thala La = Hkakabo Razi, *Burma* 29 E20
Thallon, *Australia* 43 D4
Thames, *N.Z.* 39 G5
Thames →, *Canada* 48 D3
Thames →, *U.K.* 9 F8
Thames Estuary, *U.K.* 9 F8
Thane, *India* 28 K8
Thanet, I. of, *U.K.* 9 F9
Thangool, *Australia* 42 C5
Thanh Pho Ho Chi Minh, *Vietnam* 26 B3
Thanjavur, *India* 28 P11
Thaolinta L., *Canada* 51 A9
Thar Desert, *India* 28 F8
Tharad, *India* 28 G7
Thargomindah, *Australia* 43 D3
Tharrawaddy, *Burma* 29 L19
Tharthār, Mileh, *Iraq* 30 C4
Tharthār, W. ath →, *Iraq* 30 C4
Thásos, *Greece* 17 D11
Thatcher, *Ariz., U.S.A.* 57 K9
Thatcher, *Colo., U.S.A.* 55 G2
Thaton, *Burma* 29 L20
Thaungdut, *Burma* 29 G19
Thayer, *U.S.A.* 55 G9
Thayetmyo, *Burma* 29 K19
Thazi, *Burma* 29 J20
The Alberga →, *Australia* 43 D2
The Bight, *Bahamas* 61 B4
The Coorong, *Australia* 43 F2
The Dalles, *U.S.A.* 56 D3
The English Company's Is., *Australia* 42 A2
The Frome →, *Australia* 43 D2
The Great Divide = Great Dividing Ra., *Australia* 42 C4
The Hague = 's-Gravenhage, *Neths.* 11 B4
The Hamilton →, *Australia* 43 D2
The Macumba →, *Australia* 43 D2
The Neales →, *Australia* 43 D2
The Officer →, *Australia* 41 E5
The Pas, *Canada* 51 C8
The Rock, *Australia* 43 F4
The Salt L., *Australia* 43 E3
The Stevenson →, *Australia* 43 D2
The Warburton →, *Australia* 43 D2
The Woodlands, *U.S.A.* 55 K7
Thebes = Thívai, *Greece* 17 E10
Thebes, *Egypt* 35 C12
Thedford, *U.S.A.* 54 E4
Theebine, *Australia* 43 D5
Thekulthili L., *Canada* 51 A7
Thelon →, *Canada* 51 A8
Theodore, *Australia* 42 C5
Theodore, *Canada* 51 C8
Theodore, *U.S.A.* 53 K1
Theodore Roosevelt National Memorial Park, *U.S.A.* 54 B3
Theodore Roosevelt Res., *U.S.A.* 57 K8
Thermaïkós Kólpos, *Greece* 17 D10
Thermopolis, *U.S.A.* 56 E9
Thermopylae P., *Greece* 17 E10
Thessalon, *Canada* 48 C3
Thessaloníki, *Greece* 17 D10
Thessaloniki, Gulf of = Thermaïkós Kólpos, *Greece* 17 D10
Thetford, *U.K.* 9 E8
Thetford Mines, *Canada* 49 C5
Thevenard, *Australia* 43 E1
Thibodaux, *U.S.A.* 55 L9
Thicket Portage, *Canada* 51 B9
Thief River Falls, *U.S.A.* 54 A6
Thiel Mts., *Antarctica* 5 E16
Thiers, *France* 14 D5
Thiès, *Senegal* 34 F2
Thika, *Kenya* 36 E7
Thikombia, *Fiji* 39 B9
Thimphu, *Bhutan* 29 F16
Thingvallavatn, *Iceland* 6 D3
Thionville, *France* 14 B7
Thíra, *Greece* 17 F11
Third Cataract, *Sudan* 35 E12
Thirsk, *U.K.* 8 C6
Thisted, *Denmark* 7 H13
Thistle I., *Australia* 43 F2
Thívai, *Greece* 17 E10
Thjórsá →, *Iceland* 6 E3
Thlewiaza →, *Man., Canada* 51 B8
Thlewiaza →, *N.W.T., Canada* 51 A10
Thoa →, *Canada* 51 A7
Thoen, *Thailand* 26 A1
Thohoyandou, *S. Africa* 37 J6
Thomas, *U.S.A.* 55 H5
Thomas, L., *Australia* 43 D2
Thomaston, *U.S.A.* 53 J3
Thomasville, *Ala., U.S.A.* 53 K2
Thomasville, *Ga., U.S.A.* 53 K4
Thomasville, *N.C., U.S.A.* 53 H5
Thompson, *Canada* 51 B9
Thompson →, *Canada* 50 C4
Thompson →, *U.S.A.* 54 F8
Thompson Falls, *U.S.A.* 56 C6
Thompson Pk., *U.S.A.* 56 F2
Thompson Springs, *U.S.A.* 57 G9
Thomson, *U.S.A.* 53 J4
Thomson →, *Australia* 42 C3
Thomson's Falls = Nyahururu, *Kenya* 36 D7
Thórisvatn, *Iceland* 6 D4
Thornaby on Tees, *U.K.* 8 C6
Thorne, *U.K.* 8 D7
Thornhill, *Canada* 50 C3
Thórshöfn, *Iceland* 6 C6
Thouin, C., *Australia* 40 D2
Thrace, *Turkey* 17 D12
Three Forks, *U.S.A.* 56 D8
Three Hills, *Canada* 50 C6
Three Hummock I., *Australia* 42 G3
Three Points, C., *Ghana* 34 H5
Three Rivers, *U.S.A.* 55 L5
Three Sisters, *U.S.A.* 56 D3
Three Springs, *Australia* 41 E2
Throssell, L., *Australia* 41 E3
Throssell Ra., *Australia* 40 D3
Thubun Lakes, *Canada* 51 A6
Thuin, *Belgium* 11 D4
Thule = Qaanaaq, *Greenland* 4 B4
Thun, *Switz.* 14 C7
Thunder B., *U.S.A.* 52 C4
Thunder Bay, *Canada* 48 C2
Thung Song, *Thailand* 26 C1
Thunkar, *Bhutan* 29 F17
Thüringer Wald, *Germany* 12 C6
Thurles, *Ireland* 10 E3
Thurrock □, *U.K.* 9 F8
Thursday I., *Australia* 42 A3
Thurso, *Canada* 48 C4
Thurso, *U.K.* 10 B5
Thurston I., *Antarctica* 5 D16
Thutade L., *Canada* 50 B3
Thysville = Mbanza Ngungu, *Dem. Rep. of the Congo* 36 F2
Ti Tree, *Australia* 42 C1
Tian Shan, *Asia* 24 B3
Tianjin, *China* 25 C6
Tianshui, *China* 24 C5
Tiaret, *Algeria* 34 A6
Tiber = Tevere →, *Italy* 16 D5
Tiberias = Teverya, *Israel* 33 C4
Tiberias, L. = Yam Kinneret, *Israel* 33 C4
Tibesti, *Chad* 35 D9
Tibet = Xizang Zizhiqu □, *China* 24 C3
Tibnī, *Syria* 30 C3
Tibooburra, *Australia* 43 D3
Tiburón, I., *Mexico* 58 B2
Ticino →, *Italy* 14 D8
Ticonderoga, *U.S.A.* 52 D9
Ticul, *Mexico* 59 C7
Tidaholm, *Sweden* 7 G15
Tiddim, *Burma* 29 H18
Tidjikja, *Mauritania* 34 E3
Tidore, *Indonesia* 27 D7
Tiel, *Neths.* 11 C5
Tielt, *Belgium* 11 C3
Tien Shan = Tian Shan, *Asia* 24 B3
Tien-tsin = Tianjin, *China* 25 C6
T'ienching = Tianjin, *China* 25 C6
Tienen, *Belgium* 11 D4
Tientsin = Tianjin, *China* 25 C6
Tieri, *Australia* 42 C4
Tierra Amarilla, *U.S.A.* 57 H10
Tierra Colorada, *Mexico* 59 D5
Tierra de Campos, *Spain* 15 A3
Tierra del Fuego, I. Gr. de, *Argentina* 64 G3
Tiétar →, *Spain* 15 C3
Tiffin, *U.S.A.* 52 E4
Tiflis = Tbilisi, *Georgia* 19 F7
Tifton, *U.S.A.* 53 K4
Tifu, *Indonesia* 27 E7
Tighina, *Moldova* 13 E15
Tigil, *Russia* 21 D16
Tignish, *Canada* 49 C7
Tigre →, *Peru* 62 D4
Tigre →, *Venezuela* 62 B6
Tigris = Dijlah, Nahr →, *Asia* 30 D5
Tigyaing, *Burma* 29 H20
Tijuana, *Mexico* 58 A1
Tikal, *Guatemala* 60 C2
Tikamgarh, *India* 28 G11
Tikhoretsk, *Russia* 19 E7
Tikhvin, *Russia* 18 C5
Tikrīt, *Iraq* 30 C4
Tiksi, *Russia* 21 B13
Tilamuta, *Indonesia* 27 D6
Tilburg, *Neths.* 11 C5
Tilbury, *Canada* 48 D3
Tilbury, *U.K.* 9 F8
Tilden, *U.S.A.* 54 D6
Tilichiki, *Russia* 21 C17
Till →, *U.K.* 8 B5
Tillamook, *U.S.A.* 56 D2
Tillsonburg, *Canada* 48 D3
Tílos, *Greece* 17 F12
Tilpa, *Australia* 43 E3
Tilsit = Sovetsk, *Russia* 7 J19
Timagami, L., *Canada* 48 C3
Timanskiy Kryazh, *Russia* 18 A9
Timaru, *N.Z.* 39 L3
Timber Creek, *Australia* 40 C5
Timber Lake, *U.S.A.* 54 C4
Timbuktu = Tombouctou, *Mali* 34 E5
Timimoun, *Algeria* 34 C6
Timirist, Râs, *Mauritania* 34 E2
Timişoara, *Romania* 13 F11
Timmins, *Canada* 48 C3
Timok →, *Serbia, Yug.* 17 B10
Timor, *Indonesia* 27 F7
Timor Sea, *Ind. Oc.* 40 B4
Timor Timur □, *Indonesia* 27 F7
Tin Can Bay, *Australia* 43 D5
Tinaca Pt., *Phil.* 27 C7
Tindal, *Australia* 40 B5
Tindouf, *Algeria* 34 C4
Tingo Maria, *Peru* 62 E3
Tingrela, *Ivory C.* 34 F4
Tinnevelly = Tirunelveli, *India* 28 Q10
Tinogasta, *Argentina* 64 B3
Tínos, *Greece* 17 F11
Tintinara, *Australia* 43 F3
Tioga, *U.S.A.* 54 A3
Tioman, Pulau, *Malaysia* 26 D2
Tipongpani, *India* 29 F19
Tipperary, *Ireland* 10 E2
Tipton, *U.S.A.* 54 E9
Tiptonville, *U.S.A.* 55 G10
Tīrān, *Iran* 31 C6
Tirana = Tiranë, *Albania* 17 D8
Tiranë, *Albania* 17 D8
Tiraspol, *Moldova* 13 E15
Tire, *Turkey* 17 E12
Tirebolu, *Turkey* 19 F6
Tiree, *U.K.* 10 C3
Tîrgovişte = Târgovişte, *Romania* 13 F13
Tîrgu-Jiu = Târgu-Jiu, *Romania* 13 F12
Tîrgu Mureş = Târgu Mureş, *Romania* 13 E13
Tirich Mir, *Pakistan* 28 A7
Tírnavos, *Greece* 17 E10
Tirodi, *India* 28 J11
Tirol □, *Austria* 12 E6
Tirso →, *Italy* 16 E3
Tiruchchirappalli, *India* 28 P11
Tirunelveli, *India* 28 Q10
Tirupati, *India* 28 N11
Tiruppur, *India* 28 P10
Tiruvannamalai, *India* 28 N11
Tisa →, *Serbia, Yug.* 17 B9
Tisdale, *Canada* 51 C8
Tishomingo, *U.S.A.* 55 H6
Tisza = Tisa →, *Serbia, Yug.* 17 B9
Tit-Ary, *Russia* 21 B13
Titicaca, L., *S. Amer.* 62 G5
Titograd = Podgorica, *Montenegro, Yug.* 17 C8
Titule, *Dem. Rep. of the Congo* 36 D5
Titusville, *Fla., U.S.A.* 53 L5
Titusville, *Pa., U.S.A.* 52 E6
Tivaouane, *Senegal* 34 F2
Tiverton, *U.K.* 9 G4
Tívoli, *Italy* 16 D5
Tizi-Ouzou, *Algeria* 34 A6
Tizimín, *Mexico* 59 C7
Tjeggelvas, *Sweden* 6 C17
Tjirebon = Cirebon, *Indonesia* 27 G13
Tjörn, *Sweden* 7 G14
Tlacotalpan, *Mexico* 59 D5
Tlahualilo, *Mexico* 58 B4
Tlaquepaque, *Mexico* 58 C4
Tlaxcala, *Mexico* 59 D5
Tlaxcala □, *Mexico* 59 D5
Tlaxiaco, *Mexico* 59 D5
Tlemcen, *Algeria* 34 B5
Toad →, *Canada* 50 B4
Toad River, *Canada* 50 B3
Toamasina, *Madag.* 37 H9
Toay, *Argentina* 64 D4
Toba, *Japan* 23 G8
Toba, Danau, *Indonesia* 26 D1
Toba Kakar, *Pakistan* 28 D6
Tobago, *W. Indies* 62 A6
Tobelo, *Indonesia* 27 D7
Tobermory, *Canada* 48 C3
Tobermory, *U.K.* 10 C3
Tobi, *Pac. Oc.* 27 D8
Tobin, L., *Australia* 40 D4
Tobin L., *Canada* 51 C8
Toboali, *Indonesia* 26 E3
Tobol →, *Russia* 20 D7
Toboli, *Indonesia* 27 E6
Tobolsk, *Russia* 20 D7
Tobruk = Tubruq, *Libya* 35 B10
Tobyl = Tobol →, *Russia* 20 D7

Tocantinópolis, *Brazil* 63 E9
Tocantins □, *Brazil* 63 F9
Tocantins →, *Brazil* 63 F9
Toccoa, *U.S.A.* 53 H4
Tochigi, *Japan* 23 F9
Tochigi □, *Japan* 23 F9
Tocopilla, *Chile* 62 H4
Tocumwal, *Australia* . . 43 F4
Tocuyo →, *Venezuela* 62 A5
Todd →, *Australia* 42 C2
Todeli, *Indonesia* 27 E6
Todos os Santos, B. de,
Brazil 63 F11
Todos Santos, *Mexico* . 58 C2
Tofield, *Canada* 50 C6
Tofino, *Canada* 50 D3
Tofua, *Tonga* 39 D11
Tōgane, *Japan* 23 G10
Togian, Kepulauan,
Indonesia 27 E6
Togliatti, *Russia* 18 D8
Togo ■, *W. Afr.* 34 G4
Tōhoku □, *Japan* 22 E10
Toinya, *Sudan* 35 G11
Toiyabe Range, *U.S.A.* 56 G5
Tojikiston =
Tajikistan ■, *Asia* . . 20 F8
Tojo, *Indonesia* 27 E6
Tōjō, *Japan* 23 G6
Tok, *U.S.A.* 46 B5
Tok-do, *Japan* 23 F8
Tokachi-Dake, *Japan* . 22 C11
Tokachi-Gawa →,
Japan 22 C11
Tokala, *Indonesia* 27 E6
Tōkamachi, *Japan* 23 F9
Tokanui, *N.Z.* 39 M2
Tokara-Rettō, *Japan* . . 23 K4
Tokarahi, *N.Z.* 39 L3
Tokashiki-Shima, *Japan* 23 L3
Tokat □, *Turkey* 19 F6
Tokelau Is., *Pac. Oc.* . 44 H10
Tokmak, *Kyrgyzstan* . . 20 E8
Toko Ra., *Australia* . . . 42 C2
Tokoro-Gawa →,
Japan 22 B12
Tokuno-Shima, *Japan* . 23 L4
Tokushima, *Japan* 23 G7
Tokushima □, *Japan* . . 23 H7
Tokuyama, *Japan* 23 G5
Tōkyō, *Japan* 23 G9
Tolaga Bay, *N.Z.* 39 H7
Tolbukhin = Dobrich,
Bulgaria 17 C12
Toledo, *Spain* 15 C3
Toledo, *Ohio, U.S.A.* . . 52 E4
Toledo, *Oreg., U.S.A.* . 56 D2
Toledo, *Wash., U.S.A.* . 56 C2
Toledo, Montes de,
Spain 15 C3
Toledo Bend Reservoir,
U.S.A. 55 K8
Tolga, *Australia* 42 B4
Toliara, *Madag.* 37 J8
Tolima, *Colombia* 62 C3
Tolitoli, *Indonesia* 27 D6
Tolo, Teluk, *Indonesia* 27 E6
Toluca, *Mexico* 59 D5
Tom Price, *Australia* . . 40 D2
Tomah, *U.S.A.* 54 D9
Tomahawk, *U.S.A.* . . . 54 C10
Tomakomai, *Japan* . . 22 C10
Tomar, *Portugal* 15 C1
Tomaszów Mazowiecki,
Poland 13 C10
Tomatlán, *Mexico* 58 D3
Tombador, Serra do,
Brazil 62 F7
Tombigbee →, *U.S.A.* . 53 K2
Tombouctou, *Mali* 34 E5
Tombstone, *U.S.A.* . . . 57 L8
Tombua, *Angola* 37 H2
Tomelloso, *Spain* 15 C4
Tomini, *Indonesia* 27 D6
Tomini, Teluk, *Indonesia* 27 E6
Tomkinson Ranges,
Australia 41 E4
Tommot, *Russia* 21 D13
Tomo →, *Colombia* . . 62 B5
Tomsk, *Russia* 20 D9
Tonalá, *Mexico* 59 D6
Tonantins, *Brazil* 62 D5
Tonasket, *U.S.A.* 56 B4
Tonbridge, *U.K.* 9 F8
Tondano, *Indonesia* . . 27 D6
Tone →, *Australia* . . . 41 F2
Tone-Gawa →, *Japan* 23 F9
Tonekābon, *Iran* 31 B6
Tonga ■, *Pac. Oc.* . . . 39 D11
Tonga Trench, *Pac. Oc.* 44 J10
Tongareva, *Cook Is.* . . 45 H12
Tongatapu, *Tonga* . . . 39 E12
Tongchuan, *China* 25 C5
Tongeren, *Belgium* . . . 11 D5
Tonghua, *China* 25 B7
Tongking, G. of =
Tonkin, G. of, *Asia* . 24 E5
Tongling, *China* 25 C6
Tongoy, *Chile* 64 C2
Tongres = Tongeren,
Belgium 11 D5
Tongsa Dzong, *Bhutan* 29 F17
Tongue →, *U.S.A.* . . . 54 B2
Tonj, *Sudan* 35 G11

Tonk, *India* 28 F9
Tonkawa, *U.S.A.* 55 G6
Tonkin, G. of, *Asia* . . . 24 E5
Tonle Sap, *Cambodia* . 26 B2
Tono, *Japan* 22 E10
Tonopah, *U.S.A.* 57 G5
Tonosí, *Panama* 60 E3
Tønsberg, *Norway* . . . 7 G14
Toobanna, *Australia* . . 42 B4
Toodyay, *Australia* . . . 41 F2
Tooele, *U.S.A.* 56 F7
Toompine, *Australia* . . 43 D3
Toora, *Australia* 43 F4
Toora-Khem, *Russia* . 21 D10
Toowoomba, *Australia* 43 D5
Top-ozero, *Russia* . . . 18 A5
Top Springs, *Australia* . 40 C5
Topeka, *U.S.A.* 54 F7
Topley, *Canada* 50 C3
Topock, *U.S.A.* 57 J6
Topol'čany, *Slovak Rep.* 13 D10
Topolobampo, *Mexico* 58 B3
Toppenish, *U.S.A.* 56 C3
Torata, *Peru* 62 G4
Torbalı, *Turkey* 17 E12
Torbat-e Heydārīyeh,
Iran 31 C8
Torbat-e Jām, *Iran* . . . 31 C9
Torbay, *Canada* 49 C9
Torbay □, *U.K.* 9 G4
Torfaen □, *U.K.* 9 F4
Torgau, *Germany* 12 C7
Torhout, *Belgium* 11 C3
Tori-Shima, *Japan* . . . 23 J10
Torin, *Mexico* 58 B2
Torino, *Italy* 14 D7
Torit, *Sudan* 35 H12
Torkamān, *Iran* 30 B5
Tormes →, *Spain* 15 B2
Tornado Mt., *Canada* . 50 D6
Torneå älv →, *Sweden* 6 D21
Torneå = Tornio,
Finland 6 D21
Torneträsk, *Sweden* . . 6 B18
Tornio, *Finland* 6 D21
Tornionjoki →, *Finland* 6 D21
Tornquist, *Argentina* . 64 D4
Toro, Cerro del, *Chile* . 64 B3
Toroníios Kólpos,
Greece 17 D10
Toronto, *Canada* 48 D4
Toronto, *U.S.A.* 52 E5
Toropets, *Russia* 18 C5
Tororo, *Uganda* 36 D6
Toros Dağları, *Turkey* . 19 G5
Torquay, *Australia* . . . 43 F3
Torquay, *U.K.* 9 G4
Torre de Moncorvo,
Portugal 15 B2
Torre del Greco, *Italy* . 16 D6
Torrejón de Ardoz,
Spain 15 B4
Torrelavega, *Spain* . . . 15 A3
Torremolinos, *Spain* . . 15 D3
Torrens, L., *Australia* . 43 E2
Torrens Cr. →,
Australia 42 C4
Torrens Creek, *Australia* 42 C4
Torrent, *Spain* 15 C5
Torreón, *Mexico* 58 B4
Torres, *Mexico* 58 B2
Torres Strait, *Australia* 38 B7
Torres Vedras, *Portugal* 15 C1
Torrevieja, *Spain* 15 D5
Torrey, *U.S.A.* 57 G8
Torridge →, *U.K.* 9 G3
Torrington, *U.S.A.* 54 D2
Tórshavn, *Færoe Is.* . . 6 E9
Tortola, *Virgin Is.* 61 C7
Tortosa, *Spain* 15 B6
Tortosa, C., *Spain* . . . 15 B6
Tortue, I. de la, *Haïti* . 61 B5
Toṛūd, *Iran* 31 C7
Toruń, *Poland* 13 B10
Tosa, *Japan* 23 H6
Tosa-Shimizu, *Japan* . 23 H6
Tosa-Wan, *Japan* 23 H6
Toscana □, *Italy* 16 C4
Toshkent, *Uzbekistan* . 20 E7
Tostado, *Argentina* . . 64 B4
Tosu, *Japan* 23 H5
Totma, *Russia* 18 C7
Totnes, *U.K.* 9 G4
Totness, *Surinam* 63 B7
Totonicapán, *Guatemala* 60 D1
Tottenham, *Australia* . 43 E4
Tottenham, *Canada* . . 48 D4
Tottori, *Japan* 23 G7
Tottori □, *Japan* 23 G7
Toubkal, Djebel,
Morocco 34 B4
Tougan, *Burkina Faso* 34 F5
Touggourt, *Algeria* . . . 34 B7
Toul, *France* 14 B6
Toulon, *France* 14 E6
Toulouse, *France* 14 E4
Toummo, *Niger* 35 D8
Toungoo, *Burma* 29 K20
Touraine, *France* 14 C4
Tourane = Da Nang,
Vietnam 26 A3
Tourcoing, *France* . . . 14 A5

Touriñán, C., *Spain* . . 15 A1
Tournai, *Belgium* 11 D3
Tournon-sur-Rhône,
France 14 D6
Tours, *France* 14 C4
Tousidé, Pic, *Chad* . . . 35 D9
Toussora, Mt., *C.A.R.* . 36 C4
Towada, *Japan* 22 D10
Towada-Ko, *Japan* . . . 22 D10
Towanda, *U.S.A.* 52 E7
Towang, *India* 29 F17
Tower, *U.S.A.* 54 B8
Towerhill Cr. →,
Australia 42 C3
Towner, *U.S.A.* 54 A4
Townsend, *U.S.A.* . . . 56 C8
Townshend I., *Australia* 42 C5
Townsville, *Australia* . 42 B4
Towson, *U.S.A.* 52 F7
Towuti, Danau,
Indonesia 27 E6
Toya-Ko, *Japan* 22 C10
Toyah, *U.S.A.* 23 F8
Toyama, *Japan* 23 F8
Toyama □, *Japan* 23 F8
Toyama-Wan, *Japan* . 23 F8
Toyohashi, *Japan* 23 G8
Toyokawa, *Japan* 23 G8
Toyonaka, *Japan* 23 G7
Toyooka, *Japan* 23 G7
Toyota, *Japan* 23 G8
Tozeur, *Tunisia* 34 B7
Trá Lí = Tralee, *Ireland* 10 E2
Trabzon, *Turkey* 19 F6
Tracadie, *Canada* 49 C7
Tracy, *Calif., U.S.A.* . . 57 H3
Tracy, *Minn., U.S.A.* . . 54 C7
Trafalgar, C., *Spain* . . 15 D2
Trail, *Canada* 50 D5
Trainor L., *Canada* . . . 50 A4
Tralee, *Ireland* 10 E2
Tranås, *Sweden* 7 G16
Trancas, *Argentina* . . 64 B3
Trang, *Thailand* 26 C1
Trangan, *Indonesia* . . 27 F8
Trangie, *Australia* . . . 43 E4
Trani, *Italy* 16 D7
Transantarctic Mts.,
Antarctica 5 E12
Transilvania, *Romania* 13 E12
Transilvanian Alps =
Carpații Meridionali,
Romania 13 F13
Transvaal, S. *Africa* . . 37 K5
Transylvania =
Transilvania, *Romania* 13 E12
Trápani, *Italy* 16 E5
Trapper Pk., *U.S.A.* . . . 56 D6
Traralgon, *Australia* . . 43 F4
Trasimeno, L., *Italy* . . 16 C5
Trat, *Thailand* 26 B2
Traun, *Austria* 12 D8
Travellers L., *Australia* 43 E3
Travemünde, *Germany* 12 B6
Travers, Mt., *N.Z.* 39 K4
Traverse City, *U.S.A.* . 52 C3
Travis, L., *U.S.A.* 55 K5
Travnik, *Bos.-H.* 17 B7
Trébbia →, *Italy* 14 D8
Třebíč, *Czech Rep.* . . . 12 D8
Trebinje, *Bos.-H.* 17 C8
Trebonne, *Australia* . . 42 B4
Tregaron, *U.K.* 9 E4
Tregrosse Is., *Australia* 42 B5
Treherne, *Canada* . . . 51 D9
Treinta y Tres, *Uruguay* 64 C6
Trelew, *Argentina* . . . 64 E3
Trelleborg, *Sweden* . . 7 J15
Tremadog Bay, *U.K.* . . 8 E3
Tremonton, *U.S.A.* . . . 56 F7
Tremp, *Spain* 15 A6
Trenche →, *Canada* . . 48 C5
Trenčín, *Slovak Rep.* . 13 D10
Trenggalek, *Indonesia* . 27 H14
Trenque Lauquen,
Argentina 64 D4
Trent →, *U.K.* 8 D7
Trento, *Italy* 16 A4
Trenton, *Canada* 48 D4
Trenton, *Mo., U.S.A.* . . 54 E8
Trenton, *N.J., U.S.A.* . 52 E8
Trenton, *Nebr., U.S.A.* 54 E4
Trepassey, *Canada* . . 49 C9
Tres Arroyos, *Argentina* 64 D4
Três Corações, *Brazil* . 64 A7
Três Lagoas, *Brazil* . . 63 H8
Tres Marías, Islas,
Mexico 58 C3
Tres Montes, C., *Chile* . 64 F1
Tres Puntas, C.,
Argentina 64 F3
Três Rios, *Brazil* 63 H10
Tres Valles, *Mexico* . . 59 D5
Tresco, *U.K.* 9 H1
Treviso, *Italy* 16 B5
Triabunna, *Australia* . 42 G4
Tribulation, C., *Australia* 42 B4
Tribune, *U.S.A.* 54 F4
Trichinopoly =
Tiruchchirappalli,
India 28 P11
Trichur, *India* 28 P10
Trida, *Australia* 43 E4
Trier, *Germany* 12 D4
Trieste, *Italy* 16 B5

Triglav, *Slovenia* 12 E7
Tríkkala, *Greece* 17 E9
Trikora, Puncak,
Indonesia 27 E9
Trincomalee, *Sri Lanka* 28 Q12
Trindade, *Brazil* 63 G9
Trindade, I., *Atl. Oc.* . . 2 F8
Trinidad, *Bolivia* 62 F6
Trinidad, *Cuba* 60 B4
Trinidad, *Uruguay* . . . 64 C5
Trinidad, *U.S.A.* 55 G2
Trinidad, *W. Indies* . . . 61 D7
Trinidad & Tobago ■,
W. Indies 62 A6
Trinity, *Canada* 49 C9
Trinity, *U.S.A.* 55 K7
Trinity →, *Calif., U.S.A.* 56 F2
Trinity →, *Tex., U.S.A.* 55 L7
Trinity B., *Canada* . . . 49 C9
Trinity Is., *U.S.A.* 46 C4
Trinity Range, *U.S.A.* . 56 F4
Trinkitat, *Sudan* 35 E13
Tripoli = Tarābulus,
Lebanon 33 A4
Tripoli = Tarābulus,
Libya 35 B8
Trípolis, *Greece* 17 F10
Tripolitania, N. *Afr.* . . . 35 B8
Tripura □, *India* 29 H18
Tristan da Cunha,
Atl. Oc. 2 F9
Trivandrum, *India* 28 Q10
Trnava, *Slovak Rep.* . . 13 D9
Trochu, *Canada* 50 C6
Trodely I., *Canada* . . . 48 B4
Troglav, *Croatia* 16 C7
Troilus, L., *Canada* . . . 48 B5
Trois-Pistoles, *Canada* 49 C6
Trois-Rivières, *Canada* . 48 C5
Troitsk, *Russia* 20 D7
Troitsko Pechorsk,
Russia 18 B10
Trölladyngja, *Iceland* . 6 D5
Trollhättan, *Sweden* . . 7 G15
Trollheimen, *Norway* . 6 E13
Trombetas →, *Brazil* . 63 D7
Tromsø, *Norway* 6 B18
Tronador, Mte.,
Argentina 64 E2
Trøndelag, *Norway* . . . 6 D14
Trondheim, *Norway* . . 6 E14
Trondheimsfjorden,
Norway 6 E14
Tropic, *U.S.A.* 57 H7
Trout →, *Canada* 50 A5
Trout L., *N.W.T., Canada* 50 A4
Trout L., *Ont., Canada* 51 C10
Trout Lake, *Canada* . . 50 B6
Trout River, *Canada* . . 49 C8
Trouville-sur-Mer,
France 14 B4
Trowbridge, *U.K.* 9 F5
Troy, *Turkey* 17 E12
Troy, *Ala., U.S.A.* 53 K3
Troy, *Kans., U.S.A.* . . . 54 F7
Troy, *Mo., U.S.A.* 54 F9
Troy, *Mont., U.S.A.* . . 56 B6
Troy, *N.Y., U.S.A.* 52 D9
Troy, *Ohio, U.S.A.* . . . 52 E3
Troyes, *France* 14 B6
Truchas Peak, *U.S.A.* . 55 H2
Trucial States = United
Arab Emirates ■, *Asia* 31 F7
Truckee, *U.S.A.* 56 G3
Trudovoye, *Russia* . . . 22 C6
Trujillo, *Honduras* 60 C2
Trujillo, *Peru* 62 E3
Trujillo, *Spain* 15 C3
Trujillo, *U.S.A.* 55 H2
Trujillo, *Venezuela* . . . 62 B4
Truk, *Micronesia* 44 G7
Trumann, *U.S.A.* 55 H9
Trumbull, Mt., *U.S.A.* . 57 H7
Trundle, *Australia* . . . 43 E4
Truro, *Canada* 49 C7
Truro, *U.K.* 9 G2
Truskavets, *Ukraine* . . 13 D12
Trutch, *Canada* 50 B4
Truth or Consequences,
U.S.A. 57 K10
Trutnov, *Czech Rep.* . . 12 C8
Tsaratanana, *Madag.* . 37 G9
Tsarevo = Michurin,
Bulgaria 17 C12
Tselinograd = Astana,
Kazakhstan 20 D8
Tsetserleg, *Mongolia* . 24 B5
Tshabong, *Botswana* . 37 K4
Tshane, *Botswana* . . . 37 J4
Tshela, Dem. Rep. of
the Congo 36 E2
Tshikapa, Dem. Rep. of
the Congo 36 F4
Tsiigehtchic, *Canada* . 46 B6
Tsimlyansk Res. =
Tsimlyanskoye Vdkhr.,
Russia 19 E7
Tsimlyanskoye Vdkhr.,
Russia 19 E7
Tsinan = Jinan, *China* . 25 C6
Tsinghai = Qinghai □,
China 24 C4
Tsingtao = Qingdao,
China 25 C7

Tskhinvali, *Georgia* . . 19 F7
Tsna →, *Russia* 18 D7
Tsu, *Japan* 23 G8
Tsu L., *Canada* 50 A6
Tsuchiura, *Japan* 23 F10
Tsugaru-Kaikyō, *Japan* 22 D10
Tsumeb, *Namibia* 37 H3
Tsuruga, *Japan* 23 G8
Tsurugi-San, *Japan* . . 23 H7
Tsuruoka, *Japan* 22 E9
Tsushima, *Gifu, Japan* 23 G8
Tsushima, *Nagasaki,*
Japan 23 G4
Tsuyama, *Japan* 23 G7
Tsyelyakhany, *Belarus* 13 B13
Tual, *Indonesia* 27 F8
Tuamotu Arch. =
Tuamotu Is., *Pac. Oc.* 45 J13
Tuamotu Is., *Pac. Oc.* . 45 J13
Tuamotu Ridge, *Pac. Oc.* 45 K14
Tuao, *Phil.* 27 A6
Tuapse, *Russia* 19 F6
Tuatapere, *N.Z.* 39 M1
Tuba City, *U.S.A.* 57 H8
Tuban, *Indonesia* 27 G15
Tubarão, *Brazil* 64 B7
Tūbās, *West Bank* . . . 33 C4
Tübingen, *Germany* . . 12 D5
Tubruq, *Libya* 35 B10
Tubuai Is., *Pac. Oc.* . . 45 K13
Tucacas, *Venezuela* . . 62 A5
Tuchodi →, *Canada* . . 50 B4
Tucson, *U.S.A.* 57 K8
Tucumcari, *U.S.A.* . . . 55 H3
Tucupita, *Venezuela* . . 62 B6
Tucuruí, *Brazil* 63 D9
Tucuruí, Rêprêsa de,
Brazil 63 D9
Tudela, *Spain* 15 A5
Tudmur, *Syria* 30 C3
Tudor, L., *Canada* . . . 49 A6
Tuguegarao, *Phil.* 27 A6
Tugur, *Russia* 21 D14
Tukangbesi, Kepulauan,
Indonesia 27 F6
Tukarak I., *Canada* . . . 48 A4
Tukayyid, *Iraq* 30 D5
Tuktoyaktuk, *Canada* . 46 B6
Tukums, *Latvia* 7 H20
Tukuyu, *Tanzania* 36 F6
Tula, *Hidalgo, Mexico* . 59 C5
Tula, *Tamaulipas,*
Mexico 59 C5
Tula, *Russia* 18 D6
Tulancingo, *Mexico* . . 59 C5
Tulare, *U.S.A.* 57 H4
Tulare Lake Bed, *U.S.A.* 57 J4
Tularosa, *U.S.A.* 57 K10
Tulcán, *Ecuador* 62 C3
Tulcea, *Romania* 13 F15
Tulchyn, *Ukraine* 13 D15
Tūleh, *Iran* 31 C7
Tulemalu L., *Canada* . 51 A9
Tulia, *U.S.A.* 55 H4
Tulita, *Canada* 46 B7
Tulkarm, *West Bank* . . 33 C4
Tullahoma, *U.S.A.* . . . 53 H2
Tullamore, *Australia* . 43 E4
Tullamore, *Ireland* . . . 10 E3
Tulle, *France* 14 D4
Tully, *Australia* 42 B4
Tulsa, *U.S.A.* 55 G7
Tulsequah, *Canada* . . 50 B2
Tulua, *Colombia* 62 C3
Tulun, *Russia* 21 D11
Tulungagung, *Indonesia* 27 H14
Tuma →, *Nic.* 60 D3
Tumaco, *Colombia* . . . 62 C3
Tumatumari, *Guyana* . 62 B7
Tumba, *Sweden* 7 G17
Tumba, L., Dem. Rep. of
the Congo 36 E3
Tumbarumba, *Australia* 43 F4
Tumbes, *Peru* 62 D2
Tumby Bay, *Australia* . 43 E2
Tumeremo, *Venezuela* 62 B6
Tumkur, *India* 28 N10
Tump, *Pakistan* 28 F3
Tumpat, *Malaysia* . . . 26 C2
Tumu, *Ghana* 34 F5
Tumucumaque, Serra,
Brazil 63 C8
Tumut, *Australia* 43 F4
Tumwater, *U.S.A.* 56 C2
Tunas de Zaza, *Cuba* . 60 B4
Tunbridge Wells =
Royal Tunbridge
Wells, *U.K.* 9 F8
Tuncurry-Forster,
Australia 43 E5
Tundzha →, *Bulgaria* 17 C11
Tungabhadra →, *India* 28 M11
Tungla, *Nic.* 60 D3
Tungsten, *Canada* . . . 50 A3
Tunguska,
Nizhnyaya →, *Russia* 21 C9
Tunguska,
Podkamennaya →,
Russia 21 C10
Tunica, *U.S.A.* 55 H9
Tunis, *Tunisia* 35 A8
Tunisia ■, *Africa* 35 A7

Tunja, *Colombia* 62 B4
Tunnsjøen, *Norway* . . 6 D15
Tunungayualok I.,
Canada 49 A7
Tununirusiq = Arctic
Bay, *Canada* 47 A11
Tunuyán →, *Argentina* 64 C3
Tūp Āghāj, *Iran* 30 B5
Tupelo, *U.S.A.* 53 H1
Tupinambaranas, *Brazil* 62 D7
Tupiza, *Bolivia* 62 H5
Tupper, *Canada* 50 B4
Tupper Lake, *U.S.A.* . . 52 C8
Tupungato, Cerro,
S. Amer. 64 C3
Túquerres, *Colombia* . 62 C3
Tura, *Russia* 21 C11
Turabah, *Si. Arabia* . . 30 D4
Tūrān, *Iran* 31 C8
Turan, *Russia* 21 D10
Ţurayf, *Si. Arabia* . . . 30 D3
Turda, *Romania* 13 E12
Turek, *Poland* 13 B10
Turen, *Venezuela* 62 B5
Turfan = Turpan, *China* 24 B3
Turgeon →, *Canada* . 48 C4
Tŭrgovishte, *Bulgaria* . 17 C12
Turgutlu, *Turkey* 17 E12
Turia →, *Spain* 15 C5
Turiaçu, *Brazil* 63 D9
Turiaçu →, *Brazil* 63 D9
Turin = Torino, *Italy* . . 14 D7
Turkana, L., *Africa* . . . 36 D7
Turkestan = Türkistan,
Kazakstan 20 E7
Turkey ■, *Eurasia* . . . 19 G6
Turkey Creek, *Australia* 40 C4
Türkistan, *Kazakstan* . 20 E7
Türkmenbashi,
Turkmenistan 19 G9
Turkmenistan ■, *Asia* 20 F6
Turks & Caicos Is. ■,
W. Indies 61 B5
Turks Island Passage,
W. Indies 61 B5
Turku, *Finland* 7 F20
Turlock, *U.S.A.* 57 H3
Turnagain →, *Canada* 50 B3
Turnagain, C., *N.Z.* . . . 39 J6
Turneffe Is., *Belize* . . . 59 D7
Turner, *U.S.A.* 56 B9
Turner Pt., *Australia* . . 42 A1
Turner Valley, *Canada* 50 C6
Turnhout, *Belgium* . . . 11 C4
Turnor L., *Canada* . . . 51 B7
Türnovo = Veliko
Tŭrnovo, *Bulgaria* . 17 C11
Turnu Măgurele,
Romania 13 G13
Turnu Roşu, P.,
Romania 13 F13
Turpan, *China* 24 B3
Tursāq, *Iraq* 30 C5
Turtle Head I., *Australia* 42 A3
Turtle L., *Canada* 51 C7
Turtle Lake, *U.S.A.* . . . 54 B4
Turtleford, *Canada* . . 51 C7
Turukhansk, *Russia* . . 21 C9
Tuscaloosa, *U.S.A.* . . 53 J2
Tuscany = Toscana □,
Italy 16 C4
Tuscola, *Ill., U.S.A.* . . 52 F1
Tuscola, *Tex., U.S.A.* . 55 J5
Tuscumbia, *U.S.A.* . . . 53 H2
Tuskegee, *U.S.A.* 53 J3
Tuticorin, *India* 28 Q11
Tutóia, *Brazil* 63 D10
Tutong, *Brunei* 26 D4
Tutrakan, *Bulgaria* . . . 17 B12
Tuttle Creek L., *U.S.A.* 54 F6
Tuttlingen, *Germany* . . 12 E5
Tutuala, *Indonesia* . . . 27 F7
Tutuila, *Amer. Samoa* 39 B13
Tutume, *Botswana* . . . 37 J5
Tututepec, *Mexico* . . . 59 D5
Tuva □, *Russia* 21 D10
Tuxpan, *Mexico* 59 C5
Tuxtla Gutiérrez, *Mexico* 59 D6
Tuy = Tui, *Spain* 15 A1
Tuya L., *Canada* 50 B2
Tüysarkān, *Iran* 31 C6
Tuz Gölü, *Turkey* 19 G5
Ţūz Khurmātū, *Iraq* . . 30 C5
Tuzla, *Bos.-H.* 17 B8
Tver, *Russia* 18 C6
Tweed Heads, *Australia* 43 D5
Tweedsmuir Prov. Park,
Canada 50 C3
Twentynine Palms,
U.S.A. 57 J5
Twillingate, *Canada* . . 49 C9
Twin Bridges, *U.S.A.* . 56 D7
Twin Falls, *Canada* . . 49 B7
Twin Falls, *U.S.A.* . . . 56 E6
Twin Valley, *U.S.A.* . . 54 B6
Two Harbors, *U.S.A.* . 54 B9
Two Hills, *Canada* . . . 50 C6
Two Rocks, *Australia* . 41 F2
Twofold B., *Australia* . 43 F4
Tyachiv, *Ukraine* 13 D12
Tychy, *Poland* 13 C10
Tyler, *Minn., U.S.A.* . . 54 C6

Tyler, *Tex., U.S.A.* 55 J7
Tynda, *Russia* 21 D13
Tyndall, *U.S.A.* 54 D6
Tyne ➝, *U.K.* 8 C6
Tyne & Wear □, *U.K.* .. 8 B6
Tynemouth, *U.K.* 8 B6
Tyre = Sūr, *Lebanon* .. 33 B4
Tyrifjorden, *Norway* ... 7 F14
Tyrol = Tirol □, *Austria* 12 E6
Tyrrell ➝, *Australia* ... 43 F3
Tyrrell, L., *Australia* ... 43 F3
Tyrrell L., *Canada* 51 A7
Tyrrhenian Sea,
Medit. S. 16 E5
Tysfjorden, *Norway* .. 6 B17
Tyulgan, *Russia* 18 D10
Tyumen, *Russia* 20 D7
Tywi ➝, *U.K.* 9 F3
Tywyn, *U.K.* 9 E3
Tzaneen, *S. Africa* 37 J6
Tzukong = Zigong,
China 24 D5

U.S.A. = United States
of America ■,
N. Amer. 2 B4
Uatumã ➝, *Brazil* 62 D7
Uaupés, *Brazil* 62 D5
Uaupés ➝, *Brazil* 62 C5
Uaxactún, *Guatemala* . 60 C2
Ubá, *Brazil* 63 H10
Ubaitaba, *Brazil* 63 F11
Ubangi = Oubangi ➝,
*Dem. Rep. of
the Congo* 36 E3
Ubauro, *Pakistan* 28 E6
Ubayyid, W. al ➝, *Iraq* 30 C4
Ube, *Japan* 23 H5
Úbeda, *Spain* 15 C4
Uberaba, *Brazil* 63 G9
Uberlândia, *Brazil* 63 G9
Ubon Ratchathani,
Thailand 26 A2
Ubort ➝, *Belarus* 13 B15
Ubundu, *Dem. Rep. of
the Congo* 36 E5
Ucayali ➝, *Peru* 62 D4
Uchiura-Wan, *Japan* .. 22 C10
Uchquduq, *Uzbekistan* 20 E7
Uchur ➝, *Russia* 21 D14
Ucluelet, *Canada* 50 D3
Uda ➝, *Russia* 21 D14
Udagamandalam, *India* 28 P10
Udaipur, *India* 28 G8
Udaipur Garhi, *Nepal* . 29 F15
Uddevalla, *Sweden* ... 7 G14
Uddjaur, *Sweden* 6 D17
Uden, *Neths.* 11 C5
Udgir, *India* 28 K10
Údine, *Italy* 16 A5
Udmurtia □, *Russia* .. 18 C9
Udon Thani, *Thailand* . 26 A2
Udupi, *India* 28 N9
Ueda, *Japan* 23 F9
Uedineniya, Os., *Russia* 4 B12
Uele ➝, *Dem. Rep. of
the Congo* 36 D4
Uelen, *Russia* 21 C19
Uelzen, *Germany* 12 B6
Ufa, *Russia* 18 D10
Ufa ➝, *Russia* 18 D10
Ugab ➝, *Namibia* 37 J2
Ugalla ➝, *Tanzania* .. 36 F6
Uganda ■, *Africa* 36 D6
Uglegorsk, *Russia* ... 21 E15
Ugljan, *Croatia* 12 F8
Uhrichsville, *U.S.A.* .. 52 E5
Uibhist a Deas = South
Uist, *U.K.* 10 C3
Uibhist a Tuath = North
Uist, *U.K.* 10 C3
Uíge, *Angola* 36 F2
Uinta Mts., *U.S.A.* ... 56 F8
Uitenhage, *S. Africa* .. 37 L5
Uithuizen, *Neths.* 11 A6
Uji-guntō, *Japan* 23 J4
Ujjain, *India* 28 H9
Ujung Pandang,
Indonesia 27 F5
Uka, *Russia* 21 D17
Uke-Shima, *Japan* 23 K4
Ukhrul, *India* 29 G19
Ukhta, *Russia* 18 B9
Ukiah, *U.S.A.* 56 G2
Ukmergė, *Lithuania* .. 7 J21
Ukraine ■, *Europe* ... 19 E5
Ulaanbaatar, *Mongolia* 21 E11
Ulaangom, *Mongolia* . 24 A4
Ulaanjirem, *Mongolia* . 24 B5
Ulan Bator =
Ulaanbaatar,
Mongolia 21 E11
Ulan Ude, *Russia* 21 D11
Ulcinj,
Montenegro, Yug. . 17 D8
Ulefoss, *Norway* 7 G13
Ulhasnagar, *India* 28 K8
Ulithi Atoll, *Pac. Oc.* .. 27 B9

Ulladulla, *Australia* ... 43 F5
Ullapool, *U.K.* 10 C4
Ullswater, *U.K.* 8 C5
Ullŭng-do, *S. Korea* .. 23 F5
Ulm, *Germany* 12 D5
Ulmarra, *Australia* 43 D5
Ulricehamn, *Sweden* . 7 H15
Ulster □, *U.K.* 10 D3
Ulubat Gölü, *Turkey* .. 17 D13
Uludağ, *Turkey* 17 D13
Ulungur He ➝, *China* . 24 B3
Uluru = Ayers Rock,
Australia 41 E5
Uluru Nat. Park,
Australia 41 E5
Ulutau, *Kazakstan* ... 20 E7
Ulverston, *U.K.* 8 C4
Ulverstone, *Australia* . 42 G4
Ulya, *Russia* 21 D15
Ulyanovsk = Simbirsk,
Russia 18 D8
Ulyasutay = Uliastay,
Mongolia 24 B4
Ulysses, *U.S.A.* 55 G4
Umala, *Bolivia* 62 G5
Uman, *Ukraine* 13 D16
Umaria, *India* 29 H12
Umarkot, *Pakistan* ... 28 G6
Umatilla, *U.S.A.* 56 D4
Umba, *Russia* 18 A5
Umbakumba, *Australia* 42 A2
Umbrella Mts., *N.Z.* ... 39 L2
Ume älv ➝, *Sweden* .. 6 E19
Umeå, *Sweden* 6 E19
Umera, *Indonesia* 27 E7
Umlazi, *S. Africa* 37 L6
Umm ad Daraj, J.,
Jordan 33 C4
Umm al Qaywayn,
U.A.E. 31 E7
Umm al Qittayn, *Jordan* 33 C5
Umm Bāb, *Qatar* 31 E6
Umm el Fahm, *Israel* .. 33 C4
Umm Keddada, *Sudan* 35 F11
Umm Lajj, *Si. Arabia* .. 30 E3
Umm Ruwaba, *Sudan* . 35 F12
Umnak I., *U.S.A.* 46 C3
Umniati ➝, *Zimbabwe* 37 H5
Umpqua ➝, *U.S.A.* ... 56 E1
Umtata, *S. Africa* 37 L5
Umuarama, *Brazil* 64 A6
Umzimvubu, *S. Africa* . 37 L5
Una ➝, *Bos.-H.* 12 F9
Unalakleet, *U.S.A.* 46 B3
Unalaska, *U.S.A.* 46 C3
Unalaska I., *U.S.A.* ... 46 C3
'Unayzah, *Si. Arabia* .. 30 E4
'Unāzah, J., *Asia* 30 C3
Uncía, *Bolivia* 62 G5
Uncompahgre Peak,
U.S.A. 57 G10
Uncompahgre Plateau,
U.S.A. 57 G9
Underbool, *Australia* .. 43 F3
Ungarie, *Australia* 43 E4
Ungarra, *Australia* 43 E2
Ungava, Pén. d', *Canada* 47 C12
Ungava B., *Canada* ... 47 C13
Ungeny = Ungheni,
Moldova 13 E14
Ungheni, *Moldova* 13 E14
União da Vitória, *Brazil* 64 B6
Unimak I., *U.S.A.* 46 C3
Union, *Miss., U.S.A.* .. 55 J10
Union, *Mo., U.S.A.* ... 54 F9
Union, *S.C., U.S.A.* ... 53 H5
Union City, *Pa., U.S.A.* 52 E6
Union City, *Tenn.,
U.S.A.* 55 G10
Union Gap, *U.S.A.* 56 C3
Union Springs, *U.S.A.* 53 J3
Uniontown, *U.S.A.* ... 52 F5
Unionville, *U.S.A.* 54 E8
United Arab Emirates ■,
Asia 31 F7
United Kingdom ■,
Europe 10 E6
United States of
America ■, *N. Amer.* 2 B4
United States of
America ■, *N. Amer.* 2 B4
Unity, *Canada* 51 C7
University Park, *U.S.A.* 57 K10
Unnao, *India* 29 F12
Unst, *U.K.* 10 A6
Unuk ➝, *Canada* 50 B2
Uozu, *Japan* 23 F8
Upata, *Venezuela* 62 B6
Upemba, L., *Dem. Rep.
of the Congo* 36 F5
Upernavik, *Greenland* . 4 B5
Upington, *S. Africa* ... 37 K4
Upolu, *Samoa* 39 A13
Upper Alkali L., *U.S.A.* 56 F3
Upper Arrow L., *Canada* 50 C5
Upper Foster L., *Canada* 51 B7
Upper Hutt, *N.Z.* 39 J5
Upper Klamath L.,
U.S.A. 56 E3
Upper Lake, *U.S.A.* ... 56 G2
Upper Musquodoboit,
Canada 49 C7
Upper Red L., *U.S.A.* .. 54 A7
Upper Sandusky, *U.S.A.* 52 E4

Upper Volta = Burkina
Faso ■, *Africa* 34 F5
Uppland, *Sweden* 7 F17
Uppsala, *Sweden* 7 G17
Upstart, C., *Australia* .. 42 B4
Upton, *U.S.A.* 54 C2
Ur, *Iraq* 30 D5
Urakawa, *Japan* 22 C11
Ural = Zhayyq ➝,
Kazakstan 19 E9
Ural, *Australia* 43 E4
Ural Mts. = Uralskie
Gory, *Eurasia* 18 C10
Uralla, *Australia* 43 E5
Uralsk = Oral,
Kazakstan 19 D9
Uralskie Gory, *Eurasia* 18 C10
Urambo, *Tanzania* 36 F6
Urana, *Australia* 43 F4
Urandangi, *Australia* .. 42 C2
Uranium City, *Canada* . 51 B7
Uraricoera ➝, *Brazil* . 62 C6
Urawa, *Japan* 23 G9
Uray, *Russia* 20 C7
'Uray'irah, *Si. Arabia* . 31 E6
Urbana, *Ill., U.S.A.* ... 52 E1
Urbana, *Ohio, U.S.A.* . 52 E4
Urbino, *Italy* 16 C5
Urbión, Picos de, *Spain* 15 A4
Urcos, *Peru* 62 F4
Urdzhar, *Kazakstan* ... 20 E9
Ure ➝, *U.K.* 8 C6
Ures, *Mexico* 58 B2
Urfa = Sanlıurfa, *Turkey* 19 G6
Urganch, *Uzbekistan* . 20 E7
Urgench = Urganch,
Uzbekistan 20 E7
Ürgüp, *Turkey* 30 B2
Uribia, *Colombia* 62 A4
Urique, *Mexico* 58 B3
Urique ➝, *Mexico* ... 58 B3
Urk, *Neths.* 11 B5
Urla, *Turkey* 17 E12
Urmia = Orūmīyeh, *Iran* 30 B5
Urmia, L. = Orūmīyeh,
Daryācheh-ye, *Iran* . 30 B5
Uroševac, *Kosovo, Yug.* 17 C9
Uruaçu, *Brazil* 63 F9
Uruapan, *Mexico* 58 D4
Urubamba ➝, *Peru* .. 62 F4
Uruçara, *Brazil* 62 D7
Uruçuí, *Brazil* 63 E10
Uruguai ➝, *Brazil* ... 64 B6
Uruguaiana, *Brazil* ... 64 B5
Uruguay ■, *S. Amer.* . 64 C5
Uruguay ➝, *S. Amer.* . 64 C5
Urumchi = Ürümqi,
China 20 E9
Ürümqi, *China* 20 E9
Urup, Ostrov, *Russia* . 21 E16
Usa ➝, *Russia* 18 A10
Uşak, *Turkey* 19 G4
Usakos, *Namibia* 37 J3
Usedom, *Germany* ... 12 B8
Useless Loop, *Australia* 41 E1
Ush-Tobe, *Kazakstan* . 20 E8
Ushakova, Ostrov,
Russia 4 A12
Ushant = Ouessant, Î.
d', *France* 14 B1
Ushibuka, *Japan* 23 H5
Ushuaia, *Argentina* ... 64 G3
Ushumun, *Russia* 21 D13
Usk, *Canada* 50 C3
Usk ➝, *U.K.* 9 F5
Usman, *Russia* 18 D6
Usolye Sibirskoye,
Russia 21 D11
Uspallata, P. de,
Argentina 64 C3
Uspenskiy, *Kazakstan* . 20 E8
Ussuri ➝, *Asia* 22 A7
Ussuriysk, *Russia* 21 E14
Ussurka, *Russia* 22 B6
Ust-Aldan = Batamay,
Russia 21 C13
Ust-Amginskoye =
Khandyga, *Russia* . 21 C14
Ust-Bolsheretsk, *Russia* 21 D16
Ust-Chaun, *Russia* ... 21 C18
Ust-Ilimpeya = Yukta,
Russia 21 C11
Ust-Ilimsk, *Russia* 21 D11
Ust-Ishim, *Russia* 20 D8
Ust-Kamchatsk, *Russia* 21 D17
Ust-Kamenogorsk =
Öskemen, *Kazakstan* 20 E9
Ust-Khayryuzovo,
Russia 21 D16
Ust-Kut, *Russia* 21 D11
Ust-Kuyga, *Russia* 21 B14
Ust-Maya, *Russia* 21 C14
Ust-Mil, *Russia* 21 D14
Ust-Nera, *Russia* 21 C15
Ust-Nyukzha, *Russia* . 21 D13
Ust-Olenek, *Russia* ... 21 B12
Ust-Omchug, *Russia* . 21 C15
Ust-Port, *Russia* 20 C9
Ust-Tsilma, *Russia* 18 A9
Ust Urt = Ustyurt
Plateau, *Asia* 20 E6
Ust-Usa, *Russia* 18 A10
Ust-Vorkuta, *Russia* .. 18 A11
Ústí nad Labem,
Czech Rep. 12 C8

Ústica, *Italy* 16 E5
Ustinov = Izhevsk,
Russia 18 C9
Ustyurt Plateau, *Asia* . 20 E6
Usu, *China* 24 B3
Usuki, *Japan* 23 H5
Usulután, *El Salv.* 60 D2
Usumacinta ➝, *Mexico* 59 D6
Usumbura =
Bujumbura, *Burundi* 36 E5
Uta, *Indonesia* 27 E9
Utah □, *U.S.A.* 56 G8
Utah L., *U.S.A.* 56 F8
Utatlan, *Guatemala* ... 60 C1
Ute Creek ➝, *U.S.A.* . 55 H3
Utena, *Lithuania* 7 J21
Utiariti, *Brazil* 62 F7
Utica, *U.S.A.* 52 D8
Utikuma L., *Canada* ... 50 B5
Utopia, *Australia* 42 C1
Utrecht, *Neths.* 11 B5
Utrecht □, *Neths.* 11 B5
Utrera, *Spain* 15 D3
Utsjoki, *Finland* 6 B22
Utsunomiya, *Japan* ... 23 F9
Uttar Pradesh □, *India* 28 F12
Uttaradit, *Thailand* ... 26 A2
Uttoxeter, *U.K.* 8 E6
Uummannarsuaq =
Nunap Isua,
Greenland 4 D5
Uusikaarlepyy, *Finland* 6 E20
Uusikaupunki, *Finland* . 7 F19
Uva, *Russia* 18 C9
Uvalde, *U.S.A.* 55 L5
Uvat, *Russia* 20 D7
Uvinza, *Tanzania* 36 F6
Uvira, *Dem. Rep. of
the Congo* 36 E5
Uvs Nuur, *Mongolia* .. 24 A4
'Uwairidh, Ḥarrat al,
Si. Arabia 30 E3
Uwajima, *Japan* 23 H6
Uweinat, Jebel, *Sudan* 35 D10
Uxmal, *Mexico* 59 C7
Uyo, *Nigeria* 34 G7
Uyūn Mûsa, *Egypt* ... 33 F1
Uyuni, *Bolivia* 62 H5
Uzbekistan ■, *Asia* ... 20 E7
Uzen, *Kazakstan* 19 F9
Uzen, Mal ➝,
Kazakstan 19 E8
Uzerche, *France* 14 D4
Uzh ➝, *Ukraine* 13 C16
Uzhgorod = Uzhhorod,
Ukraine 13 D12
Uzhhorod, *Ukraine* ... 13 D12
Užice, *Serbia, Yug.* ... 17 C8
Uzunköprü, *Turkey* ... 17 D12

Vaal ➝, *S. Africa* 37 K4
Vaasa, *Finland* 6 E19
Vác, *Hungary* 13 E10
Vacaville, *U.S.A.* 56 G3
Vach = Vakh ➝,
Russia 20 C8
Vache, Î. à, *Haiti* 61 C5
Vadodara, *India* 28 H8
Vadsø, *Norway* 6 A23
Vaduz, *Liech.* 14 C8
Værøy, *Norway* 6 C15
Vágar, *Færoe Is.* 6 E9
Vågsfjorden, *Norway* . 6 B17
Váh ➝, *Slovak Rep.* .. 13 D9
Vahsel B., *Antarctica* .. 5 D1
Vaigach, *Russia* 20 B6
Vakh ➝, *Russia* 20 C8
Val-d'Or, *Canada* 48 C4
Val Marie, *Canada* 51 D7
Valahia, *Romania* 13 F13
Valandovo, *Macedonia* 17 D10
Valcheta, *Argentina* ... 64 E3
Valdayskaya
Vozvyshennost,
Russia 18 C5
Valdepeñas, *Spain* 15 C4
Valdés, Pen., *Argentina* 64 E4
Valdez, *U.S.A.* 46 B5
Valdivia, *Chile* 64 D2
Valdosta, *U.S.A.* 53 K4
Valdres, *Norway* 7 F13
Vale, *U.S.A.* 56 E5
Vale of Glamorgan □,
U.K. 9 F4
Valemount, *Canada* ... 50 C5
Valença, *Brazil* 63 F11
Valença do Piauí, *Brazil* 63 E10
Valence, *France* 14 D6
Valencia, *Spain* 15 C5
Valencia, *U.S.A.* 57 J10
Valencia, *Venezuela* .. 62 A5
Valencia □, *Spain* 15 C5
Valencia de Alcántara,
Spain 15 C2
Valencia I., *Ireland* 10 F1
Valenciennes, *France* . 14 A5
Valentim, Sa. do, *Brazil* 63 E10
Valentin, *Russia* 22 C7
Valentine, *U.S.A.* 54 D4
Valera, *Venezuela* 62 B4
Valga, *Estonia* 7 H22
Valier, *U.S.A.* 56 B7

Valjevo, *Serbia, Yug.* . 17 B8
Valka, *Latvia* 7 H21
Valkeakoski, *Finland* .. 7 F20
Valkenswaard, *Neths.* . 11 C5
Vall de Uxó = La Vall
d'Uixó, *Spain* 15 C5
Valladolid, *Mexico* 59 C7
Valladolid, *Spain* 15 B3
Valle de la Pascua,
Venezuela 62 B5
Valle de Santiago,
Mexico 58 C4
Valle de Suchil, *Mexico* 58 C4
Valle de Zaragoza,
Mexico 58 B3
Valle Hermoso, *Mexico* 59 B5
Valledupar, *Colombia* . 62 A4
Vallejo, *U.S.A.* 56 G2
Vallenar, *Chile* 64 B2
Valletta, *Malta* 16 G6
Valley City, *U.S.A.* 54 B6
Valley Falls, *U.S.A.* ... 56 E3
Valleyview, *Canada* ... 50 B5
Valls, *Spain* 15 B6
Valmiera, *Latvia* 7 H21
Valognes, *France* 14 C3
Valona = Vlorë, *Albania* 17 D8
Valozhyn, *Belarus* 13 A14
Valparaíso, *Chile* 64 C2
Valparaíso, *Mexico* ... 58 C4
Valparaiso, *U.S.A.* 52 E2
Vals, Tanjung, *Indonesia* 27 F9
Valsad, *India* 28 J8
Valverde del Camino,
Spain 15 D2
Vammala, *Finland* 7 F20
Van, *Turkey* 19 G7
Van, L. = Van Gölü,
Turkey 19 G7
Van Alstyne, *U.S.A.* ... 55 J6
Van Blommestein Meer,
Surinam 63 C7
Van Buren, *Canada* ... 49 C6
Van Buren, *Ark., U.S.A.* 55 H7
Van Buren, *Maine,
U.S.A.* 53 B11
Van Buren, *Mo., U.S.A.* 55 G9
Van Diemen, C.,
N. Terr., Australia .. 40 B5
Van Diemen, C.,
Queens., Australia . 42 B2
Van Diemen G.,
Australia 40 B5
Van Gölü, *Turkey* 19 G7
Van Horn, *U.S.A.* 55 K2
Van Rees, Pegunungan,
Indonesia 27 E9
Van Wert, *U.S.A.* 52 E3
Vanadzor, *Armenia* ... 19 F7
Vanavara, *Russia* 21 C11
Vancouver, *Canada* ... 50 D4
Vancouver, *U.S.A.* 56 D4
Vancouver, C., *Australia* 41 G2
Vancouver I., *Canada* . 50 D3
Vandalia, *Ill., U.S.A.* .. 54 F10
Vandalia, *Mo., U.S.A.* . 54 F9
Vanderhoof, *Canada* .. 50 C4
Vanderlin I., *Australia* . 42 B2
Vänern, *Sweden* 7 G15
Vänersborg, *Sweden* . 7 G15
Vangaindrano, *Madag.* 37 J9
Vanguard, *Canada* 51 D7
Vanino, *Russia* 21 E15
Vanna, *Norway* 6 A18
Vännäs, *Sweden* 6 E18
Vannes, *France* 14 C2
Vanrhynsdorp, *S. Africa* 37 L3
Vansbro, *Sweden* 7 F16
Vansittart B., *Australia* 40 B4
Vantaa, *Finland* 7 F21
Vanua Levu, *Fiji* 39 C8
Vanua Mbalavu, *Fiji* .. 39 C9
Vanuatu ■, *Pac. Oc.* .. 38 C9
Vapnyarka, *Ukraine* .. 13 D15
Varanasi, *India* 29 G13
Varanger-halvøya,
Norway 6 A23
Varangerfjorden,
Norway 6 A23
Varaždin, *Croatia* 12 F8
Varberg, *Sweden* 7 H15
Vardak □, *Afghan.* 28 B6
Vardar = Axiós ➝,
Greece 17 D10
Varde, *Denmark* 7 J13
Vardø, *Norway* 6 A24
Varena, *Lithuania* 7 J21
Varese, *Italy* 14 D8
Varkaus, *Finland* 7 E22
Varna, *Bulgaria* 17 C12
Värnamo, *Sweden* 7 H16
Varzaneh, *Iran* 31 C7
Vasa Barris ➝, *Brazil* . 63 F11
Vascongadas = País
Vasco □, *Spain* ... 15 A4
Vasht = Khāsh, *Iran* .. 28 E2
Vasilevichi, *Belarus* ... 13 B15
Vasilkov = Vasylkiv,
Ukraine 13 C16
Vaslui, *Romania* 13 E14
Vassar, *Canada* 51 D9
Vassar, *U.S.A.* 52 D4
Västerås, *Sweden* 7 G17
Västerbotten, *Sweden* 6 D18
Västerdalälven ➝,
Sweden 7 F16

Västervik, *Sweden* 7 H17
Västmanland, *Sweden* . 7 G16
Vasto, *Italy* 16 C6
Vasylkiv, *Ukraine* 13 C16
Vatican City ■, *Europe* 16 D5
Vatnajökull, *Iceland* .. 6 D5
Vatoa, *Fiji* 39 D9
Vatra-Dornei, *Romania* 13 E13
Vättern, *Sweden* 7 G16
Vaughn, *Mont., U.S.A.* 56 C8
Vaughn, *N. Mex., U.S.A.* 57 J11
Vaujours L., *Canada* .. 48 A5
Vaupés = Uaupés ➝,
Brazil 62 C5
Vaupes □, *Colombia* .. 62 C4
Vauxhall, *Canada* 50 C6
Vava'u, *Tonga* 39 D12
Vawkavysk, *Belarus* .. 13 B13
Växjö, *Sweden* 7 H16
Vaygach, Ostrov, *Russia* 20 C6
Vechte ➝, *Neths.* 11 B6
Vedea ➝, *Romania* .. 13 G13
Veendam, *Neths.* 11 A6
Veenendaal, *Neths.* ... 11 B5
Vefsna ➝, *Norway* ... 6 D15
Vega, *Norway* 6 D14
Vega, *U.S.A.* 55 H3
Vegreville, *Canada* ... 50 C6
Vejer de la Frontera,
Spain 15 D3
Vejle, *Denmark* 7 J13
Velas, *C., Costa Rica* . 60 D2
Velebit Planina, *Croatia* 12 F8
Veles, *Macedonia* 17 D9
Vélez-Málaga, *Spain* .. 15 D3
Vélez Rubio, *Spain* ... 15 D4
Velhas ➝, *Brazil* 63 G10
Velika Kapela, *Croatia* . 12 F8
Velikaya ➝, *Russia* .. 18 C4
Velikaya Kema, *Russia* 22 B8
Veliki Ustyug, *Russia* . 18 B8
Velikiye Luki, *Russia* .. 18 C4
Veliko Tŭrnovo, *Bulgaria* 17 C11
Velikonda Range, *India* 28 M11
Velletri, *Italy* 16 D5
Vellore, *India* 28 N11
Velsk, *Russia* 18 B7
Velva, *U.S.A.* 54 A4
Venado Tuerto,
Argentina 64 C4
Vendée □, *France* 14 C3
Vendôme, *France* 14 C4
Venézia, *Italy* 16 B5
Venézia, G. di, *Italy* ... 16 B5
Venezuela ■, *S. Amer.* 62 B5
Venezuela, G. de,
Venezuela 62 A4
Vengurla, *India* 28 M8
Venice = Venézia, *Italy* 16 B5
Venice, *U.S.A.* 53 M4
Venkatapuram, *India* .. 29 K12
Venlo, *Neths.* 11 C6
Vennesla, *Norway* 7 G12
Venray, *Neths.* 11 C6
Ventana, Punta de la,
Mexico 58 C3
Ventnor, *U.K.* 9 G6
Ventotène, *Italy* 16 D5
Ventoux, Mt., *France* .. 14 D6
Ventspils, *Latvia* 7 H19
Ventuarí ➝, *Venezuela* 62 C5
Ventura, *U.S.A.* 57 J4
Venus B., *Australia* ... 43 F4
Vera, *Argentina* 64 B4
Vera, *Spain* 15 D5
Veracruz, *Mexico* 59 D5
Veracruz □, *Mexico* .. 59 D5
Veraval, *India* 28 J7
Verbánia, *Italy* 14 D8
Vercelli, *Italy* 14 D8
Verdalsøra, *Norway* .. 6 E14
Verde ➝, *Argentina* .. 64 E3
Verde ➝, *Goiás, Brazil* 63 G9
Verde ➝,
*Mato Grosso do Sul,
Brazil* 63 H8
Verde ➝, *Chihuahua,
Mexico* 58 B3
Verde ➝, *Oaxaca,
Mexico* 59 D5
Verde ➝, *Veracruz,
Mexico* 58 C4
Verde, Cay, *Bahamas* . 60 B4
Verden, *Germany* 12 B5
Verdun, *France* 14 B6
Vereeniging, *S. Africa* . 37 K5
Verga, C., *Guinea* 34 F3
Vergemont Cr. ➝,
Australia 42 C3
Verín, *Spain* 15 B2
Verkhnevilyuysk, *Russia* 21 C13
Verkhniy Baskunchak,
Russia 19 E8
Verkhoyansk, *Russia* . 21 C14
Verkhoyansk Ra. =
Verkhoyanskiy
Khrebet, *Russia* ... 21 C13
Verkhoyanskiy Khrebet,
Russia 21 C13
Vermilion, *Canada* 51 C6
Vermilion ➝, *Alta.,
Canada* 51 C6
Vermilion ➝, *Qué.,
Canada* 48 C5

Vermilion, B., *U.S.A.* 55 L9
Vermilion Bay, *Canada* 51 D10
Vermilion Ł., *U.S.A.* 54 B8
Vermillion, *U.S.A.* 54 D6
Vermont □, *U.S.A.* 52 D9
Vernal, *U.S.A.* 56 F9
Verner, *Canada* 48 C3
Vernon, *Canada* 50 C5
Vernon, *U.S.A.* 55 H5
Vero Beach, *U.S.A.* 53 M5
Véroia, *Greece* 17 D10
Verona, *Italy* 16 B4
Verona, *U.S.A.* 54 D10
Versailles, *France* 14 B5
Vert, C., *Senegal* 34 F2
Verviers, *Belgium* 11 D5
Veselovskoye Vdkhr.,
Russia 19 E7
Vesoul, *France* 14 C7
Vesterålen, *Norway* 6 B16
Vestfjorden, *Norway* . . . 6 C15
Vestmannaeyjar, *Iceland* 6 E3
Vestspitsbergen,
Svalbard 4 B8
Vestvågøy, *Norway* . . . 6 B15
Vesuvio, *Italy* 16 D6
Vesuvius, Mt. =
Vesuvio, *Italy* 16 D6
Veszprém, *Hungary* . . . 13 E9
Vetlanda, *Sweden* 7 H16
Vetlugu →, *Russia* 18 C8
Vettore, Mte., *Italy* . . . 16 C5
Veurne, *Belgium* 11 C2
Veys, *Iran* 31 D6
Vezhen, *Bulgaria* 17 C11
Viacha, *Bolivia* 62 G5
Viamão, *Brazil* 64 C6
Viana, *Brazil* 63 D10
Viana do Alentejo,
Portugal 15 C2
Viana do Castelo,
Portugal 15 B1
Vianden, *Lux.* 11 E6
Vianópolis, *Brazil* 63 G9
Viaréggio, *Italy* 16 C4
Vibo Valéntia, *Italy* 16 E7
Viborg, *Denmark* 7 H13
Vic, *Spain* 15 B7
Vicenza, *Italy* 16 B4
Vich = Vic, *Spain* 15 B7
Vichada →, *Colombia* 62 C5
Vichy, *France* 14 C5
Vicksburg, *U.S.A.* 55 J9
Victor, *India* 28 J7
Victor Harbor, *Australia* 43 F2
Victoria = Labuan,
Malaysia 26 C5
Victoria, *Canada* 50 D4
Victoria, *Chile* 64 D2
Victoria, *Kans., U.S.A.* . 54 F5
Victoria, *Tex., U.S.A.* . . 55 L6
Victoria □, *Australia* . . 43 F3
Victoria →, *Australia* . 40 C4
Victoria, Grand L.,
Canada 48 C4
Victoria, L., *Africa* . . . 36 E6
Victoria, L., *Australia* . 43 E3
Victoria Beach, *Canada* 51 C9
Victoria de Durango =
Durango, *Mexico* . . . 58 C4
Victoria de las Tunas,
Cuba 60 B4
Victoria Falls, *Zimbabwe* 37 H5
Victoria I., *Canada* 46 A8
Victoria Ld., *Canada* . . 49 C8
Victoria Ld., *Antarctica* 5 D11
Victoria River, *Australia* 40 C4
Victoria Str., *Canada* . . 46 B9
Victoria Taungdeik,
Burma 29 J18
Victoriaville, *Canada* . . 49 C5
Victorica, *Argentina* . . 64 D3
Victorville, *U.S.A.* 57 J5
Vicuña, *Chile* 64 C2
Vidalia, *U.S.A.* 53 J4
Vidin, *Bulgaria* 17 C10
Vidisha, *India* 28 H10
Vidzy, *Belarus* 7 J22
Viedma, *Argentina* . . . 64 E4
Viedma, L., *Argentina* . 64 F2
Vielsalm, *Belgium* . . . 11 D5
Vienna = Wien, *Austria* 12 D9
Vienna, *Ill., U.S.A.* . . . 55 G10
Vienna, *Mo., U.S.A.* . . 54 F9
Vienne, *France* 14 D6
Vienne →, *France* . . . 14 C4
Vientiane, *Laos* 26 A2
Vientiane, *Laos* 26 A2
Vientos, Paso de los,
Caribbean 61 C5
Vierzon, *France* 14 C5
Vietnam ■, *Asia* 26 A3
Vigan, *Phil.* 27 A6
Vigévano, *Italy* 14 D8
Vigia, *Brazil* 63 D9
Vigia Chico, *Mexico* . . 59 D7
Vigo, *Spain* 15 A1
Vijayawada, *India* . . . 29 L12
Vijosë →, *Albania* . . 17 D8
Vík, *Iceland* 6 E4
Vikeke, *Indonesia* 27 F7
Viking, *Canada* 50 C6
Vikna, *Norway* 6 D14
Vila de João Belo = Xai-
Xai, *Mozam.* 37 K6

Vila do Bispo, *Portugal* 15 D1
Vila Franca de Xira,
Portugal 15 C1
Vila Nova de Gaia,
Portugal 15 B1
Vila Real, *Portugal* . . . 15 B2
Vila-real de los Infantes,
Spain 15 C5
Vila Real de Santo
António, *Portugal* . . . 15 D2
Vila Velha, *Brazil* 63 H10
Vilagarcía de Arousa,
Spain 15 A1
Vilaine →, *France* . . . 14 C2
Vilanculos, *Mozam.* . . . 37 J7
Vilanova i la Geltrú,
Spain 15 B6
Vileyka, *Belarus* 13 A14
Vilhelmina, *Sweden* . . 6 D17
Vilhena, *Brazil* 62 F6
Viliga, *Russia* 21 C16
Viliya →, *Lithuania* . . 7 J21
Viljandi, *Estonia* 7 G21
Vilkitskogo, Proliv,
Russia 21 B11
Vilkovo = Vylkove,
Ukraine 13 F15
Villa Ahumada, *Mexico* 58 A3
Villa Ángela, *Argentina* 64 B4
Villa Bella, *Bolivia* . . . 62 F5
Villa Bens = Tarfaya,
Morocco 34 C3
Villa Cisneros = Dakhla,
W. Sahara 34 D2
Villa de María,
Argentina 64 B4
Villa Dolores, *Argentina* 64 C3
Villa Frontera, *Mexico* . 58 B4
Villa Hayes, *Paraguay* . 64 B5
Villa Juárez, *Mexico* . . 58 B4
Villa María, *Argentina* . 64 C4
Villa Mazán, *Argentina* 64 B3
Villa Montes, *Bolivia* . 62 H6
Villa Ocampo, *Argentina* 64 B5
Villa Ocampo, *Mexico* 58 B3
Villa Unión, *Mexico* . . 58 C3
Villacarrillo, *Spain* . . . 15 C4
Villach, *Austria* 12 E7
Villagrán, *Mexico* . . . 59 C5
Villaguay, *Argentina* . 64 C5
Villahermosa, *Mexico* . 59 D6
Villajoyosa, *Spain* . . . 15 C5
Villalba, *Spain* 15 A2
Villanueva, *U.S.A.* . . . 55 H2
Villanueva de la Serena,
Spain 15 C3
Villanueva y Geltrú =
Vilanova i la Geltrú,
Spain 15 B6
Villarreal = Vila-real de
los Infantes, *Spain* . . 15 C5
Villarrica, *Chile* 64 D2
Villarrica, *Paraguay* . . 64 B5
Villarrobledo, *Spain* . . 15 C4
Villavicencio, *Colombia* 62 C4
Villaviciosa, *Spain* . . . 15 A3
Villazón, *Bolivia* 62 H5
Ville-Marie, *Canada* . . 48 C4
Ville Platte, *U.S.A.* . . . 55 K8
Villena, *Spain* 15 C5
Villeneuve-d'Ascq,
France 14 A5
Villeneuve-sur-Lot,
France 14 D4
Villingen-
Schwenningen,
Germany 12 D5
Vilna, *Canada* 50 C6
Vilnius, *Lithuania* 7 J21
Vilvoorde, *Belgium* . . . 11 D4
Vilyuy →, *Russia* . . . 21 C13
Vilyuysk, *Russia* 21 C13
Viña del Mar, *Chile* . . 64 C2
Vinarós, *Spain* 15 B6
Vincennes, *U.S.A.* 52 F2
Vindelälven →,
Sweden 6 E18
Vindeln, *Sweden* 6 D18
Vindhya Ra., *India* . . . 28 H10
Vineland, *U.S.A.* 52 F8
Vinita, *U.S.A.* 55 G7
Vinkovci, *Croatia* 17 B8
Vinnitsa = Vinnytsya,
Ukraine 13 D15
Vinnytsya, *Ukraine* . . 13 D15
Vinton, *Iowa, U.S.A.* . . 54 D8
Vinton, *La., U.S.A.* . . . 55 K8
Virac, *Phil.* 27 B6
Virago Sd., *Canada* . . 50 C2
Viramgam, *India* 28 H8
Viranşehir, *Turkey* . . . 30 B3
Virden, *Canada* 51 D8
Vire, *France* 14 B3
Virgenes, C., *Argentina* 64 G3
Virgin →, *U.S.A.* 57 H6
Virgin Gorda, *Virgin Is.* 61 C7
Virgin Is. (British) ■,
W. Indies 61 C7
Virgin Is. (U.S.) ■,
W. Indies 61 C7
Virginia, *S. Africa* . . . 37 K5
Virginia □, *U.S.A.* . . . 52 G7
Virginia Beach, *U.S.A.* . 52 G8

Virginia City, *Mont.,*
U.S.A. 56 D8
Virginia City, *Nev.,*
U.S.A. 56 G4
Virginia Falls, *Canada* . 50 A3
Virginiatown, *Canada* . 48 C4
Viroqua, *U.S.A.* 54 D9
Virovitica, *Croatia* . . . 16 B7
Virton, *Belgium* 11 E5
Virudunagar, *India* . . 28 Q10
Vis, *Croatia* 16 C7
Visalia, *U.S.A.* 57 H4
Visayan Sea, *Phil.* 27 B6
Visby, *Sweden* 7 H18
Viscount Melville Sd.,
Canada 4 B2
Visé, *Belgium* 11 D5
Viseu, *Brazil* 63 D9
Viseu, *Portugal* 15 B2
Vishakhapatnam, *India* 29 L13
Viso, Mte., *Italy* 14 D7
Visokoi I., *Antarctica* . 5 B1
Vistula = Wisła →,
Poland 13 A10
Vitebsk = Vitsyebsk,
Belarus 18 C5
Viterbo, *Italy* 16 C5
Viti Levu, *Fiji* 39 C7
Vitigudino, *Spain* 15 B2
Vitim, *Russia* 21 D12
Vitim →, *Russia* 21 D12
Vitória, *Brazil* 63 H10
Vitória da Conquista,
Brazil 63 F10
Vitória de São Antão,
Brazil 63 E11
Vitoria-Gasteiz, *Spain* . 15 A4
Vitsyebsk, *Belarus* . . . 18 C5
Vittória, *Italy* 16 F6
Vittório Véneto, *Italy* . 16 B5
Vivian, *U.S.A.* 55 J8
Vizcaíno, Desierto de,
Mexico 58 B2
Vizcaíno, Sierra, *Mexico* 58 B2
Vize, *Turkey* 17 D12
Vizianagaram, *India* . 29 K13
Vjosa →, *Albania* . . . 17 D8
Vjosë = Vijosë →,
Albania 17 D8
Vladikavkaz, *Russia* . . 19 F7
Vladimir, *Russia* 18 C7
Vladimir Volynskiy =
Volodymyr-Volynskyy,
Ukraine 13 C13
Vladivostok, *Russia* . . 21 E14
Vlieland, *Neths.* 11 A4
Vlissingen, *Neths.* . . . 11 C3
Vlóra = Vlorë, *Albania* 17 D8
Vlorë, *Albania* 17 D8
Vltava →, *Czech Rep.* 12 D8
Vogelkop = Doberai,
Jazirah, *Indonesia* . . 27 E8
Vogelsberg, *Germany* . 12 C5
Voghera, *Italy* 14 D8
Vohimarina = Iharana,
Madag. 37 G10
Vohimena, Tanjon' i,
Madag. 37 K9
Voi, *Kenya* 36 E7
Voiron, *France* 14 D6
Voisey B., *Canada* . . . 49 A7
Vojmsjön, *Sweden* . . . 6 D17
Vojvodina □,
Serbia, Yug. 17 B9
Volborg, *U.S.A.* 54 C2
Volcano Is. = Kazan-
Rettō, *Pac. Oc.* 44 E6
Volda, *Norway* 7 E12
Volga →, *Russia* 19 E8
Volga Hts. =
Privolzhskaya
Vozvyshennost,
Russia 19 D8
Volgodonsk, *Russia* . . 19 E7
Volgograd, *Russia* . . . 19 E7
Volgogradskoye Vdkhr.,
Russia 19 D8
Volkhov →, *Russia* . . 18 B5
Volkovysk = Vawkavysk,
Belarus 13 B13
Volochanka, *Russia* . . 21 B10
Volodymyr-Volynskyy,
Ukraine 13 C13
Vologda, *Russia* 18 C6
Vólos, *Greece* 17 E10
Volovets, *Ukraine* . . . 13 D12
Volozhin = Valozhyn,
Belarus 13 A14
Volsk, *Russia* 18 D8
Volta →, *Ghana* 34 G6
Volta, L., *Ghana* 34 G6
Volta Redonda, *Brazil* . 63 H10
Voltaire, C., *Australia* . 40 B4
Volterra, *Italy* 16 C4
Volturno →, *Italy* . . . 16 D5
Volzhskiy, *Russia* 19 E7
Vopnafjörður, *Iceland* . 6 D6
Vóriai Sporádhes,
Greece 17 E10
Vorkuta, *Russia* 18 A11
Vormsi, *Estonia* 7 G20
Voronezh, *Russia* 19 D6
Voroshilovgrad =
Luhansk, *Ukraine* . . 19 E6

Voroshilovsk =
Alchevsk, *Ukraine* . . 19 E6
Võrts Järv, *Estonia* . . . 7 G22
Võru, *Estonia* 7 H22
Vosges, *France* 14 B7
Voss, *Norway* 7 F12
Vostok I., *Kiribati* 45 J12
Votkinsk, *Russia* 18 C9
Votkinskoye Vdkhr.,
Russia 18 C10
Votsuri-Shima, *Japan* . 23 M1
Vouga →, *Portugal* . . 15 B1
Vozhe, Ozero, *Russia* . 18 B6
Voznesensk, *Ukraine* . 19 E5
Voznesenye, *Russia* . . 18 B6
Vrangelya, Ostrov,
Russia 21 B19
Vranje, *Serbia, Yug.* . . 17 C9
Vratsa, *Bulgaria* 17 C10
Vrbas →, *Bos.-H.* . . . 16 B7
Vršac, *Serbia, Yug.* . . . 17 B9
Vryburg, *S. Africa* . . . 37 K4
Vryheid, *S. Africa* . . . 37 K6
Vukovar, *Croatia* 17 B8
Vulcan, *Canada* 50 C6
Vulcan, *Romania* 17 F12
Vulcano, *Italy* 16 E6
Vulkaneshty =
Vulcaneşti, *Moldova* 13 F15
Vulkaneshty . . . .
Vulcaneşti, *Moldova* . 13 F15
Vung Tau, *Vietnam* . . 26 B3
Vyatka = Kirov, *Russia* 18 C8
Vyatka →, *Russia* . . . 18 C9
Vyatskiye Polyany,
Russia 18 C9
Vyazemskiy, *Russia* . . 21 E14
Vyazma, *Russia* 18 C5
Vyborg, *Russia* 18 B4
Vychegda →, *Russia* . 18 B8
Vychodné Beskydy,
Europe 13 D11
Vyg-ozero, *Russia* . . . 18 B5
Vylkove, *Ukraine* 13 F15
Vynohradiv, *Ukraine* . 13 D12
Vyrnwy, L., *U.K.* 8 E4
Vyshniy Volochek,
Russia 18 C5
Vyshzha = imeni 26
Bakinskikh
Komissarov,
Turkmenistan 31 B7
Vyškov, *Czech Rep.* . . 13 D9
Vytegra, *Russia* 18 B6

W.A.C. Bennett Dam,
Canada 50 B4
Waal →, *Neths.* 11 C5
Waalwijk, *Neths.* 11 C5
Wabana, *Canada* 49 C9
Wabasca →, *Canada* . 50 B5
Wabasca-Desmarais,
Canada 50 B6
Wabash, *U.S.A.* 52 E3
Wabash →, *U.S.A.* . . . 52 G1
Wabigoon L., *Canada* . 51 D10
Wabowden, *Canada* . . 51 C9
Wabuk Pt., *Canada* . . 48 A2
Wabush, *Canada* 49 B6
Waco, *U.S.A.* 55 K6
Waconichi, L., *Canada* . 48 B5
Wad Hamid, *Sudan* . . 35 E12
Wad Medanî, *Sudan* . 35 F12
Wadayama, *Japan* . . . 23 G7
Waddeneilanden, *Neths.* 11 A5
Waddenzee, *Neths.* . . 11 A5
Waddington, Mt.,
Canada 50 C3
Waddy Pt., *Australia* . . 43 C5
Wadebridge, *U.K.* 9 G3
Wadena, *Canada* 51 C8
Wadena, *U.S.A.* 54 B7
Wadeye, *Australia* . . . 40 B4
Wadhams, *Canada* . . . 50 C3
Wādī as Sir, *Jordan* . . 33 D4
Wadi Halfa, *Sudan* . . 35 D12
Wafrah, *Si. Arabia* . . . 30 D5
Wageningen, *Neths.* . . 11 C5
Wager B., *Canada* . . . 47 B11
Wagga Wagga,
Australia 43 F4
Waghete, *Indonesia* . . 27 E9
Wagin, *Australia* 41 F2
Wagner, *U.S.A.* 54 D6
Wagon Mound, *U.S.A.* . 55 G2
Wagoner, *U.S.A.* 55 H7
Wah, *Pakistan* 28 C5
Wahai, *Indonesia* . . . 27 E7
Wâhid, *Egypt* 33 E1
Wahoo, *U.S.A.* 54 E6
Wahpeton, *U.S.A.* 54 B6
Waiau →, *N.Z.* 39 K4
Waibeem, *Indonesia* . 27 E8
Waigeo, *Indonesia* . . 27 E8
Waihi, *N.Z.* 39 G5
Waihou →, *N.Z.* 39 G5
Waikabubak, *Indonesia* 27 F5
Waikaremoana, L., *N.Z.* 39 H6
Waikari, *N.Z.* 39 K4
Waikato →, *N.Z.* 39 G5
Waikerie, *Australia* . . 43 E3
Waikokopu, *N.Z.* 39 H6
Waikouaiti, *N.Z.* 39 L3
Waimakariri →, *N.Z.* . 39 K4

Waimate, *N.Z.* 39 L3
Wainganga →, *India* . 28 K11
Waingapu, *Indonesia* . 27 F6
Waini →, *Guyana* . . . 62 B7
Wainwright, *Canada* . . 51 C6
Waiouru, *N.Z.* 39 H5
Waipara, *N.Z.* 39 K4
Waipawa, *N.Z.* 39 H6
Waipiro, *N.Z.* 39 H7
Waipu, *N.Z.* 39 F5
Waipukurau, *N.Z.* 39 J6
Wairakei, *N.Z.* 39 H6
Wairarapa, L., *N.Z.* . . . 39 J5
Wairoa, *N.Z.* 39 H6
Waitaki →, *N.Z.* 39 L3
Waitara, *N.Z.* 39 H5
Waitsburg, *U.S.A.* 56 C5
Waiuku, *N.Z.* 39 G5
Wajima, *Japan* 23 F8
Wajir, *Kenya* 36 D8
Wakasa, *Japan* 23 G7
Wakasa-Wan, *Japan* . . 23 G7
Wakatipu, L., *N.Z.* . . . 39 L2
Wakaw, *Canada* 51 C7
Wakayama, *Japan* . . . 23 G7
Wakayama □, *Japan* . 23 H7
Wake Forest, *U.S.A.* . . 53 H6
Wake I., *Pac. Oc.* 44 F8
WaKeeney, *U.S.A.* 54 F5
Wakefield, *N.Z.* 39 J4
Wakefield, *U.K.* 8 D6
Wakefield, *U.S.A.* 54 B10
Wakkanai, *Japan* 22 B10
Wakool, *Australia* 43 F3
Wakool →, *Australia* . 43 F3
Wakre, *Indonesia* 27 E8
Wakuach, L., *Canada* . 49 A6
Wałbrzych, *Poland* . . . 12 C9
Walbury Hill, *U.K.* 9 F6
Walcha, *Australia* 43 E5
Walcheren, *Neths.* . . . 11 C3
Walcott, *U.S.A.* 56 F10
Wałcz, *Poland* 12 B9
Waldburg Ra., *Australia* 41 D2
Walden, *U.S.A.* 56 F10
Waldport, *U.S.A.* 56 D1
Waldron, *U.S.A.* 55 H7
Walebing, *Australia* . . 41 F2
Wales □, *U.K.* 9 E3
Walgett, *Australia* . . . 43 E4
Walgreen Coast,
Antarctica 5 D15
Walker, *U.S.A.* 54 B7
Walker, L., *Canada* . . . 49 B6
Walker L., *Canada* . . . 51 C9
Walker L., *U.S.A.* 56 G4
Walkerston, *Australia* . 42 C4
Walkerton, *Canada* . . 48 D3
Wall, *U.S.A.* 54 D3
Walla Walla, *U.S.A.* . . 56 C4
Wallace, *Idaho, U.S.A.* . 56 C6
Wallace, *N.C., U.S.A.* . 53 H7
Wallaceburg, *Canada* . 48 D3
Wallachia = Valahia,
Romania 13 F13
Wallal, *Australia* 43 D4
Wallam Cr. →,
Australia 43 D4
Wallambin, L., *Australia* 41 F2
Wallan, *Australia* 43 F3
Wallangarra, *Australia* . 43 D5
Wallaroo, *Australia* . . 43 E2
Wallis & Futuna, Is.,
Pac. Oc. 38 C11
Wallowa, *U.S.A.* 56 D5
Wallowa Mts., *U.S.A.* . 56 D5
Wallula, *U.S.A.* 56 C4
Wallumbilla, *Australia* . 43 D4
Walmsley, L., *Canada* . 51 A7
Walney, I. of, *U.K.* . . . 8 C4
Walnut Ridge, *U.S.A.* . 55 G9
Walpole, *Australia* . . . 41 F2
Walsall, *U.K.* 9 E6
Walsenburg, *U.S.A.* . . 55 G2
Walsh, *U.S.A.* 55 G3
Walsh →, *Australia* . . 42 B3
Walterboro, *U.S.A.* . . . 53 J5
Walters, *U.S.A.* 55 H5
Waltman, *U.S.A.* 56 E10
Walton-on-the-Naze,
U.K. 9 F9
Walvis Bay, *Namibia* . 37 J2
Walvisbaai = Walvis
Bay, *Namibia* 37 J2
Wamba, *Dem. Rep. of*
the Congo 36 D5
Wamego, *U.S.A.* 54 F6
Wamena, *Indonesia* . . 27 E9
Wamsutter, *U.S.A.* . . . 56 F9
Wamulan, *Indonesia* . 27 E7
Wana, *Pakistan* 28 C6
Wanaaring, *Australia* . 43 D3
Wanaka, *N.Z.* 39 L2
Wanaka L., *N.Z.* 39 L2
Wanapitei L., *Canada* . 48 C3
Wandel Sea = McKinley
Sea, *Arctic* 4 A7
Wandoan, *Australia* . . 43 D4
Wang →, *Thailand* . . 26 A1
Wangal, *Indonesia* . . 27 F8
Wanganella, *Australia* . 43 F3
Wanganui, *N.Z.* 39 H5
Wangaratta, *Australia* . 43 F4
Wangary, *Australia* . . . 43 E2

Wangerooge, *Germany* 12 B4
Wangiwangi, *Indonesia* 27 F6
Wanless, *Canada* 51 C8
Wantage, *U.K.* 9 F6
Wapakoneta, *U.S.A.* . . 52 E3
Wapato, *U.S.A.* 56 C3
Wapawekka L., *Canada* 51 C8
Wapikopa L., *Canada* . 48 B2
Wapiti →, *Canada* . . . 50 B5
Wapsipinicon →,
U.S.A. 54 E9
Warangal, *India* 28 L11
Waratah, *Australia* . . . 42 G4
Waratah B., *Australia* . 43 F4
Warburton, *Vic.,*
Australia 43 F4
Warburton, *W. Austral.,*
Australia 41 E4
Warburton Ra., *Australia* 41 E4
Ward, *N.Z.* 39 J5
Ward →, *Australia* . . . 43 D4
Wardha, *India* 28 J11
Wardha →, *India* . . . 28 K11
Ware, *Canada* 50 B3
Waregem, *Belgium* . . . 11 D3
Waremme, *Belgium* . . 11 D5
Warialda, *Australia* . . . 43 D5
Wariap, *Indonesia* . . . 27 E8
Warkopi, *Indonesia* . . 27 E8
Warm Springs, *U.S.A.* . 57 G5
Warman, *Canada* 51 C7
Warminster, *U.K.* 9 F5
Warner Mts., *U.S.A.* . . 56 F3
Warner Robins, *U.S.A.* . 53 J4
Waroona, *Australia* . . . 41 F2
Warracknabeal,
Australia 43 F3
Warragul, *Australia* . . 43 F4
Warrego →, *Australia* . 43 E4
Warrego Ra., *Australia* . 42 C4
Warren, *Australia* 43 E4
Warren, *Ark., U.S.A.* . . 55 J8
Warren, *Mich., U.S.A.* . 52 D4
Warren, *Minn., U.S.A.* . 54 A6
Warren, *Ohio, U.S.A.* . 52 E5
Warren, *Pa., U.S.A.* . . 52 E6
Warrensburg, *U.S.A.* . . 54 F8
Warrenton, *U.S.A.* . . . 55 F8
Warri, *Nigeria* 34 G7
Warrina, *Australia* . . . 43 D2
Warrington, *U.K.* 8 D5
Warrington, *U.S.A.* . . . 53 K2
Warrnambool, *Australia* 43 F3
Warroad, *U.S.A.* 54 A7
Warruwi, *Australia* . . . 42 A1
Warsa, *Indonesia* 27 E9
Warsaw = Warszawa,
Poland 13 B11
Warsaw, *U.S.A.* 52 E3
Warszawa, *Poland* . . . 13 B11
Warta →, *Poland* 12 B8
Warthe = Warta →,
Poland 12 B8
Waru, *Indonesia* 27 E8
Warwick, *Australia* . . . 43 D5
Warwick, *U.K.* 9 E6
Warwick, *U.S.A.* 52 E10
Warwickshire □, *U.K.* . 9 E6
Wasagaming, *Canada* . 51 C9
Wasatch Ra., *U.S.A.* . . 56 F8
Wasco, *Calif., U.S.A.* . 57 J4
Wasco, *Oreg., U.S.A.* . 56 D3
Waseca, *U.S.A.* 54 C8
Wasekamio L., *Canada* 51 B7
Wash, The, *U.K.* 8 E8
Washburn, *N. Dak.,*
U.S.A. 54 B4
Washburn, *Wis., U.S.A.* 54 B9
Washim, *India* 28 J10
Washington, *U.K.* 8 C6
Washington, *D.C.,*
U.S.A. 52 F7
Washington, *Ga., U.S.A.* 53 J4
Washington, *Ind., U.S.A.* 52 F2
Washington, *Iowa,*
U.S.A. 54 E9
Washington, *Mo., U.S.A.* 54 F9
Washington, *N.C.,*
U.S.A. 53 H7
Washington, *Pa., U.S.A.* 52 E5
Washington, *Utah,*
U.S.A. 57 H7
Washington □, *U.S.A.* . 56 C3
Washington, *Mt., U.S.A.* 52 C10
Washington Court
House, *U.S.A.* 52 F4
Washington I., *U.S.A.* . 52 C2
Wasian, *Indonesia* . . . 27 E8
Wasilla, *U.S.A.* 46 B5
Wasior, *Indonesia* . . . 27 E8
Waskaganish, *Canada* . 48 B4
Waskaiowaka, L.,
Canada 51 B9
Waskesiu Lake, *Canada* 51 C7
Wasserkuppe, *Germany* 12 C5
Waswanipi, *Canada* . . 48 C4
Waswanipi, L., *Canada* 48 C4
Watampone, *Indonesia* 27 E6
Water Park Pt., *Australia* 42 C5
Water Valley, *U.S.A.* . . 55 H10
Waterbury, *U.S.A.* 52 E9
Waterbury L., *Canada* . 51 B8
Waterford, *Ireland* . . . 10 E3

Wrexham

Waterhen L., Canada 51 C9
Waterloo, Belgium 11 D4
Waterloo, Canada 48 D3
Waterloo, Ill., U.S.A. 54 F9
Waterloo, Iowa, U.S.A. 54 D8
Watersmeet, U.S.A. 54 B10
Waterton Lakes Nat. Park, U.S.A. 56 B7
Watertown, N.Y., U.S.A. 52 D8
Watertown, S. Dak., U.S.A. 54 C6
Watertown, Wis., U.S.A. 54 D10
Waterville, Maine, U.S.A. 53 C11
Waterville, Wash., U.S.A. 56 C3
Wates, Indonesia 27 G14
Watford, U.K. 9 F7
Watford City, U.S.A. 54 B3
Wathaman →, Canada 51 B8
Wathaman L., Canada 51 B8
Watheroo, Australia 41 F2
Watkins Glen, U.S.A. 52 D7
Watling I. = San Salvador I., Bahamas 61 B5
Watonga, U.S.A. 55 H5
Watrous, Canada 51 C7
Watrous, U.S.A. 55 H2
Watsa, Dem. Rep. of the Congo 36 D5
Watseka, U.S.A. 52 E2
Watson, Australia 41 F5
Watson, Canada 51 C8
Watson Lake, Canada 50 A3
Watsonville, U.S.A. 57 H3
Wattiwarriganna Cr. →, Australia 43 D2
Watuata = Batuata, Indonesia 27 F6
Watubela, Kepulauan, Indonesia 27 E8
Watubela Is. = Watubela, Kepulauan, Indonesia 27 E8
Wau = Wâw, Sudan 35 G11
Waubay, U.S.A. 54 C6
Wauchope, N.S.W., Australia 43 E5
Wauchope, N. Terr., Australia 42 C1
Wauchula, U.S.A. 53 M5
Waukarlycarly, L., Australia 40 D3
Waukegan, U.S.A. 52 D2
Waukesha, U.S.A. 52 D1
Waukon, U.S.A. 54 D9
Waupaca, U.S.A. 54 C10
Waupun, U.S.A. 54 D10
Waurika, U.S.A. 55 H6
Wausau, U.S.A. 54 C10
Wautoma, U.S.A. 54 C10
Wauwatosa, U.S.A. 52 D2
Waveney →, U.K. 9 E9
Waverley, N.Z. 39 H5
Waverly, Iowa, U.S.A. 54 D8
Waverly, N.Y., U.S.A. 52 E7
Wavre, Belgium 11 D4
Wâw, Sudan 35 G11
Wâw al Kabīr, Libya 35 C9
Wawa, Canada 48 C3
Wawanesa, Canada 51 D9
Waxahachie, U.S.A. 55 J6
Way, L., Australia 41 E3
Waycross, U.S.A. 53 K4
Wayne, Nebr., U.S.A. 54 D6
Wayne, W. Va., U.S.A. 52 F4
Waynesboro, Ga., U.S.A. 53 J4
Waynesboro, Miss., U.S.A. 53 K1
Waynesboro, Pa., U.S.A. 52 F7
Waynesboro, Va., U.S.A. 52 F6
Waynesburg, U.S.A. 52 F5
Waynesville, U.S.A. 53 H4
Waynoka, U.S.A. 55 G5
Wazirabad, Pakistan 28 C9
We, Indonesia 26 C1
Weald, The, U.K. 9 F8
Wear →, U.K. 8 C6
Weatherford, Okla., U.S.A. 55 H5
Weatherford, Tex., U.S.A. 55 J6
Weaverville, U.S.A. 56 F2
Webb City, U.S.A. 55 G7
Webequie, Canada 48 B2
Webster, U.S.A. 54 C6
Webster City, U.S.A. 54 D8
Webster Springs, U.S.A. 52 F5
Weda, Indonesia 27 D7
Weda, Teluk, Indonesia 27 D7
Weddell I., Falk. Is. 64 G4
Weddell Sea, Antarctica 5 D1
Wedderburn, Australia 43 F3
Wedgeport, Canada 49 D6
Wee Waa, Australia 43 E4
Weed, U.S.A. 56 F2
Weert, Neths. 11 C5
Weiden, Germany 12 D7
Weifang, China 25 C6
Weimar, Germany 12 C6
Weipa, Australia 42 A3
Weir →, Australia 43 D4
Weir →, Canada 51 B10
Weir River, Canada 51 B10
Weirton, U.S.A. 52 E5
Weiser, U.S.A. 56 D5
Wejherowo, Poland 13 A10
Wekusko L., Canada 51 C9
Welch, U.S.A. 52 G5
Welkom, S. Africa 37 K5
Welland, Canada 48 D4
Welland →, U.K. 9 E7
Wellesley Is., Australia 42 B2
Wellingborough, U.K. 9 E7
Wellington, Australia 43 E4
Wellington, N.Z. 39 J5
Wellington, Somst., U.K. 9 G4
Wellington, Telford & Wrekin, U.K. 9 E5
Wellington, Colo., U.S.A. 54 E2
Wellington, Kans., U.S.A. 55 G6
Wellington, Tex., U.S.A. 55 H4
Wellington, I., Chile 64 F2
Wellington, L., Australia 43 F4
Wells, U.K. 9 F5
Wells, U.S.A. 56 F6
Wells, L., Australia 41 E3
Wells, Mt., Australia 40 C4
Wells Gray Prov. Park, Canada 50 C4
Wells-next-the-Sea, U.K. 8 E8
Wellsboro, U.S.A. 52 E7
Wellsville, N.Y., U.S.A. 52 D7
Wellsville, Utah, U.S.A. 56 F8
Wellton, U.S.A. 57 K6
Wels, Austria 12 D8
Welshpool, U.K. 9 E4
Welwyn Garden City, U.K. 9 F7
Wem, U.K. 8 E5
Wemindji, Canada 48 B4
Wenatchee, U.S.A. 56 C3
Wenchi, Ghana 34 G5
Wenchow = Wenzhou, China 25 D7
Wendesi, Indonesia 27 E8
Wendover, U.S.A. 56 F6
Wenlock →, Australia 42 A3
Wenshan, China 24 D5
Wensleydale, U.K. 8 C6
Wensu, China 24 B3
Wensum →, U.K. 8 E8
Wentworth, Australia 43 E3
Wentzel L., Canada 50 B6
Wenut, Indonesia 27 E8
Wenzhou, China 25 D7
Weott, U.S.A. 56 F2
Weri, Indonesia 27 E8
Werra →, Germany 12 C5
Werrimull, Australia 43 E3
Werris Creek, Australia 43 E5
Weser →, Germany 12 B5
Wesiri, Indonesia 27 F7
Wesleyville, Canada 49 C9
Wessel, C., Australia 42 A2
Wessel Is., Australia 42 A2
Wessington Springs, U.S.A. 54 C5
West, U.S.A. 55 K6
West Baines →, Australia 40 C4
West Bank □, Asia 33 C4
West Bend, U.S.A. 52 D1
West Bengal □, India 29 H16
West Berkshire □, U.K. 9 F6
West Beskids = Západné Beskydy, Europe 13 D10
West Branch, U.S.A. 52 C3
West Bromwich, U.K. 9 E6
West Cape Howe, Australia 41 G2
West Chester, U.S.A. 52 F8
West Columbia, U.S.A. 55 L7
West Des Moines, U.S.A. 54 E8
West End, Bahamas 60 A4
West Falkland, Falk. Is. 64 G5
West Fargo, U.S.A. 54 B6
West Fjord = Vestfjorden, Norway 6 C15
West Fork Trinity →, U.S.A. 55 J6
West Frankfort, U.S.A. 54 G10
West Helena, U.S.A. 55 H9
West Ice Shelf, Antarctica 5 C7
West Indies, Cent. Amer. 61 D7
West Jordan, U.S.A. 56 F8
West Memphis, U.S.A. 55 H9
West Midlands □, U.K. 9 E6
West Monroe, U.S.A. 55 J8
West Palm Beach, U.S.A. 53 M5
West Plains, U.S.A. 55 G9
West Point, Nebr., U.S.A. 54 E6
West Point, Va., U.S.A. 52 G7
West Pt. = Ouest, Pte. de l', Canada 49 C7
West Pt., Australia 43 F2
West Road →, Canada 50 C4
West Schelde = Westerschelde →, Neths. 11 C3
West Seneca, U.S.A. 52 D6
West Sussex □, U.K. 9 G7
West-Terschelling, Neths. 11 A5
West Valley City, U.S.A. 56 F8
West Virginia □, U.S.A. 52 F5
West-Vlaanderen □, Belgium 11 D2
West Wyalong, Australia 43 E4
West Yellowstone, U.S.A. 56 D8
West Yorkshire □, U.K. 8 D6
Westall Pt., Australia 43 E1
Westbrook, U.S.A. 53 D10
Westbury, Australia 42 G4
Westby, U.S.A. 54 A2
Westerland, Germany 7 J13
Western Australia □, Australia 41 E2
Western Dvina = Daugava →, Latvia 7 H21
Western Ghats, India 28 N9
Western Sahara ■, Africa 34 D3
Western Samoa = Samoa ■, Pac. Oc. 39 B13
Westernport, U.S.A. 52 F6
Westerschelde →, Neths. 11 C3
Westerwald, Germany 12 C4
Westhope, U.S.A. 54 A4
Westland Bight, N.Z. 39 K3
Westlock, Canada 50 C6
Westmar, Australia 43 D4
Westminster, U.S.A. 52 F7
Westmorland, U.S.A. 57 K6
Weston, Oreg., U.S.A. 56 D4
Weston, W. Va., U.S.A. 52 F5
Weston I., Canada 48 B4
Weston-super-Mare, U.K. 9 F5
Westport, Ireland 10 E2
Westport, N.Z. 39 J3
Westport, U.S.A. 56 C1
Westray, Canada 51 C8
Westray, U.K. 10 B5
Westree, Canada 48 C3
Westwood, U.S.A. 56 F3
Wetar, Indonesia 27 F7
Wetaskiwin, Canada 50 C6
Wete, Tanzania 36 F7
Wetherby, U.K. 8 D6
Wetteren, Belgium 11 D3
Wetzlar, Germany 12 C5
Wewoka, U.S.A. 55 H6
Wexford, Ireland 10 E3
Weyburn, Canada 51 D8
Weymouth, Canada 49 D6
Weymouth, U.K. 9 G5
Weymouth, C., Australia 42 A3
Wha Ti, Canada 46 B8
Whakatane, N.Z. 39 G6
Whale →, Canada 49 A6
Whale Cove, Canada 51 A10
Whales, B. of, Antarctica 5 D12
Whangamomona, N.Z. 39 H5
Whangarei, N.Z. 39 F5
Whangarei Harb., N.Z. 39 F5
Wharfe →, U.K. 8 D6
Wharfedale, U.K. 8 C5
Wharton, U.S.A. 55 L6
Wheatland, U.S.A. 54 D2
Wheaton, Md., U.S.A. 52 F7
Wheaton, Minn., U.S.A. 54 C6
Wheeler, Oreg., U.S.A. 56 D2
Wheeler, Tex., U.S.A. 55 H4
Wheeler →, Canada 49 A6
Wheeler L., U.S.A. 53 H2
Wheeler Pk., N. Mex., U.S.A. 57 H11
Wheeler Pk., Nev., U.S.A. 57 G6
Wheeling, U.S.A. 52 E5
Whernside, U.K. 8 C5
Whiskey Jack L., Canada 51 B8
Whistleduck Cr. →, Australia 42 C2
Whistler, Canada 50 C4
Whitby, U.K. 8 C7
White →, Ark., U.S.A. 55 J9
White →, Ind., U.S.A. 52 F2
White →, S. Dak., U.S.A. 54 D5
White →, Tex., U.S.A. 55 J4
White →, Utah, U.S.A. 56 F9
White, L., Australia 40 D4
White B., Canada 49 C8
White Bird, U.S.A. 56 D5
White Butte, U.S.A. 54 B3
White City, U.S.A. 56 E2
White Cliffs, Australia 43 E3
White Hall, U.S.A. 54 F9
White Horse, Vale of, U.K. 9 F6
White I., N.Z. 39 G6
White L., U.S.A. 55 L8
White Mountain Peak, U.S.A. 57 G4
White Mts., Calif., U.S.A. 57 H4
White Mts., N.H., U.S.A. 52 C10
White Nile = Nîl el Abyad →, Sudan 35 E12
White Otter L., Canada 48 C1
White River, Canada 48 C2
White River, U.S.A. 54 D4
White Russia = Belarus ■, Europe 13 B14
White Sea = Beloye More, Russia 18 A6
White Sulphur Springs, Mont., U.S.A. 56 C8
White Sulphur Springs, W. Va., U.S.A. 52 G5
Whitecliffs, N.Z. 39 K3
Whitecourt, Canada 50 C5
Whitefish, U.S.A. 56 B6
Whitefish L., Canada 51 A7
Whitefish Point, U.S.A. 52 B3
Whitegull, L., Canada 49 A7
Whitehall, Mich., U.S.A. 52 D2
Whitehall, Mont., U.S.A. 56 D7
Whitehall, N.Y., U.S.A. 52 D9
Whitehall, Wis., U.S.A. 54 C9
Whitehaven, U.K. 8 C4
Whitehorse, Canada 50 A1
Whitemark, Australia 42 G4
Whiteriver, U.S.A. 57 K9
Whitesand →, Canada 50 A5
Whitesboro, U.S.A. 55 J6
Whiteshell Prov. Park, Canada 51 D9
Whiteville, U.S.A. 53 H6
Whitewater, U.S.A. 52 D1
Whitewater Baldy, U.S.A. 57 K9
Whitewater L., Canada 48 B2
Whitewood, Australia 42 C3
Whitewood, Canada 51 C8
Whitianga, N.Z. 39 G5
Whitney, Canada 48 C4
Whitney, Mt., U.S.A. 57 H4
Whitstable, U.K. 9 F9
Whitsunday I., Australia 42 C4
Whittlesea, Australia 43 F4
Wholdaia L., Canada 51 A8
Whyalla, Australia 43 E2
Wiarton, Canada 48 D3
Wibaux, U.S.A. 54 B2
Wichita, U.S.A. 55 G6
Wichita Falls, U.S.A. 55 J5
Wick, U.K. 10 B5
Wickenburg, U.S.A. 57 K7
Wickepin, Australia 41 F2
Wickham, Australia 40 D2
Wickham, C., Australia 42 F3
Wicklow Mts., Ireland 10 E3
Widgeegoara Cr. →, Australia 43 D4
Widgiemooltha, Australia 41 F3
Widnes, U.K. 8 D5
Wieluń, Poland 13 C10
Wien, Austria 12 D9
Wiener Neustadt, Austria 12 E9
Wiesbaden, Germany 12 C5
Wigan, U.K. 8 D5
Wiggins, Colo., U.S.A. 54 E2
Wiggins, Miss., U.S.A. 55 K10
Wight, I. of □, U.K. 9 G6
Wigston, U.K. 9 E6
Wigton, U.K. 8 C4
Wilber, U.S.A. 54 E6
Wilberforce, C., Australia 42 A2
Wilburton, U.S.A. 55 H7
Wilcannia, Australia 43 E3
Wildspitze, Austria 12 E6
Wilhelm II Coast, Antarctica 5 C7
Wilhelmshaven, Germany 12 B5
Wilkes-Barre, U.S.A. 52 E8
Wilkie, Canada 51 C7
Wilkinson Lakes, Australia 41 E5
Willandra Creek →, Australia 43 E4
Willapa B., U.S.A. 56 C2
Willcox, U.S.A. 57 K9
Willemstad, Neth. Ant. 62 A5
William →, Canada 51 B7
William 'Bill' Dannely Res., U.S.A. 53 J2
William Creek, Australia 43 D2
Williams, Australia 41 F2
Williams, U.S.A. 57 J7
Williams Harbour, Canada 49 B8
Williams Lake, Canada 50 C4
Williamsburg, Ky., U.S.A. 53 G3
Williamsburg, Va., U.S.A. 52 G7
Williamson, U.S.A. 52 G4
Williamsport, U.S.A. 52 E7
Williamston, U.S.A. 53 H7
Williamstown, Australia 43 F3
Williamstown, U.S.A. 52 F3
Willingboro, U.S.A. 52 E8
Willis Group, Australia 42 B5
Williston, Fla., U.S.A. 53 L4
Williston, N. Dak., U.S.A. 54 A3
Williston L., Canada 50 B4
Willits, U.S.A. 56 G2
Willmar, U.S.A. 54 C7
Willow Bunch, Canada 51 D7
Willow L., Canada 50 A5
Willowlake →, Canada 50 A4
Willows, U.S.A. 56 G2
Wills, L., Australia 40 D4
Wills Cr. →, Australia 42 C3
Willunga, Australia 43 F2
Wilmette, U.S.A. 52 D2
Wilmington, Australia 43 E2
Wilmington, Del., U.S.A. 52 F8
Wilmington, N.C., U.S.A. 53 H7
Wilmington, Ohio, U.S.A. 52 F4
Wilmslow, U.K. 8 D5
Wilpena →, Australia 43 E2
Wilsall, U.S.A. 56 D8
Wilson, U.S.A. 53 H7
Wilson →, Australia 40 C4
Wilson Bluff, Australia 41 F4
Wilson Inlet, Australia 41 G2
Wilsons Promontory, Australia 43 F4
Wilton, U.S.A. 54 B4
Wilton →, Australia 42 A1
Wiltshire □, U.K. 9 F6
Wiltz, Lux. 11 E5
Wiluna, Australia 41 E3
Wimborne Minster, U.K. 9 G6
Wimmera →, Australia 43 F3
Winchester, U.K. 9 F6
Winchester, Idaho, U.S.A. 56 C5
Winchester, Ind., U.S.A. 52 E3
Winchester, Ky., U.S.A. 52 G3
Winchester, Tenn., U.S.A. 53 H2
Winchester, Va., U.S.A. 52 F6
Wind →, U.S.A. 56 E9
Wind River Range, U.S.A. 56 E9
Windau = Ventspils, Latvia 7 H19
Winder, U.S.A. 53 J4
Windermere, U.K. 8 C5
Windhoek, Namibia 37 J3
Windom, U.S.A. 54 D7
Windorah, Australia 42 D3
Window Rock, U.S.A. 57 J9
Windrush →, U.K. 9 F6
Windsor, Australia 43 E5
Windsor, N.S., Canada 49 D7
Windsor, Ont., Canada 48 D3
Windsor, U.K. 9 F7
Windsor, Colo., U.S.A. 54 E2
Windsor, Mo., U.S.A. 54 F8
Windsor, Vt., U.S.A. 52 D9
Windsor & Maidenhead □, U.K. 9 F7
Windward Is., W. Indies 61 D7
Windward Passage = Vientos, Paso de los, Caribbean 61 C5
Winefred L., Canada 51 B6
Winfield, U.S.A. 55 G6
Wingate Mts., Australia 40 B5
Wingham, Australia 43 E5
Wingham, Canada 48 D3
Winisk, Canada 48 A2
Winisk →, Canada 48 A2
Winisk L., Canada 48 B2
Wink, U.S.A. 55 K3
Winkler, Canada 51 D9
Winnebago, L., U.S.A. 52 D1
Winnecke Cr. →, Australia 40 C5
Winnemucca, U.S.A. 56 F5
Winnemucca L., U.S.A. 56 F4
Winnett, U.S.A. 56 C9
Winnfield, U.S.A. 55 K8
Winnibigoshish, L., U.S.A. 54 B7
Winnipeg, Canada 51 D9
Winnipeg →, Canada 51 C9
Winnipeg, L., Canada 51 C9
Winnipeg Beach, Canada 51 C9
Winnipegosis, Canada 51 C9
Winnipegosis L., Canada 51 C9
Winnsboro, La., U.S.A. 55 J9
Winnsboro, S.C., U.S.A. 53 H5
Winnsboro, Tex., U.S.A. 55 J7
Winokapau, L., Canada 49 B7
Winona, Minn., U.S.A. 54 C9
Winona, Miss., U.S.A. 55 J10
Winooski, U.S.A. 52 C9
Winschoten, Neths. 11 A7
Winsford, U.K. 8 D5
Winslow, U.S.A. 57 J8
Winston-Salem, U.S.A. 53 G5
Winter Garden, U.S.A. 53 L5
Winter Haven, U.S.A. 53 M5
Winter Park, U.S.A. 53 L5
Winterswijk, Neths. 11 C6
Winterthur, Switz. 14 C8
Winthrop, U.S.A. 56 B3
Winton, Australia 42 C3
Winton, N.Z. 39 M2
Wirrulla, Australia 43 E1
Wisbech, U.K. 9 E8
Wisconsin □, U.S.A. 54 C10
Wisconsin →, U.S.A. 54 D9
Wisconsin Rapids, U.S.A. 54 C10
Wisdom, U.S.A. 56 D7
Wishek, U.S.A. 54 B5
Wisła →, Poland 13 A10
Wismar, Germany 12 B6
Wisner, U.S.A. 54 E6
Witbank, S. Africa 37 K5
Witham, U.K. 9 F8
Witham →, U.K. 8 E7
Withernsea, U.K. 8 D8
Witney, U.K. 9 F6
Wittenberge, Germany 12 B6
Wittenoom, Australia 40 D2
Wkra →, Poland 13 B11
Wlingi, Indonesia 27 H15
Włocławek, Poland 13 B10
Włodawa, Poland 13 C12
Wokam, Indonesia 27 F8
Woking, U.K. 9 F7
Wokingham □, U.K. 9 F7
Wolf →, Canada 50 A2
Wolf Creek, U.S.A. 56 C7
Wolf L., Canada 50 A2
Wolf Point, U.S.A. 54 A2
Wolfe I., Canada 48 D4
Wolfsberg, Austria 12 E8
Wolfsburg, Germany 12 B6
Wolin, Poland 12 B8
Wollaston, Is., Chile 64 H3
Wollaston L., Canada 51 B8
Wollaston Lake, Canada 51 B8
Wollaston Pen., Canada 46 B8
Wollongong, Australia 43 E5
Wolsey, U.S.A. 54 C5
Wolvega, Neths. 11 B6
Wolverhampton, U.K. 9 E5
Wondai, Australia 43 D5
Wongalarroo L., Australia 43 E3
Wongan Hills, Australia 41 F2
Wonosari, Indonesia 27 G14
Wonosobo, Indonesia 27 G13
Wonowon, Canada 50 B4
Wŏnsan, N. Korea 25 C7
Wonthaggi, Australia 43 F4
Wood Buffalo Nat. Park, Canada 50 B6
Wood Is., Australia 40 C3
Wood L., Canada 51 B8
Woodah I., Australia 42 A2
Woodbridge, U.K. 9 E9
Woodburn, U.S.A. 56 D2
Woodenbong, Australia 43 D5
Woodend, Australia 43 F3
Woodford, Australia 43 D5
Woodland, Calif., U.S.A. 56 G3
Woodland, Maine, U.S.A. 53 C12
Woodland Caribou Prov. Park, Canada 51 C10
Woodridge, Canada 51 D9
Woodroffe, Mt., Australia 41 E5
Woods, L., Australia 42 B1
Woods, L. of the, Canada 51 D10
Woodside, Australia 43 F4
Woodstock, Australia 42 B4
Woodstock, N.B., Canada 49 C6
Woodstock, Ont., Canada 48 D3
Woodstock, U.K. 9 F6
Woodstock, U.S.A. 54 D10
Woodsville, U.S.A. 52 C10
Woodville, N.Z. 39 J5
Woodville, Miss., U.S.A. 55 K9
Woodville, Tex., U.S.A. 55 K7
Woodward, U.S.A. 55 G5
Woody →, Canada 51 C8
Woolamai, C., Australia 43 F4
Wooler, U.K. 8 B5
Woolgoolga, Australia 43 E5
Woomera, Australia 43 E2
Woonsocket, R.I., U.S.A. 52 E10
Woonsocket, S. Dak., U.S.A. 54 C5
Wooramel →, Australia 41 E1
Wooramel Roadhouse, Australia 41 E1
Wooster, U.S.A. 52 E5
Worcester, S. Africa 37 L3
Worcester, U.K. 9 E5
Worcester, U.S.A. 52 D10
Worcestershire □, U.K. 9 E5
Workington, U.K. 8 C4
Worksop, U.K. 8 D6
Workum, Neths. 11 B5
Worland, U.S.A. 56 D10
Worms, Germany 12 D5
Worsley, Canada 50 B5
Wortham, U.S.A. 55 K6
Worthing, U.K. 9 G7
Worthington, U.S.A. 54 D7
Wosi, Indonesia 27 E7
Wou-han = Wuhan, China 25 C6
Wousi = Wuxi, China 25 C7
Wowoni, Indonesia 27 E6
Wrangel I. = Vrangelya, Ostrov, Russia 21 B19
Wrangell, U.S.A. 50 B2
Wrangell Mts., U.S.A. 46 B5
Wrath, C., U.K. 10 B4
Wray, U.S.A. 54 E3
Wrekin, The, U.K. 9 E5
Wrens, U.S.A. 53 J4
Wrexham, U.K. 8 D4
Wrexham □, U.K. 8 D5

Wright, U.S.A. 54 D2
Wrightson Mt., U.S.A. . 57 L8
Wrigley, Canada 46 B7
Wrocław, Poland 13 C9
Września, Poland 13 B9
Wu Jiang →, China .. 24 D5
Wubin, Australia 41 F2
Wudinna, Australia ... 43 E2
Wuhan, China 25 C6
Wuhsi = Wuxi, China . 25 C7
Wuhu, China 25 C6
Wukari, Nigeria 34 G7
Wuliaru, Indonesia ... 27 F8
Wuluk'omushih Ling,
China 24 C3
Wulumuchi = Ürümqi,
China 20 E9
Wundowie, Australia .. 41 F2
Wunnummin L., Canada 48 B2
Wuntho, Burma 29 H19
Wuppertal, Germany .. 12 C4
Würzburg, Germany .. 12 D5
Wusuli Jiang =
Ussuri →, Asia ... 22 A7
Wutongqiao, China ... 24 D5
Wuwei, China 24 C5
Wuxi, China 25 C7
Wuzhong, China 24 C5
Wuzhou, China 25 D6
Wyaaba Cr. →,
Australia 42 B3
Wyalkatchem, Australia 41 F2
Wyandra, Australia ... 43 D4
Wyangala Res.,
Australia 43 E4
Wyara, L., Australia .. 43 D3
Wycheproof, Australia . 43 F3
Wye →, U.K. 9 F5
Wyemandoo, Australia 41 E2
Wymondham, U.K. .. 9 E9
Wymore, U.S.A. 54 E6
Wyndham, Australia .. 40 C4
Wyndham, N.Z. 39 M2
Wynne, U.S.A. 55 H9
Wynyard, Australia .. 42 G4
Wynyard, Canada ... 51 C8
Wyola L., Australia .. 41 E5
Wyoming □, U.S.A. .. 56 E10
Wyong, Australia ... 43 E5
Wytheville, U.S.A. ... 52 G5

Xaçmaz, Azerbaijan ... 19 F8
Xai-Xai, Mozam. 37 K6
Xainza, China 24 C3
Xangongo, Angola ... 37 H3
Xankändi, Azerbaijan .. 19 G8
Xánthi, Greece 17 D11
Xapuri, Brazil 62 F5
Xátiva, Spain 15 C5
Xenia, U.S.A. 52 F4
Xi Jiang →, China ... 25 D6
Xiaguan, China 24 D5
Xiamen, China 25 D6
Xi'an, China 25 C5
Xiang Jiang →, China 25 D6
Xiangfan, China 25 C6
Xianggang = Hong
Kong □, China 25 D6
Xiangquan He =
Sutlej →, Pakistan . 28 E7
Xiangtan, China 25 D6
Xianyang, China 25 C5
Xiao Hinggan Ling,
China 25 B7
Xichang, China 24 D5
Xigazê, China 24 D3
Xing'an, China 25 D6
Xingu →, Brazil ... 63 D8
Xining, China 24 C5
Xinjiang Uygur
Zizhiqu □, China ... 24 C3
Xinxiang, China 25 C6
Xique-Xique, Brazil .. 63 F10
Xisha Qundao = Paracel
Is., S. China Sea ... 26 A4
Xixabangma Feng,
China 29 E14
Xizang Zizhiqu □, China 24 C3
Xuanhua, China 25 B6
Xúquer →, Spain ... 15 C5
Xuzhou, China 25 C6

Yaamba, Australia ... 42 C5
Yaapeet, Australia ... 43 F3
Yablonovy Ra. =
Yablonovyy Khrebet,
Russia 21 D12
Yablonovyy Khrebet,
Russia 21 D12
Yabrūd, Syria 33 B5
Yacheng, China 25 E5
Yacuiba, Bolivia 62 H6
Yacuma →, Bolivia .. 62 F5
Yadgir, India 28 L10
Yadkin →, U.S.A. ... 53 H5
Yaeyama-Rettō, Japan 23 M1
Yagodnoye, Russia .. 21 C15
Yahk, Canada 50 D5
Yahuma, Dem. Rep. of
the Congo 36 D4
Yaita, Japan 23 F9

Yakima, U.S.A. 56 C3
Yakima →, U.S.A. ... 56 C3
Yakobi I., U.S.A. 50 B1
Yakovlevka, Russia .. 22 B6
Yaku-Shima, Japan .. 23 J5
Yakumo, Japan 22 C10
Yakutat, U.S.A. 46 C6
Yakutia = Sakha □,
Russia 21 C13
Yakutsk, Russia 21 C13
Yala, Thailand 26 C2
Yalgoo, Australia ... 41 E2
Yalinga, C.A.R. 36 C4
Yalkubul, Punta, Mexico 59 C7
Yalleroi, Australia ... 42 C4
Yalobusha →, U.S.A. 55 J9
Yalova, Turkey 17 D13
Yalta, Ukraine 19 F5
Yam Ha Melaḥ = Dead
Sea, Asia 33 D4
Yam Kinneret, Israel . 33 C4
Yamada, Japan 23 H5
Yamagata, Japan ... 22 E10
Yamagata □, Japan .. 22 E10
Yamaguchi, Japan ... 23 G5
Yamaguchi □, Japan . 23 G5
Yamal, Poluostrov,
Russia 20 B8
Yamal Pen. = Yamal,
Poluostrov, Russia .. 20 B8
Yamanashi □, Japan . 23 G9
Yamantau, Gora, Russia 18 D10
Yamba, Australia ... 43 D5
Yambarran Ra.,
Australia 40 C5
Yâmbiô, Sudan 35 H11
Yambol, Bulgaria ... 17 C12
Yamdena, Indonesia . 27 F8
Yame, Japan 23 H5
Yamethin, Burma ... 29 J20
Yamma-Yamma, L.,
Australia 43 D3
Yamoussoukro, Ivory C. 34 G4
Yampa →, U.S.A. ... 56 F9
Yampi Sd., Australia . 40 C3
Yampil, Moldova ... 13 D15
Yampol = Yampil,
Moldova 13 D15
Yamuna →, India ... 29 G12
Yamzho Yumco, China 24 D4
Yana →, Russia 21 B14
Yanagawa, Japan ... 23 H5
Yanai, Japan 23 H6
Yanaul, Russia 18 C10
Yanbu 'al Baḥr,
Si. Arabia 30 F3
Yanchep Beach,
Australia 41 F2
Yanco, Australia ... 43 E4
Yanco Cr. →, Australia 43 F4
Yandoon, Burma ... 29 L19
Yangambi, Dem. Rep. of
the Congo 36 D4
Yangch'ü = Taiyuan,
China 25 C6
Yangon = Rangoon,
Burma 29 L20
Yangquan, China ... 25 C6
Yangtse = Chang
Jiang →, China ... 25 C7
Yangtze Kiang = Chang
Jiang →, China ... 25 C7
Yangzhou, China ... 25 C6
Yanji, China 25 B7
Yankton, U.S.A. 54 D6
Yanqi, China 24 B3
Yantabulla, Australia . 43 D4
Yantai, China 25 C7
Yaoundé, Cameroon . 36 D2
Yap I., Pac. Oc. 44 G5
Yapen, Indonesia ... 27 E9
Yapen, Selat, Indonesia 27 E9
Yapero, Indonesia ... 27 E9
Yappar →, Australia . 42 B3
Yaqui →, Mexico ... 58 B2
Yar-Sale, Russia ... 20 C8
Yaraka, Australia ... 42 C3
Yaransk, Russia 18 C8
Yare →, U.K. 9 E9
Yaremcha, Ukraine .. 13 D13
Yarensk, Russia 18 B8
Yari →, Colombia ... 62 D4
Yarkand = Shache,
China 24 C2
Yarkhun →, Pakistan . 28 A8
Yarmouth, Canada .. 49 D6
Yarmūk →, Syria ... 33 C4
Yaroslavl, Russia ... 18 C6
Yarqa, W. →, Egypt . 33 F2
Yarra Yarra Lakes,
Australia 41 E2
Yarram, Australia ... 43 F4
Yarraman, Australia . 43 D5
Yarras, Australia ... 43 E5
Yartsevo, Russia ... 21 C10
Yarumal, Colombia .. 62 B3
Yasawa Group, Fiji .. 39 C7
Yaselda, Belarus ... 13 B14
Yasin, Pakistan 28 A8
Yasinski, L., Canada . 48 B4
Yasinya, Ukraine ... 13 D13
Yass, Australia 43 E4
Yatağan, Turkey 17 F13
Yates Center, U.S.A. . 55 G7
Yathkyed L., Canada . 51 A9

Yatsushiro, Japan ... 23 H5
Yavari →, Peru 62 D4
Yávaros, Mexico 58 B3
Yavatmal, India 28 J11
Yavne, Israel 33 D3
Yavoriv, Ukraine ... 13 D12
Yavorov = Yavoriv,
Ukraine 13 D12
Yawatahama, Japan . 23 H6
Yazd, Iran 31 D7
Yazd □, Iran 31 D7
Yazd-e Khvāst, Iran .. 31 D7
Yazoo →, U.S.A. ... 55 J9
Yazoo City, U.S.A. .. 55 J9
Ye Xian = Laizhou,
China 25 C6
Yebyu, Burma 29 M21
Yecla, Spain 15 C5
Yécora, Mexico 58 B3
Yedintsy = Edinet,
Moldova 13 D14
Yegros, Paraguay ... 64 B5
Yehuda, Midbar, Israel 33 D4
Yei, Sudan 35 H12
Yekaterinburg, Russia 20 D7
Yekaterinodar =
Krasnodar, Russia .. 19 E6
Yelarbon, Australia .. 43 D5
Yelets, Russia 18 D6
Yelizavetgrad =
Kirovohrad, Ukraine 19 E5
Yell, U.K. 10 A6
Yellow Sea, China .. 25 C7
Yellowhead Pass,
Canada 50 C5
Yellowknife, Canada . 50 A6
Yellowknife →, Canada 50 A6
Yellowstone →, U.S.A. 54 B3
Yellowstone L., U.S.A. 56 D8
Yellowstone National
Park, U.S.A. 56 D9
Yelsk, Belarus 13 C15
Yemen ■, Asia 32 E3
Yenangyaung, Burma . 29 J19
Yenbo = Yanbu 'al
Baḥr, Si. Arabia ... 30 F3
Yenda, Australia ... 43 E4
Yenice, Turkey 17 E12
Yenisey →, Russia .. 20 B9
Yeniseysk, Russia ... 21 D10
Yeniseyskiy Zaliv,
Russia 20 B9
Yenyuka, Russia ... 21 D13
Yeo →, U.K. 9 G5
Yeo, L., Australia ... 41 E3
Yeola, India 28 J9
Yeovil, U.K. 9 G5
Yeppoon, Australia . 42 C5
Yerbent, Turkmenistan 20 F6
Yerbogachen, Russia . 21 C11
Yerevan, Armenia ... 19 F7
Yerington, U.S.A. ... 56 G4
Yermak, Kazakstan .. 20 D8
Yermo, U.S.A. 57 J5
Yeropol, Russia 21 C17
Yershov, Russia 19 D8
Yerushalayim =
Jerusalem, Israel .. 33 D4
Yes Tor, U.K. 9 G4
Yeso, U.S.A. 55 H2
Yessey, Russia 21 C11
Yetman, Australia .. 43 D5
Yeu, Î. d', France ... 14 C2
Yevpatoriya, Ukraine . 19 E5
Yeysk, Russia 19 E6
Yezd = Yazd, Iran .. 31 D7
Yi 'Allaq, G., Egypt .. 33 E2
Yiannitsa, Greece ... 17 D10
Yibin, China 24 D5
Yichang, China 25 C6
Yichun, China 25 B7
Yıldız Dağları, Turkey . 17 D12
Yilehuli Shan, China . 25 A7
Yinchuan, China ... 24 C5
Yindarlgooda, L.,
Australia 41 F3
Yingkou, China 25 B7
Yining, China 20 E9
Yinmabin, Burma ... 29 H19
Yirga Alem, Ethiopia . 32 F2
Yirrkala, Australia .. 42 A2
Yishan, China 24 D5
Yithion, Greece 17 F10
Yiyang, China 25 D6
Yli-Kitka, Finland ... 6 C23
Ylitornio, Finland ... 6 C20
Ylivieska, Finland ... 6 D21
Yoakum, U.S.A. 55 L6
Yog Pt., Phil. 27 B6
Yogyakarta, Indonesia 27 G14
Yoho Nat. Park, Canada 50 C5
Yojoa, L. de, Honduras 60 D2
Yokadouma, Cameroon 36 D2
Yokkaichi, Japan ... 23 G8
Yoko, Cameroon ... 36 C2
Yokohama, Japan ... 23 G9
Yokosuka, Japan ... 23 G9
Yokote, Japan 22 E10
Yola, Nigeria 35 G8
Yolaina, Cordillera de,
Nic. 60 D3
Yoloten, Turkmenistan 31 B9
Yom →, Thailand ... 26 A2
Yonago, Japan 23 G6

Yonaguni-Jima, Japan 23 M1
Yonezawa, Japan ... 22 F10
Yonibana, S. Leone .. 34 G3
Yonkers, U.S.A. 52 E9
Yonne →, France ... 14 B5
York, U.K. 8 D6
York, Ala., U.S.A. ... 55 J10
York, Nebr., U.S.A. .. 54 E6
York, Pa., U.S.A. ... 52 F7
York, C., Australia ... 42 A3
York, Kap, Greenland . 4 B4
York, City of □, U.K. . 8 D6
York, Vale of, U.K. .. 8 C6
York Sd., Australia .. 40 C4
Yorke Pen., Australia . 43 E2
Yorketown, Australia . 43 F2
Yorkshire Wolds, U.K. 8 C7
Yorkton, Canada ... 51 C8
Yoro, Honduras 60 C2
Yoron-Jima, Japan .. 23 L4
Yos Sudarso, Pulau =
Dolak, Pulau,
Indonesia 27 F9
Yosemite National Park,
U.S.A. 57 H4
Yoshkar Ola, Russia . 18 C8
Yotvata, Israel 33 F4
Youghal, Ireland ... 10 F3
Young, Australia ... 43 E4
Young, Canada 51 C7
Younghusband, L.,
Australia 43 E2
Younghusband Pen.,
Australia 43 F2
Youngstown, Canada . 51 C6
Youngstown, U.S.A. . 52 E5
Yozgat, Turkey 19 G5
Ypres = Ieper, Belgium 11 D2
Yreka, U.S.A. 56 F2
Ystad, Sweden 7 J15
Ysyk-Köl, Ozero,
Kyrgyzstan 20 E8
Ytyk Kyuyel, Russia .. 21 C14
Yu Jiang →, China .. 25 D6
Yuan Jiang →, China 25 D6
Yuba City, U.S.A. ... 56 G3
Yūbari, Japan 22 C10
Yūbetsu, Japan 22 B11
Yucatán □, Mexico .. 59 C7
Yucatán, Canal de,
Caribbean 60 B2
Yucatan Str. = Yucatán,
Canal de, Caribbean 60 B2
Yucca, U.S.A. 57 J6
Yuci, China 25 C6
Yuendumu, Australia 40 D5
Yugoslavia ■, Europe . 17 B9
Yukon →, U.S.A. ... 46 B3
Yukon Territory □,
Canada 46 B6
Yukta, Russia 21 C11
Yukuhashi, Japan .. 23 H5
Yulara, Australia ... 41 E5
Yule →, Australia ... 40 D2
Yuleba, Australia ... 43 D4
Yuma, Ariz., U.S.A. . 57 K6
Yuma, Colo., U.S.A. . 54 E3
Yuma, B. de, Dom. Rep. 61 C6
Yumen, China 24 C4
Yun Xian, China ... 24 C4
Yungas, Bolivia 62 G5
Yunnan □, China ... 24 D5
Yunta, Australia ... 43 E2
Yurga, Russia 20 D9
Yurimaguas, Peru .. 62 E3
Yuryung Kaya, Russia 21 B12
Yuscarán, Honduras . 60 D2
Yushu, China 24 C4
Yuxan Qarabağ =
Nagorno-Karabakh,
Azerbaijan 19 F8
Yuxi, China 24 D5
Yuzawa, Japan 22 E10
Yuzhno-Sakhalinsk,
Russia 21 E15

Zaanstad, Neths. ... 11 B4
Zāb al Kabīr →, Iraq . 30 C4
Zāb aş Şagīr →, Iraq . 30 C4
Zabaykalsk, Russia .. 21 E12
Zābol, Iran 31 D9
Zābolī, Iran 31 E9
Zabrze, Poland 13 C10
Zacapa, Guatemala . 60 D2
Zacapu, Mexico 58 D4
Zacatecas, Mexico .. 58 C4
Zacatecas □, Mexico . 58 C4
Zacatecoluca, El Salv. . 60 D2
Zachary, U.S.A. 55 K9
Zacoalco, Mexico ... 58 C4
Zacualtipán, Mexico . 59 C5
Zadar, Croatia 12 F8
Zadetkyi Kyun, Burma 26 C1
Zafarqand, Iran 31 C7
Zafra, Spain 15 C2
Żagań, Poland 12 C8
Zagaoua, Chad 35 E10
Zagazig, Egypt 35 B12
Zāgheh, Iran 31 C6
Zagorsk = Sergiyev
Posad, Russia 18 C6
Zagreb, Croatia 12 F9

Zágros, Kúhhá-ye, Iran 31 C6
Zagros Mts. = Zágros,
Kúhhá-ye, Iran ... 31 C6
Zāhedān,
Sīstān va Balūchestān,
Iran 31 D9
Zāhedān, Fārs, Iran .. 31 D7
Zahlah, Lebanon ... 33 B4
Zaïre = Congo →,
Africa 36 F2
Zaječar, Serbia, Yug. . 17 C10
Zakamensk, Russia .. 21 D11
Zakhodnaya Dzvina =
Daugava →, Latvia . 7 H21
Zākhū, Iraq 30 B4
Zákinthos, Greece .. 17 F9
Zakopane, Poland .. 13 D10
Zalaegerszeg, Hungary 13 E9
Zalău, Romania 13 E12
Zaleshchiki =
Zalishchyky, Ukraine 13 D13
Zalew Wiślany, Poland 13 A10
Zalingei, Sudan 35 F10
Zalishchyky, Ukraine 13 D13
Zama L., Canada ... 50 B5
Zambeze →, Africa .. 37 H7
Zambezi =
Zambeze →, Africa 37 H7
Zambezi, Zambia ... 37 G4
Zambia ■, Africa ... 37 G5
Zamboanga, Phil. ... 27 C6
Zamora, Mexico 58 D4
Zamora, Spain 15 B3
Zamość, Poland ... 13 C12
Zandvoort, Neths. .. 11 B4
Zanesville, U.S.A. .. 52 F4
Zangābād, Iran 30 B5
Zanjān, Iran 31 B6
Zanjān □, Iran 31 B6
Zanjān →, Iran 31 B6
Zante = Zákinthos,
Greece 17 F9
Zanthus, Australia .. 41 F3
Zanzibar, Tanzania .. 36 F7
Zaouiet El-Kala = Bordj
Omar Driss, Algeria . 34 C7
Zaouiet Reggane,
Algeria 34 C6
Zap Suyu = Zāb al
Kabīr →, Iraq 30 C4
Zapadnaya Dvina =
Daugava →, Latvia . 7 H21
Západné Beskydy,
Europe 13 D10
Zapala, Argentina .. 64 D2
Zapata, U.S.A. 55 M5
Zapolyarnyy, Russia . 18 A5
Zaporizhzhya, Ukraine 19 E6
Zaporozhye =
Zaporizhzhya, Ukraine 19 E6
Zara, Turkey 30 B3
Zaragoza, Coahuila,
Mexico 58 B4
Zaragoza, Nuevo León,
Mexico 59 C5
Zaragoza, Spain ... 15 B5
Zarand, Kermān, Iran . 31 D8
Zarand, Markazī, Iran . 31 C6
Zaranj, Afghan. 28 D2
Zarasai, Lithuania .. 7 J22
Zárate, Argentina ... 64 C5
Zard, Kūh-e, Iran ... 31 C6
Zāreh, Iran 31 C6
Zaria, Nigeria 34 F7
Zarneh, Iran 30 C5
Zarqā', Nahr az →,
Jordan 33 C4
Zarrīn, Iran 31 C7
Zaruma, Ecuador ... 62 D3
Zarzis, Tunisia 35 B8
Zaskar Mts., India .. 28 C10
Zavitinsk, Russia ... 21 D13
Zavodovski, I.,
Antarctica 5 B1
Zawiercie, Poland .. 13 C10
Zāwiyat al Bayḍā = Al
Bayḍā, Libya 35 B10
Zāyandeh →, Iran .. 31 C7
Zaysan, Kazakstan .. 20 E9
Zaysan, Oz., Kazakstan 20 E9
Zayü, China 24 D4
Zbarazh, Ukraine ... 13 D13
Zdolbuniv, Ukraine .. 13 C14
Zduńska Wola, Poland 13 C10
Zeballos, Canada ... 50 D3
Zeebrugge, Belgium . 11 C3
Zeehan, Australia .. 42 G4
Zeeland □, Neths. .. 11 C3
Zefat, Israel 33 C4
Zeil, Mt., Australia .. 40 D5
Zeila, Somali Rep. .. 32 E3
Zeitz, Germany 12 C7
Zelenodolsk, Russia . 18 C8
Zelenograd, Russia . 18 C6
Zelenogradsk, Russia 7 J19
Zemun, Serbia, Yug. . 17 B9
Zenica, Bos.-H. 17 B7
Žepče, Bos.-H. 17 B8
Zeya, Russia 21 D13
Zeya →, Russia 21 D13

Zghartā, Lebanon ... 33 A4
Zgorzelec, Poland .. 12 C8
Zhabinka, Belarus .. 13 B13
Zhailma, Kazakstan . 20 D7
Zhambyl, Kazakstan . 20 E8
Zhangaqazaly,
Kazakstan 20 E7
Zhangjiakou, China . 25 B6
Zhangye, China 24 C5
Zhangzhou, China .. 25 D6
Zhanjiang, China ... 25 D6
Zhannetty, Ostrov,
Russia 21 B16
Zhanyi, China 24 D5
Zhaotong, China ... 24 D5
Zhashkiv, Ukraine .. 13 D16
Zhayyq →, Kazakstan 19 E9
Zhdanov = Mariupol,
Ukraine 19 E6
Zhejiang □, China .. 25 D7
Zheleznodorozhnyy,
Russia 18 B9
Zheleznogorsk-Ilimskiy,
Russia 21 D11
Zhengzhou, China .. 25 C6
Zhetiqara, Kazakstan 20 D7
Zhigansk, Russia ... 21 C13
Zhilinda, Russia ... 21 C12
Zhitomir = Zhytomyr,
Ukraine 13 C15
Zhlobin, Belarus ... 13 B16
Zhmerinka =
Zhmerynka, Ukraine 13 D15
Zhmerynka, Ukraine 13 D15
Zhob, Pakistan 28 D6
Zhodino = Zhodzina,
Belarus 13 A15
Zhodzina, Belarus ... 13 A15
Zhokhova, Ostrov,
Russia 21 B16
Zhongdian, China .. 24 D4
Zhumadian, China .. 25 C6
Zhytomyr, Ukraine .. 13 C15
Zīārān, Iran 31 B6
Zibo, China 25 C6
Zielona Góra, Poland 12 C8
Zierikzee, Neths. ... 11 C3
Zigey, Chad 35 F9
Zigong, China 24 D5
Ziguinchor, Senegal . 34 F2
Zihuatanejo, Mexico 58 D4
Žilina, Slovak Rep. . 13 D10
Zillah, Libya 35 C9
Zima, Russia 21 D11
Zimapán, Mexico ... 59 C5
Zimbabwe ■, Africa . 37 H5
Zimnicea, Romania . 13 G13
Zinder, Niger 34 F7
Zion National Park,
U.S.A. 57 H7
Zirreh, Gowd-e, Afghan. 28 E3
Zitácuaro, Mexico .. 58 D4
Ziway, L., Ethiopia .. 32 F2
Zlatograd, Bulgaria . 17 D11
Zlatoust, Russia ... 18 C10
Zlín, Czech Rep. ... 13 D9
Zmeinogorsk, Kazakstan 20 D9
Zmiyev, Ukraine ... 13 D13
Znojmo, Czech Rep. . 12 D9
Zobeyrī, Iran 30 C5
Zoetermeer, Neths. . 11 B4
Zolochev = Zolochiv,
Ukraine 13 D13
Zolochiv, Ukraine ... 13 D13
Zomba, Malawi 37 H7
Zongo, Dem. Rep. of
the Congo 36 D3
Zonguldak, Turkey .. 19 F5
Zorritos, Peru 62 D2
Zouar, Chad 35 D9
Zouérate = Zouîrât,
Mauritania 34 D3
Zouîrât, Mauritania . 34 D3
Zoutkamp, Neths. .. 11 A6
Zrenjanin, Serbia, Yug. 17 B9
Zufar, Oman 32 D5
Zug, Switz. 14 C8
Zugspitze, Germany . 12 E6
Zuid-Holland □, Neths. 11 C4
Zuidbeveland, Neths. 11 C3
Zuidhorn, Neths. ... 11 A6
Zula, Eritrea 32 D2
Zumbo, Mozam. ... 37 H6
Zumpango, Mexico . 59 D5
Zuni, U.S.A. 57 J9
Zunyi, China 24 D5
Zurbātīyah, Iraq ... 30 C5
Zürich, Switz. 14 C8
Zutphen, Neths. ... 11 B6
Zuwārah, Libya 35 B8
Zūzan, Iran 31 C8
Zverinogolovskoye,
Russia 20 D7
Zvishavane, Zimbabwe 37 J6
Zvolen, Slovak Rep. . 13 D10
Zwettl, Austria 12 D8
Zwickau, Germany .. 12 C7
Zwolle, Neths. 11 B6
Zwolle, U.S.A. 55 K8
Żyrardów, Poland .. 13 B11
Zyryan, Kazakstan .. 20 E9
Zyryanka, Russia ... 21 C16
Zyryanovsk = Zyryan,
Kazakstan 20 E9
Żywiec, Poland 13 D10